JAMES WHITCOMB RILEY
THE POET AS FLYING ISLANDS OF THE NIGHT

by
Thomas Earl Williams

with primary illustrations by Katherine Kuonen

and the great assistance of Robert Tinsley
with Riley artifacts

Coiny Publishing Co., P.O. Box 585, Greenfield, IN 46140
317/462-7758

DEDICATION

Dorothy June Jackson Williams (1906-1995). James Whitcomb Riley Birthplace Hostess at Greenfield, Indiana (1957-1995).

All of the truth I know tells me you are not dead but simply away as James Whitcomb Riley's poem "Away" describes. Enjoy now the accompaniment of others rather than those who, on earth, sang to fretfully. I have experienced no wonder so great as to be in the presence of you, most wondrous woman of women.. This book is most lovingly dedicated to you. I miss you terribly, my AEo. "What'll I do when you are far way\And I am blue what'll I do?"

JAMES WHITCOMB RILEY:
THE POET AS FLYING ISLANDS OF THE NIGHT

...Squeers I
MY GRANDFATHER SQUEERS

So remarkably deaf was my Grand-father Squeers
That he had to wear lightning-rods over his ears
To even hear thunder, and oftentimes then,
He was forced to request it to thunder again.

And so glaringly bald was the top of his head
That many's the time he has solemnly said,
As his eye journeyed o'er its reflex in the glass:
"I must be out a few signs of "Keep off the Grass!""

(from Kokomo TRIBUNE May 1, 1880)

...Squeers II

THE ELDERLY SQUEERS

Such a hale constitution had Grandfather Squeers,
That although he used "Navy" for ninety-odd years,
He could still chew his fifty-cent plug every week,
With a ballast of "fine-cut" besides, in each cheek.

Then my Grandfather Squeers had a singular knack
Of sitting around on the small of his back,
With his legs like a letter Y propped o'er the grate,
Wherein 'twas his custom to ex-pec-to-rate.

(from Kokomo TRIBUNE May 22, 1880)

...Squeers III
SQUEERS - THE ANCIENT

O, my Grandfather Squeers took a special delight,
In trimming his corns every Saturday night
With a horn-handled razor, whose edge he excused,
By saying `twas one that his grandfather used.

And although deeply etched in the haft of the same
Was the ever euphonious Wostenholm's name,
`Twas my grandfather's custom to boast of the blade
As "the very best razor that Seth Thomas made!"

(from Kokomo TRIBUNE May 29, 1880)

VI. Mr. Bryce

VII. Krung

...Squeers IV

THE ANTIQUE SQUEERS

My Grandfather Squeers, when retiring at night,
Used always to thoughtfully turn up the light,
In order to see how to blow down the flue
And tell, if it busted, just what it would do.

And then it was melody, when on the ledge
Of the bed he curled up like a shaving on edge,
And snored and snorted, cavorted and pawed
With wakeful revulsions in which he just chawed.

(from Kokomo TRIBUNE June 12, 1880)

VIII. Bud

Riley's Poetry

Riley's Prose

Miscellaneous (includes selected writings of others about Riley)

JAMES WHITCOMB RILEY:

THE POET AS
"THE FLYING ISLANDS OF THE NIGHT"

An artist's 1913 conception of a "Flying Island of the Night" based upon the James Whitcomb Riley poem "The Flying Islands of the Night." Riley at 28 conceived of himself as islands of estrangement-each a personality and fragmented "self" playing a role in the despair of his intoxicated world of the night...and then set these "selves" loose to fly on the stage of his soul in a mock play to seek a strategy for the remainder of his lonely life. Never in literature has such an odd autobiography been written and the poem forms the basis of the biography of this poetic genius. Even more strangely...what came of his strategy was a poetry bearing the heart and themes of the Incarnation Theological movement (and its message that there is value and redemption in living a humble, ethically reputable life of service to others) that overwhelmed his land-with Riley as its principal poet-following the volatile period after the American Civil War. Drawing by Franklin Booth (American, New York, 1874-1948).

JAMES WHITCOMB RILEY:
THE POET AS FLYING ISLANDS OF THE NIGHT

A WAYWARD SONG

How strange! How very, very strange that the message of a song of the very earliest Christians could appear in such a way!...in poems about Nineteenth Century American farm families, Hoosier cricks and corn shocks...and children.

We remember these early Christian folk huddled together in persecution because they worshipped a crucified, humble man and thought God had something to do with His rich yet poor earthly life. They sang a "Christ Hymn" to keep up their courage. With the way the world was aflame against these early Christians, they needed a song to lift their spirits. Paul recorded it in his Letter to the Philippians. "Let this mind be in you,.."[1]

In the mid-Nineteenth Century, time decreed that this song be sung again for a new people. This folk was the confused remnant from the great

Riley around age 20.

American Civil War. After this deadly conflict pitting friend against friend, America's spirit needed lifting too.

The song that needed singing was actually an import into America. The "Christ Hymn" began being heard again as a "rallying cry" from an obscure German creed called Incarnation Theology in Germany.[2] It was a new response of the Nineteenth Century to meet the challenge of life in its time. Soon its humble message spilled over the Atlantic and into the American heartland where it was popularized in the tuneless songs of a frontier American poet born in a log cabin in Greenfield, Indiana.

I introduce the singer, James Whitcomb Riley.

Many people connect James Whitcomb Riley only with the light-hearted and happy poetry of the later years of his life. James Whitcomb Riley really was a much beloved person and his poetry was heartening. He came to be known as the "Children's Poet." His humanism, caring and depiction of children captured the Nineteenth Century America with such poems as "Little Orphant Annie."

LITTLE ORPHANT ANNIE (1885)

Little Orphant Annie's come to our house to stay,
An' wash the cups an' saucers up, an' brush the crumbs away,
An' shoo the chickens off the porch, an' dust the hearth, an'
sweep,
An' make the fire, an' bake the bread, an' earn her board-an-
keep;
An' all us other childern, when the supper-things is done,
We set around the kitchen fire an' has the mostest fun,
A-listenin' to the witch-tales 'at Annie tells about,
An' the Gobble-uns 'at gits you
 Ef you
 Don't
 Watch
 Out!...

It does not hurt to think of James Whitcomb Riley this way. He was America's poet for children of his time as his friend Rudyard Kipling was the poet for the children of the British Empire.

But Riley was so much more complicated than that. He was an enigmatic creative genius. It is almost impossible to learn about him or explain his life because he so completely related to his age that he can hardly be separated from it. We do know that Riley's life was not all joyous. He also felt deeply wrenching despair. When James Whitcomb Riley was suffering his deepest anguish about his life in the Nineteenth Century, he fell into depression and occasional alcoholism and knew great

Little Orphant Annie from a sketch by Will Vawter, Riley's favorite illustrator. Little Orphant Annie became an American national figure whose name was known by virtually every American schoolchild.

As the Twentieth Century progressed, "Little Orphant Annie" re-appeared as a Harold Gray comic strip character "Little Orhpan Annie" which evolved into a popular Broadway play whose title was populary advertised as shown and a motion picture entitled "Annie" in 1982.

dejection for many reasons. This was primarily when he was a homeless young man in his twenties.

Riley did not arise to his most popular acclaim until after his depression was brought under control-although never fully conquered. Around Riley's thirtieth birthday, he started building on the faith that helped him survive. He began singing American versions of the "Christ Hymn" in poetry. These were songs of hope and courage for living humbly.

The great poetry of James Whitcomb Riley, and those poems, particularly his early "Benjamin Johnson of Boone" poems, which made Riley the most famous poet of his time, were frontier American "Christ Hymn" masterpieces.

"Benjamin Johnson of Boone" visualized by artist Will Vawter in 1905. Although born in Virginia on April 13, 1871, Vawter moved to Greenfield, Indiana with his parents around 1880. Vawter grew up in a "permissive" home and was encouraged to paint. As a child he was known to wipe his brushes on window curtains and paint over the home's wallpaper whenever he wanted.

TO MY OLD FRIEND, WILLIAM LEACHMAN (1882)

Fer forty year and better you have been a friend to me, Through days of sore afflictions and dire adversity, You allus had a kind word of counsul to impart, Which was like a healin' `intment to the sorrow of my hart.

When I buried my first womern, William Leachman, it was you Had the only consolation that I could listen to - Fer I knowed you had gone through it and had rallied from the blow
And when you said I'd do the same, I knowed you'd ort to know.

But that time I'll long remember; how I wundered here and thare-
Through the settin'-room and kitchen, and out in the open air-
And the snowflakes whirlin', whirlin', and the fields a frozen glare,
And the neghbors' sleds and wagons congergatin ev'rywhare.

I turned my eyes to'rds heaven, but the sun was hid away;
I turned my eyes to'rds earth again, but all was cold and gray;
And the clock, like ice a-crackin', clikt the icy hours in two -
And my eyes'd never thawed out
ef it hadn't been fer you!

We set thare by the smoke-house -
me and you out thare alone-
Me a-thinkin' - you a-talkin' in a
soothin' undertone -
You a-talkin' - me a-thinkin' of
the summers long ago,
And a-writin' "Marthy - Marthy"
with my finger in the snow!

William Leachman, I can see you
jest as plane as I could then; And
your hand is on my shoulder, and
you rouse me up again; And I see
the tears a-drippin' from your
own eyes, as you say:
"Be rickonciled and bear it - we but linger fer a day!"

A log home in Hancock County, Indiana similar in construction to the Riley birth-home in Greenfield, Indiana standing at the end of the Nineteenth Century. John A. Howland photography collection.

At the last Old Settlers' Meetin' we went j'intly, you and me -

Your hosses and my wagon, as you wanted it to be;
And sence I can remember, from the time we've neghbored here,
In all sich friendly actions you have double-done your sheer.

It was better than the meetin', too, that nine-mile talk we had
Of the times when we first settled here and travel was so bad;
When we had to go on hoss-back, and sometimes on "Shank's mare,"
And "blaze" a road fer them behind that had to travel thare.

And now we was a-trottin' 'long a level gravel pike
In a big two-hoss road-wagon, jest as easy as you like -
Two of us on the front seat, and our wimmern-folks behind,

A-settin' in theyr Winsor-cheers in perfect peace of mind!
And we pinted out old landmarks, nearly faded out of sight: -
Thare they ust to rob the stage-coach; thare Gash Morgan had the fight
With the old stag-deer that pronged him - how he battled fer his life,
And lived to prove the story by the handle of his knife.

Thare the first griss-mill was put up in the Settlement, and we
Had tuck our grindin' to it in the Fall of Forty-three -
When we tuck our rifles with us, techin' elbows all the way,
And a-stickin' right together ev'ry minute, night and day.
Thare ust to stand the tavern that they called the "Travelers' Rest,"
And thare, beyent the covered bridge, "The Counterfitters' Nest" -
Whare they claimed the house was ha'nted - that a man was murdered thare,
And burried underneath the floor, er 'round the place somewhare.

And the old Plank-road they laid along in Fifty-one er two -
You know we talked about the times when the old road was new:
How "Uncle Sam" put down that road and never taxed the State
Was a problem, don't you rickollect, we couldn't dimonstrate?

Ways was devius, William Leachman,
that me and you has past;
But as I found you true at first, I find you
true at last;
And, now the time's a-comin' mighty
nigh our jurney's end,
I want to throw wide open all my soul to
you, my friend.

With the stren'th of all my bein', and the
heat of hart and brane,
And ev'ry livin' drop of blood in artery
and vane,
I love you and respect you, and I vener-
ate your name,
Fer the name of William Leachman and
True Manhood's jest the same!

The statue of James Whitcomb Riley in front of the Hancock County Courthouse, Greenfield, Indiana paid for by contributions of pennies from America's school children. The bronze life-size statue sculpted by Myra Richards was unveiled Nov. 26, 1918. Unfortunately for the sculptress, Riley died before the statue was completed. She solved the problem by hiring the actor John Drew to pose for Riley. Technically, the statue is Riley from waist up and John Drew from the waist down. (From the Barton Rees Pogue glass positive collection.)

By the time of his death, James Whitcomb Riley's folk-lore and poetry had come to personally represent America's vision of itself in humility and redemption. How this could happen is not only strange but close to miracu-lous considering the temper-ance forces at work in America at the same time as Riley's years of great popular-ity. One would have thought they would have teamed up

A Riley parade entry for 1973. Annually Greenfield, Indiana holds a Riley Festival to honor Riley on the weekend of his October birth-day. This includes an event where school children bring flowers to place on the Riley statue on Friday and a parade on Saturday with many other events. It is the second largest community festival in Indiana ranking only behind the Indianapolis "500" Festival on Memorial Day weekend in Hoosier attendance.

against Riley because of his occasional very public bouts of intoxication. They never did. Riley's "affliction" (alcoholism) was forgiven him because the age needed to be reassured by the re-singing of the humble message of the "Christ Hymn."

By the time of Riley's death, he was highly revered with celebrations of his birthday all across America. His poetry was sung in America's voice. In describing the affect of Riley's death upon the nation, Meredith Nicholson, author and Editor of the Indianapolis NEWS from 1885 to 1897, wrote, "On a day in July, 1916, thirty-five thousand people passed under the dome of the Indiana capitol to look for the last time on the face of James Whitcomb Riley. The best-loved citizen of the Hoosier commonwealth was dead, and laborers and mechanics in their working clothes, professional and business men, women in great numbers, and a host of children paid their tribute of respect to one whose sold claim upon their interest lay in his power to voice their feelings of happiness and grief in terms within the common understanding. The very general expressions of sorrow and affection evoked by the announcement of the poet's death encourage the belief that the lines that formed on the capitol steps might have been augmented endlessly by additions drawn from every part of America."

The incredible path of Riley's life which led to this outcome is the story that follows.

How did the public perceive such a poet?

The answer seems that James Whitcomb Riley was taken mainly as a humorist and entertainer in his time.

"Riley" was fun. He dealt in the healing influence of laughter and humor. He was Riley at play as a mischievous comic, "dialect singer" and entertainer. This was the perception of Riley from his days on the lyceum circuit when his "lectures" to great public audiences all around the country were managed by the great James Redpath and his Boston Redpath Bureau and by the successor "manager" Major James B. Pond of New York and his agency. Being a popular lyceum speaker gave Riley huge access to the American public in the Post-Civil War era. This was, of course, an age before electronic media. Folk went out to public lecture halls for entertainment in those days instead of watching televisions in their homes.

A "popular" picture of James Whitcomb Riley comes to us from the promotional literature about him. Called "The Autobiography of James Whitcomb Riley," it was not really written by Riley at all but rather "in fun" by Edgar Wilson Nye, Riley's great platform partner during the 1880's. It is quoted here clothed in Nye's humor:

Ticket in the possession of The Riley Old Home Society, Greenfield, Indiana

AUTOBIOGRAPHY OF
JAMES WHITCOMB RILEY
Written by Himself
Through Edgar Wilson Nye.

The unhappy subject of this sketch was born so long ago that he persists in never referring to the date. Citizens of his native town of Greenfield, Ind., while warmly welcoming his advent, were no less anxious some few years ago to "speed the parting guest." It seems, in fact, that the better they came to know him, the more resigned they were to give him up. He was ill-starred from the very cradle, it appears. One day, while but a toddler, he climbed, unseen, to an open window where some potted flowers were arranged, and while leaning from his high chair far out, to catch some dainty, gilded butterfly, perchance, he lost his footing and, with a piercing shriek, fell headlong to the gravelled walk below; and when, an instant later, the affrighted parents picked him up, he was - a poet.

The father of young Riley was a lawyer of large practice, who used, in moments of deep thought, to regard this boy as the worst case he ever had. This may have been the reason that, in time, he insisted on his reading law, which the boy really tried to do; but, finding that political economy and Blackstone didn't rhyme, he slid out of the office one hot, sultry afternoon, and ran away with a patent

A Riley Advertisement with his own last name spelled out. (Neg.C7180, IMCPL-Riley Collection, Indiana Historical Society.)

medicine and concert wagon, from the tail end of which he was discovered by some relatives in the next town, violently abusing a brass drum. This was a proud moment for the boy; nor did his peculiar presence of mind entirely desert him till all the country fairs were over for the season. Them afar off, among strangers in a strange State, he thought it would be fine to make a flying visit home. But he couldn't fly. Fortunately, in former years he had purloined some knowledge of a trade. He could paint a sign, or a house, or a tin roof - if some one else would furnish him the paint - and one of Riley's hand-painted picket fences gave rapture to the most exacting eye. Yet, through all his stress and trial, he preserved a simple, joyous nature, together with an ever widening love of men and things in general. He made friends, and money, too - enough, at last, to gratify the highest ambition of his life, namely, to own an overcoat with fur around the tail of it. He then groped his way back home, and worked for nothing on a little country paper that did not long survive the blow. Again excusing himself, he took his sappy paragraphs and poetry to another paper and another town, and there did better till he spoiled it all by devising a Poe poem fraud, by which he lost his job; and, in disgrace and humiliation shoe-mouth deep, his feelings gave way beneath his feet, and his heart broke with a loud report. So, the true poet was born.

Of the poet's present personality we need speak but briefly. His dress is at once elegant and paid for. It is even less picturesque than all-wool. Not liking hair particularly, he wears but little, and that of the mildest shade. He is a good speaker - when spoken to - but a much better listener, and often longs to change places with his audience so that he also may retire. In his writings he probably shows at his best. He always tries to, anyway. Knowing the manifold faux pas and "breaks" in this life of ours, his songs are sympathetic and sincere. Speaking coyly of himself, one day he said: "I write from the heart; that's one thing I like about me. I may not write a good hand, and my `copy' may occasionally get mixed up with the market

Riley's final resting place at Crown Hill Cemetery, Indianapolis, the highest point of land in the Hoosier capitol. This is as close to a shrine of the Hoosier people as one will find in Indiana. (From the Barton Rees Pogue glass positive collection.)

reports, but, all the same, what challenges my admiration is that humane peculiarity of mine - i.e., writing from the heart - and, therefore, to the heart."

More about this side of Riley "the humorist" and the public perception of the man will follow, but I take the biographer's prerogative of focusing on what I find the most revealing about James Whitcomb Riley first.

A "TWINTORETTE"
IN THE MORNING PAPER

To know about this enigmatic figure of the American frontier, humor and Incarnation Theology ("kenoticism"), it would have helped to open up a Hoosier newspaper, The Indianapolis Saturday HERALD," on August 24, 1878. The citizens of Indiana found one of the strangest writings in all of literature on its page 6.

What was it?

The piece called itself a "Twintorette." What was that?

It was embedded in a column calling itself: "Respectfully Declined" Papers of The Buzz Club, number IV. What was

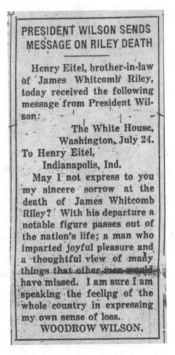

PRESIDENT WILSON SENDS MESSAGE ON RILEY DEATH

Henry Eitel, brother-in-law of James Whitcomb Riley, today received the following message from President Wilson:

The White House,
Washington, July 24.
To Henry Eitel,
Indianapolis, Ind.
May I not express to you my sincere sorrow at the death of James Whitcomb Riley? With his departure a notable figure passes out of the nation's life; a man who imparted joyful pleasure and a thoughtful view of many things that other men would have missed. I am sure I am speaking the feeling of the whole country in expressing my own sense of loss.
WOODROW WILSON.

Indianapolis (IN) NEWS, July 24, 1916

the Buzz Club? Who wrote it? The piece had a cast as a play does. Was it a play?

Time revealed that the author of "The Flying Islands of the Night" was the young Hoosier poet, James Whitcomb Riley, very early in his career and long before fame settled upon him. In this "flight" lies the answer to Riley's poetry of love, joy, peace, patience, kindness, goodness, faithfulness, gentleness, and self-control, the kenotic categories of expression of the spirit of the "Christ Hymn."

Footnotes:

1. The whole "Christ Hymn" is as follows:

"Let this mind be in you, which was also in Christ Jesus: Who, being in the form of God, thought it not robbery to be equal with God: But made himself of no reputation, and took upon him the form of a servant, and was made in the likeness of men: And being found in fashion as a man, he humbled himself, and became obedient unto death, even the death of the cross. Wherefore God also hath highly exalted him, and give him a name which is above every name: That at the name of Jesus every knee should bow..."

2. The first Incarnation theologians of the Nineteenth Century were the Germans: Thomasius, its founder, Neander, Dorner, Van Oosterzee, Pressense, Schneckenburger, Liddon, Uhlhorn, Edersheim, soon joined by such as J.P. Lange, and C.A. Ross. A primary text of the German inception is found in the Nineteenth Century lectures of Alexander Bruce, D.D, in THE HUMILIATION OF CHRIST and R.J. Cooke's THE INCARNATION AND RECENT CRITICISM. A more recent work (1965) is Claude Welch, GOD AND INCARNATION IN MID-NINETEENTH CENTURY GERMAN THOUGHT. An easy-to-read introduction to the subject is found in the OXFORD DICTIONARY OF THE CHRISTIAN CHURCH, ed. by F.L. Cross under "Kenotic theories." Interesting variations of Incarnation Theology appeared concurrently in Germany such as Hegel's conception that the Incarnation was manifest in the human race in general and not in individuals. Even at the theological level, Incarnation Theology engaged the age's social Darwinism. SEE: Herbert Spencer's SYNTHETIC PHILOSOPHY, "First Principles," part 1, in which God is seen as an unknown and unknowable substratum of all phenomena rather than one known through human appearance. These should get started someone interested in Nineteenth Century theology such as became expressed popularly by James Whitcomb Riley's poetry. None of course explains the phenomenon of the Incarnation because, as theologian Edward Towne says, "What is a mystery if it can be dissolved away in an explanation?"

3. "Kenoticism" is a more technical name for Incarnation Theology of the Nineteenth Century. It is an idea of "emptying out oneself." It derives from the Greek adjective "kenos" - the adjective used in the Philippian's "Christ Hymn" to describe Jesus's act of casting off pride, advantage and power to find satisfaction in a humble life.

James Whitcomb Riley

Nellie Millikan Cooley

The two-person cast of The Flying Islands Of The Night

Riley as Krung

Riley as Amphine

Riley as Crestillomeem

Riley as Jucklet

Riley as Spraivoll

Nellie as Dwainie

THE FLYING ISLANDS
OF THE NIGHT

Oil painting on canvas of Riley (1903) by John Singer Sargent
(American, 1856-1925). Sargent waived his usual commission of
Five Thousand Dollars to have the opportunity to paint this foun-
dation piece of the collection of the Indianapolis Museum of Art.
Copyright Indianapolis Museum of Art, Painted on Commission
from the Art Association of Indianapolis.

INTRODUCTION TO:
THE FLYING ISLANDS OF THE NIGHT

Marcus Dickey, the secretary of James Whitcomb Riley once wrote, "It was not the habit of the Hoosier Poet to explain. Again and again his friends saw him as through a glass darkly. At times he took conspicuous pride in concealing his thought and his way of doing things. My assumptions concerning him remained assumptions. The more his friends sought to know his history the more capriciously he concealed it."

In the cryptic poem that follows Riley revealed his own life in the form of an autobiography with himself in his various "soul-selves" as the cast except for the woman who was his great encourager and "soul partner."

Riley at the time of writing "The Flying Islands of the Night." A photograph from a tintype of Riley enclosed in a letter of October 10, 1879 to Elizabeth Kahle. Note how the mustache gives Riley the appearance of wearing a huge "frown." For this reason I think of it as Riley unhapy with himself for being under the influence of "Crestillomeem."

JAMES WHITCOMB RILEY:
THE POET AS FLYING ISLANDS OF THE NIGHT:

A BRIEF INTRODUCTION TO
RILEY'S AUTOBIOGRAPHICAL POEM

It is a simple fact that James Whitcomb Riley tended to write out of his own experiences. There is not a single poem where Riley's fantasies are not based on some projection out of his life. Riley's prodigious imagination used himself always to create his poetry.

If this is so, where does Riley's "The Flying Islands of the Night" fit in? It is certainly obscure at places. It stands out so in the body of his poetry like a sore thumb because of its length as well as its oddity.

The only answer appears to be that Riley made it obscure for a reason. It was the most "personal" poem he ever wrote. The poem describes the groping of his own soul. It is the last rush of the madness from his impetuous youth. Then, Riley sheltered his soul from criticism by obscuring his poetic expression of it.

Riley's autobiographical poem (from age 28-but revised at intervals) originally contained two great themes and a minor one. The most important was Riley's "dark play" on his own dire alcoholism. The language is a combination of Middle English spiced with American folklore, and "intoxicatese" creating a fantastic and wildly "astronomically" extravagant imagery. The origins of all of this will be explained later.

For now we need only remember Riley's fear of his alcoholism as its most basic theme.

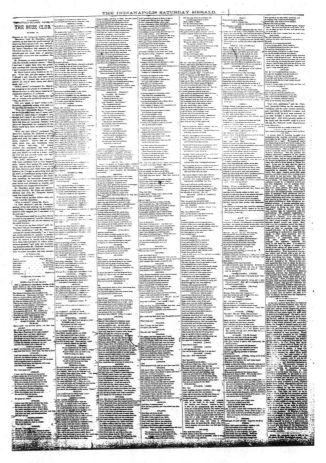

The single page in the Indianapolis Saturday HERALD newspaper on which Riley's poem The Flying Islands of the Night originally appeared on August 24, 1878.

Riley portrays himself "married" to alcoholism personified as the "nasty" Queen Crestillomeem. Riley is first introduced as his minstrel self called Jucklet. This is Riley's "survival self" at the soul level. Jucklet has to live "underground" and he can only "peep out" when Crestillomeem permits.

Riley lived by his wits and was often penniless during the period of his "minstrel wandering" twenties. He had begun consoling himself from tragic events in his life with overuse of alcohol. This poem tells us of the outcome of all of this. You will be very surprised.

In "The Flying Islands of the Night" Riley must experience the effects of alcoholism. The "night" in the title is a reference to alcohol addiction. Riley's contemporary of the related book FIFTEEN YEARS IN HELL, Luther Benson, says: "...From time to time until I tried to break the terrible chain...of intemperance, my life was one long, hopeless, blank, black night." Riley's alcoholism was his night too. He feared himself sinking into a "night" of depression, delirium and madness.

The second great theme is Riley's groping for salvation from his alcoholism. As his mind turns to recollections of loving encouragement and true friendship he has known, he remembers Nellie Millikan Cooley, a married friend, who has just died in Illinois critical

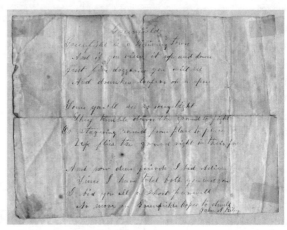

A comical poem entitled "Greenfield" by John A. Riley, the poet's brother. ("Greenfield is a thriving town/And if you view it up and down/Just five dozzens you will see/And drunken loafers on a spree./Some you'll see so very tight/They tumble down the ground to fight/On staggering round from place to place/Up flies the ground right in their face/And now dear friends I bid adieu/Since I have told both you and zois/I bid you all a short farewell/No more on Greenfield hopes to dwell.") (Courtesy of The Riley Old Home Society, Greenfield, Indiana.)

days before the poem was written. Nellie is the only other character in the original play which is not a Riley "personified personality breakdown." Nellie is "Dwainie" who tells the fearfully drunken Riley she will continue to encourage him and love him even though she is now dead.

How can this be? Another surprise is in store!

The version of "The Flying Islands of the Night" which follows was the original one. In a later expansion of the original play for a book, Riley adds his mother, Elizabeth as "AEo" as an encourager along with Nellie. Dwainie will eventually convince Riley in the poem that she is still encouraging him in spirit and this gives Riley the strength to produce the Godly poetry of "Spraivoll," the "tune fool" of Riley's cast of self-characters.

A minor comical but tragic theme is the "Murphy" pledge that temperance ladies were requiring young men to sign at the time the play was written. This pledge committed a person not to drink intoxicants. Riley had recently seen how futile such a pledge was and enjoyed harpooning it. His brother, Hum (Reuben Alexander Humboldt Riley), took one as revealed in this letter to brother John Riley, in 1877: "... within the last few days, on the evening of the 4th of July, I commenced a work that will in time make me more money than any other work I could engage in. I think it is the most honorable work a young man can engage in. I celebrated the 4th in a better way than I ever did before. On that morning I signed the Murphy Pledge and have been at work ever since in that great cause and hope before a great while to bring a great many more into the ranks and try and bring the cause to a great and glorious end. We have already taken in some of the boys such as Jim Walsh, John Huley, John Skinner and his father and many others too (sic) numerous to mention. When I went up to take the pledge Father Wilson kissed me and told me to stick to it. I told him I would try..."

Hum couldn't make it. Disastrous drinking soon followed. The Murphy pledge was a joke. Signing a pledge proved not a real commitment to anything. Hum became an alcoholic so severely that often he would disappear without word requiring his family to try to locate him wherever they could find him. In this same year Riley was dealing with his own alcoholism. He saw what alcoholism was doing to his brother Hum. A letter contemporaneous to Riley's "The Flying Islands of the Night," reads:

Friend "Meeks" —

Hum left on noon train to-day and as he was "full", and none of us knew where he started for, we are all greatly distressed. He went east, and it has occurred to me that possibly he had gone to see you — thence this letter of inquiry. And now, dear Jim tell me if he is with you, and if so I charge you, with all earnestness, do what you can to keep him from whisky - for he is killing himself and breaking all our hearts at home. He is good, and wouldn't act as he does could he realize what he is doing — and I trust and believe that you will do all in your power to turn him from it. I tried to see him before he went, and was at the depot, but he slipped me somehow. I wanted to tell him that if he got hard up to write to me for money — I will raise it if he needs it, and if you see him you must tell him so for me. If he is not with you try to find him along the line by telegraphing, and I will compensate you for your trouble. It may be that he has not gone far, but let me know at once if you know anything of him.

Very truly yours
J.W. Riley.

Hum's fitful life continued. We know he was in Indianapolis in Feb., 1881, and wrote sister Mary to send him "his things" by express train in a telegram of Feb. 25th. Hum died November 24, 1881 at 5 a.m. at age 25 from severe hemorrhage of the bowels according to the Riley family Bible at the Riley Birthplace in Greenfield, Indiana. Someone noted underneath the entry "typhoid fever," but the suspicion is a complication of alcoholism. Hum's funeral was apparently on the Friday following. Hum isn't mentioned thereafter in family correspondence.

Crestillomeem got his younger brother and now the alluring siren was after James Whitcomb Riley!

The version of "The Flying Islands of the Night" which follows is the first one published. The poem seems an excellent point of departure for a biography of the poet's life. I apologize if "The Flying Islands of the Night"

Hum Riley, the poet's brother, in a last photograph, dying at 25. The Riley Family Bible lists him with four names as Reuben Alexander Humboldt Riley.

is sometimes hard to follow. Riley wrote it that way to cause it to be mysterious and secretive to protect his very fragile ego. Just remember that Riley was all the characters in the cast that follows except "Dwainie."

Only a creative genius might conceive of himself in such an odd but imaginative way. This was James Whitcomb Riley.

His poem continues into Three Acts which we will examine in greater detail as an aid in unraveling the knot of his life - a chapter per character at a time.

Perhaps we should allow Riley to introduce his own autobiography as he did at his "Buzz Club" newspaper article - through Mr. Clickwad - one of the fictional members-who says of the piece: "This is an affliction," continued Mr. Clickwad, unrolling an enormous manuscript, "too great for me to bear alone, and I ask your succor and assistance as humbly and earnestly as ever beggar asked for alms."

ACT I
THE FLYING ISLANDS
OF THE NIGHT

THE FLYING ISLANDS OF THE NIGHT.
A Twintorette.

Dramatis Personae[1]

KRUNG...King of the Spirks
CRESTILLOMEEM................................The Queen
SPRAIVOLL......................................The Tune Fool
AMPHINE...Son of Krung
DWAINIE..Of the Wunks[2]
JUCKLET..Dwarf
CREECH..Nightmares
GRITCHFANG................Counselors, Courtiers, Etc.

1. The names of the characters have loosely evocative associative qualities. Krung is Riley's triumphant public reputation- or his hopes about it, a sober and rational personality in respon-

Rumor's Flutter

sibility, success and empowerment. It is Riley as Cronus (or "Kronus"), the Titan, and "King." Spraivoll is the poetic "tune-fool" Riley. It is Riley the "Christ hymn" poet. The aspect of poetry has the feminine gender, as Calliope, the muse of poetry was feminine. Amphine evokes Riley as a lover like Amphion, son of Zeus and Antiope, who, in Greek legend, built Thebes by music of lute which he played so melodiously that the stones danced into walls and houses. Riley played the guitar and violin for romantic purposes. Dwainie is his inspirational friend, recently deceased at the time of the first writing of "The Flying Islands," Nellie Millikan Cooley, wife of George B. Cooley. "Dwainie" suggests the Old English word "Dwine" meaning waste away. Nellie was recently dead when "The Flying Islands" was first written in August 1878. Riley shared the author Thomas Chatterton's fascination with old English sounding names. Chatterton's writings were major inspiration for this poem. "Jucklet", the dwarf, is Riley as self-admitted prankster but also Riley's survival self since Riley can only survive by his wits. The name evokes juggler from the Latin joculator, a jester, or joker in the Middle Ages. Jugglers of those days accompanied minstrels and troubadours and added entertainments to musical performances, e.g. sleight of hand, antics, feats of musing prowess and a staple of tricks. The form is in the diminutive just as Riley was small. The nightmares suggest interior aspects of creed for Creetch and dreads of novel encounters or depressive events where Riley is "greenhorn" and engaged or bitten as by fangs as Gritchfang. That the names are not entirely imaginative, but rather referential and elliptical is supported by some evidence. The poet in his 1898 edition of "The Flying Islands" added a footnote to additions to

Chorus of Swarming Faces

"Spirk and Wunk Rhymes," saying, "So, too, in numberless other aspects, must the reader's fancy freely-play- even as the writer frankly confesses his own has done,- in such particulars, for instances, as fancying the "ont-l-dawn-bird" of the Flying Islanders is our nightingale; their "trance-bird" our humming-bird; their "echo-bird" our mocking-bird, etc., etc., ad infinitum."

2. A wunk is a Hoosier folklore figure. It is not what it appears to be. It is like a ghost that can take on outward appearance at night of anything or any-one it wishes to.

ACT I

SCENE - THE FLYING ISLANDS Scene I. - Spirkland at Moondawn - Interior of the King's Court - A star burns dimly in the dome above the throne- Enter Crestillomeem.

CRESTILLOMEEM.

The throne is throwing wide its gilded arms
To welcome me. The throne of Krung! Ha! ha!
Leap up, ye lazy echoes, and laugh loud!
For I, Crestillomeem, the queen - ha! ha!
Do fling my richest mirth into your mouths
That ye may fatten ripe with mockery!
I wonder what the kingdom would become
Were I not here to nurse it like a babe,
And dandle[1] it beyond the silly reach
Of sycophants and serfs. Ho! Jucklet, ho!
`Tis time my twisted warp of nice anatomy
Were here to weave away upon our web -
Of silken villainies. Ho! Jucklet, ho!

1."Dandle" is something like dangle and handle mixed up.

(Lifts a secret door to the pave, and drops a star-bud through the opening. Enter Jucklet.)

JUCKLET.

Spang sprit[1]! my gracious queen, but thou hast
*   scorched*
My left ear to a cinder, and my head
Rings like a ding-dong on the coast of death!
For, patient hate! thy hasty signal burst

Full in my face as thitherward I came;
But though my lug[2] is fried to a crisp, and my
Singed wig stinks like a little sun-stewed wunk,
I stretch my fragrant presence at thy feet,
And kiss thy sandal with a blistered lip.

1. "Sprit" is Chatterton's representation of the verb for "gives spirit" at "AElla," 2.1332. Chatterton, living in the century prior to Riley, wrote poetry which he fraudulently claimed was written by a monk named Rowley of the 15th Century. Chatterton sold these forgeries for income. The poetry was actually rather good and came to be much admired by Riley. There was no such monk as Rowley, of course, and Chatterton killed himself with arsenic at the age of 17 when his deception was discovered.
2. The external ear in this use.

CRESTILLOMEEM.

Hold! rare-done fool, lest I may call the cook
And bake thee brown! How fares the king by this?
JUCKLET.

I left him sleeping[1], but uncorked his nose,
And o'er the odorous blossom of his lips[2]
I squeezed the tinctured sponge, and felt his pulse
Come staggering back to regularity.
And four hours hence his highness will awake
and Peace will take a nap.

1. The setting is Riley sleeping off intoxication which becomes subject to delirium in Act II, with recovery in Act III.
2. "Liquor breath."

CRESTILLOMEEM.

Ha! what mean you?
JUCKLET.

I mean that he suspects our knaveries.
Some traitor spy is burrowed in the court
Whose unseen eye is ever focused fine
Upon our actions, and whose hungry ear
Eats every crumb of counsel that we drop
In these our secret interviews -for he -
The king - thro' all his talking-sleep to-day
Has jabbered of intrigue, conspiracy,
And treachery and hate in fellowship,
With dire designs upon his royal self,
To oust him from the throne.
CRESTILLOMEEM.

He spoke my name?
          JUCKLET.
I never hear him speak but that thy name
Makes melody of every sentence. Yes, -
He thinks thou art as true to him as thou
Art fickle, false and subtle! O how blind,
and lame and deaf and dumb, and worn and weak,
And faint and sick, and all-commodious
His dear love[1] is!

1. Riley's love of alcohol.

          CRESTILLOMEEM.

Wilt thou wind up thy tongue
Nor let it tangle in a knot of words!
What said the king?
          JUCKLET.
He said: "Crestillomeem -
O that she knew this great distress of mine!
For she would counsel with me, and her voice
Would flow in limpid wisdom o'er my wounds,
And, like an ointment, lave my hidden grief,
And heal my bleeding heart;" and so went on
Spinning the web of love in which he lies
Bound hand and foot and buzzing helplessly.
          CRESTILLOMEEM.
And did he drop no hint of his distress,
And how, and when, and whence his trouble came?
          JUCKLET.
He spoke as the tho' some woman talked with him -
Full courteously he said: "In woman's guise
Thou comest, yet I think thou art indeed
But woman in thy form; they words are strange,
And I am mystified! I feel the truth
Of all thou hast declared, and yet so vague

And shadow-like thy meaning is to me,
I know not how to act to ward the blow
Thou say'st is a hanging o'er me even now."
And then, with open hands held pleadingly,
He asked, "Who is my foe?" and o'er his face

A sudden pallor flashed like death itself,
As tho' if answer had been given it
Had fallen like a curse.

CRESTILLOMEEM.

I'll stake my soul
`Tis Dwainie[1], of the Wunks, who peeks and peers
With those fine eyes of hers in our affairs,
And carries Krung, in some disguise, these hints
Of our intent! See thou that silence falls
Forever on her lips, and that the sight
She wastes upon our secret action blurs
With gray and grisly skum that shall for aye
Conceal us from her gaze while she writhes blind
And fangless as the fat worms of the grave.
Here, take this tuft of downy druze, and when
Thou comest on her, fronting full and fair,
Say "Sherzham!" thrice, and fluff it in her face.

1. Nellie Millikan Cooley, Riley's beloved married friend, who died shortly before the publication of this piece.

JUCKLET.

Thou knowest little magic, O, my queen,
But all thou dost is very excellent.
And now for Amphine - he, too, doubtless, has
Been favored with an outline of our scheme.
And I would kick my soul all over hell
If I might juggle his fine figure up
In such a shape as mine.

CRESTILLOMEEM.

Then this: if thou
Canst ever find him bent above a flower,
Or any blooming thing, and thou canst slip
Behind and reach it first and touch it fair,
And with thy knuckle strike him on the breast,
Then his fine form will shrink and shrivel up
As warty as a toad's - so hideous
Thine own will seem a marvel of rare grace,
Tho' idly speakest them of mystic skill
`Twas that which won the king for me - `twas that

Bereft him of his daughter[1] ere we had
Been wedded for a month; she strangely went
Astray one morning from the palace steps;
And when the dainty vagrant came not back
And all the spies in Spirkland in her quest
Came straggling empty-handed home again
Why, then the wise king wiped his rainy eyes
And sagely tho't the little toddler strayed
Out to the island's edge and tumbled off.
I could have set his mind at ease on that;
I could have told him when she tumble off.
I tumbled her, and tumbled her so far
She tumbled in another land, from which
But one charm known to art can tumble her
Back into this.

1. Spraivoll, Riley's poetic self, in this delirium tremens attack from alcoholic binge.

JUCKLET.

Ay, true enough, perhaps!
But dost thou know that rumors float about
Among thy subjects of thy sorceries?
And if my counsel is worth aught to thee,
Then have a care thy charms do not revert
Upon thyself!

CRESTILLOMEEM.

Ha! ha! no fear of that
While Krung remains -
(She pauses abruptly, and a voice of exquisite
melody is heard singing.)

VOICE.

When kings are kings, and kings are men -
And the lonesome rain[1] is raining -
O who shall rule from the red[2] throne then,
And who shall wield the scepter when -
When the winds[3] are all complaining?

When men are men, and men are kings -
And the lonesome rain is raining -
O who shall list as the minstrel sings

Of the ermine robes and the signet rings
when the winds are all complaining?

1. Rain most often refers to God's judgment on sinners in frontier American poetry. Such imagery often derives from scripture in this case possibly Ez. 38.22.

2. Red is the color of sin in frontier American Protestant folklore. This probably derives from Isaiah 1.18. The sin in this use would be the overuse of alcohol.

3. The wind is often a depiction of the operation of the Holy Spirit within the world in the same folklore tradition. John 3.8. In light of the imagery of Spraivoll's initial poem, we would suspect the answer to the poem's question is no one.

CRESTILLOMEEM.
Whence flows that sweetness, and
whose voice is that?
JUCKLET.
The voice of Spraivoll if mine ears
are tuned.
CRESTILLOMEEM.
And who is Spraivoll, and what song is that she
sings?
JUCKLET.
Spraivoll, the Tune Fool is she called
By those who meet her in her nightly rounds.[1]
She comes from Wunkland, as she so declares,
And has been roosting round the palace here
For half a moon.

1. Riley only wrote poetry at night.

CRESTILLOMEEM.
And pray, where is she perched?
JUCKLET
Under some dingy cornice[1], like enough.
She is no woman, tho' - and yet, indeed
She is licensed idiot, and drifts
About as restless, and as useless, too,
As any lazy breeze in summertime.

I'll call her forth to greet your majesty -
Ho! Spraivoll! Ho! my plumeless bird, flit here!

1. Riley was writing most of his poetry at this time in a place he called the "Morgue," an upstairs space in row office buildings in downtown Greenfield, Indiana.

(From behind a group of statuary Spraivoll enters.)

SPRAIVOLL. (Singing[1])

Ting-along aling-ting! Tingle-tee! Ting-aling,
aling-ting! Tingle-tee!
The world runs round and round for me;
Wind it up with a golden key
Ting-aling, aling-ting! Tingle-tee!

1. Spraivoll's songs contain ellided and unintelligible words because, we remember, Riley cannot write poetry while he is intoxicated as he is in Acts I and II. Spraivoll does much better in Act III when she is "herself" or rather Riley "himself."

JUCKLET.

Who art thou, woman, and what singest thou?

SPRAIVOLL. (Singing.)

What sings the breene[1] on the wertling-vine[2],
And the tweck[3] on the bamner-stem[4]?
The song they sing is the same as mine,
And mine is the same to them.

1. Probably a brown wren. Under Chatterton's "Rowley" technicalities, any word that can take a terminal "e" does so. Riley's poem has elements of Chatterton "takeoff."

2. Wert, wyrt, wairt, wurt, wort (as in liverwort) refers to a herb in Middle English. A "wertling-vine" is possibly a herb-vine.

3. Probably suggestive of a "twaddling" (or silly) "peck" or "woodpecker" although the "tw" might refer to the Middle English twecche (twitch).

4. A "bamner-stem" is possibly a "runner bamboo stem" or some such.

JUCKLET.

Your majesty may be surprised somewhat,
But Spraivoll cannot talk; her only mode
Of speech is melody; and thou might'st put
The gifted fool a-thousand questions, and
In full return, receive a thousand songs,
Each set to different tunes - as full of naught
As space is full of emptiness.

CRESTILLOMEEM.

A fool?
A fool, and with a voice so strangely sweet?
A fool?

JUCKLET.
Ay, warranted! Around the world
She walks unrivalled, and a queen of fools -
Eh, Spraivoll?
SPRAIVOLL. (Singing.)
O, Aye! Tho' Spirkland has grown great
    In foolish ways, I ween
Her greatest fool will intimate,
    He bows to me as queen.

CRESTILLOMEEM.
So! my Jucklet finds his peer!
Come hither woman, and be not afraid,
For I like fools so well I married one.
And since thou art a queen of fools, and he
A king, why I've a mind to bring you two
Together in some way. Canst use thy tongue
in such a wise thy hearer can but list?

SPRAIVOLL. (Singing.)
If one should ask me for a song
    And I should answer, then my tongue
Would twitter, trill and troll along
    Until the song was done.

Or should one ask me for my tongue,
    And I should answer with a song,
I'd trill it till the song was sung
    And troll it all along.

CRESTILLOMEEM.
Thou art indeed a fool, and one I
    think
To serve my purpose well. Give
    ear to me!
And Jucklet, thou go to the
    king and wait
His waking; then repeat
    these words: "The queen
Impatiently awaits his majesty,
    And craves his presence in the

Tower of Stars,[1]

> That she may there express all tenderly
> Her great solicitude and" - there, say this:
> "So much she bade, and drooped her glowing face
> Deep in the shadows of her unbound hair,
> And with a flashing gesture of her arm
> Turned all the moonlight pallid, saying, "Haste!"

1. A "tower of stars" is the prison of his hopes for success. In Riley's personal symbolism, a tower is a place of bondage where one is made a prisoner. SEE: Contemporaneous Riley letter to the Cooleys and his beloved married friend, Nellie Cooley, dated October 28, 1877 "...take me your prisoner and `fasten me down forever in the round tower of your heart; and I'll never murmur for release till heaven dawns thro the gates." In Riley imagery, stars have to do with success. In a letter to his brother John of Nov. 16, 1874, Riley states, "In those dark hours (of drifting while a sign painter), I should have been content with the twinkle of the tiniest star."

JUCKLET.

> And would it not be well to hang a pearl
> Or two upon thy silken lashes?

CRESTILLOMEEM.

> Go! (Jucklet disappears.)
> Now fool, I'll furnish thee a topic for
> A song: A woman once, with angel in
> Her face and devil in her heart, had cause
> To breed confusion to her sovereign lord,
> And work the downfall of his haughty son -
> The issue of a former marriage, who
> Inspired her hatred from the very first;
> Thro' her the king is haunted with a dream
> That he is soon to die, and so prepares
> The throne for the ascension of the son.
> The woman now has won the husband's love,
> And by her craft and wanton flatteries
> Sways him to every purpose but the one
> Most coveted. And so, to serve that end
> She would make use of thee, and if thou dost
> Her will as her good pleasure shall direct.
> Why, thou shalt sing at court, and thy sweet voice
> Shall woo the echoes of the listening throne.
> At present does the king lie in a sleep
> Drug-wrought and deep as death - the after-phase

Of an unconscious state in which each act
Of his throughout his waking hours is so
Rehearsed in manner, motion, deed and word
Her spies may tell her of his very tho't,
And should he come upon the throne to-night
Where his wise counselors sit waiting him,
Then has she cause to think her purposes
Will fall in jeopardy; but if he fail,
Thro' any means, to lend his presence there,
Then, by a former mandate, is his queen
Empowered with all sovereignty to reign
And work the royal purposes instead.
Therefore the queen has set an interview
With him that will occur at noon to-night -
One hour ere the time the throne convenes -
And with her thou shalt go, and lie in wait
Until she signal thee to sing, and then
Shalt thou so work upon his mellow mood With that
unearthly magic of thy voice -
So dazzle all his serious tho't with dreams -
The queen may, all unnoticed, slip away,
And leave thee singing to a throneless king.

    SPRAIVOLL. (Singing.)
And who shall sing for the haughty son
   While the good king droops his head?
And will he dream when the song is done
   That a princess fair lies dead?[1]

1. If he is drunk, can he forget about his dead friend, Dwainie (Nellie) recently deceased?

    CRESTILLOMEEM.
The haughty son has found his "song"
   sweet curse
And may she sing his everlasting dirge!
She comes from that near-floating
   land of thine,
And with her fairer skin and finer ways,
Has caught the prince between her
   mellow palms And
stroked him flutterless. Didst ever hear

Of Dwainie, of the Wunks?
   SPRAIVOLL. (Singing.)[1]
Ay, "Dwainie! My Dwainie!"
  The lurloo[2] ever sings,
  A tremor in his flossy crest
  And in his glossy wings,
And "Dwainie! My Dwainie"
  The winnow welvers call,
But Dwainie hides in Spirkland
  And answers not at all.

The teeper[3] twitters "Dwainie!"
  The tcheucker[4] on his spray
Teeters up and down the wind
  And will not fly away;
And "Dwainie! My Dwainie:"
  The drowsy oovers[5] drawl;
But Dwainie hides in Spirkland
  And answers not at all.

O Dwainie! my Dwainie,!
  The breezes hold their breath;
The stars are pale as blossoms,
  And the night as still as death;
And "Dwainie! My Dwainie!"
  The fainting echoes fall;
But Dwainie hides in Spirkland
  And answers not at all.

1. A poem of Riley's anguish over his separation from his great soul-mate, Nellie Cooley, so recently deceased. Spraivoll, Riley's poetic self, cannot reach Nellie; only Amphine, Riley's manifestation of love, can as we will soon discover.
2. Dwainie (Nellie Cooley) is evoked to Riley by an alluring but hidden spirit. "Lurloo" is a name in intoxicated onomatopoeia through formation of allegorical qualities rather than from animal sounds. The name probably derives from the archaic form "lure" in the sense of an enticement or allure and the loo which suggests a masking of an appearance as in the loo or mask a woman wore to avoid tanning her complexion. The fantastic bird creatures of "Dwainie" are spirits, a common Riley catachresis extending the obvious "bird" word into a proper poetic, as in "Song of the Rain."
3. Something which "tees" draws, tugs, pulls. Such a spirit twitters about Dwainie. Possibly

a tree-toad which is said to "twitter" in Riley's poem "A Treat Ode" of roughly contemporaneous time. ("Scurious-like!" said the tree-toad, - \"I've twittered for rain all day...")
4. A tcheucker has the intoxicatese onomatopoeic ring of a squirrel's call.
5. oover suggests a compaction of "owl hooting overhead" giving its "hooooooooot."

CRESTILLOMEEM.

A melody ecstatic, and thy words
Altho' so meaningless, seem something more -
A vague and shadowy something, eerie-like,
That makes me catch my breath all tremulous,
But save thy music! Come, that I may make
Thee ready for thy royal auditor. (Exeunt).

ACT II

ACT II

Scene 2. - A garden of Krung's palace, screened from the moon and lighted with star flakes. An arbor, near which is a table spread with a repast. A fountain, near which Amphine sits thrumming a trentoraine.[1]

1. "Thrumming" is like strumming with his thumb. Trentoraine, is probably something like a "trembling instrument sounding like rain" or some such, most likely Riley's guitar with which he entertained Nellie on many evenings in his early twenties.

AMPHINE.

O warbling strand of silver, where, oh where
Hast thou unraveled that sweet voice of thine,
And left its silken murmurs quavering
In spasms of delight? O golden wire,
Where hast thou spilled thy precious twinkerings
What thirsty ear ear has drained thy melody
And left me but a wild, delirious drop
To tincture all my soul with vain desire?
O, Trentoraine, how like an empty vase
Thou art - whose clustering blooms of song have drooped

And faded, one by one, and fallen away
And left to me but dry and tuneless stems,
And crisp and withered tendrils of a voice
Whose thrilling tone, now like a throttled sound
Lies stifled, faint, and gasping all in vain
For utterance. (Enter Dwainie[1], unperceived)
O empty husk of song,
If deep within my heart the music thou
Hast stored away might find an opening,
A fount of limpid laughter would leap up
And gurgle from my lips, and all the winds
Would revel round me riotous with joy;
And Dwainie in her beauty would lean o'er
The battlements of night, and like the moon,
The glory of her face would light the world,
For I would sing of love,

1. Riley's beloved - and dead - Nellie appears in spirit. Riley elsewhere calls her his "truest friend on earth, or now in heaven" in a letter to Nellie's daughter, Mrs. Emma Cox, on April 10, 1885. He adds, "God bless us always with the sweetness of her memory!"

DWAINIE. (Concealed.) *And she would hear,*

And reaching overhead among the stars
Would scatter them like daisies at thy feet.

AMPHINE.

O voice, where art thou floating on the air?
O angel-soul, where art thou hovering?

DWAINIE.

I hover in the zephyr of thy sighs,
And tremble lest thy love for me shall fail
To buoy me thus forever on the breath
Of such a dream as heaven envies.

AMPHINE

Then
Thou lovest! O my angel, flutter down
And nestle to the warm home of my breast
So empty are my arms, so full my heart
The one must hold thee or the other burst.

DWAINIE.

(Throwing herself in his embrace.)
I think the hand of God has flung me here;
O hold me that he may not pluck me back.

AMPHINE.

So closely will I hold thee that not e'en
The hand of death shall separate us.

DWAINIE.

So,
May sweet death find us, then, that, woven thus
In the corolla of a ripe caress,
We may drop light, like twin plustre-buds[1],
On Heaven's star-strewn lawn.

1. Buds which are purely lustrous.

AMPHINE.

So do I pray,
But tell me, tender heart, as thou dost love,
Where hast thou loitered for so long?
For I have ordered merl[1] and viands to be brought
For our refreshment here, where all alone
I might sip with thee words as well as wine. Why
hast thou kept me so athirst, for I

Am jealous of the very solitude
In which thou walkest. (They sit at table.)

1. Merl is an alcoholic beverage, probably wine, and named after a fictional character of
Riley poetry. SEE: Riley's poem of 1879, "To the Wine-God Merlus" (the "God" of "drink"
who "blowest all my cares.")

DWAINIE

Nay, I will not tell,

Since, if I did a thousand questions more
Would vex our interview with idle tho't
And speculation vain. Let this suffice -
I talked with one who knew me long ago
In dreamy Wunkland,[1] *talked of mellow nights And*
long, long hours of golden olden times
When love lay like a baby in my arms.
And life was like a tinkling toy. We talked
Of all the past, ah, me, and all the friends
That now await my coming and we talked
Of many, many things, so many things
That I forget them all in dreams of when,
With thy warm hand clasped close in this of mine
We walk the floating bridge that spans the gulf
Between this isle of strife and gloom, and doubt,
And my most glorious realm of joy and peace,
Where summer-night reigns ever, and the moon
Hangs ever ripe and lush with radiance
Above a land were roses gloat on wings
And fan their fragrance out so lavishly
The winds dive out of heaven to bathe in it.

1. Earthly life. In Hoosier folklore, Wunkland persons are those who have been "wunks" on
earth, personalities or selves or souls within shapes and sizes of humanity for homes.

AMPHINE

O empress of my listening soul, talk on,
And tell me all of that rare land of thine,
For even tho' I reigned a peerless king
Within mine own, I think I could fling down
My scepter, signet, crown and royal robes,
And so walk naked down the path of life,
If at the dwindling end my feet might touch

Upon the shores of such a land as thou
Dost paint for me. O tell me more of it,
And tell me if thy sister-woman there
Is like to thee - but nay! for it thou didst
These foolish eyes would not believe - but thou
Canst tell me of thy brothers. Are they great,
And can they grapple with God's arguments,
And cipher out the problems of the stars?
          DWAINIE.
Aye, they have leaped all earthly barriers.
`Twas Wunkland's son[1] that voyaged round the moon,
And talked with Mars, and buckled Saturn's belt;
`Twas Wunkland's son that bent the rainbow
straight.
And walked it like a street, and so returned
To tell us it was made of hammered shine,
Inlaid with strips of selvedge[2] from the sun,
And burnished with the rust of rotten stars.
`Twas Wunkland's son who comprehended first
All grosser things, and took the world apart
And oiled its joints with new philosophies;
For now our goolores[3] say, below these isles
A million million miles are other worlds -
Not like to ours, but round, as bubbles are,
And like them, ever reeling on thro' space,
And anchorless thro' all eternity;
Not like to ours, for our isles,[4] as they say
Are living things that fly about at night,
And soar above, and cling, throughout the day
Like bats, beneath the rafters of the skies:
and I myself have heard, at dawn of moon,
A liquid music filtered thro' my dreams,
As tho' a thousand trilling voices pent
In some o'erhanging realm, had spilled themselves
In streams of melody that trickled thro'
the chinks and crannies of a crystal pave
Until the wasted juices of harmony,
slow-leaking o'er my senses, drowned my soul

With ecstacy divine. And afferhaiks [5]
Who scour our coasts on missions for the King,
Declare our island's shape is like the zhibb's [6]
When lolling in a trance upon the air,
With open wings upslant and motionless.
O such a land it is - so all complete
In all wise habitants, and knowledge, lore,
Arts, sciences, perfected government -
In kingly wisdom, worth and majesty -
So furnished forth in all things lovable,
O Amphine, love of mine, it lacks but thy
Sweet presence to make it a Paradise.

1. Riley seeks the soul within as rendering those in earthly bodies as "wunks" and the earth as we know it as "wunkland." Persons in the "beyond" will have activities including universal explorations, musical enjoyments, ministerial functions for God, etc.
2. Variant spelling of selvage, an edge of woven material which prevents ravelling out of the weft.
3. Probably an ellipse of "good lores" or "best books."
4. Riley confirms to us that "The Flying Islands" are lives that he lives at night. These are himself in fragmented souls or selves.
5. A haik is worn by an Arab explorer into the deserts. It is an outer cloth. "Afferre" is Latin meaning "to conduct inward." Afferhaiks may refer to functionaries in the universal sphere.
6. An inventive creature of Riley's vivid imagination possibly striped as a zebra and thus "ribbed" or some such.

(Takes up the Trentoraine.)

And shall I tell thee of the home [1] *that waits*
For thy glad coming, Amphine? Listen, then -

1. After describing the people of the "beyond" and their activities, Dwainie now tells Riley of the land itself in song in an imaginative fanciful vision in which Riley and Nellie can live together. Dwainie gives Amphine to know that their "heaven" is a garden-party.

SONG

A palace veiled in a gleaming dusk;
    Warm breaths of a tropic air,
Drugged with the odorous Marzhoo's [1] *musk*
    And the perfumed cynchottaire [2]*; Where the*
trembling hands of the lilwing's [3] *leaves*
    The winds caress and fawn,
As the dreamy starlight idly weaves
    Designs for a damask [4] *lawn.*

Densed in the depths of a dim eclipse

Of palms in a flowery space,
A fountain leaps from the marble lips
   Of a girl with a golden vase
Held atip on a curving wrist,
   Drinking the drops that glance
Laughingly in the gleaming mist
   Of her crystal utterance.

Archways looped o'er blooming walks
   That lead thro' gleaming halls;
And balconies where the tune-bird talks
   To the tipsy waterfalls.
And easements gauzed with a filmy sheen
   Of a lace that sifts the sight,
While a ghost of bloom on the haunted screen
   Drips with the dews of light.

Weird, pale shapes of sculptured stone,
   And marble nymphs agaze
Ever in fonts of amber sown
   With seeds of gold, and sprays
Of emerald mosses ever drowned,
   Where glimpses of shell and gem
Peer from the depths as round and round
   The nautilus nods at them.

Faces blurred in a mazy dance
   And a music wild and sweet,
Spinning the threads of a mad romance
   That tangles the waltzer's feet:
Twining arms, and warm swift thrills
   That pulse to the melody,
Till the soul of the dancer dips and fills
   In the wells of ecstacy.

Eyes that melt in the quivering ore
   Of love, and the molten kiss
Bubbling out of the hearts that pour

Their blood in the molds of bliss;
`Tis worn to a languor slumber-deep,
The soul of the dreamer lifts
A silken sail on the gulfs of sleep,
And into the darkness drifts.[5]

1. Possibly an ellipse of "martyrs of the Hoosiers" or such.
2. "Sin-choked air" or such.
3. Possibly "Littlest winged cupid" kind of thing.
4. A lawn of ornamental variegated pattern as is damask.
5. What kind of place is Riley heading as Dwainie tells him his destination? Is this overblown, sensation-sated place described with bawdy house parlor accouterments a delirium-evoked description of where Riley is really heading due to his alcoholism, i.e. hell?

(The instrument falls from her hands; and Amphine in a gust of passionate delight, embraces her.)

AMPHINE

Thou art not all of earth, O angel one!
I do not wonder me those eyes of thine,
Have peeped above the very walls of Heaven!
What hast thou seen there? Hast thou looked on God
And did he fling as bright a smile as thine
Back to thee as he beckoned thee within?
And tell me, didst thou meet an angel there
Alinger at the gates, nor entering
Till I, her brother, joined her?[1]

1. Riley's sister, Martha Celestia, born February, 1847, died as a baby in 1851, two years after Riley was born.

DWAINIE

Why, hast thou
As sister dead? Truth, I have heard of one
Long lost to thee - not dead?

AMPHINE

Of her I speak.
She strayed away from us long, long ago,
But I remember her - wondering eyes
That seemed as tho' they ever looked on things
We could not see, as haply so they did,
For she went from us all so suddenly,
So strangely vanished, that I of times think
She found a pathway leading back to God,
And bent her steps therein and slipped away

Unseen of earthly eyes.
DWAINIE
Nay, do not grieve
Thee thus, O loving heart! Thy sister yet
May come to thee in some sweet way the fates
Are planning, even while thy tear-drops fall;
so calm thee while I speak of thine own self.
And I have listened to a whistling bird
That pipes of waiting danger. Did'st thou note
No strange behavior of thy sire of late?

AMPHINE
Ay, he is silent, and he walks as one
In some deep melancholy, or as one
Asleep.

DWAINIE
And does he never speak with thee,
Nor ask thy counsel?

AMPHINE
Once he stopped me on
The palace stairs, and whispered, "Lo! my son,
thy reign draws near - prepare!" and so passed on
And vanished like a ghost - so pale he was.

DWAINIE
And didst thou never reason on this thing?
Nor ask thyself "What dims my father's eye,
And makes a sullen shadow of his form?"

AMPHINE
Why, there's a household rumor that he dreams
Death lurks forever at his side, and soon
Will signal him away.[1] But Jucklet says
Crestillomeem has said the leeches say
There is no cause for serious concern;
As so I am assured it is nothing more
Than childish fancy; so I laugh, ha! ha!
And wonder, as I see him gliding past,
If ever I shall waver as I walk
And stumble o'er my beard, and knit my brow,
And o'er the dull mosaics of the pave

Play checkers with mine eyes.[2] *Ho, ho! Ah,ha!*

1. A possible subtle hint of a Riley suicide plan if he cannot get himself together enough to write poetry. SEE: the contemporary poem in Hoosier dialect, "Lines to an Onsettled Young Man." ("An' what is Death?" - W'y, looky hyur -\ Ef Life an' Love don't suit you, sir, \Hit's jes' the thing yer lookin' fer!"). At this point, Riley's poetry contains the theme of the relief from life that comes with nihilation. SEE the 1879 poem "Death," with its final line "Soh, bless me! I am dead!"

2. Riley is in a stupor and the fears he will die while intoxicated in tremens if he cannot come to. His intoxicated self, Crestillomeem, however, doesn't deter him from alcohol consumption. Riley notices himself tumbling about glancing in distraction as do checkers jumping about on a board, square by square.

DWAINIE (Aside)

How dare I tell him? Yet, I must - I must?

AMPHINE

Why, art thou, too, grown childish, that thou canst
Find crazy pleasure talking to thyself,
And staring frowningly with eyes whose smiles
I need so much?

DWAINIE

Nay, rather say their tears, poor thoughtless
prince!

AMPHINE

What mean you?

DWAINIE

Why, I mean, one hour agone,
The queen, thy mother -

AMPHINE

Nay, say only "queen!"

DWAINIE

The queen, one hour agone, as so I learn,
Sent message craving audience with the king
At noon to-night, within the Tower of Stars.
Thou knowest one hour later that the throne
Convenes, and that the king has set his seal
Upon a mandate that proclaims the queen
Shall there preside if he do not appear.[1]
And therefore she, as I have been apprised,
Connives to hold him absent purposely
That she may claim the vacancy - for what
Covert design I know not, but I know

It augurs danger to you both.

1. If Riley can't get over his alcoholism, he will consign himself to a life as an alcoholic under Crestillomeem's control.

AMPHINE
I feel
Thou speakest truth, and yet how know you this?

DWAINIE
Ask me not that; my lips are welded close,
And more - since I have dared to speak, and thous
To listen - Jucklet is accessory,
And even now is plotting for thy fall -
But, passion of my soul, think not of me,
For nothing but sheer magic was avail
To work me harm; but look thee to thyself!
For thou art blameless cause of all the hate
That rankles in the bosom of the queen.
So have thine eyes about thee, that no step
May steal behind thee ever - for in this
Unlooked of way thy enemy will come.
This much I know, but for what fell intent
And purpose dire I dare not even guess;
So look thee, night and day, that none may come
Upon thee from behind.

AMPHINE
And thou, O precious heart!
How art thou guarded, and what shield hast thou
Of safety?

DWAINIE
Fear thou not for me at all;
Possessed am I of wondrous sorcery -
The gift of holy magic at my birth,
My enemy must face me as he comes
And I will know him at one utterance,
And then I may disarm him tho' he be
A giant and of thrice a giant's strength,
But hist! What wandering minstrel comes this way?

VOICE (In the distance.)
The drowsy eyes of the stars grow dim;

The wamboo roosts on the rainbow's rim,
   And the moon is a ghost of a shine:
The soothing song of the crool[1] is done,
But the song of love is a sweeter one,
   And the song of love is mine.
Then wake! O wake!
For the sweet song's sake,
Nor let my heart with the morning break!

1. Crooning oriole or some such.

AMPHINE

Some serenader, but what does he in
The gardens here at glare of noon? Let us
Conceal ourselves within the bower and watch.

   (They go within.)

   VOICE. (Drawing nearer.)

The mist of the morning, chill and gray,
Wraps the night in a shroud of spray,
   The sun is a crimson blot:
The moon fades fast, and the stars take wing;
The comet's tail is a fleeting thing,
   But the tale of love is not,
Then, wake! O wake! For the sweet song's
sake, Nor let my heart with the morning break.

   (Enter Jucklet.)

JUCKLET

Ho! ho! what will my dainty mistress say
When I shall stand knee-deep in the wet grass
Beneath her window, and with upturned eyes
And swaying head, and all-melodious tongue
Out-lolling like the clapper of a bell,
Fling her a song like that? I wonder now
If she will not put up her finger thus,
And say, "Hist! heart of mine! the angels call
For thee!" Ho! ho! Or will her blushing face
Light up her dim boudoir, and from her glass
Flare back to her a flame upsprouting from
The red-hot socket of a soul whose light
She tho't long since had guttered out - Ho! ho!

Or, haply, will she chastely bend above -
A parian phantom with its head atip,
And twinkling fingers dusting down the dews
That glitter on the tarpysma vines
That riot round her casement, gathering
Their blooms to pelt me with, as I below
All winkingly await the fragrant shower?
Ho! ho! how jolly is this thing of love!
But how much richer, rarer, jollier
Than all the loves is this rare love of mine!
Why, my sweet mistress does not even dream
I am her lover; for, to tell the truth,
I have a way of wooing all my own,
And waste no speech in creamy compliment,
And courtesies all gaumed with winy words.
In fact, I do not woo at all. I win!
How is it now the old duct glides off?

                    SONG[1]
  How is it you woo? and now answer me true, -
    How is it you woo and you win?
  Why, to answer you true, - the first thing to do
    Is simply, my dear, to begin.
  But how can I begin to woo or to win
    When I don't know a Win from a Woo?
  Why, cover your chin with your fan or your fin
    And I'll introduce them to you.

  But what if it drew from my parents a view
    With my own in no manner akin?
  No matter, - your view is the best of the two
    So I hasten to usher them in.

  But stay! Shall I grin at the Woo or the Win?
    And what will he do if I do?
  Why, the Woo will begin with "How pleasant it's
  been"
    And the Win with "Delighted with you."

Then supposing he grew very dear to my view?
  I'm speaking, you know, of the Win?
Why, then you should do what he wanted you to,
  And now is the time to begin.

The time to begin? O then usher him in -
  Let him say what he wants me to do!
He is here - he's a twin of yourself, - I am Win,
  And you are my darling - my Woo.

1. An amusing song-poem of courtship and marriage in which Jucklet contemplates his hope of marriage with Dwainie (Nellie, already married of course.) One who "woos" is an object of courtship and one who "wins" gets married. When Jucklet says, "I am win" he is expressing his confidence that he can become a groom. The phrase is found in an early 1971 Riley courtship poem, the "Unexpected Result," as a "casual" phrase for the ritual of courtship and marriage. ("...If I were you/ I'd marry that woman, that's what I'd do,/ As certain as one and one make two!/ Or ain't you much on the marry now?/ Well, she's a mighty fat take anyhow!"/ "Well now, you can bet she ain't so slow,/ Hang it! I won't play off on her so!/ Where's my overcoat? I'm going to go!/ And you needn't sit up till I come in,/For I am right on the `woo' and the `win!'")

That song I call most sensible nonsense;
And if the fair and peerless Dwainie were
But here with that sweet voice of hers, to take
The part of "Woo," I'd be the happiest "Win"
On this side of futurity! Ho! ho!
        DWAINIE. (Aside to Amphine.)
What means he?
        AMPHINE.
Why he means that throatless head
Of his needs further chucking down between
His ugly shoulders!
(Starts forward, Dwainie detains him.)
        DWAINIE.

Nay, thou shalt not stir!
See; now the monster has discovered our
Repast, so let us mark him further.
        JUCKLET.
What!
A roasted wheffle and a toe-spiced whum[1] -
Tricked with a larvey and gherghling's tail

And, sprit me²! wine enough to swim them in!
Now I should like to put a question to
The guests, but as there are none, I direct
My interrogatory to the host:
Am I behind time?

1. A "wheffle" is probably something like a waffle and a truffle mix and a "whum" a wheat bun or some such.
2. Give me spirit.

    (Showing humbly.) *Then I can but trust*
My tardy coming will be overlooked
In my most active effort to regain
A gracious tolerance by
      service now:
Directing the attention to
      the fact
That I have brought my
      appetite along,
I can but feel - ahem! that
      further words
Would be a waste of time.

(Sits at table, pours out wine,
and eats voraciously)

There was a time
When I was rather backward in my ways;
But somehow, as I think I have outgrown
The nice, shy age, wherein one makes a meal
Of two estardles and a fork of soup.
Hey, Sanaloo; but my starved stomach stands
With mouth agape, awe-stricken and aghast
Before the rich profusion of this feast;
So will I lubricate it with a glass of merl
And coax it on to more familiar forms
Of fellowship with these delectables.
(Pours out wine and holds up the goblet.)
Mine host - thou of the viewless presence and
Hush-haunted lip - thy most imperial,
Ethereal, and immaterial health!
Live till the sun dries up, and comb thy cares
With star-prongs till the comets fizzle out

And fade away and fall and are no more!
  (Drinks and refills the goblet.)
And if thou wilt permit of the remark, -
The gleaming shaft of spirit in this wine
Goes whistling to its mark, and full and fair
Zipps to the target center of my soul.
Why, now, I am the veriest gentleman
That ever buttered woman with a smile,
And let her melt and run, and drip and ooze
All over and around a wanton heart;
And if my mistress bent above me now,
In all my hideous deformity,
I think she would look over, as it were,
The hump upon my back; and so forget
The kinds and knuckles of my crooked legs
In this enchanting smile, that she would leap
Love-dazzled, and fall faint and fluttering
Within these open, all-devouring arms
Of mine! Ho! ho! and yet Crestillomeem
Would have me blight my dainty mistress with
This feather from the Devil's wing, but I
Am far too full of craft to spoil the eyes
That yet shall pour their love like nectar out
Into my own, and I am far too deep
For royal wit to wade my purposes.

        DWAINIE.
What can he mean.
        AMPHINE.
I will rush forward and
Tear out his tongue, and slap it in his face!
        DWAINIE.
Nay, nay! It's what he says!
        JUCKLET.
How big a fool -

How all magnificent an idiot -
I would be to blight her, when I have power
To crush the only object that now lies
Between her love and mine! Ho! ho! ho! ho!

I wonder, when she sees the human toad
Squat at her feet, and cock his filmy eyes
Upon her, and croak love, if she wilt not
Call me to tweezer him with two long sticks,
And toss him from her path - O, ho! ho! ho!
Hell bend him o'er some blossom quick, that I
May have one brother in the flesh! (Nods drowsily.)

DWAINIE. (Aside)

Ha! See!
Look, Amphine, he grows drunken; bide a spell
And I will vex him with my sorcery¹;
Then will we leave him, for the hour draws on
When all our arts and strategies must needs
Be called in action.

1. The spirit of Nellie and her faith in Riley's poetic possibility invests Jucklet, Riley's survival personality, with awareness that his drunkenness may kill him.

Jucklet yawns drowsily, stretches, and gradually sinks at full length on the sward.¹ Amphine and Dwainie come forward. Amphine is about to place his foot contemptuously upon the sleeper's breast, but is held back by Dwainie, who motions him to turn away and hide his face; this time, she unbinds her hair, and throwing it forward over her face, and bending till it trails the ground she lifts to the knee her dress,and so walks backward round the sleeper, crooning to herself an incoherent song.² Then pausing, letting fall her dress, and rising to full stature, waves her hands above the sleeper's face, and runs to Amphine, who turns about and looks upon her wonderingly.

1. A grassy surface.
2. A song of reminder of her faith in Riley which will soon combine with the terror of dementia tremens from his alcoholism to reform Riley and wake him out of the poem's delirium.

DWAINIE.

Now shalt thou look on
Such misery as thou hast never dreamed.

(As she speaks a chorus of unearthly voices is heard chanting
to strange discord.)

CHANT

When the fat moon smiles
And the comets kiss,
And the Spirkland elves rejoice,
The whanghoo twunkers¹

A tune like this,
And the nightmare nips the royce²:

1. "whanghoo twunkers" is possibly an ellipse for a wailing spirit evoking a "twang" or "plunk" sound.
2. Possibly an ellipse for "royal arse." (As these words die away, a comet-freighted with weird

shapes, dips from the sky, and trails near the sleeper's feet, while from it two nightmares, Creech and Gritchfang, alight; the comet hisses, switches its tail and disappears, while the two goblins hover over Jucklet, who stares at them with starting eyes and horribly comforted features.)

CREECH (To Gritchfang.)

Buzz! Buzz! Buzz! Buzz!
Flutter your wings like your grandmother does,¹
Tuck in your chin, and wheel over and whir
Like a dickerbug fast in the web of the wurr,
Reel out your tongue and untangle your toes,
And rattle your claws o'er the bridge of his nose;
Tickle his ears with your feathers and fuzz,
And keep up a hum like your grandmother does.

(Jucklet moans and clutches at the air convulsively.²)

1. In Middle English mythology, the "nightmare" was a female monster supposed to settle upon people and animals in their sleep producing a feeling of suffocation or great distress from which the sleeper vainly tries to free one's self. The grandmother of nightmares would be the ultimate ancestral nightmare herself.
2. An account of Riley's "survival self" in tremens.

AMPHINE (Shuddering)

Most horrible! See how the poor worm writhes!

DWAINIE

But good will come of it, a far voice sings.

GRITCHFANG (To Creech.)

Let me dive down in his nostriline caves,
And keep an eye out as to how he behaves;
Fasten him down while I put him to rack,
And don't let him flops from the flat of his back.

(Shrinks to minute size, disappears in the sleeper's nose, and calls gleefully from within:)

Lo! I have bored thro' the floor of his brains,
And set them all writhing with torturous pains;
And I shriek out the prayer as I whistle and whizz,
I may be the nightmare that my grandmother is!

(Appears, and assuming former shape, crosses to Creech, and they dance on the sleeper's stomach in broken time to chorus.)

CHORUS

Whing! whang! so our ancestors sang,
And they guzzled hot blood and blew up with a bang;
But they ever tenaciously clung to the rule
To only blow up in the hull of a fool -
To fizz and explode like a cast-iron toad
In the cavernous depths where his victuals were
stowed -
When chances were ripest and thickest and best
To burst every button-hole out of his vest.

(They pause, float high above, and fussing together into a ponderous iron weight, they drop heavily upon the chest of the sleeper, who moans piteously.)

AMPHINE (Hiding his face.)

Ah! Heavens! take we hence!

(Dwainie leads him off, looking backward as she disappears and waving her hands.)

CREECH (To Gritchfang.)

Zipp! Zipp! Zipp! Zipp!
Sting his tongue raw and unravel his lip:
Grope, on the right, down his windpipe, and squeeze
His liver as dry as a petrified flea's.

(Gritchfang bows, shrinks and disappears.)

Throttle his heart till he's black in the face,
And bury it down in some desolate place,
Where only remorse in her agony lives
To dread the advice that your grandmother gives.

(The sleeper struggles convulsively, while the voice of Gritchfang calls from within.)

Ho! I have clambered the rounds of his ribs,
And riddled his lungs into tatters and dribs;
And I turn up the tube of his heart like a hose
And squirt all the blood to the end of his nose;
I stamp on his stomach, and caper and prance,
With my tail tossing round like a boomerang lance,
And thus may success ever crown my intent

To wander the way that my grandmother went.
(Appears, falls hysterically in Creech's outstretched arms. They dance and chorus.)

CHORUS

Whing! Whang! so our ancestors sung.
And they snorted and pawed, and they hissed and
they stung,
And they took a terrific delight in their work
On the fools that they found in the lands of the
Spirk.
And each little grain of their powders of pain
They scraped up and pestled again and again,
And they mixed it in doses for gluttons and sots
Till they strangled their dreams with abdominal
knots.

(The comet again trails past, upon which the nightmares leap and disappear. Jucklet staggers to his feet, glares frenziedly about him, and with a wild, unearthly howl of agony, rushes off.)

ACT III

JAMES WHITCOMB RILEY:
THE POET AS FLYING ISLANDS OF THE NIGHT

ACT III

Scene I. - Court of Krung -The royal ministers and counselors in session - Crestillomeem, in royal attire presiding - She signals to herald on her right, who steps forward - Blare of trumpets, greeted with loud murmurings and tumult from without.

HERALD.

Hist, ho! Ay,ay! Ay,ay! Her majesty,
The all glorious and ever gracious queen
Crestillomeem, to her most loyal, leal [1]
And right devoted subjects, greeting sends -
Proclaiming, in the absence of the king,
Her royal presence, as by him empowered
To sit upon the throne in sovereign state
And work the royal will. (Confusion)
Hist, ho! Ay,ay! Ay,ay!
And be it known, the king, in view of his
Approaching dissolution -
Hath decreed The reading of this royal document.

1. A Middle English word meaning "true." (Sensation among the counselors, etc. within and wild tumult without; cries of "Long live the king!" and "Down with the sorceress!") (Unrolls a scroll with royal seal attached. Sensation in court - wild tumult without, and cries of "Plot!" "Conspiracy!" "Down with the Queen!" "Down with the sorceress!")

CRESTILLOMEEM. (Wildly)

Bring me the traitor-knave who dares to cry
"Conspiracy!"

(Wild confusion without - sound of rioting, and a voice, "Let me be taken!" Enter officers, dragging Jucklet, wild-eyed and hysterical.)

CRESTILLOMEEM. (Starting.)

Why bring you Jucklet here?

OFFICER.

Because `tis he who cries "conspiracy!"
And who incites the mob without with cries
Of "Plot" and "Treason!"

CRESTILLOMEEM.

Ha! Can this be true?
I'll not believe it! Jucklet is my fool,
But not so great a fool that he would tempt
His sovereign's ire. Let him be freed. Come here,
My Fool.
      JUCKLET. (Wildly)

Thy fool? Ho! ho! Why, thou art mine!
(Confusion. Cries of "Strike down the traitor!")
      JUCKLET.
Back! all of ye! I have not waded Hell
That I should fear your puny enmity!
But I will give you proof of what I say.
(Presses toward the throne, hurling his opposers left and right.
Crestillomeem sits as tho' stricken speechless, waving him off, while Jucklet
folds his arms and stands before her.)
      JUCKLET. (To the throng)
Lo! do I here defy her to lift up her voice
And say this is a lie that Jucklet speaks.
(The queen motions to officers, who, unperceived, close behind Jucklet.)
And further - I pronounce the document [1]
That craven herald there holds in his hand
A forgery - a trick - and dare the Queen
Here in my listening presence to command
Its utterance.

1. Probably an anti-temperance Murphy pledge to remain alcoholic rather to remain sober.

      CRESTILLOMEEM. (Wildly rising to her feet)
Hold, hireling! traitor! fool!
The Queen thou dost in thy mad boasts insult
Will utter first thy doom.
(Jucklet is seized from behind, and hurled, face upward on the dais at her feet, while a minion, with a drawn sword pressed against his breast, stands over him.)
Ere we proceed
With graver matters let this demon-knave
Ben sent back home to Hell. Give me the sword -
The insult has been mine - so even shall
The vengeance be!
(As she bends forward with the sword, Jucklet, with a super human effort

frees his hand and with a sudden motion, and an incoherent muttering, flings something[1] at the queen, who staggers, dropping the sword, and with her arms tossed wildly aloft, totters forward and falls prone upon the pave. In the confusion following, Jucklet mysteriously disappears, and as the bewildered and awe-stricken courtiers lift the fallen queen, a clear and piercing voice is heard singing.)

1. Sobriety which will change Riley from Crestillomeem's influence in drunkenness to Krung a respectable person in society.

VOICE.

The pride of noon must wither soon,
   The dusk of death must fall;
Yet out of darkest night the moon
   Shall blossom over all.

(For an instant a dense cloud envelops the throne, then slowly lifts, discovering Krung seated in royal state, with Jucklet in the act of presenting the scepter to him. Blare of trumpets, and chorus of courtiers, ministers, heralds, etc.)

CHORUS.

All hail! All hail! All hail! Long live the King!

KRUNG.

Thro' God's great providence, together with
The intervention of an angel whom
I long ago tho't lost to earth and me,[1]
Once more, as your sovereign, do I greet
And tender you my blessing. Until late
I have been subject of the baleful spells
And witcheries[2] of this poor woman here[3]
Who grovels at my feet, blind, speechless, and
So stricken with a curse herself designed
Should light upon hope's fairest minister.
Remove her from my sight.

1. Nellie.
2. Intoxication.
3. Crestillomeem, Riley's drunken self.

(As the queen is led away Spraivoll appears in royal attire. She kneels and kisses the king's hand; in return he kisses her upon the brow, and lifts and seats her at his side.[1])

1. Spraivoll, Riley's "versifier" self can now write humble poetry.

Behold in this sweet woman here my child, who,

when a babe,
The cold, despicable Crestillomeem -
(He bows his head within his hands and shudders)
By spells
And wicked necromancies spirited
To some strange real, where, happily
A Wunkland princess[1] found her, and undid
The spell by a most potent sorcery[2]
She doth possess, God-given, to right wrong.
Lo! let the peerless princess now appear!

1. "Dwainie-Nellie."
2. The power of encouragement and love.

(He lifts his scepter, and a gust of melody, unearly beautiful, sweeps through the court. The star above the Throne drops slowly downward, bursting like a bubble on the scepter-tip, and issuing therefrom Amphine and Dwainie, hand in hand, full at the feet of Krung, who bends above them with his blessing, while Jucklet capers wildly round the group.)

JUCKLET.

Ho! ho! but I could shriek for very joy -
For tho' fair Amphine even now bends o'er
A blossom, I, ho! ho! have no desire
To meddle with it, since with but one eye
I slept the while she backward walked around
Me in the garden.

(Amphine laughs gaily, Jucklet blinks and leers, and Dwainie bites her finger.)

KRUNG.

Peace! good Jucklet, peace!
For this is not a time for juiceless wit -
Tho' I have found restored to me my life -
Tho' I have found a daughter, I have lost
A son - for Dwainie, with her sorcery,
Will, on the morrow, carry him away.[1]

1. Riley's bond with Nellie causes his "lover-self" to go live with Nellie in her grave or perhaps heaven as her "soulmate."

SOME COMMENTS ON THE POEM
FROM THE TIME OF ITS FIRST PUBLICATION

Riley never talked about the substance of the poem. There is an account of a Riley acquaintance of the time, Minnie Belle Mitchell, who was in her brother-in-law, George F. Hauck's Greenfield Grocery in 1878 when the Saturday HERALD arrived with "The Flying Islands" in it. Riley's brother, Hum, working in the store as a clerk received the newspaper from the paper carrier and spread it out on a counter. While she and Hum were reading it, Riley and his friend Frank Hayes came into the store. Minnie Belle remembers saying to Riley, "It's wonderful, simply marvelous," with her teen-age exuberance. She continued, "It's beautiful to look at too, but do you know, I can't understand a word of it - I don't know what it's all about."

She adds, "My extravagant remarks were followed by an explosion of laughter from the three young men, and I knew instantly that I had said the wrong thing and my face was scarlet."

Riley's autobiographical poem was a lark to him at the time. He was "Thomas Chatterton" putting forth a prank poem but without so serious an intent as to try to make any money out of a Middle English "forgery" as Chatterton had tried.

Riley eventually replied, "Well, Minnie Belle, I have to confess-I don't know what that poem is all about myself. It was given to me, you know." Riley was not about to tell his young friend that it was a soul journey while he was intoxicated.

The public was just as confused about "The Flying Islands of the Night" as was Minnie Belle Mitchell.

The Kokomo TRIBUNE published the following about "The Flying Islands of the Night" on September 26, 1878. Our young friend, J.W. Riley, has covered himself all over with glory by his "The Flying Islands of the Night" recently published in the Indianapolis HERALD. Never since the days of Poe has there been such a fanciful piece of versification written. It is so unique and purely original that any attempt to describe it or criticize it would result in a miserable failure. It must be read to be appreciated. Mr. Riley has been before the public but for a short time, but in that time his poems have placed him at the head of the poets of the West. For sublimity, originality, conception and purity of diction, Mr. Riley ranks the leading literary lights of the state. His sonnet on the death of Mr. Philips was one of the grandest concepts that was ever penned. Christ hears the wailing of the tired soul, and reaching down from Heaven, takes him by the hand and helps him up. We are pleased to learn Mr. Riley's engagements to lecture are numerous and financially his prospects are bright."

Yes, but what about the subject matter?

The poem was really a play. The play was about Riley's life. The strange thing about it was that Riley was all the characters except for Dwainie.

THE FLYING ISLANDS AS THEATER

There is something like the great Shakespearian explanation that "All the world's a stage" in Riley's autobiographical poem.

Riley loved to act and was considered a great actor in his time.

We might digress to talk about Riley and the theater in his life. Riley was a great actor. We have the testimony of other actors to confirm this. Riley played in the soul-roles he described in his poem.

At a dinner given in London for Riley by Sir Henry Irving, the great Nineteenth Century actor of England, with Coquelin, the great actor of France present, Coquelin remarked to Irving upon hearing Riley, "This Monsieur Riley has by nature what you and I have spent twenty years to acquire." This remark was made on Riley's famous summer trip of 1891 through Scotland to see Robert Burns' "wee cot" that ended up in London.

Riley was a great American actor as well as poet. He lived in a play cast of himself on the stage of his soul.

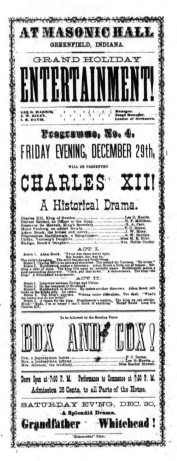

Riley performed in numerous local theater productions as a young man sch as this one.

ALCOHOLIC'S CONFESSIONAL GENRE LITERATURE

What about the plot?

Who would have guessed that Riley's genius had produced the most novel use of a purely American genre in all of literature.

Riley had transformed the Alcoholic's Confessional Genre of literature into poetry. He had come close to strangling it. He used it absurdly. Literature had never seen such a mischievous minstrel as Riley before.

One of the most original aspects of Riley's writing of "The Flying Islands of the Night" was the use he made of the Alcoholic's Confessional Genre. In that genre generally, an alcoholic describes himself as a despicable alcoholic. Then along comes a "saving soul" or perhaps the "agent of salvation." It is a special person to the doomed alcoholic who pleads to the deranged intoxicated person and inspires them to escape their drunkenness while in tremens or delirium of one sort or another. Presto! The alcoholic is saved and a "new person."

This genre was very popular in Riley's time when great temperance movements swept the country. However no other poet made even the slightest use of the genre. Nor does it appear that any other author followed Riley's lead in applying it to autobiographical poetry. "The Flying Islands of the Night" is really a very complex puzzle. Once we see that Poe's "Scenes from Politian" and mock Thomas Chatterton trumpery were sources of form and language, then we must look to the movement of Riley's piece. Alcoholic's Confessional Genre literature provides that more dominant influence.

The key to the genre is an initial description of alcoholic "hell" followed by the saving influence of somebody and then a final scene where sobriety triumphs. In Riley's autobiographical use of the genre, the spirit of the dead Nellie Cooley, his married inspiration of days gone by, is the saving force. Later, during his revisions for subsequent publications, Riley adds his mother's love as AEo as a saving force too.

Riley's triumph is that of Krung in achieving great fame and respectable status.

We find the alcoholic's confessional genre in the prose of Luther Benson's FIFTEEN YEARS IN HELL. In that book, which Riley was reading at the time he wrote "The Flying Islands of the Night," Benson describes the following sequence in his life in which his mother saves him. "My wild revel was protracted for days out of dread of the awful sorrow and remorse that I knew must surely come on my getting sober. My mother appeared to me in my troubled dreams, and talked to me as in life. Many times in my slumber, and in my waking fancies did I see her pale, troubled face, with her pitying eyes looking on me as from that bed of pain and death, and at such times I reached out my hands toward her in mute pleading for forgiveness, forgetting or not knowing that she was dead."

Riley looked on Benson with awe and reverence. But was he for real? Was he just another "charlatan" with a product to sell - piety and salvation - as did Docs McCrillus and Townsend sell "miracle cures." Luther was someone of national significance as can be seen in two representative press reports of his time.

From the Pittsburgh (Pennsylvania) GAZETTE:

Luther Benson, Esq. of Indiana, has just closed one of the most powerful temperance lectures ever delivered here. The house was one solid mass of people, with not one spare inch of standing-room. For nearly two hours he held the audience as any magic. At the close a large number signed the pledge, some of them the hardest drinkers here. The people are so delighted

Luther Benson (1847-1989), great lecturer on the evils of alcohol and reformed alcoholic who counseled Riley on his alcoholism and took him along with him on a lecture trip near the time Riley wrote "The Flying Islands of the Night". Benson had been confined to a "madhouse" and jails because of his delirious visions from tremens bout.

with his good work that they have secured him for another lecture Wednesday evening."

From the Manchester (New Hampshire) PRESS:

"Smyth's Hall was completely filled, seats and standing room at two o'clock Sunday afternoon, with an audience which came to hear Luther Benson. The officers of the Reform Club, clergymen and reformed drunkards occupied seats upon the platform. Mr. Benson is a native of Indiana, and says he was a drunkard from six years of age. He was within three months of graduation from college when he was expelled for drunkenness. Then he studied for a lawyer, and was admitted to practice, being drunk while studying and drunk while engaged in a case. At length he reduced himself to poverty, pawning all he had for drink. At length he started to reform and though he had once fallen he was determined to persevere. Since his reformation two years ago, he gave temperance lectures. He is a young man, a powerful, swinging sort of speaker, with a good command of language, original with peculiar intonation, pronunciation and idioms, sometimes rough, but eminently popular with his audiences. He spoke for an hour and a half steadily, wiping the perspiration from his face at intervals, taking up the greater part of his address with his personal experience. He said he had delirium tremens several times, once for fifteen days, and gave an exceedingly minute and graphic description of his

John Hatfield (1851-ca. 1936), "The Hoosier Evangelist," reformed drinker and friend of James Whitcomb Riley about whom it was said: "John Hatfiled can preach longer and louder, and keep at it longer, and shout more, and jump higher, and get more people to the alter, and pray longer and harder, than any man that walks on the ground."

torments. A number of men signed the pledge at the close of the meeting. Among them was one man, who sat in front of the audience and kept drinking from a bottle he had evidently in a spirit of bravado, but at the conclusion of the address he signed the pledge, crying like a child."

In another example of the genre, THIRTY-THREE YEARS A LIVE WIRE, the autobiography of John T. Hatfield, another reformed alcoholic was incidentally a childhood friend of James Whitcomb Riley who went on to lecture on holiness, the Act II stage (the saving agency) is referred to as an "Anointing." Instead of a "Dwainie" as with James Whitcomb Riley or a "doting mother" as with Benson, Hatfield's inspiration is Christ.

Riley was as much aware of Hatfield's writing in the genre as he was Benson's.

As to their boyhoods together, Hatfield writes, "James Whitcomb Riley and myself were boys together. We were in the same class at school, and at the same "swimming hole," since made famous in one of Mr. Riley's poems. During the Civil War we marched the streets together with tin pans for drums and broomsticks for guns. Little did passers-by imagine, as they cast indifferent glances at us little dust-begrimed urchins out in the road playing soldier, that, in the coming years, little Johnnie Hatfield would bless his

A camp meeting of John Hatfield's at the Cleveland Campgrounds which John Hatfield called "My home camp" outside Greenfield, Indiana, a place where souls were saved by the intervention of the Holy Spirit.

country as John T. Hatfield, "The Hoosier Evangelist," and little Jim Riley would be known the world over as James Whitcomb Riley, "The Hoosier Poet."

Hatfield held revivals country-wide as a primary speaker of the American "Holiness movement" and founded a religious college in Pasadena, California.

From his boyhood memorials, he says, "My father, in those days, frequently kept a bottle of "Old Kentucky Rye" in the cupboard and its contents were offered to both children and guests. This custom of the home had something to do in kindling to great intensity my appetite for strong drink, and at the age of twenty years I was frequenting saloons and seeking companionship among the vile, soul-destroying influence of saloon life. (Biographer's Note: This crowd probably included James Whitcomb Riley.) Like a meteor in the night I was fast going down, and nothing less powerful than the mighty attraction of heavenly gravitation could reverse my hellward course and draw me to the heights of noble Christian manhood. Thank God, the Holy Spirit interposed, the blood of Christ was supplied, and my young life was transformed from a disgraceful career of drunken profligacy to one of eminent usefulness in the cause of the Lord Jesus Christ."

Strangely enough, James Whitcomb Riley's life passage had the same result.

An anointing incident which saves Hatfield from his life of sin is described as occurring at a typical Midwestern camp-meeting of the period. Hatfield says, "People who witnessed the scenes of that day declared that they saw flashes of Divine light appear over the congregation as wave and wave of heavenly power descended upon the assembly of thousands." After the meeting, Hatfield went to a farmer's home exhausted and went to bed, but couldn't sleep until "I again closed my eyes and there appeared before me a vision. I saw a silver horn lined with gold, the large end resting upon my breast. It appeared to be many feet in length from the large end to the mouthpiece which appeared to be quite small. I looked up from the large end, and had never held anything so indescribably beautiful. Suddenly the opening at the small end was darkened and there appeared a halo of light, which seemed to envelop a fast-approaching figure. As nearer and nearer the lovely vision approached, I soon recognized the central figure as that of Jesus and the beautiful halo proved to be a band of bright, shining angels. All the angels were singing and such exquisite tones cannot be described, neither can they be compared to any earthly melodies. In a short time, Jesus stood close beside me, and looked down upon me with an expression that, in clearer tones than words, spoke of tenderest love, then He disappeared. At the same time I felt a sensation in my throat as though I was swallowing something. Then the horn passed away, the angels disappeared and the music ceased. I opened my eyes and then closed them again, hoping that the vision would appear one more, but I waited and listened in vain." The call was for Hatfield to preach just as James Whitcomb Riley's call from his deceased Dwainie was inspiration for him to write poetry and recite it from the lyceum circuit stages around the country.

Whether Riley was intoxicated while writing "The Flying Islands of the Night" is unknown. There is this possibility. Recent study by Mark Brunke and Merv Gilbert in "Alcohol and Creative Writing" in PSYCHOLOGICAL REPORTS (1992, 71, 651-658) found that alcohol facilitates creative writing and specifically the use of novel figurative language. The testing of the hypothesis had intoxicated persons write brief stories or streams of con-sciousness, all of which were fictional. There were significantly more novel tropes while intoxicated than sober. Subjects also wrote significantly more words when intoxicated. There is obviously very marked used of figurative language and novel trope use in "The Flying Islands of the Night." Nevertheless, the writing bears great sense as an autobiographical exposi-tion under the circumstances of its writing. Whether Riley wrote the piece while intoxicated is debatable but unnecessary to know for its value in this biography.

We cannot fully explore "The Flying Islands of the Night" in this pref-ace to the life of the most important of the late Nineteenth Century American

poets, James Whitcomb Riley. We must however confirm its autobiographical nature as the basis of this biography. Crestillomeem, Krung, Jucklet and
others are the self-visualization which Riley embodied in his wonderfully
"astronomically" impossible vision of self- alienation and personality fragmentation he called "The Flying Islands of the Night" which will govern the
biography to follow.

Why bother with such an impossible person?

There may be other reasons for a study of Riley - and some of them will
be explored - but ultimately the very mix of his personality, and the eventual triumph of his poetic self, "Spraivoll," (usually) was brought about by
an intervening instrumentality of spirituality that I find so compelling it
must be written about. At its point of greatest flourish, this aspect of Riley
became transforming to Riley's poetry as well as literally "saving" him from
Crestillomeem. At its very best the quality in his life became kenotic poetry. Kenotic poetry is the finest poetry of Post-Civil War American literature
and Riley wrote its greatest singing verse. The reason it is the finest poetry
of the period is that it connected ecstatically with the American soul and

"Civil War Company A" recruited from Greenfield, Indiana, Riley's hometown. Great social trauma accompanied the
end of the war. Reuben Riley is the front left soldier.

expressed its song.

Some mention of the obscure kenotic theological movement originating
in Germany must be interwoven into this account and also its odd peripatet-
ic journey into the American mid- continent where Riley wrote his poetry.
This will come with a discussion of Riley as Spraivoll later on in this biography.

But for now let us meet Riley as a cast of himself as he knows himself
to be at the level of his soul.

There is simply no way of accounting for the life ofJames Whitcomb
Riley without meeting his dialoguing "self- cast" play partners. We will
introduce them in the chapters that follow and see how their individual lives
were lived.

JUCKLET

HOW CAN RILEY SURVIVE IT ALL? JUCKLET, A MINSTREL WHO ANSWERS THE CALL WITH MISCHIEF IN MIND

HOW CAN RILEY SURVIVE IT ALL? -
JUCKLET, A MINSTREL WHO ANSWERS THE CALL
WITH MISCHIEF IN MIND

Among the play characters Riley sees himself playing in his autobiographical "The Flying Islands of the Night," is Jucklet, the mischievous "jongleur," dialect singer, story teller and Riley's survival self. It would be a grave mistake to consider this Riley "self" as some sort of happy idiot. Jucklet kept his eyes open and his genius was searching out American life.

Jucklet was probably the role that people enjoyed the most about Riley. Some of his clever shenanigans, such as his "blind painter" act when he was wandering around Indiana as an itinerant house and sign painter, are firmly lodged in American folklore.

THE BLIND PAINTER
PRANK

The "blind painter" prank occurred in August, 1872 with his traveling friends- also itinerant craftsmen or vagrants calling themselves "The Graphics" - who knew of Riley's genius for mimicry. The group decided to have some fun with the town folk of Peru, Indiana. The young men hinted around

An illustration of Riley's "blind painter" hoax at Peru, Indiana with folk in the background wondering how Riley could paint the sign being blind. Illustrator, R.J. Campbell.

town that a "blind sign painter" was outside trying to paint a sign on a building. Soon half the town came out to witness. How could a blind man paint a sign? Riley assumed the patient, weary look of a blind man, groping about and upsetting a can of paint, whereupon his associates jeered him and made terrible fun of him. Then another would say, "Look at that poor blind man. Isn't it a shame the way folks make fun of him!" In the meantime, Riley climbed the ladder, fumbled for a few minutes, and, at last, without laying out the letters, as a sign painter customarily did, he produced a beautifully done free-hand sign on the side of the building while his friends laughed and poked each other below. In the meantime, people chirped, "He isn't blind!

How could he do that if he were blind!" while the Graphics solemnly insisted, "Oh, yes he is!" This Riley, the "blind sign painter," was classic Jucklet.

THE VOICE FROM THE CELLAR PRANK

My favorite prank performed by Riley was done with John Hoover in a small town in the heat of summer of 1874. Bill Moore, hot and fat, plodded the main street which was baking in a scorching sun. In front of the dry goods store, a pleading voice reached his ear. "Bill, help, Bill! Lift up the cellar door. I am trapped in the cellar. I can't see in here!" Bill put his hands under the cellar door and tugged and pulled and teased but the cellar door failed to move when along came another person, Lee Trees. Lee was wearing a new white suit and was the town "dandy." "Lee, Lee. Help!" the voice called out from the cellar. "Please lift up the cellar door. I'm in here and I can't get out." Both men pulled and tugged and teased. Dripping with perspiration they went inside the dry goods store and came out with

John Q. Hoover of Lafayette, Indiana shortly before his death in 1927. Riley friend and traveling companion in youth and the source for many tales about Riley widely reported in Hoosier newspapers.

candles to look through a window into the dark cellar. They saw that the cellar door was locked with chains from the inside. When they went back into the dry goods store, the merchant scratched his head and rocked on his heels and said he didn't know how anyone could get down there in the first place. Then, from next door in the hardware store, they heard James Whitcomb Riley and John Hoover laughing hysterically and holding their sides. Upon further investigation they found Riley holding a hose the other end of which went through an iron grating and down into the cellar. The voice from the cellar door came from the lips of James Whitcomb Riley in the hardware store through the hose. Jucklet was just having some fun.

TAKE RADWAY'S READY RELIEF PRANK

I should add that Riley himself was not simply pranking playing Jucklet, he was also surviving in the character role. Sometimes the two mixed. There is a story of Jucklet, while a young man traveling through the countryside painting signs. On a new gate between Kennard and New Castle, Riley noticed a farmer had displayed on its top board: "What will you do to be saved?" With no one in sight, Riley painted underneath it, "Take Radway's

Ready Relief!" This was a common laxative of the time. Some days later, he passed the same farm and on the bottom board the farmer had added, "And prepare to meet thy God!"

Jucklet was also a poet. His greatest writing is found in the "Poetical Gymnastics" series and "Respectably Declined Papers of the Buzz Club" series published originally in the Indianapolis Saturday HERALD. This body of Riley's work represents Riley in unburdened creativity and mischievous orientation. In these great series, Riley writes the poem "On Quitting California." No, this poem is not about moving away from the great Pacific coastal state. It is about giving up a "California" brand of cheap "red-eye" whiskey. Riley is quitting a crummy brand -not giving up alcohol entirely.

Cleverness and humor are marks of Jucklet. Jucklet is the usual story teller. There seems to be an easy, casual and honest relationship between Riley and Jucklet.

Occasionally one finds Jucklet lapsing into the "dots" and "disses" of his native Hoosier Deutsch culture. Here is one of Riley's stories from his "Buzz Club" writings.

UNAWANGAWAWA;
OR, THE EYELASH OF THE LIGHTNING (1878).

It was the noble red man, from the land of the setting sun, in company with some half dozen members of his tribe, under management of "Captain Rigby Knowles," who, as the big bills went on to state, had been "nine years a captive among the wild, untutored wanderers of the western wilderness," and was now "a missionary, disseminating knowledge, and the advantages of education, to his dusky brothers, as well as enlightening the civilized world regarding the manners and customs of the poor Indian."

Unawangawawa

They were billed to show "for one night only," at the one church in our little village, the Thursday evening prayer meeting having been postponed for their accommodation, and "the clergy" complimented. I shall never forget their visit to our school that afternoon, for I was then a lad of ten orthereabout; so I leave you to infer the aching sense of my own inferiority as they stalked stoically into the school room, in full bloom of war-paint, wampum, bead moccasins and feathers, and headed by the redoubtable "Captain Rigby Knowles" himself, looking, for the world, like an enlarged facsimile of the "Daniel Boone" in Monteith's geography, only excepting the melancholy and the deceased deer at his feet.

The arithmetic class, in fractions, hurried to its seat, and the silence of death fell upon the room, while the blanched faces of the "scholars" contrasted vividly with those of their tawny visitors as "the famed interpreter and guide," after a wheezy conversation with the teacher, in which the latter only nodded his head submissively at every proposition - seized suddenly hold of a stalwart warrior, and with the bloodcurdling remark of "Pombee steel-ah da be-bee wah-wah!" or words to that effect, wheeled him before us with the following introduction:

"He iss a big chief. He come to make some talk wiss you. He iss a much, heap, smart man. He will make you big Injun speech dot you don't could understand, and den we told you w'as he say. He no talk white talk. He on'y talk much very Injun. He talk Choctaw - he talk Mohawk - he talk Chippavay - he talk effry all style of Injun talk, on'y he no talk white talk. He iss awful smart! Me talk, like big chief, effry all style of Injun-talk, on'y me talk United States also. He iss - O, he iss awful smart, big, very, posted Injun gentlemans. Now he iss go to speak big Injun speech, unt den I say it explain, so dot you know wass he say." Then, turning to the big chief, he touched him off with the following fuse: "De ah-ghee-ghah bee-gah wah-way!" at which the chief at once opened fire in deep, lazy guttural, accompanying the utterance with that facial contortion indicative of an acute attack of cholera morbus. This incoherent mastication had occupied but a brief interval of time when the interpreter jerked the tail of the warrior's shawl, and with a spasmodic "Chow," and a "Ching-ching," he stopped as abruptly as a German music-box. The interpreter explained:

"He say dot you must oxcuse him - dot he don't know he was go to speak. He say dot he ain't much fix on the de subjec', but dot he try to drop some small, leedle, few remarks dot come to hiss mind." Then, prodding the big chief between the shoulders with a rigid thumb, the noble red man lumbered off again in a complexity of verbal chow-chow that put the listener's ears on edge, and thrilled the speculative fancy with a nameless dread, as the ever-widening stream of conglomerated eloquence dashed into savage meaning, fiercely defined by gestures that swung invisible war-clubs, hurled toma-

hawks, and manipulated the gory scalping-knife. And it was sometime before the fearless interpreter could check this impassioned burst. He had jerked at the tail of the warrior's shawl like a school-boy at the string of a limber-jack, and with pretty much the same result. The "scholars" were wild- eyed, and pale with fright. The teacher had one leg thrown careless-ly over the window sill, and with an air of careless indifference was pruning his trembling nails with the big blade of his knife, while the girls in actual terror hid their pallid faces behind their desk-lids, and pencils and pen-holders rained from their places, some, piercing with their barbed points the floor, stood bolt upright and quivered with affright. It was a critical moment for us all; but the daring interpreter, with a presence of mind worth a Van Amburg, threw open his blouse, disclosing a magic something lurking in an inner pocket which the savage reached for with a pacified "Ugh! give some, me dry up!" while the small boys whispered they bet it was a pistol! They bet he'd killed lots o' Indians! They bet he wasn't afraid!, etc. etc. And so we listened with unusual interest as the interpreter explained:

"You mustn't don't get sceert: he won't hurt noting. He wass on'y yoost say dot he for hissef iss sorry dot he don't gone to school when he wass been a leedle childrens like you. But he say when he was leedle like dot, he roll unt dumble in de grass, unt go mitout hiss clothes, unt kick hiss heels like a jaybird. He say dot he not got some advantages ober he would gone to school now off he wass a leedle boy wonce. He was yoost told you how he wass a leedle poor Injun boy, unt don't gone to Sunday school. He say when he wass leedle, heap, awful naughty Injun boy he wass one time play mit hiss leedle brutters mit seesters in de big wasser, unt he want to comed out unt dey wont let um, unt sling um wiss mud, unt dot make um heap-much-brave, so dot he kill um unt scalp um. Den when he goned home his folks dey said: "Where iss your leedle brutters unt seesters?" Unt he say: "Dey at de swim-min-hole." Unt when gone to found um, dey all was scalped unt dead, unt dey hands cut off, unt dey nose cut off, unt dey ears unt eyes cut off. Den hiss folks say: "Who wass done it?" Unt he say: "I don't could lied about it; I do it wiss my leedle hatchet!" Unt den his folks dey say: "Dot's goot! Dot boy will been on de war-path ober he been twelf moons of age!" Unt den he say dot make um feel like big warrior, so dot he can't wait, unt got impul-siff, unt kill also de rest of his folks, unt gone on de war-path unt kill heap-much of ladies unt gentlemens. But he say dot he won't done it now - dot he iss sorry cos off he would a saved his leedle brutters unt seester he would took um to Sunday school wiss um. "Ugh gee bebah wah-wah!" This con-

cluding sentence of the interpreter, abruptly addressed to the warrior, evidently conveyed to him instructions to simmer down, and close his peroration in some conciliatory and complimentary fashion, for the noble savage smiled like a genial hippopotamus, and thumped his breast like a bass drum.

His remarks now seemed to be particularly addressed to the fairer portion of his audience, and his gesticulation at was so palpably indicative of love and affection the big girls blushed and giggled, and the small boys whistled aloud. Only once did he cause a tremor of trepidation to thrill the bosoms of his gentle auditors, when in a triumphant burst he tossed his arms aloft, an, with a glory of inspiration lighting up his dusky features, gave vent to the impassioned utterance, "Shoot-pop-bang!" and then, shortly after, he drew his shawl tightly about him, slapped his chest so vehemently it jarred a feather from his head-gear, and, with the pompous exclamation, "Me big chief, wah!" he folded his arms, and stood stoical and silent.

The interpreter, quivering with an inward paroxysm, after prefacing the interpretation with the chuckling observation, "Bet you don't know whas he say!" went on in this wise"

"Well he say dot he would like to marry a few off you girls. You notice he hold up hiss hand like dot? Well, dot mean five; he say he would like to marry five off you girls You notice he hold up de also both hands? Well, dot mean dot he would have ten wife - off de both kind - five injun, unt five white squaw. He say he tink dot make things lifely off his domestics unt hiss leedle quiet wigwam. He say dot off you marry him he make you all a good husband, unt dot he took you to de land of de setting sun, where you to do nothing - only yoost work. He say he will done all de huntin' hisself, unt dot he will "shoot-pop-bang," like he say, de mussrat unt possum, unt cath um by the tail unt bring um home; den all you had to done wass build de fire, unt peel um, unt cook yoost a leedle, unt he will eat um. Den he say he will give you all de rest. He say you will suit de climate - he say it iss so healdy dot you live more as a hundred years old off you gone wiss him once, unt a tree don't fall on you. He say it iss so healdy out dere dot hiss grandpa iss livin' yet, unt he iss over four tousand year old, unt ain't a gray hair in his head. He say dey also no hair in his head. He say he chaw tobacker all hiss life unt don't hurt um. He say he is healdy dot you wouldn't know um off you see um. He say dot you got in for fifteen cent, unt de leedle children's five cent tonight at de meetin' house."

As Spraivoll's friends are ministers, primarily Myron Reed and Robert Burdette, or fellow kenotics such as Lew Wallace author of "Ben Hur," as

Crestillomeem's are fellow alcoholics such as James McClanahan, Clint Hamilton, and Luther Benson, as Krung's friends are establishment figures such as Dr. Wycliffe Smith, Booth Tarkington and Benjamin Harrison, Jucklet's friends are the mischievous and daring nonconformists and "funsters" such as John Skinner, Bill Nye and Mark Twain.

Here is an incident that reveals how Riley as Jucklet often mischievously made his way through life before he became famous minstrelizing. The incident is one recalled by Minnie Belle Mitchell.

TRIP TO CHARLOTTESVILLE

"The struggle and disappointments endured by the Hoosier poet in his effort to arouse public interest in his poems would have discouraged fainter hearts. But each succeeding failure made him more determined to carry on. He had for some time been reading his poems at home and church entertainments and social gatherings (from his early twenties). Public offerings at first failed completely.

Then another opportunity presented itself when the trustee of the Charlottesville one-room school came to Greenfield and Riley saw his chance to offer a public entertainment there. After Riley explained to the school trustee his plan, the trustee appeared interested. The fellow not only have his consent to the enterprise, but agree to have the schoolhouse warm and lighted and to see that a large audience would greet him.

Minie Belle Mitchell (to the left), Greenfield author and Riley biographer shown in the backyard of her home, now the Riley Museum in Greenfield, Indiana.

Thinking this would be fun, Riley and his friend and roommate, John Skinner, prepared a variety show with a few guitar numbers and reading of poetry by Riley.

Charlottesville was eight miles east of Greenfield and the two young men in their twenties, never doubting that a full house would mean a big income, ordered a horse and buggy from Greenfield's liveryman, a Mr. Morgan. The only problem was that the only road to Charlottesville was a toll road at the time. To get there a tollgate had to be passed and neither Riley nor Skinner had any money to get through. When the two reached the tollgate, they got the toll gate keeper to agree to await payment until they returned with their receipts from the entertainment.

The two arrived at Charlottesville and went to the schoolhouse but found it dark. Everyone in Charlottesville was in bed. The two drove their team to the trustee's home and found him in bed too. He forgot his promise to broadcast publicity about the entertainment. He did, however, get up and go open the schoolhouse. About a dozen people were rousted up. The collection to pay for the show at the end of the program amounted to only thirty-five cents. The trustee said he and his family should not have to pay.

The two boys were in a quandary since they had to pay the tollgate keeper to get home and the liveryman.

When the two reached the tollgate, they found the tollhouse was dark - the tollgate keeper was in bed and the pole across the road was tied down. There was just one thing to do. John Skinner got out and cut the rope and up flew the pole from across the road. Then he got back in and the two flew down the road towards Greenfield as if chased by bandits.

When the two got to the livery stable, Riley found a boy in charge. Riley as Jucklet, ever resourceful, asked the boy if he could change a twenty dollar bill. The boy said "No," and told them young men they would have to pay for the horses in the morning when Mr. Morgan was there.

The Guyman Inn, an inn on the National Road in Greenfield, Indiana, long since torn down. Riley took a room here after his return from his escapade with Doc McCrillus and his traveling miracle medicine show.

Then the two returned to their lodgings at the Guyman Inn in Greenfield where they spent their "take" from the entertainment on cheese and crackers sinking behind the potbelly stove in the tavern office. While they were relaxing, there was a great knocking on the tavern door, and the irate tollgate keeper came in, fuming and swearing. He asked the night clerk if he had heard a rig pass by the tavern traveling at high speed. The clerk said he didn't remember any such thing and then listened as the tollgate keeper told his tale of somebody running the tollgate and probably driving on to Indianapolis. He said, "I think I know who they were. Two young men looking awful suspicious went through earlier and said they would pay on their way back through. They were wearing white collared shirts and looked like city fellers."

As Riley and Skinner slumped deeper and deeper into their chairs on the other side of the stove, the clerk confirmed that young men like that were probably city "fellers" as the tollgate keeper left."

Getting started as a poet and platform artist was made much easier for Riley because, as Jucklet, he appreciated and enjoyed mischief and the occasional humor of the perverse.

There is something to be said that Riley's Jucklet character has the good humor and sense of fun of his Hoosier Deutsch ancestors. Central Indiana is sometimes referred to as the land of the "Hoosier Deutsch." Riley was predominantly of Hoosier Deutsch cultural influence. Riley's father, Reuben, spoke Deutsch in his boyhood home and did not learn to speak English until after his childhood even though he came from Irish roots. Riley's ancestors kept alive many of the old folktales and stories of their lives. Few of these Deutsch tales survive. I myself preserved one in a book called THE WILD BULL OF BLUE RIVER.

The records are very, very scant about the hardy Deutsch settlers of Central Indiana. Their language was once spoken on the street corners of Greenfield. Cultural influences discouraged it. For example, in Riley's own Bradley Methodist Church of Greenfield, Indiana those who spoke German were consigned to the back of the church since it was deemed only the English speaking Methodists could derive benefit of the English sermons. Balconies were built in some such churches so that the Deutsch might see what was going on at the altar since they could not be expected to understand the service verbally. The Deutsch language was slowly lost in Indiana until the time of the First World War. In fact Deutsch was made illegal in Greenfield schools by an ordinance of the Greenfield City Council during World War One and was rarely spoken after that.

One of the Deutsch poems was preserved by Riley. It was called "Lullaby," and was published in Riley's famous column in the Indianapolis Saturday HERALD called "Poetical Gymnastics" in 1879. Its subtitle says "From the German." It has never been included in Riley's COMPLETE WORKS apparently because Riley translated it and it was not an original composition. Riley did write another "Lullaby" but it was not his Hoosier Deutsch translation.

HOOSIER DEUTSCH LULLABY

Leedle dutch baby haff gome to town!
Jabber and jump till der day goes down;
Jabber unt schpluter, unt blubber unt phizz
Vot a dutch baby dees lannsman is!
I dink dose mout vas leedle too vide
Obber you laugh fon dot also-side;
Haff got blenty of deemple unt vrown?
Hey, leedle dutchman gome to town.

Leedle dutch baby, I dink me proud
Obber your fader can schquall dot loud
Ven he vos leedle dutch baby like you,
Unt yoost don'd gare like he always do;
Guess ven dey vean id on beer you bet
Dots der reason he don'd vean'd yet -
Vot you said off he drink you down,
Hey, leedle dutchman gome to town.

Leedle dutch baby, yoost schquall avay -
Schquall fon breakfast till gisterday:
Better you all-time gry unt shoud
Dan schmile me vonce fon der coffin oud!
Vot I gare off you keek my nose
Downside-up, mit you heels unt toes -
Downside-up, or sideup-down
Hey! leedle dutchman gome to town.

The kitchen at the Riley brithplace, Greenfield, Indiana, where Riley was born.

Riley enjoyed being a Hoosier Deutschman as we can tell from this recollection of one of their poems. The Hoosier Deutsch were a playful, happy people who enjoyed life as well as industry. They were wanderers. Jucklet sprang from predominantly Deutsch culture although not entirely from Deutsch roots.

Andrew A. Riley, Irish grandfather of James Whitcomb Riley, was born in Bedford County, Pennsylvania in a Deutsch speaking community. Andrew's parents were Rebecca Harvey, born July 11, 1769 in England who died in Montgomery County, Ohio on Sept. 7, 1849, and James (or John

"William") Riley born 1752 in Torsnagh, Cork, Ireland who died in Bedford, Pennsylvania before 1820. The source of this pedigree is listed in the acknowledgements. James Riley had married Rebecca Harvey about 1775 at Reading Berks, Pennsylvania.

Scene at a Kee-wau-nay village of 1837. Sketch by George Winter. Indiana historians generally find Indian removals from Indiana occurred by tribes with the Delaware leaving in the 1820's as required by the Treaty of St. Mary's or "New Purchase Treaty of 1818," the Potawatomi in the 1830's on the "Trail of Death of 1838," and the Miami in the 1840's mostly from those left in the Ft. Wayne area around 1847.

Andrew was the second child. The firstborn was Samuel Riley, born 1790. After Andrew came James Anderson Riley, born 1796 who died in Nov. 1840; Isaac Riley, born about 1800; Henry Riley, born about 1803; George Washington Harvey Riley, born Dec. 19, 1807 who died May 22, 1868; Sarah Riley, born about 1810 in Pennsylvania who married George Roudebush; and Mary Ann Riley, born 1813 who died in 1887.

Andrew's wife, Margaret Slick, was the daughter of John Slick born about 1769, the son of Philip Slick born about 1740 in Germany, and Elizabeth Wilson. Andrew A. Riley and Margaret Slick were married in Bedford, Pennsylvania, but the Family Bible gives no date. It must have been around 1820 since they started West soon after that date. They stopped first near Cincinnati, Ohio and then at Richmond and finally located on a farm a short distance southeast of Windsor in the western part of Randolph county on what was later known as the Joshua Swingley farm, with Andrew remaining there and running a tavern until the time of his death about November 29, 1840. He was also the local justice of peace for Stoney Creek Township until 1837 according to the bond records of the county. The farm was on a knoll along Stoney Creek. Coming to frontier Indiana was a daring family trip. During the 400 mile journey from Pennsylvania, Andrew sold all of his belongings for $30 except a horse, a "carry-all" and some clothing. He and his older sons walked while the mother and daughters rode in the wagon. Reuben Riley was one of those sons who walked. He was the fifth in a family of 14 children. During this westward trek, the family lived in the open, building campfires in the woods at night. In the Allegheny foothills, their fare was slight. When they reached Randolph County, Indiana, they were able to find a bounty of food from wild deer, black bear, squirrels, wild turkey and wild vegetables growing along Stoney Creek.

Andrew and Margaret had the following children: Sarah Ann Riley, born about 1815 who married Tom D. Shepherd; Job Harvey Riley, born about 1816; John Sleek Riley (Dr.) born Dec. 12, 1817; Reuben (the poet's father) born June 2, 1819; Andrew Pinckney Riley, born 1820 who married Elizabeth Cline; James Anderson Riley born about 1821; George Washington Harvey Riley born about 1823 who married Emma C. Nex; Joseph Sleek Riley, born about 1824; Benjamin Frank Riley born about 1826 who married Elizabeth Patterson; and Martin Whitten Riley born about 1828 who married Elizabeth Dodson.

A field cleared for crops with the stumps still in.

Andrew's agricultural labor produced large crops and one winter it is said he helped save a tribe of starving Miami Indians by loading their ponies with corn. In another time of scarcity, a stockman offered him 75 cents a bushel for his corn, but he chose to sell it to needy neighbors for 25 cents a bushel. Shortly before his death, Andrew said, "I have never intentionally wronged any man. I have not been vulgar or profane. I have tried to do right. I do not fear to die."

Not all Hoosiers could say the same.

Reuben Riley reached Hancock County, Indiana, within a few scant years of the departure of the last native Americans from Indiana. Many were wrenched away in a horrible episode in Indiana history. The last of the Potawatomi, those who had not accepted "white folks ways" or left before were rounded up and removed by the county militiamen of Indiana called up to state service for that purpose by the Governor in 1838.

These native Americans were forced to take the infamous "Trail of Death" out of Indiana during September of that year.

A militia officer, General Tipton, was placed in charge of the roundup of the Hoosier Indians. Many tried to escape into the woods but were arrested and made prisoners. Indian children were left in the woods by parents in the hope that they, at least, might be able to stay in the native lands if they could survive. Many stories exist of such children being adopted by "white European" families when they were discovered.

No sad story stopped General Tipton. He was not cruel but he knew what the Hoosier Governor's orders were and that was to round up the remaining Indians and get them out of the state. Here is an excerpt of one of his written accounts, "Many of the Indian men were assembled near the chapel when we arrived, and were not permitted to leave camp or separate until matters were amicably settled and they had agreed to give peaceable possession of the land sold by them." If Indians had weapons, these were taken away.

Squads of militia fanned out to collect the remnants of the tribes who had refused to move out of Indiana by that time.

By September, Tipton had gathered the last 859 which contained many old people and young. One of the Catholic missionaries, Father Petit, who had lived with the tribes describes his final Christian worship service since he was not permitted to go on the Trail of Death. "At the moment of my departure I assembled all my children to speak to them for the last time. I wept, and my auditors sobbed aloud. It was indeed a heartrending sight, and over our dying mission we prayed for the success of those on their way to the new hunting grounds. We then with one accord say, `O Virgin, we place our confidence in thee.' It was often interrupted and but few could finish it. After the Indians were sequestered, the soldiers were under orders to burn and destroy the huts and cabins of the Indians to erase temptation to return to Indiana.

When the Indian march order was given on the early morning of September 4th. The weather was very hot and dry. The ordinary sources of water were dried up by then and malaria started infecting the Indians because water supplies were stagnant. The native Americans were marched single file on foot to cross Indiana, Illinois and the Mississippi. Few made it. Even by the time they reached the pioneer settlement at Logansport many died. Their camp there was described as "a scene of desolation; on all sides were the sick and dying." The militiamen too were getting sick and many were permitted to return to their homes. The few Indians with Indian ponies were compelled to give them up for these departing militiamen to return to their families.

On the way through the Wabash Valley, the suffering increased so much that General Tipton relented and allowed the Indians to call for Father Petit to come to them. Despite his own delicate health the good father went and says, "On Sunday, September 16, I came in sight of my poor Christians, marching in a line, and guarded on both sides by soldiers who hastened their steps. A burning sun poured its beams upon them, and they were enveloped in a thick cloud of dust. After them came the baggage wagons into which were crowded the many sick, the women and children who were too feeble to walk... Almost all the babies, exhausted by the heat, were dead or dying. I baptized several newly-born happy little ones, whose first step was from the land of exile to heaven." Soon the militiamen tired of walking and chose to ride in the baggage wagons forcing the Indian

Bishop Brute preaching to the Hoosier Potawatomi Indians on September 9, 1838 just prior to their dispatch from Indiana on the "Trail of Death." Sketch by George Winter.

women and children out to walk and die all the quicker.

Many stories remain. There is one of a hundred year old Indian woman, the mother of a Chieftain, who pleaded with her tribe to put her to death in Indiana. She knew she had no hopes of surviving a long trek and wished to be buried in the land of her ancestry. The tribe refused the old woman's wish to kill her. She was buried along the trail four days later. Not a single baby made the trip.

The Hoosier people live with the memories of their history. These memories mix with those of the settlers like Andrew Riley who came to Hoosier forests.

There are no records of Andrew's death in the Family Bible and his date of death in 1840 is derived from the records in the Randolph County probate court records of that date. A Dr. Dynes was the attending physician during Andrew Riley's last illness. Dr. Dynes made daily calls for some days prior to November 20, 1840. His itemized claim filed against the estate shows a charge each day up to and including November 19th for a call and medicine left. On the 20th day a charge is made for just the call - no medicine. This was the doctor's last call so Andrew probably didn't need the doctor anymore. Andrew Riley was buried on the farm where he lived.

In the probate court order book of Randolph County, vol. 2, page 139 is this entry:

"Be it remembered that on the fifteenth day of December in the year of our Lord, one thousand eight hundred and forty; letters of administration of all and singular the goods and chattels, rights, credits, monies and effects which were of Andrew Riley late of Randolph County in the State of Indiana, deceased, was granted by George W. Monks, clerk of the probate court in and for said county to Reuben A. Riley,he, the said Reuben A. Riley, having first filed bond in the sum of fifteen hundred dollars with Lewis Remmel and Smoot securities and he was duly affirmed as such administrator."

Reuben Riley's authority to handle his father's estate was later revoked by this entry:

"In the matter of Reuben A, Riley, administrator of the estate of Andrew Riley, deceased. It appearing to the satisfaction of the court, from the affidavit of Margaret Way, late Margaret Riley, widow and relict of said Andrew Riley, that the said Reuben A. Riley has emigrated to and is now a citizen of Iowa Territory. It is ordered and adjudged by the court that the letters of administration heretofore granted by the clerk of this court to the said Reuben A. Riley, on the estate of said deceased, be and the same are hereby revoked and nulled and made void. Whereon on application of the said Margaret, it is further ordered by the court that administration de bonis non of said estate is hereby committed to Thomas W. Reece, and thereupon said Thomas W. Reece appears in open court and accepts said appointment and files bond in the sum of twelve hundred dollars, with William Dickson and George W. Smithson as his securities."

What became of Margaret?

Margaret (Slick) Riley remained Andrew's widow for only about a year and a half and then in March 1842 she married Thomas Way. Little is known about this arrangement. Eventually Margaret moved from the Windsor neighborhood to Greenfield, Indiana, as a single woman, and lived near her son Reuben Riley until 1868. She died October 3, 1884 at the home of her son Dr. A.J. Riley in Muncie. The funeral notices were sent out under the name of Margaret Riley. The notice read: "Mrs. Margaret Riley was born in Bedford County, Pa. October 23rd, 1793, died at the home of her son, Dr. A.J. Riley in Muncie, Indiana, Monday evening, Oct. 3rd, 1884, aged 87 years, 11 months, and 10 days. Her funeral will take place tomorrow, Wednesday, October

Riley's grandmother, Margaret Riley (Way), "rouser" of frontier Hoosier Methodists. (Neg.C7178, IMCPL-Riley Collection, Indiana Historical Society.)

5th at the grave yard near Windsor, Randolph County, at 2 o'clock P.M. The funeral cortege leaving Muncie at 8 o'clock A.M. The funeral services will be conducted by Rev. F.D. Simpson. The friends of the family are invited." The dates have to be wrong because if correct she died at 90.

The burial places of Andrew and Margaret Riley are in the Clevenger Cemetery about a mile south of Windsor. The exact spots are no longer locatable. The lettering of the stones is mostly erased in this cemetery, vegetation has overgrown it and most tombstones are broken or at least half-buried. Windsor might well have become the birth home of James Whitcomb Riley. Reuben Riley owned a lot there and was licensed to practice law there in 1842 but Riley's stay was short and he sold his lot in Windsor to Andrew West on August 18, 1842.

After his father's death, Reuben had gone to a prairie village in Iowa, been admitted to the bar there, but had only achieved a very limited practice. He subsequently returned to Randolph County. He was tall, black eyed and considered to be an eloquent debater.

Reuben Riley became reacquainted with Elizabeth Marine at a Fourth of July gathering in Neeley's Woods, near Windsor, in 1843 after his return from Iowa. The occasion was a grand barbecue of pigs, an ox and five lambs. Reuben danced with Elizabeth and the two were said to have decided to get married instantly.

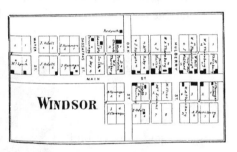

An 1865 plat of Windsor, Indiana. Reuben Riley owned Lot 5 in Block 1 of Windsor (corner of Main and Mulberry) until he sold it for $40 on August 18, 1842 to go to Iowa. Reuben Riley's parents lived on a farm in the vicinity of Windsor and are buried near this Hoosier town.

Reuben Alexander Riley and Elizabeth (Marine) Riley, parents of the poet, were married March 15, 1844 at Union Port, Randolph county, by Rev. Thomas Leonard, minister of the Methodist church. Elizabeth's brother Jonathan and Emily Hunt stood up for the two. Elizabeth wore a pale pink silk wedding dress with a long white veil and white kid gloves and shoes. Her "in-fair" dress was of gray poplin, and she wore a leghorn bonnet when she rode away with Reuben the next day. They went immediately to Greenfield and occupied a log cabin. The marriage license of Reuben A. Riley and Elizabeth Marine was issued by the Clerk of the Randolph Circuit Court on the 18th of Feb. but they were not married until about a month later, March 15, 1844.

Elizabeth Marine Riley's father was John Marine. In the Riley family Bible she spells his last name M-E-R-I-N-E. John Marine's father was Jonathan Marine and his mother was Mary Charles who lived in the Carolinas. Mary Charles Marine died in Wayne County, Indiana, and was buried in Randolph County. Jonathan Marine was buried in the New Garden churchyard about nine miles from Richmond. Mary Charles Marine lived to be ninety-six years old.

Elizabeth was the tenth in a family of 11 children and a descendent of persecuted French Huguenots and English Quakers. She claimed birth in Rockingham, North Carolina in 1823.

Probably Reuben's first work was on his father's farm and in his tavern. Reuben Riley became the school teacher in the little one-room schoolhouse at the east end of Union Port on the south side of the road. Soon after marriage the Rileys went to Greenfield to Hancock county to make their future home.

Greenfield was at that time a little village of a few scattered log houses with puncheon floors and oil paper windows. Reuben Riley was said to have built the log cabin and equipped it with furniture which he had made. The main advantage of the site was that it was located on the National Road that stretched from Cumberland, Maryland across country to the trails to the Pacific Coast.

A pioneer wagon on the National Road.

It was here in their original log cabin that their six children were born. The Riley children were John Andrew Riley, born Dec. 11, 1844 who married Julia Wilson and died Dec. 11, 1911; Martha Celestia Riley, born Feb. 21, 1847; James Whitcomb Riley, born Oct. 7, 1849 and died July 22, 1916 in Indianapolis, Indiana, Elva May Riley born Jan. 1856 and died in 1909 in Indianapolis, Indiana; Humboldt Alexander Riley born Oct. 15, 1858 and died Nov., 1887; and Mary Elizabeth Riley born Oct. 27, 1864 who married and divorced Frank C. Payne and died in 1936.

There is speculation that James Whitcomb Riley's genius came from John Marine, the probable father of Elizabeth and an outstanding character in the early history of Randolph and Delaware counties. John Marine loved poetry and, like his famous grandson, was said to have written his autobiography in rhyme. He also was said to write and write. He wrote a book, now lost, on religion urging all Christians to unite. He also wrote sermons in verse and delivered them to Methodist camp meetings. None of these works survive. John had lost his modest fortune speculating in weaver-sleighs two years after Elizabeth's birth and came to Indiana.

James Whitcomb Riley was one of those many great men who have been unusually fond of their mothers. There was the artist Whistler whose most famous work was a portrait of his mother. Then there was George Washington. No matter how far his surveying took him from Virginia, he kept in touch with Mary Washington. To this list, we must add James Whitcomb Riley whose primary love was Elizabeth Marine Riley, his lovely mother. His first poem was a valentine written to his mother.

As a child, she had come in a one-horse buggy with her parents the 700 miles from North Carolina to Indiana. They came over the Cumberland Gap, the usual route through the Allegheny Mountains. Then on through the endless forests where all sorts of wild animals lurked. There were about 400 in their party which finally found its way to Randolph County Indiana. The party found only wilderness without any inhabitants or built up places or village.

After brief stops at New Garden and one or two points in Wayne County, he settled with his family in Randolph County and built a cabin on a high bank of the Mississinewa River a few miles below Ridgeville and a mill nearby.

James Whitcomb Riley thought that his mother had led an ideal life as a young person. The Marine cabin was on the banks of a beautiful stream, called by an Indian name, the Mississiniwa River. She had grown to become a beautiful young woman. One of Elizabeth's interests was discovering new things.

The Marines were flat boat builders, millers and poets. John laid out the defunct town of Rockingham on the Mississinewa and advertised lots in verse. It

"Rockingham," Indiana. A plat of a town drawn out by Elizabeth Riley's father. It was never inhabited except for the brief tenure of a store set on the high bluff on the south side of the Mississiniway (sic) River. The plat was recorded by J. Merine (sic) as Agent on March 31, 1836 in Randolph County, Indiana.

did no good. The town failed to attract settlers.

John also was a preacher and teacher. He advocated the union of all churches, a dangerous thing to do in those days. He and the poet's grandmother, Margaret Riley, were leaders in the camp meetings of Randolph and Delaware Counties.

William A. Thornburg, an elderly neighbor who remembered the Marines living nearby, told Marcus Dickey, an early Riley biographer, that "Elizabeth Marine was remarkably pure- minded. I never saw anyone so beautiful in a calico dress. She loved to wander along streams and wander in the green

Marcus Dickey, the secretary of James Whitcomb Riley and his earliest biographer.

woods. She was always seeing things among the leaves." Elizabeth met Johnny Appleseed who planted apple cores among the settlements and liked to listen to his accounts of his wanderings and his views on Christianity one of which was that folk do not die but "go right on living."

Every boy has an early determination - a first one - to follow some exciting profession, once he grows up to man's estate, such as being a policemen or a performer on the high trapeze. Riley was not interested in these nor in being the "People's Laureate," but the Greenfield baker, had his fairy godmother granted his "boy-wish."

Here is how Riley remembered his "wish" in his later life.

"AN IMPETUOUS RESOLVE" (1890)

When little Dickie Swope's a man,
He's going to be a sailor;
And little Hamey Tincher, he's
A'going to be a Tailor;
Bud Mitchell, he's a'going to be
A stylish Carriage-Maker;
And when I grow a great big man
I'm going to be a Baker.
And Dick will buy his sailor-suit
Of Hame; and Hame will take it
And buy as fine a double rig
As ever Bud can make it;
And then all three'll drive round for me,

And we'll drive off together
Slinging pie-crust along the road
Forever and forever.

To Riley, running a bakery "seemed the acme of delight," using again his own expression. Happiness was "to manufacture those snowy loaves of bread, those delicious tarts, those toothsome bon-bons. And then to own them all, to keep them in store, to watch over and guardedly exhibit. The thought of getting money for them was to me a sacrilege. Sell them? No indeed. Eat `em - eat `em, by tray loads and dray loads! It was a great wonder to me why the pale-faced baker in our town did not eat all his good things. This I determined to do when I became owner of such a grand establishment. Yes, sir. I would have a glorious feast. Maybe I'd have Tom and Harry and perhaps little Kate and Florry in to help us once in a while. The thought of these play-mates as `grown up folks' didn't appeal to me. I was but a child, with wide-open eyes, a healthy appetite

Elmer Swope. One of Riley's "gang" as a boy.

and a wondering mind. That was all. But I have the same sweet tooth to-day, and every time I pass a confectioner's shop, I think of the big baker of our town, and Tom and Harry and the youngsters all."

The Hancock County courthouse at the time of the Civil War. (From the Barton Rees Pogue glass positive collection.)

As a child, Riley often went with his father to the courthouse where the lawyers and clerks playfully called him "Judge Wick, Jr." Here as a privileged character he met and mingled with the country folk who came to sue and be sued, and thus early was exposed to the dialect, the native speech, the quaint expressions of his "own people." How frontier folk spoke took firm root in the fresh soil of his young memory.

Why was he called "Judge Wick, Jr.?"

William Wick was Circuit Judge of Hancock County from 1850 to 1853. It was during his tenure, James Whitcomb Riley came to have the nickname, "Judge Wick, Jr." The nickname came about when Reuben Riley made James Whitcomb Riley, about four years old, a suit of clothes identical in style and cloth to that worn by the Judge. The boy was given to wear a long swallowtail coat and matching trousers. When Riley first wore that outfit going with his father to court, he earned the name "Judge Wick, Jr." The judge gave him this name. It stayed with Riley through early adolescence when he hated it so much no one dared call him it anymore. While his father was in court, the poet listened and played in the back or in the window sills where he could see what was going on while cases were being tried.

The "rafter room" of the James Whitcomb Riley birthplace in Greenfield, Indiana where the poet slept as a child.

At about this time, he made his first poetic attempt in a valentine which he gave to his mother. Not only did he write the verse, but he drew a sketch to accompany it, greatly to his mother's delight, who, according to the best authority, gave the young poet "three big cookies and didn't spank me for two weeks. This was my earliest literary encouragement."

Oliver P. Morton, Indiana's Civil War Governor. Starting out as a hatter's apprentice, he went on to become a lawyer in Wayne County, Indiana before becoming Indiana's most important governor. During the Civil War, when the Hoosier legislature refused to appropriate funds, Morton borrowed millions of dollars on his own signature and without security to keep Indiana's government operating and on the side of the Union.

1856 was a critical year for the Riley family. It was the year Reuben Riley joined his friend Oliver P. Morton in forming a new political party in Indiana. Then, as the 1860 presidential election loomed, Reuben was an Indiana delegate at the Chicago convention that nominated Lincoln for the Presidency. After this convention, Reuben arrived home in the middle of the night to announce what had happened at the Chicago convention. Abraham Lincoln, the "Emancipator," had been nominated in part through Reuben's efforts in the Indiana delegation. Hancock County did not share Reuben's enthusiasm for Lincoln. Lincoln failed to carry Hancock County in the crucial 1860 election. Nevertheless, much of the rest of Indiana was solidly in the majority for Lincoln as was the tier of Northern states sufficient to elect Abraham Lincoln to the presidency. Reuben Riley was named a Lincoln "elector" to vote Indiana's selection of Lincoln for electoral college purposes.

Before throwing in his lot with Oliver Morton and Abraham Lincoln, Reuben Riley had been Hancock County Prosecutor in 1844, Representative in the Indiana Legislature in 1845 (Reuben was the youngest member of the state legislature at the time) and 1848, published a newspaper, The INVESTIGATOR in Greenfield for six months in 1847, was prominent in the county Democratic conventions since 1845, and in 1852 became Greenfield's first mayor. This in effect made him a judge and enforcer of the city's ordinances, mainly against things such as assaults and batteries.

What did Riley remember of his earliest days in the log cabin at Greenfield? He recalled the first time the family had a night lamp. Here came Reuben Riley bringing home a lamp and chimney in one hand and a bottle of coal oil in the other. The family tinkered with it the whole evening. Riley said, "To us it gave forth marvellously lustrous light..I was then reading the "Arabian Nights," wholly enraptured with that magic story, and had come to the tale of the Wonderful Lamp and the cry of new lamps for old. Well, the smell of that coal oil became associated in my mind with Aladdin and his Wonderful Lamp, and to this day I cannot smell coal oil without recalling the old delights of the story and feeling myself lying prone on my stomach reading, reading, and reading by the hour."

A story survives of how Riley wandered after older boys toward the "Ole Swimmin' Hole" before he could swim. His father learned of this and ran toward the crick in a great panic. Upon arriving at the banks, his worst fears were realized. Riley was out in the middle splashing in the water. Only after Reuben jumped in and got out to save his son did he discover the poet was in no danger. He had been holding on to a submerged root that extended out from a huge tree.

What about Riley's dismal school record?

Mrs. Neill's was the first to try. She did not teach in a free public school, but rather a private pay one. The school began in the early Spring. Mrs. Neill had no experience as a teacher but enrolled students after advertising in a local Greenfield newspaper, "Mrs. Neill will open school at her residence on Monday next. This lady has had much experience and will, no doubt, render good service." Mrs. Neill taught as a mother would rather than as a formal teacher. She encouraged good behavior for a week by hanging a bright silver dollar around the scholar's neck until the bad behavior stopped. Mrs. Neill did not tolerate either lying or tattle-telling. Lying resulted in getting one's mouth washed out with lye soap and tattle-telling earned wearing a card with "tattle tale" in large letters. If a child was restless she took the child into her kitchen and gave him a cookie from the cookie jar or if thirsty permitted the child to go to the well and drink from a yellow gourd from a bucket drawn up with its cool water. All drank from the same gourd. On Friday afternoons she passed out small cardboard rings with holes in the center and brought out a box of colored yarn. The yarn was drawn in and out of the hole until filled and then the children had fluffy, colored balls to take home for the weekend. If a child fell asleep she took the child into her sitting room to a pallet beside her blind husband who sat on a rocker day in and day out rocking monotonously.

After attending Mrs. Neill's school, Riley went on to attend the Greenfield Academy in the late 50's. The school was first taught by a Greenfield Presbyterian Minister, Rev. David Montfort to supplement his salary. Reuben Riley was the secretary of this school. At the Academy, Riley was not comfortable. He didn't join "gangs" very easy because the boys did robust things that required more stamina than he had. He always lost in races. He sometimes went off by himself in depression. Reuben Riley wished his son to be more of a competitor. It is not believed Riley was able to rise above the Primary Department because of his difficulty with mathematics. Later in 1861, the Greenfield Academy moved to the Methodist Church where Lee O. Harris became the teacher after he got back from 90 days service. Then this private church-housed school ceased to operate because of the Civil War. Lee O. Harris had enlisted in the Fifth Indiana Cavalry for a three year term. During this period, Riley is recalled as being truant in school, but it was more anti-social than anti-intellectual. He was said to be a persistent truant and to go off by himself into the woods.

Lee O. Harris, Riley's childhood teacher, cavalry officer in the American Civil War and noted poet.

Probably recalling this period, Riley wrote of truanting "Out to Old Aunt Mary's in his later days:"

OUT TO OLD AUNT MARY'S (1884)

Wasn't it pleasant. O brother mine,
In those old days of the lost sunshine
Of youth - when the Saturday's chores were through,
And the "Sunday's wood" in the kitchen, too,
And we went visiting, "me and you,"
Out to Old Aunt Mary's? -

"Me and you" - And the morning fair,
With the dewdrops twinkling, everywhere;
The scent of the cherry-blossoms blown
After us, in the roadway lone,
Our capering shadows onward thrown -
Out to Old Aunt Mary's!

It all comes back so clear to-day!
Though I am as bald as you are gray, -
Out by the barn-lot and down the lane
We patter along in the dust again,
As light as the tips of the drops of the rain,
Out to Old Aunt Mary's.

A country road with rail fence aside in Hancock County, Indiana, in the late Nineteenth Century. Such a road would have led "Out to Old Aunt Mary's." John A. Howland photography collection.

The few last houses of the town;
Then on, up the high creek-bluffs and down;
Past the squat toll-gate, with its well-sweep pole,
The bridge, and the "the old 'baptizin'-hole,'"
Loitering, awed, o'er pool and shoal,
Out to Old Aunt Mary's.

We crossed the pasture, and through the wood,
Where the old gray snag of the poplar stood,
Where the hammering "red-heads" hopped awry,
And the buzzard "raised" in the "clearing"-sky
And lolled and circled, as we went by
Out to Old Aunt Mary's.

Or, stayed by the glint of the redbird's wings,

or the glitter of song that the bluebird sings,
All hushed we feign to strike strange trails,
As the "big braves" do in the Indian tales,
Till again our real quest lags and fails -
Out to Old Aunt Mary's. -

And the woodland echoes with yells of mirth
That make old war-whoops of minor worth!...
Where such heroes of war as we? -
With bows and arrows of fantasy,
Chasing each other from tree to tree
Out to Old Aunt Mary's!

And then in the dust of the road again;
And the teams we met, and the countrymen;
And the long highway, with sunshine spread
As thick as butter on country bread,
Our cares behind, and our hearts ahead
Out to Old Aunt Mary's. -

A "trundle bed" where young children slept. The bed was pulled out at night.

For only, now, at the road's next bend
To the right we could make out the gable-end
Of the fine old Huston homestead - not
Half a mile from the sacred spot
Where dwelt our Saint in her simple cot -
Out to Old Aunt Mary's.

Why, I see her now in the open door
Where the little gourds grew up the sides and o'er
The clapboard roof! - And her face - ah, me!
Wasn't it good for a boy to see -
And wasn't it good for a boy to be
Out to Old Aunt Mary's? -

The jelly - the jam and marmalade,
And the cherry and quince "preserves" she made! And the
sweet-sour pickles of peach and pear,
With cinnamon in 'em, and all things rare! -

And the more we ate was the more to
    spare,
   Out to Old Aunt Mary's!

Ah! was there, ever, so kind a face
And gentle as hers, or such a grace
   Of welcoming, as she cut the cake
   Or the juicy pies that she joyed to make
   Just for the visiting children's sake -
    Out to Old Aunt Mary's!

The honey, too, in its amber comb
One only finds in an old farm-home;

The spinning wheel of the Riley's, a truly pioneer Hoosier family.

  And the coffee, fragrant and sweet, and ho!
  So hot that we gloried to drink it so,
   With spangles of tears in our eyes, you know -
   Out to Old Aunt Mary's.

And the romps we took, in our glad unrest! -
Was it the lawn that we loved the best,
   With its swooping swing in the locust trees,
   Or was it the grove, with its leafy breeze,
   Or the dim haymow, with its fragrancies -
   Out to Old Aunt Mary's.

Far fields, bottom-lands, creek-banks - all,
We ranged at will. - Where the waterfall
   Laughed all day as it slowly poured
   Over the dam by the old mill-ford,
   While the tail-race writhed, and the mill-wheel roared -
   Out to Old Aunt Mary's.

But home, with Aunty in nearer call,
That was the best place, after all! -
   The talks on the back porch, in the low
   Slanting sun and evening glow,
   With the voice of counsel that touched us so,
   Out to Old Aunt Mary's.

And then, in the garden - near the side
Where the beehives were and the path was wide, -
  The apple-house - like a fairy cell -
  With the little square door we knew so well,
  And the wealth inside, but our tongues could tell -
    Out to Old Aunt Mary's.

And the old spring-house, in the cool green gloom
Of the willow trees, - and the cooler room
  Where the swinging shelves and the crocks were kept,
  Here the cream in a golden languor slept,
  While the waters gurgled and laughed and wept -
    Out to Old Aunt Mary's.

And as many a time have you and I -
Barefoot boys in the days gone by -
  Knelt, and in tremulous ecstasies
  Dipped our lips into sweets like these, -
  Memory now is on her knees
    Out to Old Aunt Mary's -

For, O my brother so far away,
This is to tell you - she waits to-day
  To welcome us: - Aunt Mary fell
  Asleep this morning, whispering, "Tell
  The boys to come"...And all is well
    Out to Old Aunt Mary's.

The dress Riley wore on his first day of school on display at the Riley birthplace, Greenfield, Indiana.

Some think that "Aunt Mary" was "Aunt Rachel Loehr," the relative of Almon Keefer, an older neighbor boy as the "Aunt Mary." Riley visited her often as a vagrant child escaping his poverty-stricken adolescent home. The Loehr and Riley families visited each other as well. Minnie Belle Mitchell provides an idealized picture of Riley's youth going to Aunt Rachel's as follows:

"...the three boys, Bud, John and Hum with Almon Keefer would go to Aunt Rachel's alone, walking the entire distance, loitering along country roads....cutting through time land, playing games of make-believe, giving Indian and catbird calls and gathering hackberries and haws along the way.

But all weariness disappeared when Aunt Rachel's home was reached and they were welcomed...The country home...had its gourd vine climbing to the roof... It had its windless well, its little spring house where the milk and butter and all sorts of good things were kept cool and fresh. There hollyhocks at the windows and a swing hung from an apple tree. And after the children had taken their usual bareback ride on the old mare, slid down the hay stack, and had visited the traps where robber rabbits and foxes were caught...Aunt Rachel would call them to dinner. The boys recalled the wild scramble to the well for the hasty washing of hands and faces, the "jellies, jams and marmalades," the usual cherry cobbler or custard pie with plenty of milk to drink.

The poem is nominally written to Riley's brother, John, which helps to date its first writing. Riley used an original four stanzas for "Old Aunt Mary's" from the letter in his early platform appearances.

New stanzas were added over the years. In a special edition of the poem in 1904, the poem was completed with twelve additional stanzas.

Riley's great poetic characters were all "composites." There were actually many "Aunt Mary's." Aunt Mary was a "character type" of warm-hearted persons who cared for children. Possibly a new such person contributed every time Riley revised the poem which was often. Additionally every time an older person died, she seems to have been eulogized by obituary and funeral sermon as the kindly "Aunt Mary" of Riley's poem if Riley had only a remote connection to the decedent.

One version of how the poem "Out to Old Aunt Mary's" happened to be written has Riley and friend, "Haute" Tarkington, later Mrs. Ovid Butler Jameson, preparing to accompany Haute's little brother, Booth, who lived at Indianapolis, on a week-end visit with the grandparents and his Aunt Mary. Sunday came and with it, the prospect of a visit to Aunt Mary but it had to be postponed. On hearing of this disappointment Booth began to cry over the unexpected failure of his plan. This suggested a theme for the poet, who, with his characteristic genius wrote one of his best poems -"Out to Old Aunt Mary's." The poem was first published in

Possible "Aunt Mary." Mary Tarkington Alexander from Harding's HISTORY OF DECATUR COUNTY, INDIANA.

the Indianapolis JOURNAL and later revised. This Mary was Mary Tarkington Alexander and she lived in Greensburg, Indiana. Her portrait shows a warmly "pudgy" faced woman with friendly eyes, wide smile a close cropped white hair in a matronly gown. She was a person any child wanted to embrace in a hug. Among other candidates of aunt's" were "blood" aunts in Mooresville and Martinsville, Indiana. The family of Riley's mother, the Marines, were very close. Riley visited their families often as a child, adolescent and in his later years.

When a childhood friend heard Riley recite the poem in later years, he noted that the poem had changed and wrote Riley to enquire about it after which the following letter was returned:

Ann Arbor, Mich. Oct. 29, 1893

(Dear Clint Hamilton:) This, as I read it in public, is the "completion" of "Old Aunt Mary's." By joining these four stanzas, at fifth one of printed form, thereafter following in order as here written until last stanza of printed is reached - then using that still as closing stanza. Keep this copy, so hastily done, in your possession.

The jelly - the jam, and the marmalade,
And the cherry and quince "preserves" she made! -
And the sweet-sour pickles of peach and pear,
With cinnamon in 'em, and all things rare!
And the more you ate was the more to spare,
Out to old Aunt Mary's!

And then, in the garden, near the side
Where the bee-hives were, and the path was wide, -
The apple-house, like a fairy cell,
With the little square door we knew so well -
And the wealth inside but our tongues could tell -
Out to old Aunt Mary's!

Clinton Hamilton

And the old spring-house, in the cool green gloom
Of the willow trees, - and the cooler room
Where the swinging shelves and crocks were kept,
Where the cream in a golden languor slept,

Where the waters gurgled and laughed and wept -
Out to Old Aunt Mary's!

And as many a time have you and I
Barefoot boys in the days gone by -
Knelt, and with tremulous ecstacies
Dipped our lips into sweets like these, -
Memory now is on her knees
Out to old Aunt Mary's!

Very truly your old friend,
- James Whitcomb Riley

Here is Riley's picture of a life lived meaningfully in service to others.

Riley's niece by marriage, Harriet Eitel Wells remembered Riley telling her this incident from his schooling as she related in the Indianapolis STAR of October 7, 1934. When Riley's teacher asked him once where Christopher Columbus went on his second voyage, Riley asked his teacher who was Christopher Columbus? Then Riley admitted he didn't know where the fellow went on the first trip. Math went in one ear and out the other. Riley's math teacher once commented "He doesn't know which is more - Twice ten or Twice Eternity."

Riley was Jucklet in his early schooling. He was an errant scholar and traveler even before he got Riley into mischief in many other ways. He loved fun. As a scholar, Riley knew how to slide a piece of wood under the old school clock and get it out of plumb so it ran faster, shortening the school hours which seemed far too long. This way Riley caused his school to be dismissed early from time to time pleasing the other pupils, especially his `swimmin'-hole' buddies. Riley was often a hero of his schoolmates. If caught on any of his pranks, he took his "licking" like a boy should, and did not try to lay the blame on someone else.

William B. Davis recalls it was in the winter of `59 that he first saw and met Jim Riley. He was in the rear of the old music hall at Greenfield working on a horizontal bar. "He was the quickest fellow - boy -that I ever saw. He was just like a squirrel going round and round in a cage. He was 10 years old then - and he could turn either backward or forward." Riley often went out to the Davis's farm because Reuben kept his horse there.

There is another incident about Riley's schooling of this period. Inside his big geography and held down under a rubber band, Riley frequently had a copy of Longfellow's poems which he read surreptitiously. When Riley's

instructor, Lee O. Harris passed up and down the aisles between the rows of
desks and came near Riley's desk, he always pretended not to see the book
of poems. How it would delight this old professor to know that toward the
end of this little pupil's life he would
receive so many college degrees that he
would remark he would have to stop writing
poetry so as to remember his degrees.

When the Greenfield Academy fizzled
out due to the Civil War, Riley went to
study at the home of Rhoda Houghton
Millikan who arrived in Greenfield in 1862
and opened a school in her home. Rhoda
Millikan was the daughter of a Superior
Court Judge and a native of Vermont. She
was a cultured, educated lady and possessed
many talents. She was the widower of a
man who had left his family in Ohio to
prospect for gold in Calfornia during the
"gold rush." The husband never returned
leaving Rhoda Millikan to raise five children - two girls and three boys. She taught
school to make ends meet.

An example of Riley's early "horrible" penmanship. (From "Man's Devotion"). Riley's
first poems are found in a small note-book
containing twenty-four poems some of which
were written when Riley was a boy. This one
is signed Jay Whit.

Riley practically moved into the Millikan home. One of the daughters
was Nellie Millikan who was "Dwainie" of "The Flying Islands of the
Night." Nellie was slightly older than Riley and enchanted him with her
playing of the piano and guitar. One of the boys, Jesse, became Riley's best
friend.

Rhoda Millikan's family were readers and had many books. They were
musical and both girls played and sang.

Riley held the mother in great esteem. She had a bright schoolroom, pictures which she painted on the walls, and wooden benches for the students
to sit on. She kept hanging jars filled with garden flowers in summer and in
winter, parlor ivy and wandering jew trailed about. The woods were visible
from her back yard to offer shade for a recess playground.

She directed Riley's studies along the lines of his interest, art, literature
and poetry. Riley was memorizing verse she discovered. She gave him
prominent parts in Friday afternoon exercises and allowed him to recite
poems he memorized from his mother.

Mrs. Millikan - who was an artist - began a Saturday afternoon class in painting and drawing. Riley became a pupil and found he could draw almost anything and easily became her star pupil.

An incident from Riley's adolescence in Mrs. Millikan's school survives.

As a young self-conscious teen, Riley's face was covered with freckles and he was called "Spotted Face" by friends. As an adolescent he became very conscious of these. He tried many things, buttermilk, vinegar and salt and was often washing his face with lye soap. He took an old custom seriously and prayed for May to wash his face in its due which he was told would get rid of them. One day his mother sent him to the store to get sugar for 50 cents and he bought a bottle advertised "A sure cure for freckles, - Balm of a thousand flowers" instead. He charged the sugar, went home to deliver the sugar, and stopped at a deserted barn to coat his face with the Balm of a Thousand Flowers without reading the instructions. When he arrived at school, Ms. Millikan was angry and while the schoolmates laughed took him from the room to look at his face as yellow as a pumpkin. The Balm was supposed to be washed off almost immediately after being put on. His face was stained for several days and when it came off the freckles and also a layer of skin came with it. He never again had freckles.

There really is no play character from Riley's autobiographical poem "The Flying Islands of the Night" who relates to Riley's adolescence except Nellie Millikan Cooley, "Dwainie," in Riley's life. This reflects the great unhappiness and poverty Riley knew as an adolescent.

Riley was not a happy teenager. He ascribed his lack of a social life to a "poor start" from those days. He claimed frustration from the very first. When he wished to escort his first sweetheart to a party, Riley said he dressed very carefully and knocked at his first love's door. Her father opened it, eyed him critically and demanded: "What you want, Jimmy?"

When Riley said, "Come to take Bessie to the party," the father snorted, "Humph! Bessie ain't goin' to no party; Bessie's got the measles!"

Riley knew very well she didn't.

As the Civil War came to a close, Greenfield reopened the Academy. In fact, Reuben Riley was chosen as the president of the public meeting called to plan its operation. This school began in 1866 and ran a fourteen week session. Riley started this school but attended in a very haphazard manner. He was truant as much as he was present. During one such truancy, his father beat him severely. It did not help. Riley quit school at sixteen.

After Riley was a drop out, his reputation in Greenfield slipped lower and lower. The other boys weren't to be around him. In a youthful letter to a friend who has been told to stay away from him, the sixteen year old Riley comments,"Your father forbids your associating with me. Well, with his understanding of my character, he did what was right. Well, so long as he thinks me a mean boy, just so long you must abide his law, for he thinks it for your good. Sometime, maybe, I can show him my real character..."

THE BOY LIVES ON OUR FARM

BY JAMES WHITCOMB RILEY

Riley book covers became such works of art that some were removed and framed for Hoosier homes as was this one.

Riley did not attend another school for several years but he was present on January 26, 1870 when Greenfield opened its first public school with 236 students. The school ran from January to May. Lee O. Harris was one of the teachers. Riley distinguished himself as an editor of one of the two school newspapers, his being The CRITERION.

Meredith Nicholson, Riley's friend in later life and noted American author, believes that Riley "would have been injured rather than benefited by an ampler education. He was chiefly concerned with human nature, and it was his fortune to know profoundly those definite phases and contrasts of life that were susceptible of interpretation in the art of which he was sufficiently the master."

Riley's education best came from riding his horse about the American woods and towns and from contacts with the popular culture of America itself.

Riley's first employment was as a decorator of the shaving mugs that ornamented and did service to the customers of the barbershop of a black barber of Greenfield, George Knox. Knox says he received "35 cents per mug, for which there never was a time he did not seem duly grateful and appreciative. ...during five years, in return for the many services rendered in the line of his trade (painting), I kept him "shaven and shorn" without price or remuneration save as he paid me in the manner indicated above."

We remember that Riley lived in a poverty stricken home after his father was discharged from the Civil War as a disabled man. The sting of poverty never left Riley. As an old man, he refused to take change from any newsboy after buying a newspaper and when asked about this he explained that he remembered when he was that age when "coins were scarce."

Knox has written, "I nicknamed (Riley) Mr. Jones and we played at imagining that he was a rich farmer of eccentric ideas, and fixed impressions of his importance and standing as a tiller of the soil. I would frequently say to him: "Well, Mr. Jones, how does it happen that you are in town so late today," and he would reply in the dialect of the Hoosier farmer, accompanied with the peculiar nasal twang that have made his recitations famous - "Wal, I kum into town to-day, intendin' to go right back as soon as possible, and what did they do but pop me on the jury first thing. I put up at the tavern and there was so much noise about I couldn't sleep, so I got up about 4 o'clock this mornin' and bought me a cegar - two fer five you know - they last longer. I kum over to git a shave; how much do you ask for a shave, George." I would say ten cents. "Now, that's too much; I'll give you five cents for a shave." etc., etc."

George Knox, Riley's benefactor and Greenfield barber.

George Knox remembered the neighbors "sneered at him (Riley), (spoke) derisively of him and declared him no good."

Riley escaped into literature to avoid his wretched poverty as a teenager. He read more out of school than in. He came to love the literature of Charles Dickens most of all. Jucklet seized upon Dickens even though Dickens was not known for his poetry but rather for his prose. Meredith Nicholson, commented: Riley "knew his Dickens thoroughly, and his lifelong attention to "character" was due no doubt in some measure to his study of Dickens's portraits of the quaint and humorous."

Early in his schooling, Riley ran away when Dickens's "The Death of Little Nell" was read. "It was a matter of eternal wonder to me, how the other children could go strong- voiced and dry-eyed through those tragedies that almost broke my heart," he once said.

DEATH OF LITTLE NELL
(From McGUFFEY'S ECLECTIC READER)

She was dead. No sleep so beautiful and calm,
so free from trace of pain, so fair to look upon.
She seemed a creature fresh from the hand of God,
and waiting for the breath of life; not one who had

lived, and suffered death. Her couch was dressed
with here and there some winter berries and green
leaves, gathered in a spot she had used to favor.
"When I die, put near me something that has loved
the light, and had the sky above it always." These
were her words.
    She was dead. Dear, gentle, patient, noble
Nell was dead. Her little bird, a poor, slight
thing the pressure of a finger would have crushed,
was stirring nimbly in its cage, and the strong
heart of its child mistress was must and motionless
forever! Where were the traces of her early cares,
her sufferings, and fatigues? All gone. sorrow
was dead, indeed, in her; but peace and perfect
happiness were born, imaged in her tranquil beauty
and profound repose..."

A strange thing happens when we read about the life of Charles Dickens.
It begins to sound like Riley's.

We review the facts of the life of Charles Dickens, 1812-1870, to note
the great parallels of the lives of Jucklet and him. Dickens was born in
Portsmouth, but spent nearly all his life in London. It would turn out that
Riley, born in Greenfield, would spend most of his adult life in Indianapolis.

Dickens's father was a conscientious man, but lacked capacity for earning a livelihood. This reminds one of Riley's father. In consequence,
Dickens's youth was much darkened by poverty as was Riley's. Dickens
began his activelife as a lawyer's apprentice; but soon left this employment
to become a reporter. Riley did the same. Dickens followed this employment from 1831-1836. Dickens's first book was entitled, "Sketches of
London Society, by Boz." This was followed, in 1837, by the "Pickwick
Papers," a work which suddenly brought much fame to the author. His other
works followed with great rapidity, and his last was unfinished at the time
of his death. Riley's books of poetry were very popular from the first and
Riley kept on writing them. He wrote on and on and on.

Dickens visited America in 1842, and again in 1867. During his last visit,
he read his works in public in the principal cities of the United States. This
was what Jucklet came to have in mind for Riley to do.

The resources of Dickens' genius seemed exhaustless. He copied no
author, imitated none, but relied entirely on his own powers. He excelled

especially in humor and pathos. He gathered materials for his works by the most careful and faithful observation. And he painted his characters with a fidelity so true to their different individualities that, although they sometimes have a quaint grotesqueness bordering on caricature, they stand before the memory as living realities. His writings present very vividly the wants and sufferings of the poor and encourage kindness and benevolence.

Finally, somehow, despite his poverty-striken youth, Dickens came to great fame and, when he died, was honored with burial in Westminster Abbey, London.

Here was a live route for Riley to follow.

Riley's life parallels that of Dickens. I think this is intentional. Riley looked to Dickens as a role model. Out of such devotion, Riley gave to America figures as compelling as Dickens did for his Englishmen.

Dickens gave to England "Little Nell," while Riley gave to America "Little Haly" of "On the Death of Little Mahala Ashcraft" (1882).

"Little Haly! Little Haly!" cheeps the robin in the tree;
"Little Haly!" sighs the clover, "Little Haly!" moans the bee;
"Little Haly! Little Haly!" calls the killdeer at twilight;
And the katydids and crickets hollers "Haly!" all the night.
The sunflowers and the hollyhawks droops over the garden fence;
The old path down the garden walks still holds her footprints' dents;
And the well-sweep's swingin' bucket seems to wait fer her to come
And start it on its wortery errant down the old beegum. ...

Riley took from Dickens the impetus to get close to his own people in order to reflect them in his writing.

Riley learned from Dickens in the novel way that Riley did things. He made a play about Dickens' characters and got his chums to act them out in their lives in Greenfield. The shoeshop of Thomas Snow was "base." In fact, the cobbler, a recent immigrant from England who knew his Dickens, was the "stage manager." The adolescent boys mixing it up with Riley in this Dickens "life production" of Riley's called themselves the "Fagan Club."

Occasionlly, things got out of hand as when the Fagan Club members acted as Fagan's thieving band of children and literally stole everything they could "pickpocket." It was fun and Riley was learning how to become Dickens. They did not get caught often enough to get thrown in jail.

As the years continued, Riley probed the perimeters of Dickens's precedents.

To be as Dickens was, Riley felt it necessary to write publicly at every opportunity. This included writing letters to the editor of newspapers. In 1873 A friend in Mooresville, A.W. Macy, suggested Riley write a letter from Anderson to the Mooresville paper about his life in Anderson and Riley did so. Doc Marigold was the name Riley used in a correspondence letter published in the May 8, 1873 issue of the Mooresville ENTERPRISE. In one of Dickens' short stories a vendor of cheap articles was named "Doc Marigold. "Riley's letter was written at Anderson, April 24, 1873.

"Dear ENTERPRISE: I have been intending to write you a letter, but have deferred it from day to day until I could bestow more attention to it than has been at my command for some time. I have not been still in one place long enough to write my "John Hancock" in a legible manner on hotel registers; and now that I have at last "found a level, I am not certain that I can interest you; for I know so little of general importance that, was there nothing else to write about, my little would be as brief as the tail of Tam O'Shanter's mare.

Anderson is a very handsome little city of about five thousand inhabitants - good people, speaking generally, though, of course, "It takes all kinds of people," etc ...

The Methodist church is in strong power here; and noble and energetic ministers and mem-

"The James Whitcomb Riley," the deLuxe Coach Streamliner train." This train drawn by a steam locomotive was named for the poet and made daily trips between Cincinnati, Indianapolis and Chicago on the New York Central rail line in the Mid-Twentieth Century.

bers are doing great and good work. The leading business men here are principally workers in the church - as I believe they are in every thriving place. The city has one flaw it is its Courthouse - that looks really lost and out of place and uncomfortable, surrounded as it is with beautiful business blocks..."

In keeping with the scheme of Dickens to write of what he knew, Riley studied the Hoosier landscape very carefully and noted its many moods. Jucklet kept his eyes open if he was going to have Riley survive as a writer.

The strained mind of the adolescent Riley saw in the life of Dickens not just a man, but the range of characters that Dickens was able to portray.

Possibly out of this observation, Riley began to create his own characters, those he could see around him. Some of them were even promising "selves" for roles for him to become.

During Riley's twenties, Jucklet also very much liked hoaxes. Riley was familiar with practically all of such literature of every age. The Jucklet in him chose out the fantastic and weirdly amusing from it. One can imagine Riley overjoyed at coming across Poe's great hoax writing called "The Balloon Hoax." Riley no doubt wondered if the American public of 1878 would appreciate the sensational as had Poe's reading public. Poe's "The Balloon-Hoax" opened with the headline: "ASTOUNDING NEWS BY EXPRESS, VIA NORFOLK! - The Atlantic Crossed in Three Days! - Signal Triumph of Mr. Monck Mason's Flying Machine! -Arrival at Sullivan's Island, near Charlestown, S.C., of Mr. Mason...in the Steering Balloon, Victoria..." This was of course impossible in Poe's day but the fun of concocting a hoax as Poe had done no doubt played on Jucklet's mind. Riley was determined to outdo Poe!

Riley's poetry came to bear the mischievousness of Jucklet.

WHAT SMITH KNEW ABOUT FARMING (1871)

There wasn't two purtier farms in the state
Than the couple of which I'm about to relate; -
Jinin' each other - belongin' to Brown,
And jest at the edge of a flourishin' town. ...
(Smith, a rich town merchant with no knowledge of agriculture
decides to buy one, live in the country "where the air is
free" and take up farming, disastrously from a financial
point of view.)
...Mr. Smith found he was losin' his health
In as big a proportion, almost, as his wealth;
So at last he concluded to move back to town
And sold back his farm to this same Mr. Brown
At very low figgers, by gittin' it down.
Further'n this I have nothin' to say
Than merely advisin' the Smiths fer to stay
In their grocery stores in flourishin' towns
And leave agriculture alone - and the Browns.

There is something to be said about simply surviving. As James Whitcomb Riley grew to maturity, it was obvious that he was not going to survive easily. He was simply not born to be a domineering, noticeable person. Riley was a "shrimp" of a boy and man. He was not physical. He was not some macho study either. Most women took one look at him and said good-bye.

There is a letter Riley's friend, Nellie Cooley, wrote to him after she moved to Illinois. In the letter, Nellie tells him she has heard from a friend that Riley "has gone to the dogs." To which she replies that she "raved" about him as loyal Nellie always did. Nellie was the exception as she always was for Riley. Perhaps total loyalty and friendship blinded her.

Only by his wits did Riley survive. Riley needed to play Jucklet badly. As alcoholic as he was becoming, his wits remained. Some part of Riley needed to deal with his ever- increasing dependence upon alcohol.

How does an alcoholic survive?

Riley acknowledges in his autobiographical poem, "The Flying Islands of the Night," that he did it by relying upon his mischievous minstrelsy persona he calls Jucklet. Jucklet, in the autobiographical poem, is the "tool" of Crestillomeem for survival purposes. However, when Riley understands he must be sober for

The "Seminary" - The Reuben Riley family home after he lost Riley's boyhood home to creditors - with the Riley family standing in front.

some reason or another, he turns to his Jucklet role. When it comes to survival, Jucklet takes over the transformative role in the poem, "The Flying Islands of the Night." When it is necessary to "ditch" Crestillomeem, his dependency on alcoholism, Jucklet defies Crestillomeem and takes over.

From the third act of "The Flying Islands of the Night," we find the following:

"(General sensation within, and growing tumult without, with wrangling

cries of "Plot!" "Treason!" "Conspiracy!" and "Down with the Queen!".
"Down with the usurper!" Down with the Sorceress!")

Crestillomeem (Wildly)
Who dares to cry
"Conspiracy!" Bring me the traitor-knave!

(Growing confusion without - sound of rioting, - Voice, "Let
me be taken! Let me be taken!" Enter Guards, dragging Jucklet
forward, wild-eyed and hysterical - the Queen's gaze fastened
on him wonderingly.)

Crestillomeem
Why bring ye Jucklet hither in this wise?

Guard
O Queen, 'tis he who cries "Conspiracy!"
And who incites the mob without with cries
Of "Plot!" and "Treason!"
Crestillomeem (Starting)

Ha! Can this be true?
I'll not believe it! - Jucklet is my fool,
But not so vast a fool that he would tempt
His gracious Sovereign's ire. (To guards) *Let him be freed!*

(Then to Jucklet, with mock service)

Stand hither, O my Fool!

Jucklet (To Queen)

What! I, thy fool?
Ho! ho! Thy fool? -ho! ho! Why, thou art mine!"

Jucklet is not merely the survival force at work within Riley's alcoholism,
but also Riley's savior. Riley saw his wit and capacity to be humorous and
to "minstrelize" as a pathway to salvation from his alcoholism and to get by.

Riley's father sought out a more concrete way of getting by for his son when he arranged that Riley take up house and sign painting.

The former slave George L. Knox recalled, "One evening as I sat in my (barber) shop I heard three men talking. They seemed very much interested in their boys. One suggested that the carpenter's trade would be a good trade for his son to learn, another thought the painter's a good trade. The parents of the three boys finally concluded that they would have their sons learn the painter's trade. The men were Captain (Reuben) Riley, Morris Pierson and Mr. Lipskin. It seemed strange to me to hear these white men talk of putting their boys out to learn trades, as where I came from (the South) white boys did not have to work. The boy who was most indulged and petted and did the least was thought the most of. I wondered why three men took such an interest in their boys, as I thought to teach the white boys to work was out of the question. One of the boys who was to learn painter's trade was James Whitcomb Riley, now the Hoosier Poet, another Wm. Pierson, now Dr. Pierson of Morristown, and the other Harry Lipskin. They all learned their trade from a man by the name of Kiefer who could paint all kinds of pictures. He was thought quite an artist by the people of Greenfield. Some of the boys were more successful in their trade than the others. Young Riley seemed the most apt. He could drawn anything and would take up his pencil and a piece of paper and make a perfect picture of anything he wanted to. The boys, when they were out of the shop (Keefer's) would come to my place of business to lounge and idle the time away. James Whitcomb used to come quite often. He seemed different than the other boys and did not choose his associates from among the boys, but the men, such as Dr. Milligan, Ed Milligan and others. The other boys would keep coming, and bother me more or less, while young Riley would come around, but seldom bothered me or got in the way. I said to him one day, "J.W." I always called him that "you can come around to the shop when you desire; I like to have

Riley sign painted for a Greenfield, Indiana bank.

you; you are not like the other boys." He gradually became a frequent visitor at my place."

When we think of Riley in his twenties, we think of Riley traveling around Indiana living as a wanderer. He often returns to Greenfield, his hometown, but he rarely stays. He has learned to be a painter. Employments are casual and transitory. He paints a barn or a sign to earn enough money to go someplace else.

What kind of signs was Riley painting?

In the Post-Civil War Era, it was customary for every merchant to have his windows ornamented with a neatly worded sign done in different colors and always in a sort of scroll design with many fancy letters, mostly in script. An example of one is recorded by Henry Miller, a retired merchant who painted with Blowney's at South Bend, Indiana, at the same time James Whitcomb Riley did. A Riley sign in South Bend was at George Muessel's grocery store on the two lower lights of each window which consisted of four large panes and on the two lower ones he painted the following signs: "G.C. Muessel-queensware and crockery," and on the other two panes, "G.C. Muessel -groceries and provisions." The sign was done with Riley's usual flourish and many colored paints.

Riley stayed where he could. He grew a long red mustache. The pace is quick. Riley needs money so he travels from town to town in search of painting jobs. He returns to Greenfield as we know he did in February, 1873 but then heads back to Anderson where he and his friend, Jim McClanahan branch out into the Graphics, named after the NEW YORK GRAPHIC MAGAZINE, a periodical popular with designers. The Graphics consist of no less than three but sometimes more living on craftsmanship services offered to residents of the Indiana towns they pass through. These gentlemen lived freely and easily.

The Graphics did many odd-jobs. Frank Spear dressed silk hats while Riley painted signs. Others of the Graphics and what happened to them

Riley and the "Graphics." Riley is seated with the droopy mustache. It is believed Jim McClanahan is in the middle of the back row. Between the ages of 22 and 25 Riley grew a fine, droopy, dark red mustache while his hair was so blond it was almost white. Eventually he cut it off saying "I look like a walrus." (From the Barton Rees Pogue glass positive collection.)

were remembered in an Anderson IN Morning HERALD article on the death of Frank Spear of Jan. 4, 1895. Edward Lemon committed suicide in a newspaper office at Nellsville, Wisconsin. Jim McClanahan, who Riley called "The Poor Man's Friend," lived in Anderson. He subsequently died of exposure after being found drunk. Will Ethell was an artist of prominence and Turner Wickersham ended up in Kansas City.

Life with the Graphics was an "off and on" employment for Riley for four years - from 1873 until the Spring of 1877. The Graphics modus operandi for making a living was worked out slyly and mischievously. They would dress fashionably and enter a town and entertain especially the girls and get contracts to make signs from merchants. Farm wives along the roads would give them pies. They would then survive having the fun of it all while they travelled togeth-er. In this journey, Riley found his way to South Bend, Indiana in July 1873, where the Graphics dis-banded for a time and each went his own way until reforming again the next Spring. Riley stayed in South Bend for several days. One of Riley's most famous projects was the making of a mural about the

An interurban named "The James Whitcomb Riley" of the T.H.I & E. Traction Line is draped with an American Flag at the time of Riley's death. Interurbans or "streetcars" operated on electric power from over-head lines until they discontinued service at the commencement of the Great American Depression. This line quit in 1931.

progress of South Bend that took two weeks to finish. In 1873, After five weeks, Riley heard his father married again to a Quaker woman from a farm near Pendleton. In November, 1873 Riley went back to Anderson to work for Doc McCrillus but went home to Greenfield shortly afterwards to see his father and meet his father's new bride. Riley stayed in Greenfield in late 1873 to help start up a theatrical troop, the Adelphians, to put on plays in Greenfield during the winter. Lee O. Harris, Riley's old teacher, was still in Greenfield and they worked together on theatricals. Riley continued to write during this period of time and sent a poem to the Danbury Connecticut NEWS published in its February 25, 1874 issue. Originally the concept of painting advertising signs outside the stores, on barns, fences, or prominent places was profitable. Sign painting was a new medium. As the group traveled around Indiana, Jim McClanahan was able to bring in many new jobs. New helpers were brought in. The Graphics made great profits. Soon, however, new advertising "firms" sprang up. Competition grew fierce. New jobs became scarce and profits were just a memory. The business of "The Graphics" dwindled away until nothing when in the spring of 1877 Riley and McClanahan returned to Anderson insolvent where they knew they had room and board at least in Mother McClanahan's household.

Riley was a witty and companionable associate. The "Ho!", often repeated as "Ho! Ho!" or Ha!, etc., in the autobiographical poem "The Flying Islands of the Night" is an identifier of Jucklet, the "minstrel" Riley persona. Perhaps it likens Riley "To the Wine-God Merlus" of a poem of that name subtitled, "A Toast of Jucklet's" wherein the "Ho! Ho!" represents Jucklet's state when "the jolly god, with kinked lips and laughter-streaming eyes," has "liftest me up."

As Riley's years with the Graphics ended, he wrote his "Craqueodoom" for the Anderson DEMOCRAT of June 1, 1877. In the newspaper world there was great consternation. What did it mean? Craqueodoom" was exchanged with other newspapers and reached other audiences.

CRAQUEODOOM (1877)

The Crankadox leaned o'er the edge of the moon
And wistfully gazed on the sea
Where the Gryxabodill madly whistled a tune
To the air of "Ti-fol-de-ding-dee."
The quavering shriek of the Fly-up-the creek
Was fitfully wafted afar
To the Queen of the Wunks as she powdered her cheek
With the pulverized rays of a star.

The Gool closed his ear on the voice of the Grig,
And his heart it grew heavy as lead
As he marked the Baldekin adjusting his wing
On the opposite side of his head,
And the air it grew chill as the Gryxabodrill
Raised his dank, dripping fins to the skies,
And plead with the Plunk for the use of her bil
To pick the tears out of his eyes.

The ghost of the Zhack flitted by in a trance,
  And the Squidjum hid under a tub
As he heard the loud hooves of the hooken advance
  With a rub-a-dub-dub-a-dub-dub
And the Crankadox cried, as he lay down and died,
  "My fate there is none to bewail,"
While the Queeen of the Wunks drifted over the tide
  With a long piece of crape to her tail.

At Kokomo, the Editor Oscar Henderson published not only the poem but also two queries to the poet as to the meaning. William Croan, Riley's Editor at the Anderson DEMOCRAT, passed the queries along to Riley who went on to draft a reply subsequently published in "The DISPATCH."

Riley's reply was evasive and mysterious.

"Although in endeavoring to reply to the above query, I feel that I place myself in rather a peculiar position, I can but trust, in so doing, to escape the incessant storm in inquiries haled so piteously upon me since the appearance of the above mentioned poem - of whatever it is.

As to its meaning - if it has any I am as much in the dark, and as badly worried over its incomprehensibility as anyone who may have inflicted himself with a reading of it; in fact more so, for I have in my possession now not less than a dozen of similar character; and when I say they were only composed mechanically, and without apparent exercise of my own thought, I find myself at the threshold of a fact that over which I cannot pass.

I can only surmise that such effusions emanate from long and arduous application - a sort of poetic fungus that springs from the decay of better effort. It bursts into being of itself, and in that alone from the decay of better effort. It bursts into being of itself, and in that alone do I find consolation.

The process of much composition may furnish a curious fact to many, yet I am assured that every writer of either poetry or music will confirm the experience I am about to relate.

After long labor at verse you will find there comes a time when everything you see or hear, touch, taste, or smell, resolves itself into rhyme, and rattles away until you can't rest. I mean this literally. The people you meet upon the streets are so many disarranged rhymes, and only need proper coupling. The boulders in the sidewalks are jangled words. The crowd of corner loungers is a mangled sonnet with a few lines missing. The farmer and his team an idyl of the road, perfected and complete when he stops at the picture of a grocery and hitches to an exclamation point.

This is my experience and at times the effect upon both mind and body is exhausting in the extreme. I have passed as many as three nights in succession without sleep - or at least without mental respite from this tireless something which

"Beats time to nothing in my hand
From some old corner of the brain."

I walk, I run, I writhe and wrestle with it, but I cannot shake it off. I lie down to sleep and all night long it haunts me. Whole cantos of incoherent rhyme dance before me, and so vividly at last I seem to read them as from a book. All this without will power of my own to guide or check; and then secure a stage of repetition - when the matter becomes rhythmically tangible at least, and shapes itself into a whole of sometimes a dozen stanzas, and goes on repeating itself over and over till it is printed indelibly in my mind.

This stage heralds sleep at last, from which I wake refreshed and from the toils of my strange persecutor; but as I have just said, some senseless piece of rhyme is printed on my mind and I go about repeating it as though I had committed it from the pages of some book. I often write these jingles afterward, though I believe I never could forget a word of them.

This is the history of the "Craqueodoom." This is the history of the poem I give below. I have theorized in vain. I went gravely to a doctor on one occasion and asked him seriously if he didn't think I was crazy. His laconic reply that he "never saw a poet that wasn't." is not without consolation.

I have talked with numerous writers regarding it, and they invariably confirm a like experience, only excepting the inability to recall these Gypsy changelings of a vagrand mind."

Riley's father thought his son was out of his mind for traveling with the Graphics and no doubt writing such strange poetry as "Craqueodoom," and got him home to learn lawyering.

Reuben Riley was a lawyer who taught many others to become lawyers in the county seat of Greenfield. We find in the county histories of Hancock County many members of the Hancock County Bar Association admitted on his motion.

On many occasions we find James Whitcomb Riley drawn to his father's law office. Now came one of those times. The father's hope no doubt was that James Whitcomb Riley was apprenticing himself for the law. The fact was simply the opposite.

While the father was away, Riley wrote poetry or fiddled around draw-ing funny pictures in his father's somber lawbooks. In the back of Riley's mind must always have been the expectation that he might return to finish apprenticing as a lawyer to take over his father's law practice. Mainly, I believe, he preferred his writing and was also rebellious against the law and order lawyering upheld. There are those in the legal profession who attempt to move the recalcitrant legal system into another posture usually failing miserably. Riley took a wider road toward humanitarian lifework.

Reuben A. Riley himself was a product of the legal apprenticeship sys-tem and was admitted to the Hancock County Bar after reading in Randolph county. Upon moving to Greenfield, Reuben was admitted to the Hancock Bar on motion of R. M. Cooper August 19, 1844. The Motion of Reuben to admit his son as a qualified reader in his office never came. Lawyers admitted to the Hancock County Bar on the Motion of Reuben Riley includ-ed Gustavus N. Moss, August 18, 1845; William P. Davis, August 10, 1847; Nimrod Johnson, August 10, 1847; Michael Wilson, August 10, 1857; William R. Hough, August 10, 1857; Joseph R. Silver, May 26, 1859; William H. Pilkinton, February 15, 1860; Brayan C. Walpole, February 1860; Oliver P. Gooding, August 15, 1865; Augustus W. Hough, February 13, 1866; W.W. Kersey, February 13, 1866; John H. Popps, August 21, 1866; Prestly Guymon, February 15, 1867; Matthias M. Hook, February 15, 1867; W.S. Denton on June 4, 1877; Richard A.M. Black, October 15, 1877; Samuel B. Waters, March 26, 1878; William C. Barrett, June 13, 1881, etc.

Since the party who moved the admission of the bar member was most often the master of the apprentice, it can be seen how active Reuben Riley was in educating new lawyers in Greenfield. He didn't get the job done with his son.

And so Riley's life in his twenties went...never very seriously...mostly as Jucklet truanting about in carefree poverty with friends.

Eventually, Riley settled down at Anderson, Indiana to write for a news-paper, the Anderson DEMOCRAT. Riley had taken odd jobs with newspa-pers before, but the Anderson DEMOCRAT offered him the steadiest work and the chance for a journalism career. We will note what happened to this position with the story of "Leonainie."

Riley's play character Jucklet deviously arranged for Riley to come to great fame in the way that the scheming, ludicrous minstrelsy of this char-acter would do such a thing: through a "hoax" more outrageous than any "hoaxer" had ever "pulled" before.

In July, 1877, shortly after Riley had composed the poem "Leonainie" and shortly after poetry he had sent to an Eastern magazine for publication had been rejected, Riley spoke with anguish to friends. He angrily proposed the theory that his poetry was rejected by

A Riley drawing of Tom Snow's shoeshop where teenagers loitered. (From the Barton Rees Pogue glass positive collection.)

national publications in the Eastern cities simply because his name was unknown, not because his poetry was not good enough.

A representation of what "Leonainie" would have looked like to Nineteenth Century Americans taken from "sheet music" of the poem.

To prove the theory, Riley proposed to pass off his poem "Leonainie" as one written by Edgar Allan Poe. His hypotheses was that the poem would be immediately successful because its author was known to fame.

Riley's friend, William H. Croan, Junior Editor of Riley's newspaper, the Anderson DEMOCRAT, and a journalist from the competing Anderson newspaper, William Kinnard of the Anderson Herald, together with Mrs. D.M. Jordan, a contributor to the Richmond "Independent" were the initial conspirators about the project. The three decided on the Kokomo DISPATCH as the newspaper to approach about initially printing the hoax poem. Riley wrote the Editor of that paper, Oscar Henderson, the following letter:

Office of The Anderson DEMOCRAT

Todiman and Croan   Anderson, Indiana July 25, 1877
    Proprietors
Editor DISPATCH - Dear Sirs:
    I write to ask a rather curious favor of you. The dull times[1] worry me, and

I yearn for something to stir things from their comatose condition. Trusting to find you of like inclination, I ask your confidence and assistance.

This idea has been haunting me: - I will prepare a poem - carefully imitating the style of some popular American poet deceased, and you man "give it to the world for the first time" thru the columns of your paper, - prefacing it, in some ingenious manner, with the assertion that the original MS. was found in the album of an old lady living in your town - and in the handwriting of the poet imitated - together with signatures etc. etc. - You can fix the story - only be sure to clinch it so as to defy the scrutiny of the most critical lens. If we succeed, and I think sheer audacity sufficient capital to assure that end, - after "working up" the folks, and smiling over the encomiums of the Press, don't you know; we will then "rise up William Riley,²" and bust our literary bladder before a bewildered and enlightened world !!!

I write you this in all earnestness and confidence, trusting you will favor the project with your valuable assistance. It will be obvious to you why I do not use our paper here. Should you fall in with the plan, write me at once, and I will prepare and send the poem in time for your issue of this week. Hoping for an early and favorable response, I am,

Very truly yours, J.W. Riley

1. Some might argue the times were not so dull. At the time of this letter, America was in the midst of a crippling and bloody railroad strike from Illinois to the Atlantic Coast, Indiana's current Senator and former Civil War Governor, Oliver Morton, was seriously ill. In Utah, Brigham Young, the founder of the Morman Church, was dying. Then, too, the Russians and Turks were in a desperate war.

2. The expression "rise up William Riley" was a reference to "Riley songs," old English or Irish ballads preserved by mountaineer bards of Tennessee and Kentucky. One began "Rise up, William Riley, you must appear this day\ The lady's oath will hang you, or else will set you free..."

The Editor of the Kokomo DISPATCH wrote back the following:

The DISPATCH Kokomo, Ind., July 23, 1877

J.W. Riley,
My Dear Sir:

Your favor of this date is just received. Your idea is a capital one and is cunningly conceived. I assure you that I "tumble" to it with eagerness. You are doubtless aware that newspaper men, as a rule, would rather sacrifice honor, liberty, or life itself, than to deviate from the paths of truth - but the idea of getting in a juicy "scoop" upon the rural exchanges, causes me to hesitate, consider, yea, consent to this little act of journalistic deception. Yes, my dear Riley, I am with you boots and soul. But hadn't I better forestall the poem by a "startling announcement" or something of the sort one week before its publication? The public would then be on the tip-toe of expectancy, etc. I merely offer this as a suggestion. We would hardly be able to publish the poem, if of any great length, this week. Copy is well in for Thursday's issue now, same some local paragraphs. Send copy as soon as you can and we may print next week. If you like, you may also write the preface as you have indicated. Perhaps you could do better than I. I enclose this letter in a plain envelope to disarm suspicion. Let me hear from you. Fraternally,

"Mum's the word."   J.O. Henderson

Riley read the Henderson letter and communicated its good news to Croan and Kinnard and wrote to the out-of-town member of the conspiracy, Ms. Jordan, as follows:

Anderson, Ind. July 25, 1877

Dear Friends:

I write - not in answer to your letter, for I haven't time to do that justice now - but to ask of you a very special favor.

I have made arrangements with the editor of the Kokomo DISPATCH that he shall publish the poem "Leonainie," under the guise of its being the work of Poe himself. Henderson is to invent an ingenious story of how the original manuscript came into his possession, and when it appears with a hurrah from the DISPATCH, I shall copy and comment upon it in the DEMOCRAT - in a way that will show that I have no complicity and I want you to review it, if you will, favorably, in the Independent - I don't want you to really admire it - but I do want you to pretend to, and eulogize over it at rapturous length, and as though you were assured it was in reality the work of Poe himself - as the DISPATCH will claim. Our object is to work up the "Press" broadcast if possible, and then to unsack the feline, and let the "secret laughter that tickles all the soul" erupt volcanically. The "Ring" around the literary torpedo as it now lies includes but four persons, including yourself, and it must be the unwavering resolved of every member to hold the secret safely fastened in the bosom quartette till time shall have ripened the deception, and the slow match had reached the touch-hole of success.

Now will you do this for me at once, for I shall not be thoroughly happy till the answer which I believe, in your great kindness, you will give, reaches me.

How are you, anyway? Happy, I trust, as I am to sign myself
Your friend, J.W. Riley
Riley also replied to Henderson:
Anderson July 26, `77

Dear Henderson:
Your letter did me good, and as I am something of an enthusiast, I am more than ever assured of the ultimate success of our detour. You ask me to fix up the story, and although I have two or three in crude design, I think it will be better, since the poem is to be unearthed at Kokomo, that you manufacture it to suit the surroundings; beside, were I to do it, the trick might be betrayed in some peculiarity of composition - no matter how trifling; for if the ruse succeeds at all, it will certainly receive most rigid scrutiny, and that too of a keenness that will probe to deepest limits. No, I think you will concede the propriety of weaving that fabric on your own loom, I will make suggestions, however, which you may use or ignore as they may be adapted to your surroundings, "In time of peace prepare for war" - that is get ready for afterclaps - or in other words fix a firm foundation. I would get some old woman, we'll say who does washing, or something of that sort, and if she hasn't got an old album, she's got an old book of some kind from which can be torn a blank leaf. Tell her frankly that you want to create a little sensation , and ask her to assist you by saying - should anyone inquire of her as to the truth of it - "that there some poetry written in the book, and that you had noticed it, and asked where the book come from, and she had said it was a book her grandmother used to have; then you had asked her if you mightn't tear out the poetry and print it, and she had acquiesced." Or, - hunt out an old wood-sawer, or an old chap who lives alone, and give him a good send off of some kind - swear him, and then tear a leaf from some old book of his - or if he hasn't got an old book, get him one and let him say "his mother gave it to him fifty year ago - that he don't know where she got it, only that he'd heard her say a young feller about twenty stayed at their house one night, and acted strange like, and looked pale, and paced the floor till morning, and the book was in his room, and when he went away she found the poetry written in it and signed simply E.A.P." -for I have selected Poe to imitate from. And now can you find anything in these suggestions you can utilize - or does not your own fancy suggest a better plan. think. there are a thousand ways, select the most feasible, and nip it at once - taking care to make it anything but complicated or sensational, -and right here while I

think of it: You will be called on to produce the M.S. - say simply that you have sent it to W.D. Howells, of The Atlantic," or some other eminent critic for inspection; and if Will Siddell is in your office, let him into it, and he can have seen it, and set from it - but don't let too many know it - only a very few in whom you can repose every confidence.

And now my dear Henderson, I have worried you enough. I turn the whole thing over to you - feeling you will get all out of it there is in it. When you publish it, I will copy and review it in a manner that shall evince most thoroughly that I have no complicity with it; and do not be surprised if I exhibit, in what I shall have to say, a covert jealousy of the "DISPATCH" - I'll do anything to throw unfavorable comment out o' gear. It might be well, as you suggest, to prepare the people for it in some startling way. Do nothing tho' without mature deliberation. Copy the poem with every care and don't omit a mark, for I have taken every precaution to imitate the most minute characteristics of the erratic original. Write me that this is received O.K. and what you think of it. Another thing, preserve our correspondence. Yours   J.W. R.

—- LATER —-It might be well for you to refresh yourself in Poe history - for such material cannot fail to be of most effective service in the "tangled web we weave." By such a course you will be enabled to locate the old lady at whose house the wild-eyed stranger stayed and penned the "Matchless lines;" and also to most minutely describe the poet's chirography.

Write me at once - if only a line, for I am interested.
                    J.W.R.

"State that the original M.S. has not a single word crossed out, nor sign of erasure - and is copied exact in all particulars. Henderson received Riley's letter that same day and had Will Siddell, his head type-setter, set up the poem "Leonainie" in type and strike off a galley proof to enclose with a letter to Riley reading as follows:

The DISPATCH

J.W. Riley   Kokomo, Ind., July 27, 1877

My Dear Sir:

Your favor and poem received yesterday. Your suggestion is good. Will publish poem next Thursday. It is really Poetical in every word and line - a superbly written and matchlessly conceived poem It certainly would not detract from Poe's transcendental genius to father the fugitive. I assure you it is withal a marvelous and rare creation, honoring you and the State as well. Have not yet matured my story but will have it in due time. Have you any additional suggestions? We have your "Kalamazoo!" Sargeant a left- handed dig in the ribs this week in the DISPATCH, but do not wish to antagonize the DEMOCRAT. Can't you favor us with a poem written over your own signature, sometime "when you have nothing else to do?" Our readers are quite well acquainted with "Riley the Poet," already.

> Fraternally,
> J.O. Henderson

1. "Kalamazoo" was the nickname of a baseball player named Sargeant who played for the Anderson baseball team and was called a notoriously "dirty player" in another article in the Kokomo DISPATCH.

Riley responded to Henderson's letter as follows:

OFFICE OF THE ANDERSON DEMOCRAT

Todiman and Croan   Anderson, Indiana, July 30, 1877
     Proprietors

Dear Henderson:

Your letter has furnished me special pleasure, as it indicates that you are sanguine of success. You ask if I have any more suggestions; None I believe - unless it be to say that the typographical form of the poem is faulty in the regard of architectural construction; tho' doubtless you have already remedied the defect, i.e. - it is not properly indented. Have you noticed? If not, repair if this reaches you in time. Nothing more - only "Courage, Courage, Mon Comrade!" We'll drive 'em bald-headed I'm sure.

> Yours, J.W. Riley

The Kokomo DISPATCH printed the following story in its issue of August 2, 1877, at the top of the fourth column of editorial page 2:

POSTHUMOUS POETRY

A Hitherto Unpublished Poem of the Lamented Edgar Allan Poe -

Written on the Fly-Leaf of an Old Book now in Possession of a Gentleman in this city —— The following beautiful posthumous poem from the gifted pen of the erratic poet, Edgar Allan Poe, we believe has never before been published in any form, either in any published collection of

Poe's poems now extant, or in any magazine or newspaper of any description; and until the critics shall show conclusively to the contrary, the DISPATCH shall claim the honor of giving it to the world.

That the poem has never before been published, and that it is a genuine production of the poet who we claim to be its author, we are satisfied from the circumstances under which it came into our possession, after a thorough investigation. Calling at the house of a gentleman of this city the other day, on a business errand, our attention was called to a poem written on the back fly-leaf of an old book. Handing us the book he observed that it (the poem) might be good enough to publish, and if we thought so, to take it along. Noticing the initials E.A.P., at the bottom of the poem it struck us that possibly we had run across a "bonanza," so to speak, and after reading it, we asked who its author was, when he related the following bit of interesting reminiscence: He said he did not know who its author was, only that he was a young man, that is, he was a young man when he wrote the lines referred to. He had never seen him, himself, but had heard his grandfather, who gave him the book containing the verses, tell of the circumstances and the occasion by which he, the grandfather, came into possession of the book. His grandparents kept a country hotel, a sort of wayside inn, in a small village called Chesterfield, near Richmond, Va. One night, but before bed-time, a young man, who showed plainly the marks of dissipation, rapped at the door and asked if he could stay all night, and was shown to a room. That was the last they saw of him. When they went to his room the next morning to call him to breakfast he had gone away and left the book, on the fly-leaf of which he'd written the lines given below.

Further than this our informant knew nothing, and, being an uneducated, illiterate man, it was quite natural that he should allow the great literary treasure to go for so many years unpublished.

That the above statement is true, and our discovery no canard, we will take pleasure in satisfying any who care to investigate the matter. The poem is written in Roman characters, and is almost as legible as print itself, though somewhat faded by the lapse of time. Another peculiarity in the manuscript which we notice is that it contains not the least sign of erasure or a single inter-lineated word. We give the poem verbatim - just as it appears in the original.

Here it is:

LEONAINIE

Leonainie - angels named her;
  And they took the light
Of the laughing stars and framed her
  In a smile of white:
    And they made her hair of gloomy
    Midnight, and her eyes of bloomy
    Moonshine, and they brought her to me
  In the solemn night.

In a solemn night of summer,
  When my heart of gloom
Blossomed up to meet the comer
  Like a rose in bloom;
    All the forebodings that distressed me
    I forgot as joy caressed me —
    (Lying joy that caught and pressed me
  In the arms of doom!)

Only spake the little lisper
  In the angel-tongue;
Yet I, listening, heard her whisper, -
  "Songs are only sung
    Here below that they may grieve you -
    Tales are told you to deceive you -
    So must Leonainie leave you
  While her love is young."

Then God smiled and it was morning,
  Matchless and supreme;
Heaven's glory seemed adorning
  Earth with its esteem:
    Every heart but mine seemed gifted
    With the voice of prayer, and lifted
    Where my Leonainie drifted
  From me like a dream.

A "slip" of "John C. Walker" (James Whitcomb Riley pseudonym) poem from the Kokomo TRIBUNE. A "slip" was a separate printing of an original newspaper piece sent by one newspaper to another as a courtesy. Slips similar to this one of the poem "Leonainie" and articles about it were sent by the Kokomo DISPATCH all over the country.

The next morning Henderson sent Riley a copy of the story of the hoax clipped from the DISPATCH with a letter:

The DISPATCH

Dear Riley: Kokomo, Ind. Aug. 3, 1877
    We published the poem yesterday. The net-work enveloping the old book, ignorant possessor, etc., you will observe, has been altered materially, for the best, we think. We have our man, a Mr. Hurd, formerly of Va. all posted, primed, etc. The ruse works. Our people think it the "finest poem" Poe ever wrote. Those best acquainted with him declare "Leonainie" to be Poetical in every detail. It is success here. We have sent marked copies to Cincinnati, Indianapolis, Boston, New York, Chicago, and Louisville papers. Also to the Monthlies - Atlantic, Harpers, Scribners, etc. The thunder of their voices will soon be reverberating through the length and breadth of the commonwealth. Do you want any extra copies of the DISPATCH If so, will send you. What do you think of it? How are you pleased with it, etc. Answer.
                        Fraternally,
                        J.O. Henderson

    Riley received Henderson's letter the same day it was written and immediately did two things to avoid suspicion of himself. He composed a squib for insertion in that days "DEMOCRAT" August 3, as follows:
    The Kokomo DISPATCH of yesterday "startles the nation and the hull creation" by publishing a posthumous Poe poem clamorously claiming the honor of its first presentation to the world. Lack of space prevents us from further remark; but we will say, however, that of all the Nazareths now at large, Kokomo is the last from which we would expect good to come."
    Secondly, Riley wrote Henderson a post-card, purposely worded to convey a message if read by the curious at Anderson or Kokomo, as follows:
                                        Anderson, Ind. August 3, 1877
Editor DISPATCH
Kokomo, Ind.
Dear Sir:
    Some literary thug has gobbled our DISPATCH containing your Poe discovery. Please send me two or three extra copies. What does it mean? Are you in earnest? I would like to enter into a correspondence with you regarding it, for even though you be the victim of a deception I would be proud to

know your real author. Do I understand from your description that the manuscript is written like printed letters? Write me full particulars and I will
serve you in response in any way in my power. Very truly, J.W. Riley

The next day, Riley wrote another letter:

Anderson Aug. 4, 1 `77
Dear, dear Henderson - and I've a notion to call you darling,-
Your Leonainie
introductory is superb, and as for the leading paragraph, a neater, sweeter lie
was never uttered. I fancy Poe himself leans tiptoe o'er the walls of Paradise
and perks an eager ear to listen and believe. There may be a feature or two
open to attack, but that's at it should be, for once the excitement of controversy started, a thousand hydra-headed critics will rise up in its behalf - if
only to be contrary.

I am well pleased; and especially grateful for the evident interest you
bestow upon it. Let me caution you again to guard the imposition with most
jealous care. Let no one know it - not even your mother-in-law, if you possess so near and dear a relative. Nor would I seem over-anxious to convince
unbelievers, for they will strive to run you thro' the gauntlet on that very
point; - excuse me for useless suggestions, but I am so fearful of detection a
shadow scares me, and I find myself
> "Like one that on a lonesome road
> Doth walk in fear and dread,
> And having once turned round walks on
> And turns no more his head,
> Because he knows a frightful fiend
> Doth close behind him tread."

And so, dear Henderson, walk with me, "and the devil may pipe to his
own" till our designs shall have ripened into the fullest bloom of victory, -
then we'll have our day.

I sent you a postal yesterday which will understand and use perhaps to
advantage. And now let me post you in regard to those who are assistants
in the deception, - for you might be approached by persons claiming to be
into the secret falsely, and by so doing catch you off guard. Mrs. D.M.
Jordan, of the Richmond INDEPENDENT, and Mr. Kinnard here, of the
HERALD, are the only ones outside yourself and DEMOCRAT who know
of it. The former - Mrs. J. - will be of greatest value to the success of the
scheme, and the latter -Mr. Kinnard - in his way, will be no less effective

and valuable. So now you are fortified on that point, and all you have to do is smile inwardly, "and with a lack-luster, dead blue eye" await the unfoldings of it at least a curious future.

I believe I have said as little and as much as now is necessary: but you must write me in the meantime, and keep me lubricated with the oily experience which I can but fancy will be yours. Send extra papers.

I shake your hand in silence and in tears; and in the language of Artemus Ward, - "I am here; I think so. Even of those." J.W. Riley

The fact was also that another person knew of the conspiracy. Riley also told his roommate, Jim McClanahan of all the details.

On Monday, Riley wrote Henderson again:

Anderson, Ind. Aug. 6

Dear Henderson:

This from the Indianapolis NEWS of the 4th is rather pointed. Yet I trust it will not have the effect of discouraging you in the least. We can't expect the public to gulp it whole, you know; for they are bound to suspect the "worm" contains a hook. "Patience and shuffle the cards!" The singular reticence of the other dailies may auger good - or bad - time only will disclose; and bear in mind no critic has as yet pronounced upon it. We will give them "a long pull - a strong pull, and a pull all together," and in the meantime let me assure you that my ardor is not in the least dampened. Mrs. Jordan's review will soon prod them, and your humble servant's likewise, and should you receive letters or coms., select quotations etc. etc., and publish good and bad alike, in order to show your willingness to abide by the public decision - in a measure at least. I find it necessary for surrounding circumstances, to claim in my review that you may perhaps be the victim of a clever deception, and also to rend the tender fabric of the poem to some extent. I do this for the double purpose of directing the attention from your complicity, and to draw attention from my own; and although I evidently strive to condemn the poem, I indirectly furnish more praise than blame - but you understand. Let nothing discourage you, I shall not. I shall watch carefully for any new points, and in case I "drop" on anything, will alter criticism to suit the public appetite.

Write me if any new developments - write anyhow, and tell me you are not discouraged. Yours fraternally,

J. W. Riley

—- LATER —-In case my review of the poem should cause any public comment to its detriment, I will furnish you with a private letter in which I will express the belief that the poem is certainly genuine, and you may answer my article by reproducing it - see?

It will be well, perhaps, for you to give me a slur of some kind this week - in response to our notice in last issue. Make it hot - call us jealous, etc. etc.

I notice Harding of the HERALD steps round it as carefully as he would a torpedo. If he'd only bit I could die resigned.

I have examined two or three here with regard to it -but they're wary, and don't want to commit themselves.

Our best literary man says its a GRAND thing, and reads it like a Murdoch. Prof. Hamilton pronounces it a fine thing, but thinks it yours. He knows you, and is almost satisfied that it is your composition. This is all "fruit" for me, you know, and after an interview of this character, I generally "wind up" my face and let it "run down" the other way. I notice that it worries `em, and that's a good sign -a good sign! Another feature, - everybody would like to believe- they want to the worst way, and all we have to do is to exercise proper policy; and as the old man has it "We study to please."

Let nothing shake your first convictions, and although we eventually cry Peocavi, the "euchered" public will be forced not only to forgive, but render homage.

And now whatever you do, write to me - Write, and keep me informed as to the welfare or the dangers attending our orphan venture - Very truly, J.W. Riley

The Indianapolis NEWS item referred to by Riley read, "The Kokomo DISPATCH publishes for the first time a poem said to have been written on the fly-leaf of an old book, by Edgar Allan Poe. The poem bears no internal evidence of such paternity." The Harding referred to is Reverend George C. Harding, owner and editor of the Indianapolis Saturday HERALD, one of Indiana's most distinguished editors. The Saturday HERALD commented, "The Kokomo DISPATCH prints what it claims to be an unpublished poem of Edgar A. Poe."

Henderson replied to Riley's letter, saying:

THE DISPATCH

Dear Riley: Kokomo, Ind., Aug. 7, 1877.
    Your very kind letter was received yesterday. I admire your zeal and join

you heartily in the hope of ultimate success. Our people here believe the poem a "true bill." The TRIBUNE folks have interviewed me and I believe I succeeded in "stuffing" them to the muzzle. They feel a trifle jealous of our journalistic "scoop" - hence their reticence. That's their way. If they doubted the genuineness of the story or poem, they would stand on their hind legs and howl furiously. Please send us every extract or notice of the poem you find in the prints with the name of the paper in which you find it. Next week perhaps we will publish all "comments of the press" etc. concerning it. This week will be too early to hear from them. Be sure to send me Mrs. Jordan's notice. We don't get the INDEPENDENT. I will keep you posted. Do the same with me. Write. Fraternally, J.O. Henderson

On August 9th, the Kokomo DISPATCH published an item stating "Our Edgar Allan Poe poem, published in last week's DISPATCH, is creating quite a flutter over the country. The literary critics are giving it the closest scrutiny." Henderson continued to risk his professional prestige and that of his newspaper in participating in this hoax.

The same day, he wrote Riley as follows:

THE DISPATCH

Dear Riley: Kokomo, Ind. Aug. 9, 1877.

The dawn of success is breaking, and every day brings us fresh evidence of ultimate triumph. Glory! The N.Y. HERALD of last Friday, Aug. 5, is before me and it has nibbled. It republished the entire article from The DISPATCH, comments on poem and credits it to The DISPATCH; so did The N.Y. SUN last Tuesday. The Rochester UNION-SPY (Ind.) also publishes the entire article. Soon we shall hear its thunder reverberating through the length and breadth of the Union! It is a success. The plot or story that we told in introducing the poem seems to somewhat disarm criticism. Think of the N.Y. HERALD, the grandest journal in Christendom, gulping it down! Riley, your fame is assured! You are destined to become a second Thomas Chatterton! Shake!

I am sanguine and overjoyed for your sake. I feel that the poem has merit that should place it in the front ranks of poetry in America. Hail, conquering hero! Fraternally, J.C.

Henderson

P.S. The reticence of the Cincinnati papers is strange indeed. I sent them all copies. Keep on the lookout and write me every paper that refers to it. J.C.H.

The only comment of the New York HERALD was in its headline: "EDGAR ALLAN POE - An Indiana Journal Professes to Have Exhumed a Hitherto Unpublished Poem - Inscription on an Old Fly-Leaf." The New York SUN published a condensed version of the DISPATCH story and the complete poem, but without any headlines or comments.

Riley wrote Henderson a letter the same day with this letterhead:
—-WILLIAM R. MYERS —-
————————
ATTORNEY AND COUNSELOR AT LAW
COLLECTIONS MADE A SPECIALTY

"All claims entrusted to his care will be
attended to without fear, favor or affection.
Anderson, Ind. Aug. 9, 1877

Dear Henderson:

The JOURNAL this morning "nibbles," and other papers
will zip it - in consequence the J. will be forced to
champion the poem. I can't tell you how sanguine of success
I now am. I can only exclaim, in the delirious eloquence of
the gifted Poe, -
" W H O O P ! " A steady nerve is all that is now required.

Keep me informed of any new phases. I will send you Richmond paper
when it appears.

Have only time to write this. Yours, J.W. Riley

The next day, Riley wrote to Henderson again:

Anderson, Aug. 10
Dear Henderson:
— 1877 —

I presume you have seen New York SUN of the 7th., and Cincinnati GAZETTE of yesterday - both got it - bad! The SUN reproduces a portion of your editorial, and the poem entire, but ventures no comment of its own. The GAZETTE heads article "An Old Poem by Poe." It must surely bring some critic to the fore ere long.

I have written my review in a way that will be apt to awaken a reply from some quarter, and I shall mark the article and ship it to the four winds.

Why don't you write? I hope you are not losing faith, or becoming "tired now and sleepy too" - for - God bless us - we are certainly at the very threshold of success! I am eager for the fray. That the poem has merit is established, you see, and all we have now to do is "Hold the Fort!" till our own good time, and in the meantime aggravate controversy from every possible quarter. Can't you come over and see me. If we could talk for one square hour we could make ourselves believe it! That's what we want - is to get together -Come over to-night or tomorrow - or Sunday - anytime that will suit you - only come. Yours "Till death us do part."

    J.W, Riley

That same day Riley finished his review of "Leonainie" for publication in his own newspaper, The Anderson DEMOCRAT. As the day progressed, Riley's review was set up in type, placed in the form and was waiting press time when Riley decided to withdraw it from that day's issue. He then added a section to Henderson's letter before mailing:

    —- LATER —-

I have "weakened" at the last moment. I have been afraid of my review, - I mean the effect of it - Is it right or wrong? I have withheld it from this issue. I will be sure I'm right before I go ahead. I send proof of it for your inspection. Examine carefully - mark what new points may strike you - suggest - etc. etc., and I'll hash it over for next issue - `Twill be better maybe for the delay: tho' I much regret that I am not better assured of the success of the article. You know the object of it all - now criticize it impartially, and tell me how I may improve it. I do wish you would come over - Come, in god's name if possible.

    Yours etc. J.W. Riley

Riley's request that Henderson come to Anderson should be put into perspective. Henderson was a co-owner of the Kokomo newspaper and Riley was an Associate Editor of his, merely an employee. Henderson simply couldn't leave his newspaper to come to Anderson.

Both the Anderson HERALD and DEMOCRAT were published on Fridays. Kinnard when he learned of the "Leonainie" story in the DISPATCH of August 2d then wrote the following for his newspaper, The HERALD:

"We expect a rhapsody of jealous censure from the jingling editor of the sheet across the way, and shall wait with the first anxiety ever experienced for the appearance of the DEMOCRAT. We look for an exhausting and damning criticism from Riley, who will doubtless fail to see "Leonainie's" apocryphal merit, and discover its obvious faults. As it is, we were led to believe "Leonainie," to quote from Riley, is a "superior quality of the poetical fungus, which springs from the decay of better thoughts." No doubt our young friend Riley will belittle this poem and say it is not the work of Poe. But it is Poe, and Poe's best manner.'"

At the last minute, Riley decided to publish his review of the poem and stopped the press, already printing that week's issue, to make room for his review. This did not endear Riley to the press foreman. The review reads as follows:

THE POET POE IN KOKOMO

An alleged important literary discovery was announced by The Kokomo DISPATCH in its issue of last week, in which the following extract from a lush and juicy article occurs: (Riley repeated the full Kokomo DISPATCH article and poem, "Leonainie.")

We frankly admit that upon first reading the article, we inwardly resolved not to be startled; in fact we resolved to ignore it entirely; but a sense of justice due - if not to Poe, to the poem - has induced us to let slip a few remarks.

We have given the matter not a little thought; and in what we shall have to say regarding it, we will say with purpose far superior to prejudicial motives, and with the earnest effort of beating through the gloom a path-way to the light of truth.

Passing the many assailable points of the story regarding the birth and late discovery of the poem, we will briefly consider first - IS POE THE AUTHOR OF IT?

That a poem contains some literary excellence is not assurance that its author is a genius known to fame, for how many waifs of richest worth are now afloat upon the literary sea whose authors are unknown and whose nameless names have never marked the graves that hid their value from the world; and in the present instance we have no right to say, -"This is Poe's work - for who but Poe could mould a name like LEONAINIE?" and all that sort of flighty flummery. Let us look deeper down, and pierce below the glare and gurgle of the surface, and analyze it at its real worth.

Now we are ready to consider, - IS THE THEME of the poem one that Poe would have been likely to select? We think not; for we have good authority showing that Poe had a positive aversion to children, and especially to babies. And then again, the thought embodied in the very opening line is not new - or at least the poet has before expressed it when he speaks of that "rare and radiant maiden whom the angels name Lenore," and a careful analysis of the remainder of the stanza fails to discover a single quality above mere change of form or transposition.

The second verse will be a more difficult matter to contest; for we find in it throughout not only Poe's peculiar bent of thought, but new features of that weird facility of attractively combing with the delicate and beautiful, the dread and repulsive - a power most rarely manifest, and quite beyond the bounds of IMITATION. In fact, the only flaw we find at which to pick, is the strange omission of capitals beginning the personified words "joy" and "doom." This,however, may be an error of the compositor's, but not probably.

The third stanza drops again. True, it gives us some new thoughts, but of very secondary worth compared with the foregoing, and is such commonplace diction the Poe-characteristic is almost entirely lost.

The first line in the concluding stanza, although embodying a highly poetical idea, is not at all like Poe; but rather so UNLIKE, and for such weighty reasons we are almost assured that the thought could not have emanated with him.

It is a fact less known than remarkable that Poe avoided the name of the Deity. Although he never tires of angels and the heavenly cherubim, the word God seems strangely ostracized. That this is true, one has but to search his poems; and we feel we are safe in the assertion that in all he has ever written the word God is not mentioned twenty times. In further evidence of this peculiar aversion of the poet's, we quote his utterance, -

"'Oh, Heaven! oh, God!

How my heart beats in coupling those two words."

The remainder of the concluding verse is mediocre till the few lines that compete it - and there again the Poe-element is strongly marked.

To sum up the poem as a whole we are at some loss. It most certainly contains rare attributes of grace and beauty; and although we have not the temerity to accuse the gifted Poe of its authority, for equal strength of reason we cannot deny that it is his production; but as for the enthusiastic editor of the DISPATCH, we are not included, as yet, to the belief that he is wholly impervious to the wiles of a deception. J.W. Riley

Paul Henderson, the author and compositor of this series of letters, newspaper articles and background of notes, calls this review by Riley "a masterpiece of subtle chicanery. Setting the scene with his sly reference to the poem's merit: "...a sense of justice due - if not to Poe - to the poem," Riley had the impudence to refer to his own pet theory: "...that a poem contains some literary excellence is not assurance that its author is a genius known to fame!"'" Riley then analyzes the poem revealing his own great knowledge of Poe's style as well as acclaiming his own poem as one "of grace and beauty."

The next day, Riley wrote Henderson:

Anderson, Aug. 11 `77

Dear Henderson:

"I wrote you yesterday that I would not publish my review this week, but receiving a letter from a literary friend in Indianapolis, enclosing "Leonainie," I stopped the press in time to insert my article for benefit of more notable exchanges at least. I think it was best, for my criticism will do everything to throw them from the agent. And now do you think it will be a good idea for me to write you a "put up" letter, praising the poem and expressing a belief in its genuineness? Write me at once - or come over. Id' come to you - but can't possibly leave work out before me.

Yours in the bonds -J.W. Riley

"Will send Richmond papers as soon as they appear."

Henderson then wrote Riley a letter on the next Monday afternoon:

THE DISPATCH Kokomo, Ind.,

Dear Riley: Aug. 13, 1877.

Your two letters Saturday received. I would like to visit you ever so well but can't get away for two weeks at least. My brother and partner has gone to Baltimore, Md., and per consequence I am tied at home. Have you seen notice in N.Y. WORLD, TRIBUNE, POST; Chicago TRIBUNE, INTER-OCEAN, Cincinnati papers, COURIER JOURNAL? I am saving all notices and will publish them this or next week. Your notice in DEMOCRAT is capital; so is HERALD'S, but it sounds like you all over.

Our plot is developing rapidly. The ball is now fairly in motion and will not stop until it reaches every State in the Union. No article was ever published in a "country" paper in the State that has had such a run as this has and will have. The end is not yet. I am anxious to see The ATLANTIC, SCRIBNER'S MONTH, etc. They are the critics. Send me all extracts you find. Get WORLD'S if possible. We do not get the paper here. Would be happy to receive a visit from you if only for one night.

Fraternally, J.O. Henderson

It should be noted that the two had not yet figured out how they would release the secret of the hoax.

It should also be noted that we know Riley was at the point of physical collapse at this point in his life. He was both writing and editorializing at his regular work for The DEMOCRAT and trying to cope with the strain of his hoax.

On Wednesday morning, the Editor of The DEMOCRAT, Croan, sensing Riley's near breakdown, suggested that Riley go to Kokomo to work out a definite plan. He could take the Panhandle railroad connection at 1:20 P.M. and get to Kokomo a couple of hours before Henderson's newspaper went to press. A problem was the manuscript on the fly-leaf of an old book. Croan suggested he take a book with him to Kokomo and selected out of a small book-case beside his desk an Ainsworth's Latin Dictionary with a blank fly-leaf. Croan also knew of a facsimile of Poe's handwriting from a back issue of Scribner's Magazine. Croan went to see a friend he knew who kept back issues of Scribner's and found the facsimile poem in the September 1875 issue by tracing through the annual index of the previous December. The poem was "Alone" and was said to have been written when Poe left West Point in 1829 - at about the time Riley would have been about twenty.

Riley needed a forger and knew where to find one in an artistic friend of his. Riley went to see his friend Sam Richards at his boarding house but Sam had gone to Indianapolis and wasn't due back until late that night. Riley left a note with the boarding house owner to be given to Richards the minute he returned to Anderson and then went to see his Graphics friend, Will Ethel. Riley didn't want to buy the "pale ink of a bluish tinge" himself and needed a friend to buy it for Sam to use on his forgery which Ethel did.

The next morning, Sam Richards came to The DEMOCRAT office. Riley gave him the book with the fly-leaf, his own copy of "Leonainie" and the bottle of ink from Will Ethel. He also gave him the facsimile poem of Poe's as a model. Riley said he had to have the poem on the flyleaf by 1:20 to take to Kokomo. Initially, Richards tried to do the job at The DEMOCRAT office but Riley hovered over him so he couldn't do it and said he was going to take it back to his own room to work on. Riley agreed but said he was coming up to see how he was doing in an hour. When Riley went, Richards said he was still practicing on Poe's handwriting and wasn't going to do it without "perfection." Meanwhile Riley was pacing around because he had to make a train to Kokomo with the forgery at 1:20.

After Riley left, Richards went back to work. He showed up at Riley's office at The DEMOCRAT to say he had not been able to get more than the first verse done on the fly-leaf. Although Riley was taken aback and very disappointed, a coincidence happened. A compositor of Henderson's own newspaper, the DISPATCH, happened to be visiting Riley's newspaper to talk to a friend who was a pressman there. The man, Will Siddell, had come to Anderson to see his sick mother and decided to stop in for a visit. When Riley learned of this he decided not to go to Kokomo until the next day but instead to have this Will Siddell tell Henderson about the forgery. Will Siddell took notes that would permit Henderson to write up the forgery document for his next issue. Riley told him about the Ainsworth's Latin Dictionary, the pale, blueish ink on both sides of a single sheet, or fly-leaf, taken from the back of the book, writing remarkably clear, can be read as easily as print, though dimmed by time and exposure. Riley told Siddell to make sure Henderson knew he himself would be over with the forged document on the next day's train.

On the next morning, Thursday, August 16th, Henderson got a letter from a Boston publisher and sent Riley a letter about it. Henderson's letter was hasty because he wanted Riley to have it that day. This meant he had to post it on the 9:35 "Panhandle" train to Anderson for Riley to get it at about 1:00 P.M. when the train would arrive at Anderson.   Henderson knew something must be done. Disastrous exposure of the hoax would surely follow if no manuscript was in his hands.

THE DISPATCH J.W. Riley   Kokomo, Ind.,
                                                                                    Aug. 16, 1877

I have just received a letter from WM. F. GILL & CO., Publishers, at Boston, requesting me to forward original MSS, of our Poe's poem. Mr. Gill has just written and published a "Life of Poe" and writes that he has the MSS. of his "Bells." He says he can identify his MSS beyond cavil and such identification would be of value to me. I send you his letter and notice of his book which please return to me at once. What shall I write him! Where is original MSS? Notices still come in - latterly from the South, Baltimore, etc. Send me all your clippings. I will need them by Friday or Saturday to publish in next week's DISPATCH - outside. I would like to see you but can't leave office until my brother returns. "Nothing succeeds like success," and this is a success. Watch "Monthlies" closely. Write.

Fraternally, J.O.

Henderson.

Henderson then had his office boy take the letter to the train for dispatch to Anderson. Later that day, Will Siddell arrived from Anderson with

Riley's message that he would be over the next day with the forged poem and its description. Based on Siddell's notes, Henderson edited in the description to a previously written article for his newspaper as follows:

"The furor over our discovery of Poe's remarkable and hitherto unpublished poem - the sweet and beautiful "Leonainie," is just not in its insipiency. The poem is traveling like wild-fire all over the country, and the ablest critics in the land have leveled their lenses upon it. If we have been the victim of a deception, we are as willing as anybody to know it. We believe in the paternity of the poem and can await with complacency the verdict of the reading public. The original MS., together with the book from which the leaves were torn, are now in our possession. The book is one of an old edition of "Ainsworth's Dictionary," considerably time-worn. The poem is written in pale ink of blueish tinge on the fly-leaf taken from the back of the book. The chirography is remarkably clear and can be read as easily as print. Of course it is somewhat dimmed by time and exposure. It is written on both sides of a single leaf. The MS will be sent East to critics for examination and judgment. The poem is indeed remarkable, and its accidental discovery is a valuable contribution to American literature."

Henderson slipped up here by saying he had the MS "now" since in the original announcement he stated he took the MS into his possession which would have been two weeks previous.

Another article in the same DISPATCH newspaper edition was an "out and out" lie. Referring to the Friday previous, Henderson wrote the enclosed article for publication:

J. W. Riley, the Hoosier poet, was in the city last Friday, and of course called at the DISPATCH office. He is a bright, sparkling conversationalist, and a more excellent elocutionist. Riley writes rhymes as easily as he writes prose. He is probably the ablest poet in Indiana. He is considerably "shook up" over our Poe's poem discovery. While he shakes his head in seeming doubt, it is evident that he believes "Leonainie" to be worthy of Poe. While here he examined the original MS., and a perplexed expression o the countenance told he was considerably worried over it, if not entirely "at sea".

Later that same Thursday, Richards brought Riley the completed forgery of the poem on the fly-leaf. It was a beautiful piece of work identical with the facsimile of Poe's writing from Scribner's. Riley showed the forgery to Croan and both agreed that Riley could spend Friday night in Kokomo, perhaps with Charley Philips, the Editor of the rival newspaper to the DISPATCH. Then Riley said he would go down to Greenfield to spend the weekend with his family.

The next afternoon, Friday, Riley got on the 1:20 "Panhandle" train to Kokomo carrying the old Dictionary wrapped in brown paper with "Leonainie" on its fly-leaf. Once in Kokomo, Riley took a round-about path to the DISPATCH office which was on the second floor of the Kokomo "opera house" block on Railroad Street at the North-West corner of Court House Square, facing the Square. He did this to avoid being seen by his good friend, Charles Philips, whose Kokomo TRIBUNE office was also on Railroad Street. When Riley arrived at the office, he met Henderson for the first time. The session was a "great time" with both laughing gleefully and with great chuckles at how everyone was deceived.

Later the two however began to argue about how to bring closure to the hoax. Riley proposed that Charles Philips of the Kokomo TRIBUNE, Henderson's great rival, be contacted and that the hoax be revealed through that newspaper. Henderson exploded. He did not like the plan and told Riley that he was the one who would have to live in the town after the hoax was over. The two agreed to think of another plan. Henderson asked Riley to spend the night since there was no train back to Anderson that night, but Riley declined. He was going to see his friend Charles Philips and antici-pated spending the night there as he had on many occasions.

When Riley looked up Charles Philips at the TRIBUNE office, Charley asked him what he was doing in Kokomo. Riley said he came to see the "Leonainie" MS. Riley told Charley that he saw it and Henderson kept it in his office safe. Riley further said the poem certainly sounded good enough for Poe. Then Riley spent the night at Charles Philips home. While staying in Kokomo, Riley wrote his Anderson girlfriend, Kit Myers, saying:

Dear Kit: Kokomo, Ind. August 18, 1877

I write to tell you how happy I am, and yet how miserable; happy that I find my pet schemes here in such lovely working order, and miserable that I can't tell you about them verbally - never mind - I'll have whole cantos to tell you when we meet again, and soon.

I have only time now to write you these few words, for I'm to take a jaunt this morning thro' Ko-ko-mo, the new way of saying it - behind the laziest horse the market affords. The eds. of both papers are making a lion of me, which you, knowing my weakness, will accept as the best of reasons for my present blissful condition and brevity of letter talks.

Write to me at once, won't you, at Greenfield, for I will be there Monday at the fartherest. Love to all my friends, and for yourself, the warmest love of `Mr. Riley'

From that day's Kokomo TRIBUNE, Charles Philips had written the following personal:

J.W. Riley, of the Anderson DEMOCRAT, the author of the strange and fantastical poem, "Craquedoom," published in these columns several weeks ago, is in the city, and gave us a pleasant call last evening. Riley is becoming well-known throughout the country for his original compositions and he has a bright future before him.

Riley left for Greenfield on late Saturday afternoon. He was so close to complete physical exhaustion that his short holiday extend to nearly two weeks in Greenfield.

The next Monday, August 20th, was a critical day in the life of the "hoax." Metcalf, Kinnard's partner at the Anderson HERALD had learned that Riley wrote "Leonainie" from a person he called a "young man" and came into the HERALD office to see Kinnard. He was determined that they should expose the hoax. Kinnard was forced to tell Metcalf that he knew of the hoax and could not reveal it in their newspaper. Despite every argument, Kinnard refused to budge. The news spread around Anderson, however, that Riley was the author of "Leonainie." When Riley's Editor, Croan, heard the rumors he wrote Riley that he needed to get back to Anderson, but this day Riley had decided to go to Indianapolis to visit his friend, George Harding, Editor of the Indianapolis Saturday HERALD. During the visit, Riley told Harding of seeing the "poe" manuscript. Riley was trying to build up discussion of the "manuscript." This visit did result in a the following notice in The Indianapolis Saturday HERALD:

The HERALD was favored on Monday last with a call from one of Indiana's favorite poets - Mr. J.W. Riley, of the Anderson DEMOCRAT. Mr. Riley had just returned from a trip to Kokomo, where he had gone for the purpose of investigating the authenticity of the alleged Poe poem, discovered by the editor of the Kokomo DISPATCH. Mr. Riley reports favorably to the honesty of the claim put forward by the editor of the DISPATCH. Whatever may be the facts, he firmly believes in the authenticity of the poem and guards it with jealous care. The book, on the fly leaves of which the poem is written, is kept under double lock and key, and it was only by tearful pleading that Mr. Riley was permitted a sight of it. The discoverer stood uneasily by while Riley studied the faded manuscript, and heaved a great sigh of relief when the precious volume was once more locked up in the safe." On Tuesday, Metcalf still could not convince his partner that the

Anderson HERALD should expose the hoax and so he wrote the full details of the hoax to Charles Philips of the Kokomo TRIBUNE. Apparently he decided that if his newspaper couldn't benefit by exposure of the hoax, he would give the benefit of it to another newspaper, the Kokomo TRIBUNE. Also Metcalf did not tell his partner Croan that he had written the letter.

At this point it should be mentioned that the poem "Leonainie" had traveled from coast to coast and particularly in the press of the East. Once the publicity about the poem had reached the East, it was re-published from the great Eastern newspapers of New York, Boston, Philadelphia, and Baltimore to those newspapers that fed on their exchanges. Between August 2d and August 25th, 1877, the Kokomo DISPATCH story with the "Leonainie" poem in it was reprinted in at least thirty-five cities in seventeen of the nation's then thirty-eight states exclusively of Indiana. Literally, from Boston to Portland, Oregon, from New York to San Francisco, from Philadelphia to Richmond and Savannah, from Chicago to Nashville, the poem "Leonainie" was printed. Not one of the newspapers in any of these places accompanied the article with editorial comment. Most tellingly however was the fact that not one of the newspapers also believed that Edgar Allan Poe had actually written "Leonainie." Not one was fooled.

From the New York EVENING POST of August 7th, '...a poetic sin has been laid at (Poe's) door..."

From the Philadelphia COMMONWEALTH of August 8th, "...The gin mills of Maryland and the Old Dominion never turned out liquor bad enough to debase the genius of Poe to the level of these wretched verses..."

From the New York WORLD of August 8th came the suggestion that a renegade of young men in a boisterous literary club called "The Perforators" were probably behind the hoax.

From the Baltimore AMERICAN of August 9th, "...The unfortunate poet (Poe) was no doubt guilty of many indiscretions, but it is hard to suppose that in his most eccentric mood he could ever have penned such wretched doggerel as that which is now attempted to be fastened on him under the name of "Leonainie..."

From the Brooklyn DAILY EAGLE of August 9th, "The composition is wild enough to have been written under the influence of Egyptian or Terre Haute whiskey, and possesses, therefore, what an eminent journalist of this city defines as a local flavor..."

From the Philadelphia PRESS of August 9th, "...If Poe wrote it, he probably intended to call it `La Inane.'"

From the Nashville DAILY AMERICAN of August 10th, "(Poe) will surely pay his respects to the scalp of the Indiana man who brought it out."

From the Richmond ENQUIRER of August 10th, "It is fair to presume that the discoverer of `Poe's Unpublished Poem' wishes that he had kept his secret..."

From the New York DAILY GRAPHIC of August 15th, "Set your non-sense to music and announce that it is copied from Edgar A. Poe's lost memorandum book, and it will travel from the South Pole to Symme's Hole and excite the wildest enthusiasm."

From the Denver ROCKY MOUNTAIN NEWS of August 16th,"... Now we can easily imagine the ebon darkness of the maiden's hair, but the `bloomy moonshine' of her eyes is what troubles us. Were they white eyes, shining in the night?"

From the Detroit FREE PRESS of August 16th, "...`Bloomy moonshine.' One sees that kind best while hanging on to the lamp post."

From the Oakland DAILY TRANSCRIPT of August 19th comes the thought that "Leonainie" should have been signed "Pooh!' instead of with the initials E.A.P.

Nevertheless, in almost every account there is the statement of the hoax that the poem "fooled even William Cullen Bryant." This singular misstatement comes from the fact that Bryant, even though in his eighty-third year at the time, still wrote regular reviews and probably wrote the one for the New York EVENING POST.

The "grand expose" appeared on Saturday morning. It was written in the Kokomo TRIBUNE, the rival newspaper of Henderson's DISPATCH. The article was written by the doughty owner and fire-eating senior editor of the TRIBUNE, Theophilus C. Philips, who had been anxious for some time to "take down" Henderson, who he called the fresh "collegiate boy editor." On page four of the August 25th TRIBUNE appeared the following headline:

LEONAINIE
—
EXPOSE OF A CONTEMPTIBLE FRAUD.
—
A RISING YOUNG MAN IN A
SMALL BUSINESS.
—

A KOKOMO NEWSPAPER, SEEK-
ING FAME, SUCCEEDS IN COV-
ERING ITSELF WITH INFAMY.

———

THE MOST ASTOUNDING LYING
ON RECORD.

The columns of this paper are witnesses that we have attributed to young
J.W. Riley, of Anderson, or rather of Hancock County, talent beyond one of
his age and experience. We regret sincerely to expose him in a piece of fraud
that will let him down many notches in the estimation of his former friends.

A few weeks ago, after writing and re-writing the poem, `Leonainie,' imi-
tating the style of Poe, he conceived the idea that if he could get it out upon
the world as Poe's production and afterwards establish himself as the author,
he would make a world-wide fame at one jump. But the effort to reach fame
by such a deception shows that his talent is more than ever balanced by his
lack of moral perception and mother wit. Having concocted his plans, he
looked about for an obscure paper in which to bring out the poem, for the
more obscure the paper the less likely that the fraud would be suspected.
Mr. Riley found in The DISPATCH, of this city, a willing tool, a paper anxious for fame and unable to reach it by climbing in the regular way. It was
a bold attempt. If it succeeded all would be well, and they, the young man,
author and editors, in the exuberancy of their youth, never dreamed but that
the deception would take like wild-fire. As the verdant young man who
picks up a pair of boots in a store and takes them away without paying for
them, only to be caught and sent to jail, these youths attempted a bold trick,
but one as gauzy as bobinet.

But to come to the story: Mr. Riley put "Leonainie" into the hands of The
DISPATCH. On August 2d, inst., they published it under head-lines and the
positive statements, that they believed it written by Poe. They pledged their
honor to the truth of all they said in regard to it.

After it was out, under the direction of Mr. Riley, copies of The DIS-
PATCH were sent to all the leading newspapers, magazines, and authors of
the country. The answer that was returned just about crushed Mr. Riley.
The DISPATCH did not seem aware of its misery, but actually paraded the
criticisms in its columns, changing some of them that pronounced positively against the fraud, so as to make them read like quasi endorsements. Those
who saw the criticisms must have noticed that everybody who had intelligence and discernment recognized the fraud, while a few inexperienced per-

sons, who probably never read Poe, waxed enthusiastic over the poem. Mr. Riley himself wrote a criticism in which he admitted some of the lines were, indeed, Poeish.

But the worst of the story is yet to come. One of the eastern publishers to whom the paper, containing the poem was addressed, wrote the editors of The DISPATCH to send them the original manuscript, saying they were familiar with the lamented poet's chirography, etc., and they offered to pay all expenses, and to faithfully return the same to Kokomo. Here was a dilemma. The DISPATCH folks decided at once what they would do. They sent a letter to Anderson with a request. There, a very old copy of Ainsworth's dictionary was procured and an expert penman placed the poem on the fly-leaf in writing as near like Poe's as possible, a recent number of Scribner's Monthly containing a facsimile of the poet's chirography. Mr. Riley carried that book to this city, himself, on Friday of last week for the purpose of having it forwarded east.

Much might have been written about this attempt at a swindle but we have only sorrow and pity for all concerned and are willing to let the matter rest. Every honorable person will be astonished that such a trick should have been attempted. Had Mr. Riley published the poem as his own it would have given him additional credit, for it is really good for a young man just beginning a literary course. Hereafter, whatever he writes, no matter how good, will go out at a discount, and no poem bearing his name will be incontrovertible with pure literary currency. Had the DISPATCH published `Leonainie' without the flourish of so many trumpets, it might have crawled out of its present position by announcing the poem as quiet joke. But it has placed it in one scale and its honor, reputation, classical knowledge and truthfulness in the other. `Great literary treasure,' for the present, farewell. We know exactly what The DISPATCH and Mr. Riley will say; we know the testimony they will adduce. When they are through, we shall puncture their bubble again.

P.S. Since J. Oscar first got the old book from a gentleman in this city, whom he says is `unlearned and illiterate' and had Riley's `Leonainie" place on a fly-leaf, how does it happen that a second old Ainsworth had to be procured at Anderson in order to have a copy sent East?

Boys, how do you feel? Have you sent Gill a copy yet? Never mind, this week's TRIBUNE will suit him as well.

J.W. Riley hit the nail on the head when he selected The DISPATCH as a paper willing to pledge its brains and honor to a falsehood and swindle, but we are surprised that he didn't know there was another paper here smart enough to gather in every point of the attempted fraud. Poor boys, we really feel sorry for them.

Also in this issue of The TRIBUNE was another bite: "'Leonainie,' poor girl, has already fallen into the arms of doom...'Leonainie' has evaporated into 'bloomy moonshine.'" "...It was with tears in his eyes that J.W. Riley told us he 'had come all the way from Anderson to see that manuscript of Poe's(?) poem, but he was afraid J. Oscar wouldn't let him look at it." " ...'The angels framed 'Leonainie' in a smile white, but the boys lay her out on the fly-leaves of two old dictionaries" "...For silly, lying, verdant deception, and gauzy smartness, the 'Leonainie' fraud beats anything we ever saw..." "The comments on 'Leonainie,' which The DISPATCH editors published this week are a total 'give-away' for that paper, one of the extracts have been garbled and remodled until the editors have manufactured indorsements out of burlesque paragraphs."

This is the article which the Editor of the DISPATCH, Henderson, saw as he read the Saturday morning rival newspaper. He wasted little time and went down to the Court House Square and then over to the rival newspaper to Talk to Charley Philips. Philips greeted him derisively and Henderson acknowledged that the joke on him. He confirmed the truth of the statements in The TRIBUNE and then said it was fun while it lasted. Philips did tell Henderson that a letter from Anderson two or three days before gave him the details of the hoax. Henderson tried to find out who wrote the letter but Philips would only say the writer was "young man" who was a most intimate friend of Riley.

Henderson wrote Riley upon his return to the newspaper office.

Aug. 25, '77

"Saturday, 10 A.M.

Dear Riley:

The Tribune of this city, this morning, published the enclosed Expose of 'Leonainie.' They tell me that they never 'tumbled' until they received a letter from a gentleman at Anderson the other day 'exposing' the poem. They say the 'exposer' is a young man - a most intimate friend of yours. It is Mr. K., I presume. You see they seem to think they have earned a place in glory for their 'expose.' What shall we do? Of course, we must explain the matter next Thursday - but how? In order to scoop The TRIBUNE again, would it not be well to acknowledge the poem, plea manly and turn the joke on them?

In this wise: Say that J.W. Riley is the father of the poem; that he selected The DISPATCH as the proper medium which he would send his poem to the world; he selected The DISPATCH on account of its high merit as a weekly paper, its well known literary tastes, and above all, its wide-extended circulation; that we entered into the plot and helped to play the ruse merely as a clever journalistic coup de main, that the poem is worthy of Longfellow, Poe, etc.; praise it and you very highly; say that you had a half dozen men as witnesses, with three more at Anderson, of the genuineness of the poem; that you and I arranged with a friend in Anderson to write to The TRIBUNE under cover of secrecy and `expose' the ruse, knowing that they would do it heartily and with all their soul, hoping thereby to `get even' with The DISPATCH; that thus we made a cat's-paw out of The TRIBUNE and accomplished our end, etc. - and then take a hearty laugh over the ruse, The TRIBUNE'S dilemma, etc. What say you, Riley? Don't you think it a capital idea? You know we must`fess up' next Thursday anyway. Let us turn the laugh. Write me immediately. If you please you may also write or block out reply to TRIBUNE and I will compare with mine. Do this at once and write me. I would like very much to have a poem from you, over your own signature written for The DISPATCH. It would help us to pacify the public mind and extricate ourself from the charge of duplicity, etc. Please write something for The DISPATCH as soon as possible. I feel that much is due the paper, don't you? Our readers would laugh heartily over the little ruse, forgive us for our part, and love you the more when they should read a poem openly by you in The DISPATCH. I would suggest that you write a parody or something after the style of `Leonainie,' poking fun at The TRIBUNE and `exposing' the `Expose' of `Leonainie.' Such a poem would come in capitally. Write me at once.

Fraternally, J.O. Henderson

Riley received the letter in Greenfield on Monday, August 27, 1877. He remained in Greenfield instead of going back to work in Anderson because he was unable to control his drinking or depression. He did however walk to the Greenfield post office where he found Henderson's letter with The TRIBUNE's expose. He read it after he got back to the Riley home at the Seminary. He also read The Indianapolis JOURNAL editorial of that day stating:

The Kokomo TRIBUNE , of Saturday, exposes a fraud on the part of The DISPATCH of that city, and J.W. Riley, the poet of the Anderson DEMOCRAT. Some time ago The DISPATCH claimed to have found in that city, on the fly-leaves of an old book, a poem by Edgar A. Poe, hitherto unknown, which it published under the title `Leonainie.' The TRIBUNE claims that his was written by J.W. Riley for the purpose of enabling him to achieve a little reputation, by claiming the authorship after the prose had pronounced a favorable verdict. But the favorable verdict was not awarded and now the whole plot, in all of its littleness, is exposed. The facts given by The TRIBUNE are corroborated by private information of the JOURNAL from Anderson.

That same day Riley wrote to Henderson, as follows:

Greetings: It's a trifle warm!

Greenfield, Aug. 27 - `77

Dear Henderson:

Unfortunately your letter of Saturday did not reach me till too late for me to strike to-day's mail - in consequence this may not reach you till too late to be of any service. I will say briefly that I do not like the idea of being compelled to confess the fraud before real critical testshave been applied.

It has not gone too far - The TRIBUNE'S expose can be successfully refuted even tho' you have verbally acknowledged its truth. You can claim that their story was manufactured for them by me, and for the purpose of claiming a poem whose excellence I envied - don't you see. Treat the matter with the same complacency that has marked your past course, and express regret that one so full of promise could stoop to such a depth, and all that sorto'stuff. Claim that my visit to Kokomo was to hatch the scheme with the Philips, and that you suspected some trickery of me and treachery from my first appearance in your office. Another thing you can mystify the Philips with but it must be done indirectly. let someone, apparently his friend, tell him that Riley has put up the job on him, for if the Anderson man was my friend why did he give me away - say that it rather looks like he - Philips - had bit at the very thing I wanted. O we can mystify anything they can pit against us! I have a friend here who has written a letter to the SENTINEL, Indianapolis,which will perhaps appear in tomorrow's issue - look for it, and I think you'll find a cue for a better course than yet to confess. When we get ready we'll confess, and I really think we can select our own good time. Yours in the bonds,

J.W. Riley

Write me in plain envelopes. My course will perhaps be silence dark and deep.

—-LATER —-

I have just written to have a letter `cooked' at Anderson, which if it reaches its proper destination will bother the public wonderfully, and be particularly unwholesome for Metcalf of the HERALD, and the TRIBUNE. It will be claimed that Metcalf is my tool, and that the story he gives The TRIBUNE is of my own manufacture - for I am satisfied that Metcalf and not Kinnard gave them the story. That I am right I think you will agree when I tell you I had word direct from Anderson last week that Metcalf had threatened to give full expose in HERALD - Well, he didn't - why? - because Kinnard wouldn't have it, and so he sneakingly sends it to The TRIBUNE, and posts them to tell you that they got it of a young man, and my intimate friend in order to make you acknowledge - see?

Well, if this ruse works and I'm almost certain it will - it will cripple them too badly to ever smile again. Then we can go on till our own good time.

Yours ever,

J.W. Riley

In the meantime to more confuse the listening public, you hatch up a letter from Kokomo to The Indianapolis JOURNAL in which you shall claim that the whole plot was concocted by The DISPATCH and TRIBUNE jointly for the purpose of notoriety to each, and that it was originally written by Judge Biddle, and never published till several years and years ago in Logansport PHAROS - and that the copy - doctored somewhat-is now in your possession - you being a civilian, and sign bogus name. Do this and we have another barricade from danger.

Here is Jucklet at work big time! Here is a mischievous minstrel piping up great court intrigue. Here is a jester who simply does not wish his jest to cease. There is also in this a great push to drain every ounce of publicity out of the great controversy that Riley can. He wants his `Leonainie' to bring him "fame." He does not seem to care a great deal about the consequences to any of the newspapers with which he is dealing. His manipulations do not reveal a great regard for reality to say the least and one senses Crestillomeem is confusing his perceptions of what reality is. To a half-drunken man, staggering can seem walking a straight line.

This day, Riley also wrote a "pseudonymous" letter - which he signed "W," his middle initial - to the Indianapolis SENTINEL which in fact was published the next day:

To the Editor of The SENTINEL:

Sir - I notice in this morning's Indianapolis JOURNAL a covert attempt to claim for their poet, J.W. Riley, of this place, the authorship of the lately discovered poem of Edgar A. Poe, the beautiful and mysterious `Leonainie' which has for some weeks been bewildering the literary world. The article referred to apparently sides with an article taken from The Kokomo TRIBUNE, savagely jealous of the good future of the rival paper that discovered the poem. Whether it is indeed Poe's I do not undertake to state, but this much I am assured of, that the well laid plan of Riley, The Kokomo TRIBUNE and The JOURNAL is altogether too thin a proposition to go down in the community. Riley may possess some genius for verse making, but he can't mislead with equal grace, and a recent visit of his to Kokomo points directly to his complicity with The TRIBUNE'S story of the poem's paternity. I have not seen the article as originally published, but that it was written by his own hand I am confident, and guarantee that an inspection of it will testify the fact.

Greenfield, Ind. Aug. 27.   W.

Nor was Riley so incapacitated that he did not take Henderson's suggestion that he write a poem parody poking fun at "Leonainie." Riley did not however write only one parody. Instead, he wrote two. Writing verse was absolutely no trick at all to him. He wrote doggerel verse all the time for advertising as well as personal instance. When, for example, he would go to visit someone and the person wasn't there, he would often leave a rhymed note to state his reason for the visit or some other thought. Many evidences of this survive.

The first of the doggerel "parodies" he sent not to his fellow conspirator Henderson, but rather to his friend Charles Philips who had just participated in the "expose." If Philips published it, the "spoof" would mean even more publicity for Riley. Then he wrote another for The Indianapolis Saturday HERALD. Riley had not told Henderson he was sending the parody to his rival newspaper so Riley wrote Henderson a second letter with this information.

The parody he wrote for The Kokomo TRIBUNE was called "Leoloony":

LEOLOONY

Leoloony, angels called her,
  And they took the bloom
Of the tickled stars and walled her
  In the nom de plume,
    And they made her hair of plaited

Midnight, and her eyes of grated
Moonshine, and with her inflated
Me with solemn gloom.

With a solemn gloom of frenzy
  For my heart of sin
Blossomed up with influenza
  When they brought her in.
    Every phase of dissipation
    I indulged at this donation —
    (For I knew of no foundation
    For a joke so thin.)

Only spake the small pretender,
  Angel-like and calm,
Yet I, listening, heard her render
  "Mary's Little Lamb;"
    And she closed the lines by saying
    I'd no further need of praying,
    For she knew `twas useless playing
    Longer such a sham.

Then I grinned, for I was grateful
  As a jolly Thug.
And the loss of one so hateful
  Overflowed my mug —
    Every grain of pain I sifted
    From the dust of sin was lifted
    As my Leoloony drifted
    From me like a bug.

    The second parody Riley wrote that day he sent to The Indianapolis Saturday HERALD which published it the following Saturday, September lst:

LEONAINIE

Leonainie - Riley named her,
  And he took the glow
Of the `laughing stars,' and framed her

In the style of Poe;
* And he chuckled with the notion*
* Of her voyage of commotion*
* O'er the literary ocean*
With his fame in tow.

He was but a local poet
* Full of coy deceit,*
And, tho' many didn't know it,
* He was `out o' meat;'*
*   And this Leonainie fever*
*   Struck him as the magic lover*
*   To uptip the world and heave her*
Worship at his feet.

Only spake the rhythmic lisper
* In a jingly strain,*
That to critics seemed to whisper -
* "All pretense is vain.*
*   I'm too thin for public diet*
*   And I long for calm and quiet*
*   Where unnoticed I may lie at*
Rest from every pain!"

Then we smiled at this conclusion -
* Pocketed our grief -*
Thankful Riley's dread delusion
* Had a life so brief.*
*   Every heart but his seemed gifted*
*   With a joy the breezes lifted*
*   Where his Leonainie drifted*
Like a withered leaf.

The events of Monday after the expose of the hoax were not over. Up in Anderson, Metcalf ran into Riley's roommate, Jim McClanahan on the street. In the course of the conversation, the hoax was brought up and Metcalf suggested to McClanahan that Kinnard had told The TRIBUNE. McClanahan immediately went to Riley's boss at the Anderson DEMOC-

RAT, Croan. Croan then wrote Riley at Greenfield with the entire conversation's contents.

Meanwhile the evening Indianapolis newspaper carried the following story:

The Kokomo TRIBUNE publishes a long expose of the fraud attempted to be played upon the public by The DISPATCH, in publishing `Leonainie' as a new found poem of Edgar A. Poe. It was very thin imitation by a local poet named Riley who can do much better untrammeled by a model. The joke was harmless and foolish enough, but it was complicated by an eastern publisher, who sent for the original. The TRIBUNE vows that Riley then got an old copy of Ainsworth's dictionary and had the lines copies into it, and sent the book east. If he did it, it was an exceedingly foolish act, if nothing worse.

The next morning, Riley found Coran's note of the night before at the Greenfield Post Office. When he had returned home he wrote his girlfriend in Anderson:

Dear Kit: Greenfield, Ind., August 28, 1877

I fear one thing has saddened you, and made you anxious on my account. I refer of course to the premature exposure of my Poe imitation. But there is not the slightest fear on that account. I was, I admit, greatly worried when I first heard of the treachery of some pretended friend, but now I am so fortified that I can laugh at the poor weak dupes who sought to injure me. I have been assured that Mr. Kinnard exposed the whole affair, but I do not believe it, and I want you, my dear Kit, to go to him and tell him that I do not doubt him in the least. I like him and my faith in him is perfect as the day I held his hand and said good-bye.

I have not been well for many days or would have written a letter for The DEMOCRAT. So you see I have not forgotten my old love. Whew! but I have bitter enemies in Anderson! I once suspected it, but now I know! and won't I make 'em scringe! My ire is like the storm-scourged surf in that light-house poem for I "hold it up and shake it like a fleece!"

In my defense I've been forced to take the most peculiar position imaginable, but I shall not fail! And if you should read some very bitter `Leonainie' squibs, just fancy I'm the author of them all, and know what I'm about. I have written a most atrocious parody or two in which I attack myself with a savageness the world will wonder at; but remember, Kit,
Out of the darkest sorrow -

Out of the deepest night -
Into the peaceful morrow
Flows the purest light!

All this you must keep strictly secret, and that all will yet go well, rest assured.

I will not write you more now, for I do not wish to worry you with never ending "Leonainie" venture. I have too many irons in the fire to think of better things. I shall expect a letter from you tonight, but if disappointed will hope at least that all is well with you. My regards to your good folks; my love to Jess, Mr. Croan and to your brother Will. Devotedly yours, J.W. Riley.

That afternoon, Riley wrote his "Card" to the General Public, confessing his part in the hoax and explaining his reasons for concocting it.
To the Public:

Having been publicly accused of the authorship of the poem, "Leonainie," and again of the far more grievous error of an attempt to false-ly claim it, I deem it proper to acknowledge the justice of the first accusa-tion. Yes, as much as I regret to say it, I am the author,\; but, in justice to the paper that originally produced it, and to myself as well, I desire to say a few words more.

The plan of the deception was originally suggested to me by a contro-versy with friends, in which I was foolish enough to assert that 'no matter the little worth of a poem, if a great author's name was attached, it would be certain of success and popularity,' and to establish the truth of this propo-sition, I was unfortunate enough to select a ruse, that, although establishing my theory, has been the means of placing me in a false light, as well as those of my friends who were good enough to assist us in the scheme, for when we found our literary bombshell bounding throughout the length and breadth of the Union, we were so bewildered and involved we knew not how to act. Our only intercourse had been by poet, and we could not advise together fairly in that way; in consequence, a fibrous growth of circumstances had chained us in a manner, and a fear of unjust censure combined to hold us silent for so long.

To find, at last, a jocular explosion of the fraud, we thoughtlessly employed a means both ill-advised for ourselves and others. And now, trusting the public will only condemn for the folly, and hold me blameless of all dishonorable motives wherein I have feigned ignorance of the real authorship of the poem, etc. etc., I am,

Yours Truly

Anderson, August 28   J.W. Riley

This card was printed in The Indianapolis JOURNAL on August 30th.
On the same day the Kokomo DISPATCH published its own reply to the expose.

LEONAINIE

A CLEVER RUSE SUCCESSFULLY PLAYED

J.W. RILEY THE AUTHOR OF THE POEM

HOW THE KOKOMO TRIBUNE WAS USED AS A TOOL TO FURNISH THE EXPOSE

WHAT PART THE DISPATCH PLAYED

"On the 23rd of July, we received a letter from Mr. J.W. Riley - then connected with the Anderson DEMOCRAT, but now residing in Greenfield - in which a proposition was made to furnish The DISPATCH with an original poem a parody on Poe, subject to these conditions: We were to envelope the poem with additional interest by clothing it with a fictitious net-work of own fabrication, in which we should loosely and in the most flimsy manner charge its paternity to Poe. It was also distinctly agreed that in the course of a few weeks, after the poem had had audience with the ablest literary critics in the land, that we would explain the ruse and declare Mr. Riley the real author of the poem. But this was not to be done until some other journal, innocent of the plot, should be duped into making a `thrilling expose' from facts furnished indirectly by Mr. Riley's friends. This, of course, would attract greater attention to Mr. Riley than if we should make the exposure ourselves. Owing to its morbid and inordinate jealously of The DISPATCH, The Kokomo TRIBUNE was selected as the paper to be used as the tool to further Mr. Riley's and our purpose. A friend in Anderson was posted and the job was handsomely set up. The friend, a pretended enemy of Mr. R., disclosed the `terrible secret' to The TRIBUNE under the strictest bond of secrecy. That paper was not to 'give its informant away,' etc., d'ye see? But to return to our part of the play: Everything was in readiness and The DISPATCH of August 2nd, published the poem. We then lay quiet and laughed in our sleeves at the comments of the press - and The TRIBUNE'S silence. That paper was thunderstruck, and for two weeks never opened its mouth. It believed the story and was just dying with jealousy, envy and pique. In the meanwhile, the poem was traveling over the country from the Pacific to the Atlantic. Eminent critics had written us concerning it. Last week we published nearly three columns of comments. The opportune moment had arrived, and the 'Expose' trap was sprung. The TRIBUNE greedily jumped at it like a bull-frog at a red flannel bait. The plot has worked admirably. All The DISPATCH wished for has been done. We have only to say, that in behalf of Mr. R., we heartily thank The TRIBUNE for its valuable, yet unwittingly rendered aid in the ruse. We have been on the inside all the time while The TRIBUNE has been in the dark on the outside. Its jealousy has for once served a useful purpose, and we can readily forgive it for past displays of this hateful passion. Really we feel like embracing The TRIBUNE for its stupidity in this matter, for we were apprehensive that it would certainly 'tumble' to it, but it didn't. Mr. Riley is so grateful that he has written and forwarded to The TRIBUNE a parody of 'Leonainie,' which that paper will probably publish this week - if it doesn't get too mad when it sees what a booby it has been. The TRIBUNE really deserves a sugar tit, and we are glad Mr. Riley has been so grateful as to forward one in the shape of a parody. It has richly earned two parodies for its assistance in this matter. The TRIBUNE will never forget 'Leonainie.'

We are sure our readers will forgive us for the part we played in this ruse. Our object was two-fold, both of which have been accomplished: First, to perpetrate a quiet, pleasant joke - which we would afterward explain; secondly, to give Mr. Riley's genius as a poet a fair, full and impartial test before the ablest critics in the land, uninfluenced by local prejudice or sectional bias. The only fiction about the transaction was the Poe story. The poem possesses a vast deal of merit and would do no violence to the reputation of our more pretentious bards of today. Although it has been pretty roughly criticized in certain quarters, it has been praised as a work of genius in others. No poem ever passed through a more relentless gauntlet of criticism than this. No one has ever had a more general reception by the press of the United States. Mr. Riley is a young poet of great promise, and will, we predict, yet make his mark as one of the sweetest singers of his age.

Riley wrote back on August 31st to Henderson in part, "I have just rec'd your letter of today, and am glad at heart.'..."

Kinnard of The Anderson HERALD wrote on August 31st:

"Upon our first page we present The TRIBUNE'S exposure of the poetical fraud `Leonainie.' We are sorry that Mr. Riley should have proven himself so mendacious, and sorrier still that he is the author of the poem. We might have forgiven him his want of veracity, but it is hard to condone `Leonainie.' The Kokomo DISPATCH, however, has sacrificed every claim to truth, and hereafter every statement it may make, no matter how trivial or commonplace, must be taken with a wide margin left for falsehood.

The Indianapolis Saturday HERALD'S loyal editor, Rev. George Harding, reprinted Riley's card of confession of the hoax in its September lst issue and added: "J.W. Riley, in a note to the JOURNAL, admits the authorship of the `Leonainie' poem, but disclaims any dishonorable intention. He only wanted to see if a poem of no merit could be floated into popularity by attaching a distinguished name to it. The rage of the fools who swallowed the bait is comical."

When Riley felt well enough, on September lst, to return to Anderson, he was told by Todiman, the co-proprietor of The Anderson DEMOCRAT that "his services were no longer required." Riley later described this by saying "The paper on which I gained my meagre living excused me."

Two weeks later The Kokomo DISPATCH had the announcement of a rosy little girl born weighing ten pounds who was named Leonainie Titus. She died about a year later, and Riley memorialized her death with another "Leonainie" poem "To Leonainie," which was published in The Kokomo TRIBUNE of February 1, 1879.

TO LEONAINIE (1879)

In memory of Leonainie, infant daughter of W.B. and Lotta Titus, these line are tenderly inscribed.

> *"LEONAINIE!" angels missed her -*
> *Baby angels - they*
> *Who behind the stars had kissed her*
> *E'er she came away;*
> *And their little, wandering faces*
> *Drooped o'er Heaven's hiding-places*
> *Whiter than the lily-vases*

On the Sabbath day.

"Leonainie!" crying, crying,
Crying through the night,
Till her lisping lips replying,
Laughing with delight,
Drew us nearer yet, and nearer
That we might the better hear her
Baby-words, and love her dearer
Hearing not aright.

Only spake the little lisper
In the Angel-tongue,
Fainter than a fairy-whisper
Murmured in among
Dewy blossoms covered over
With the fragrant tufts of clover,
Where the minstrel honey-rover
Twanged his wings and sung.

"Leonainie!" - And the glimmer
Of her starry eyes
Faded and the world grew dimmer
E'en as Paradise
Blossomed with a glory brighter
Than the waning stars, and whiter
Than the dying moon, and lighter
Than the morning skies.

Children have always been at the center of Hoosier family life. From the author's Ora Myers glass negatives collection of Hancock County, Indiana subjects.

After the "Leonainie" hoax received continuing great comment throughout the United States, many other "Poe" poems were found. One, allegedly found etched on a barn door, read:

MARIENNEY

Mary Ann her parents named her,
But SHE wrote it Marienney;
And though angels have not claimed her

She's as fair as any.
  For her eyes are dark and gloomy,
  And her nose is sort o' bloomy,
  And her mouth is rather roomy, —
  And have angels whispered to me,
    Marienney?
    No, not any
etc.   *E.A.P.*

The New York comic magazine "Puck" in its September 12, 1877 issue reported the arrest of "The young lady without an abdomen" who was arrested on the Bowery under the poetic name of "Melusine," for fraud carrying a Poe forgery of a poem of her name signed E.A.P. The poem reads in part, "Melusine, so they named her\ Stomachless, but beauteous bright!\ In a looking-glass they framed her\ To deceive the people's sight.\ But the angels wouldn't stand it,\ `Move on, Mellie!" they commanded,\ Melusine's biz was stranded,\ And she vanished ere the night. etc.

"Leonainie" was set to music in March 14, 1879 by Will H. Ponthius of Cincinnati.

The Ainsworth's Latin Dictionary containing the Poe forgery was sold for twenty-five dollars to a New York book dealer, Charles B. Foote. Following Foote's death, a Cleveland, Ohio collector of Riley, Paul Lemperly, bought the forgery. Following his death in 1939, Scribner's Sons purchased it.

Riley eventually included "Leonainie" in his volume of poems entitled "Armazindy," published October 7, 1894. The Indianapolis SENTINEL in reviewing the book repeated the details of the hoax, commenting that "It was extensively copied, and so clever was the imitation that American and English reviewers, and even an eminent authority like Edmund Clarence Stedman pronounced it genuine; and when the name of the real author was disclosed, Mr. Stedman still maintained that the poem was unquestionably written by Poe."

For many years, "Leonainie" reappeared in various places in the world as a "previously unpublished" poem of Poe's such as in the The New York CRITIC of April 8, 1886. On June 5, 1886, an article printed in the Paris, France newspaper THE AMERICAN REGISTER recounted "Leonainie" was widely known in Italy as a poem of Poe's. The London FORTNIGHT-LY REVIEW of February, 1904 brought it forth as a new poem of Poe's, etc. etc.

There is an element of the "Leonainie" hoax that might easily be overlooked if we did not examine it here. Riley was perpetrating the hoax within a tradition Riley enjoyed immensely. Riley enjoyed the poetry of the "master hoaxer" Thomas Chatterton. There was once this angry, suicidal young man, fatherless early in life, originally thought an idiot from birth, named Thomas Chatterton. Actually, Thomas Chatterton was a creative and literary genius in Riley's view. Born in Bristol on November 20, 1752, Chatterton's father, a teacher, died shortly after his son's birth. The mother took in

Drawing of Thomas Chatterton, "Despair Offering a Bowl of Poison to Chatterton," from British museum, London. Chatterton died an arsenic suicide at the age of 18.

sewing and ran a "home school" to support herself and child. Chatterton refused to play with other children nor communicate. His first school expelled him for being a dullard. Chatterton then chose to lock himself often in the attic of the family home where he found ancient paper which his father had brought home as waste paper. The paper had been old music folios the father had come across while a sub-chanter at the Church of St. Mary Redcliff in Bristol. The father brought the old papers home with him for his wife to use as sewing-patterns, or for himself as bookbindings. Chatterton made use of these old papers in quite a different way.

Chatterton became a forger. With reading materials limited to a huge family Bible, a bad printing of Chaucer, and borrowed "faulty" dictionaries and glossaries, Chatterton produced literary pieces he proposed as the works of a 15th Century monk named Thomas Rowley (Rowleie). They were Chatterton's own poems, of course, written on dad's purloined sheets of music folios.

We remember that Chatterton was only in his early teenaged years and not considered very bright so when he started selling these works of the Middle English monk, Thomas Rowley, they were considered a great "find."

Chatterton was desperate for funds. He was unhappily apprenticed to an attorney when all else failed him. This position drove him even more suicidal and he began drawing and writing poetry in the lawyer's office until the attorney found a suicide note dated for the next day unless the attorney released him from his apprenticeship. He did. Chatterton left for London where he hoped to make his mark as a poet. Hunger and poverty awaited him in London and he died by poisoning himself with arsenic at the age of seventeen.

Two of those most influenced by this strangely possessed boy were William Wordsworth, an English poet who extolled him in poetry as "The marvellous boy,\ The sleepless soul that perished in his pride" and James Whitcomb Riley, the American poet. Chatterton's poetry and particularly his faked "Rowley poems" in fact had great literary merit as Riley recognized.

Even though the poems were certainly not medieval manuscripts, they are very richly decorative pieces filled with mystery and "gut" emotion. Modern critics call Chatterton the first "Romantic" poet. Not just Riley and Wordsworth, but also Keats and Byron acknowledged indebtedness to his poetry. Riley took from Chatterton's works a love of their richness of imagery and great technical dexterity.

We must not forget Chatterton as an influence on Riley's "The Flying Islands of the Night," written the year after "Leonainie." Chatterton's "AElla" is similarly written in play form. It concerns a pre-Norman conquest warrior named AElla whose wooing of his beloved Birtha is interrupted by a Danish invasion of England. Believing Birtha is taken into the arms of another man, AElla commits suicide ("stabbeth hys breste") with his sword. Just before his death, a noble Danish warrior, Hurra, who respects AElla's honor brings Birtha to him. She chooses to die with AElla saying, "Oh! ys (is) mie (my) AElla dedde?\ O! I will make hys (his) grave mie (my) vyrgyn (virgin) spousal bedde." Riley's subject matter in "The Flying Islands of the Night" goes in quite another direction. Both "plays" are impossible to produce and set in the strange Chaucerian style.

And so ends our journey through the "Leonainie" hoax through correspondence, references, clippings and recollections.

We think of Riley as being a journalist, or perhaps a newspaper poet, as well as lyceum circuit "lecturer" during the 1880's. Jucklet was with Riley in both his newspaper office and on the platform tours.

Riley loved to play practical jokes while working as a "staffer" at the

Indianapolis JOURNAL. One of them he used often he called the "lung tester" which he rigged up. There was an electric call box in the newspaper's editorial offices. To engage it, the message sender pushed over a lever, released it and it returned with considerable clatter. Riley rigged the call box so he could push the lever over and release it at will. Then he attached a tube to it and put the nipple from a baby's bottle on the end of the tube. When a friend came in, he would slap him on the back, compliment him on his vigorous health, ask him how his lungs were, and finally suggest that he try them out on the office lung tester. The friend would put the baby nipple in his mouth, blow lustily, Riley would release the lever and it would clatter to the end of the slot. The friend would swell up with pride until the device was loosed again without the aid of any lung power and reveal that the clatter had nothing to do with the man's lungs.

Jucklet was in Riley's very soul throughout his life.

That Riley was able to have his chance to excel on the Lyceum Circuit was due to Jucklet. Jucklet was the minstrel in Riley who loved to tell stories and entertain people with witty anecdotes.

One of Riley's favorites was "The Object Lesson." This was a tale Riley repeated so often he fully mastered its presentation.

One of the tellings of this story occurred at the Indianapolis JOURNAL office where Riley was employed at a time when many people were present. One of those present was a friend who Riley had recently met named Robert Burdette, a man already on the Lyceum Circuit and billed as "Hawkeye Man."

Benjamin Harrison, 23rd President of the United States and Riley crony.

Burdette was so impressed by the recitation that he became convinced Riley could succeed on the platform. In a sense, then, this recitation would later become responsible for Riley's getting his chance at a platform career. Marcus Dickey, Riley's secretary and early biographer, relates the incident. "Burdette was one of a group in a back corner of the Journal office, when Riley recited "The Object Lesson.""That audience," said Burdette, "beat any public one that ever drew a a watch on me or coaxed me into silence by their slumbers. There were brilliant men in it, among them a future president of the United

States (Benjamin Harrison)" Burdette was so certain after hearing it that Riley could magnetize a public audience that he went home and wrote the following, which he sent abroad to lecture bureaus and committees, and had printed in many newspapers:

Office of "The Hawkeye," Burlington, Iowa

It has been my pleasure to listen to Mr. J.W. Riley and I never heard him say a tiresome word or utter a stupid sentence. I would walk through the mud or ride through the rain to hear him again. I would get out of bed to listen to him. If I have a friend on a lecture committee in the Untied States, I want to whisper in his ear that one of the best hits he can make will be to surprise his audience with J.W. Riley and his "Object Lesson." Riley is good clean through. His humor is gentle; it is not caustic. It is pure and manly, and the people that will once listen to him will want him back again the same season.

/S/ Robert J. Burdette

What follows is a written representation of one of Riley's always varying recitations of his famous platform piece.

THE OBJECT LESSON[1]

Barely a year ago I attended the Friday afternoon exercises of a country school. My mission there, as I remember, was to refresh my mind with such material as might be gathered for a "valedictory," which, I regret to say, was to be handed down to posterity under another signature than my own.

There was present, among a host of visitors, a pale young man of perhaps thirty years, with a tall head and bulging brow and a highly-intellectual pair of eyes and spectacles. He wore his hair without roach or "part" and the smile he beamed about him was "a joy forever." He was an educator - from the East, I think I heard it rumored - anyway he was introduced to the school at last, and he bowed, and smiled, and beamed upon us all, and entertained us after the most delightfully edifying manner imaginable. And although I may fail to reproduce the exact substance of his remarks upon that highly important occasion, I think I can at least present his theme in all its coherency of detail. Addressing more particularly the primary department of the school, he said: -

"As the little exercise I am about to introduce is of recent origin, and the bright, intelligent faces of the pupils before me seem rife with eager and expectant interest, it will be well for me, perhaps, to offer by way of preparatory preface, a few terse words of explanation.

"The Object-Lesson is designed to fill a long-felt want, and is destined, as I think, to revolutionize in a great degree, the educational systems of our land. - In my belief, the Object-Lesson will supply a want which I may safely say has heretofore left the most egregious and palpable traces of mental confusion and intellectual inadequacies stamped, as it were, upon the gleaming reasons of the most learned - the highest cultured, and the most eminently gifted and promising of our professors and scientists both at home and abroad.

"Now this deficiency - if it may be so termed - plainly has a beginning: and probing deeply with the bright, clean scalpel of experience we discover that - "As the twig is bent, the tree's inclined." To remedy, then, a deeply-seated error which for so long has rankled at the very root of educational progress throughout the land, many plausible, and we must admit, many helpful theories have been introduced to allay the painful errors resulting from the discrepancy of which we speak: but until now, nothing that seemed wholly to eradicate the defect has been discovered, and that, too, strange as it may seem, is, at last, found emanating, like the mighty river, from the simplest source, but broad-

"The Educator" as I would picture him. Drawing by Frank Beard.

ening and gathering in force and power as it flows along, until, at last, its grand and mighty current sweeps on in majesty to the vast illimitable ocean of-of-of- Success! Ahem!

"And, now, little boys and girls, that we have had by implication, a clear and comprehensive explanation of the Object-Lesson and its mission, I trust you will give me your undivided attention while I endeavor - in my humble way - to direct your newly acquired knowledge through the proper channel. For instance: -

"This little object I hold in my hand - who will designate it by its proper name? Come, now, let us see who will be the first to answer. `A peanut,' says the little boy here at my right. Very good - very good! I hold then, in my hand, a peanut. And now who will tell me, what is the peanut? A very simply question - who will answer? `Something good to eat,' says the little girl. Yes, `something good to eat,' but would it not be better to say simply that the peanut is an edible? I think so, yes. The peanut, then, is - an edible - now, all together, an edible!

"To what kingdom does the peanut belong? The animal, vegetable or mineral kingdom? A very easy question. Come, let us have prompt answers. `The animal kingdom,' does the little boy say? Oh no! The peanut does not belong to the animal kingdom! Surely the little boy must be thinking of a larger object than the peanut - the elephant, perhaps. To what kingdom, then, does the peanut belong? The v-v-veg-The vegetable kingdom,' says the bright-faced little girl on the back seat. Ah! that is better. We find then that the peanut belongs to the - what kingdom? The `vegetable kingdom.' Very good, very good!

"And now who will tell us of what the peanut is composed. Let us have quick responses now. Time is fleeting! Of what is the peanut composed? `The hull and the goody,' in vulgar parlance, but how much better it would be to say simply, the shell and the kernel. Would not that sound better? Yes, I thought you would agree with me there!

"And now who will tell me the color of the peanut! And be careful now! for I shouldn't like to hear you make the very stupid blunder I once heard a little boy make in reply to the same question. Would you like to hear what color the stupid little boy said the peanut was? You would, eh? Well, now, how many of you would like to hear what color the stupid little boy said the peanut was? Come now, let's have an expression. All who would like to hear what color the stupid little boy said the peanut was, may hold up their right hands. Very good, very good - there, that will do.

"Well, it was during a professional visit I was once called upon to make to a neighboring city, where I was invited to address the children of a free school - Hands down, now, little boy, - founded for the exclusive benefit of the little newsboys and bootblacks, who, it seems, had not the means to defray the expenses of the commonest educational accessories, and during an object lesson identical with the one before us now - for it is a favorite one of mine - I propounded the question, what is the color of the peanut? Many answers were given in response, but none as sufficiently succinct and apropos as I deemed the facts demanded; and so at last I personally addressed *a ragged, boy, as I then thought, a bright-eyed little fellow, when judge of my surprise, in reply to my question, what is the color of a peanut, the little fellow, without the slightest gleam of intelligence lighting up his face, answered, that `if not scorched by roasting, the peanut was a blond.' Why, I was almost tempted to join in the general merriment his inapposite reply elicited. But I occupy your attention with trivial things; and as I notice the time allotted me has slipped away, we will drop the peanut for the present. Trusting the few facts gleaned from a topic so homely and unpromising will sink deep in your minds, in time to bloom and blossom in the fields of future usefulness - I-I—I thank you."*

1. An Object Lesson from going to a county teacher's institute in Anderson in late 1872.

Riley and Bill Nye had a standard lark when they went on lecture tours. On entering a town, Riley or Nye would enter the best bookstore in town, take the proprietor to one side and in a whisper inquire as to whether he could sell them an unexpunged edition of Felicia Hemans. Of course the bookstore owner could not, and then the two would meet outside and have a good laugh at the unsophisticated bookseller. But one day, Riley thought he would have a little fun at Nye's expense so before they arrived at Milwaukee, Wisconsin, Riley wrote ahead to one of the prominent book-stores acquainting the proprietor with all the facts and asking him to prepare a special title page and insert it in a volume of Mrs. Heman's poems. On arriving at Milwaukee, it was Nye's turn to try to secure the unexpunged edition of Mrs. Hemans's poems.

Riley remained outside while Nye went through the usual program and offered the bookseller $5 if he could secure for him such an edition. In a whisper, much to Nye's surprise, he told him he had such a book, produced it, and Nye was forced to lose his $5 and when they met later at the hotel, for Riley did not remain outside this time, Riley certainly had a good laugh at Nye's discomfort.

Jucklet was always a great entertainer even when he reached fame. He was fun to be with socially. Stories about him always portray him as warm nd companionable.

Riley liked to begin stories with friends and then have them carry through with its story line. He would reach a point in a story and then ask a friend to carry it on. The only point at which Riley would object would be if some-one wanted to kill off one of the heroes of Riley's invention. He called anyone wanting to do not only a person of no imagination but also a blatant murderer. Such a person did not understand that there could be no death to literary characters so they must be allowed to live forever.

An Indianapolis street scene in 1891.

Even so, around his friends, Riley was not always humorous and generous to persons he did not like. Haute Jameson recalled that Riley did not like some of the young men who joined the social group with Riley who often gathered at the Tarkington home. He did not like a man's beard to be parted and to one young man who called while there he said "a beard like that may be becoming to his style of character, but to me it places him in the garden, not as flowering product, but as a nice pleasant, comforting woolly worm. Maybe a caterpillar would be a better word, but woolly worm is the way I think of him." Haute recalled Riley said he felt "fuzzy" when in the man's presence. Another man Riley did not like he called "aboriginal" and said the man's head was "meat clear through."

This Riley was the witty socialite who took Indianapolis society by storm upon his move there. The Indianapolis scene was a welter of busy, busy activity compared to the life he knew in his hometown of Greenfield, Indiana.

Riley was able to play the great "literatus" and find a place in the most reputable and socially expanded circles. Jucklet continued to write amusing anecdotal stories through this period.

THE FISHING PARTY (1890)

Wunst[1] we went a-fishin' - Me
An' my Pa an' Ma, all three
When they wuz a picnic, 'way
Out to Hanch's Woods, one day.
An' they wuz a crick out there,

Where the fishes is, an' where
Little boys 'taint big an' strong
Better have their folks along!

My Pa he ist fished an' fished!
An' my Ma she said she wished
Me an' her was home; an' Pa
Said he wished so worse'n Ma.

Pa said ef you talk, er say
Anything, er sneeze, er play
Hain't no fish, alive er dead,
Ever go' to bite! he said.

Purt'[2] nigh dark in town when we
Got back home; an' Ma, says she,
Now she'll have a fish for shore!
An' she buyed one at the store.

Nen at supper Pa he won't
Eat no fish, an' says, he don't
Like 'em - An' he pounded me
When I choked!...Ma, didn't he?

From the author's Ora Myers glass negatives collection of Hancock County, Indiana subjects.

---

1. Once.
2. Variant of "pretty," a Hoosier expression denoting proximity.

Was Jucklet's mischievous minstrelsy involved in Riley's elderly years? Yes, Jucklet seems to have lived with Riley as a favorite self until the end.

In these last years, we recall the great honors bestowed upon Riley. These years were the years as in 1902 when Yale College, New Haven, Connecticut conferred upon Riley at age 52 the honorary degree of Master of Arts. Or the next year, 1903 when Wabash College at Crawfordsville, Indiana presented Riley at age 53 with another Honorary Master's Degree. Or the next year, in 1904, when the University of Pennsylvania, Philadelphia, Pennsylvania honored Riley at age 54 with a degree of Doctor of Letters, or in 1907, when Indiana University, Bloomington, Indiana granted Riley at age 57 the degree of Doctor of Laws.

It was Jucklet that had earned these degrees more than any of the other roles Riley played in his life. Riley had survived to achieve great honor as a mischievous jongleur, dialect singer, and story teller.

Appropriately, it was a poem of Jucklet's that Riley recited at Yale on the occasion of his receiving his honorary degree from that institution.

NO BOY KNOWS (1902)

There are many things that boys may know -
Why this and that are thus and so, -
Who made the world in the dark and lit
The great sun up to lighten it:
Boys know new things every day -
When they study, or when they play, -
When they idle, or sow and reap -
But no boy knows when he goes to sleep.

Boys who listen - or should, at least, -
May know that the round old earth rolls East; -
And know that the ice and the snow and the rain -
Ever repeating their parts again -
Are all just water the sunbeams first
Sip from the earth in their endless thirst,
And pour again till the low streams leap. -
But no boy knows when he goes to sleep.

The library at Riley's Lockerbie Street home where he resided upon writing this poem.

A boy may know what a long, glad while
It has been to him since the dawn's first smile,
When forth he fared in the realm divine
Of brook-laced woodland and spun-sunshine; -
He may know each call of his truant mates,
And the paths they went, - and the pasture-gates
Of the 'cross-lots home through the dusk so deep. -
But no boy knows when he goes to sleep.

O I have followed me, o'er and o'er,
From the flagrant drowse on the parlor-floor,
To the pleading voice of the mother when

I even doubted I heard it then -
To the sense of a kiss, and a moonlit room,
And dewy odors of locust-bloom -
A sweet white cot - and a cricket's cheep. -
But no boy knows when he goes to sleep.

Toward the end of his life, and after suffering a crippling stroke, Riley kept himself very busy with a huge correspondence. Jucklet was at work in this voluminous daily correspondence.

One of his letter found after he died was to a child who wrote him to say she enjoyed the poem "Orphant Annie" and "The Runaway Boy."

Dear Little Friend. - One time an old middle-aged man, a very middle-aged man, who from his childhood had been playing that he was a poet - got some sure-enough books of poetry- pieces printed, at last, and sprinkled them over his friends like salt on cantaloupes; and then leaned back and waited for applause and laughed to himself so that he would not miss any voice of praise out of the vast chorus of the world at large. And - he is listening still - though, like the bass kings in the O-r-tao-r-o,

> He thinks it not becoming
> To be found in idle funning
> So his laugh is ver-ee L O W -
> H A ——————————— H A!

And yet not quite in vain has he been listening all these years, for now and then faint murmurous accents like yours reach his almost starving senses; and as he hears them, the old man's fancies find his Youth again and all the childish joys that once were his. So veritably young he is that he goes danc-ing back to his old make-believes and plays that he's a poet, just as then.

> Miss Medairy Dory Ann
> Cast her line and caught a man,
> But when he looked so pleased aback!
> She unhooked and plunked him back,
> "I never like to catch what I can,"
> Said Miss Medairy Dory Ann.

—-(Biographer's Note: This letter was never completed.)

At Christmas times, Riley's correspondence was said to rival Santa Claus's. On his last birthday, October 7th 1915, ten thousand cards came many of them containing greetings of an entire class of school children. One child wrote, "I think Indiana should be proud of such a child as you. Not only Indiana, but the United States should be proud of you. I am proud of you myself." Another wrote "I tell you what, Mr. Riley, I was surprised to learn that you was living because I thought all poets was dead." Another wrote, "I have read so many of your poems that I have a strong taste of poetry myself."

JUCKLET'S LAST TRICK

Indiana's U.S. Senator Harry S. New told the ghost story that follows about Riley at the time of the poet's death. The Senator knew Riley intimately from being a young reporter of the Indianapolis JOURNAL when Riley was on its staff and later as the same newspaper's Managing Editor who valued Riley's contributions exceedingly.

"The Riley home was in East Lockerbie street in Indianapolis, and it was there that the poet died. His death came in the afternoon and it was still early when the undertaker, that individual most repellent to Riley in his lifetime, arrived to perform the preliminary services of those of his kind. The room in which the dead man lay was on the second floor and was a modest apartment with but a single door and a window opposite, which looked out on a narrow side yard. In that room what was left of the sensitive poet was alone with the creature he despised, and if the soul of the dead lingers near the mortal clay, it may be conceived that Riley's spirit had a bad half hour with the follower of the grim reaper. But that half hour passed and the servitor of the departed soft-footedly went his way, silently closing the door behind him.

This was but part of the work of the undertaker. He was to return some hours later to finish his task. He returned as the day was drawing to its close, and mournfully climbed the Riley stairs. He applied the cautious pressure of a silent hand to the Riley door knob which he had deftly turned but a few hours earlier. The knob refused to turn. The door declined to open.

Evidently, said the methodical worker, some member of the family has locked the death chamber. He summoned those in the house and asked for the key. He was told that the door had not been locked. No one had been in the second floor room since his former visit.

Nevertheless, he assured them, the door was locked. So the family bunches of keys were produced and the journey of the undertaker, this time not alone, wound again to the second floor. But there it halted at the poet's door. One after one the keys were tried in the lock. None would enter the keyhole. The door might not be unlocked.

A delicacy was felt in doing violence to the door of the dead. As there was no other entrance to the room except the window, the party went into the yard, procured a ladder and the undertaker climbed it and entered the room of the departed through the window.

When he had gained an entrance he investigated carefully and found that the door was locked from the inside, and that the key had been left in the lock.

Those who knew Riley best, his penchant for a practical joke, his dis-

Riley died in this bedroom at Lockerbie Street, Indianapolis. Did his ghost lock the door to this bedroom from the undertaker?

like for undertakers, his belief in the ministration of the spirits of the departed, are willing to admit that here was a prank quite characteristic and to be expected - the sort of thing that might be done by the ghost of him who was gone, if ghosts were a matter of fact."

Although Jucklet was not Riley's most enduring role, and certainly was not the character in Riley's life who produced his finest poetry, nevertheless Jucklet must receive credit for a job successfully done. Riley survived on his inner laughter.

A Hoosier farm scene of Riley's era. From the author's Ora Myers glass negative collection of Hancock County, Indiana subjects.

AMPHINE

WHERE IS LOVE FOR RILEY?
AMPHINE'S WOMAN PROBLEMS
AND CAPACITIES FOR GREAT
FRIENDSHIPS

WHERE IS LOVE FOR RILEY?
AMPHINE'S WOMAN PROBLEMS AND
CAPACITIES FOR GREAT FRIENDSHIPS

There is at least one event in everyone's life which"tears you up." In Riley's great poem of self-scrutiny "The Flying Islands of the Night," Riley is "torn up" because of love. He can know it only at the level of the soul with an already married woman. How could a poetic genius have been driven to such an impasse? What foul fate fickled him?

Riley's self that bears this scar is Amphine, the Riley who can love. Riley wants to know love very badly. He needs his soulmate. Amphine is the lover who seeks reunion with his recently deceased married friend, Nellie Millikan Cooley who died in the days before he wrote "The Flying Islands of the Night."

No, Riley's relationship with Nellie Millikan Cooley was no ordinary one. Would we expect the tapestry of Riley's romance to be woven as traditional cloth? Riley's affair with Nellie was a combination silver, gold and diamond friendship of souls.

Riley is dealing with his emotional self in great turmoil in the poem "The Flying Islands of the Night." Where is love? Where can he find love now that his beloved soul-mate Nellie Millikan Cooley is dead? Riley is dealing with the essential sensibility of a

Nellie Millikan at 18 (1864) short months before her marriage to George Cooley. (Neg. C7173, IMCPL-Riley Collection, Indiana Historical Society.

poet, love, a "feel" of warmth, of passion, of happiness, of fulfillment, occasions of loving and being loved in the past and future as well as the present. There is no definition of love but it does have a root meaning which can be expressed in descriptions of qualities and expressions, never matters of intention or demand, but always in happening and gift. It has to do with affection but is not limited to spheres of affections but rather finds its expression in relationships and the yearning to be with another. Riley knew this great love for Nellie Cooley, the source of his great inspiration. That is why it had the worth of silver, gold and diamond.

Riley as Amphine was also a play character of love who expresses Riley's need for companionship with men as well as women. This is love which the Greeks referred to as "philia" rather than "eros." Riley was capable of assuming the role of Amphine, the lover and man of affectionate relationships, with ease. The company of others often saved him from his deep depression which we will consider in a following section on Crestillomeem, Riley's dejected and alcoholic self in the poem and in his life.

The company of Amphine probably leaves Riley at the end of "The Flying Island of the Night." Riley sought relief from his heavy depression in alcohol on many occasions. Riley "drowned" his sorrow as some refer to it. We are reminded of an effect of alcohol from Shakespeare's "Macbeth," Act II, iii29-40, where Macbeth's porter made the following remark to a houseguest:

"Macduff: What three things does drink especially provoke?

Porter: Marry, sir, nose-painting, sleep, and urine. Lechery, sir, it provokes and unprovokes. It provokes the desire, but it takes away the performance. Therefore much drink can be said to be an equivocator with lechery. It makes him and it mars him, it sets him on and it takes him off, it persuades him and disheartens him, and makes him stand to and not stand to; in conclusion, equivocates him in a sleep, and giving him the lie, leaves him."

Modern science supports Shakespeare's observation.

Amphine did not depart Riley other than as impotence might have resulted from too great a consumption of alcohol. Possibly such problems marred every single one of Riley's later attempts to find a marriage partner. Most of the women Riley seems to have courted after his thirties cited Riley's alcoholism as a reason why they did not wish to marry him. We simply do not

CONCERT

Tuesday, Nov. 18.

PROGRAMME.

1—Opening Chorus, Star Spangled Banner.
2—Prayer.
3—Instrumental Solo .... Minnie Sebastian.
4—Comic Solo, Courting in the Rain. .... John Skinner.
5—Solo and Quartette, Beautiful Girl of the South, Fannie Branham, Julia Mathers, Otis Ridgeway, Ed. Millikan.
6—Solo, Near the Old Plantation. .... Emma Cooley.
7—Instrumental Solo, Falling Leaves .... Lydia Martin.
8—Solo and Quartette, Kiss me and I'll go to Sleep .. Hattie Thayer, Nellie Cooley, O. N. Ridgeway, E. Millikan.
9—Solo, Kathleen Mavourneen .... Minnie Sebastian.
10—Solo and Quartette, I'm Waiting ... Callie Offutt, Fannie Branham, O. N. Ridgeway, Ed. Millikan.
11—Comic Recitation. .... James W. Riley.
12—Instrumental Duet, Home, Sweet Home. .... Lydia Martin, Anna Chittenden.
13—Solo, Maggie's Secret. .... Mellie Ryan.
14—Vocal Duet, In the Days of Long Ago ...... Nellie Cooley, O. N. Ridway.
15—Solo and Quartette, Pulling Hard Against the Stream.
16—Select Reading, The Blind Boy (by request). .. Dr. Thomas.
17—Instrumental Duett, Helter Skelter Gallop. .... Mrs. Cooley and Daughter.
18—Solo, Not for Gold or Precious Stones ...... Hattie Thayer.
19—Instrumental Solo, Blushing Morn. ..... Annie Chittenden.
20—Vocal Solo, Castles in the Air. .... Nellie Cooley.
21—Vocal Solo, We will have to get the Style. .... Lizzie Ryon.
22—Instrumental Duet .... Jennie Conover, Ellie Branham.
23—Comic Solo. .... J. W. Riley.
24—Instrumental Solo, Silver Thistle. ...... Minnie Sebastian.
25—Tableau.

Doors open at 7.00; Concert at 7.45.

The Riley "gang" in one of their town entertainments Note: Riley gives a "Comic Recitation" and "Comic Solo," while Nellie sings "Kiss Me and I'll Go to Sleep," "In the Days of Long-Ago" and "Castles in the Air." Riley's pal John Skinner even sings "Courting in the Rain." (Courtesy of The Riley Old Home Society, Greenfield, Indiana.)

know what this meant.

Riley retained the great capacity for affectionate relationships. Anyway, Riley's "affair of the souls" with Nellie Millikan Cooley was enough to remember. It was a North Star to guide Riley's emotions even after her death.

We have so very, very little to go on to recreate the setting of the great "soul-level" love of James Whitcomb Riley's for Nellie Millikan Cooley. Those in Greenfield who gossiped after noticing Riley's horse tethered at Nellie's house so often are long gone but their tales have lived on to the present time in folklore. Riley retreated to Greenfield from wherever he wandered when he "felt bad." The soul-mate who shared this escape to find comfort in an unfriendly world who helped him survive such bouts was Nellie Millikan
Cooley.

We know that Nellie, married to another man, George Cooley, was taken from Greenfield by her husband to a far point in Illinois after many years of rambunctious youth for Riley and his Nellie together. Prior to that must have occurred the moments of sharing that brought Nellie and Riley into such great union of souls. Nellie and her husband, George Cooley, remained married for only a short time in Illinois -about two years -before Nellie died there. She was brought back to Greenfield for burial and Riley wrote a great emotionally draining obituary shortly before writing "The Flying Islands of the Night." Were it not for this autobiographical poem and "taking stock of himself after Nellie's demise" we would probably have nothing at all from Riley about this great soul-love of his life. Riley would never have brooked causing Nellie's reputation to suffer because of their relationship.

The poem "The Flying Islands of the Night" contains much speculative material about this relationship which will be considered further in this section on the life of Amphine, Riley's romantic self, but for now we read a letter of Nellie's sent to Riley from her exile with her husband in Illinois.

LETTER FROM NELLIE COOLEY
January 13, 1877

Jim dear boy —-...We have been too true and loving friends to say "Good Bye" and let that be all. How many times I have thoughts of you, how many good things I have read and wished you could read it. Oh, how many times I have only asked for one more evening like those happy ones spent in old

G... when you would come over and bring your violin and perhaps have one of your charming poems in your pocket to read to us and when it would rain and I would send the beggar maid to see you home. Jim, when your letter was brought to me yesterday, I was sitting reading over some of your poems and some of our correspondence, very strange "was noted." Sometimes you appear to me in a dream and how we do talk and laugh, and always we are the same warm friends that we have been for so many years and every evening I play over the same waltzes and sing the same songs but alas there is a missing link. I sound A in vain, but I still play them all the same...

Your devoted friend til death
Nellie M. Cooley

Nellie's standard farewell was, "Your devoted friend," as in another letter extant of June 1, 1877. The distance of Riley from Nellie after George took her to Illinois apparently did not cool their "soul companionship." Forgive me for a little quote that comes to mind from Shakespeare's 116th Sonnet:

"Let me not to the marriage of true minds
Admit impediments. Love is not love
Which alters when it alteration finds..."

This seems to describe how Riley felt about Nellie wherever she might be. Riley's soul found a home in the encouragement of Nellie. Even death did not sever Riley's cord of regard for Nellie.

We also have a poem from one letter from Riley to Nellie preserved by her daughter, Emma Cooley Cox, which was brought to light in 1878 about eight years after Nellie's death. It attests to Nellie's encouragement to Riley.

A LETTER TO A FRIEND (To: Nellie Cooley)

The past is like a story
I have listened to in dreams
That vanished in the glory
Of the Morning's early gleams;
And - at my shadow glancing -
I feel a loss of strength,
As the Day of Life advancing
leaves it shorn of half its length.

But it's all in vain to worry

At the rapid race of Time -
And he flies in such a flurry
   When I trip him with a rhyme,
I'll bother him no longer
   Than to thank you for the thought
That "my fame is growing stronger
   As you really think it ought."

And though I fall below it,
   I might know as much of mirth
To live and die a poet
   Of unacknowledged worth;
For Fame is but a vagrant -
   Though a loyal one and brave,
And his laurels ne'er so fragrant
   As when scattered o'er the grave.

Nellie's daughter, Emma Cooley Cox, mentioned this poem to the editor (Ochiltree) of the Indianapolis Saturday HERALD who thereafter published it many years after Nellie's death. Riley included the poem in a letter to Nellie in which Riley responded to Nellie's saying she felt his fame was growing stronger as she thought it ought.

In the original poem, "The Flying Island of the Night" as it appeared in the Indianapolis Saturday HERALD in 1878, Amphine, Riley's romantic and affectionate self, loved only the one woman, Dwainie, recently deceased as far as earthlife was concerned. Nellie was only dead weeks at this time. Dwainie is Nellie.

Nellie Millikan Cooley with daughter Emma . (Neg. C7175, IMCPL-Riley Collection, Indiana Historical Society.)

Dwainie - Nellie Millikan Cooley - was a woman married to another man whose life we shall connect with Riley's as Amphine grew into adolescence and with Nellie into his mid-twenties. Now, by the time Riley wrote his autobiographical poem, Nellie had died. Nellie was the great foe of Crestillomeem of the poem. While Crestillomeem plotted Riley's downfall, Dwainie, steeped in love for Riley, returned to Riley from the dead to save his great life-plan to achieve fame. Crestillomeem early in the poem recognizes Dwainie:

> 'Tis Dwainie of the Wunks who peeks and peers
> With those fine eyes of hers in our affairs
> And carries Krung, in some disguise, these hints
> Of our intent! See thou that silence falls
> Forever on her lips, and that the sight
> She wastes upon our secret action blurs
> With gray and grisly scum that shall for aye
> Conceal us from her gaze while she writhes blind
> And fangles as the fat worms of the grave!

Nellie Millikan Cooley was not simply the woman who Riley loved, she was his great booster and encourager. Her death preceded the writing of the poem "The Flying Islands of the Night" bears Riley's otherwise unexpressible grief at her passing. Without Nellie, his love interest became alcohol, the Crestillomeem of the poem. His soul had lost its mate and needed another. Crestillomeem sought Riley's courtship.

"The Flying Islands of the Night" tells us that Riley loved Nellie Cooley. That is not to say that he did not have affection for others or even encounters "on the run" in his years of early manhood. These seem extremely probable. But with Nellie Cooley did Riley indulge in his great "soul" love affair. "The Flying Islands of the Night" written during R iley's great grief following Nellie's death, contains what this biographer considers the finest love lyric in all of literature. One recognizes echoes from Riley's obituary of Nellie alive in "Warm depths of azure skies, where merry birds, afloat on waves of sunshine, poured out their sweetest songs, and so baptized the world with sweetest melody..."

AY,DWAINIE! - MY DWAINIE

Spraivoll (Singing)

Ay, Dwainie! - My Dwainie!
The lurloo ever sings,

A tremor in his flossy crest
And in his glossy wings.
And Dwainie! - My Dwainie!
The sinno-welvers call; -
But Dwainie hides in Spirkland
And answers not at all.

The teeper twitters Dwainie! -
The tcheucker on his spray
Teeters up and down the wind
And will not fly away:
And Dwainie! - My Dwainie!
The drowsy oovers drawl; -
But Dwainie hides in Spirkland
And answers not at all.

O Dwainie! - My Dwainie!
The breezes hold their breath -
The stars are pale as blossoms,
And the night as still as death:
And Dwainie! - My Dwainie!
The fainting echoes fall; -
But Dwainie in Spirkland
And answers not at all.

The death of a beloved can never make more sense than Riley gives to this Dwainie poem of "The Flying Islands of the Night." Love blurs reality and takes its imagery from absurdity or from such alienation as delirium dreams.

There is only scant evidence of the life of Nellie Millikan Cooley. Although Riley's obituary of her shows her burial in Greenfield's Park Cemetery, no stone remains to mark the spot nor record of where she is buried. Nor does the cemetery have record of it. The winter of the writing of this biography, 1997, the biographer located the grave with cemetery personnel from Greenfield's Riley Park Cemetery using a probe into the soft early winter earth. Only the pea gravel which covered the wooden coffin gave the tracings of the spot of her burial. I placed a wreath of the usual variety on the grave once located. It will probably never be of interest hereafter. The thought of my causing a "probe" to be sent into the ground to disturb her grave causes me horrible regret. Nellie, "Dwainie," forgive my curiosity.

Riley sent his soul down into that grave I found to marry his Dwainie there. Marriage with any other was impossible.

In the 1870 United States census, Nellie is listed as living in Greenfield, Indiana in the household of George B. Cooley, age 30, as Nellie M. Cooley, age 25, "keeping house" and born in Ohio. Her children are listed as Emma, age 4, and Susannah, age 1. Also listed in the household of George B. Cooley is the mother, Rhoda Millikan, Riley's art and "home school" tutor from Riley's youth. She is listed as being age 50 and as an "artist."

The Millikans are not recorded in the 1860 United States census as being residents of Hancock County, Indiana.

"Dwainie's currently unmarked grave. According to cemetery officials, the grave of Nellie Millikan Cooley is in a small row of lots purchased by her husband George when Greenfield, Indiana first opened its Park Cemetery. Only the resistance to a probe of pea gravel placed around the wooden coffins in those days permitted its location by a cemetery ground crew. I placed my jacket on the spot.

They arrived shortly after the American Civil War began and Nellie Millikan's mother, Mrs. Rhoda Millikan, took up schooling in Greenfield from the opportunity that the local school had disbanded when its men teachers went off to war.

Shortly after her arrival with her family in the year 1862, Nellie Millikan - as a girl - joined the Ladies Saxhorn Band which apparently took the place of the men's group after it enlisted en masse to become a regimental band for a Hoosier Civil War Regiment.

While still a young girl, Nellie married George Cooley on February 22, 1865. George was in advertising and often traveled.

History tells us that Nellie, and sometimes her husband, George, were members of many casts of the Adelphians, a Greenfield dramatic club. The Adelphians put on plays at the Greenfield Masonic Hall. James Whitcomb Riley was very active in this group in the early 1870's and was said to have made most of the stage scenery and backdrops while Nellie provided piano accompaniments. Other familiar faces mentioned in Riley poetry or within his circle of friends who were in the casts were Lee O. Harris, George A.

Carr, War Barnett, E.P. and Jesse Millikan.

"Mother" Rhoda Millikan died October 2, 1903 after returning to Greenfield Indiana. She had lived with her son Jesse Millikan, born the same year as James Whitcomb Riley, who died the month before on September 1st.

While Jesse Millikan lay on his deathbed shortly before his death, James Whitcomb Riley went to see him and tried to cheer him up saying, "Jesse, I just met old Fate up on the street and I knocked him the other way: he is going east now." Jesse was not able to do much more than smile and died shortly afterward.

George Cooley, husband of Nellie Millikan Cooley. George Brewer Cooley was born Jan. 3, 1840 and died Sep. 1893. A Civil War veteran, he had seen action at Chicamauga where he was promoted to Captain on the battlefield. He also carried a bullet in his side from that battle for the rest of his life. (Neg. C7179, IMCPL-Riley Collection, Indiana Historical Society.)

Riley loved the Millikans as his own family because they were in his mind his own family through his soul-love for Nellie. When Nellie died in Riley's late 20's his world was shattered. Nellie's brothers, Ed Millikan, a Greenfield painter, and Jess Millikan, a Greenfield shoemaker, remained among Riley's closest friends throughout their long lives. After Riley bought his boyhood home in Greenfield, he left a standing order with Nellie's brother Ed to paint it once a year - "twice a year if you have time." When Nellie's brother Jess got sick, Riley cheered him by saying, "Hurry and get well, Jess, and if you haven't any leather in your shop, I'll see to getting some if I have to tan my own old hide," and to Jess's doctor, he said, "You've got to cure this man - I don't care what it costs." Riley paid for the care including an extended hospital bill.

Let us pose what Riley's life was like with Nellie. Can we imagine Riley serenading her? Serenading was very popular in the days of Riley's and Nellie's youth. Riley played the violin, mandolin, guitar, banjo and anything else he could lay his hands on. Did they make fudge, pull taffy or pop popcorn? Their moments together are shrouded in oblivion.

The finality of the death of Nellie Cooley in 1878 left Riley with only the dreams of a life a woman with whom he could share his life's goals and aspirations, love and affection. But let us return to the earlier days in Riley's 20's when he returned to Greenfield on so many occasions to be with Nellie.

Gone seemed all of the truanting days of his young manhood.

His life when Nellie was alive included croquet parties, ice cream festivals on the courthouse lawn, dancing at the Twilight Club. They acted together in Adelphian plays and private entertainments. He played violin on moonlit nights with Nellie at the stone culvert over the Bradywine where the boys and girls of Greenfield went for privacy. Public appearances included other women. Alice Thayer took Riley as a date to a February party and he acted like a skittish girl. Then after the fun and socializing, if he didn't feel the urge to write and if he felt the need to bare his genius- soul, he went to Nellie's. George, who travelled selling advertisements, was perhaps not always around. Or perhaps he was. George did not get in the way.

The final stanza of "The Flying Islands" seems to indicate Riley's determination to love only Nellie and be content with these dreams of her even after her death.

> *"Tho' I have found restored to me my life -*
> *Tho' I have found a daughter, I have lost*
> *A son - for Dwainie, with her sorcery,*
> *Will, on the morrow, carry him away."*

The dead Nellie took Riley's life of his soul-love as one feels for a true mate to the grave with her. Riley married Nellie in heaven.

Riley once dismissed his failure to marry in another way as, "Should he find the right woman she would fail to find him the right man." But we suspect some altogether different reason. Nellie was the only woman he fully loved.

He seems to have enjoyed relationships with other women but these were simply encounters. There were no more Nellies.   Content with his dreams permitted great imaginative contacts with her, one of which was Riley's poem, "An Old Sweetheart of Mine," written in 1875 before Nellie left Greenfield with her husband or Nellie was resettled by her husband in Illinois.

It is useless to speculate why Nellie left Greenfield with her husband at about the time Riley also left Greenfield. Did George become jealous about Riley and his wife's relationship at a soul level which he could not share?The relationship of Riley and the Cooleys in the lonesome letters that Riley later wrote to Nellie do not indicate any strain in Riley's friendship with George.

Riley's sadness at Nellie's departure is reflected in poetry of the Amphine of 1876 who wrote romantic and narrative verse. His was a stifled inspiration most often drawn from recollection and personal experience. On the other hand some of Amphine's themes are borrowed from literary sources. Unlike Spraivoll's great kenotic poetry, inspired by an indirect route from the great Lutheran German theologians, Amphine's inspiration comes from Riley's heart. Here is a poem written after Nellie's departure from Greenfield when she was taken to Illinois by her husband.

ONLY A DREAM (1876)

Only a dream!
       Her head is bent
Over the keys of the instrument,[1]
While her trembling fingers go astray
In the foolish tune she tries to play.
He smiles in his heart, though his deep, sad eyes
Never change to a glad surprise
As he finds the answer he seeks confessed
In glowing features, and heaving breast.

Only a dream!
       Though the fete is grand,
And a hundred hearts at her command,
She takes no part, for her soul is sick
Of the Coquette's art and the Serpent's trick, -
She someway feels she would like to fling
Her sins away as a robe, and spring
Up like a lily pure and white,
And bloom alone for him to-night.

Only a dream
       That the fancy weaves.
The lids unfold like the rose's leaves,
And the upraised eyes are moist and mild
As the prayerful eyes of a drowsy child.
Does she remember the spell they once
Wrought in the past a few short months?
Haply not - yet her lover's eyes
Never change to the glad surprise.

Only a dream!
He winds her form
Close in the coil of his curving arm,
And whirls her away in a gust of sound
As wild and sweet as the poets found
In the paradise where the silken tent
Of the Persian blooms in the Orient, -
While ever the chords of the music seem
Whispering sadly, - "Only a dream!"

1. Nellie often played the piano while Riley sang or played his violin or guitar.

For two years the Cooleys lived in Belleville, Illinois where Riley wrote them this letter in Oct. 28, 1877.

Dear Friends -
`Mother,' Nell, George:

I have neglected writing to you for so long that I come to you at last with my apologetic features elongated and stretched to their utmost tension. If you can forgive me for my long silence do so in God's name, and if you can't w'y take me your prisoner and `fasten me down forever in the round tower of your heart' and I'll never murmur for release till heaven dawns thro' the gates.

I am so glad today - so `sure-enough' glad - that you must join me in my joy, and become a portion of that fat and rare old sentiment - `W'ats the hodds so long as you're happ!" I've a thousand things to tell you, and a thousand things to ask: but first I would suggest - by way of casual introductory - the propriety of your getting together the accessories of instant response, for I shall expect a reply by return mail.

Everything has changed here - everything - except, perhaps, old Johnny Rardin - who won't die, and don't care a cuss who knows it. Yes, Johnny is as "bright" as ever and as thoroughly up with the styles. I saw him blow past awhile ago in a cloud of leaves, but as he had taken precaution before, leaving home to have his straw hat firmly strapped on his head, that - valuable adornment will doubtless plug up some window of the future or furnish fodder of facts for some historian yet unborn. Speaking of old Johnny - you wouldn't know the old street passing his palatial residence - the old road home, you know. W'y it's had all the twists taken out of its vertebra, and dug down and filled up till it's as level as a brickyard from A to Izzard; a lovely sidewalk on either side, and a stone and iron fence occasionally - well, in fact it's the `boss' thoroughfare in the city - no mistaking. But then, for all that, it can never be so good a friend to me as when in the old days - it led me through its ruts and puddies to the Cooley mansion. And as I write the words, a gust of memories blown from the Long Ago comes like a fragrance o'er my yearning heart and thrills me with-

"A feeling of sadness and longing
  That is not akin to pain
And resembles sorrows only
  —- as the mist resembles the rain."

   You were better friends to me than I could know - or appreciate then - but now - now when great blank miles and miles of cruel separation intervene I can but reach with empty hands and fancy they are pressed again with that old warmth of hale regard that still burns in your bosoms I am sure -but pardon! "My heart grows as weak as a woman's" and it "behooves me to fend off such puerile tho'ts and turn to manlier things - the girls for instance. I was at "the Club" last night (Terpsichorean)...(I'd like to give in this connection a genuine Hartpence local[1], but - space forbids, and thank God, that "Space" is still in our midst!"

   Well, I've rattled away here for an hour or more, and have said nothing of importance or interest yet forgive me for my intentions were the best. Before I close I want to ask if you don't think it would do you all good to come home here for awhile. I want to see you - your friends want to see you, and in fact Greenfield as an individual would greet you with open arms. I have been building castles of a visit to you, but the Fates won't hear to it yet awhile. I will come tho' the very minute my incoming `ship' sticks her nose against the shore...

   I have been quite busy with my literary studies, and am progressing with every promise of success. I have in course of construction now a work I'd like to read to mother and Nell before the great eyes of the public - get a peek. Whatever you do write to me and write now and kiss the children for your old friend.

J. W. Riley

---

1. "Hartpence local" would be a local news account for William Hartpence, the Editor of the Greenfield NEWS to which Riley contributed (and later edited) until it folded.

The very subtitle of "The Flying Islands of the Night" reflects Nellie and Riley's love for her. In the original publication of "Flying Islands of the Night" in the Buzz Club series, Number IV of August 24, 1878, the poem was subtitled "A Twintorette."

What is a "Twintorette?"

As in many other instances, one can look to other writing of Riley for assistance in interpretation. A poem entitled "A Twintorette" was first published in 1881 but no doubt was written much earlier.

A TWINTORETTE

Ho! my little maiden
*   With the glossy tresses,*
* Come thou and dance with me*
*   A measure all divine;*
Let my breast be laden
*   With but thy caresses -*
* Come thou and glancingly*
*   Mate thy face with mine.*

Thou shalt trill a rondel,
*   While my lips are purling*
* Some dainty twitterings*
*   Sweeter than the birds';*
And, with arms that fondle
*   Each as we go, twirling,*
* We will kiss, with twitterings,*
*   Lisps and loving words.*

"Twinning," as this poem proposes, has to do with romantic joinder. It refers to intimate union of two things. Torrid is suggestive of the depth of the "twinning" and "ette" simply means a short poem. Flying Islands was originally of course, published on a single page, Page 6 of the Indianapolis Saturday Herald of August 24, 1874.

A "twintorette" seems to be a poem in which a lover and beloved are rejoined. The two who are the subjects of this poem are Riley and his beloved Nellie Cooley, recently deceased by a bare two months, at the time of the writing.

Riley wrote to Mrs. Emma Cox, Nellie's daughter, on April 10, 1885 in response to the publication of a poem Riley had written to Nellie which Nellie's daughter had published.

Dear Friend: -

It is Sunday, but to write you as I do is like a prayer, - Your beautiful tribute in the HERALD touched me deeply, recalling so tenderly your absent mother's kindliness when she was here; her brave, glad nature; the noble generous gentlewoman that she was; the truest friend on earth, or now in Heaven - God bless us always with the sweetness of her memory!

I can say no more now - only, my dear friend, I am very proud of your friendship, and of your talents - in music - composition - every way, and God bless us everyone!'

Gratefully and always, as ever, your friend.

J.W. Riley

Literary friends of Mrs. Rhoda Millikan, Nellie Cooley's mother, asked her, during the summer of 1902 (a year before her death) to write her first impression of Mr. Riley. Though 83 years old she was still a constant reader, her mind was clear and her handwriting easily legible. Her recollections were reported in the Indianapolis STAR of October 4, 1931.

Rhoda Millikan, Riley's teacher at the time of the American Civil War, and daughter, Nellie Cooley, as a child. (Neg. C7174, IMCPL-Riley Collection, Indiana Historical Society.)

AN IMPRESSION OF JAMES WHITCOMB RILEY

"I have been requested by some friends of Mr. James Whitcomb Riley to write my first impressions of that much admired poet, humorist and artist. My first impression of Mr. Riley was vague and uncertain. When I first saw him I was a middle-aged woman. He was a small boy, quiet, shy and modest. When I came to Greenfield, I was a stranger. I took charge of a school there. I had some of my own children with me. They soon became quite well acquainted with `Jim' Riley. It was a great treat to them to hear him talk and they were constantly telling me something concerning what he had said to them. I soon became interested and requested them to bring their admired companion to my room. I soon saw he was trying to become a writer. After a time he could be found willing to read some of his poems and prose sketches to me. I was greatly surprised when I heard them though I had a hard time to make him believe they were of any merit.

After a while some of his poems were published in some of the Greenfield papers. They were not copied in papers outside of Greenfield. This was discouraging to our very young writer. He came to talk to me about it and said he would write no more. I told him that was what young writers might look for. Greenfield was then quite a small place, and editors of magazines were not looking for gems in smallcountry papers. I talked a good deal to him at this time as he was not much encouraged by his father, a lawyer of decided ability, who was anxious to have James study law...

Mr. Riley was in the way of coming in sometimes of an evening. He never was much inclined to talk very much, but what he did say counted. He nearly always had a pencil in his hand, and when he left the house we would find some of the most comical drawings or the queerest little poems imaginable.

One night, I remember, a Japanese fan had been left on the table. The picture on the fan was quite as ridiculous as are usually found on fans of that kind. It represented an impossible bridge, with three Chinamen in undress costume fishing on from the bridge. My daughter had just been singing Kingsley's "Three Fishers." We saw Mr. Riley writing something on the fan which proved to a parody on the first verse of "The Fishers' -

"Three fishers came walking out of the west.
Out of the west when the sun went down: -
And so they came almost undressed
To be prepared if the bridge broke down"

Well, time when on. I have lived eight-three years in this world and have seen many people, but I have never met any one that I felt was like James Whitcomb Riley. He stands quite alone. His writings are a strange mixture of humor and pathos blended with a strong element of unexpectedness which is a fascination of itself. I have been made happy by his success. I have able to exclaim with the famous old lady, "I told you so." Rhoda H. Millikan

While Nellie Millikan Cooley lived, it seems that Riley was able to use the verse of Longfellow as inspirational models to produce ballad like poetry of a similar ilk to Longfellow's. After Nellie died the possibility of Longfellow lyric also departed. Perhaps its lilt and feel were simply no longer possible in Riley's life.

Riley's earliest published poetry seems to have the ring of Longfellow about it. Much of his earliest poetry, published in local Greenfield newspapers such as the Greenfield COMMERCIAL, is lost but we do have the early "Amphine" poem "Man's Devotion" of 1872 published in The Indianapolis Saturday MIRROR to look at. Its theme is romantic in that we find the departures or separations of innocent first lovers is an inexplicable but necessary life situation.

MAN'S DEVOTION (1872)

A lover said, "O Maiden, love me well
*   For I must go away:*
And should another ever come to tell
*   Of love - What will you say?"...*

(The Maiden promises to remain faithful to him until he returns, keeps his picture, but eventually after "years -dull years -in dull monotony" she marries another who eventually dies. The young wandering man\lover returns after much time, but the "Maiden" must admit she has been married.)

And as she kneeled there, sobbing at his feet
*   He calmly spoke - no sigh*
Betrayed his inward agony - "I count you meet
*   To be a wife of mine!"*

And raised her up forgiven, though untrue;
*   As fond he gazed on her,*
She sighed, - "So happy!" And she never knew
*   He was a widower.*

I suppose we recall that about this time, Riley was leaving Nellie Cooley behind in Greenfield for jaunts out into the countryside to paint barns or signs and also to travel in the medicine shows. His theme explores how attachments between lovers change and marital conditions become inevitable drawbacks to the permanency of stolen initial innocent love. Nevertheless personal ties, "vows," remain real and circumstances may later permit the first lovers to resume a more permanent residence together. In the poem the woman marries another but eventually the two again find each other and resume life together again. It sounds like a "pipe-dream" but Riley perhaps had the youthful thought in his head, as evidenced by the poem, that he could leave Greenfield and come back to find the woman he loved a widow and then marry her.

After Nellie's death, the lyric of Longfellow's romantic ballad's was pretty much stilled. While Nellie lived, and was close, he could write "An Old Sweetheart of Mine," with its sentimental strain of satisfaction in a loving home he could conjure up with Nellie. Then Nellie left and we have no more such "Longfellow" type ballads.

Much has been made of the relationship of the early James Whitcomb Riley and Henry Wadsworth Longfellow. This derives from Riley's recollections that Riley read Longfellow poetry from an early age. Riley's early ballad narratives do seem to bear this influence. His "Longfellow" poetry also seems to bear on his relationship with Nellie in the early period of Riley's twenties. Perhaps the figure in this poem was the Riley who never married because the woman he loved was already married. Perhaps one day they might marry. Perhaps we can see a little of Nellie as "Mary" and Riley in this one. In 1874, Riley wrote

FARMER WHIPPLE - BACHELOR (1874)

It's a mystery to see me - a man o' fifty-four,
Who's lived a cross old bachelor fer thirty year' and more -
A-lookin' glad and smilin'! And they's none o' you can say
That you can guess the reason why I feel so good to-day!

I must tell you all about it! But I'll have to deviate
A little in beginnin', so's to set the matter straight
As to how it comes to happen that I never took a wife -
Kindo' "crawfish" from the present to the Springtime of my life!

I was brought up in the country: Of a family of five -
Three brothers and a sister - I'm the only one alive, -
Fer they all died little babies; and 'twas one o' Mother's ways,
You know, to want a daughter; so she took a girl to raise.

The sweetest little thing she was, with rosy cheeks, and fat-
We was little chunks o' shavers then about as high as that!

But someway we sort o' suited-like! and Mother she'd declare
She never laid her eyes on a more lovin' pair

Than we was! So we growed up side by side fer thirteen year',
And every hour of it she growed to me more dear! -
W'y, even Father's dyin', as he did, I do believe
Warn't more affectin' to me than it was to see her grieve!

I was then a lad o' twenty; and I felt a flash o' pride
In thinkin' all depended on me now to pervide
Fer mother and fer Mary; and I went about the place
With sleeves rolled up - and workin', with a mighty smilin' face, -

Fer somepin' else was workin'! but not a word I said
Of a certain sort o' notion that was runnin' through my head, -
"Some day I'd maybe marry, and brother's love was one
Thing - a lover's was another!" was the way the notion run!

I remember onc't in harvest, when the "cradle-in'" was done,
(When the harvest of my summers mounted up to twenty-one),
I was ridin' home with Mary at the closin' o' the day -
A-chawin' straws and thinkin', in a lover's lazy way! And
Mary's cheeks was burnin' like the sunset down the lane:
I noticed she was thinkin', too, and ast her to explain.
Well - when she turned and kissed me, with her arms around me - law!
I'd a bigger load o' Heaven than I had a load o' straw!

I don't p'tend to larnin', but I'll tell you what's a fac',
They's a mighty truthful sayin' somers in a' almanac -
Er somers - 'bout "puore happiness"- perhaps some folks'll laugh

At the idy - "only lastin' jest two seconds and half." -
But it's jest as true as preachin'! - fer that was a sister's kiss,
And a sister's lovin' confidence a-tellin' to me this: -
"She was happy, bein' promised to the son o' Farmer Brown."
And my feelin's stuck a pardnership with sunset and went down!

I don't know how I acted, and I don't know what I said, -

Fer my heart seemed jest a-turnin' to an ice-cold lump o' lead;
And the hosses kind o' glimmered before me in the road,
And the lines fell from my fingers - And that was all I knowed -

Fer - well, I don't know how long - They's a dim rememberence
Of a sound o' snortin' horses, and a stake-and-ridered fence
A-whizzin' past, and wheat-sheaves a-dancin' in the air,
And Mary screamin' "Murder!" and a-runnin' up to where

I was layin' by the roadside, and the wagon upside down
A-leanin' on the gate-post, with the wheels a-whirlin' roun'!
And I tried to raise and meet her, but I couldn't, with a vague
Sort o' notion comin' to me that I had a broken leg.

Well, the women nussed me through it; but many a time I'd sigh
As I'd keep a-gettin' better instid o' goin' to die,
And wonder what was left me worth livin' fer below,
When the girl I loved was married to another, don't you know!

And my thoughts was as rebellious as the folks was good and kind
When Brown and Mary married - Railly must 'a' been my mind
Was kind o' out o' kilter! - fer I hated Brown, you see,
Worse's pizen - and the feller whittled crutches out fer me -

And done a thousand little ac's o' kindness and respec' -
And me a-wishin' all the time that I could break his neck!
My relief was like a mourner's when the funeral is done
When they moved to Illinois in the Fall o' Forty-one.

Then I went to work in airnest - I had nothin' much in view
But to drownd out rickollections - and it kep' me busy, too!
But I slowly thrived and prospered, tel Mother used to say
She expected yit to see me a wealthy man some day.

Then I'd think how little money was, compared to happiness -
And who'd be left to use it when I died I couldn't guess!
But I've still kep' speculatin' and a-gainin' year by year,
Tel I'm payin' half the taxes in the county, might near!

Well! - A year ago er better, a letter comes to hand
Astin' how'd I'd like to dicker fer some Illinois land -
"The feller that had owned it," it went ahead to state,
"Had jest deceased, insolvent, leavin' chance to speculate,"-

And then it closed by sayin' that I'd better come and see." -
I'd never been West, anyhow - a'most too wild fer me,
I'd allus had a notion; but a lawyer here in town
Said I'd find myself mistakend when I come to look around.

So I bids good-by to Mother, and I jumps aboard the train,
A-thinkin' what I'd bring her when I come back home again -
And ef she'd had an idy what the present was to be,
I think it's more'n likely she'd 'a'went along with me!

Cars is awful tejus ridin', fer all they go so fast!
But finally they called out my stoppin'-place at last:
And that night, at the tavern, I dreamp' I was a train
O' cars, and skeered at somepin', runnin' down a country lane!

Well, in the morning airly - after huntin' up the man -
The lawyer who was wantin' to swap a piece o' land -
We started fer the country; and I ast the history
Of the farm - its former owner - and so forth, etcetery!

And - well - it was interestin' - I su'prised him, I suppose,
By the loud and frequent manner in which I blowed my nose! -
But his su'prise was greater, and it made him wonder more,
When I kissed and hugged the widder when she met us at the door! -

It was Mary:...They's a feelin' a-hidin' down in here -
Of course I can't explain it, ner ever make it clear. -
It was with us in that meetin', I don't want you to fergit!
And it makes me kind o' nervous when I think about it yit!

I bought that farm, and deeded it, afore I left the town,
With 'title clear to mansions in the skies," to Mary Brown!
And fu'thermore, I took her and the childern - fer you see,

They'd never seed their Grandma - and I fetched 'em home with me.

So now you've got an idy why a man o' fifty-four,
Who's lived a cross old bachelor fer thirty year' and more
Is a-lookin' glad and smilin'! - And I've jest come into town
To git a pair o' license fer to marry Mary Brown."

While Nellie was alive, Riley might imagine a hopeful future. With Nellie in Greenfield, Riley could visualize his arrangement with her almost as a married life. He included the thought in poetry, thinking of her as the companion he had grown up with and the wife she might have been or could one day become after her more elderly husband's death, one of which is the following:

AN OLD SWEETHEART OF MINE [1] (1875)

An old sweetheart of mine! - Is this her presence here with me,
Or but a vain creation of a lover's memory?
A fair, illusive vision that would vanish into air
Dared I even touch the silence with the whisper of a prayer?

Nay, let me then believe in all the blended false and true -
The semblance of the old love and the substance of the new, -
The then of changeless sunny days - the now of shower and shine -
But Love forever smiling - as that old sweetheart of mine.

This ever-restful sense of home, though shouts ring in the hall. -
The easy chair - the old book-shelves and prints along the wall,
The rare Habanas in their box, or gaunt church-warden-stem
That often wags, above the jar, derisively at them.

As one who cons at evening o'er an album, all alone,
And muses on the faces of the friends that he has known,
So I turn the leaves of Fancy, til, in shadowy design,
I find the smiling features of an old sweetheart of mine.

The lamplight seems to glimmer with a flicker of surprise,

As I turn it low - to rest me of the dazzle in my eyes,
And light my pipe in silence, save a sigh that seems to yoke
Its fate with my tobacco and to vanish with the smoke.

'Tis a fragrant retrospection, - for the loving thoughts that start
Into being are like perfume from the blossom of the heart;
And to dream the old dreams over is a luxury divine -
When my truant fancies wander with that old sweetheart of mine.

Though I hear beneath my study, like a fluttering of wings,
The voices of my children and the mother as she sings -
I feel no twinge of conscience to deny me any theme
When Care has cast her anchor in the harbor of a dream -

In fact, to speak in earnest, I believe it adds a charm
To spice the good a trifle with a little dust of harm, -
For I find an extra flavor in Memory's mellow wine
That makes me drink the deeper to that old sweetheart of mine.

O Childhood-days enchanted! O the magic of the Spring! -
With all green boughs to blossom white, and all bluebirds to
sing!
When all the air, to toss and quaff, made life a jubilee
And changed the children's song and laugh to shrieks of ecstasy.

With eyes half closed in clouds that ooze from lips that taste, as well,
The peppermint and cinnamon, I hear the old School bell,
And from "Recess" romp in again from "Blackman's" broken line,
To smile, behind my "lesson," at that old sweetheart of mine.

A face of lily beauty, with a form of airy grace,
Floats out of my tobacco as the Genii from the vase;
And I thrill beneath the glances of a pair of azure eyes
As glowing as the summer and as tender as the skies.

I can see the pink sunbonnet and the little checkered dress
She wore when first I kissed her and she answered the caress
With the written declaration that, "as surely as the vine

Grew 'round the stump," she loved me - that old sweetheart of mine.

Again I made her presents, in a really helpless way, -
The big "Rhode Island Greening ²" - I was hungry, too, that day! -
But I follow her from Spelling, with her hand behind her - so -
And I slip the apple in it - and the Teacher doesn't know!

I give my treasures to her - all, - my pencil - blue-and-red; -
And, if little girls played marbles, mine should all be hers, instead!
But she gave me her photograph, and printed, "Ever thine"
Across the back - in blue-and-red - that old sweetheart of mine!

And again I feel the pressure of her slender little hand,
As we used to talk together of the future we had planned, -
When I should be a poet, and with nothing else to do
But write the tender verses that she set the music to...

When we should live together in a cozy little cot
Hid in a nest of roses, with a fairy garden-spot,
Where the vines were ever fruited, and the weather ever fine,
And the birds were ever singing for that old sweetheart of mine.

When I should be her lover forever and a day,
And she my faithful sweetheart till the golden hair was gray;
And we should be so happy that when either's lips were dumb
They would not smile in Heaven till the other's kiss had come.

But, ah! my dream is broken by a step upon the stair,
And the door is softly opened, and - my wife is standing there:
Yet with eagerness and rapture all my visions I resign, -
To greet the living presence of that old sweetheart of mine."

1. This poem was one of Riley's most popular. It was said to have earned him $500 a word
- a princely sum in Riley's day. A story set in New York City demonstrates its popularity, A
vagabond named McGlaughlin was brought to Court on an October day charged with loitering and vagrancy. In defending himself he said that he was an actor and simply out of work.
"To prove I'm an actor just give me a poem to recite. I'll orate any piece you choose." The
judge said if he could recite "An Old Sweetheart of Mine" he would acknowledge that he was
no "bum." McGlaughlin did so and his reading was so good that the judge not only dismissed
the charges but also had a collection taken up for the man in his courtroom.

2. Apples were the most commonly mentioned food in Riley's poetry and the variety known as Rhode Island Greening is the most obscure of Rileyana.

Shortly after the writing of this poem, Nellie was taken from Greenfield by her husband to exile in Illinois. Others have vied ever since for the honor of being Riley's "Old Sweetheart of Mine."

One of the most unseemly debates in all of literature is that over who was the woman pictured in the poem "An Old Sweetheart of Mine."

It seems that almost every otherwise "reputable" Greenfield family of the last century tried to publicize some one or other of its oth-

The Walker Block Building located at the Northwest corner of State and Main Streets, Greenfield, Indiana, long since removed. On the second floor of this building, in Reuben Riley's law office at the time, the poem "An Old Sweetheart of Mine," was composed.

erwise modest and chaste daughters as having sultry, wildly adulterous or loose affairs with Riley in order to have them pictured as the "Sweetheart." Some even published books to have a daughter deemed the one, unconcerned that their daughter's reputation might suffer a little in the process. It seems hard to imagine the mothers and fathers fighting so to have a daughter deemed promiscuous with James Whitcomb Riley, but they went at it with "unadulterated" frenzy.

Of course the poem was the most widely known poem of the last century and made Riley rich, but that hardly seems like a good excuse to slander an otherwise nice young daughter.

I think this genre of books, pushing a woman's claim to having had an affair with Riley, is the strangest of any ever published, but apparently the goal of having the woman declared the "Sweetheart" offered the gift of fame beyond any wish to keep the more private things of life about a family member under wraps, assuming an encounter between Riley and any of the girl candidates ever did occur with any of the many proposed "Sweethearts."

It seems to me we ought to leave all of these candidates to their own little private reminiscences as to what did or did not happen with James Whitcomb Riley. Although I do not believe any one woman is the model for the "Sweetheart," I agree with Minnie Belle Mitchell, one of the poet's great biographers, that the most important female influences on his life, and thus probably in his mind in picturing the Sweetheart, would have been his own mother, Elizabeth Riley, Nellie Millikan Cooley, and Adda Rowell Barber, both of the latter being early Riley girlfriends who married other men.

Having said that, let us remember the poem itself, not because it made Riley the most wealthy poet who ever lived, or because it has been the most widely published American piece of poetry in history, or for any other reason than to indulge in a picture of American homelife by Amphine's most hopeful vision of love itself within the intimacy of lover's fantasy sheltered from the world outside.

While it seems that Nellie Cooley was Riley's only fully beloved woman, Nellie's husband was also a friend of Riley's and perhaps never aware how intimate Riley and Nellie were. George Cooley wrote Riley letters of encouragement as did Nellie.

LETTER FROM NELLIE COOLEY'S HUSBAND, GEORGE

Bellesville, IL Jan 1, 1877 (Holiday Eve)

My Dear James,

I have had my letters but seldom one as welcome as yours to myself and Nellie. Those lines to Nellie were beautiful indeed. You have a talent - that is bound to meet with its first reward. Should you live a few years (Greenfield notwithstanding). Go on my Boy. Never look backward. It is in you. I only wish it was in my power to point you to a shorter and lazier road to fame than that you seem to have been compelled to travel but as before said, pass on. Look forward. Work - be determined and despite all back biting and jealousy, such as has been displayed with Hancock. Take my word for it. The time will come when it won't be Jim Riley, but James W. Riley, Esq. one of America's Famous Poets.

He goes on to encourage Riley to write both or either himself or Nellie and states Nellie will be writing him the next day.

As the poem "The Flying Islands of the Night" comes to an end, Riley comments how Dwainie takes Amphine with him into the grave.

Riley's memorial to Nellie was not just his written obituary to her or his poetry to her but also his play/poem, "The Flying Islands of the Night." This poem, with all of its many revisions and additions and editings, retained the references to Nellie as its core.

Linger, my Dwainie! Dwainie! lily-fair,
Stay yet thy step upon the casement-stair [1] *-*
Poised be thy slipper-tip as is the tine
Of some still star. - Ah, Dwainie - Dwainie mine,
  Yet linger - linger there!

1. A casement is a window-frame. For it to be a stair would refer to it as an access down from heaven through it, or possibly, the reference is to the stair leading to Riley's place of writing at "The Seminary" where the Riley family lived called the "Crow's Nest" where Riley wrote much of this poetry.

Thy face, O Dwainie, lily-pure and fair,
Gleams i' the dusk, as in the dusky hair
The moony zhoomer [1] *glimmers, or the shine,*
Of the swift smile - Ah, Dwainie -Dwainie mine,
  Yet linger - linger there!

1. Summer in intoxicatese.

With lifted wrist, where round the laughing air
Hath blown a mist of lawn and clasped it there,
Waft finger-thipt [1] *adieus that spray the wine*
Of they waste kisses toward me, Dwainie mine -
  Yet linger -linger there!

A fanciful illustration by Adrian Marcel of the line "Linger, my Dwainie! Dwainie, lily fair..." from the Homestead Edition of "The Flying Islands of the Night" as published 1908 by Charles Scribner's Sons.

1. (tipped) - language in simply intoxicated thickly uttered speech.

What unloosed splendor is there may compare
With thy hand's unfurled glory, anywhere?
What giant of dazzling dew or jewel fine
May mate thine eyes? -Ah, Dwainie - Dwainie mine!
  Yet linger - linger there.

My soul confronts thee; On thy brow and hair

It lays its tenderness like palms of prayer -
It touches sacredly those lips of thine
And swoops across thy spirit, Dwainie mine,
  The while thou lingerest there.

The recollection of Nellie did not dim over the years. Riley added the following poem to the text of "The Flying Islands of the Night" many years after her death during a later revision:

Ah, help me! but her face and brow
Are lovelier than lilies are
Beneath the light of moon and star
That smile as they are smiling now -
White lilies in a pallid swoon
Of sweetest white beneath the moon -
White lilies in a flood of bright
Pure lucidness of liquid light
Cascading down some plenilune [1]
When all the azure overhead
Blooms like a dazzling daisy-bed -
So luminous her face and brow,
The luster of their glory, shed
In memory, even, blinds me now.

1. Something like plenteous lunar rays in intoxicatese.

Nellie remained Riley's salvation over the many years of his life. Nellie, from her dead state, continually intervened to encourage Riley over the years and fend off Crestillomeem.

By the time "The Flying Islands of the Night" was revised thirteen years later and placed into book form in 1891, Riley chose to add another beloved from his life to join the cast with Dwainie, Nellie Millikan Cooley. This was AEo, Riley's mother. The name derives from the centered letter "E," the abbreviated first letter of his mother's name surrounded by the Greek alpha and omega substitutes signaling his mother meant to him the beginning and end of his love.

The tombstone of James Whitcomb Riley's mother, Elizabeth Riley, at Greenfield, Indiana's Park Cemetery reflects that she lived from 1823 until

1870, "the year the mother died." Her grave on a hill overlooks Brandywine Creek meandering through the Hoosier landscape, the same "crick" on which was James Whitcomb Riley's "Old Swimmin' Hole" was located to the north near the old "National Road."

Her name was Elizabeth Marine before she married Reuben Riley and bore James Whitcomb Riley as her third child.

We can elaborate more upon the life of Riley's beloved mother. Elizabeth's family had come to America to avoid persecution in Europe. This seems to be the case with most of our ancestors which is why I find it so hard to understand how any American can have prejudice toward any member of another church, creed or race. Elizabeth's Marine (or Merine) grandparents were Welch Quakers who came to America when Quakers were being persecuted in England. The Marine grandmother's family had fled to England to avoid Protestant persecution in France. Their son, John, married Elizabeth'smother, Fanny. They were living on the border between North Carolina and South Carolina, near Rockingham, when Elizabeth, their tenth of eleven children, was born.

When Elizabeth was only two, her parents left North Carolina broke. By the time the family fled over the Blue Ridge Mountains and into Indiana, their total resources were a wagon pulled by a single horse. Elizabeth's parents became pioneer settlers of a Randolph County farm. At this place, Elizabeth became acquainted with Johnny Appleseed personally and had listened to the tales he told the pioneer children. Most people know of Johnny Appleseed's quaint habit of wearing a cooking pot for a hat and for planting apple trees wherever he went, but not everybody remembers that Johnny was also a gospel carrying preacher. Elizabeth believed him when he said you grow old on earth but you grow young again in heaven. You can find traces of Johnny's preachings in the poetry of James Whitcomb Riley, Elizabeth's son. As a child Elizabeth went to school obediently to her parents' wishes, but she enjoyed most wandering through the Hoosier woods.

Her father tried to turn part of his farm into a town called Rockingham after the town in North Carolina he had fled. The project failed and the platted town remains farmland to this day except for what was to be the town cemetery without stones in one of whose graves rests Elizabeth's mother, Fanny.

After her mother died, the Marines moved to a settlement on Cabin Creek near the Mississinewa River. At a Fourth of July picnic in 1843, Elizabeth met Reuben Riley. There was an Indian trail between the creek Elizabeth lived on and the one where the family of Reuben Riley resided, Cabin Creek. After the two, Elizabeth and Reuben, met at the picnic, it is said this trail got worn down by Reuben's use. In Feb. 1844, Elizabeth married Reuben in a beautiful pioneer wedding performed by the local Methodist preacher. Pioneer Indiana was not so backwoodsy and crude as many think. Elizabeth wore a long white veil, white kid gloves and shoes, and a pale pink silk dress. She was a truly beautiful woman.

Elizabeth and her new husband left for Greenfield five months after the wedding to settle in Greenfield. In the year 1844, Greenfield was a settlement of about 300 people. The legislature had only "created" Hancock County 16

THE FIRST HOME OF CAPTAIN RILEY IN GREENFIELD AND BIRTH PLACE OF JAMES WHITCOMB RILEY, THE POET.

Drawing by Will Vawter, Greenfield-born artist, of the birthome of the poet. Vawter was 21 years younger than Riley. The two first collaborated when Vawter illustrated the poem "Armzindy."

years before. The town was mainly cabins and a few frame houses and businesses around the "public square." The Riley Home, then a cabin, was on the West edge of Greenfield and the Hoosier woods was behind it.

Elizabeth Riley was said to be gentle, kindly, sympathetic, tolerant, and patient. She and her son were on the same wave length at all times. Both were poetic, imaginative. If one saw fairies in their walks through the woods the other saw them too and each wove fanciful stories. Both were dreamers to live above the sordid impoverishment of their daily lives. She was the only one who fully recognized his talents and visualized the heights he could attain. Some have stated Elizabeth Riley was over-solicitous of James Whitcomb Riley. They note that on September 4, 1851, when he was two, his older sister, Martha Celeste died and that as sometimes happens after a child's death, the mother becomes extra extra careful about the next child.

What is clear is that Riley leaned heavily upon his mother's sympathetic encouragement and understanding and love and clung to her as strongly as he clung to his goal of being a writer. She was necessary to his very existence. He wished his success for her. Then one day she died.

The death of his mother gave Riley a deep abiding sympathy and pity for those who suffered bereavement and he wrote

SINCE MY MOTHER DIED (1879)

"Since my mother died, my face
Knows not any resting-place,
Save in visions, lightly pressed
In its old accustomed rest
On her shoulder. But I wake
With a never-ending ache
In my heart, and naught beside,
Since my mother died. ...

What was her legacy to the boy?

A psychologist of my century, Jerome Kagan, teaches that an intelligent person is not necessarily creative but a creative person is generally intelligent with creativity based on three key characteristics: they have a mental set to search for the unusual, they take delight in generating novel ideas and they are not unduly apprehensive about making mistakes. A creative person is one whose life is not subject to humiliation upon failure. The caregiver has given such a person great freedom to try, to succeed, and to fail. High-risk solutions can be tried without fear of their potential. This describes Elizabeth Riley's strategy for her son, James Whitcomb Riley. She encouraged each of the three characteristics. Elizabeth Riley was the source of the poet's strength and courage as well.

In Riley's "Poem of the Seven Faces" comes the confession of a "face" of a character who is not one of the "Flying Islands" of the cast. The faces of the poems are those vivid recollections that confront Riley's life every day and often drive him into the relief of intoxication. The "Second Face" of the poems speaks of someone other than one of Riley's play-characters representing a fragmentation of himself. This "Second Face" says of Crestillomeem, Riley's alcoholic self:

I knew her - long and long before
High AEo loosed her palm and thought:
"What awful splendor have I wrought
To dazzle earth and Heaven, too!"

Elizabeth Riley, Riley's mother who died in the midst of the poverty stricken years when Riley was 20, confesses from her seat in heaven that her departure has precipitated Riley's initial descent into alcoholism. From heaven, AEo can only be horrified at Riley in the throes of Crestillomeem.

Riley's mother was with him as a living presence throughout his life as the poem acknowledges.

Jucklet

In one strange phase he spake
As though some spirited lady (AEo[1]) talked with him. -
Full courteously he said: "In woman's guise
Thou comest, yet I think thou art, in sooth
But woman in thy form. - Thy words are strange
And leave me mystified. I feel the truth
Of all thou hast declared, and yet so vague
And shadow-like thy meaning is to me
I know not how to act to ward the blow
Thou sayest is hanging o'er me even now."
And then, with open hands held pleadingly,
He asked, "Who is my foe?" - And o'er his face
A sudden pallor flashed, like death itself,
As though, if answer had been given, it
Had fallen like a curse.

1. AEo, Riley's mother, now dead tries to caution him against his drunken lifestyle.

A letter is preserved which Riley wrote as an old man to a child, James L. Murray, confirming his mother was still very much in his thoughts.

Dear Little Boy, -No-sir-ee! I couldn't write verse when I was nine years old like you. But, as you do, I could get verses "by heart," for speeches at School - only I always got pale and sick and faint when I tried to speak `em - and my chin wobbled, and my throat hurt, and then I broke clean down and cried. Oughtn't I been ashamed of myself? I bet you ain't goin' to cry - in the Second Room of the A Grade!

I was sorry to hear your mother died when you were only one year old. My mother is dead, too; and so I wouldn't be surprised if your mother and my mother were together right now, and know each other, and are the best friends in their World, just as you and I are in this. My best respects to your good father and teachers all.

Ever your friend, James Whitcomb Riley

Riley's finest set of complete works was published 1915 with dedication to his mother as the Elizabeth Marine Riley Edition. Original watercolors are inserted as illustrations in many of the limited edition of 150. From George Richman, a Hancock County historian we learn that Riley's mother was a "woman of rare strength of character, combined with deep sympathy and a clear understanding." Others recalled her as being a gardener and a writer of verse.

Speaking to his nephew and secretary, Edmund Eitel, Riley commented on the death of his mother when asked about it and after a long period of silence. "Sometimes I think mentality is developed by such things. Some terrible experience comes and worries and worries you until your mind seems stretched like the head of a drum. Well, you bear up bravely, and say to yourself, I can stand just this - but no more. Then some greater horror comes and turns the screws and turns the screws until you feel that your mind is surely strained to breaking...and so on, and so on, and if it doesn't break, it becomes very strong. "

The same Edmund Eitel added, "(Riley's mother, Elizabeth) alone understood the boy, Riley, and sympathized with him. Riley said, "I was her child in color of hair and eyes, in heart and soul. I worshiped her, and to see her in poverty and suffering was agony for me -and a mother so worthy of the best!"

Riley's mother probably did not know of his great love of Nellie Cooley in real life, but Riley imagined she must know of it from her vantage in heaven. She would also know of her son's great anguish at Nellie's departure from Greenfield and then death. After the death of Nellie Cooley, great sadness must have stroked Riley's life. Nellie did not outlive her husband, George, so that Riley might rush to Illinois, find her a widow with children, marry her and bring her back to Indiana to find happiness in the way envisioned in the 1974 poem, "Farmer Whipple-Bachelor."

The only memory Riley had was of his stolen love with Nellie as a married woman. This relationship might otherwise have been a sordid affair except that Riley knew that the "mother's heart" of Elizabeth understood his needs and situation and approved it. He writes of this in his autobiographical poem's Act II when speaking to the dead spirit of Nellie, he says:

"Amphine
        Then,
Thou lovest! - O my homing dove, veer down

And nestle in the warm home of my breast!
So empty are mine arms, so full my heart
The one must hold thee, or the other burst.

Dwainie (Throwing herself in his embrace)

AEo's own hand methinks hath flung me here;
O hold me that He may not pluck me back!"

Riley felt his mother must have understood how much he needed Nellie. Her "own hand" encourages the relationship.

There was an earlier love interest of Riley than Nellie Cooley that we should speak of.

Adda Rowell was Riley's first romantic interest in his teens. The year was 1868. Adda was 16 when her family moved to Greenfield, arriving in town shortly after the Civil War. John Rowell, the father, was a New Englander and he was accompanied by his wife, a son, Edward, and the beautiful daughter, Adda. Riley was nineteen and fresh from an apprenticeship with John Keefer, the village sign painter. According to the memoir of Minnie Belle (Alexander) Mitchell, Riley had not before had an "affair of the heart" before Adda. Mitchell remembers, "Little Adda Rowell slipped easily into the social life of the village. She attended parties, shared in charades and tableaux, attended plays in the old Masonic Hall where the Riley youth displayed his unusual histrionic talent and, as a crowning glory, she heard him play the trap drum in the old Adelphian Band."

I repeat the account of this romance in the words of Mitchell who witnessed the events.

"All through the gay glad summer, young Riley worshiped at the shrine of winsome Adda, singing, rhyming and absorbing from her the art of playing the guitar. They had long walks down by Brandywine Creek, loitering in shady places and with Adda's little sunbonnet handing by a string...

At that early period a culvert made of rough hewn stone spanned a small brook which intruded through the heart of the village. Its low graceful arch was topped on either side by broad stone balustrades which provided sea0ts for weary travelers, as well as trysting place for lovers. It was, indeed, a beautiful spot and a favorite resort of Bud's since it was an integral part of the old road which his father had glorified in his stories of early pioneer days. So the old stone culvert easily lured Bud and the fair Adda still with a smile in her eyes, to its broad sides where the moonlight tunneled its way through borders of willow reeds and fell benignly upon the lovers.

The guitar, of course, shared in the scene and the lovers played and sang, she exchanging her eastern melodies for the lad's "Lilly Dale," "Sweet Belle Mahone," "Laurena," "Sweet Genevieve" and other songs of the day." Mitchell accounts this romance one from May, when Adda arrived in Greenfield, to Autumn. She recalls Riley re-naming Adda as the "Airy Fairie Lillian" and being very desperately in love with her.

The romance ended in the fall when John Rowell took his family from Greenfield to go to the Northwest. Riley and Adda exchanged letters for a time. Riley's were sometimes in rhyme.

Eventually Adda married and became Adda Barber living in Oregon and their letters ceased. She was later widowed with two daughters. Riley's last letter to Adda, written in 1906, just ten years before his death, was addressed in care of her brother, Edward, in Michigan. It contained two books, volumes of "Rhymes of Childhood," so Riley must have found out

Mr. Phillipson and sign painted by Riley in Warsaw, Indiana. (Neg. C7180, IMCPL-Riley Collection, Indiana Historical Society.)

his Adda had two children, with the following inscription, "For Mrs. Adda Rowell Barber, From her old Hoosier friend and fellow townsman of the days of our youth at Greenfield, Indiana, where Jess and Nell and Alice were living - now, alas, long gone. James Whitcomb Riley."

Even though he returned often to Greenfield, and apparently to Nellie Cooley, Riley did not feel constrained from seeking the company of many young women in the places he visited.

The recollections of James Whitcomb Riley by friends and letters support the probability that Riley, like many other unsettled young men of his time and ours, expressed his sexuality "on the run."

From every town where Riley traveled in his early days of his twenties and as he traveled from town to town painting signs and composing poetry on the sly, there seems to be a legend about an eligible young lady "left behind."

An example comes from when Riley lived in Peru, Indiana earning his way as a sign painter. An acquaintance, A. William Neff, recalled a casual love affair Riley had while there. This was in the year 1872. Riley's partner named "Smith" was also a resident. They set up their shop on the second floor of a two story building over a livery stable owned by John and Ben E. Wallace located on East Third Street between Broadway (the main street of Peru) and Wabash Street. The business prospered and they became known in the community. Soon Riley became interested in a young woman named Catherine Musselman, an Irish girl. The year before, she had gone to live with the Neffs and lived there about five years. Riley dated her and called at the Neff residence on the corner of East Third and Wabash only half a block from his workshop. Most of his evenings in Peru were spent in her company and usually at the Neff home.

Another recollection of Neff's should be recorded. A. William Neff remembered Riley spending rainy days painting signs and pictures very skillfully. A few years younger than Riley, Neff remembered spending time watching him point and he was also Riley's messenger boy to take messages to Catherine. Eventually, Riley gave Neff several pictures as he painted them which remain in Peru and have been exhibited from time to time. One of the scenes was a farm scene with a young couple in a hay field with arms intertwined, the girl with a rake in her left hand the boy holding a hay fork,.. In the background was a cabin and dense woods. The boy was kissing the girl and a caption read, "Making Hay While the Sun Shines." Another picture was the head of a beautiful school girl in a low cut blouse, large white beaded necklace and wide brimmed hat. The picture was painted on poplar board and has "Riley and Smith" on the top for signature. It is believed they are on display at the Miami County Historical Museum.

While in Peru, it is remembered that Riley belonged to a social club known as the Academy Club of Peru. The club was composed of young men and had a dancing room and club room on the third floors of adjoining buildings at Second street and Broadway connected by a doorway. The club employed Riley to paint and redecorate the rooms. Riley frescoed the club room.

Eventually, Riley simply up and left. Catherine had no more explanation than anyone else. Eventually a letter came to Catherine and in it was a poem, "The Little Town of Tailholt," which Riley had just written and sent to her. Catherine Musselman was saddened at his departure. She was not the only one left behind. All the rest joined her in this situation.

Another recollection of Riley from roughly the same period - but a little later - has him at South Bend.

In South Bend, Riley worked for Major Blowney who was a painting contractor and had a number of men in his employment. As Henry Pershing remembers it, there were always many girls hanging around in Blowney's shop talking to the boys while they worked. Riley liked to talk if there was anyone to listen while he painted signs in the shop. Riley was considered a "jolly short of fellow and everybody liked him; in fact, he was regarded by everyone as a hail fellow, making friends easily." In particular an incident is recalled in which Riley was sitting after his lunch hold-

Major Blowney's South Bend "boys." Riley in middle of row. (From the Barton Rees Pogue glass positive collection.)

ing a newspaper in his hand, while the fellows were eating their lunch, he read to them. On this occasion, Riley began to read out loud so all could plainly hear him giving all the details about a disastrous fire over in Mansfield, Ohio, where the house of a "Henry Bronson" was burned to the ground and how the owner was barely saved by the firemen from a terrible death in the burning building. Riley read it with all the details of how Mr. Bronson was carried out by the firemen, when up jumped Jim Bronson, one of Riley's fellow workers who had been sitting in the circle listening, exclaiming, "My God, that's my father." Riley's reading had produced the affect desired and that was what he wanted and they all had a good laugh when Riley told them he was simply making it up as he went along. Riley had the reputation of being quite a joker. Jucklet was in Riley's heart.

Henry Miller, a friend working at Blowney's with Riley, does not remember Riley paying much attention to the girls in South Bend. When he called on the daughters of a Mrs. Harper, a prominent family in South Bend society, Miller reports that Mrs. Harper was not impressed enough with him to permit her girls to see Riley.

He was apparently not, at least in South Bend, Indiana, a steady lover.

It is possible that Riley's sexuality was expended on casual sexual acquaintances both before and after the writing of "The Flying Islands of the Night." The record from "before" is far the greater.

A letter of McClanahan preserves the casual nature of the casual morality practiced by at least that close friend.

The letter is addressed to Riley from McClanahan in Ackley, Iowa, and is dated February 25, 1876. McClanahan is with a woman he calls "Baby." She has been sick. "I'm blue as hell to night." He says "Baby" is taking all his "sugar." He mentions things were fine when Baby was working and paying bills. Then in August, 1876, Mack is writing Riley from Dearborn Street in Chicago, sans "Baby." Then in December he is over with Doc. Townsend traveling with another medicine show. He says he doesn't feel well. In fact he feels like someone "after taking a few drops of Dock's balsam tonight while I am smoking a `bald head.'" Such was the life of the best friend of Riley's early 20's.

While we must be true to Riley's autobiographical understanding of his own life, we shall expand the activities of Riley as Amphine to include those other persons for whom he showed affection - correspondents and friends - particularly the many close friends who bore such close camaraderie with Riley.

Among his closest friends during his teenaged years and early twenties were the members of the Adelphians theatrical troupe. The Adelphians began as a band of musicians in 1868 during a political campaign. The group purchased a band wagon manufactured locally and while its driver, James Cox, maneuvered the bandwagon in political parades, the uniformed band members, William Davis, Ed Millikan, War Barnett, Thomas Carr, Charles Warner, Jesse Millikan, Isaac Davis, John Davis, John Guymon, Fred Hafner, Emsely Wilson, Hiram Riley and Riley's brother John played rousing musical numbers. Riley and his friends, Clint

The Adelphian band in horse-drawn wagon.

Hamilton and Fred Beecher, also occasionally played in this band. Later in
Riley's life, in   1890, Riley composed a poem about his days as a musician
in the Adelphians or sometimes called the Davis Brother's Band as follows:

THE OLD BAND (1890)

It's mighty good to git back to the old town, shore,
Considerin' I've b'en away twenty year and more.
Sense I moved then to Kansas, of course I see a change,
A-comin' back, and notice things that's new to me and strange;
Especially at evening when yer new band—fellers meet,
In fancy uniforms and all, and play out on the street -
...What's come of old Bill Lindsey and the Saxhorn fellers - say?
    I want to hear the old band play.

What's come of Eastman, and Nat Snow? And where's War Barnett at?
And Nate and Bony Meek; Bill Hart; Tom Richa'son and that
Air brother of him played the drum as twic't as big as Jim;
And old Hi Kerns, the carpenter - say, what's become o' him?
I make no doubt yer new band now's a competenter band,
And plays their music more by note than what they play by hand,
And stylisher and grander tunes; but somehow - anyway,
    I want to hear the old band play.

Sich tunes as "John Brown's Body" and "Sweet Alice," don't you know;
And "The Camel Is A-Comin'," and "John Anderson, My Jo";
And a dozent others of 'em - "Number Nine" and "Number 'Leaven"
Was favor-rites that fairly made a feller dream o' Heaven.
And when the boys 'ud saranade, I've laid so still in bed
I've even heerd the locus' blossoms droppin' on the shed
When "Lilly Dale," er "Hazel Dell," had sobbed and died away
    ...I want to hear the old band play.

Yer new band ma'by beats it, but the old band's what I said -
It allus 'peared to kind o' chord with somepin' in my head;
And, whilse I'm no musicianer, when my blame' eyes is jes'
Nigh drowned out, and Mem'ry squares her jaws and sort o' says
She won't ner never will fergit, I want to jes' turn in

And take and light right out o' here and git back West ag'in
And stay there, when I git there, where I never haf' to say
   I want to hear the old band play.

About two years later, in April 1870, many of the members of the old Adelphians or Davis Brothers Band decided to put on entertainments at the Old Masonic Hall in Greenfield. They called their club "The Adelphi" and themselves "The Adelphians." The group became best known for dramatic performances which continued for several years. James Whitcomb Riley and his beloved Nellie Millikan, later Mrs. George Cooley, were very prominent in these productions. Other members of the Adelphians were Lee O. Harris, George Carr, War Barnett, A. Ford, Nellie's brothers Ed and Jesse, George B. Cooley, O. N. Ridgeway, John Skinner, H. McGruder, Clint Hamilton, Angie Parker, Mary Dille, and Kate Geary and others from time to time. Riley commonly painted backdrops and produced the stage scenery used in the plays. The group seems to have continued until about 1875, mainly being active in the Christmas seasons and winters.

Thomas Carr, "Tuba Tom" of the Adelphian Band.

The Adelphians' combined talents produced entertainments and plays for several years in Greenfield. Most were given at the Old Masonic Hall catycornered from the Bradley Methodist Church. I detail an early program for one from Nov. 28, 1869, calling itself

A GRAND ENTERTAINMENT
THE PROCEEDS OF ONE EVENING'S
PERFORMANCE TO BE GIVEN TO
—THE POOR —
THE OTHER ASIDE FROM EXPENSES

WILL GO TO THE BENEFIT OF
—THE GREENFIELD CORNET BAND —
General Manager, J. W. Riley
Stage Manger, Lee O. Harris
Leader of Orchestra, I.R. Davis.

Greenfield, Indiana's Masonic Hall built in 1854 where many Riley entertainments were performed. Greenfield's former Presbyterian Church since replaced by a new building in 1906, is in the background. (From the Barton Rees Pogue glass positive collection.)

There was a general musical introduction followed by "The Great Moral and Domestic Drama of the Chimney Corner."   If James Whitcomb Riley developed stage presence and dramatic and comical stage skills someplace, it came from living and breathing on his hometown's stage.

Adolescence became the time when Riley learned enough about characters to be able to play the parts he later assumed. His character types were a wide number of persons many from the world of literature and art. He spent more time reading Dickens at Tom Snow's and read poetry such as Keats, Herrick, Tennyson, Longfellow and Poe. Snow had bought fragments of the old township library and Jim borrowed Lives of Eminent Painters and Sculptors. He poured over the work and life patterns of artists.

At 20, Riley was into theatrical plays, chewed tobacco, loved the girls, and possessed neither skill nor job.   He played Solomon Probity, in

November, 1869, of that year in "Chimney Corner." In playing this part, Riley followed Jimmy Rarden, an old man, around town for a week, watching him sit and stand, walk and talk. He constructed the fireplace for the set and had a good time. In that one year, from Dec. 26 through the holidays at the end of the year, this group put on "Child of Waterloo," "The Rough Diamond," "More Blunders Than One," "Charles the XII," "The Obstinate Family," "Box and Cox," and "Grandfather Whitehead." James Whitcomb Riley took a part in every one of these many plays and in many he had the leading part.

Although Riley's adolescence was not notable for being happy in his life, it was perhaps the most important epoch in the respect that during this time Riley learned to live life by acting out play characters. This came about through Riley's experiences as an actor in plays and productions in his

Riley in one of his favorite roles-an "old man" - at center - stage at the Greenfield Masonic Hall, Greenfield, Indiana.

hometown of Greenfield, Indiana. The Christmas season of 1869, his troupe presented seven plays. "Child of Waterloo" written by Lee O Harris was the first one.

Riley sharpened his awareness of play acting by attending plays wherever he happened to wander. We know he attended plays at White's Hall while at Marion in 1872.

The entertainments in those days were mostly local productions. Few traveling companies journeyed through the Midwest. Townspeople put on the plays as the enterprising among them conceived and did them. Riley was a major actor in his adolescent years. He kept on acting when he left the stage and continued on and on, doing the parts, throughout his life. He memorializes his most important parts in his great autobiographical poem, "The Flying Islands of the Night."

The early experiences of acting contributed materially to Riley's later success. Booth Tarkington, says, "In Mr. Riley's `platform career,' during those years when he went about the country "reading," his poems he saw with his eyes, and heard with his ears, what people thought of him.

"Never any other man stood night after night on stage or platform to receive such solid roars of applause for the `reading' of poems - and for himself.

"He did not read his poems; he did not recite them either; he took his whole body into his hands; as if were, and by his wizard mastery of suggestion left no James Whitcomb Riley at all upon the stage. Instead, the audience saw and heard whatever the incomparable comedian wished them to see and hear. He held literally unmatched power over them for riotous laughter or for actual copious tears and no one who ever saw an exhibition that power will forget it - or forget him." Remember Greenfield as it was then a village, twenty miles away from Indianapolis, but still very isolated. There were no libraries and no telephones and no autos for quick transportation and so in Greenfield a group composed of the school teachers and others joined in literary groups to share experiences. Books and magazines were passed along with may comments on their margins. The ones James Whitcomb Riley passed added thumbnail sketches of the characters. A former city resident, Mrs. Charles E. Cox, formerly Emma Cooley, Nellie's daughter, remembered one on "Mrs. Weatherbee's Quilting Part" a story by Alice Carey included in the old "Clovernook Sketches."

Perhaps the medium most attuned to Riley as Amphine was raw art of which his sign painting was a commercial variant. It is said he loved to draw from childhood. When he was 5, he drew valentines and is said to have written verses on them for his friends for which his mother praised him greatly. Little of this survives.

In an "approved" sketch of his life, Riley gave his nephew, Edmund Eitel, information for the following account.

"Shortly after his sixteenth birthday, young Riley turned his back on the little schoolhouse and for a time wandered through the different fields of art, indulging a slender talent for painting until he thought he was destined for the brush and palette, and then making merry with various musical instruments, the banjo, the guitar, the violin, until finally he appeared as bass drummer in a brass band. "In a few weeks," he says, "I had beat myself into the more enviable position of snare drummer. Then I wanted to travel with a circus, and dangle my legs before admiring thousands over the back seat of a Gold Chariot. In a dearth of comic songs for the banjo and guitar, I had written two or three myself, and the idea took possession of me that I might be a clown, introduced as a character-song-man and the composer of my own ballads."

My father was thinking of something else, however, and one day I found myself with a 'five-ought' paint brush under the eaves of an old frame house that drank paint by the bucketful, learning to be a pointer. Finally, I graduated as a house, sign and ornamental painter, and for two summers traveled about with a small company of young fellows calling ourselves 'the Graphics,' who covered all the barns and fences in the state with advertisements."

Another possibility he explored was working as a printer and working in the village print-shop and a later ambition was acting, encouraged by the good times he had in the theatricals of the "Adelphian Society of Greenfield.""In my dreamy way," he afterward said, "I did a little of a number of things fairly well - sand, played the guitar and violin, acted, painted signs and wrote poetry. My father did not encourage my verse-making for he thought it too visionary, and being a visionary himself, he believed he understood the dangers of following the promptings of the poetic temperament. I doubted if anything would come of the verse- writing myself."

Many stories survive of a possible love affair of James Whitcomb Riley with Clara Bottsford, a teacher and poet in her own right who once lived with the Riley family in "The Seminary" and went on to teach and write much poetry. Her sister, Lotta M. B. Cooper, has written a book documenting this relationship called CLARA LOUISE. She commences her account with the statement: "It is well known in Greenfield and Hancock County that James Whitcomb Riley and Clara Louise Bottsford were at one time lovers for some years." The connections are numerous and can be seen in the very subject matter of Riley poetry. Clara Louis Bottsford and Riley were said to be seeing each other when she was teaching near the "Little Town of Tailholt" and was living in the family of "My Old Friend, William Leachman."

Her sister writes:

"The dark-eyed girl had overflowing vitality, and unbounded enthusiasm for the things she liked, and the attraction grew to be the love of the poet's life, and of hers, the living, ardent expression of which lasted through a period of nearly eight years, in which they walked and talked, and read and sang, and laughed together. They read the poets endlessly, it seemed to us, and much history and mythology. In this time, too, the poet's father loaned the girl books and talked to her about them...

It is impossible for strangers to know, to see, or to feel the personal charm of a poet in his youth and intimate associations. This poet was also a musician as the Troubadours were so. He played the guitar and sang with fine effect the old love songs.

We lived, a group of young people in the midst of an acre of trees, where had been our father's and mother's home, (Biographer's note: Clara Louise's parents died much earlier and shortly after they purchased a farm along Sugar Creek in Hancock County, Indiana, in 1860. The Bottsford children, with Clara Louis as the eldest and her father's administratrix, stayed on the farm and raised themselves.) On summer nights with the moon shining through the branches, the soft air vibrated with tenderness as he sang:

"Unloose the snood that you wear, Jeanette,
    Let me tangle a hand in your hair, my pet,
For the world to me holds no daintier sight
    Than your brown hair veiling your shoulders white.
Than your brown hair veiling your shoulders white."
Another of the Riley's favorite songs she recalls was "Juanita:"
"Nita, Jaunita, let me linger by thy side,
    Nita, Juanita, be my own fair bride."

The courtship was open and admitted, though unannounced. The family were included or disregarded as it might happen, she being the oldest. It was not a matter of moment to the pair who sat with them, or didn't, though the youngest brother spent much time with them; he was a lovely boy and a favorite with both...

"Jim" liked to do caricature, too, and when he sang:
"If there's any girl here wants a kiss from me
    She'll find me as young as I used to be."
...I think it was along here that he tried lecturing, giving entertainments, but he suffered from a disability which in his day was common to temperamental men and plainer ones as well. (Biographer's note: alcoholism.)

...About this time it was that the young brother one day, having gone part way with Mr. Riley to the railroad station, came close to the grown-up sister and said almost in a whisper, "You don't know what he said to me. He said the one thing in all the world he wanted was to succeed at something so that you and he could be married."

(Clara Louise) answered, smiling, "And was it news? I've known that for a long time."

In all poetic justice, they should have married and been happy; but poesy was never known to take account of that which men call justice, and the element of chance, which so sore afflicts mankind may be to the gods, opportunity. Who knows.

Time went on and lengthened out. Success seemed no nearer. With discouragement and uncertainty, the poet's propensity for following Bobby Burns (Biographer's note: alcoholism) in his best known characteristic grew stronger and finally brought the end of the love story."

What do we know of this alleged lover? Miss Clara Louise Bottsford was a native of Johnson County and moved to Sugar Creek Township when she was a child. Her parents, E.S. and Lorinda Bottsford, died within one year of each other leaving an orphaned family of seven children including Clara Louise, one child having died earlier. Clara Louise taught in the schools of Greenfield and boarded in the home of Reuben A. Riley where she met and was allegedly courted by James Whitcomb Riley. The Bottsford daughters and sons kept the farm home, living there in the summer and teaching in the winter, until the youngest was grown up. John H. Binford, author of the first HISTORY OF HANCOCK COUNTY, knew her in the first normal school of the county and as superintendent of the Greenfield graded schools licensed her to teach. She first wrote with a nom de plume in the county papers, then in FRANK LESLEY MAGAZINE, CHIMNEY CORNER, and The New York LEDGER and then, after 1882, wrote over her own signature in the Indianapolis JOURNAL and HERALD, Chicago INTER-OCEAN, New York SUN, and other metropolitan newspapers.

The following poem has been popularly said to have been inspired by her:

"DREAM" (1878)

Because her eyes were far too deep
And holy for a laugh to leap

Across the brink where sorrow tried
To drown within the amber tide;
Because the looks, whose ripples kissed
The trembling lids through tender mist,
Were dazzled with a radiant gleam -
Because of this I called her "Dream."

Because the roses growing wild
About her features when she smiled
Were ever dewed with tears that fell
With tenderness ineffable;
Because her lips might spill a kiss
That, dripping in a world like this
Would tincture death's myrrh-bitter stream
To sweetness - so I called her "Dream."

Because I could not understand
The magic touches of a hand
That seemed, beneath her strange control,
To smooth the plumage of the soul
And calm it, till, with folded wings,
It half forgot its flutterings,
And, nestled in her palm, did seem
To trill a song that called her "Dream."

From the author's Ora Myers glass negative collection of Hancock County, Indiana subjects

Because I saw her, in a sleep
As dark and desolate and deep
And fleeting as the taunting night
That flings a vision of delight
To some lorn martyr as he lies
In slumber ere the day he dies -
Because she vanished like a gleam
Of glory, do I call her "Dream."

In 1950, a folk-recollection of Riley and his connection with Clara Bottsford is found in the pamphlet THE PRINCE AND PRINCE'S LAKES by Joan Lattimore. When the area of Johnson County, Indiana, south of Indianapolis where Clara Bottsford's family once lived, was being developed and lakes were created, the developer, Howard Prince, published a newsletter for the residents called "Prince's Lakes News" that contained the following article.

"BELOVED HOOSIER POET LOST FIANCEE AT HISTORIC HOUSE NEAR ENTRANCE."

"Some may have wondered what we intended to do with the old house at the entrance across from our administration building. Frankly there have been many other things more urgently in need of immediate attention that this.

However we do intend to repair this old house and paint it up, but we do not intend to radically change its appearance on account of its historical background.

We are informed by Mrs. Earl Wilks who used to live in this house, that a second cousin of hers, Clare (sic) Louise Bottsford was the fiancee of James Whitcomb Riley and the inspiration for his poem "An Old Sweetheart of Mind."

Mrs. Wilks says that Riley courted her cousin and became engaged to her here at this old house. On the day they were to be married he came to the house intoxicated and she broke off the engagement. Later on they began going together again and again became engaged. On the day set for the wedding he again came intoxicated and this time Miss Bottsford broke off the engagement for good.

Mrs. Wilks informs us that Riley then made the statement that he would never marry, which vow we all know he kept..."

Later it was decided the house should be torn down.

Greenfield folk considered Clara to be Riley's mistress for many years. The relationship continued sporadically for the later years after the departure of Nellie Cooley for Illinois in 1875 until 1883. In that year, responding to his sister Mary's insistence, Riley allegedly made arrangements for a quiet wedding to Clara and hired a minister and a church in Indianapolis. Clara turned

Clara Bottsford, Riley's fiancee, who refused to marry him because of his alcoholism.

down this offer. Later she married a bartender and her last years were lived without notoriety.

This strange development is recorded in the autobiographical poem as Crestillomeem indicates how she will foil Riley's attempts at love by shriveling him up so that she marries another man whose sire Riley knows. This situation is detailed in the "expanded" 1892 version of the poem in which Riley refers to his loss of a "princess."

"She strangely went
Astray one moonset from the palace-steps -
She went - nor yet returned. -Was it not strange? -
She would be wedded to an alien prince
The morrow midnight - to a prince whose sire [1]
I once knew, in lost hours of lute and song,
When he was but a prince - I but a mouth
For him to lift up sippingly and drain
To lees [2] *most ultimate of stammering sobs*
And maudlin [3] *wanderings of blinded breath.*

1. When Clara married her bartender, Riley knew his sire, "red eye." Clara Bottsford was allegedly lost to Riley because of his alcoholism. "Sire" is a catchword of Riley's referring to one who exercises dominion or rule, one's lord or sovereign, the business of alcohol in this context.
2. A lee is a place of protection or resting place. Possibly the lee was a tavern where both Clara's new husband and Riley shared alcohol.
3. A term used to refer to a stage of drunkenness in which one is tearful and effusively sentimental.

After the Clara Louise episode, it appears that Riley gave up any hope of marriage. There is no record of any later offer of marriage. His women friends after Nellie are "dreams." He means this proabably literally as well as sarcastically. He sometimes addresses "hopefuls" just that way. They really are dreaming if they think they are going to marry James Whitcomb Riley! He admits his feeling of futility about love in his introductory letter to Elizabeth Kahle of Feb. 21, 1879, "...I am a young man and unmarried. I write sentimental verses occasionally, simply because I don't believe in love and am anxious to convince myself of my error, possibly - I don't know why else."

Riley associated with many other women in many different respects. Some are as literary correspondents, some are "Nellie" or "Clara" substi-

tutes or hopefuls. Another one written to at the same time as Elizabeth Kahle was Ella Wheeler, an eligible woman for marriage, correspondent and
poet of Wisconsin. Unfortunately, when Riley met her in Wisconsin when he went there with his friend Rev. Myron Reed on a hunting trip in June 1880 both were disgusted with each other.

Elizabeth Kahle, Riley's Pennsylvania correspondent of his late 20's to whom Riley worte revealing letters-sometimes called 'love letters." The relationship was literary and after Elizabeth first met Riley three years later, the relationship cooled and Elizabeth quickly remarried another suitor without telling Riley.

How strange Riley's relationships with these "literary lovers" was! For example, during the months Riley was living in Anderson, sharing an apartment with his friend, James McClanahan, and dating a lawyer's sister, Kate Myers who he called "Kit," he was also writing Elizabeth Kahle "love letters" in Pennsylvania and Ella Wheeler "love letters" in Wisconsin. While Riley was going with Kit to picnics, dances and parties, and composing his poems, as he did in bed at night next to Jim McClanahan in the double bed they shared, Riley was also writing letters of great romantic intention to "My dearest friend," Elizabeth Kahle. Riley's correspondence with Elizabeth went on three years before Riley even met her and after he did their relationship cooled to ice.

Neither Elizabeth Kahle nor any of the other literary correspondent companions could be the "soul partner" that Nellie Cooley was so they all faded away into fantasy holding on tightly to letters written to them by Riley preserved with great hope for later publication. In this category we find "love letters" to Ella Wheeler, Edith Thomas, Evaleen Stein, and many others. Some of the latter are known through self- promoted "gossip" as that of Elizabeth Fisher Murphy, a married lady in Delphi who for years claimed to have been Riley's lover when he visited Dr. Smith in Delphi. She was another self-promoting "Old Sweetheart of Mine" candidate too.

Since James Whitcomb Riley never married, his various courtships - none resulting in marriage - have been highly debated. Who did he really love?

I believe "The Flying Islands of the Night" pretty much answers the question. His hope for married love in the traditional sense in home and family was destroyed because his "partner chosen for him in heaven," Nellie Cooley, was already married.

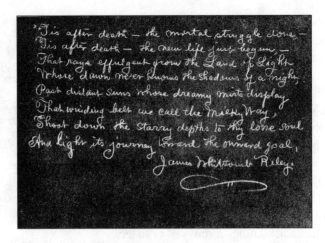

" A spirit writing" on slate of a Riley poem allegedly written by Riley to his friend, Elizabeth Kahle, a year after Riley died. Elizabeth was a spiritualist who happened to be at a seance held by a Professor Pierre L.A.O. Keller when she requested a message from her friend of former years, James Whitcomb Riley, and asked that he be summoned to give her a last poem to add to his correspondence to her to make a book. Elizabeth wanted the title of this last poem to be "After Death." During a subsequent seance, the writing of this poem allegedly appeared by Riley's "crossed over" spirit.

> 'Tis after death - the mortal struggle done, -
> 'Tis after death - the new life just begun,-
> That rays effulgent from the Land of Light
> Whose dawn ne'er knows the shadows of a night,
> Past distant suns whose dreamy mists display
> That winding belt we call the Milky Way
> Shoot down the starry depth to thy lone soul
> And light is journey toward the onward goal,
> James Whitcomb Riley

Perhaps due to impotency from his alcoholism and with the exception of occasional intimacies, Riley seems to have concentrated more socially on making friends with men and women than with investing in romantic dalliances.

One measure of his success in making friends is found in his work for the Kokomo Saturday TRIBUNE when Riley was its Home Editor in 1879. As such Editor, Riley rounded up literary contributions for the newspaper from among his friends. Here is a list of those who wrote poetry for Riley for an issue of December 27th, 1879: Maurice Thompson, Lee O. Harris, Mary H. Krout, Sarah T. Bolton, Louise V. Boyd, Emily T. Charles, Frank Mayfield, Asa Burrows, M.E. Harmon, H.W. Taylor, Mrs. O.B. Hewitt, Luther G. Riggs, W. J. Lampton, Dan L. Paine, H.S. Taylor, B.S. Parker, D,M. Jordan, Clara Louise Bottsford, John W. Tindall, John N. Taylor, Horace P. Biddre, Frank Winter, Celeste M.A. Winslow, Lilla N. Custhman, L.E.F.R. with prose by Mary Dean, Margret Holmes, Mary A. Cornelius,

Mrs. T.C. Vickrey, J.P. Charles, W.C. Cooper, Dr. P. Baldwin, Mary F. Tucker, R.H.J., Mary H. Catherwood, Amy E. Dunn, "Christie," N.L. NBraffett. Kittie Knox, Willard G. Nash, Smith Griffith, and "G.P." Riley had many, many friends who wrote pieces for him to publish.

Who were some of his closest friends?

Riley sought out friends. One was Meredith Nicholson. Nicholson's verses had been picked up in a Cincinnati newspaper as Riley discovered. Riley investigated to find where Nicholson worked and went to meet him. When they met, Nicholson was employed in a law office where he copied legal documents, ran errands, and scribbled verses in his spare time. Nicholson says, "He was the most interesting as he was the most amusing and the most lovable man I have known." Some of Nicholson's other comments about Riley should be recorded. They point out how peculiar was this fellow Riley to his friends. "(Riley) was always curious as to the origin of any garment or piece of haberdashery displayed by his intimates, but strangely secretive as to the source of his own supplies. He affected obscure tailors, probably because they were likelier to pay heed to his idiosyncrasies than more fashionable ones. He once deplored to me the lack of attention bestowed upon the waistcoat by sartorial artists. This was a

Hautie Tarkington, courted by Riley, later Mrs. Ovid Butler Jameson. In her brother's, Booth Tarkington's autobiography is the entry, "(Riley's) manner with my sister, like hers with him, was of the liveliest mock coquetry; they were having a tremendous affair in which their was nothing-nothing but gaiety."

garment he held of the highest importance in man's adornment." Nicholson adds, "He inspired affection by reason of his gentleness and inherent kindliness and sweetness. The idea that he was convivial person, delighting in boon companions and prolonged sessions at table, has no basis in face. He was a domestic, even a cloistral being; he disliked noise and large companies; he hated familiarity, and would quote approvingly what Lowell said somewhere about the annoyance of being clapped on the back. Riley's best friends never laid hands on him; I have seen strangers or new acquaintances do so to their discomfiture."

Riley and Nicholson liked to loaf together at a common bookstore where once Riley noted many copies of a Nicholson book. Later when Nicholson returned he learned that Riley had furtively purchased seventy-five of them to distribute widely to friends. Riley often did that for authors he liked. He was beloved within the literary community because he boosted others careers.

In the course of time, Riley's fame as a poet and platform speaker brought him recognition from many of the best writers of his era. They wrote him letters that he was glad to answer in his inimitable style and through correspondence and personal contacts there was established a lasting friendship with such writers as Mark Twain, Joel Chandler Harris, John Burroughs, Rudyard Kipling, William Dean Howells, John Hay, William Lyon Phelps and many others.

James Whitcomb Riley had a phenomenal gift of making and keeping friends. One of his oldest was John Skinner. Riley and Skinner knew each other from school days on through Riley's years of early great alcoholism. In fact they lived together more often than not when Riley was not off wandering on some nomadic escapist venture.

Riley knew Skinner as a train dispatcher in Butler, Indiana during later years, but in the former years, both shared living in Room Eleven in the Dunbar House, a hostelry. The basis of the arrangement began in teenaged years. Skinner and Riley were both "printer's devils" for the rival newspapers of Greenfield. Their job was to "roll" the presses with printer's ink.

This connection with newspapers, as lowly as it was, was the starting point for each to become interested in newspaper work. In their final year of "graded" school, in 1870, both undertook editorial supervision of the "Criterion," the Greenfield school newspaper. The two edited this newspaper there in the room at the Dunbar House working through the night to put out its issues.

Riley had a genius for friendship and bound his friends to him with `hoops of steel' as his secretary, Marcus Dickey, once said. To some extent the phrase would be better put as with "hoops of red eye." Riley's closest friends were almost always those whose indulgence approached his own. Almon Keefer and Clint Hamilton share Riley's inscriptions in the records of the Greenfield Mayor's Court for public intoxications. His closest friend of his wandering days, Jim McClanahan was hopelessly alcoholic and eventually died after a binge of exposure. Even Charles Holstein, into whose house Riley moved at 528 Lockerbie Street, was initially Riley's friend from being a drinking companion. Riley was a prolific letter writer and in consequence there are several collections of letters written to various friends, each correspondence revealing some one of the many diverse sides of his lovable nature.

Strangely, and in conflict with the obvious strength of his many friendships, Riley apparently believed he had more enemies than friends. He wrote in a letter to Elizabeth Kahle on February 21, 1879, "I have many friends, but more enemies, and can scarcely tell which I most enjoy - for I really enjoy being hated by some people. I am cynical in a marked degree, and disagreeable at time, I most frankly admit. Socially I move in the best circles, - not, -perhaps, because I was `to the manor born,' but because - because - well, I recite dialectic poems acceptably, sing comic songs and make funny faces, all of which seems to please everybody but myself, for when I seem the happiest is when I feel the most like crying - though there are times I could take the whole world in my arms, and love it as I would a great, fat, laughing baby with a bunch of jingling keys..."

Riley apparently believed he had friends only so long as he was entertaining and funny. This is not a man who is comfortable with who he really is.

Riley certainly loved his family and particularly his sisters. His greatest tenderness was extended to those who were vulnearable as was his sister Mary. Riley was very tender-hearted towards his sister, Mary, as she thought, to make up for the lack of a mother's care in growing up. He earned very little at first, but after Mary was grown and married and moved to Chicago, and other places, Here is a letter Riley wrote to his sister while on a platform tour:

Oskaloosa, Iowa
March 25, 1889

My Dear Sister Mary:

Your last letter, just read, seems as though some rainy Sunday at our dear old home. I had spit on my hands and written it myself. You take a Riley, for instance, and mix him up with a Marine - and Lord! - don't we make a combination!..As to your doctor's doleful prognostications, I know the profession too well to believe a word of it. All you want is some decided change and sensible care of yourself...Anyway in the world, and I am now, comparatively wealthy, that I can serve you, my Mother's dearest child, don't you know how it would please me who have done so little good and in so poor a way?

When I neglect you, writing - it's because only I've neglected everybody else and everything else in this final struggle to get some good green dollars sucked into the bank - enough at least that I can lie down and die without folk's tearin' out the tail-gate of my bed for a headstone. And now at last I'm accumulating money, nothing would better please me than for you to enjoy any share of it you choose. Have been thinking very seriously of buying the old original home at Greenfield, if I can get it. How would you like that - to go back there and live? Or any other place in your fancy I could supply or help to ....

`So I want you to feel utterly secure in the love of a brother now so better able than ever before to prove myself so, without stint of material wealth, as wealth of affection.

As ever, with tenderest love, your bro.,

Jim

Riley was compassionately tender together with an inimitable sense of humor that never deserted him even during the strain of years of greatest struggle. Crestillomeem was his "pressure valve" when tenderness and humor failed.

Riley's own alcoholism placed him in sympathetic relationships with others who greatly influenced his writing both in character and subject matter. Especially the "intoxicatese" of such people was a well-spring of humor and source of "golden lines." Old Sport, William Stafford, provided a persona for the John Walker series. John W. Campbell was another gentleman who Riley liked to imitate with friends. He was a rural Hancock farmer but had a penchant for coming in to town to get drunk and chat with friends in the bars of Greenfield. Campbell was a hunter on land he owned in Arkansas. Riley enjoyed his amusing stories about his exploits as a hunter down on his Arkansas reserve. When he was intoxicated, the Greenfield boys, including Riley, would taunt him, "When are you going to Arkansas?" The kindly old farmer sometimes replied, "I'll be ready to strike out when the frost is on the punkin and the fodder's in the shock." This was repeated in Riley's story telling and eventually became the "golden line" in his famous Benjamin Johnson poem of that name.

Perhaps we should detail James McClanahan's life who we have mentioned incidentally earlier. Let us see what happened to him. He was Riley's sign painting "partner" from Riley's early twenties.

Jim McClanahan was born May 5, 1855 in Indiana. His father was T.J. McClanahan, a Marylander, as was his mother Harriet Settor. James McClanahan appears to have considered Anderson his domicile all his tragic life. He however leaves few traces. He shows up in the Emerson's City Directory of Anderson of 1876-7 listed as a "traveling agent" with a room at the corner of Bolivar and Jackson. Not until the 1891-2 city directory does he re-appear, this time as James "McClenehen" residing in a house at 84 W, 9th Street. No intervening or later city directory lists him at all. His obituary is on page one of the newspaper not because he was notable but because he was connected with the life of James Whitcomb Riley, then world-famous.

A wife, May McClanahan, was indicated on his death certificate at the Madison County (Indiana) Health Department. She is listed as deceased. The obituary had said she was dead thirty years. Unfortunately no record of her exists anywhere. Wherever she slipped away, it made insufficient splash to be recorded.

According to his obituary in the Anderson HERALD of Sunday morning, July 27, 1913, James McClanahan was found dying in the Anderson City Park and expired at Anderson's St. John's hospital the evening of July 26th, just before midnight. He died at 58 leaving only two half sisters. It does not seem too hard to speculate that a similar end to James Whitcomb Riley might have occurred.

The newspaper article relates, "In a dying condition Mr. McClanahan was found lying in a shed in the City Park, formerly the fair ground, yesterday afternoon by workmen who were tearing down the sheds. Police were notified and the patrol wagon and Patrolman Beeman took Mr. McClanahan to the county jail. There it was discovered that the man was very ill and he was transferred to St. John's hospital."

Apparently Jim McClanahan, Riley's comrade beginning thirty years before, had been passed out there in a ramshackle building, and probably been trying to live there, sick for at least since the prior Wednesday. One suspects alcoholism had drained his will to live. The building had formerly been the animal show barn of the Madison County Fair where livestock were exhibited until the place had been turned into a

DEATH JAMES M'CLANAHAN

INTIMATE FRIEND OF JAMES WHITCOMB RILEY FOUND. DYING IN CITY PARK.

EXPIRES AT HOSPITAL

Two Half-Sisters Only Surviving Relatives—Incident of Riley's Recent Visit Recalled.

James McClanahan, age 58, intimate friend of James Whitcomb Riley since their sign painting days about thirty years ago, died shortly before last midnight at St. John's hospital. The body was removed to Bells Bros.' morgue. Funeral arrangements will be made today and Mr. Riley will be advised of the death of his old friend.

In a dying condition Mr. McClanahan was found lying in a shed in the City Park, formerly the fair ground, yesterday afternoon by workmen who were tearing down the sheds. Police were notified and with the patrol wagon Patrolman Beeman took Mr. McClannahan to the county jail. There is was discovered that the man was very ill and he was transferred to St. John's hospital.

In Shed Since Wednesday.

It is thought that Mr. McClannahan had lain in the sheds, formerly used for exhibition of live stock, since Wednesday afternoon when he was seen in City Park. Since that time it is thought he had been ill without food and exposed to the weather. He was barely able to speak when taken to the hospital and gradually lapsed city park. Jim McClanahan had had no food and been exposed to the weather there and when found and arrested could hardly speak and soon lapsed into unconsciousness before dying.

The medical records of that admission show that a doctor first saw him on the Saturday of his death, July 26 at 3:10 P.M. He was brought to the hospital from the jail in an ambulatory condition where he had been taken after a vagrancy arrest. At first there was no room for him at the hospital, but he was taken to Ward 2 of the hospital eventually. The only thing noted about him is that he was 58 and died the next day at 2 A.M. apparently without any treatment by the hospital staff. The hospital records do not reflect he was an alcoholic. The doctor's note says, "Ailment. Supposed to be overcome by heat and hunger." The man's death certificate at the Madison County Health Department gives the cause of death as "Exhaustion following acute alcoholism." /s/ Dr. Elmer S. Albright. Death Record CH9, page 23. Undertaker Earl Sells then took over.

McClanahan had apparently been married to someone whose name escaped mention in his obituary - although it shows up in the death certificate as "May" - probably because she had died thirty years before, around the time he and James Whitcomb Riley had become friends, and he had never re- married. His rambling, nomadic life had included the times with "Baby" and no doubt others.

We can trace Jim McClanahan and James Whitcomb Riley through the years with Doc McCrillus and the year after the McCrillus summer together. They both were members of a group called the Graphics who painted signs along with Will Ethell, who would move to Washington, D.C. This sign painting consortium would give Riley cause to travel all over the State of Indiana mainly painting barns and fences in the countryside and buildings in many cities and towns.

The path of McClanahan diverged after these ventures with Riley and Ethell and the Graphics characters whose lives we will soon explore. James Whitcomb Riley went into writing. Will Ethell went into business. McClanahan had no such enterprising design and took whatever odd jobs he could find. He must have been very dispirited. He mainly worked about hotels, barber shops or livery barns cleaning up.

Throughout the years, Riley contributed to Jim's income although McClanahan always maintained that he had never asked his soon-to-become wealthy friend for even a cent of charity.

The parting of the intimate friends is described from just the prior month before McClanahan's miserable death. Anderson had held a week-long "Made in Anderson" Week honoring James Whitcomb Riley. The city could rightfully claim that Riley was their product. He had really begun his serious writing at that place. During one of the entertainments of the week, at the home of Mr. and Mrs. T.N. Stilwell, Riley insisted that he must see James McClanahan, his friend from the Doc McCrillus medicine show days and the Graphics capers. Half an hour later, it is said the Jim McClanahan was brought to Riley from a hotel office where he was working.

What a strange meeting this must have been. Riley was by this time nationally prominent many times over, wealthier than any other writer in America, obviously fawned over and highly reputed. McClanahan would have been almost the antithesis. One can imagine the man, alcoholic and unshaven, someone who doesn't raise his eyes from the ground very often. Death was probably in those eyes even then.

The two drew apart from the crowd of Riley well-wishers and spent the next minutes together again as they had been thirty years before. They said their good-byes. As Jim left Jim, it was recalled that McClanahan had given a wave. That was the last time they would ever see each other. (I should note that the last name of Riley's intimate friend is spelled in many ways in many accounts often within the same reference. I have stuck to the spelling "McClanahan" although I find it spelled McClannahan or M'Clanahan or M'Clannahan. Apparently he was considered so nondescript that he was not even worth having a consistently spelled last name.)

Riley chose not to attend the funeral of this traveling companion of his youth who he had helped support over the years. There is absolutely no clue on which to speculate why. What can we really know about the man, Jim McClanahan, or whatever his name really was? We know that he was Riley's traveling companion with Doc McCrillus during his first summer away from home. We also know in the next years he and Riley formed a partnership to paint signs and barns and that both later became members of "The Graphics" about which more will come later. All of this is unfortunately very little.

The shadowy and illusive Jim McClanahan seems to have existed in history only as a friend and traveling companion to James Whitcomb Riley and then fallen back into the obscurity of a man who took odd jobs cleaning horse stables, being a handyman, sweeping up barber shops, painting from time to time, or performing maintenance at Anderson hotels. He apparently lived where he could, if he could afford it, and in his last years, anywhere with even scanty shelter such as the abandoned animal barn at the Madison City Park where he was found after a bout with intoxication which cost him his life.

This man may not have lived much of a life and certainly his life is not celebrated in many ways. But it certainly is in the poetry of James Whitcomb Riley.

THE RAGGEDY MAN (1890)

O The Raggedy Man! He works fer Pa;
An' he's the goodest man ever you saw!
He comes to our house every day,
An' waters the horses[1], an' feeds 'em hay;
An' he opens the shed - an' we all ist laugh
When he drives out our little old wobble-ly calf[2];
An' nen - ef our hired girl says he can -
He milks the cow[3] fer 'Lizabuth Ann. -
*   Ain't he a' awful good Raggedy Man?*
*   Raggedy! Raggedy! Raggedy Man!*
W'y, the Raggedy Man -he's ist so good,
He splits the kindlin'[4] an' chops the wood;
An' nen he spades in our garden[5], too,
An' does most things 'at boys can't do. -
He clumbed clean up in our big tree
An' shooked a' apple[6] down fer me -
An' 'nother 'n' too, fer 'Lizabuth Ann -
An' 'nuther 'n' too, fer The Raggedy Man. -
*   Ain't he a' awful kind Raggedy Man?*
*   Raggedy! Raggedy! Raggedy Man!*
An' The Raggedy Man one time say he,
Pick' roast' rambos[7] from a' orchurd-tree,
An' et 'em - all ist roast' an hot! -

The "Raggedy Man" could be counted on to take the stinger from a bee out of a boy's hand. Drawing by Will Vawter.

An' it's so, too! - 'cause a corn-crib got
Afire one time an' all burn' down
On "The Smoot Farm," 'bout four mile from town -
On "The Smoot Farm"! Yes - an' the hired han'
'At worked there nen 'uz The Raggedy Man! -
*   Ain't he the beatin'est Raggedy Man?*
*   Raggedy! Raggedy! Raggedy Man!*

The Raggedy Man's so good an' kind
He'll be our "horsey," an "haw" an' mind
Ever'thing 'at you make him do -
An' won't run off - 'less you want him to!
I drived him wunst way down our lane
An' he got skeered, when it 'menced to rain,
An' ist rared up an' squealed and run
Purt' nigh away! - an' it's all in fun!
Nene he skeered ag'in at a' old tin can...
　　Whoa! y' old runaway Raggedy Man!
　　Raggedy! Raggedy! Raggedy Man!
An' The Raggedy Man, he knows most rhymes,
An' tells 'em, ef I be good, sometimes:
Knows 'bout Giunts, an' Griffuns, an' Elves,
An' the Squidgicum-Squees 'at swallers the'rselves:
An', rite by the pump in our pasture-lot [8],
He showed me the hole 'at the Wunks is got,
'At lives 'way deep in the ground, an' can
Turn into me, er 'Lizabeth Ann!
Er Ma, er Pa, er The Raggedy Man!
　　Ain't he a funny old Raggedy Man?
　　Raggedy! Raggedy! Raggedy Man!
An' wunst, when The Raggedy Man come late,
An' pigs [9] ist root' thru the garden-gate,
He 'tend like the pigs 'uz bears an' said,
"Old Bear-shooter'll shoot 'em dead!"
An' race' an' chase' 'em, an' they'd ist run
When he pint his hoe at 'em like it's a gun
An' go "Bang!-Bang!" nen 'tend he stan'
An' load up his gun ag'in! Raggedy Man!
　　He's an old Bear-Shooter Raggedy Man!
　　Raggedy! Raggedy! Raggedy Man!
An' sometimes The Raggedy Man lets on
We're little prince-children, an' old King's gone
To git more money, an' lef' us there -
And Robbers is ist [10] thick ever'where:
An' nen - ef we all won't cry, fer shore -
The Raggedy Man he'll come and "splore

From the author's Ora Myers glass negative collection of Hancock County subjects.

The Castul-Halls," an' steal the "gold" -
An' steal us, too, an' grab an' hold
An' pack us off to his old "Cave"! - An'
   Haymow's the "cave" o' The Raggedy Man! -
   Raggedy! Raggedy! Raggedy Man!
The Raggedy Man - one time, when he
Wuz makin' a little bow-'n'-orry [11] fer me,
Says "When you're big like your Pa is,
Air you go' to keep a fine store like his -
An' be a rich merchunt - an' wear fine clothes? -
Er what air you go' to be, goodness knows?"
An' nen he laughed at 'Lizabuth Ann,
An' I says "'M go' to be a nice Raggedy Man!"
   I'm ist go' to be a nice Raggedy Man!
   Raggedy! Raggedy! Raggedy Man!

1. Every home needed a well for water obtained by hand pump, sole source of water for drinking, cooking and washing. Grooming horses was a daily task. Draft horses were the tractors and vehicle motors of the nineteenth-century.
2. A bull calf raised as a steer was sometimes kept or "fed out" by a family to provide meat for the family.
3. Every morning and evening, a family's cow had to be milked in the late Nineteenth Century. Each family commonly kept a cow, even those in the towns, in a barn or shed behind the home. The ordinary breed was a Shorthorn, a dual purpose breed good for both milk and beef.
4. Most homes kept "kitchen" gardens in the mid-Nineteenth Century. With the exception of sugar, coffee and tea, most food that a family ate was raised at home.
5. Apples were a fruit staple. They were eaten fresh, kept in cellars (precursors of basements), sometimes canned, or dried for use in pies.
6. Kindling are finer strands of wood or material to initially take flame to start a fire. Keeping a good supply of firewood was a year-round task and a woodlot was in most Hoosier back-yards.
7. Rambo refers to a large cooking apple and apple variety that has a coat streaked with red.
8. From early Spring, domestic animals no longer had to be fed hay and grain but could be sustained on grass in pasture- lots.
9. Pigs were tended by men and boys in the Hoosier gender scheme of division of chores. Black and white Poland China pigs were the most popular Hoosier breed in the Nineteenth Century, a breed originated in southwest Ohio during the mid-Nineteenth Century.
10. Just
11. Pioneer children played "settler and Indian" with the bow and arrow being the Indian weapon of choice.

As all of Riley's poems are, "The Raggedy Man" is a composite of many characters that Riley had known. I think one of them was Jim McClanahan. Another was a man who had worked for Walter Smoot, a farmer near Greenfield, whose name is lost. The "Raggedy Man" is the archetypical good-hearted handyman and helper of every child or vulnerable person one seems to find in Riley's poetry. He is warm, hale, friendly, even if he is also worthless by worldly criterion of wealth or family reputation people. He is a Riley invention who entertains us with lack of sophistication on the way the world has passed him by or driven him down, lacking ambition to overcome the temptations of the world, such as alcoholism. But down deep we know such people are us, could have been us, or might be us.

Bumbling, good-for-nothing, Jim McClanahan is worth a shout of joy about life, not because he is someone who we are better than, but because we know in the scheme of things to the vulnerable ones of this world does God show equal favor as to any other.

Let us turn our attention to Luther Benson.

Riley came to laugh at himself for ever having anything to do with the odd temperance speaker, Luther Benson. That was a great failing on the part of Riley. Luther Benson gave Riley to be able to deal with Crestillomeem after the death of Nellie Cooley as Riley clearly was unable to do before. In fact, Riley came to actively mock this American temperance figure. One of his platform sketches became "Benson Out-Bensoned." In this sketch, Riley made himself into a sadly laughable caricature of a "floundering drunken do gooder." The sketch was not well-received at the time and there is no record of its content which survives.

Who was Luther Benson? His life spanned the years 1847-1898, and he was a temperance movement figure. THE ENCYCLOPEDIA OF BIOGRAPHY OF INDIANA, 1899, gives this record of the man's life:

"Any biography of this man is necessarily a record of one of the greatest triumphs ever achieved by mortal in his life-and-death struggle with abnormal appetite. This appetite was undoubtedly inherited from his maternal grandfather and was fostered and strengthened by the customs of the day, spirituous liquors being kept and freely used by every family. Luther Benson was one of a family of nine children, seven of whom were boys. His father, John Harley Benson, was born Mar. 2, 1802... In 1835 he left Kentucky with his family and located in Rush County, Ind... Here his son Luther, destined to become so singularly distinguished, was born Sept. 9, 1847, and grew to manhood assisting with the work of his father's farm. He obtained the rudiments of an education in two little log school-houses- one standing by a stream called Hood's Creek, the other on the site of the present Ammon's mill. When sixteen years of age he began attending school at the little village of Fairview...His education was completed at Moore's Hill College near Cincinnati, after which he began the study of law; but the time had come when the onward current of his expanding young life was to receive a fearful check and its sweet and wholesome waters be turned to bitterness. His passion for drink had come upon him; and although he afterward entered college, his attendance was of short duration. Henceforth his best efforts must be expended in fighting the fiend that threatened his destruction. Of his moral sense and moral stamina his later years of triumph gave abundant proof; but that triumph came only after a long season of misery and humiliation to himself, his family and friends.

On Jan. 21, 1877, he experienced a profound revulsion to his manner of life and determined to raise above his weakness. This seeming conversion occurred at Jeffersonville, Ind., and was the forerunner of his permanent conquest of a few months later at Fowler, although a period of relapse to his pitiful thralldom intervened. During the ten years prior to this time he had been engaged in the practice of law, a vocation to which in some ways he was admirably adapted, having, when not under the influence of liquor, a logical intelligence and eloquent flow of language. He had begun his legal studies in the office of Hon. John S. Reid, at Connersville, and had subsequently opened one on his own account at Rushville, where he practiced with good success until, himself released from the tyranny of strong drink, he felt impelled to devote his remaining days to the rescuing of like victims. Imbued with the moral courage of a lofty purpose, the chosen scene of his first lecture was Raleigh, whose inhabitants had been eye-witness to his most reckless dissipations. After this he proceeded from one to another of the principals towns of Indiana until, within three years, he had delivered nearly five hundred lectures in his home State. Subsequently he made a tour in the East...his efforts meeting everywhere with much appreciation and enthusiasm...

In 1883 or 1884 Mr. Benson received the Democratic nomination for Congress from the Sixth District, but in a manly letter declined the nomination, not wishing actively to enter into political life...In 1884 Mr. Benson was married to Anna C. Slade. His domestic life was made beautiful by a wealth of affection, and his death which occurred June 21, 1898, was deeply and widely deplored...

Not only with oral eloquence did Mr. Benson labor for the cause of temperance; he toiled with pen as well. FIFTEEN YEARS IN HELL is the significant title of a book of which he is the author and which has had a phenomenal sale throughout the country; and Mrs. Benson holds for publication the manuscript of her husband's autobiography, completed shortly before his death..."

One of those who read this autobiography was James Whitcomb Riley. The life of Luther Benson must have seemed so similar to his own at the time.

James Whitcomb Riley's poem "Luther Benson," was written in 1878 at approximately the same time as the composition of "Flying Islands" which it parallels in many respects. "The Flying Islands of the Night" is Riley's autobiography just as the one Riley was reading of Luther Benson's.

LUTHER BENSON[1] (1878)
(After reading his Autobiography)

Edward Munch "Melancholy" (1896).

Poor victim of that vulture curse[2]
That hovers o'er the universe,
With ready talons quick to strike
In every human heart alike,
And cruel beak to stab and tear
In virtue's vitals everywhere, -
You need no sympathy of mine
To aid you, for a strength divine
Encircles you, and lifts you clear
Above this earthly atmosphere.

And yet I can but call you poor,
As, looking through the open door
Of your sad life, I only see
A broad landscape of misery,
And catch through mists of pitying tears
The ruins of your younger years,
I see a father's shielding arm
Thrown round you in a wild alarm -
Struck down, and powerless to free
Or aid you in your agony.

I see a happy home grow dark
And desolate - the latest spark
Of hope is passing in eclipse -
The prayer upon a mother's lips
Has fallen with her latest breath
In ashes on the lips of death -
I see a penitent who reels,
And writes, and clasps his hands, and kneels,
And moans for mercy for the sake
Of that fond heart he dared to break.

And lo! as when in Galilee
A voice above the troubled sea
Commanded "Peace; be still!" the flood
That rolled in tempest-waves of blood
Within you, fell in calm so sweet
It ripples round the Savior's feet;
And all your noble nature thrilled
With brightest hope and faith, and filled
Your thirsty soul with joy and peace
And praise to Him who gave release.

1. This poem could almost be an outline of "The Flying Islands of the Night."
2. Alcoholism, which curse struck Riley too.

Luther Benson wrote Riley a letter of encouragement upon hearing of
Riley's alcoholism. Riley went to meet him. Benson was Riley's age and
like Riley, a bachelor. In November, 1877, Riley toured Northern Indiana
for a short time with Luther Benson and then returned to Greenfield with a
copy of Benson's autobiography which he studied and pondered.

As his biographer, I would have to say that Riley was greatly informed
about the alcoholics confessional genre of writing from his experience with
Luther Benson. The friendship with Benson continued. Before his winter
tour of 1884 commenced, Riley had to borrow money because he was no
longer employed by the Journal. He went to Luther Benson to borrow $80.
He gave him a note which Riley never repaid. In Jan. 1888, Riley went to
Luther Benson's home to give readings for his guests. Benson wrote out that
the $80 he loaned him before was repaid. Riley did say he would repay him

"when he got ahead." After Riley's success, Benson sued Riley for the $80 in 1892 except Riley had kept the paper showing the debt repaid and produced it in court. Benson lost.

How closely Riley could feel about a friend is revealed in a letter to Charles Philips.

The Morgue, midnight, August 15, 1879

Dear Charles,

I wrote you last evening, requesting especially, that you should answer me to-night, and looked certainly for a reply - for you have never failed me. But there was none. I can not tell you the depth of my disappointment and anxiety- for all evening I have gone about with a strange feeling of heaviness, and last it has grown intolerable and I have just risen from my sleepless bed to write you this. In my letter of last evening I fear I unintentionally wounded you, and that you are "striking back" with silence. I wrote hurriedly, I know, but it was with the very warmest feeling of brotherly regard. What I said, I distinctly said for the effect of force more than elegance, but it was not meant to hurt -neither was it as I thought an undue license in one as warmly interested in you as your own true character compels me to be. When I like any one, perhaps it is my fault to enter too deeply into their personal affairs, or, in other words - am inclined to meddle with matters that do not concern me. If I have done this with you, I earnestly ask you to regard it as an insane burst of affection, for at worst it is that. I don't think you understand my real nature. I have thought different at times, but as I write, I fear with a regret there is no name for, that like the grand majority, you misjudge me. I do not blame you if you do, only it hurts, my dear friend, just to wade on through existence as I do with no one soul of all the world's wide millions that well see me as I am. I try very hard to laugh down this idea of mine that I am being eternally misinterpreted, but every fresh experience only seems more firmly to fix and rivet the truth of it within me. When I tell my friend I love him, I love him. There is no play in the grooves of my affection. And when a friend slides in my heart he fits there and the bony hand of Death can not jostle him. Maybe I do you wrong to doubt the strength of your regard, but I want such giant strengths of friendship that sometimes I think my own will never be matched here - that it is more than I could ask or expect. In any instance I am what I am. God made me so, and if I do not pass for my full value here, Heaven will be brighter comprehending it.

Tomorrow I go down to Indianapolis. I may not hope to see you then as I desired; but wherever you are through life and death fell always that my love is with you.

J. W. Riley

Such a letter betrays such deep emotion the mood is nearly romantic. Who would Riley write such a letter to? Who is this man Charles Howard Philips? He was a young man like Riley who Riley had met during his Graphics wandering days. His biography was published along with his death notice in the Kokomo TRIBUNE when Charles Philips died at the young age of 25. It read: "Charles Howard Philips, Born June 6th, 1856 Died November 5th, 1881, Age 25 years, 4 months, 29 days. His death resulted from consumption, after a severe attack of typhoid fever. For over a year he had been an invalid, traveling North and South, hoping for a healthful climate. His death was quiet and painless. Philips was an accomplished journalist. Three years before his death, he married Kate Kennedy October 17, 1878 who died in Florida in the Spring 1880. The mother lingered and eventually died from complications of the birth. The child, a daughter, Kate, died during the summer of 1881, just weeks before Charles Philips' death. He had received a common school education until the age of 13 when he began doing editorial work and typesetting on his father's newspaper. He became a partner in the Kokomo TRIBUNE his family's newspaper when the father died in July 1878."

One wonders if the above letter is simply "fawning" to gain a position on the Kokomo TRIBUNE. We do know Riley as a man desperate for fame. We also know that Philips was Editor of the Kokomo TRIBUNE who eventually placed Riley in charge of his Kokomo TRIBUNE column, "Home Department."

At Philips' untimely death, Riley published a poem in memoriam:

CHARLES H. PHILIPS (1881)

Obit November 5th, 1881

O Friend! There is no way
To bid farewell to thee!
The words that we would say

Above thy grave to-day
Still falter and delay
And fail us utterly.

When walking with us here,
The hand we loved to press
Was gentle, and sincere
As thy frank eyes were clear
Through every smile and tear
Of pleasure and distress.

In years, young; yet in thought
Mature; thy spirit, free,
And fired with fervor caught
Of thy proud sire, who fought
His way to fame, and taught
Its toilsome way to thee.

So even thou hast gained
The victory God-given -
Yea, as our cheeks are stained
With tears, and our souls pained
And mute, thou hast attained
Thy high reward in Heaven!

Riley's poem was in the genre of "In Memoriam" poems of the time.
Another example of the type is one by Frank Winter in the Kokomo TRI-
BUNE of November 12, 1881 titled "In Memoriam. Charles Howard
Philips."

November's chilling winds had come.
  The falling leaves on hill and dale:
Gave Nature a sad look at home
  And told our hearts a deathly tale.
A noble man, tho' young in years,
  Had sought the guilded halls of Fame;
Thro' joys and sorrows, hopes and fears,
  Had won himself an honored name.

(three further stanzas.)

Riley's great feeling toward friends is reflected in the feeling of blessedness as we find in a roughly contemporaneous poem "To H.S.T." with the subheading, "The Morgue, Midnight, July 3, 1879." This poem was published in the Indianapolis Saturday HERALD in Riley's "Poetical Gymnastics" column of July 12, 1879.

TO H.S.T.

Friend of a wayward hour, you came
Like some good ghost, and went the same;
And I within the haunted place
Sit smiling on your vanished face,
  And talking with - your name.

But thrice the pressure of your hand -
First hail - congratulations - and
Your last "God bless you!" as the train
That brought you snatched you back again
  Into the unknown land.

"God bless me?" Why, your very prayer
Was answered ere you asked it there,
I know - for when you came to lend
Me your kind hand, and call me friend,
  God blessed me unaware.

Here is a poem of a friendly visit to Riley that provides us a picture of Riley friends and friendliness. This friend who we know was H.S. Taylor, an author, came from Illinois to Greenfield, where the "Morgue" was located, shook Riley's hand three times, first to greet him, then to congratulate him, and then with a farewell blessing. The handshakes give us to know the substance of the visit. We do not need to hear the conversation.

The importance to a biography of Riley from this poem derives from its climaxing thought. With friends behind him, Riley was confident God was blessing his poetic activity. Riley did not even need to know others were thinking kindly of him. His work was a product of hopes for his success by others. He felt the power of friendship as an energy. We do not speak of the direction of the "push." Riley simply knew his audience of well-wishers appreciated him. The thrill of this recognition presaged his resolution of what to do with himself. His immersion into kenotic poetry followed. Perhaps the spotlight of fame nudged him into a humbling response. Support of friends encouraged him to take his poetry out from narrative and romantic themes and into a realm of desperate illusion as we found in "Flying Islands" where Riley gained the self-vision of his personal fragmentation that permitted self-conversation and dialogue.

Riley and Eugene V. Debs were very friendly in the days when Riley was employed at the "Indianapolis Journal" and Debs was Terre Haute's elected city clerk, state legislator and union organizer. In 1880 Debs arranged three Riley appearances in Terre Haute sponsored by the Occidental Literary club. Often Debs would close an issue of his union's (then called a "Brotherhood") magazine, BLF MAGAZINE with a Riley poem, including one called "Terry Hut," in which Riley describes Debs as a man "as warm a heart that ever beat Betwixt here and the Mercy Seat." This was many years before Debs was incarcerated during the Pullman labor strike, ran for President on socialist tickets or became a cause celebre by being incarcerated for ten years upon conviction under the American "Espionage Act" in 1918 for speaking in Canton, Ohio about the relationship between capitalism and the First World War, the uneven burden of the war on workers, and the injustice of the government's loyalty program.

Riley knew Debs as an active Terre Haute citizen rather than a labor unionist, a radical and a militant fighter against the social order of his time. He was a kindly soul, had a heart of gold, and he appeared to Riley mysteriously. Riley never thought of him as a politician although Debs was a Socialist candidate for President of the United States several times, but he did admire the character and loved the man. Riley's poem "Regardin' Terry Hut," is about Debs. In fact it is "Debs." Riley exercises his kenotic discernment to describe how Debs can live in Terre Haute, Indiana feeling the way he does about an American society which does not credit its conscience with concern for the worker, the poor and the socialist agenda for the vulnerable.

He says no town
"beats old Terry Hut!"
"It's more'n likely you'll insist
I claim this 'cause I'm predjudist,

Bein' born'd here in old Vygo
In sight o'Terry Hut; but no,
Yer clean dead wrong! - and I maintain
They's nary drap in ary vein
O'mine but what's as free as air
To jes' take issue with you there! -
`Cause, boy and man, fer forty year,
I've argied ag'inst livin' here..."

Eugene Debs in 1897.

Much has been said of Riley's friendship with Debs but not a great deal of effort, excepting mutual admiration, was expended on maintaining the early warm friendship in latter years when the two took divergent paths. Riley supported his friend when he was incarcerated as a result of the Pullman strike and no doubt would have stood by him during his incarceration from a conviction in the "red scare" period following Riley's death. I am not aware of a single instance in which Riley violated a bond of friendship formed during his own early vulnerable life. The press of fame caused him not to be able to cultivate many potential friendships or preserve earlier ones. Turning his back on a friend was not in Riley's nature.

Riley's friendship with Dr. Wycliffe Smith went back many years. It began when Riley delivered a lecture at Delphi. After the lecture, Riley walked the streets alone until he saw a stranger ahead and asked him for a match. It was Dr. Wycliffe Smith. "Come up to my office, but up the stairs," the doctor said. Turning into a dark stairway, he did so. Riley followed and the two men, Riley and "Doc" Smith, were soon getting acquainted. The poet sat in the doctor's office where the two talked over many worldly things and found each other's acquaintance worth cultivating. Many considered Dr. Smith to be gruff and plain-spoken, but he was every inch a man, and friend of the down-

Riley with his friend Dr. Wycliffe Smith of Delphi, Indiana. In the front is the boy nicknamed "Smallpox" Sneathen. He was the sole survivor of a family of smallpox victims treated by Dr. Smith who took the boy in and raised him. His given name was Joseph. Riley "escaped" from his life as a high profile author and lecturer by visiting Dr. SMith on many happy occasions in the mid-1880's.

trodden and poor. Dr. Smith suggested Riley "rest awhile" in Delphi and they would take trips into the country. The two, poet and physician, began a long friendship whereby the two rambled through Carroll county, usually on horseback. They became a familiar sight, both riding along in Prince Albert coats and plug hats. Dr. Smith rode his stallion, "Dexter," and Riley rode his mare, "Hanky Panky." Many of the poems of the Riley poetry volume called "Green Fields and Running Brooks" depict Carroll County and arose from Riley's jaunts with Dr. Smith.

One of Dr. Smith's memorable deeds was his effort to save a Delphi family from death by smallpox. He fought the battle alone, but was unable to do more than save one child, Joe Sneathon, whom he practically adopted. The boy became known as "Smallpox" Sneathen. A famous picture of the boy with Riley and Dr. Smith was taken by the two on a lark.

While riding with Dr. Smith, the poet met a Deutschman named Herr Weiser and wrote a poem commemorating him on August 18, 1884. The two were often visiting the fascinating man, an old gunsmith, on his thickly wooded farm.

HERR WEISER (1884)

Herr Weiser! - Threescore years and ten, -
A hale white rose of his countrymen,
Transplanted here in the Hoosier loam,
And blossomy as his German home -
As blossomy and as pure and sweet
As the cool green glen of his calm retreat,
Far withdrawn from the noisy town
Where trade goes clamoring up and down,
Whose fret and fever, and stress and strife,
May not trouble his tranquil life!

Breath of rest, what a balmy gust! -
Quit of the city's heat and dust,
Jostling down by the winding road,
Through the orchard ways of his quaint abode. -
Tether the horse, as we onward fare
Under the pear trees trailing there,
And thumping the wooden bridge at night

With lumps of ripeness and lush delight,
Till the stream, as it maunders on till dawn,
Is powdered and pelted and smiled upon.
Herr Weiser, with his wholesome face,
And the gentle blue of his eyes, and grace
of unassuming honesty,
Be there to welcome you and me!
And what though the toil of the farm be stopped
And the tireless plans of the place be dropped,
While the prayerful master's knees are set
In beds of pansy and mignonette
And lily and aster and columbine,
Offered in love, as yours and mine? -
What, but a blessing of kindly thought,
Sweet as the breath of forget-me-not! -
What, but a spirit of lustrous love
White as the aster he bends above! -
What, but an odorous memory
Of the dear old man, made known to me
In days demanding a help like his, -
As sweet as the life of the lily is -
As sweet as the soul of a babe, bloom-wise
Born of a lily in Paradise.

At Delphi, Riley often was seen at the home of Mrs. Elizabeth Fisher Murphy. She was a grand person who adopted three daughters and lived to be 92. She and Riley were said to be lovers.

Dr. Smith one time persuaded Riley and Bill Nye to come to the small town of Delphi. Riley cancelled other engagements to accommodate the request of his friend. When they arrived in town, they were surprised to find Doc Smith had plastered the town with huge yellow posters saying his friend was going to be at the opera house that night. The evening was one of the more memorable ones in Delphi history. Riley introduced Nye as follows: "This entertainment, is composed of a poet and a lyre. I am the poet." With a nod at Nye, the entertainment began.

Riley came to adopt Delphi as a second home. When Walter Whistler, a Carroll county youth who was with the Greeley expedition to the North Pole, died and was returned to Delphi for burial, Riley went "home" to

Delphi for the funeral. In the meantime, Dr. Smith was hired by the family to perform an autopsy. Without food, the polar exploration party reportedly agreed to cannibalism to survive on the basis of the drawing of lots. When a name was drawn, the party would use that person's body for food. The grandparents had heard this rumor and wondered if their grandson's name had been drawn. Dr. Smith performed the autopsy and upon opening the metallic casket found unmistakable evidence that the boy had in fact been the victim of cannibalism.

The friendship of Dr. Smith and Riley lasted until the doctor got killed at a roadway intersection with the Wabash railroad, west of Delphi. A train struck his buggy which he was sharing with a little Filipino boy, Francisco Sousa, who Dr. Smith brought home with him from the Spanish-American war. Riley was so touched by the death of his physician friend that he wrote a tribute to him, "The Noblest Service." In the poem, Riley lauded him saying, "universal good he dreamed and wrought..."

Two of Riley's friends in Lafayette were Evaleen Stein, a poet and artist fourteen years his junior, and her brother, Orth Stein. Some have linked Riley romantically with Ms. Stein. He not only wrote her but also attended a literary banquet in her honor at Purdue in 1907. Riley perhaps met her at one of his two stage appearances at Lafayette or when he performed at the opening of a rollerskating rink there in 1885. The connection with Ms. Stein's brother Orth Stein is less clear. Orth Stein was a brilliant illustrator and writer of fiction. Unfortunately he was also a white collar criminal leaving a trail of bad checks and confidence games from Baltimore to San Jose. He had also shot and killed a man in a fight over a woman in Kansas City in 1882. How Riley and the roving Orth Stein were in contact no one knows but when Orth Stein died of consumption in 1901 at a New Orleans hotel, an autographed book of Riley poems lay at his bedside. It was "Poems Here at Home" and Riley's written inscription bears a hauntingly beautiful and mysterious message intended to be personal and special:

And the sense caught through the music
Twinkles of dabbling feet;
And glimpses of faces in covert green
And voices faint and sweet;

And back from the lands enchanted
When my earliest mirth was born,

The trill of a laught was blown to me,
Like the blare of an elfin horn.

There is a novel of pleasant reading by Meredith Nicholson called THE
POET published in 1914. The poet of the book is clearly a representation of
James Whitcomb Riley, the friend of the author. The novel opens with a
child, Marjorie, in dejected play. The poet sees her and says, "The lonesomeness of that little girl over there is becoming painful...I can't make out
whether she's too dressed up to play or whether it's only shyness." The
child's father, Miles, turns out to be a securities dealer who the poet knew
earlier in his life as an aspiring artist. The father gave up art to become
wealthy in business. This broke up his family. His wife, Marian, the mother
of Marjorie, left him because she could not stand the fanatical "money-grub-
ber" that he had become. Marjorie, the child, was withdrawn. Her nurse
commented to the poet, "She's always like that...and you can't do anything
with her."

Maybe most people would not even bother. But Nicholson's "poet" is not
an ordinary man. He orchestrates visits to the father, Miles, and mother,
Marian, and forces each to recall their obligation to the child. Marian presses on with divorce proceedings. Fate intervenes when a securities issue
Miles is involved in is found to be fraudulent. Though Miles makes good all
losses, he is broken financially. When his pursuit of money fails, he finds
the strength to seek a return to his former happier life as an artist with his
reunited family, his wife, Marian, and his child. The poet has been the kind
counselor, reconciler and sound adviser about life and morality throughout
the alienating period of their lives.

The "friend in deed" is really the true life picture of James Whitcomb
Riley as one sees him in the eyes of his friends. This was the caliber of the
man as his friends perceived him. Nicholson knew this "helper" Riley from
experience. Nicholson was having little luck getting his first work recognized when Riley, already established in 1890, wrote the editor, Charles
Warren Stoddard this praise of Nicholson: "By this time you doubtless have
his first book of verse, wherein he says such things as though God some new
hymn had writ and whispered it from star to star."

George Ade, a Hoosier humorist and dialectician, spoke at a Memorial
Services for Riley at the Indiana Society of Chicago, October 29, 1916.

RILEY'S STYLE OF FRIENDSHIP

"Riley shrank from idle and promiscuous friendships. He selected for his confidences those who met him fairly and acknowledged the brotherhood without protesting the same. He made his own ratings and never consulted the social register. He loved to sit into the night talking with Benjamin Harrison, a former President and his great friend. Also he was given to long and intimate confabulations with a negro barber who showed a devouring interest in the stories brought to him by Riley. These stories concerned a certain Frank who lived at Fortville, Indiana; also his wife, Minnie, a most courageous and resourceful character. Frank and Minnie were of the adventurous sort; taking many railway journeys, adopting unusual trades and professions and overcoming all sorts of adverse circumstances. Of course, they had no existence except in the bubbling imagination of Riley but he continued the fascinating serial year after year. An author's best reward is one good listener and Riley gave reams of manuscript to the spell-bound colored brother. Just three days before he died, Riley sat in the barber chair and told how Frank had gone to the Mexican border with one of the Indian regiments and was in charge of the cook tent and having his own troubles with tarantulas and bandits. Think of a man sixty-seven years old delightedly weaving these make-believe yarns, just for the satisfaction of pleasing an humble audience. That was Riley.

But how he could get under cover and stay under cover when his canny instinct told him that some one was trying to exploit him or exhibit him. He was the best platform entertainer of his time, always idolized by the public and yet he dreaded these public appearances and always suspected that he was about to fail and disappoint his audience. Once I heard him say "Every morning when I wake up the first thought that comes to me is, `This is the day they get on to me.'"

He was the best story-teller I ever heard because his character impersonations were vivid and accurate and convincing beyond all belief. Henry Irving (a famous contemporary English actor) was right when he said that Riley would have been one of the few truly great character actors of the English speaking stage. Take his well-known verses, "Good bye, Jim, take keer of yourself." I have heard them recited by Sol Smith Russell, Maurice Barrymore and David Warfield (the most noted contemporaneous American actors) and they put into their renditions the skill of the trained reader - every trick of the actor's trade and each gave to the reading the strength and warmth of a genuine personality, but after you heard Riley recite those won-

Riley at the famous Fairbanks "Tea Party." It is well known that alcohol did not sit well with President Theodore Roosevelt. When Rossevelt came to Indianapolis on May 30, 1907, his Hoosier Vice-President, Charles Fairbanks hosted a lawn party at his mansion unaware that his household employee found the punch had no alcohol in it and had gone to the Columbia Club and returned to "spike it." Roosevelt was furious. When the press learned of this, Fairbanks was dubbed "Cocktail Charlie," and it is said failed to win renomination the following year as a result. The irony was that Fairbanks was a strict prohibitionist. Seated guests are (L-R): Mrs. John N. Carey, Dr. Mary A. Spink, James Whitcomb Riley, Sen. Albert J. Beveridge, Gov. J. Frank Hanly, Vice-Pres. Charles W. Fairbanks, President Theodore Roosevelt, Cornelia Cole Fairbanks, James A. Hemingway, Rear Admiral George Brown. Standing fifth from the left is Meredith Nicholson.

derful verses which reveal the real Hoosier - saturated with sentiment but ashamed to be sentimental - and you felt the lump coming into your throat and your eyes began to blink, you knew that our friend had gifts and graces which I really believe were not given to nay other man of his generation."

Riley loved to visit George Ade at his home, "Hazelden" at Brook in Newton County. During those visits Riley most enjoyed napping to rest and meditating in the shade of a giant hickory tree there. It is said when the old hickory tree finally died and had to be removed Riley stopped visiting saying the place wasn't the same home without its meditating tree.

In his very last years, and particularly after his 1910 stroke, Riley spent much time re-visiting the places in his life where he had known love and friendship of former days. His automobile, a "Peerless" gave him this opportunity. He took daily rides in this automobile which he purchased in 1911 and most often when his chauffeur would ask him the question, "Where do you want to go?" Riley answered, "Let's go to Greenfield."

As your biographer completes this short recount of Riley's life as Amphine, the starkness of it strikes me to the core. Where is there justice in the facts? Where is there equity in life? Was it necessary that Riley should truly find comfort only with a woman already married? Is there justification in his later love of so many in affectionate regard and expression? We sim-

ply have no answer except to recall that love and justice concepts are baf-
flingly conflicting always.

RILEY WITH OTHER SPIRITS

Nellie Cooley (Dwainie) and Elizabeth Riley (AEo) were not the only
two "dead souls" with whom Riley lived and communicated. There were
many stories of others. Riley was firmly commited to the belief in ministra-
tions from the spirit world.

One story had to do with Robert Louis Stevenson, Riley's friend and fellow author. When Stevenson died, the publisher of his books wrote Riley
and asked him to prepare an appreciation. Riley readily complied. In a few
days a very liberal check came in the mail from the publisher. Riley returned
it saying he could not possibly accept a check for paying a tribute to so dear
a friend. The the publishers wrote back that they would like to send Riley
Stevenson's books in appreciation. Riley wrote back to accept the gesture
providing the books were of a modest binding. But the books never came.
Riley wondered and wondered what had happened to them. Then on his
birthday, they arrived. Bright and early on that morning an expressman
came whistling up the walk and delivered them. Riley commented to many
people that he was sure his friend had had the delivery delayed until his
birthday to give the gift special meaning.

Another dead friend who intervened in Riley's life was fellow author and
reader Eugene Fields. Riley had written a memorial poem about Fields when
he died. A joint friend, the opera singer Francis Wilson, sent Riley a book
of Fields's poems and asked Riley if he would inscribe his memorial poem
to Fields inside and return it to his hotel in Cincinnati. Riley did so. Then the
book was lost. The opera singer wrote Riley if it was recovered to send it to
another address but of course Riley could not do so. About a year later, the
opera singer was in Chicago and went into a bookstore that Riley was not
aware of. The bookstore manager recognized Wilson and said he had a pack-
age for him. It was the Fields poetry inscribed by Riley. When Riley was
informed of this he thought nothing of it. "Eugene Fields did that," he said.

Another member of his cast of "dead souls" who lived with Riley after
their deaths was his long time lyceum partner, Bill Nye. Every time Riley's
luggage was missing while Riley was traveling by train - which was almost
always- Riley would dismiss it as Bill Nye pulling another trick on him.
Friends from the other world helped Riley avoid loneliness and despair.

CRESTILLOMEEM

DRUNKENNESS AND DELIRIUM TREMENS AS A LADY TRYING TO RUIN RILEY'S LIFE

CRESTILLOMEEM
DRUNKENNESS AND DELIRIUM TREMENS AS A LADY
TRYING TO RUIN RILEY'S LIFE

In the Preface we first met Crestillomeem.[1] She is the naggy depression and drunkenness that threatens Riley. She is Riley's "Queen." She has taken charge of him in his late 20's when "The Flying Islands Of the Night" was written. Riley calls her his "Second Consort" in the later "book" editions of the poem. His first and foremost "Consort" was his beloved "soul-mate" Nellie who died shortly before the poem was first composed.

1. We remember her name is an elision of "crestfallen" (dejected), "ill" and "me" backwards and forwards.

Crestillomeem is the Riley who goes crazy about life sometimes and becomes a binge drinker before pulling himself out. She is also the scary tremens and torporous deliriums of alcoholism. These are, of course, the vision of Riley's great autobiographical poem "The Flying Islands of the Night." Crewstillomeeem is the nasty Queen of Riley's life trying to destroy its meaning and hope for success.

Riley in the clutches of "Crestillomeem." A court record of a Riley arrest and conviction of public intoxication in Greenfield, Indiana, the poet's hometown, on Dec. 27, 1877, within the few months prior to writing "The Flying Islands of the Night."

Crestillomeem is one of Riley's "Flying islands." Flying Islands are Riley's lives in the poem. They are not a singular island. Riley, with great insight, knew himself as an archipelago afloat in "red eye" whiskey at the time of the writing of "The Flying Islands of the Night." All of the islands make up Riley's conception of his own life as a man in great alienation acting through life as a cast of players. Riley was a great enough actor to get by with this. He simply was not a single "himself."

Islands are lonely images. They are by themselves and don't have "connections." Riley must have felt so very, very lonely at times to take upon himself this representation of himself in his imagination. I suspect this loneliness was the cause for becoming Crestillomeem at times. Most often, Riley retreated to Greenfield when he fell under Crestillomeem's spell and "waited her out" among friends and family.

We see Riley using this depressed and sometimes drunken aspect of himself most often in his John C. Walker poems which we will discuss later in this book. For now, we might want to get a taste of how this persona wrote poetry:

JOHN GOLLIHER'S THIRD WOMERN [1] (1879)
(From the Kokomo Saturday *TRIBUNE* of Dec. 27, 1879)

I'm a-talkin' - not adzac'ly in the old-maid kindo way
O' sayin' things onpleasant `cause there're plenty sich to
say: -
`Ner cause I am a womern `ats tuck sich manly part
In Tempernce institutions as to spile her womern's heart:-

But I `low `at married people, as a rule, all has their sheer
O' troubles and vexations. - Yet theyr're one example here
`At some folks find confusin' - seein's how they used to say
John Golliher's third womern wouldn't be alive today!

You see, John's ben a drinker - jest a SOAKER thue and thue!-
As his daddy was afore him, and his old grandaddy, too! -
W'y, the Golliher's, I reckon, ef you'd stand `em in a row,
Would make a string o' drunkards clean from here to Jericho.

John was drunk at his first weddin', But his wife had made her brags

She'd have him, drunk or sober, ef she had to dress in rags,-
And thems the kind o' clothin' she dome to `fore she died,
And laid `em down forever, thanking God, and saisfied.

John's sobered up a little after that; and found a place
For the little girl still left him - like her mother in the face;
And fer-well, a year and better, he kep' straight enough, I guess
Til he met a widder womern `at upset him more or less.

He was warned agin the womern -she was warned agin the man,-
And ef that won't make a weddin', w'y there're nothin' else `at can!
And when THAT couple married, they was some `at even bet
The widder would out-last him, but - John's a-livin yet!

Things was might bad, I tell you, at that funeral o'hern!-
No serous indications o' very deep concern-
Except the tears `at Mary his grow'd-up dorter shed
Fer the crazy wretch with tremans howlin' there beside the dead!

W'y the preachers worked their sermints out o' that!- and women wrung
Their empty hands in meetin! and shouted, cried and sung:
And little sleepy childern was shuck awake to pray,
With "Golliher'll git ye fer neglectin' that-away!"

They was no one else to `tend him, so I staid there -more on
Account of Mary's feelin's than fur any keer o' John, -
Fer that fust thing, when he rallied so's he knowed me, I- says- I-
"I'm mighty feered the chances is you aint a-goin' to die!"

O I said it! and I meant it! and was jest a stoopin' down
To bathe the feller's forred when he whispered, with a frown,-
"Don't, then! I'll DIE - A DRUNKARD! and the womern who can say
As mean a thing as that is, ortn't tetch him! GO AWAY!"

It was afterwards `at Mary told me she was peekin' thue
The kitchen-door, and saw me, knelln'- like I used to do
In public meetins' - on'y, the prayer, she said was more
Full o' lovin' stren'th `an any `at she'd ever heerd afore.-

And, railly, I reckon the girl's opinion was
About as nigh pefection as they git `em now - because,
Her father he forgive me- quit his drinkin'- and is- Well,
John Golliher's third womern ain't got nuthin' else to tell.

1. This poem parenthetically points out the difficult life of women in Riley's day. Life was literally a woman-killer. A man might marry the first time for love, resulting in several children. To bring up the children, he might marryseveral more times "for convenience." Riley describes housework of women in "My First Womern:"

"Fer I'm allus thinkin' - thinkin' Of the first one's peaceful ways.
A bilin' soap and singin' of the Lord's amazin' grace.
-And I'm thinkin' of her constant, Dyin' carpet-chain and stuff
And a makin' up rag carpets,
When the floor was GOOD ENOUGH!
And I'm allus thinkin' of her reddin' up around the house;
Er cookin fer the farm hands; er drivin' up the cows.
- And there she lays out yander By the lower medder fence.
W'y they ain't no sadder thing
Than to think of my first womern, and her funeral last spring."

Crestillomeem's spell on Riley really wasn't so humerous as John C. Walker portrayed. She brought about Riley's depression or was at least a product of it. But she is also a uniquely important person in the life of James Whitcomb Riley because she impels him through dialogue to see her as a consequence to him if he does not pursue the only other goal for his life that James Whitcomb Riley could imagine more powerful - the lust for fame (another figure in Riley's imaginative self-life who Riley thinks of as an equally clearly defined "flying island" named Krung. We shall meet Krung later on in this book. The happy result of it all was, however, to allow Spraivoll, yet another character, to sing poetically. This conforms to the common description of alcohol as "the great exciter of the Yes function in people."

It was about himself as the sinful persona dominated by his alcoholic Crestillomeem that Riley's 1878 poem, "The Flying Islands of the Night," was written in the turmoil of one of his greatest periods of intoxication and tremens and possible concern over impotency.

In the "Flying Islands of the Night," Riley knows that Crestillomeem, his alcoholism, is constantly beckoning him. She seeks to destroy him and even seek his death. Crestillomeem demands Riley toe her line and meet her demands. She invites him to imprison himself in the tower of servitude to alcoholism and its fantasies. We read:

> *"The Queen (Crestillomeem)*
> *Impatiently awaits his Majesty*
> *And craves his presence in the Tower of Stars,*
> *That she may there express full tenderly*
> *Her great solicitude."*

In alcoholics' confessional genre literature the curse of alcohol manifest in a person, here Crestillomeem in James Whitcomb Riley, always leads to self-destructive behavior. As the great temperance mediator Luther Benson states in Fifteen Years in Hell, "(to go out on an alcoholic spree) "is to quench the light of ambition, to crush hope, entomb joy, lay waste the powers of the mind, neglect duty, desert the family and commit in the end suicide."

In the poem, "The Flying Islands of the Night," Riley is able to cast her off. In reality Riley never was able to fully subdue his alcoholism. Riley's capacity to physically love was probably affected by Crestillomeem. One suspects that impotence was her legacy, possibly manifest about the time he began writing "The Flying Islands of the Night" and after the death of Nellie Cooley, the only woman Riley had loved as a soul-mate.

The Crestillomeem character of Riley's fragmented life is "roughly" referenced in verse in James Whitcomb Riley's poem "Luther Benson" contemporaneously written with "Flying Islands" as the poem's subtitle says, "After reading his autobiography." The poem describes alcoholism as the "vulture curse, That hovers o'er the universe, With ready talons quick to strike In every human heart alike." Benson's autobiography, Fifteen Years in Hell, like Riley's play/poem, marks how Benson was wasted in alcohol addiction, reformed,and went on to "lecture" extensively throughout Indiana and the nation as a temperance speaker. The parallel to the movement of the acts of "Flying Islands" is pronounced as is the eventual progress of Riley's own life...although Riley's"cause" was not temperance but the spread of humanistic and "kenotic" themes. His dependency makes of his dissolute and alcoholic nature the relationship of something wedded to him as a queenly wife as well as curse. Possibly "Flying Islands" was originally intended as an extensive farcical account of the life of Benson, based on Benson's autobiography, in the nature of Riley's comical imitation of Benson on the platform called "Benson Out-Bensoned" but if so Riley's realization that the alcoholic addiction was similar to his own probably changed the story line and the play\poem into Riley's own autobiography. Benson does not seem to be remembered much these days, but his book *Fifteen Years in Hell* describing his alcoholic years was a national best-seller in the 1880's.

A major event in Riley's life must have been his first encounter with tremens from his alcoholism. This was the most dispiriting aspect of play with himself as Crestillomeem. I am informed that such tremens come only to one of lengthy and alcoholic lifestyle.

Riley admits his writing is "under the influence" in his Sixth and Final episode of the Buzz Club Papers in which series "The Flying Islands of the Night" appears. When writing "The Flying Islands" the author was stated to be under the "baleful influence of intoxicants...driving reason from her Throne." The work is the product of "old crime."

Riley was, of course, notorious for using pseudonymous names for his writings. The ostensible writer of the original "The Flying Islands of the Night" is Mr. Clickwad, a member of the "Buzz Club" whose poetry is deliberately questioned in the very first of the "Respectfully Declined" Papers of the Buzz Club. Another member asks: "The gentleman who has just favored us," said Mr. Plempton, "is a weird cuss, but if he'll pardon my curiosity I should like to inquire if he was ever troubled with the tremens?" The answer is obvious. "The Flying Islands of the Night," appearing in the fourth installment of the "Respectfully Declined" series, is introduced as Mr. Clickwad's work.

Riley knows of the tremens. He experienced them. He also wrote of them in such prose accounts as "Jamesy" where he refers to them as "jim jams." At one point in that short narrative appears the following colloquy which might relate to one of James Whitcomb Riley's own experiences:

"Liable to what?" said I
"Liable to jist keel over - wink out, you know - cos he
has fits, kindo jim jams, I guess. Had a fearful old matinee
with him last night! You see he comes all sorts o' games on
me, and I have to put up for him - cos he's got to have
whisky, and if we can on'y keep him about so full he's a
regular lamb, but he don't stand no monkeyin' when he wants
whisky, now you bet!.."

Riley must have felt enraged because intoxication was not supposed to have such a down side! As Riley's teenaged years dawned alcohol use was only beginning to questioned. When Riley was 11, a newspaper article published in the Hancock DEMOCRAT of July 3, 1861 stated, "It was at one time generally believed that the use of alcoholic liquors was positively necessary and beneficial to all men...Physicians recommended such beverages and regular daily rations of rum were provided in all armies and navies. These notions are still entertained by many persons, and very generally there is a want of correct information on the subject. It is very common for soldiers of all classes to indulge in the use of alcoholic beverages...By close observation and many experiments, it has been found that the tissues and the blood of drunkards, as well as those who continually tipple in beer and whisky, but do not get drunk, are generally in a state of degeneration. Alcohol passes into the blood and retards the elimination of waste and injurious matter from the body and thus tends to produce disease, especially fever..." The effects of alcohol were obviously unclear in Riley's time.

Eventually, Riley came to see his alcohol addiction to personify the activity of a person he called Crestillomeem and took her vision of himself as his own to see what it meant. This was done in "The Flying Islands of the Night." Crestillomeem never left Riley but came to become a pretty much subdued lady except for many private but also a few highly publicized incidents such as one recurrence in Louisville, Kentucky in February 1890 which caused the breakup of his stand-up comedy partnership with Edgar Nye.

Crestillomeem did not produce poetry. Riley wrote no poetry when he was in delirium. Crestillomeem did, however, provide the delirious subject matter of a small body of very important poetry to a biographer. She gave Riley "An Adjustable Lunatic" with its vision of a lover in another dimension whose ethereal connectedness is an otherwise mad man's only touch with reality.

FANTASY (1878)
(FROM "AN ADJUSTABLE LUNATIC")

(a poem written by a fictional author in a Riley sketch, a man who subsequently committed suicide within the story line and who described himself as "an adjustable lunatic" by profession. The sketch from which this poem derives portrays the writer of "Fantasy" as a penniless bachelor, the owner of a painting of a mysteriously enchanting woman in his room.
The poem reveals an impossible romantic attachment so real and yet so

imaginary that it severs the man from his senses. As a biographer, I find the story bears relation to Riley's relationship with his married friend, Nellie Cooley, so recently dead at the time of its writing.)

A Fantasy that came to me
   As wild and wantonly designed
As ever any dream might be
   Unraveled from a madman's mind, -
A tangle-work of tissue, wrought
   By cunning of the spider-brain,
   And woven, in an hour of pain,
To trap the giddy flies of thought -.

I stood beneath a summer moon
   All swollen to uncanny girth,
And hanging, like the sun at noon,
   Above the center of the earth;
   But with a sad and sallow light,
   As it had sickened of the night
And fallen in a pallid swoon.
Around me I could hear the rush
   Of sullen winds, and feel the whir
Of unseen wings apast me brush

A tavern of the 1880's.

   like phantoms round a sepulcher;
And, like a carpeting of plush,
   A lawn unrolled beneath my feet,
   Bespangled o'er with flowers as sweet
   To look upon as those that nod
   Within the garden-fields of God,
   But odorless as those that blow
   In ashes in the shades below.

And on my hearing fell a storm
   Of gusty music, sadder yet
   Than every whimper of regret
That sobbing utterance could form,
   And patched with scraps of sound that seemed
   Torn out of tunes that demons dreamed,

And pitched to such a piercing key,
It stabbed the ear with agony;
And when at last it lulled and died,
I stood aghast and terrified.
I shuddered and I shut my eyes
    And still could see, and feel aware
    Some mystic presence waited there;
And staring, with a dazed surprise,
    I saw a creature so divine
    That never subtle thought of mine
    May reproduce to inner sight
    So fair a vision of delight.

A syllable of dew that drips
From out a lily's laughing lips
Could not be sweeter than the word
I listened to, yet never heard. -
For, oh, the woman hiding there
Within the shadows of her hair,
Spake to me in an undertone
So delicate, my soul alone
But understood it as a moan
Of some weak melody of wind
A heavenward breeze had left behind.

A tracery of trees, grotesque
    Against the sky, behind her seem
Like shapeless shapes of arabesque
    Wrought in an oriental screen;
And tall, austere and statuesque
    She loomed before it - e'en as though
    The spirit-hand of Angelo
    Had chiseled her to life complete,
    With chips of moonshine round her feet.
And I grew jealous of the dusk,
    To see it softly touch her face,
    As lover-like, with fond embrace
It folded round her like a husk:

A brewery ad which commonly was hung on tavern
walls in Riley's epoch.

But when the glitter of her hand
  Like wasted glory, beckoned me,
  My eyes grew blurred and dull and dim -
  My vision failed - I could not see -
I could not stir - I could but stand,
  Till, quivering in every limb,
  I flung me prone, as though to swim
  The tide of grass whose waves of green
  Went rolling ocean-wide between
  My helpless shipwrecked heart and her
  Who claimed me for a worshiper.

And writhing thus in my despair,
  I heard a weird, unearthly sound,
  That seemed to lift me from the ground
  And hold me floating in the air.
  I looked, and lo! I saw her bow
  Above a harp within her hands;
A crown of blossoms bound her brow,
  And on her harp were twisted strand
Of silken starlight, rippling o'er
With music never heard before
By mortal ears; and, at the strain,
I felt my Spirit snap its chain
And break away, - and I could see
It as it turned and fled from me
To greet its mistress, where she smiled
To see the phantom dancing wild
And wizard-like before the spell
Her mystic fingers knew so well.

A cartoon of Riley's era.

What is it? Who will rightly guess
If it be aught but nothingness
That dribbles from a wayward pen
To spatter in the eyes of men?
What matter! I will call it mine,
  And I will take the changeling home
And bathe its face with morning-shine,

And comb it with a golden comb
Till every tangled tress of rhyme
Will fairer be than summer-time;
And I will nurse it on my knee
And dandle it beyond the clasp
Of hands that grip and hands that grasp
Through life and all eternity!

Something like this vision became Act II of Riley's great delirious, auto-biographical play\poem "The Flying Islands of the Night." The other subject matter is in such poetry as "Quitting California." The poem is not, of course, about the State of California at all, but rather about a brand name of whiskey. While one is led by the poem to believe that the poem's writer is becoming temperate and giving up alcohol, the poem playfully concludes that the writer is merely changing to another brand of cheap whiskey and not giving up whiskey at all.

Crestillomeem's friends.

ON QUITTING CALIFORNIA (1879)

O rare old drink, the oldest, strongest far
  Of which the house can boast,
Whose guardian, smiling, betteth at the bar
  On who can drink the most -

How art thou conquered - tamed in all the pride
  Of average beauty still!
How brought, O painter of the human hide,
  To know thy master's will!

No more the shallow goblet is baptized
  Until it overflows;
No more thy liquid blushes are capsized,
  And succored by the nose.

For now the wild oats thou hast helped to till
  In pain are harvested,
And, as the boss presents his little bill,
  The gleaner droops his head.

Yet at thy shrine shall thousands kneel again
  Beneath thy mystic spell;
O mother-in-law of great and mighty men,
  Thou do'st thy mission well!

Thy newer children shall restore the right
  I force you to resign
And future years yield up an appetite,
  Perchance as wild as mine.

Though order, justice, social law shall scowl
  On all the works reveal,
And art and science shake their heads and howl
  With unabated zeal,

The marble, shaken from its glassy sheath,

Shall twirl and palpitate
For those of fiery eye and potent breath
Who take their whisky straight.

The cornless cob shall drain its warmest blood -
The still its blackest lees,
And all transfusive percolations flood
Thy swollen arteries,

Till "Tremens," as he hides himself away
Within thy depths, shall wink
As victims pour him down from day to day
At fifteen cents a drink.

When Mr. Clickwad is finished his friends congratulate him at least on agreeing to quit alcohol. Mr. Clickwad denies this intent and admits that he is only quitting the one brand indicated. He remains an unrepentant alcoholic which is his nature.

While the poetry of Crestillomeem is small in volume, Riley considered it his personal record of the hell of his life and treasured it inordinately. One finds his poem "The Flying Islands of the Night" being published again and again from 1878 to the end of his life. None of the printings was popular. Most contained changes as Riley considered and reconsidered its autobiographical cryptic subject matter. The poem came to have a strange life of its own because of its beautiful lyrics and of course authorship by the famous James Whitcomb Riley.

Riley simply hid himself in this poem. No one except possibly his alcoholic brother Hum (who died three years after "The Flying Islands of the Night's" composition) and friend, Dr. Frank Hays, knew the poem was a delirium.

Why?

Among the reasons why Crestillomeem was not a visible presence was Riley's later popularity and commercial posture. But another reason was that Crestillomeem lurked within his soul. Riley couldn't account for this himself. His vision of life included a simple belief that ultimately life was inexplicable. When his father died, Riley had engraved on the Riley family marker in the little Greenfield cemetery where he was buried, "God is his own interpreter and will someday make things clear." Riley's alcoholism like his father's death was a part of life that God alone understood. Nevertheless there was an expectation that it fit in with some greater plan.

Crestillomeem was Riley in his uneasiness about his alcoholism. Benjamin Franklin, in his autobiography, declared uneasiness was the central human motive. Riley was constantly in a state of uncertainty about himself. His incentive to survive despite his alcoholism required great mental work, emotionality and activity. After a person's biological needs are satisfied, time and energy are next spent in a narrow space of mind bounded on the right by boredom and ordinarily on the left by terror of the bizarre. Riley often lived in this region of the bizarre and actually knew it as a comfort. He often lived in the nurture of Crestillomeem. Others have commented that Riley's "weakness" was even beneficial. Rev. Finley Sapp, minister of a Greenfield Protestant Church from 1904-1906 and knew Riley, has written: "James Whitcomb Riley touched the heart of humanity as only a few have. "Jim" was really more "'ligious" when "lit up" a little, than most of the saints at camp meeting." (From page 54, A HISTORY OF THE GREENFIELD CHRISTIAN CHURCH, Dorothy June Williams).

So who is Crestillomeem? She is the one whose life is explained in The Flying Islands as an entourage of faces. She is the soul breaking apart in Riley's "Poem of Seven Faces." In tremens deliriums, Riley encounters faces swarming around him telling him all about Crestillomeem.

CRESTILLOMEEM'S
STORY IN A CHORUS OF SWARMING FACES

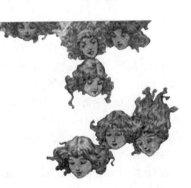

First Face

And who hath known her - like as I
Have known her? - since the envying sky
Filched from her cheeks its morning hue,
And from her eyes its glory, too,
Of dazzling shine and diamond-dew.

Second Face

I knew her - long and long before
High AEo[1] loosed her palm and thought:
"What awful splendor have I wrought

To dazzle earth and Heaven, too!"

1. AEo is Elizabeth, Riley's mother, who died when he was twenty. The E is her initial surrounded by the alpha and omega representing the scope of Riley's affection for her from beginning of life to end. Riley idolized his mother causing deep agony upon her death and Riley's initial need for consolation and escape in alcoholism.

Third Face

I knew her - long ere Night [2] was o'er -
Ere, AEo yet conjectured what
To fashion Day of - ay, before
He sprinkled stars across the floor
Of dark, and swept that form of mine
E'en as a fleck of blinded shine,
Back to the black were light was not.

2. Night is related to the past in the alcoholics confessional genre of literature such as "The Flying Islands of the Night." SEE: Benson, Fifteen Years in Hell, (night as a black, unlighted past).

Fourth face

Ere day was dreamt, I saw her face
Lift from some starry hiding-place
Where our old moon was kneeling while
She lit its features with her smile.

Fifth Face

I knew her while these islands [3] yet,
Were nestlings - ere they feathered wing,
Or e'en could gape with them or get
Apoise the laziest-ambling breeze;
Or cheep, chirp our, or anything!
When time crooned rhymes of nurseries
Above them - nodded, dozed and slept,
And knew it not, till, wakening.
The morning stars agreed to sing
And Heaven's first tender dews were wept.

3. Riley's fractured lives are the "flying" islands, disassociated "play/cast" entities, of the poem.

Sixth Face

I knew her when the jealous hands
Of Angels set her sculptured form
Upon a pedestal of storm
And let her to this land with strands
Of twisted lightnings.

Seventh Face

   And I heard
Her voice ere she could tone a word
Of any but the Seraph-tongue. -
And O sad-sweeter than all sung -
Or word-said things! - to hear her say,
Between the tears she dashed away: -
"Lo, launched from the offended sight
Of AEo! - anguish infinite
Is ours, O Sisterhood of Sin!
Yet is thy service mine by right,
And, sweet as I may rule it, thus
   Shall Sin's myrrh-savor taste to us -
   Sin's empress - let my reign begin![4]*"*

4. After his mother's death and then Nellie's death, Riley fell to pieces and launched a life of abandonment to alcoholism supported by meager casual employments.

RILEY'S FOUR GREAT ENCOUNTERS
WITH CRESTILLOMEEM

There were four great encounters Riley had with Crestillomeem. Each led to a new era in Riley's life and the crises were closer together in years in his 20's than later on. Each proved devastating and led to great life changes for the sensitive poet. The first occurred as Riley was faced with the death of his mother on Aug. 9, 1870 when Elizabeth Riley died of heart disease. Riley floundered after this and eventually took to the road with a traveling miracle medicine show of Doc McCrillus.

After returning to his home to settle down, a second event occurred when he was in his 20's which thoroughly unsettled him. This was a "black lynching" by a band of masked Hancock County men who broke into the Greenfield jail to drag a presumably innocent black man out for his date with a rope at the local fairgrounds. Riley again left his hometown for a second trip with a traveling medicine show, this time the one of Doc Townsend.

Again returning to Greenfield after a time, he learned of the death of his soul-mate he most loved, Nellie Cooley, and after writing her obituary and burying her back in Greenfield, he again entered into a period of great despondency resulting in his eventual move to Indianapolis to work for a newspaper there.

It was after this third great "depressing" circumstance that Riley wrote his autobiographical poem, "The Flying Islands of the Night."

By this time, Riley was brought in contact with kenotic teachers and was taking to the platform. His great Benjamin Johnson of Boone poems were written during a period of recovery.

The fourth great onset of depression culminated in 1890 when Riley could not take the strain of constant platform touring any longer and was found drunk and with the "shakes" in public. This ended Riley's lyceum circuit days as they had been. The event did however usher in a gentler time when Riley wrote most of his annual books and became "The Children's Poet." We will examine each of these periods of Riley's great bouts with Crestillomeem in turn before getting into his great poetry written as Spraivoll of the play/poem "The Flying Islands of the Night."

CRESTILLOMEEM'S FIRST GREAT ENCOUNTER
WITH RILEY AFTER THE DEATH OF HIS MOTHER

At what point in Riley's life he became severely depressed we do not know. His experience with alcohol tells us nothing about this. We remember Riley was from a Hoosier Deutsch family. The Hoosier Deutsch were very lenient in regard to alcohol use.

The Hoosier Deutsch were a very industrious farming people in central Indiana. Their farms, distinguished because their farm houses were often

Among the most prominent places of business in Riley's hometown were taverns. The most famous, the Gooding Tavern, located across the street from the Courthouse, was frequented not only by townspeople but by travelers such as former President Martin VanBuren and Presidential candidate Henry Clay.

built in the middle of their land rather than along the roads, were very prosperous. Nothing was wasted. Whiskey was made from their excess corn crops and all of their holidays and weddings involved great drinking of whiskey.

Deutsch-run taverns were in every locale where the Deutsch settled in Indiana and were places of common social and even family gathering. Whiskey was kept in homes and children were given it for medicinal reasons at the drop of a hat. Riley no doubt had tasted corn whiskey or "red eye" on many, many occasions as a child. In adolescence we hear of Riley's drunken times with friends.

Riley once admitted, "I've went more (miles) so's to come back by old Guthrie's still-house where minors got liquor providing we showed him that Old folks sent for it from home."

The occasions were social and the stories from these times are humorous. One night when John E. Davis, met "Uncle" Billy Davis (not related) and Riley, Davis got his nickname "Durbin." The three were "whooping" it up on Greenfield streets. They had just stopped in at a Deutsch tavern in Greenfield, the "Last Chance," but found it closed for the night. Riley led the three to another place to get a drink, a water pump that Riley sighted. According to Davis, "Riley grabbed hold of the pump handle, clapped me on the back and said, "I want you to meet Mr. Durbin. Now Mr. Durbin, I want the boys to have all they want. It's on the house, boys."" Davis continued, "We drank water and pumped and drank again. And ever since, they've called me after a kind of pump manufactured in those days known as the Durbin pump." Davis also mentioned another story. As a boy, Durbin said, Riley "always had a pocketful of poems even when we swam down on the Brandywine. I've seen him turn somersaults, recite a poem, and then jump clean over the muddy bank into the swimmin' hole. He knowed all of Charles Dickens' works by heart." As a boy, "Uncle" Davis said Riley wasn't much of a swimmer but preferred to loiter in the shade while the other swam. "We'd go in nat-

John Davis one of Riley's pals as a young man. His nickname was "Durbin." Friends called Riley and him the "49'ers" from the year of their birth.

ural and many's the time we'd tie each others clothes into knots and throw mud at each other. He used to make up poems down there and recite them to us while we swam around. There were some dandies all right. There's

The Riley family lot at Park Cemetery, Greenfield, Indiana as it appeared in 1997. The exact grave in which the poet's mother lies is unknown since there are no records of such things kept by the cemetery at the early date of Elizabeth's death. Riley's infant sister Celeste and brother Hum are buried to the left of the large Riley stone. Brother John and his wife Julia are buried immediately behind.

one of them I'll never forget. I only wish it could be printed."

After Riley quit school at 16, he apparently fooled around with alcohol. The casual attitude toward drinking by the young men of the time is revealed by a story contemporary with this period in Hancock County in which a young man riding home one night slightly "bour bonized" looked at the moon with great contempt and said, "You needn't be so proud, Madame Moon. You are full once a month and I every night."

In any case, Riley was familiar with alcohol use even before his first great encounter with Crestillomeem.

THE DEATH OF HIS MOTHER CAUSED RILEY'S
FIRST GREAT PERIOD OF INTOXICATION

The death of Riley's mother Elizabeth was publicly announced in the Hancock DEMOCRAT of Thursday morning, August 11, 1870 as follows:

SUDDEN DEATH

On Tuesday morning last our citizens were much astounded to hear that Mrs. Elizabeth Riley, wife of Capt. R.A. Riley, of this place, had died very suddenly and unexpectedly that morning, about half past seven o'clock, of heart disease. Some time during the latter part of the night, she felt unwell and got up from her bed without awaking any of the family. In a short time Capt. Riley was aroused by someone falling on the floor. He soon discovered that it was his wife who had fallen as if in a swoon. The alarm was given and the neighbors and physician sent for. No serious danger was at the time apprehended, but toward daylight she begun to grow worse and died as we have stated above. She was buried in the new cemetery on yesterday morning. A large

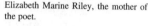

Elizabeth Marine Riley, the mother of the poet.

number of our citizens were present at the funeral services, conducted by Rev. J.W. Lacy, and all sympathized deeply with the bereaved family. We tender our condolence to our friend, Capt. Riley, and his bereaved and afflicted children. In the death of the one they loved so well, we can truthfully say that she was a kind and good woman and that is the best epitaph that can be written upon the tomb of a departed wife and mother.

Brother John wrote in his diary of that day, "What shall we do with Jim now that mother is dead?"

The answer was that nothing on this earth could console Riley except alcohol.

Riley was very "tied to his mother's apron strings."

Here is a little poem Riley wrote that shows his depth of affection for his mother remembered even in his older age.

A BOY'S MOTHER (1890)

My mother she's so good to me,
  Ef I was good as I could be,
I couldn't be as good - no, sir! -
  Can't any boy be good as her!

She loves me when I'm glad er sad;
  She loves me when I'm good er bad;
An', what's a funniest thing, she says
  She loves me when she punishes.

I don't like her to punish me, -
  That don't hurt, - but it hurts to see
Her cryin', - Nen I cry; an' nen
  We both cry an' be good again.

Flowers of dyed wool made into a wreath by Elizabeth Riley, the poet's mother on display at the Riley birthplace, Greenfield, Indiana.

She loves me when she cuts an' sews
  My little cloak an' Sund'y clothes;
An' when my Pa comes home to tea,
  She loves him most as much as me.

She laughs an' tells him all I said,
  An' grabs me up an' pats my head;
An' I hug her, an' hug my Pa
  An' love him purt' nigh as much as Ma.

Riley's secretary, Marcus Dickey, has recorded how Riley recollected his reaction to his mother's death. "The bereavement caused a complete change in his life. It sent him into the world to make his own living, and in numerous ways it was a forlorn road he had to travel. A few hours after her death he walked alone through a cornfield to a favorite retreat south of the railroad to an old clearing. "I was alone," he said, "till as in a vision I saw my mother smiling back upon me from the blue fields of love - when lo! she was young again. Suddenly I had the assurance that I would meet her somewhere in another world. I was gathering the fruit of what had been so happily impressed on me in childhood. I had seen that the world is a stage. Now I saw that the universe is a stage. Another curtain had been lifted. My mother was enraptured at the sight of new scenery. It was the dream of Heaven with which `Johnny Appleseed' had impressed my mother in the Mississinewa cabin."

James Whitcomb Riley about age 20 when his mother, Elizabeth, died. (Neg. C7170, IMCPL-Riley Collection, Indiana Historical Society.)

The first thing Riley did after his mother died was to go to Rushville to sell Bibles with some man unknown in history. Reuben Riley was very skeptical about this enterprise and did not know the Bible salesman Riley had taken off to Rushville with. On December 19, 1870 we find the father writing to the son,

"I have been patiently waiting for a letter from you and have received none. Scarcely an hour passes without my thinking of you and wondering how you are getting along? how you are doing? how you are managing? I have had much more experience in the world than you. It is all important that you associate with none but those of good character, that you be self-reliant and aim high and suffer no stain to attach to your conduct. I would like to counsel and advise with you. Please write me fully and confidently, and all reasonable assistance in my power I will render..."

"It turned out," said Riley, "that citizens of Rushville had all the Bibles they needed; they had not time to read those they had." Soon Riley was back in Greenfield apprenticed to Almon Keefer's uncle, John Keefer, a painter by trade. Reuben paid for the apprenticeship. Soon Riley was armed with a Number 5 paint brush and a bucketful of paint under the eaves painting houses in Greenfield. Riley worked at painting houses for two summers while he learned the more delicate art of painting signs. Eventually Riley rented a paint shop above a drugstore which he called the "Morgue" and slept there much of the time because he did not want his family to see how intoxicated he often became.

The Editor of Century Magazine, Hewitt Hanson Howland, claimed Riley's life was dominated by two fears, the fear of life and the fear of death.

"From my earliest recollection of him, he would, on the death of a friend, take on an added air of confidence, almost of gaiety. `You can't make me believe he isn't around here somewhere,' he would say, `probably listening to us now and chuckling over our distress.'" I thought of him then as whistling in the dark; today we'd call it defensive mechanism. But by whatever name, Riley always gave the departed the best of the bargain." The death of his mother left him outside her physical presence ut with the hope that she was still with him and had gone right on living.

When Riley wrote poetry he was in a way still participating in an activity with his mother. Riley told Hamlin Garland in an interview that he got his verse-writing from his mother's family, the Marines. A characteristic of the whole family was their ability to write rhymes, but all unambitiously. "They wrote rhymed letters to each other, and joked and jim-crowed with the Muses." This family love of poetry was the legacy of the poverty stricken mother to her son. She had nothing else to give him.

After the mother's death, poverty in the Riley home continued to render life there miserable. Riley's brother, Hum, and sisters remained. The period was one of great privation. Reuben Riley was not a good provider at any time following his very brief Civil War service. Riley's younger brother gives evidence of this in a brief plaintive letter to brother John who left home to live and earn an income in Indianapolis. Riley's brother, Hum at 13, wrote his brother John,

"Dear Brother,

I want you to send me a cap if you pleas (sic) by tomoro (sic) evening. I have none but one old one and it is not fit to wear to the festival a cheap one will do so it looks well.

Yours truly,

/s/ Hum

The boy hadn't funds to wear the cap that the other boys had.

Another letter from Riley himself to his brother, John explains Riley's poverty.

July 14, 1871
Dear Bro.:

Yesterday morn I failed to write to you - I found "the folks" all well - that is, "on their pins," but all pretty blue and no wonder. There is no one to help May, who still continues to "gaze in vacancy" the greater part of the time.

I "waked" her for a little time yesterday by reading a sketch or two from Dickens. Father is chief-cook-and bottle washer. I was going to say but Hum washes the dishes. Father has to go to the court house and be fined $10 for contempt of court. John, I tell you, our noble House is on the wane - everything is going - going - the same old carelessness marks our "progress."

...I am going to work for Harris in a day or two. Father, I guess don't want to get, or keep a girl to assist May - economy, you know. I've been laughing forced laughs and dancing forced jigs till I'm about gone up - they don't appear to take - it will take a deeper trick - "simulating" happiness, to be a success.

Augustus and Marie were up last evening and Dora from Pendleton - we had a pleasant time in our front parlors - the kitchen door open and father with his sleeves rolled up to his knees, getting supper for his clamor of offspring who ate crackers and water for dinner - maybe I don't talk right- I can't say other way -Your affectionate bro. Jim.

Elva May Riley, at fourteen, took the mother's place in the family. Harris was Riley's school master. In his schoolhouse in Lewisville, Riley and Harris spent half the night studying the poetry, especially Tennyson, and writing verse.

The Reuben Riley family bible on display at Greenfield birthplace. Photo courtesy of Roger Looney, staff of Greenfield Daily Reporter. This bible legally establishes Riley's date of birth.

The first poems were printed in Greenfield in local newspapers about this time. Riley wrote them under the name Edyrn, taken from Tennyson's IDYLLS OF THE KING.

Although Elva May Riley assumed the role of the mother of the bereaved family, the younger crippled child, Mary, was left in great inconsolable sorrow by the death of her mother.

Following Elizabeth's death, Riley took to the habit of coming to his sister Mary's side at night after she had been put to bed to recite Tennyson and Longfellow. Both came to know some of these poems by heart and she remembered her brother particularly tried to emulate the musical cadence of the "The Lady of Shalott". She recalled him as loving Keats best of all, but "he did not repeat those poems to me as a girl."

Mary and Riley formed a special bond during this period. Often Riley came home to the Riley homestead drunk and the little girl came down to assist him get to his room.

Throughout the remainder of his life Riley considered his sister, Mary, as a special charge and supported her and her daughter, Leslie, financially through many travails. Born during the Civil War, Sister Mary suffered from spinal meningitis and was 15 years younger than Riley. His financial help kept her in a rather expensive standard of living. She and her daughter, Lesley, lived in Paris, France, for many years dependent upon the assistance of the poet who gladly provided whatever resources were needed. Riley did this in memory of his mother as well as out of love for his sister. His sister's life was as shattered by Crestillomeem as was his own.

Eventually, still in grief at his mother's death, Riley left Greenfield, his boyhood home, in May 1872, when he was twenty-two by joining the traveling medicine show of Dr. Samuel Brown McCrillus. As the Twentieth Century ends, we can hardly imagine such a wild and strange event as the appearance in town of a medicine show. But to the folk of Greenfield and the little towns of Indiana in the decade following the Civil War, the coming of a patent medicine wagon offered an occasion for fun and excitement.

Dr. McCrillus was not just a "doctor" who made his own prescription in Anderson - the one principal remedy for almost every illness to hear him tell it - McCrillus' European Balsam - he was also an entertainer back in the days when folk with that duo proclivity would take to the roads and sell medicine at medicine shows.

Imagine yourself in the Greenfield of the decade after the Civil War. Supper is over and the women are busy with a sinkful of dishes and the children are finishing their chores for the day. The men are out on the front porches having an after-dinner chaw of tobacco. Only the buzz of a persistent fly breaks the lazy silence of the warm summer evening.

Suddenly, this halcyon scene is broken by a near-deafening blast of a trumpet. The Greenfield folk rush out of their houses to see what is going on.

Down State Street from the direction of Anderson come a pair of matched, plumed horses pulling a gaily decorated wagon. It is painted in gaudy reds and blues and is embellished with curlicues in gold. Is it a circus wagon? No. Even so all the kids of the town, cheering and pushing to get close, rush toward it and circle it as it heads down to the courthouse square.

Dr. McCrillus has brought his medicine show to Greenfield once

Your author could not find a photo of either a Dr. McCrillus or a Dr. Townsend patent medicine show wagon but an example of the type is pictured from Minnesota at the turn of the century.

again as he did every year during this era.

We would all know him. Dr. Samuel Brown McCrillus is one of the most notable men in this part of Indiana. He has made sure he is well known by hiring an "advance man" to paint his advertisements for his patent medicines in Greenfield on every available barnside, post and rock.

Dr. McCrillus sits on the wagon seat, dignified and smiling, and he waves his hat to the men and bows and lifts his hat in a mannerly way to the ladies along the way. He is a great humanitarian who takes the tributes of the crowd in stride. After all not everyone has curing the sicknesses and ailments of folk in their hearts like the good Quaker doctor.

After encircling the town square, Dr. McCrillus stops his bright wagon and climbs down. Soon he is joined by the young man with him, Jim McClanahan, who will present an evening performance on the tailgate of the wagon in the flickering late summer light along the Greenfield downtown Main Street.

Frequent commercials were interjected into the entertainments. Dr. McCrillus would signal for silence and a hush would encompass the crowd. "Friends and neighbors, " he would say, "let's get one thing clear at the beginning. I don't want your money. I have come to Greenfield to help you." He really meant it. Then he would give his 19th Century hard sell, a pitch for "McCrillus European Balsam" and it worked, probably unlike the medicine itself.

One observer of this has recorded Dr. McCrillus's standard introduction of himself, as follows: "I have been engaged in the medicine business ever since I can recollect. I made pills by the day when only a boy of ten years. For the past thirty-eight years, I have been engaged in putting up what is known as Dr. McCrillus' popular standard remedies, European Balsam, Tonic Block Purifier, Oriental Liniment, and Hoarhound Expectorant. They are sold by druggists. I could offer thousands of genuine certificates, but I am willing to leave the great public to judge of their merits. I have adopted for my special use a trade mark, whereby the public may be protected against fraud and imposition. Relief has been obtained by thousands of sufferers by the use of my medicines and they in turn have recommended them to others. In this way, I am making living advertisements for myself and medicines. Be sure the name of Dr. S.B. McCrillus, Anderson, Indiana, is on every bottle, otherwise it is a fraud." (As found in the Madison County Historical GAZETTE of October, 1979.)

Dr. McCrillus worked all winter making pills and preparing his tonic in his laboratory. Then in the summer he would pack them all up in a bright wagon driven by his two sorral horses and travel all over Central Indiana putting on these little shows to cause people to congregate.

When Doc McCrillus left Greenfield on this occasion, he took James Whitcomb Riley with him.

When James Whitcomb Riley left Greenfield at the age of twenty-two to join a traveling patent medicine show, he had not just hooked up with a simple charlatan. Doc McCrillus was a patent medicine manufacturer who believed in his products and traveled around Indiana in the summers peddling his cures with vim and vigor. The Doc would give wondrous programs from his wagon to extol the virtues of his many cures. Somehow he also kept open a little medicine shop on the south side of Anderson's public square during this era according to the EMERSON AND WILLIAMS ANDERSON CITY DIRECTORY of 1876-77.

In a way, Riley was lucky that Doc McCrillus took him on. Jim Riley tried to talk his way into the good doctor's traveling miracle medicine show on the basis that he could do a good public relations job. Riley had experience painting signs - Riley's dad apprenticed him to a Greenfield signmaker at an early age to keep the boy from being a juvenile delinquent - and he told Doc McCrillus he would advance to the next towns on the circuit and make signs for his show. The problem is that Doc McCrillus already had one sign painter, a young man named James McClanahan also from the doctor's hometown of Anderson.

The more Riley talked though, the more the doctor felt favorably inclined to include the young man in his travels. Like many others, Doctor McCrillus knew Reuben Riley, Jim's dad, and knew his father, a lawyer, was a good showman in his own way. Then he asked Riley to see some of his signs. Riley sighted him to a bridge where he had painted an eagle and a flag. With the boy's father's permission, James Whitcomb Riley was off on his first adventure away from Greenfield and home.

Doc McCrillus's visit to Greenfield was the first of the patent medicine man's stops in the summer of 1872. Actually, the Doc took his two Jims back to Anderson and to his home at 3 East Lincoln Street there on its historic brick street that still remains after the Greenfield trip to prepare for the entertainments for the rest of the summer. Jim Riley and Jim McClanahan learned to perform many acts together. Riley had brought with him his guitar and banjo along with his natural gift of wit and novelty. The program would provide a forum for Doc McCrillus to spiel out his philosophic approach to his patent medicines, then the three would sing a trio and other entertainments would follow. In this summer, Riley became a comedian and give recitations and also sang, as well as went on ahead of the medicine show to the oncoming towns to paint signs advertising the show to come.

It is a shame that Doctor McCrillus has faded into such obscurity as a historical figure. No obituary of him survives. We only know that he was born in Dubois County on June 27, 1830 and died at the age of 70 in Anderson on Feb. 12, 1901. His wife was from Southern Indiana. Her name was Helen Coningore and the two married in 1861 in Paoli. The doctor's parents were Aaron Bailey and Sarah (nee Brown) McCrillus. We know from the standard Dubois County Histories of the Nineteenth Century that Dr. Samuel McCrillus was educated in a pioneer school - his only education that I could uncover-in the front room of a "Professor Cheaver on the southeast corner of the public square of Jasper, and was elected as the first Auditor of Dubois County before he was twenty-one under Indiana's Second Constitution, before migrating to Anderson in 1861 for some unknown reason and taking to patent medicine manufacture. Medical School anywhere is not in his resume. I suppose he had learned as Auditor of Dubois County that to be a medical doctor in this period of history one only had to register as such with the County Auditor where you wished to be an M.D. Among the places his children settled was Wilkinson, in Hancock County.

This was the man who would spirit James Whitcomb Riley away from Greenfield and offer him the chance to become an entertainer and meet many characters.

None of this may particularly sound like a background experience for a young man who would help define what an American home and its life would involve. But James Whitcomb Riley was a young man who "itched" to move right then.

Whether he knew it or not, James Whitcomb Riley was on a quest to understand the meaning of his life as well as to understand his Greenfield home where he had lived in his youth, a home whose coup he had now flown. His quest would cause him to write extensively and famously and he would explore every element of what others might think were elements of his dream. Strangely he would never have a home such as he would formulate as an ideal for his readers and listeners.

In a newspaper interview about taking on James Whitcomb Riley to join his patent medicine show, Doc McCrillus once said, "This patent medicine business was not organized then like it is today." (I suppose he meant after the passage of laws like the Pure Food and Drug Act regulating what could be sold as "drugs.") "I did as big a business as any one. All of us then had great, fine wagons and would load up with our medicines and drive from town to town. We would carry a sign painter along and as we jogged from place to place would stop and paint signs on fences or barns. I would take part of the pay for the medicines in paint."

Riley with sign he painted in his early 20's taken by traveling chum John O. Hoover of Lafayette.

"We got to Greenfield...(His "sign painter," James McClanahan was present at this interview too)... "and when I was over at the drug store, Jim McClanahan, who was my painter, scraped up an acquaintance with this fellow Riley, who was a red-head, sorry-looking young fellow."

"Yes, (McClanahan said,) Doc had gone over to the drug store and I had let down the back and was looking over the supply of paint when this feller Riley came up and commenced to talk to me. He told me he was a painter, too. I sized him up and shot back - 'Yes, I see as how you're a blin' painter,' and I pointed out some green paint on his clothes - the green that we used to daub the blinds with. That was the worst thing you could say to a painter, and Riley blushed and said that he could paint more than blinds and houses and he pointed out a sign or two. When Doc came back to the wagon I told him the young fellow wanted to go with us, that he had paint-

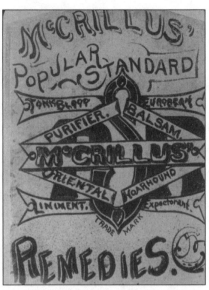

The "trade mark" of Doc Sameul McCrillus. (From the Barton Rees Pogue glass positive collection.)

ed those signs; and that he said he could play the guitar and the fiddle - Riley never liked the word fiddle. Doc took him on to help me out and to help him in his lectures. Riley was a fast painter and his lettering was good, and he helped McCrillus entertain the crowds in the street." (From a newspaper interview found in loose papers at the Indiana University library at Indianapolis.)

It is easy to say that Riley's career began on Doc McCrillus's gaudy "show wagon." The entertainments that Riley performed to gather crowds for Doc McCrillus were the start of his public career as a showman him-self...and entertainer from the stage.

After his death, a contemporary American author of Riley's, Hamlin Garland, would say of him, "...in truth his success did not come so much in print as through his own reading of his lines from the platform. He had in him something of the minstrel. He possessed notable power to charm and move an audience, and everywhere he spoke he left a throng of friends. To hear him read - or recite - "A Song of the Airly Days" was to be moved in a new and unforgettable way. His vibrant individual voice, his flexile lips, his droll glance, united to make him at once poet and comedian - comedian in the sense which makes for tears as well as for laughter." (From

"Commemorative Tribute to James Whitcomb Riley" by Hamlin Garland, read in the 1920 Lecture Series of the American Academy of Arts and Letters.)

Riley's "minstrelsy" or showmanship may have been an offshoot of Doc McCrillus's, or at least substantially influenced by him. People would come to listen and be entertained by the patient medicine man and his young men consorts. At most these audiences were a "testing ground" for the young James Whitcomb Riley to learn his craft of entertaining and amusing audiences. There is a tendency to think this shallow and not necessarily significant. That conclusion would be dead wrong.

There is not just a "give" but rather a "give and take" in the performing arts. James Whitcomb Riley participated in the life of these audiences around the brightly painted patent medicine wagon. The crowds became a part of the entertainer who would write down his poetry from time to time. What the crowds found "right" in Riley's poetry became Riley's subject matter. Since establishing homes was the main thrust of the small town populaces Riley entertained, ideas of home abound in Riley's poetry.

Riley's trip with Doc McCrillus was a start on a journey which would take him through his life and even take his life at the end. It was a tragic quest which was buried in humor and hopeful sentiment. It was a journey to find love and to try to be loved in the life of his Hoosier people. Its meaning would boil down to a concept of home. Unfortunately, the meaning was one which proved a truce by which American homelife could become established and normalized and permit the thriving of others, but not for himself. A lonely death in a small upper apartment of an Indianapolis house would be James Whitcomb Riley's lot.

In the Biographical Edition of his poetry, Riley described his employment with Doc McCrillus, the traveling miracle medicine man with whom Riley escaped Greenfield:

"My duty was the manipulation of two blackboards swung at the sides of the wagon during our street lecture and concert. These boards were alternately embellished with colored drawings illustrative of the manifold virtues of the nostrum vended. Sometimes, I assisted the musical olio with dialect recitations and character sketches from the back steps of the wagon."

In describing his getaway from the memories of this death with a medicine man selling his cure-all, Riley said "I rode out of town with that glittering cavalcade," the poet said, "without saying good-bye to anyone, and though my patron was not a diplomaed doctor, as I found out, he was a man of excellent habits and the whole company was made up of good, straight, jolly, chirping vagabonds like myself." Riley fitted easily into this roving company as a black board and colored chalk artist, illustrating the virtues of the medicine vended, supplemented with a repertoire of songs, jokes and original recitations. After a wonderful tour, the poet returned to Greenfield with pockets as empty as they were when he left.

In May 31, 1872 Riley wrote his brother,

"... I have been advertising for the Farmer's Grocery for three or four days and am feeling pretty sore, physically - but quite the contrary mentally for I have now removed a load of about $6 from my mind and so -

"Patience and shuffle the cards," - and I'll soon be out of debt.

John, I have an offer from a young advertiser, who was attracted by my card in the post-office, to travel and do Medicine advertising and such, and I believe I will go. I can be at home as often as you. I guess: so we won't be broken badly. I think it will be the best thing I could do: I'll be in the open air all the time, and I do like advertising - especially where I have a chance of making $5 and $6 a day. I send you a photograph of my card. - How do you like? - I received a complimentary squib in both our worthy papers. The young man i am going with is a good business agent and sharp as the proverbial tack. He is not much on the letter, but knows how to get work and handle "expenses" and all that. He is entirely stranger to me - but he is from Anderson, and refers me to dozens of the best men the town contains. We will do general advertising: he has had experience and knows all about it - I will go as partner or not at all. If we succeed it won't be a great while before I show advertisers what advertising is like the card I send you for instance - I can design them and we can have them engraved and furnish cards novel, new and unique for so much a thous - look out!

Yours &c Jim

Then on July 17th 1872, he wrote his brother that he was about to start on a week's trip to neighboring towns.

When Riley and McClanahan traveled by themselves to paint, they entered a town to great theatrical display. Riley said, "On entering a town, McClanahan went first to the livery stable and with unfailing instinct picked out the best horses. It was not long before we were in the good graces of the livery-man and had as our reward the best team in the barn free of charge for the afternoon. Then the two made a dashing appearance into town to talk to the leading merchants proposing to advertise them on every barn fence and boulder on each of the roads leading into town. Riley remembered saying "these signs will stand as long as the fence or barn or stone remains...Why, you spend that much each year on newspaper advertising and, what is more, your newspaper allows your competitor to advertise in the very next column in a more conspicuous place. He can't do that on the road, because you'll have every fence and barn, and if you don't take the contract he will, you bet."

Their business card proposed "all styles of signs and painted advertisements and original designs in fancy cards and bulletins and banner signs of all kinds and ends is in rhyme,

"We strive in each particular to give our fellow man entire Satisfaction.
        Riley and McClanahan

Life on the road was not easy. Riley did not conserve what money he did make. In the winter of 1872-3, Riley spent the winter in Marion. He recalls, "I didn't have enough covers on my bed, only a counterpane. (Biographer's note: coverlet). I laid newspapers in between that and the sheet to keep out the cold. Oh, I was living in an old rat-trap and didn't see where the money for my Saturday's board was coming from. And I was homesick. One day a letter came from my small brother `Hum,' a boy letter about "Nuisance," our dog, who had died. When I got that broken-hearted letter I simply crawled away to my room, threw myself on the bed and cried." This was the winter when "Dot Leedle Boy of Mine," was written. Riley said, "Writing verse was the only fun I had."

We know that Riley left Greenfield to join Doc McCrillus and therafter to travel with Jim McClanahan painting at just about the time the temperance movement was strengthening and young men Riley's age were being asked to sign Murphy pledges not to drink alcoholic beverages. Near this time of Riley's period of greatest inebriations after his mother's death, the Indiana Women's Christian Temperance Union was just getting organized. When Mrs. Zerelda Wallace, its first President, and stepmother of General Lew Wallace, author of BEN HUR, took her first temperance petition before the Indiana legislature, she was informed that, since her petition was from women who couldn't vote, it "amounted to no more than the tracks of so many mice." This aroused Mrs. Wallace to become a public speaker throughout the state on temperance and women's vote issues. Other women joined in the fight. Soon women were lining up, two abreast, in great processions after church services to enter the taverns of Hoosier towns to ask saloon keepers to close down and seek the reformation of the drinkers inside. Tavern keepers could do little about these invasions. They could not throw out the ladies who would yell, "Unhand me, Sir!" or remind them that "No one but a coward touches a woman save in kindness." No lady could be removed from the bar door when they chose to sing temperance songs outside. It is said that huge and brutal looking barkeeps quailed to the pure womanhood while their potential patrons left or walked away without entering their usual haunts.

The resistance of the saloon keepers of the Hoosier Deutsch - those of Riley's stock - was greater than the others. Sometimes a thick accented German wife of a barkeep fetched her small children and fed them beer in full sight of the temperance women. Many times those of Hoosier Deutsch heritage were subject to derision for special sinfulness and foreign barbarism. It was more common for the Deutsch saloon owners to resist. They drove the women out of their establishments by opening doors and windows in the winter, throwing pepper on the stoves to cause them to sneeze and cry, flooding the floor with filthy water, putting out the fires in their stoves or just plain plugging the stovepipe to smoke them out. Occasionally, drinkers would throw tobacco juicy sawdust from the bar floors at the ladies. If fights did break out, few ladies feared being convicted of disorderly conduct or such charges.

A poem by Elizabeth T. Wills of the Wabash, Indiana, Women's Christian Temperance Union describes the temperance activity of the time. It should be remembered that Riley and his friends were what these ladies would call "rummies." The antagonistic but pious mood toward alcoholics in Indiana is expressed in this poem.

THE TEMPERANCE CRUSADE

Away back in the Seventies
A long, long time ago,
We women went out in the old crusade
When the ground was covered with snow.
Now what do you mean by the old crusade?
We would like to hear you explain
Was the fight just for popularity
Which we women were hoping to gain?
No, we mothers had sat in rum ruined homes
And mourned o'er the wreckage the rum fiend had made
It was rum, rum with its withering curse,

That's what started the Temperance Crusade. Rum had
robbed us of husband, had robbed us of sons
And of all, which the heart holds most dear
So we women went out, in this battle for home
Without the least tremor of fear.
In Hillsboro, Ohio, the Crusade first broke out
And the first soon kindled to flame.
it flew to the south, the north, east and west
Just like a tornado it came.
This fire had been smoldering for years and for years
Just waiting and ready to catch.
It was fed by wrecked manhood and orphan's sad tears
All it lacked was just touching the match.
We met in the churches, met three times a day
To form resolutions, to talk, sing and pray.
Just women in daytime, men kept out of sight
But they joined in our mass-meetings held every night.
Then while all the church bells were ringing at once
and all the whistles were blowing,
We started right out with our hymn books in hand
To visit saloons - we were going.
We caused much excitement as we marched two abreast
Through the crowded and awe-stricken street But with
heads quite erect and courage unchecked
Did we march with the snow on our feet.
We marched right in to the open saloon
And begged of the men to desist
But some grew angry and cursed us
And came at us with shaking fist;
And some of them told us we'd better go home
And men our husband's sox; We appointed committees to
sit out in front,
To keep the men out of saloons.
I imagine we felt a little like men
When they finally tree their 'coons;
And we couldn't help but sorter wear
A half-way satisfied grin
To see the men we were keeping out

That wanted so much to go in.
Then while at this stage in the conflict
After first excitement was through,
we organized the little band
called the W.C.T.U,
And the ball has kept rolling and rolling
with its purity banner unfurled,
Till now our white-ribbon army
Is teaching and belting the world.
So pin on the white ribbon, sisters,
And we will keep plugging away,
Till we win in the fight and put rummies to flight
Some Glad Day.

I suppose to some extent the young Riley was "put to flight" by the temperance ladies and their talk about such young men as Riley who drank too much.

Riley did not consider his alcoholism as some disease or unconscious decision. Riley wanted to indulge in alcohol and become intoxicated as a young man following the death of his mother. He did not want any temperance movement person interfering for the escape he found in drinking alcoholic beverages.

This admission is made in his autobiographical poem, "The Flying Islands of the Night" where Jucklet explains this to Crestillomeem, Riley's alcoholism. The "wife" and "love" is alcohol.

He thinks thee even true to him as thou
Art fickle, false and subtle! O how blind
And lame, and deaf and dumb, and worn and weak,
And faint, and sick, and all-commodious
His dear love is! In sooth, O wifely one,
Thy malleable spouse doth mind me of
That pliant hero of the bald old catch
"Thy Lovely Husband." - Shall I wreak the thing?

(Sings[1] - with much affected gravity and grimace)

O a lovely husband he was known,

He loved his wife and her a-lone;
She reaped the harvest he had sown;
She ate the meat, he picked the bone.
  With mixed admirers every size,
  She smiled on each without disguise;
  This lovely husband closed his eyes
  Lest he might take her by surprise,

(Aside, exclamatory)

Chorious uproarious!

(Then pantomime as though pulling at bell-rope - singing in
pent, explosive utterance)

Trot!
Run! Wasn't he a handy hubby?

What
Fun
She could plot and plan!

Not One
Other such a dandy hubby
As this lovely man!

---

1. The 1898 edition of "The Flying Islands" contains a score for this song. Riley set the song
to music for this edition.

This part of the poem borders on pathos rather than humor.

Nellie Cooley (Dwainie) tried on many occasions to set Riley free from
his alcoholism, none with any success during her lifetime. Only after her
death did she come to him in the delirious account chronicled in "The Flying
Islands of the Night," and succeed in this effort.

Riley not only began his life of alcoholism after his mother's death, but
he also most earnestly began his writing of poetry to express his feelings.
Riley began his nocturnal life. Riley's poems were mostly written at night
because he once said, "Then angels listen to the whisper of his pencil as I
write." This habit came early and from the days he painted signs. Often too

intoxicated to return home, he slept many places. One of them was at the station of the night watchman of the Greenfield Bank. The night watchman was happy for the company because he could sleep at night knowing Riley was awake by a dim lamp with a pencil and tablet in hand.

Most of his early life, he recalled hearing a clock strike four.

How did Riley consider his life?

There can be no more discordant event than the death of a caregiving mother. There is no place to go for reassurance and to avoid anxiety more satisfying than to one's mother. One does not feel unworthy when a mother gives acceptance. Parental love is the great shield of apprehensiveness.

The next year saw Riley traveling the State of Indiana again with McClanahan.

Riley's friends shared his general love of the drunken life. Nov. 26, 1873, apparently written while Mack (James McClanahan) was drunk. The letter starts out, "Answer soon for God's sake. Don't make fun of me. This is written on the letterhead of Harvin and Booker, Frankfort. "O dam the pin I can't write fast enough. Damd if I ever felt good in my life. Good God I'm off my feet. Would to God that I could see you NOW. You ask me why don't I write. That's damn fine talk ain't it...Oh, my God, but I do feel Hob. Hob hell. That don't express it. Can you read this?...." McClanahan is writing Riley in desperation. The woman he is living with is apparently giving him Hell. McClanahan says he has given people the impression the woman he is living with and he are married but they aren't.

There are records from friends in newspaper recollections that are revealing:

From Riley's South Bend life comes the recollection of Frank Murphy. Just across from Blowneys was a saloon and Riley was said to dearly love to have a glass of beer there with innumerable friends, Bill Allen, Al Stockford, Frank Murphy. On one occasion, when Riley and Bill Allen, a drinking buddy of Riley's, were painting the outside of the old St. Joseph hotel, the scaffolding they were standing on fell and both of them were hurt, but not seriously. Later, when Riley was famous and was lecturing in South Bend, Bill Allen went to see Riley at his hotel and Riley refused to see him. In Riley's "Pipes o' Pan at Zekesbury," Riley mentioned many of his South Bend friends and in particular "the Wild Irishman," Frank Murphy, a genial, jovial Irishman, loud of speech, warm in friendship and who could improvise poetry and enjoy a glass of whisky or any other concoction accompanied with plenty of hilarity and good fellowship, which was exactly to young

Riley's temperamental liking and as a result the two were good friends til death took them. Riley called him Tommy in his sketch and says he sings at one of their convivial gatherings in the Andrews saloon:

"But R-R-Riley, he'll not go I guess
Lest, he'd get losht in the wil-der-ness,
And so in the city he will shtop
For to curl his hair in the barbershop."

Of the Andrews Saloon where Riley frequently quenched his thirst and was always welcome, he sings,

"Of the Andrews brothers they'll be there
Wid good sy-gars and wine to spare,
They'll treat us here on fine champagne
And when we're there, they'll treat us again."

Whenever Murphy went to Indianapolis, he would look Riley up and they would have a good time recalling the days when Riley was a sign painter in South Bend. Maj. Blowney did not mind Riley writing verses and gave him a blank book to write them in.

It is to this early period of Riley's wandering life following the death of his mother, that Riley refers in his autobiographical poem when he portrays Crestillomeem (his alcoholism) and his minstrelsy play-self (Jucklet) in happy companionship and shared delight.

Semblance of Jucklet (Sings)

Crestillomeem!
     Crestillomeem! Soul of my slumber! - Dream of
my dream!
Moonlight may fall not as goldenly fair
As falls the gold of thine opulent hair -
Nay, nor the starlight as dazzlingly gleam
As gleam thine eyes, 'Meema - Crestillomeem! -
     Star of the skies, 'Meema -
          Crestillomeem!

Semblance of Crestillomeem (Sings)
O Prince divine!
     O Prince divine!
Tempt thou me not with that sweet voice of thine!

Though my proud brow bear the blaze of a crown,
Lo, at thy feet must its glory bow down.
That from the dust thou mayest lift me to shine
Heaven'd in thy heart's rapture, O Prince divine! -
   Queen of thy love ever,
                O Prince divine!

   Semblance of Jucklet (Sings)

Crestillomeem! Crestillomeem!
Our life shall flow as a musical stream[1] -
Windingly - placidly on it shall wend,
Marged with mazhorra-bloom banks without end -
Word-birds shall call thee and dreamily scream,
"Where dost thou cruise, 'Meema - Crestillomeem?
   Whither away, 'Meema? -Crestillomeem!

1. *Jucklet, Riley's pranking and jocular self, can express*
himself along quite well in intoxicated state.

            Duo

(Vision and voices gradually failing away)

Crestillomeem!
          Crestillomeem!
Soul of my slumber! - Dream of my dream!
Star of Love's light, 'Meema - Crestillomeem!
   Crescent of Night, 'Meema! -
   Several incidents from Riley's travels are remembered.
   Once Riley suspended himself by a rope from a bridge and painted a sign
on the bottom of the bridge inverting the letters so the approaching traffic
would see the advertising on the surface of the water. He painted many
barns on his travels in the years of his early twenties.
   When he returned home to Greenfield occasionally he did some odd jobs
for Greenfield folk. He did cards for War Barnett and went to a Greeley
meeting and "ogled some terribly damp Goddesses of Liberty, etc."
   Riley saw Brett Harte read while in South Bend in the fall 1873 but did

not go speak to him although they stood close to each other after the performance. "I wanted to speak to him for he had been a great inspiration to me, but some fear within restrained me."

1874 was another year of restless wandering about Indiana with Jim McClanahan and friends. Riley's family were not supportive. They wished him settled down. They did not like his wanderings around with his carefree drinking friends. A letter Riley sent to his brother John, dated Nov. 16, 1874, states:

"...In reply to a question of yours-McClanahan is not with me now, nor hasn't been for months, and in lieu of myself -as per lady-book-statement, -is traveling in the Vinegar Recipe line and making big money. He controls a party of 13 agents who sell recipes while he is employed selling Territory.

I have been working for McCrillus, principally, since my return to Anderson, but have surprised the folks occasionally with a sign: I am at work now on an advertising card that will be superior! I won't enter in to a description of it - wait till it's done and I'll show it to you - it will be my masterpiece as I have "mixed my colors with brains." Oh, it's artistic - not letters in gold alone, but the "female form divine" graces the center of the design, while the letters around her twine and glimmer and gleam and shine

> Like the limpid, laughing waters
> Of the Classic Brandywine."

The picture from the poetry and the situation of the departure with the good Doc's patent medicine show is of a young man, Riley, simply on the run from the death of his mother steadily seeking the companionship of Crestillomeem but holding his own in the sign painting and medicine show business.

Perhaps his relationship with his married friend, Nellie Cooley back in Greenfield further encouraged both his departures and exacerbated alcohol use. Upon his returns to Greenfield he inevitably sought Nellie's company and this was not a situation Riley's family was very happy about either. Nellie was, after all, a married woman. It was not a good sign that she was the woman he was paying attention to. For now we simply repeat the last stanza of this poem:

A POET'S WOOING (1872)

What can I do to make you glad -
  As glad as glad can be,
    Till your clear eyes seem
    Like the rays that gleam
And glint through a dew-decked tree? -
  Will it please you, dear, that I now begin
  A grand old air on my violin?"
And she spoke again in the following way, -
  "Yes, oh yes, it would please me, sir;
I would be so glad you'd play
  Some grand old march - in character, -
  And then as you march away
I will no longer thus be sad,
But oh, so glad - so glad - so glad!"

Was Nellie discouraging Riley's attentions as well as encouraging them driving Riley crazy?

Life with Doc McCrillus was a pleasant and diverting life. To gain the flavor of the Doc McCrillus patent medicine enterprise, it may be helpful to consider the product Riley was selling. One of the testimonials to Doc McCrillus's patent medicine has come down to us from two Anderson, Indiana men who otherwise are unknown to history, E. Sipe and Sam Pence, self-styled as "Horse Dealers." They witness as follows: "We speak whereof we have seen and know about Dr. S.B. McCrillus' European Balsam. We believe it to be a valuable medicine in the cure of horse disease -epizootic -as a disinfectant, and also a great relief to the horse when sick by burning it on coals in the stable and letting the horses inhale the Balsam." (Found in loose folders on Riley in the Anderson City Library).

This testimonial would be rather "backhand" since Doc McCrillus's miracle cures were intended for humans.

As you would look at the darkly ominous bottle of the good doctor's chief product, you would immediately know it was something very special. A trumpeting baby elephant was on the label on whose back was a huge leather satchel as big as the elephant containing the word's "McCrillus' European Balsam."

The Balsam's label contained other information in different sized print: "The Acknowledged Excelsior System Renovator. Cures WEAK BACK. It Cures Bronchitis, Palpitation of the Heart, Laryngitis, Sore Throat, Phthisic(sic), Weak Breast, Coughs and Colds, Female Complaints, Liver Complains, Dyspepsia, Chronic Rheumatism, Etc." In much smaller print along the sides of the label are the statements, "This Balsam, composed exclusively of vegetable matter, has attained for itself an almost cosmopolitan celebrity. In its successful treatment of all diseases of a nervous and inflammatory nature, and for a weak state of the system. It heals the lungs, strengthens the stomach, rectifies its disorders and regulates the bowels. It allays inflammation externally and internally. Dissolves the secretions of the urinary glands, and cures grave and WEAKNESS OF THE KIDNEYS."

Just dreaming up such a mess of quasi-medical gobbledegook such as this must have taken the good Doc much time. Incidentally, the good Dr. McCrillus's death certificate on file with the Madison Co. Health Department shows his cause of death as "acute pneumonitis" which we tend to call pneumonia. Did the doctor not take his own cure? Lung ailments were supposed to be overcome by his European Balsam. Or could it have been that he wished his own remedy worked a little better as he was slipping away?

In any case, the summers in which James Whitcomb Riley left home to join Doc McCrillus and paint and travel were pleasant and fun-filled interludes and adventures Riley and McClanahan were said to have performed many acts together from the show wagon. Riley always took his guitar and banjo with him, and much entertainment was verbalized with recitation of entertaining stories. When Riley was on the road with Doc, he would interject his philosophy of medicine and the virtues of his cures and then sometimes the three would sing as a trio. Eventually, James Whitcomb Riley is said to have become very popular with demands for encores for his recitations and even singing.

After these surrealistic summer experiences, James Whitcomb Riley returned with the Doc to Anderson to idle away time. He lived either with Doc or in boarding houses in Anderson or nearby towns where he went to paint signs or houses or with mom McClanahan in Anderson. Everywhere he went, Riley spent time on street corners talking to the people of Anderson or wherever he was and writing seriously, filling the bureau drawers of his board rooms and trunks with papers until they were stuffed.

Only when Riley ran out of his "summer" or "sign" money did he return to Greenfield, his boyhood home.

1874 was the year McGeecy, editor of the Danbury, Connecticut, NEWS, accepted Riley's poetry encouraging him greatly. This was also the year Riley worked out the elocution and performance points for "The Bear Story" and "Tradin' Joe." Riley read these in occasional school houses and churches.

These early years of young manhood also saw Riley produce much whimsical doggerel verse for advertising including this "advertisement" for his friend the good Doc McCrillus:

"Wherever blooms of health are blown,
McCrillus' Remedies are known;
Wherever happy lives are found
You'll find his medicines around,
From coughs and colds and lung disease
His patients find a sweet release
In using his Expectorant
That cures where even doctors can't.
His Oriental Liniment
Is known to fame to such extent
That orders for it emanate
From every portion of the State,
His European Balsam, too,
Send blessings down to me and you;
And holds its throne from year to year
In every household far and near,
His purifier for the blood
Has earned a name fair and good
As ever glistened on the page
Of any annals of the age.
And he who pants for health ease
Should try these Standard Remedies."

There is both prose and poetry written reflecting Riley's wandering life with Crestillomeem. It is mostly poetry of the 1870's, Riley's period of great production in which no topic of his life was "off limits."

We have the poet who would one day - after he comes to kenoticism - be known as "The Children's Poet" taking the classic "Little Red Riding

Hood," and turning it into the story as told by an alcoholic - maybe Riley's friend "Old Sport."

"LITTLE RED RIDING HOOD"

"Wonst they was a leetle-teeny dirl, an' she was named Red Riding Hood, toz her ma maked her a leetle red cloak `at torned up over her head - an' it was all thist one piece of red cardnal like the dreat long stockin's `at the storekeeper's dot. O! it was the nicest cloak in this town! An' - an' - an' so one day her ma she put it on her. It was Sunday, coz the cloak was too nice to wear thist all the time. An' so her ma she put it on her, an' told her not to dit no dirt on it; an' nen she dot out her little basket `at ole K'is b'inged her, an' filled it full o' whole lots o' good fings t'eat, an' told her to take `em to her dran'ma, an' not spill `em, toz her dran'ma'd spank her ef she did, maybe.

An' so little Red Riding Hood she promised to be tareful, an' tossed her heart she wouldn't spill`em for six-five-ten-two hundred bushel dollars. An' nen she kissed her ma dood bye, an' went a skippin off through the dreat big woods to her dran'ma's - no she didn't do a skippin' nedver coz that 'ud spill the dood fings. She thist went a walkin'along like a little lady, she did - as slow an' purty- like she was a marchin' in the Sunday school kassession.

An' so she was a goin' along an' along through the dreat big woods - toz her dran'ma lived a way fur off from her ma's house, an' you had to do through the dreat big woods to dit there.

An' little Red Riding Hood had mostest fun when she'd do there - a listenin' to the purty burds, an' pullin the purty flowers at drowed around the stumps - an' catchin' butterflies an' drasshoppers, an' stickin' pins through 'em-I thist `said' that! coz she was dood. She'd this catch `em, an' leave their wings on `em thist like they was, an' let 'em do adin, toz she was a "boss girl" - my pa said she was!

An' so she was a doin' along an' doin' along, an' purty soon they was a old wicked wolf jumped out; an' he wanted to eat her up, but there was a big man a choppin' wood wite

those there, an' you could hear him, an' so th' old wolf was
afeared to tackle her this then - feared the man ud kill him,
you know; an' so he `tended like he was a dood friends to
her, an' he says, "Dood morning, little Red Riding Hood!"
this like that. An' nen little Red Riding Hood she says,
"dood morning," this as kind - like her ma learnt her - coz
she didn't know th' old wolf wanted t'eat her up.

Nen th' old wolf says, "Where are you doin' to?"

Nen little Red Riding Hood says, "I'm doin' to my
dran'ma's -coz my ma said I might." An' nen she told him that
th' old wolf skipped out an' dot to her dran'ma's first, an'
she didn't know he did.

Nen when th' old wolf dot to her dran'ma's he knocked at
the door. An' nen th' old wolf he knocked adin, an' little
Red Riding Hood's dran'ma she says, "Who's there?"

Nen th' old wolf 'tended like he was little Red Riding
Hood, you know, an' so he says, "W'y, it's me, dran'ma; I'm
little Red Riding Hood, an' I'm tome to see you!"

Nen little Red Riding Hood's dran'ma she says, "Thist
walk in, nen, an' make yousef at home, toz I'm dot the
'raigy, an' tuvered up in bed, an' I tan't open the door fur you!"

An' so the old wolf thist walked in an' shut the door,
an' hopped up on th' bed an' et old Miss Ridinghood up 'fore
she could take her specs off, he did! Nen th' old wolf put
on her nightcap an' tovered up in bed like she was, you know,
an' purty soon her tome little Red Riding Hood, an' she
knocked at the door. Nen th' old wolf says, "Who's there?"
thist like he was her dran'ma, you know, an' she thought he
was, an' so she says, "W'y its me, dran'ma; I'm little Red
Riding Hood, an' I'm tome to see you."

Nen th' old wolf says "Thist walk in an' make yousef at
home, toz I dot the 'raigy an' tovered up in bed, an' I tan't
open the door for you."

An' so little Red Riding Hood she opened the door an'
tomed in; an' the old wolf told her to set down her basket
an' take off her fings an' tome an' set on the bed wif her.

An' little Red Riding Hood she didn't know it was th'
old wolf, an' so she set down her basket an' tooked off her

fings, an' dot a chair an' thumbed up on the bed wif her an'
she thought th' old wolf had more whiskers'n her dran'ma, an'
dreat bigger eyes too, an' she was skeered, an' so she says:
"Oh, dran'ma, what big eyes you dot!"

Nen th' old wolf says: "They're thist big toz I'm so
dlad to see you."

Nen little Red Riding Hood she says: "O! dran'ma, what a
big nose you dot."

Nen th' old wolf says: "It's thist big thataway toz I
smell the dood fings you bringed in the basket."

An' nen little Red Riding Hood she says: "O! dran'ma,
what long, sharp teeth you dot."

Nen th' old wolf he says: "Yes, an' they're thist
thataway t'eat you up wif!" an' nen he made a jump at her,
an' she hollered an' the big man that was a choppin' wood he
tomed in there wif his axe, an' he split th' old wolf's
brains out from ear to ear, an' killed him so quick it made
his head swim, an' little Red Riding Hood wasn't hurt at all,
an' the big man tooked her home, an' her ma was so dlad she
div'd him all the dood fings in the basket an' told him to
call adin - an - an- that's all of it."

Alcoholism rendered Riley like an "adjustable lunatic." He must have feared the consequences of public intoxication displays greatly after public intoxication arrest. The main character in his story, "An Adjustable Lunatic," explains why. He says, "I don't make a business of insanity, or I wouldn't be running at large here on the streets of the city." He continues at a later point, "...I'm glad to assure you of the fact that I'm as harmless as a baby-butterfly. Nobody knows I'm crazy, nobody ever dreams of such a thing - and why? -Because the faculty is adjustable, don't you see, and self-controlling. I never allow it to interfere with business matters, and only let it on at leisure intervals for the amusement it affords me in the pleasurable break it makes in the monotony of a matter-of-fact existence. I'm off duty to-day - in fact, I've been off duty fir a week; or, to be franker still, I lost my situation ten days ago, and I've been humoring this propensity in the mean-while..."

A poem of the period reads:

BELLS JANGLED (1879)

I lie low-ceiled in a nest of dreams;
    The lamp gleams dim i' the odorous gloom,
And the stars at the casement leak long gleams
    Of misty light through the haunted room
Where I lie low-coiled in dreams.

The night-winds ooze o'er my dusk-drowned face
    In a dewy flood that ebbs and flows,
Washing a surf of dim white lace
    Under my throat and the dark red rose
In the shade of my dusk-drowned face.

There's a silken strand of some strange sound
    Slipping out of skein of song:
Eerily as a call unwound
    From a fairy-bugle, it slides along
In a silken strand of sound.

There's a tinkling drip of faint guitar;
    There's a gurgling flute, and a blaring horn
Billowing bubbles of tune afar
    O'er the misty heights of the hills of morn,
To the drip of a faint guitar.

And I dream that I neither sleep nor wake -
    Careless am I if I wake or sleep,
For my soul floats on the waves that break
    In crests of song on the shoreless deep
Where I neither sleep nor wake.

That there are pieces describing Riley's intoxicated situation is not to say they were not transforming pieces. Such poetry challenge thought patterns. But deep down they touch on Riley's greatest fear. This was the fear that he was the psychotically wounded Edgar Allan Poe in reincarnation. This fear was grounded in the birth of James Whitcomb Riley at precisely the morning in October, 1849, when the tormented Edgar Allan Poe died in

Baltimore in delirium tremens. It was as if Riley took up the air of life that Poe expired. Did he also inherit his alcoholism?

At some point it seems, Riley, similarly demonically possessed in alcoholism as Poe took his former incarnation's "Scenes from `Politian" and was in the process of completing them when a strange thing happened-the recollection of the recently deceased Nellie Cooley entered the strange world of Riley's demonic delirium while Riley was writing "The Flying Islands of the Night." Nellie Cooley, we remember, was the young married woman and friend whose encouragement had kept Riley from total breakdown after his mother's death until her husband moved her away to Illinois and away from Riley in 1875 when both left Greenfield after a black lynching there.

Edgar Allan Poe's melancholy or joyless themes were combined with mastery of verse. Riley devoted many hours to studying Poe's verse and read "The Rationale of Verse," Poe's essay on the subject, thoroughly. The memory of Nellie kept him from Poe's thematics.

Riley did not just study Poe's manner, he also wrote Poe-like poems. His "A Dream of Long Ago," was given the metre and cadence of Poe's "The Raven," with a slightly different verse structure. The sounds of Poe were easily mirrored with the liquid and musical sounds of the alphabet.

Crestillomeem was a great admirer of Poe. In a letter of March 4, 1883 written to Dr. James Newton Matthews, Riley said:

Edgar Allan Poe. 1809-1949. Riley was born on the same Sunday morning that Poe died of delirium tremens in Baltimore, Maryland. Riley sometimes feared he was a reincarnation of Poe probably because they shared alcoholism and Poe's "hoodoos."

"...In the Poe sonnets, the work is splendid - masterly in parts - only the theme is joyless - and that hurt the success of such an effort, however deserving in all other qualities. It is what hurt Poe, and will always drape his memory with gloomy speculations and unsatisfying contemplations. He was a marvelous intellect perhaps as much estranged from himself as from all of his kind. Anyway, he seems, always, to me, unhappy, and his influence always cheerless. If I ever get to Heaven, I will doubtless love him better there where all `will be unriddled.' All melancholy themes are pets of mine - positively; but I am growing to avoid them as much as possible for I am more and more satisfied of their hurtfulness every new one I indulge."

"Poe was hoodooed all his life. I took up the hoodoo where he left off," Riley once said. We know Riley studied Poe because of the famous "Leonainie" incident in Riley's life. Riley wrote the poem in the style of Poe and perpetrated the hoax in concert with a friend who was the editor of the Kokomo Dispatch upon the representation that it was a newly discovered manuscript of Edgar Allan Poe published in the Kokomo DISPATCH on August 12, 1877.

How Riley described writing "Leonainie": "I studied Poe's method. He seemed to have a theory, rather misty to be sure, about the use of m's and n's and mellifluous vowels and sonorous words. I remember that I was a long time in evolving the name of `Leonainie,' but at length the verses were finished and ready for trial. A friend, the editor of the Kokomo Dispatch, undertook the launching of the hoax in his paper; he did this with great editorial gusto, while, at the same time, I attacked the authenticity of the poem in the Democrat. That diverted all possible suspicion from me. the hoax succeeded far too well, for what had started as a boyish prank, became a literary discussion nation-wide, and the necessary expose had to be made. I was appalled by the result. The press assailed me furiously, and even my own paper dismissed me because I had given the `discovery' to a rival."

How much Riley knew about the orphaned, tragic Edgar Allan Poe is not known. Poe's death in delirium tremens was widely reported. Discovered by a printer named Walker in a Baltimore tavern called Gunner's Hall on an Election Day for members of Congress, Poe was in great distress. Taken to Baltimore's Washington Medical College in stupor, he was admitted at five in the afternoon. He remained in stupor until three o'clock the next morning when he entered a stage of busy delirium, talking constantly and deliriously addressing spectral and imaginary objects on the walls. The next day Poe revived somewhat but was basically incoherent before lapsing into violent delirium resisting the efforts of nurses to keep him in bed. His doctor, a man named Dr. John J. Moran, mentions him raving for nearly a day and calling out an unrecognizable name until three o'clock the next morning when Doctor Moran noted: "quietly moving his head he said `Lord help my poor soul' and expired." Poe died a drunk. Dr. Moran attributed his death to delirium tremens on the basis of Poe's profuse perspiration, trembling and hallucinations. Others have since sought to find less disgraceful causes of death such as "exposure." Poe's great admirer, the French poet Charles Baudelaire, called the death "suicide" which is probably much closer to the truth.

Riley studied Poe extensively. He thought of himself as Poe at times. His forgery of Poe's name to the poem, "Leonainie," may not have even seemed like forgery. Riley's "Tale of a Spider" in which a spider takes on the life of a doomed communicant and "An Adjustable Lunatic" of a maniacal disappearing and suicidal stranger seem clearly composed under Poe's gothic influence. It is not clear if Riley wrote poetry while intoxicated as Poe did. One remembers that "The Bells" was written by an Edgar Allan Poe who did not even remember he wrote it the next morning. Riley's "The Flying Islands of the Night" was, we know, written by an alcoholic seeking to understand himself. Some of it bears the same throbbings and excesses of "intoxicatese" writing that Poe's does. One thing seems clear. If Riley had not written his "The Flying Islands of the Night" and gained through it a self-understanding and feeling of great encouragement to himself from the beyond from his dead mother and dead Nellie Cooley one could speculate he might have died as Poe did. The strange death-birth connection between Poe and Riley contributed to Riley's unease about the fate for which he was destined. The poetry and alcoholic life-style of Edgar Allan Poe were definite dynamics in Riley's self-perception. One does not fear being a reincarnation of someone without great tremor. Probably for this reason, Riley avoided admitting he was born when he was. The comparisons of alcoholism by two kindred poets was already too vivid in Riley's mind.

There was in fact great talk of Riley being Poe's reincarnation as in an article in the Chicago TRIBUNE of December 16, 1894 under the title: "Plagiarism or Reincarnation?" The many points of similarity of the writing of Riley and Poe brought forth the author of this article, George Harper, to find evidence for the Hindoo theory of transmigration of souls, or reincarnation. When Riley as Crestillomeem wrote, Poe was affixed in his mind.

In the meantime, Riley slipped further and further into alcoholism. Riley, the alcoholic, was considered a no-good in Greenfield during much of his early life, but he was not reviled.

To understand this requires a brief review of the temperance movement in Indiana of the time.

Whiskey was easily availability in the corn growing regions of Indiana where Riley grew up. Whiskey was a corn product after all. Liquor traffic was always a source of revenue to Hancock County from the founding of the county. The first meeting of the county's government, through its board of commissioners, was held April 7, 1828 and the first license to sell liquor was granted by them less than a month later. As the years went along, whisky was sold not just at saloons but also in grocery stores. Every home had supplies. Children drank whisky and it was a popular medicine used for colds or pain reduction.

In the 1860's movements to control alcoholism, then an epidemic, began. Citizens began to remonstrate against the granting of licenses to sell whiskey. Reuben Riley and Joseph B. Atkison were usually the two Greenfield lawyers who represented the remonstrators.

As Riley entered manhood, the temperance battle against alcohol use reached the level of a crusade, just as James Whitcomb Riley, was firmly established as an alcoholic.

A Ladies' Temperance Alliance was organized at Greenfield's Methodist Episcopal church in 1874. The goal was to obtain pledges of Hancock County men not to drink intoxicating liquors. Other meetings were held in area churches and soon the ladies began visiting liquor establishments causing many of them to close or else begin serving sodas. Lists were made of signatories of the Murphy pledge and circulated. Applicants for liquor licenses were hounded into withdrawing them. Prosecutions were sought of intoxicated persons or any proprietor who served liquor to an intoxicated person. As stated elsewhere, Riley himself was prosecuted for intoxication. Candidates for office were screened to ensure they were not subject to intoxication. The local bar was invited to a meeting and the demand was made that none represent alcoholic interests or the intoxicated. Lawyers were urged to sign a pledge not to but the majority of the members refused. Mass meetings were organized and among the local speakers against intoxicants was Reuben Riley, the poet's father. Richman described one of March 7, 1874 at the Greenfield Christian Church. Later in the 1870's Red Ribbon Societies were organized in which persons who had signed the "pledge" wore red ribbons. Another temperance group wore "blue ribbons." A county convention was organized of the Christian Temperance Union in 1879. Temperance picnics and the like were sponsored. A "secret" organization also spread devoted to terrorist tactics for the cause bragging of "cells'in every township. The only saloon in New Palestine was burned to the ground during this period by such a secret "cell."

It was in the mood of a county with such temperance activity that James Whitcomb Riley was often found drunk in different places around the city.

Reuben Riley, the poet's father, and remonstration attorney, refused to assist his son under any such circumstances. Nor would the "Captain" pay fines or bonds when the poet was arrested and charged with public intoxications during his youth. The Riley family was greatly ashamed of the poet. Stories are told of Riley sneaking into the home, led by the hand up to his bedroom to sleep off a drunk, by his little sister, Mary, fifteen years his junior. The two, Mary, who also suffered from alcoholism later in life, as well as the brother between them, Hum, often relied upon each other in a world hostile to them because of their propensity to liquor overuse.

As the early 70's proceeded, the temperance movement gained more and more force. Riley's father, Reuben Riley, became a leader of it further distancing himself from Riley because Riley was, after all, "wedded to Crestillomeem."

Greenfield saw a great temperance movement arise in 1874. As a part of this movement, mass meetings of citizens were called. One such meeting was sponsored by the Temperance Alliance, a ladies' organization, held in the Methodist Episcopal Church on Sunday evening, March 8, 1874. The church was filled to overflowing with hundreds of people and many of the lawyers of the town were present. At one point in the meeting, the ladies distributed the usual temperance pledges for the attendees to sign. In addition, the ladies had a special pledge they wished the attorneys to sign. This pledge contained an agreement not to defend any person charged with a violation of the liquor laws. When the majority of the lawyers refused to sign the pledge, the ladies called for them to explain themselves. The first to speak was the lawyer, Ephraim Marsh who stated "All criminals were entitled to a fair and impartial trial, and to be heard in person or by counsel, This being the case, I as a lawyer cannot consent to place myself in a position not to accept employment in any case at bar if I desire to do so." Another lawyer, Charles G. Offutt, responded to the call to sign the pledge saying, "I declined to sign it and I still decline. So far as I know but two members of the bar have signed it. I hold that an attorney has the right to engage in the defense of any man, woman, or child charged with a crime without being liable to just censure from any quarter. The fundamental law of the land declares that in all criminal prosecutions the accused shall have the right to be heard by himself and counsel, and that the presumption of innocence is in his favor. Sir, because a man is charged with a violation of law, be it the "Baxter bill" or any other, it doesn't necessarily follow that he is guilty, not by any means."

As Offutt continued his reasons for not signing the pledge, his words reveal the mild attitude against alcoholics such as Riley which then prevailed in Greenfield.

"As far as the temperance question is concerned, I think it is admitted by all candid men that temperance is right and intemperance wrong. It is not necessary that I should stand here and declaim against the evils of intemperance. All men everywhere admit it to be the great foe of mankind. The veriest wretch that ever drank destruction to his own soul will tell you that his course is not to be approved or followed. No man can engage in the use of intoxicating liquor to an excess, and not finally destroy his constitution. It shatters the physical man and lays the mind in ruins, and whatever others may say, I know that no man in this audience would more heartily rejoice over the success of any plan that would stay the fearful tide of intemperance sweeping over the land, than I. And, sir, I think this is the most favorable time for the ladies to accomplish great good. No political party, as my friend, Captain Ogg, has said, is opposing their movements. Good people everywhere are wishing them success, and if they go about their work in the spirit of Christianity, love and kindness their efforts may be crowned with success. It won't do to proscribe men or treat them harshly for their views, but reason with them, treat them kindly, convince them that it is to their interests to be sober and upright, that the good of society demands that they should give up a business which yields only poverty, disgrace and crime, and, my word for it, your success will be great."

It is said that this lawyer's speech was roundly applauded at the ladies temperance meeting in this year before the community consented to other mob action, the breaking in of the Hancock County Jail and the lynching of the black taken out from there at the county fairgrounds so soon to occur. Despite the castigation and shame cast on alcoholics such as Riley, they were not to be the subject of violent personal attacks. The bars they frequented were. The sellers of alcoholic products were. The talk was much against them. None were, however, lynched. One wonders where Messers Marsh and Offutt were when the black man, William Kemmer, was lynched the next year with their lofty beliefs in rights to trial, an attorney, a presumption of innocence and a semblance of a right to defense.

CRESTILLOMEEM'S SECOND GREAT ENCOUNTER WITH RILEY AFTER THE LYNCHING OF KEMMER

One does not imagine Riley's first great encounter with Crestillomeem as involving more than "bouts" with depression ever more serious but only occasional lapses into intoxications. This was the period after his mother's death until his return to Greenfield in 1875 prepared to settle down.

Crestillomeem was under wraps after Riley returned to Greenfield in his mid-twenties. She had not succeeded in keeping him from marginal employments, pleasant associations with friends and moments of inspiration with Nellie in the Millikan-Cooley household. Riley was surviving and maturing as a man. Could he even consider permanently staying at home in Greenfield? Perhaps he might conform to his father's wishes and even become a lawyer?

These thoughts were no doubt in his mind as the year 1875 dawned. Riley was back in town from his McCrillus medicine show trips and from his Graphics adventures.

Kemmer to his reward. Illustration from "The Flying Islands Of The Night".

Early 1875 was the year Riley's poem "A Dreamer" appeared in HEARTH AND HOME MAGAZINE. Ik Marvel, its Editor, not only accepted it but sent Riley a check of the first money he received for a poem. Riley did not remember how much it was he spent it so fast. In a letter dated April "foolest," 1875, Riley wrote his brother John, "...I have had and still have plenty to do in signwork -I've got old Greenfield spangled off like a

At an unkown spot in this clup of trees and wild brush in the middle of a field lie the remains of William Kemmer, lynched by a mob of masked vigilantes buried with the noose still around his neck. The spot was a "pauper cemetery" mainly for the indigent living in a county home or "Infirmary" across the National Road from the site.

circus clown... I am improved to some extent in a moral particular. I am a confirmed Sunday-school goer - Yes! did Secretary business for two Sundays, and blackboard lesson - You just ought to see me clothe a blackboard in artistic raiment and yaller chalk -

Last Sunday's was as good as a magic-lantern show to the children. The trustees talk of an admission fee. Well, here's the "best of the wine"! I yesterday received a letter, with check enclosed, paying for poem published in Hearth & Home of April 10. I want you to secure for me a few extras as they cannot be had here. Write to me and "told me all about it." Jim."

After this fact, he says, "I thought my fortune made. Almost immediately I sent off another contribution, whereupon to my dismay, came this reply `The management has decided to discontinue the publication and hopes that you will find a market for your worthy work elsewhere."

As to Riley's Sunday School Secretary tenure there is a story that survives. When no one else was at Riley's Methodist Church to take minutes of the meetings, Riley was asked to do so. The result was so flowery with such items as "Mrs. Pinkney wore a large pink feather-trimmed hat," that he was never again asked to do such duties.

But Riley was busy with other things.

One can now see James Whitcomb Riley on his way into his father's legal profession. Reuben was the trainer of many young lawyers. The list of those entered on the roll of the Hancock County Bar Association on the Motion of Reuben Riley is very extensive. Reuben taught young men the law. Law

Riley's last sign, "A.J. Banks," painted for a downtown Greenfield Building at the time of his writing of "An Old Sweetheart of Mind" in 1875. (From the Barton Rees Pogue glass positive collection.)

schools were not established in Indiana at this time. Barristers became lawyers by "reading" with older lawyers such as Reuben Riley. Now James Whitcomb Riley had finally begun the process. Often, when James Whitcomb Riley was expected to be reading Blackstone, his book was laid down while his pen was busy at poetry. One of the poems written in his father's law office during this period of apprenticeship was the famous "An Old Sweetheart of Mine" which would one day become the most commonly known poem in America.

Along with his legal apprenticeship, in mid-June, 1875, Riley decided to try a program of readings and instrumental music outside Greenfield with his friend, John Moore. These evening engagements were a break from "reading the law." Riley and Moore chose Kokomo as a location for an evening entertainment. John borrowed the Prince Albert coat needed for wardrobe from the store of his father. The first night's show was totally disastrous and such a crushing failure financially that the two were unable to pay for their overnight lodging. The bill was paid for by painting the next day. This truncated tour is mentioned in the Hancock DEMOCRAT. Riley was friendly with its editor who reported in its June 24th issue, "Every place they have visited they met with great success." Ha, ha!

Riley was on the verge of becoming a county seat lawyer. The days of apprenticeship continued on until one of the most telling details of the history of the poet's hometown occurred, the hanging of William Kemmer.

This was a lynching of a black man and it shook Riley down to the soul. All of the country had been shocked that such events were occuring in the North. That such lynchings were going on in the South was less of a surprise. In fact there were twenty such lynchings of black men without trial in Indiana between 1865 and 1903 according to HANDBOOK ON INDIANA HISTORY, page 91, Edited by Donald Carmony. None of the others however was so close to Riley as this one. I believe he must have witnessed it or at least some of it.

The lynching of William Kemmer in Greenfield caused Riley to become aware that social institutions matter hugely. This revolution in the thought of James Whitcomb Riley caused him to leave Greenfield again for a "spell" of wandering. He took off to join a "second" traveling "miracle medicine show." He apparently was not about to settle down in a place of "mob rule" and "lynching." He took off on another spur of the moment decision as he had left on the first shortly after history records this lynching in Riley's hometown of Greenfield.

Although no photo has survived of the Kemmer hanging that the sensitive frontier poet Riley probably observed, this photo of a similar vigilante lynching of the era does.

Eventually Riley would find an answer to his alienation from this event in kenotic ideas and taking refuge withinits hope of salvation in a "humble" redeeming Jesus. Racism, in particular, was a hated thing to him arising from his sight of it from this black lynching in his hometown. Riley also nurtured a hatred for all intolerance as a result of this event. Riley was nudged more and more toward love for the humble people he had come to know in his travels with Crestillomeem. Riley wrote in the poem "To Uncle Remus,"

> "The Lord who made the day and night,
> He made the Black man and the White;
>> So, in like view,
>> We hold it true
> That He hain't got no favorite."

Although the life of James Whitcomb Riley was tumultuous in many respects, the one great event of his life which fueled his flight into kenotic poetry was an event never mentioned in all of his poetry except his cryptic autobiographical poem, "The Flying Islands of the Night." Riley simply stayed away from controversy in order to secure for himself a standing on which to make kenotic points for a public needing encouragement to live peacefully and "neighborly" with each other. The following is an excerpt from his autobiographical poem:

"THAT AIRY PENALTY"

Jucklet (Aside)
Twigg-brebblets! but her Majesty hath speech
That doth bejuice all metaphor to drip
And spray and mist of sweetness!

Crestillomeem (Confusedly)
                    Where was I?
O ay! ...
... - That airy penalty
The jocund Fates provide our love-lorn wights
In this glad island: So for thrice three nights
They spun the prince his lien and marked him pay
It out (despite all warnings of his doom)
In fast and sleepless search for her - and then
They tripped his fumbling feet and he fell - UP! -
Up! - as 'tis writ - sheer past Heaven's flinching walls
And toppost cornices. - Up - up and on! -

And, it is grimly guessed of those who thus
For such a term bemoan an absent love,
And so fall upwise, they must needs fall on -
And on and on - and on - and on - and on!
Ha! ha!

Jucklet
      Quahh! but the prince's holden breath
Must ache his throat by this!

Jucklet, or James Whitcomb Riley who survives to tell his story in min-strelsy, tells us of the metaphoric happening of a lynching incident in his hometown which could not have been otherwise described.

The vagabond who "strangely went" as the result of this hanging was none other than himself, James Whitcomb Riley. He left Greenfield, Indiana, his hometown under the circumstance of a shocking hanging. The lynching is a ghost of the American Reconstruction period following the American Civil War. It was a typical example of not just racism but also the social Darwinist impulse. A black man was simply being selected out a lit-tle quicker than evolution would inevitably have provided anyway. Riley was sickened and ran.

The Kemmer hanging was on the front page of the Indianapolis JOUR-NAL of Monday morning, June 28, 1875 under the huge headline, "Judge Lynch," A first sub-headline read, "Hanging of a Negro Ravisher by an Armed Mob.", with a second reading "Swift Punishment Meted Out to an Inhuman Fiend - Greenfield in a State of Wild Excitement." The article was attributed to information from an unnamed "Special Correspondent." Was it Riley? Later, the Journal was pressed for who this "correspondent" was but the newspaper never revealed the informer's name. The account differs from the way the event was reported in Greenfield by the Hancock DEMOCRAT and is quoted.

JUDGE LYNCH

This account reads in part, "...While Mr. Vaughn, a farmer, was at work in the fields, about a half a mile away, a Negro entered the house and delib-erately outraged the person of the wife, who was at that time lying sick and defenseless on her bed, with no companion but her two-year old son. The burly brute entering the house, proceeded without a moment's hesitation to the commission of the awful crime, and escaped from the house just in time to avoid the husband, who had been summoned by his little son, who had ran toward him and attracted his attention....(Kemmer) was overtaken in Rush County, and for the time being confined in the Rushville jail, but threats of lynching having been freely indulged in, he was removed to the a jail in Greenfield, the crime having been perpetrated within the confines of Hancock County. The people were in a state of wild excitement and demanded that an indictment be returned against the brute at once, that his trial and punishment might not be delayed an instant. But the authorities in their wisdom decided to wait till the indigna-

The location at which Riley may have observed the lynching of Kemmer. This field was the location of the "Floral Hall" and the Hancock County Agricultural Fairgrounds where Kemmer was lynched in 1875.

tion had subsided somewhat and as a consequence measures were taken with the utmost secrecy and dispatch to execute summary vengeance upon the prisoner. The quiet community was thoroughly aroused and a look of deep determination was on every face. Everybody knew something was on foot, but none could say who were engaged in it. The husband of the outraged woman was in a perfect frenzy that nothing could appease and every where he met with the spontaneous sympathy of good and true citizens who could only be worked up the commission of an unlawful act by some such an emergency as this, Mrs. Vaughn was lying at the very point of death from the effects of her injuries, and it was determined to rid the world of a monster ere his victim passed to the other shore. Accordingly on Friday night, a band of one hundred and sixty disguised men met at an appointed rendezvous between Rushville and Greenfield and without a sound marched toward the latter place, passing on their way long enough to take a vote as to whether their intended victim should be hung, burned or cut to pieces. With grim ferocity, forty men balloted for the cutting process and thirty-two for the burning, but eighty-eight votes were cast for the less brutal yet equally certain means of transit out of the world. A squad of seventy remained on the outskirts to act as a reserve in case their services were needed while the remainder of the battalion moved silently in the direction of jail wherein Kemmer was confined.

A detail of twenty of the vigilants noiselessly effected entrance by means of an aperture in one of the windows and made their way to the sheriff's quarters, where a demand was made upon him for the keys to Kemmer's cell. The plucky office refused to deliver them but he was quickly overpowered and the keys were taken from him but as the invaders were to them they were of little value, and crowbar agency was resorted to with eminent success. Kemmer remained in his bed quietly until his door was opened when he sprang to his feet and with a heavy club, commend a furious battle for his life, striking right and left with destruction. The leader, a large and powerfully built man, received a terrific blow on the head but in a trice his assailant was disarmed, bloodily beaten into submission, bound and taken to a wagon and hastily carted to the fair-ground, the place designed for his execution. In "Floral Hall" a rude gallows was improvised by means of a rafter and noose, a very simple yet effective contrivance. The wagon containing Kemmer was then backed up under the rafter, the noose adjusted about his neck, and the other end securely fastened to an immovable object.

The wretch was then given a chance to say something for himself, but his sole response to an inquiry from the chief was "Men, you are doing wrong."

"If that's all you have to say," was the angry reply, "the quicker you die the better," and at the word the wagon was drawn from under the ravisher's feet and he was left to die of strangulation, the shock not having been sufficient to break his neck. The rope was a new one and, with the heavy weight attached, stretched until Kemmer's great feet touched the earth but the ground was scooped out by a dozen willing hands in less time than it takes to tell it.

In twenty minutes the man was pronounced dead, and shortly thereafter the vigilants under orders from the chief, took the back track, but not until the score or so of citizens standing about had been ordered to go home and make no attempt to follow or ascertain their identity. The body was allowed to hang till morning, and when it was cut down the following verdict written on an envelope was found pinned to his back:

"It is the verdict of 160 men from Hancock, Shelby and Rush, that his life is inadequate to meet the demands of justice.

The Coroner empanneled a jury Saturday and after hearing the evidence of all persons who claimed to have knowledge of the affair, returned a verdict in accordance with the facts as above narrated.

Kemmer is well known in Indianapolis where he has lived for several months and gained an unenviable reputation. Together with a woman whom he claimed was his sister, he occupied a tenement owned by John E. Foundray in the northwestern part of the city. On the night previous to the day he committed the crime for which he was hung, he stole a horse from Mr. Springer, an employee of Daggett & Co., confectioners, and left the city."

The Hancock DEMOCRAT in Greenfield, William Mitchell, Editor, also carried a report of the incident in its issue of July 1, 1875:

THE FORCIBLE HANGING OF THE NEGRO MAN...

"In the Democrat of last week, we published an account of the ravishing of Mrs. Vaughn, wife of Wm. N. Vaughn, of Blue River township, by a negro man named William Kemmer, and his subsequent arrest in Rush county, and legal transfer to this county. It is now our duty to record the summary death at the hands of a large number of outraged but unknown citizens of Rush, Shelby and Hancock on Saturday morning last, and we will endeavor to discharge that duty without unnecessary varnish or sensational literature, keeping as near the facts of the summary proceeding as possible, considering the secrecy of the transaction.

At about 12:30 A.M. on Saturday morning, June 26, 1875, a party of armed and masked men, numbering about 125, quietly and orderly entered our town from the East and without unnecessary preliminaries surrounded the new jail building. An entrance from the front and south doors was soon and easily effected by probably twenty-five of the party. Once in the building, the next step was to get the keys of the jail house. Search was made for the room in which Mr. Thomas, the Sheriff and jailor, was sleeping. This was soon found by the answer of Mr. Thomas to the demand for admission, as his voice was probably well known. To this demand Mr. Thomas positively and persistently refused. Seeing that he could not be roused to depart from a sworn duty, the necessary means were soon brought to bear to open the door by force. This was easily done, as it was a pine door, and the splinters flew in every direction in the room. Mr. Thomas was soon face to face with an armed, masked, and of course, unknown lot of men, who resolutely and determinedly demanded the keys of the jail and to whose demand Thomas as resolutely refused to surrender the keys. He was informed that they did not desire to injure him or the building, and that they did not want to be injured themselves; but that they would have the keys or they would go through the walls of the jail They wanted the incarcerated negro, had come for him and would have him at all hazards. Thomas still refused and stood in silence before his armed and powerful opponents. Seeing that he would not surrender, he was caught and forced back against the wall where he was soon relieved of the coveted keys. Once in their possession, the object of the mission seemed half accomplished; but they did not know they had the right keys, and if so, they were uncertain how to use them. Thomas was then asked if they were the right keys, but he said not a word, but stood silent and mute as a marble statue. The next move was to get him to go down and open the doors leading to the object of their midnight mission; but this was stoutly refused. Then he was taken up by four of the most stalwart men in the room and carried head first down the front stairs. Thomas now began to feel his oats, and said it was useless to try to force him to do that which a plain violation of his official duty, and he emphasized it by saying that he would be d-d if he would. Satisfied that they were losing time on Thomas, they sent him back to his room, saying that they would endeavor to open the fail themselves. There are two separate locks to the doors one of which opens out and other in. A little practice soon resulted in the opening of these doors. They were now in the main part of the jail, but there was another bolt to throw before the prisoner could be reached, and this they did not at first understand, for they forced by main strength and crowbars the upper fastening of the cell door. When this bolt was broken off, the lower bolt not being damaged, it looks as if some one had pulled the lever below that operates the bolt above. While the men were working at the door, our information is, but we have no idea that it is mere guess work, that the negro lay still on his bed on the lower bunk. When the cell door was thrown back, the same authority says, and equally creditable, that the negro sprang forward and leveled two of his assailants. It is probably that by this time he was in the hall aiming for the door on the west of the cells, which leads to the lower floor of the jail. At this point it is very probable the negro was knocked senseless by some of the men in which condition he was securely bound, taken below and placed in a spring wagon standing at the south door of the jail. It is not true that the negro had a bar of iron in his cell. The bar of iron alluded to and found in the negro's cell the next morning, was evidently taken there by one of the masked me, as, after the negro was locked up for the night, it was standing outside the jail part of the building. The negro was a very powerful and physically courageous man, and with such an implement for defense, he would have bloody work for at least some of the men. The statement of its presence in the cell is merely sensation and coined in the brain of some reporter to lengthen out his piece to regular city limits. But we must return to our narrative.

In possession of the subject of their search, and seeing him securely tied and lying in the bottom of the wagon and surrounded by a few of their trusty friends, the masked men gave vent to their feelings by repeated shouts of apparent joy. The leader of their party then gave the word to move on as they had entered the town in regular order and in true military style. The order was speedily and quietly executed and the march of death was commenced for this victim of a hellish and unbridled lust. Around the jail building the solemn procession moved toward Main street and approaching which street the negro began to mourn and make piteous appeals to his Master above whose laws he had so cruelly and wantonly violated. Turning into Main street, the procession moved silently toward the east, followed by a rear guard to keep off all intruders. Reaching the toll-house, the procession turned to the south when the Fair Grounds was soon reached, into which the procession moved with unerring precision toward the south end of the old Floral Hall, as if it had been previously selected for the expiation of the criminal's evil and outrageous deed of crime. The preparation for the last act of the tragedy was soon completed, by the fastening of a rope to the joists of the hall. A neat and judicious hangman's knot was soon place at the other end, and the wagon in which the doomed man lay was backed under. Standing between the certainties of earth and the uncertainties of the future, with the dark waters of death in full view to the eyes of him who was soon to pass over, the guilty culprit was asked if he had anything to say, and his reply was..." Men, you are doing a great wrong!" which he repeated several times. He was asked if he had nothing more to say: if not the end was near. Saying nothing more, the wagon was driven from under, and William Kemmer, the negro ravisher, danced an air jig suspended between heaven and earth. Thus ended the career of an evil and corrupt scoundrel, whose vicious tastes and unbridled lust brought him a just and ignominious death. After hanging until he was dead and beyond the reach of the pains and pangs of this world, a placard, written upon the glued side of an envelope was pinned upon his breast by some one who fully understood the use and force of his mother tongue, from which we made the following copy:
"- It is the verdict of one hundred and sixty men from Hancock, Shelby and Rush that his life is inadequate to the demands of justice." ...

When life was pronounced extinct, some one in the masked crowd rose and announced in slow and measured tones, in substance as follows:

"The act just committed was done in no spirit of bravado or malice, but to vindicate, in a small degree, an outrage upon an innocent and unprotected woman, and to give protection in the future to your wives, as well as mine; that if any one, be he officer or citizen, divulge the secrets of this night he shall suffer (pointing to the suspended negro) in the same way."

With this benediction, the crowd was dispersed from the Fair Ground and the inanimate form of William Kemmer was left suspended in mid-air..."

Another article mentioned the Coroner's Inquest over the Dead Body of William Kemmer. On Saturday morning, January 26, 1875, Harrison I. Cooper, Coroner of Hancock County, hearing that the dead body of a negro man was suspended in the old Floral Hall on the Fair Ground, east of Greenfield, repaired to the scene with a dray to remove the body to town. He found the body suspended by the neck with a small cotton cord doubled and looking quite natural. The mouth and eyes were closed, and, beyond a slight hemorrhage at the nose, the man looked as if nothing unusual had happened. The cord around the neck was sunk beneath the skin, but so far as could be seen the skin was not broken. Two small holes in the scalp on the back of the head were visible, but they evidently did not

Doc Townsend, "traveling medicine man" and "U.S. Grant lookalilke." (Neg. C7177, IMCPL-Riley Collection, Indiana Historical Society.)

do much harm, beyond a stun at the time of being made, as the skull was not broken. The Coroner cut him down, placed him on the dray and moved him to town, leaving the noose still around his neck, and with which he was buried. He was placed in a coffin at the undertaking establishment of Wills and Pratt, where he remained during the day, being visited by thousands of citizens and strangers. Some difficulty was experienced in getting a place to deposit his remains, his father, at Carthage, having refused to a special messenger from the Coroner to have anything to do with them. Not being a citizen of Greenfield, he could not be interred in the New Cemetery without the payment of the required fee, two dollars. There was no one to advance the money, and Mr. Cooper had to look elsewhere for a place to deposit the body of Kemmer. About dark the box was placed in a wagon, and the Coroner, and the grave-digger, Buffalo Bill, it was driven to the county poor farm, where the remains of William Kemmer, the negro ravisher, were deposited about 11 p.m. in their last resting place, "unwept, unhonored, and unsung."

After the lynching of Kemmer, James Whitcomb Riley "strangely went" from town.

Shortly after the Kemmer incident, Riley composed his little remembered poem, "Death."

DEATH

"Lo, I am dying! And to feel the King
Of Terrors fasten on me, steeps all sense
Of life, and love, and loss, and everything.
In such deep calms of restful indolence,
His keenest fangs of pain are sweet to me
As fused kisses of mad lovers' lips
When, flung shut-eyed in spasmed ecstasy,
They feel the world spin past them in eclipse,
And so thank God with ever-tightening lids!
But what I see, the soul of me forbids
All utterance of; and what I hear and feel
The rattle in my throat could ill reveal
Though it were music to your ears as to
Mine own. - Press closer - closer - I have grown
So great, your puny arms about me thrown
Seem powerless to hold me here with you; -
I slip away - I waver - and - I fall -
Christ! What a plunge! Where am I dropping? All
My breath bursts into dust - I can not cry -
I whirl - I reel and veer up overhead,
And drop flat-faced against - the sky -
Soh, bless me! I am dead!"

This seems to be a projection of how William Kemmer must have felt.

So began another period of wandering which continued for the next two years.

How did Riley leave Greenfield?

When Riley slipped down the stairs from his father's law office having decided to skip out "for his own reasons", he observed Dr. Townsend at the town square bowing and introducing himself on a little back platform, stetson hat lifted, frock coat flapping and hair and beard trimmed to make him appear like a double to General U.S. Grant. Behind him were three young men wearing linen dusters each playing two musical instruments playing martial music interspersed with loud organ recitals of hymns from an organ within the wagon. That night a "free concert" was promised "at early- candlelite." Riley talked his way into this crew and left Greenfield with "the glittering cavalcade" without saying good-bye to anybody.

Riley later wrote in doggerel,
"Why let pain your pleasure spoil
For want of Townsend's Magic Oil?"

The Wizard Oil Co. left Greenfield for Fortville and places beyond with Riley on board and several young men. The boys laughed at his stories and enjoyed his drawing, calling him "Little Man." He taught them new songs and did blackboard illustrations for Doc Townsend who he called "Doxy." The Wizard Oil co. boys arrived in town about noon announcing their presence with great showers of music. Then the boys would distribute handbills and Doc Townsend would lecture on his medicines afternoon and evening. In the evenings, by torchlights, Riley would entertain too. He did original recitations, impersonations, and readings of poetry. When there was a week-long county fair, the Wizard boys would stay in town the whole week and participate in the parades and fair entertainments. The boys being exciting and mysterious vagabonds had many girls chasing them. Riley's depression about Greenfield was lifted. A "rainbow" was in the sky. The times were never dull. By October the group reached Lima, Ohio, where Townsend resided and kept his laboratory. The group made Lima the center for the last flings around Ohio before winter set in. Riley made many friendships and was invited often to read his poems. While Townsend spent the days making his medicines, Riley was living in the Townsend home and preparing new advertising. Riley kept no regular schedule. He is remembered by the child of Doc Townsend as studying Buckles' HISTORY OF CIVILIZATION and deToqueville's DEMOCRACY IN AMERICA during this period. A few weeks before Christmas, Riley decided to return back home to Greenfield.

During the "dark half" of 1875 after Riley "ran" from the Kemmer lynching, Riley wrote relatively little poetry. Nellie's departure from Greenfield as well as his own were horribly wrenching events. He escaped from Crestillomeem with Doc Townsend and his ridiculous "patent medicine" touring show.

While James Whitcomb Riley was on the run from Greenfield, his mind yet returned to his life there. Here is a letter Riley wrote to his equally mischievous friend, John Skinner from Lima, Ohio October 7, 1875 during this "dark half" of the year of the Kemmer lynching: "After my long waiting your letter came at last....."I tho't this place without an equal in regard to its "increase in crime", but I must knock under for the present to old Greenfield. A saloon keeper was shot here last week and no particular stir made about it, nor the man missed...Day before yesterday we were furnished an entire `change of program' by our funny man -the one you know. They had a warrant for him and he run (sic) like a little man-the whole town ran after him. They wore him out at last and bro't him up a-standin'". He had seduced a girl here - a Miss Vananda - and not having compromise money enough, or a hankering after prison wall -he did what he ought to have been man enough to do without compulsion -married her. She is fifteen and he eighteen and both in the family way. By the way there is a slashin' lot of girls here, and they do hold a man off too "purty". I have only made the acquaintance of two or three, and they're the very ones I didn't care to know, but I will make it Hot for 'em shortly: I'm handling "wires" now that'll fetch 'em. "Confound my time" "I stand in" with the best men of the town, and am rapidly growing in public favor - I'll be out in book form yet. I wish you were here to room with me at the bobbiest little boarding house in the world - everything is perfect even to the old girl, "the hostess." She wears a crutch, but I don't know how many of her legs are off. She capers under the jocund patronymic of "Aunt Jane" - everybody calls her that, so if she Aunt Jane who is she? Speaking of Boarding
Houses - how's the Test House? I would like to strike old 13 to-night with its exchanged bed - I need something of that kind now, but I shall not excite your sensitive nature with visions of "sweet faces, rounded arms and bosoms prest to little harps of gold" not waken in the drowsy channels of your inmost soul, the fire of "Kisses sweet as those by hopeless fancy feigned
On lips that are for others".
To Mrs. Test give my especial regards, and thank her for remembering me so kindly. Tell Minnie I could be happy once again could I hear her one plaintive melody. I think of you often, and of the rare old times we had, and I still nurse a hope that we may have a grand Rehearsal of them again. Say to Angie that she haunts me (a casual romantic interest)..." Yours truly, Jim
Give my love to George and Nell - not forgetting Jesse and Nett.

Apparently Riley left Greenfield under "sudden need" during this month after the Kemmer hanging. Riley was never far from newspaper reporting. Earlier in the year that Kemmer was hung Riley had edited and contributed to the Greenfield COMMERCIAL and NEWS. After those newspapers folded, Riley did occasional assignments for what had been the rival newspaper, the Hancock DEMOCRAT. Minnie Belle Mitchell, wife of its later editor, recalled, Riley spending hours in the office of the Hancock DEMOCRAT where William Mitchell, the kindly old editor, sensing Riley's genius, would share with him a corner to write. The editor gave him assignments such as reporting current events or social events or writing advertisements for the local columns. Sometimes these would end up "rhymed."

One can imagine that Riley may have contributed or written the Hancock DEMOCRAT article detailing the events of the lynching of Kemmer. If he witnessed the events, he might have lived precariously. The perpetrators would have known his name. When other detailed versions of the incident - less favorable to the action - began being leaked to other newspapers, Riley might well have felt the heat of suspicion directed at him.

Another letter to John Skinner - from Union City, Sept 14, 1876.

At first he admits "dying of loneliness" striking Fortville after he joined the group at Greenfield. He must have had to leave very quickly and desperately. Then things changed for the better.

"I am having first rate times considering the boys I am with - they, you know, are hardly my kind, but they are pleasant and agreeable...We sing along the road when we tire of talking, and when we tire of that and the scenery, we lay ourselves along the seats and "dream the happy hours away", as blissfully as the time-honored "baby in the sugar trough." "I made myself thoroughly solid with "Doxy" (a playful patronymic I have given the proprietor) by introducing a blackboard system of advertising, which promises to be the best card out. I have two boards about 3 ft. by four, which - during the street concert - I fasten on the sides of the wagon and letter and illustrate during the performance and throughout the lecture. There are dozens in the crowd that stay to watch the work going on that otherwise would drift from the fold during the dryer portion of the Doctor's harangue. Last night at Winchester I made a decided sensation by making a rebus of the well-known lines from Shakespeare: -

"Why let pain your pleasure spoil,
For want of Townsend's Magic Oil?"

with a life sized bust of the author, and at another time, a bottle of Townsend's Cholera Balm on legs, and a very bland smile in its cork, making the "Can't come it" gesture at the skeleton, Death, who drops his scythe and hour-glass and turns to flee. Oh: I'm stared at like the fat woman on the side-show banner..."

Riley talks about his departure from Greenfield being "serious enough."

After the lynching incident, the poet's small hometown went into a period of great anguish and self-scrutiny. Should the law condone the lynching? Obviously it had to since all of the county had either participated in it or done nothing about it. The attention of the State was focused on what the lynch mob had done. Self-righteously believing it had done the "right thing," the town drew its collective energy into internally defending its action. Any criticism within the town was dealt with. Anyone who claimed the town should not have lynched an "untried" man was suspicious. Folk closed ranks against all dissenters. No one from the town was supposed to even talk to outsiders. We find an Editorial in the Hancock DEMOCRAT on July 15th condemning the fact that someone has "broken" the code of silence about the conspiracy to hang Kemmer and talked to the Indianapolis newspapers.

This Editorial demands the Indianapolis JOURNAL to "surrender" the name of the Greenfield "traitor" who provided their information. The goal is to ensure that "all respectable people might not be contaminated by the presence and society of this moral leper."

Shortly after this Editorial we find Riley making a desperate departure from Greenfield on a medicine wagon similar to his departure escapade with Doc McCrillus after his mother's death.

Not only did Riley leave after the lynching of Kemmer, but also Riley's married friend, Nellie Cooley, soon left Greenfield.

Riley's poem, "The Flying Islands of the Night," went through many editions and changes over Riley's life but in the 1892 book of it appeared Riley's addition of the lines about the "airy penalty" when a fellow fell "up" to heaven. Riley viewed death as "dropping upward." SEE: "Death," composed contemporaneously with "The Flying Islands of the Night": "My breath bursts into dust - I can not cry - I whirl - I reel and veer up overhead, And drop flat-faced against - against - the sky - Soh, bless me! I am dead!"

As I drove by the long abandoned site of the county fairgrounds of the 1870's in this year as the 20th century closed, I could hardly imagine that I was looking at the place where masked men had lynched a black man for allegedly raping a white woman. But it was true. What is now a cornfield on Morristown Pike just south of the lane leading back to the Greenfield

Country Club was once the Hancock County Fairgrounds, a scene of proud livestock shows and country entertainment. The deed from Samuel Milroy to the "Hancock Agricultural Society" was given March 9, 1863 and is recorded in Deed Record V, page 165 in the Office of the Recorder of Hancock County, IN. The eight acre tract served as the county fairgrounds during the 1860's and 1870's.

On this site a "Floral Pavilion" had been built by the society for the ladies to display their floral bouquets, gardening produce and canning at the fair. Unfortunately this pavilion had burned in 1871 and was a ruins - but still standing - shortly after midnight June 26, 1875. On that date and at that time, the "old" Floral Pavilion achieved its most notorious use. It was around a joist of this building in ruins that the mob of masked men threw a cotton rope to hang the Negro man named William Kemmer. The rope was fashioned into a noose at its end tightly coiled around the black man's throat.

The scene must have been eerie indeed as the men approached the fairgrounds that night. The hanging party came to the place surrounding a spring wagon drawn by a gray horse in which the Negro man who had been plucked out of the Hancock County Jail lay. According to observers the only
light came from torches and oil street lamps "confiscated" by the mob as it rode through town in disciplined order. The night was pitch black.

It seems impossible that the scene with bound man being fitted for hanging and piteously begging for his life in the midst of close to two hundred masked men is now merely a field filled with corn stubble since the crops have been harvested.

On U.S. 40 outside of Greenfield to the East on the north side, in a field across the road from what was the old County Home, or "Infirmary" between 400 and 500 East, there appears a strangely inappropriate stand of tall trees in the middle of a field. These trees represent a graveyard without markers of any kind. It was once the place where the county poor were taken to be buried into anonymity. William Kemmer, the lynched Negro, is buried here at some unknown place in this solitary and isolated site. He was buried with the noose with which he had been lynched still around his neck.

Riley must have often felt like the last child of Abraham Lincoln and the American Civil War.

LINES ON HEARING A COW BAWL
IN A DEEP FIT OF DEJECTION, ON THE
EVENING OF JULY 3, A.D. 1879

Portentous sound! mysteriously vast
And awful in the grandeur of refrain
That lifts the listener's hair as it swells past,
And pour in turbid currents down the lane.

The small boy at the woodpile, in a dream,
Slow trails the meat-rind [1] o'er the listless saw;
The chickens roosting o'er him on the beam
Uplift their drowsy heads with cootered [2] awe.

The "gung-oigh!" of the pump is strangely stilled;
The smoke-house door bangs once emphatic'ly
Then bangs no more, but leaves the silence filled
With one lorn plaint's despotic minstrelsy.

Yet I would join thy sorrowing madrigal,
Most melancholy cow, and sing of thee
Full-hearted through my tears, for, after all,
'Tis very kine [3] in you to sing for me.

1. meat-rind, a humorous description of the appearance of a beef cow. Rind is skin in reference to an animal.
2. The image is of chickens swaying their heads into an arch as do the coots, birds which stiffly arch their necks prior to a dive into waters to fish.
3. "Kine" is an old plural form of the "cow," a substitute for the word "cattle." Riley employs paronomasia. His play on the word for "kine" is humorously intended to suggest "kind" as in the expression "How kind (thoughtful, pleasant) of you."

Who is the boy?

No flight of fancy is needed to recognize the boy at the woodpile as Abraham Lincoln, the "log-splitter." The poem simply describes how Abraham Lincoln might have felt in contemplation of the 4th of July in the year 1879.

Riley clearly indicates the place where his poem is composed. It is "The Morgue," the name he gave to his second floor paint shop in downtown Greenfield, Indiana . The place of the poem is thus Greenfield in racial turmoil. Greenfield was not a happy place for Riley during the years immediately following the Kemmer lynching. The Sheriff who had offered so little resistance, a prosperous farmer of Brandywine Township born in 1840, was elected just the year prior to the lynching, and was re-elected the year later. He did not seek re-election in 1878, but supported his deputy, William H. Thompson, who was elected that year. Greenfield's mood was out of kilter with Lincoln's vision of a free American nation.

Blacks were treated in Greenfield, as elsewhere, literally as "cattle." We read from an account by George Knox, Greenfield's famous black barber of Riley's epoch of an incident of the kind to which Riley may refer in 1879 while the country was still reeling under the impact of the American Civil War.

"The Morgue," in Greenfield, Indiana. On the second floor was Riley's paint shop where he painted signs, composed poetry and often slept. Much of "The Flying Islands of the Night" was composed in this den.

Reconstruction of the South was a primary need in those days since the economy there had been based upon the intolerable system of slavery. But what of the blacks from the South? Many migrated north. In this year the four o'clock train arrived in Greenfield with a car load of blacks. Riley's good friend and benefactor George Knox said, "I shall not forget as long as I live, the sensation the news made in the city (Greenfield) and the querulous and anxious and frequently condemnatory looks that were leveled at me from all sides." Knox was approached by a "colored man" (Knox's words) coming with an envelope to the barbershop having been directed there somehow. He handed Knox the envelope and said he had "twenty seven head." The letter was addressed to someone named Jones that Knox did not know. When Knox asked him what he meant by "twenty seven head," the man indicated he meant a wide assortment of ages of black folk.

Knox recalled that when he got to the depot a large and angry crowd were gathering. "The excitement was reaching fever heat." The black folk were in desperate circumstances. Some were barely clothed. All were homeless and hungry.

Knox took charge of them and kept them in the depot the first night. He also talked to a white Christian storekeeper of the town who provided food for the destitute homeseekers. None of this went over very well with Greenfield and this store keeper's store was burned shortly afterwards.

What can be done about the dejected singing of the cattle, as the blacks were treated in Riley's hometown? Who would listen to the bawl of one of the kine? Who could speak up for the lynched Kemmer? Lincoln could not. He was dead and "in a dream." Those of tender and disposing sensibilities realized the bawl was a song of the nation. The shame of it comes from the juxtaposition of the "portentous sound"..."awful" on the day before Fourth of July holiday, the day when America celebrated its national independence, values and worth.

Crestillomeem for all of her hellishness cried for Kemmer and these "kine."

CRESTILLOMEEM'S THIRD GREAT ENCOUNTER WITH RILEY AFTER THE DEATH OF NELLIE COOLEY

Riley's third great encounter with Crestillomeem was his most serious and resulted in delirious experiences. The great expression of the encounter was the writing of Riley's autobiographical piece, "The Flying Islands of the Night." The immediate event causing this delirious flight into fancy was the death of Nellie Cooley, Riley's great encourager. Whereas earlier encounters had been episodic and at generally increasing levels, Riley's alcoholism following Nellie's death was so pronounced that Riley was physically unable to work and deemed himself "ill" which generally meant suffering such serious depression and alcoholism that he often could not leave his bed.

When Nellie Cooley died, Riley truly lost his true soul-partner. Only to Riley and her family was Nellie's death so devestating. So strange it is that there is no record of her death in Belleville, Illinois, the county seat where she died. Nor is there any record of her burial in Greenfield where her body was brought for final rest on July 29, 1878. Riley's writing of her is our only written proof of the dates of such things.

The young poet's reaction to this bereavement, his grief and sense of loss, is expressed in her obituary which Riley wrote and had published in the Hancock DEMOCRAT.

MEMORIAL - NELLIE M. COOLEY

Died, at Belleville, Illinois, July 27, 1878, Nellie M. Cooley, wife of George B. Cooley. Interred at Greenfield, her old home, July 29, 1878. Her life was like a dreamy summer day, made up of bright things only. Warm depths of azure skies, where merry birds, afloat on waves of sunshine, poured out their sweetest songs, and so baptized the world with sweetest melody: where morning walked the dewy paths that led through Nature's fairest haunts, and laid her shining hand on all things loveable; where meadowlands lay basking in the sun and clover-blossoms shook their fragrance out on every passing breeze and flavored all the air with sweetness and delight; where the laughing brook

Nellie Millikan at 16 (1862) when James Whitcomb Riley knew her before her marriage to George Cooley. (Neg. C7172, IMCPL-Riley Collection, Indiana Hisorical Society.)

leaped from its shady hiding-place, low-nestled in among the cool grasses growing in the dusky woods, and, while the lilies leaned their wondering face o'er the brink, and the weeping willows trained their slender hands within the wave, went loitering along its winding way, and babbling limpid music as it went.

We can imagine Riley and his married friend, Nellie Cooley, in song together at this organ with Riley playing the violin. A scene in the Riley birthplace, Greenfield, Indiana.

Her life was like a dreamy sunny day; and, as always was her wish, on such a day she laid aside the weary task of life, and out across "the all-golden afternoon" she walked on and on into her Father's open arms, and where fell upon her brow the sister kiss of Heaven's happiest angel.

The fairest gifts of womanhood were hers - a child's pure faith, a maiden's hope, a woman's charity. Her heart was soundless in its depths of love; her soul was boundless in its breadth of nobleness; she wore the bond of Friendship loyally, and ever held a gracious hand of welcome to distress. Her home was Joy's abiding place, and Patience, Peace and Love walked ever at her side, as now they walk, appareled in the raiment of the Lord's approving smile, and waiting with her loved ones lingering here.

Riley also appended a poem to his Hancock DEMOCRAT obituary for Nellie.

A DREAM UNFINISHED

Only a dream unfinished; only a form at rest
With weary hands clasped lightly over a peaceful breast.

And the lonesome light of summer through the open door-way falls,
But it makes no laugh in the parlor - no voice in the vacant halls.

It throws no spell of music over the slumbrous air;
It meets no step on the carpet - no form in the easy chair.

It finds no queenly presence blessing the solitude
With the gracious benediction of royal womanhood.

It finds no willowy figure tilting the cage that swings
With the little pale canary that forgets the song he sings.

No face at the open window to welcome the fragrant breeze;
No touch at the old piano to waken the sleeping keys.

The idle book lies open, and the folded leaf is pressed
Over the half-told story while death relates the rest.

Only a dream unfinished; only a form at rest,
With weary hands clasped tightly over a peaceful breast.

The light steals into the corner where the darkest shadows are,
And sweeps with its golden fingers the strings of the mute guitar.

And over the drooping mosses it clambers the rustic stand,
And over the ivy's tresses it trails a trembling hand.

But it brings no smile from the darkness - it calls no face
from the gloom -
No song flows out of the silence that aches in the empty room.

And we look in vain for the dawning in the depths of our despair,
Where the weary voice goes wailing through the empty aisles of prayer.
And the hands reach out through the darkness for the touches
we have known
When the icy palms lay warmly in the pressure of our own.
When the folded eyes were gleaming with a glory God designed
To light a way to Heaven by the smiles they left behind.

Only a dream unfinished; only a form at rest
With weary hands clasped lightly over a peaceful breast. "

Was Riley's attachment romantic? We can only speculate about such things. Why did Riley never mention such a thing if that was his feeling and he truly loved her?

Honor. Honor. Honor.

To a Nineteenth Century American, honor required giving respect to a married person as such. Honor required one to regard married people as inviolably matched. In private Riley might love Nellie dearly, but his sense of honor did not permit him to break up their marriage. In addition, Riley seems to have loved Nellie's husband almost as much as Nellie fraternally.

After Nellie's death, honor seemed to Riley much less of an excuse for not having Nellie in his life. His dedication quotation to a later edition of "The Flying

"Dwianie's" currently unmarked grave. According to cemetery officials, the grave of Nellie Millikan Cooley is in a small row of lots purchased by her husband George when Greenfield, Indiana first opened its Park Cemetery. Only the resistance to a probe of pea gravel placed around the wooden coffins in those days permitted its location by a cemetery ground crew. I placed my jacket on the spot.

Islands of the Night" berates honor as "A thynege of wychencref, an idle dreme..." This comes from Thomas Chatterton's "AElla," lines 536-7 where a frustrated "other man" contemplates the situation of a betrothed woman taken by a friend. Riley was equally frustrated by honor which kept Nellie Cooley from his arms. George Cooley was his friend.

This death of his beloved shortly before the writing of "The Flying Islands of the Night" is represented in "Wraith- Song of Spraivoll" at the commencement of Act III of "The Flying Islands of the Night." A "wraith" has a 1500's sense of an immaterial spectral appearance of a living being, portending the person's death. Here, Riley the poet, is close to death from alcoholism depressed over the death of his beloved Nellie Cooley. Spraivoll, the poet's poetic self, bemoans his despair at the situation of Riley having lost Nellie to the hand of death.

WRAITH-SONG OF SPRAIVOLL

I will not hear the dying word
    Of any friend, nor stroke the wing
Of any little wounded bird.
    ...Love is the deadest thing!
I wist not if I see the smile
    Of prince or wight, in court or lane. -
I only know that afterwhile
    He will not smile again.

The summer blossom, at my feet,
    Swims backward, drowning in the grass. -
I will not stay to name it sweet -
    Sink out! and let me pass!

I have no mind to feel the touch
    Of gentle hands on brow and hair. -
The lack of this once pained me much,
    And so I have a care.

Dead weeds, and husky-rustling leaves
    That beat the dead boughs where ye cling,
And old dead nests beneath the eaves -

Love is the deadest thing!

Ah! once I fared not all alone;
  And once - no matter, rain or snow! -
The stars of summer ever shone -
  Because I loved him so!
With always tremblings in his hands,
  And always blushes unaware,
And always ripples down the strands
  Of his long yellow hair.

I needs must weep a little space,
  Remembering his laughing eyes
And curving lip, and lifted face
  Of rapture and surprise.

O joy is dead in every part,
  And life and hope; and so I sing:
In all the graveyard of my heart
  Love is the deadest thing!

There is a recollection of Minnie Belle Mitchell about Riley with Nellie and her family.

... IN HIS TEENS WHEN THE MILLIKAN FAMILY CAME FROM THE EAST.

"James W. Riley was in his early teens when the Millikan family came from the east and settled in Greenfield. Mrs. Millikan, a widow with three sons and two daughters, brought with her Greenfield's first piano. Because young Riley possessed another gift, a talent for music, he was at once attracted to the family, especially to the younger daughter, Nellie, who not only played the piano, but also that sentimental instrument, the guitar.

Bud was intrenched into the Millikan family. He and the youngest son, Jesse, established an intimate friendship which grew with each year until the latter's death.

But the lad's friendship for Nellie was different. She was a gay, vivacious, fun-loving girl and young woman. Her music delighted him. She shared in the boys' games, helped young Riley with his studies and laughed sympathetically at his wild antics and mimicry. She was the personification of a satisfying friend and enough older than him to exercise a sister's prerogative of advising, criticizing and rebuking him when the need arose.

The intimacy and freedom of the Millikan home established in those early days remained unchanged on through Nellie's courtship and marriage to George Cooley, who shared in the family's affectionate regard for the sixteen year-old lad.

All through the years of the young poet's diligent writing and struggle for recognition, Nellie remained his staunch friend and critic. Her standards were high. She not only encouraged and praised his poetic efforts but she chided him at times when a passing weakness turned his faltering steps away from his coveted goal. She, with a mother's intuition, sustained him with her impelling faith in his ultimate success and started him again upon the upward grade.

The happy times with the Millikans did not end, however, with Nellie's marriage. She and her husband with young Bud and Jesse attended the dancing club which was an integral part of all social gatherings and they were always the life of the crowd. Bud and Nellie also led in charade parties which finally developed into parlor dramatics. Later young Riley, with a group of friends, organized a dramatic club known as "The Adelphians." It was in this organization that he found his greatest pleasure - he was a born actor. The years he had spent in character study and mimicry stood him well in hand and the Cooleys and other intimates formed an enviable cast.

In 1875, Mrs. Millikan's family and the Cooleys moved to Illinois. There were later two small children in the Cooley family. The frequent letters that were exchanged, especially Nellie's bright, encouraging ones, cheered the young poet in a way, yet his loneliness was great. An intimacy extending over many years could not be broken without a pull at heart strings. Finally after three years absence, the faithful friend whose love and interest was much like that of a mother, passed away at Belleville, Illinois, on July 27, 1876. She was brought back to Greenfield for burial."

Riley's response to Nellie's death was a lapse into even more continuous intoxications with attendant occasional deliriums. Riley's call for Crestillomeem (his alcoholism) to take over his life is found in his autobiographical poem, "The Flying Islands of the Night," where Riley admits:

THIS THICK DISTRESS OF MINE

He said: "Crestillomeem -
O that she knew this thick distress of mine! -
Her counsel would anoint me and her voice
Would flow in limpid wisdom o'er my woes
And, like a love-balm, lave my secret grief
And lull my sleepless heart! " (Aside) And so went on,
Struggling all maudlin in the wrangled web
That well-nigh hath cocooned him!

That Riley was parted with Nellie he had come to accept. That he was consigned never to live with Nellie was never accepted. Her death sealed that fact. It literally "cocooned" him. He took to the night only as a place where he might function away from people.

In another part of the poem, Crestillomeem, Riley's alcoholism, acknowledges that but to achieve fame can Riley choose to live and avoid suicide.

...the Queen, doth rule the King in all
Save this affectionate perversity
Of favor for the son whom he would raise
To his own place. - And but for this the King
Long since had tasted death and kissed his fate
As one might kiss a bride!

If his debauched nature can put an end to the reputable "Krung", then the triumph of debauchery will be complete and Riley must succumb to utter despair and suicide.

With the death of Nellie Cooley, Riley faced a bleak future. There would never be the affection or essential signs of love, the expectation of embrace and kiss or physical affection. Gone was the great "backer." This lack generated great anxiety. The goal of happiness becomes unattainable. If one is of a great loving nature, the expression of it becomes frustrated. The anger must be released. When the death is of one's great soul-partner there is no one with whom to express the depth of the separation. Nellie was this soul-partner of Riley.

Without Nellie to encourage him he was like "The Singer" of his poem of that name:

THE SINGER (1879)

While with ambition's steadfast flame
He wastes the midnight oil,
And dreams high-throned on heights of fame
To rest him from his toil. -
Death's Angel, like a vast eclipse,
Above him spreads her wings,
And fans the embers of his lips
To ashes as he sings.

Nellie was dead and after her death, fame seemed meaningless. Who could share Riley's joy with the polish of a word or turn of a phrase or being published? Death takes the triumph out of success.

Riley's reputation was also a terrible problem now that he was falling deeper into addiction.

"RUMOR'S FLUTTER"

But dost thou know that rumors flutter now
Among the subjects of thy sorceries? -
The art being banned[1], thou knowest; or, unhoused
Is unleashed pitilessly by the grim,
Facetious body of the dridular[2]
Upon the one who fain had loosed the curse
On others. - An my counsel be worth aught,
Then have a care thy spells do not revert
Upon thyself, nor yet mine own poor hulk
O' fearsomeness!

1. Intoxication is a crime in Indiana as James Whitcomb Riley came to know from being convicted of it.
2. Dridular is a prohibitionist agitator. The word is suggestive of a "dry dealer" in "intoxicatese" or the opposite of alcohol dealing.

There are two Riley poems following Nellie's death which contemplate suicide.

LINES TO AN ONSETTLED YOUNG MAN (1879)

"O what is Life at last," says you,
'At woman-folks and man-folks, too,
Cain't oncomplainin', worry through?

"An' what is Love, 'at no one yit
'At's monkeyed with it kin forgit,
Er gits fat on remembern hit?

"An' what is Death?" - W'y, looky hyur -
Ef Life an' Love don't suit you, sir,
Hit's jes' the thing yer lookin' fer!

In 1879. Riley, considering himself as Jucklet of his play, composed "A Toast of Jucklet's," in similar Chattertonian bawd to his writing in "The Flying Islands," "To the Wine-God Merlus"

Ho! ho! thou jolly god, with kinked lips
And laughter-streaming eyes, thou liftest up
The heart of me like any wassail-cup,
And from its teeming brim, in foaming drips,
Thou blowest all my cares. I cry to thee
Between the sips: - Drink long and lustily;
Drink thou m ripest joys, my richest mirth,
My maddest staves of wanton minstrelsy;
Drink every song I've tinkered here on earth
With any patch of music; drink! and be
Thou drainer of my soul, and to the lees
Drink all my lover-thrills and ecstasies;
And with a final gulp - ho! ho! - drink me,
And roll me o'er thy tongue eternally.

Actually, in the poem itself, Crestillomeem is the Riley "self" who enchants Riley into alcoholism and delirium tremens. ("At present doth the King (Riley) lie in a sleep Drug-wrought and deep as death - the after-phase of an unconscious state...") The poem is in the ostensible form of a "play," because this most fanciful of Riley's poems is a "play" on his life. It is written as a takeoff of a 15th century play such as Thomas Chatterton, the fantastic forger- boy would have written and passed off as play of the non-existent monk Rowley. It probably owes its form more to the gloom Poe fitted into his "Scenes from Politian." But Riley's "play" is not dreamish humorous or despairing however clever and entertaining or dishonest as a forgery on life it might be or as it may appear or be. "The Flying Islands of the Night" is boldly delirious-appropriate to Riley's hellish perception of his existence without ordinary love.

Riley intimately knows this cast member, Crestillomeem, a pushy, slutty lady-this possibly mannish cross-dressing queen of a fantasy horror show who slurs words and lurks behind him ready to take over his life at every juncture. She is the foil of a W.C.T.U. crusader of Riley's late Nineteenth Century era, a type of personality who has haunted Riley and hunted him out for persecution as a youth to ridicule him and call him a "no-good" in his adolescence, to drive him under and sign a pledge not to drink. The fact is Riley's "Crestillomeem" is on the other side of the issue of alcoholism but just as determined a lady as any temperance "bitch." "Crestillomeem" wants Riley drunk and delirious. She doesn't want him writing poetry. She likes him suicidal. She is the reincarnation of the poison that Thomas Chatterton took when his forgeries became known. Crestillomeem wants Riley dead if not drunk and insists he sign a "pledge" to stay drunk just as her "purer" W.C.T.U. counterparts want Riley to sign a pledge to abstain from alcohol! Will Riley sign on to alcoholism's "Murphy" pledge? His autobiographical poem, "The Flying Islands of the Night" tells us.

She wants him to die as did Thomas Chatterton, the poet whose life was such a fascination to Riley - the boy who ditched an apprenticeship in the law, wrote forgeries, but then committed suicide horribly through taking arsenic rather than face life after exposure of his forged poems. Following the condemnations of Riley for forging "Leonainie," Riley must have considered the same course of suicidal action.

Riley was afflicted with terrible suicidal depression as well as alcoholism. This is not beyond expectation. Creative writers are much more often afflicted by disabling personality traits as well as alcoholism, and writers are more than twice as likely to have affective disorders as other high achievers according to the recent psychiatric study by the British Psychiatrist Felix Post in his article, "Verbal Creativity, Depression and Alcoholism," in the BRITISH JOURNAL OF PSYCHIATRY 1966.

Soon Riley was in rebellion with all of poetry as well as his life situation.

Something had to change. Something had to help.

Riley's life demanded he find an answer to his dilemma about seeking fame as a poet.

So came Riley's "Declaration of Independence" from prior American poetry, particularly that of Henry Wadsworth Longfellow. This conclusion was announced in a letter to the editor carried in the Kokomo TRIBUNE of April 5, 1879. The letter was signed by Riley's nom de plume John Walker. The letter to the newspaper was entitled, "USE AND ABUSE OF THE POETIC THEME."

USE AND ABUSE OF THE POETIC THEME

"Poetry," said Johnson, "is the next best thing to prose." And in my belief had Johnson lived on until the present day and age, that utterance would now read, "Poetry is the next best thing to nothing."

The poetry of to-day is altogether too lush - too "sobby," I may say; too much sap, and not enough timber, you understand. It's just as refreshing, perhaps, to those who never use it as it ever was; but to those who liked myself have the smoldering embers of poetic fire forever gasping the fuel true genius alone can supply, the poetry of to-day only serves to smother and depress the flickering flames that otherwise would leap up roaringly, and illuminate the whole heart like a torch-light procession.

Poets who will persist in writing the poetry of to-day ought to be bucked and gagged, and rolled up like a ball of stale pop-corn and thrown out of the car-window of modern advancement. And yet how many unfettered hands do we daily see lifted in this most unholy practice.

Nor is the Press of our land wholly guiltless of lending furtherance to this most crying wrong; for it not only passively submits to these constantly recurring atrocities of rhyme, but - indirectly it may be - it aids and abets the evil by publishing and reproducing the very "poems" which otherwise would drop at once into the famishing oblivion which pants for them in vain. Where is the boasted justice of our broad Republic? Where is the Red-eyed Law we boast of? And "where, may I ask, is the Grand Jury of our land?"

This train of thought has been most painfully inflicted on my mind by a recent "poem," still going the rounds of the press, entitled "The Chamber Over the Gate," and openly claimed by its author, Henry W. Longfellow.

Now, personally, I have nothing but the kindliest feeling toward Mr. Longfellow, but, in justice to the demands of the strictly literary element of

Howard county, and Kokomo in particular, I must affirm that the really "suggestive and inviting theme he has selected, has not only met with neglect at his hands, but positive abuse. Yet like the thousands like it that are daily flaunted in our faces by the public press, it is copied, reproduced, and duplicated till the path of progress is literally strewn and choked with the rank dead leaves of poetical ruin and literary woe.

I cannot comment at length upon a subject so glutted with disaster and so bleared and bloated with the highwires of distress, but I will add, by way of admonition to Mr. L. that an author, and poet in particular, cannot be too cautions in his encroachments on the public weal. There are, I am frank to admit, certain points in "The Chamber over the Gate" that would warrant me in advising Mr. L. to continue, for a time at least, in the exercise of his poetical inclinations, but even this advice I must withhold, unless, indeed, the audacious aspirant will curb his ambition, and adopt in future for each succeeding effort of his pen, a fresh nom de plume. This, in a measure, would advance anything of worth he might chance to produce, while it would shield him as well from the pain and humiliation he must necessarily feel in reading such criticisms as the one my duty now calls on me to lay before the world. And now that I have gone so far in pointing out this glaring discrepancy, and directing at least one wandering upon his pilgrimage to the Great Perhaps, it becomes my further duty to illustrate, both to the unfortunate poet, and to my many admirers, the real principle involved in the poetical management of the theme he has so ruthlessly distorted and abused.

I subjoin a hastily arranged though mainly perfect copy of the poem as it should be treated by a master hand.

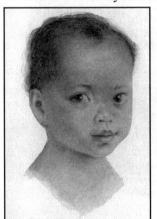

GIVEN-NAME is 'MANCIPATION,
An' sir-name is PROCLAMATION—
'Dopted, Lincoln's ministration,
Ho de god=child of de Nature

Riley never forgot that the African-American barber of Greenfield, George Knox, employed him and provided the little money Riley had to live on as an adolescent.

Faces of Hoosiers Riley would have known. From the author's Ora Myers glass negative collection of Hancock County, Indiana subjects.

Here is something very new in the life of James Whitcomb Riley. Yes, he wanted to be a poet. He had always wanted to be a poet. Yet his life had driven him into despair, confused depression and alcoholism. Poetry was going to save him if anything could. Here would be his fun as well as his life itself.

To find his voice it was necessary for him to transform poetry itself. This meant first and foremost to break awayfrom the mainstream "Longfellow-type romantic" poetry which he had previously most admired.

Riley needed to write alcoholic poetry before he could write kenotic poetry.

He wrote poetry as "Old Sport" wrote doggerel for awhile. This was Riley's John Walker poetry. "Who is Old Sport?" "Old Sport" was where Riley was coming from.

We look briefly at where Riley was coming from.

Let us first consider the "elevated" poetry of America's poet laureate prior to Riley's advent. "The Chamber Over the Gate" was a poem of the elderly Longfellow written October 30, 1878. Longfellow wrote it to accompany a letter of condolence written to a Protestant "Bishop" of Mississippi, Rev. Duncan C. Green, whose son had died in Greenville, Mississippi serving victims of an outbreak of yellow fever.

We compare Longfellow's and Riley's "John Walker" rearrangement:

THE CHAMBER OVER THE GATE

LONGFELLOW'S	RILEY'S
Is it too fine for thee	*Is it too fine for thee*
To drop onto, and see	*To drop onto, and see*
In the chamber over the gate	*In the chamber over the gate*
That old man hesitate -	*That old man hesitate -*
Watching and waiting there	*Watching and waiting there*
To swoop down unaware?	*To swoop down unaware*
O Absalom, my son!	*O Absalom, my son!*
Is it so long ago	*Is it so long ago*
That cry of human woe	*That in the street below*
From the walled city came,	*Thou hungst there on the gate*
Calling on his dear name	*While the clock banged on from eight*

That it has died away
In the distance of to-day?
O Absalom, my son!

There is no far or near,
There is neither there nor here,
There is neither soon nor late,
In that Chamber over the Gate,
Nor any long ago
To that cry of human woe,
O Absalom, my son!

From the ages that are past
The voice sounds like a blast
Over seas that wreck and drown,
Over tumult of traffic and town;
And from ages yet to be
Come the echoes back to me,
O Absalom, my son!

Somewhere at every hour
The watchman on the tower
Looks forth, and sees the fleet
Approach of the hurrying feet
Of messengers, that bear
The tidings of despair,
O Absalom, my son!

He goes froth from the door,
Who shall return no more.
With him our joy departs;
The light goes out in our hearts;
In the Chamber over the Gate
We sit disconsolate.
O Absalom, my son!

That 't is a common grief
Bringeth but slight relief;

Till thy footsteps died away
Into the dawning of the day?
O Absolam, my son!

There is no near or far.
There is neither here nor thar.
There is neither soon nor late
In that chamber over the gate
Nor any long ago
To that wail of human woe,
O Absalom, my son!

In dreams of the van shed past
The voice comes like a blast
Over the window-sill
Thou hears it howling still.
And in nightmares yet to be
Will its echoes tackle thee
O Absolam, my son!

He goes forth from the door
Who shall return no more:
With him the flower-pot goes
And the boot a spector throws
From the chamber over the gate
Where the old man lies in wait
O Absalom, my son!

That tis a common grief
Bringeth but slight relief;
Her's is the bitterest loss-
For the old man is the boss -
And forever the cry must be:
Would I had fled with thee
O Absalom, my son!

Ours is the bitterest loss,
Ours is the heaviest cross;
And forever the cry will be
"Would God I had died for thee,
O Absalom, my son!

Riley turns the Longfellow subject matter over to a humble life situation. John Walker does not know a noble father who grieves for a deserving son. John Walker knows a boy who must leave of his home because of an impaired father. He knows this boy to be thrown out of his house with a flower pot and boot thrown out after him to make sure he goes on his way and knows he can't come home. This, according to Riley, would be a much more likely scenario for the writing of a poem about a "chamber over the gate."

In his late twenties, Riley is abandoning Longfellow as a trusted guide to American life and throwing his support to the weltershung of his fellow alcoholic "Old Sport."

John C. Walker, the pseudonym which Riley used here, was "Old Sport" according to his friend and biographer, Minnie Belle Mitchell. The John Walker poems were done in imitation of an alcoholic "corduroy" poet whose real name was William Stafford. She says of him, "The boys about town called Bill Stafford "Old Sport." When sober he sold a patent sieve from door to door, but when he was drinking, "Old Sport" made verses which were the merest doggerel. He would sing to the tune of a weird old Irish song. While thus engaged he would sit bent over on a box outside a store with arms crossed tight, legs dangling and head down, making these rhymes and singing them dolefully. Sometimes his rhymes were of a local nature, again they would soar into the realm of imagination and become weird and
mournful. "Old Sport" was, indeed, a favorite character for Mr. Riley to imitate when in a jolly crowd. The poet would make up his own doggerel and sing it to the same Irish tune and every little while would say under his breath in "Old Sport's" same cracked voice, "God - what a doleful tune!" The following is an example of "Old Sport's" artful rhyming -

"I will not be a farmer
Nor longer till the sod,
I will not hitch another team
Nor hop another clod."

Mitchell believes this very doggerel inspired Riley's first John C. Walker poem as published in the Kokomo TRIBUNE called "Tom Johnson's Quit."

Riley's Bible reading was well known. I find the references to John, the apostle of humility, and Riley's assumption of the name Johnson ("John's son") so often more than coincidence.

We do not find this character in Riley's poetry to even have a first name in Riley's use of the appellation in "Use and Abuse of the Poetic Theme."

In Riley's contemporaneous "Buzz Club," we find another use of the name Johnson. It is a boy who everyone seems to condemn, but who finds peace in being John's son despite the humility the condition has had on his life.

Here is Mr. Plempton's poem, "Johnson's Boy:"

JOHNSON'S BOY

The world is turned ag'in me,
  And people says, "They guess
That nothin' else is in me
  But pure maliciousness."
I git the blame for doin'
  What other chaps destroy;
And I' jist a-goin' to ruin
  Because I'm "Johnson's Boy"

That ain't my name - I'd ruther
  They'd call me Ike or Pat. -
But they've forgot the other -
  And so have I, for that!
I reckon it's as handy,
  When "Nibsy" breaks his toy,
Or some one steals his candy,
  To say 'twas "Johnson's Boy."

You can't git any worter
  At a pump, and find the spout
So durn chuck full o' mortar
  That you have to bore it out;
You tackle any scholar

In Wisdom's wise employ,
And I'll bet you half a dollar
    He'll say its "Johnson's Boy."

Folks don't know how I suffer
    In my uncomplainin' way!
They say I'm gittin' "tougher"
    And "tougher" every day.
Last Sunday night, when Flinder
    Was a-shoutin' out for joy
And some one shook the winder
    He prayed for "Johnson's Boy."

I'm tired o' bein' follered
    By farmers every day
And then o' bein' collared
    For coaxin' hounds away.
Hounds always plays me double -
    It's a trick they all enjoy
To git me into trouble
    Because I'm "Johnson's Boy."

From the author's Ora Myers glass negative collection of Hancock County, Indiana subjects.

I'm tired o' havin' fellers
    Tie strings across the floor,
And havin' bloody "smellers"
    A layin' at my door;
And people intimatin'
    It's a life that I destroy
If a feller drownds a skatin'
    When he's out with "Johnson's Boy."

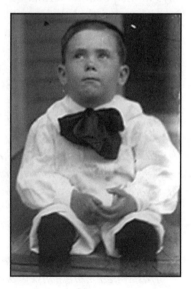

But if I git to Heaven,
    I hope the Lord'll see
Some feller has been perfect,
    And lay it on to me;
I'll swell the song sonorous
    As I clap my wings for joy,
And sail off on the chorus -

"Hurray for Johnson's Boy."

How strange it is that the self-professed victim here, the boy, is always associated with dire events? Can we believe him when he says he is always the victim of circumstances? How strangely necessary it is that he continue to profess his innocence. Is it credible that he is charged with causing tragic happenings on so many occasions just because he is Johnson's boy? Did he kill the boy he was skating with? We certainly do wonder. Riley employs antistrophe in repeating Johnson's Boy at the end of each stanza so that the whole weight of the horribles seems to rest upon the boy's shoulders in reality.

The point seems to be the redemption that nevertheless comes later because the boy has hope for redemption as John's son.

Life is not, even for the Riley of Crestillomeem, without the hope of redemption to a son of John. Riley uses this name Johnson so frequently it must have had special significance to him. We remember that eventually it will be his poems under this name that betoken his finest kenotic poetry, these being the poems of Benjamin Johnson of Boone. Then again when his life is depicted on the Broadway stage in New York, Riley suggests his character be called "Jim Johnson." "Ways is devius.." to the creative Riley as he says in his poem to William Leachman.

Then we find the groping with alcoholism a major subject in James Whitcomb Riley's poetry. Can we see here a step into redemption through kenoticism?

TOM JOHNSON'S QUIT (1879)

A passel o' the boys last night -
  An' me amongst 'em - kind o' got
To talkin' Temper'nce left an' right,
  An' workin' up "blue-ribbon, " hot;
An' while we was a-countin' jes'
  How many hed gone into hit
An' signed the pledge, some feller says, -
  "Tom Johnson's quit!"
We laughed, of course - 'cause Tom, you know,
  Has spiled more whisky, boy an' man,
And seed more trouble, high an' low,

Than any chap but Tom could stand:
And so, says I, "He's too nigh dead
Fer Temper'nce to benefit!"
The feller sighed ag'in, and said -
"Tom Johnson's quit!"

We all liked Tom, an' that was why
We sort o' simmered down ag'in,
And ast the feller ser'ously
Ef he wa'n't tryin' to draw us in:
He shuck his head - tuck off his hat -
Helt up his hand an' opened hit,
An' says, says he, "I'll swear to that -
Tom Johnson's quit!"

Well, we was stumpt, an' tickled, too, -
Because we knowed ef Tom hed signed
There wa'n't no man 'at wore the "blue"
'At was more honester inclined:
An' then and there we kind o' riz -
The hull dern gang of us 'at bit -
An' thr'owed our hats and let 'er whiz, -
"Tom Johnson's quit!"

From the author's Ora Myers glass negative
collection of Hancock County, Indiana subjects.

I've heerd 'em holler when the balls
Was buzzin' 'round us wus'n bees,
An' when the old flag on the walls
Was flappin' o'er the enemy's,
I've heerd a-many a wild "hooray"
'At made my heart git up an' git -
But Lord! - to hear 'em shout that way! -
"Tom Johnson's quit!"

But when we saw the chap 'at fetched
The news wa'n't jinin' in the cheer,
But stood there solemn-like, an' reched
An' kind o' wiped away a tear,
We someway sort o' stilled ag'in,

And listened - I kin hear him yit,
His voice a-wobblin' with his chin, -
    "Tom Johnson's quit!"

"I hain't a-givin' you no game -
    I wisht I was!...An hour ago,
This operator - what's his name -
    The one 'at works at night, you know? -
Went out to flag that Ten Express,
    And sees a man in front of hit
Th'ow up his hands an' stagger - yes, -
    "Tom Johnson's quit!"

Riley places the character of "Old Sport" through the mental gymnastics of abstinence of alcohol. In the same Mayor's Court docket book where one finds Along with James Whitcomb Riley's arrest for Public Intoxication in Dec. 1878, one finds many, many arrests of William Stafford for the same thing. Those dates of arrest are followed up by incarcerations for public intoxication because "Old Sport" had to "lay out his fines." (One got credit for fines on a per diem basis of incarceration if one didn't have the money to pay the fine.) It seems clear that Riley from the late 1870's and at least until his turn into kenoticism delves into the life of shamed alcoholics like himself to not only explore what intoxication and the life causing it but also how a poetry of such a man might be written. Riley's poetry changes subject matter and also technique with flights into ellipse, "intoxicatese" orthography and diction, and imaginative dissembling such as one finds in "The Flying Islands of the Night."

I do find that Riley always seemed to come to identify with those who, like himself, suffered public shame by public intoxication arrests to include friends like Clint Hamilton, Luther Benson, Almon Kiefer and even Riley's friend John Mitchell, whose wife was Minnie Belle Mitchell, the author and biographer of Riley whose intimacy with the facts of his life are so very helpful. In fact it almost seems to be a necessity that one be an alcoholic for Riley to dedicate a book of his poetry to the person. It is a very rare volume of Riley's poetry that is not dedicated to an alcoholic.

Riley realized there is nothing about God's love which bars any alcoholic or anyone else from being a child of the gentle and beloved John.

1. There simply is not enough information to determine a more formal diagnosis of what Riley's situation was regarding alcohol use at the time of the writing of "The Flying Islands of the Night." Did the writing occur while Riley was alcohol dependent or withdrawing from alcohol use? Was his condition one of dementia rather than delusion? Did he suffer hallucinosis or a spot of amenstic disorder? Was he alcohol dependent at all or merely a "poor little lamb, out on a spree, doomed from here to eternity." We just don't know. He might have been having fun with us by just spoofing being drunk as he says he was when writing "The Flying Islands of the Night" in the dialogue of the Buzz Club members. We just don't know. I close my DSM-III-R with a violent thud.

The finest of the "Crestillomeem" Riley's works were his Buzz Club papers. They were a "fun" series with taunts at the temperance prudes from the start. The meetings always conclude with resort to alcohol somewhere as if the members were not under the influence during the meetings themselves. The Buzz Club consisted of something like an alcoholic's support group in which each of the three members would try to better himself by producing something of literary merit. The results were semi-comical but oddly beautiful pieces of writing and poetry and stand-up comedy or drama in varying degrees of "intoxicatese," of which "The Flying Islands of the Night," has proven to be the most cryptic yet enchanting.

The pieces were published in the Indianapolis Saturday HERALD as follows: Respectfully Declined Papers of the Buzz Club No. I, May 11, 1878; Respectfully Declined Papers of the Buzz Club No. II, June 15, 1878; Respectfully Declined Papers of the Buzz Club No. III, July 6, 1878; Respectfully Declined Papers of the Buzz Club No. IV, August 24, 1878; Respectfully Declined Papers of the Buzz Club No. V, September 28, 1878; and Respectfully Declined Papers of the Buzz Club No. VI, November 16, 1878.

The first of the series opens with an explanation that the club, originally of twenty-five members, is now down to three and one of the members, Mr. Clickwad, moves that the club be disbanded and "I shall insist upon either a second or a duel...As Sancho Panza says...in God's name let us abandon the enterprise while we have enough members left to vote. If it runs this way there'll be no one but the janitor here next meeting..." Such anacoluthon gives us to know the members of this club are simple drunks. We are not given to expect much but grammatical inconsequence and intoxicated inconsistency in expression by the group. Occasionally, we are not entirely disappointed.

Crestillomeem is at work. She is the poet who writes in the sing-song "intoxicatese" of dissyllabic iambs. The gentlemen of the Buzz Club are at an unrepentent antitheticalAlcoholics Anonymous meeting drunk.

Mr. Clickwad delivers the first poem we encounter in the series:

A DREAM (1878)

I dreamed I was a spider
A big, fat, hungry spider;
A lusty, rusty spider
  With a dozen paisied limbs
With a dozen limbs that dangled
Where three wretched flies were tanglea
And their buzzing wings were strangled
  In the middle of their hymns.

And I mocked them like a demon;
A demoniacal demon
Who delights to be a demon
  For the sake of sin alone.
And with fondly false embraces
Did I weave my mystic laces
Round their horror stricken faces
  Till I muffled every groan.

And I smiled to see them weeping,
For to see an insect weeping,
Sadly, sorrowfully weeping,
  Fattens every spider's mirth;
And to note a fly's heart quaking,
And with anguish ever aching
Till you see it slowly breaking
  Is the sweetest thing on earth.

I experienced a pleasure,
Such a highly flavored pleasure,
Such intoxicating pleasure,
  That I drank of it like wine
And my mortal soul engages
That no spider on the pages

Of the history of ages
  Felt a rapture more divine.

I careened around and capered -
Madly, mystically capered -
For three days and nights I capered
  Round my web in wild delight;
Till with fierce ambition burning,
And an inward thirst and yearning
I hastened my returning
  With a fiendish appetite.

And I found my victims dying,
"Ha," they whispered, "we are dying!"
Faintly whispered, "we are dying!
  And our earthly course is run."
And the scene was so impressing
That I breathed a special blessing,
As I killed them with caressing
  And devoured them one by one."

Riley continues, "There was a wild, unearthly light in Mr. Clickwad's eyes as he closed the poem and glared defiantly upon his hearers."

We have heard a mock delirium tremens vision in lyric trimeter. The next member, Mr. Plempton, continues with his own as a stand-up narrative. He "dreams" he is in a deserted banquet hall all alone. A feast was on the table and he was very hungry. There were chickens roasted, fried and broiled, dumplings and peach cobblers, pies etc. Whenever he tried to eat anything it became alive. He harpooned a fat apple dumpling and it squealed like a pig when he stuck it. He then took a chicken leg and all the chickens on the feast table got up and fluttered away. Even the chicken from whom he had wrenched the leg got up and hopped away on its remaining leg while the other chickens screamed at him, "He's got the chicken leg." He defiantly tried to eat it, but it was as steel and the fowl laughed at him, "He can't eat it. He can't eat it." Mr. Plempton says he then swallowed it metallic though it was after which the chicken on one leg hopped over to him and told him he had "swallowed a navy revolver, loaded with mugs to the sluzzle." Any movement and it would go off. The jelly then asked him if he had "any little earthly matters to clear up." Trembling, all Mr. Plempton could do was pray, "Jesus, tender shepherd, hear me;\Bless thy little lamb tonight" - to which the Jelly replied, "Oh, what a little lamb!" and later while Mr. Plempton was praying Jesus to keep him safe, the jelly shrieks, "Time's up, Make ready! Take aim! Fire!" The shot that got Mr. Plempton also wounded the jelly, who murmured, "A random shot, but we can at least die together."

The final member delivers a more metered piece, again in fantasy, ".../Dreamer, say, will you dream of love\That lives in a land of sweet perfume,\ Where stars drip down from the skies above\In molten spatters of bud and bloom..." To cries of "Splendid," the meeting adjourns with them all going out for a bottle of burgundy at Mr. Hunchley's. So ends our first acquaintanceship with the antithetical Buzz Club.

In the second Buzz Club meeting, we learn what degenerate reprobates the members are. The subject upon which each is to produce a literary piece is childhood. The example of Mr. Clickwad will suffice. He leads off with an incident in which he was tricked by a child who he is trying to entice to sit on his lap. While visiting in Terre Haute Clickwad is taken into a drawing room to await the coming of a friend he wishes to meet when a sweet-faced little girl peeps in. Clickwad asks her name and she says, "I'm mama's yitty angel."'"Ah!" I exclaimed rapturously, "and you are a little angel, to be sure!" And then telling her of my passionate love for little angels, "I patted my knee with a most seductive air." The little girl takes a nickel to come closer but won't sit on his lap for that because another gentleman "divs me one-five-two mucher'n that." Eventually she will sit on his lap for all of his money and plays with his possessions, sticking her doll down his vest. Eventually while trying to open his watch, she strikes herself on the head and rushes off to return with mother yelling this man tried to kill her. When he got up to defend his honor, the legs of the doll protruded from his vest.

There is only "The Flying Islands of the Night," offered by Mr. Clickwad, in the fourth episode.

In the fifth episode, where imitations were to be undertaken, two lengthy pieces are presented: "An Idyl of the King" is told by Mr. Plempton on the order of Tennyson. (The title is Old Hec's Idolatry as found in Riley's Complete Works, Biographical Edition.) Then Mr. Hunchley reads his offering in prose, "Twiggs and Tudens" in imitation of Dickens.

The sixth episode contains Mr. Bryce's imitation of an old man reciting "Farmer Whipple - Bachelor" followed by Mr. Clickwad's offering.

Clickwad tells the group at this last meeting, that he intends to quit drinking after the evening and its drunken party afterward.

Riley's "intoxicatese" becomes childlike, fantastic and "Lewis Carrollish" in "A Wrangdillion." Riley would have been particularly joyish in finding a writer such as Carroll along about the time this poem was written since Carroll was a "truant" name for the real author, Charles Lutwidge Dodgson.

A WRANGDILLION (1877)

Dexery-Tethery! down in the dike,
Under the ooze and the slime,
Nestles the wraith of a reticent Gryke,
Blubbering bubbles of rhyme;
Though the reeds touch him and tickle his teeth -
Though the Graigroll and the Cheest
Pluck at the leaves of his laureate-wreath,
Nothing affects him the least.

He sinks to the dregs in the dead o' the night,
And he shuffles the shadows about
As he gathers the stars in a nest of delight
And sets there and hatches them out:
The Zhederrill peers from his wtery mine
In scorn with the Will-o'-the-wisp,
As he twinkles his eyes in a whisper of shine
That ends in a luminous lisp.

The Morning is born like a baby of gold,
And it lies in a spasm of pink,
And rallies the Cheest for the horrible cold
He has dragged to the willowy brink,
The Gryke blots his tears with a scrap of his grief,
And growls at the wary Graigroll
As he twunkers a tune on a Tiljicum leaf
And hums like a telegraph pole.

The poet of wanderings in the American life of Indiana and Ohio over the last seven years since his mother's death, with the experiences of its ways, began recording his personal views driving him into alcoholism into a figurative speech appropriate to his condition. And yet the world- for a time- did not care to see what he was doing to be able to drive him into conformity and banality. While the influence of Charles Dickens was very pronounced not just in Riley's point of view but also in his life plan, the English poet, William Blake, and of course Riley's preinacarnation self, "Edgar Allan Poe," seem to me to be the most important writers to Riley's career as Crestillomeem.

I am not taking Riley's writing career step-by-step. Nevertheless, chronologically, Riley was aware of "inspired spiritualism" in poetry from an early age. I attribute Riley's study of William Blake for encouragement as the great freeing verse. Blake's poetry best adapted to a poetry of tremens-inspired visions such as "The Flying Islands of the Night," to spiritually inspired poetry such as Riley's greatest poetry, his kenotic poetry, and finally to his imaginative poetry of the variety commonly called Riley's children's poetry.

As we have noted, delirium is an essential feature of alcohol withdrawal. "The Flying Islands of the Night" seems a delirium account. While Riley sank into great alcoholism after the death of his mother and to escape Greenfield again after the Kemmer lynching with another medicine man, this time Doc Townsend, he does not appear to have grown delirious from these experiences. We find evidence of delirium tremens only after the death of Nellie. Delirium tremens often comes very quickly as within a week after withdrawals. It consists of marked autonomic hyperactivity, with tachycardia and sweating. This is "delirium tremens," or "tremens," as referred to in the Buzz Club papers. The associated feature of tremens are vivid hallucinations. Delusions and agitated behavior accompany these deliriums. A more modern diagnostic description is organic alcohol hallucinosis which is described in the American Psychiatry Associations "DSM III-R" as "The essential feature of this disorder" in which vivid and persistent hallucinations develop shortly (usually within 48 hours) after cessation of or reduction in alcohol ingestion by a person who apparently has Alcohol Dependence. The hallucinations may be auditory or visual. The auditory hallucinations are usually voices and, less commonly, unformed sounds such as hissing or buzzing. In the majority of cases, the content of the hallucinations is unpleasant and disturbing...The voices may address the person directly, but more often they discuss him or her in the third person." In discussing delirium, the note is made that "The duration of an episode of Delirium is usually brief, about one week; it is rare for Delirium to persist for more than a month." Recovery is usually complete although a more stable organic mental disorder may result. Diagnostic Criterion are reduced ability to maintain attention to external stimuli, disorganized thinking, rambling, irrelevant, or incoherent speech, and the occasional perceptual disturbance, illusion, misinterpretation, hallucination, disorientation to time, place, or person, and episodic memory impairment.

Crestillomeem is the Riley suffering from alcoholism, its delusions, and tremens upon withdrawal. She is the ranting bitch that schemes at his success or composure as a poet. She also is a person with remarkable powers of assessment who seems to see Riley the most clearly of all of his fragmented selves. She is not the "essential Riley." She is however his nightmare of himself.

On August 14, 1879, Riley wrote his friend, Elizabeth Kahle, "I am now furnishing four papers with contributions, besides writing a partnership book, and perfecting an original programme for readings the coming season. So you will see I am indeed overwhelmed, and I must throw in, too, by way of good measure, the fact that I'm in rather ill health." He meant he was mostly drunk these days.

Riley admitted this poem ("I loved her, why I never knew-\Perhaps, because her face was fair;\Perhaps, because her eyes were blue,\ And wore a weary air.") was about his vision of his own love of "dissipation" in a letter he wrote to Elizabeth Kahle of July 6, 1880. She knows it as "Delilah" because Riley had not yet fitted it into "The Flying Islands of the Night," his autobiographical poem. About it he says, "I must not let you think that I ever have loved seriously visions only; one part of my life has been seriously scarred with dissipation -as I think I have often intimated to you, because I would never willfully attempt the denial of any fact, however unpleasant the acknowledgment of it would be."

Riley's last letter from Elizabeth Kahle of June 26, 1884, sent to Riley just before she married and became Mrs. Brunn, was a nasty one in which Elizabeth, Riley's correspondent and lover by mail only, "volunteered some advice as to his one failing." Thereafter, Riley tried to keep up a correspondence but was not given her address.

Meredith Nicholson recalled that Riley took pains to escape from any company where he found himself the centre of attraction. He resented being "shown off" (to use his phrase) like "a white mouse with pink eyes." How could such a bashful person hope to live a life of great public fame? He required the company of Crestillomeem. Riley never knew what to do with himself when alone or unoccupied on the road during his lyceum years. He often drank out of loneliness.

ANOTHER LIFE PATH FOR A DEPRESSED FRIEND

There is a small stone to mark a grave at Park Cemetery, Greenfield, Indiana, Riley's hometown, only large enough for four letters, A-N-N-A. It is near a much larger family stone, Chittenden. The A-N-N-A lies not so far from the Riley family memorials at the same cemetery.

Here lie the remains of a woman known to generations of kids who have borrowed children's books from the Greenfield Public Library in Riley's hometown. My recollection is that the children's corner of the former "Carnegie" Greenfield library in use in Greenfield during the majority of the Twentieth Century bore a

The little stone on the left says "Anna" and marks the grave of Anna Chittenden at Park Cemetery, Greenfield, Indiana. She and Riley joined the Greenfield Reading Club together in 1879. Her depression and alcoholism got her committed to a sanitarium and hospital for the insane whereas Riely's path with the same diagnoses brought him national fame.

plaque which dedicated the area to her. Some of its children's books were purchased out of a fund bequeathed by her. In December, 1996, the Greenfield Library Board voted to terminate this fund established in 1926 and use the remaining principal to purchase shelving. No longer will Anna be the benefactress of children's books but it was a seventy year ride of benefiting the children of Anna Chittenden's hometown.

Anna and James Whitcomb Riley knew each other well. Both were in the Greenfield Literary Club founded in Greenfield in 1879. They were the only two unmarried members of one of the divisions of the club. They must have spent pleasant afternoons together discussing literature with the other few intimate members of that division. There is another connection however. Both suffered horribly from depression and alcoholism.

Anna Chittenden was a school teacher for some time but the sad fact is that Anna Chittenden lived a life of torment beyond description which causes me to consider hers to be one of the saddest stories I have ever heard. Her life history represents what might have become of James Whitcomb Riley. Eventually neither Riley nor Anna Chittenden could handle their own property or make decisions for themselves.

A little woman of 5'2" and frail appearing at just over 100 pounds, with hazel eyes, light brown hair, and a light complexion, Anna began life in 1856, before the Civil War, on the sour note of having no father to raise her. Her father, Giles, died in 1855 of a stroke before she was born. Her mother, Margaret Chittenden, survived until 1895 and lived out her life on the corner of North and School Streets in Greenfield. Anna's mother died of an "abscess of the brain." Anna had no brothers or sisters either. One died of paralysis and three others died within a couple of years of birth. Anna was the last child born and lived a long life. Eventually she would die at 70 of tuberculosis with her body described as "emaciated" at the inquest. She had suffered from pulmonary tuberculosis for the last fourteen years of her life.

During her youth, Anna Chittenden appeared to have every chance for success. Aside from having "scrofula" as a child, she did fine in school and graduated from the Greenfield schools at the age of eighteen. She decided on entering the teaching profession and got a little more education to qualify her for that.

Soon she was teaching in various parts of the state and did so for the next ten years. The only school in Hancock County where she taught that I could find was Fortville where she taught school in 1882 under M. Caraway, Principal along with two other teachers, A.E. Cummins and Alice Cory. Nevertheless, by all accounts, Anna Chittenden was a fine teacher and considered one of the best teachers in every community where she taught. It is said she was frequently able to discipline pupils "when other teachers failed entirely".

Then came 1890 and her school board of that year did not renew her contract. At 34 and unmarried, she apparently flew off the deep end and attempted suicide. Alcoholism lurked into her life. She couldn't get it out of her mind that she was fired because the other teachers conspired against her. For the next five years, her family boarded her in a private sanitarium in Oxford, Ohio. Upon her return home to Greenfield in 1895, she was more than her sick mother could handle. According to Commitment Proceedings begun in the Hancock Circuit Court, her uncle, a Greenfield, Indiana, medical doctor by the name of Warren R. King described her as "filthy, violent, abusive, thinks her best friends are her enemies, writing letters that have no intelegent(sic) construction, while she is well educated and when in good health refinement about her person and clothing." Thus began her first commitment to Central State Hospital for the Insane. She was released after ten months in Dec. 1895 and termed "much improved." Her mother had died in the interim and she was the recipient of her mother's estate of about $5,000.

For ten years, Anna Chittenden survived outside the state's mental hospital mainly by her wits. However, according to John P. Black, M.D. who signed a Proceeding to Re-Commit her, "she wanders about the streets and exposes herself." Apparently her alcohol problem intensified although was called only a borderline alcoholic. Anna, at 49, had reduced her standard of living to the point that she was found living in a hut without heat in winter according to Central State records, paying someone $2.00 a week for rent. Her uncle, Dr. King, by this time her legal guardian, again headed for Hancock Circuit Court to have her committed to Central State. This second admission would be from Jan. 27, 1905 until June 30, 1908. It got her out of the hut and into a warm place for the next three years. The Court papers call her "violent and abusive at times. Unable to adopt herself to environment." Once again she was released.

A little over a year later would spell the end of Anna Chittenden's life outside of the institution for the insane. On Nov. 25, 1910, the Judge of the Circuit Court again committed her - this one the third such commitment- and Anna's life would never again see freedom. It was said Anna Chittenden had again been found "restlessly wandering" around Greenfield and this time she was committed to Central State Hospital where she remained until she died.

Usually, I find her described in hospital records as having chronic melancholia which to us means depression. But sometimes there is a statement such as "well systematized delusions of persecution. She believed that parties were plotting against her to deprive her of property...Has had numerous hallucinations. Has heard people plotting against her..."

There is much more, but the fact is that a will of hers was found at the Fortville Bank executed just before her first commitment leaving her property to her mother then aunts and if none of them were around to the public library in Greenfield. With all dead, the library got her estate after a will contest was lost by Anna's more distant relatives. And that is why for all the years since 1926, terminating only in 1996, that the kids of Greenfield have benefited with children's books from the life of a woman who suffered such agony that few could bear. And the lesson is further that something like this might very well have happened to James Whitcomb Riley due to his alcoholism.

CRESTILLOMEEM ENCOUNTERS RILEY ON THE ROAD

The writing of "The Flying Islands of the Night" resulted in a truce in the life of James Whitcomb Riley. Perhaps he no longer had Nellie as a font of encouragement and strength, but Riley felt her presence with him. She was a "heavenly consort." She encouraged the Godly songs of Spraivoll who confronted Crestillomeem from above and dazed her with the mystical entrancement of the Philippian's Christ Hymn.

Then there came about Riley's great travels for platform lecturing and Crestillomeem often began to accompany Riley in his trips. Riley took consolation in alcohol from his loneliness in his travels to distant places. Occasionally Crestillomeem took over.

Rumor's Fluter

Indianapolis journalist Robert Kyle told the story about Riley when he resided at the Dennison Hotel in Indianapolis during this period. Responding to a knock on his door one day, Riley was confronted by a young "hopeful" who introduced himself as "Albert Beveridge, a candidate for United States Senator."

"Young man, I've had enough `beveridges' today!" the poet snorted, slamming the door in the face of a man destined to become one of America's most distinguished public servants.

Everyone knew of Riley's drinking problem and most tried to help him avoid falling prey. There is another story of his trials and temptations. Once when Riley was trying to avoid drinking, he had the hotel lock him in his room so he couldn't get out to buy whiskey. Then he got thirsty and bemoaned his hasty action. To accomodate his self-imposed prohibition he rang for a bellboy to bring a bottle of bourbon and a straw to the door of his room. Once there, it was a simple matter to have the boy insert one end of the straw into the open bourbon bottle and the other end through the keyhole.

A publicity photo for the lyceum circuit team of James Whitcomb Riley (on the left) and Edgar Wilson ("Bill") Nye (on the right.)

Crestillomeem once went completely out of control. She caused great harm to Riley and the breakup of his most famous platform partnership- the one with Bill Nye.

One generally thinks of Riley as being in command of his alcoholism from the time of the writing of "The Flying Islands of the Night." There were many instances of illness noted about Riley. One suspects these incidents reflect depression as much as anything. The overall picture does not portray a disabling situation of severe alcoholism.

There is one time of great public occurrence however when Crestillomeem clearly got the upper hand.

The breakup of his lecturing partnership with his friend, Bill Nye was a very public divorce.

The Louisville COURIER-JOURNAL published the following article after the Louisville incident of early Feb., 1890.

THE POET'S SIDE OF IT

Mr. James Whitcomb Riley's Brother-in-Law
Talks of the Split with Nye.
The Hoosier Bard Had Been in Bad Health for
Months and a Little Liquor Was Too Much

Mr. James Whitcomb Riley still keeps his room at the Galt House, but sees no one save his brother-in-law, Mr. Henry Eitel, of Indianapolis, who come(sic) down yesterday for the purpose of taking the poet home as soon as he is able to travel. Mr. Riley is much prostrated, and is in a bad state of mind over the recent unfortunate breaking up of his joint tour, in which matter he considers that he has to some extent been badly treated, being saddled with the entire responsibility of the affair.

Mr. Eitel, in the course of a conversation with a COURIER JOURNAL reported last night, said that Mr. Riley's condition was not so much the result of his drinking as of mental worry over it. "Mr. Riley," said Mr. Eitel, "is a man of nervous temperament and very high-strung or he couldn't be a poet if he wasn't and has been in rather bad health for some time. His throat has troubled him a good deal, and, being a careless eater, his stomach is frequently out of order. As a consequence, (sic) he has been much worn out with constant travel and has at times felt the necessity of taking something to brace him up. His condition has been such that it took but little to affect him. He couldn't stand much liquor. The main trouble seems to be that he did not like to be watched, and was much exasperated at Mr. Walker's way of handling him, giving out orders at hotels that he was to have no whisky, following him around and all that, and finally kicked over the traces. He and Mr. Walker had some pretty hot words about it, and no doubt both of them said things they were sorry for. He had several disagreements before reaching here."

"Mr. Walker was very strict, was he?"

"Yes, very - inclined to be arbitrary, in fact. Of course, he was looking after his own interests, but I can't blame him for that. I think he handled Riley too severely. He had a contract with him for five years, and was continually shaking it over Riley's head. That exasperated him also, and so things went on until the breach here. Mr. Riley had been out four months and had missed but one engagement, at Madison, Wis. I think both Nye and Riley needed rest. It was intended that they should have a day off every week, but Major Pond either booked the time full or kept them on long trips, so that they got no rest at all.

"They should have taken Riley to his room when they saw his condition, instead of leaving him to sleep in a public place, but I suppose they were in a heat and did not think. Mr. Riley doesn't like to have the idea go out that all the trouble was because of his fondness for drink."

"Mr. Nye has gone, has he not?"

"Yes, he left for New York to-night. He went up and told Riley good-bye, and they parted good friends. Both regret the affair very much. I will take Riley home to-morrow afternoon, if he is able to travel, as I suppose he will be. His nerves are all unstrung, and he needs rest. No, he has formed no new plans as yet. He has several books to revise, and there are several publishers who want him to write, so that he will probably rest and resume his literary work, which has been much interrupted. He now feels much hurt at the false position in which he has been placed, as if he were to blame for the whole affair, especially because he had missed but one date up the time he reached here - a period of four months. I will take him home at 2 o'clock tomorrow afternoon, if possible."

Delirium tremens can be a nightmarish thing.

In later years, Riley told his nephew, Edmund Eitel, how he felt being in a lecture tour. "Imagine yourself on a crowded day-long excursion; imagine that you had to ride all the way on the platform of the car; then imagine that you had to ride all the way back on the same platform; and lastly, try to imagine how you would feel if you did that every day of your life, and you will get a glimmer- a faint glimmer -of how one feels after traveling about on a reading or lecturing tour." Riley sought relief in alcohol consumption.

Bill Nye, a lyceum stage partner, told how Riley's habit of drinking too much was handled while they were on tour. At their hotel, the manager was warned that nothing "but clean shirts and farinaceous food" was to be sent up to "No. 182." This was Riley's room. The poet, however, found that his room communicated with the next one, No. 180. Also he discovered the man in that room had left for the evening. Nye comments, Riley stepped in and "at odd times used the bell of No. 180 with great skill, thereby irritating his manager so much that he returned to New York on the following day." Crestillomeem was a very dangerous "play-partner" to Riley but he often simply couldn't avoid the temptation to join her games.

The report of Riley's Louisville public episode with Crestillomeem was spread throughout the nation because by 1890 Riley was a very famous American.

Among those friends of Riley's who shared concern for his mental health was Henry Woodfin Grady, Henry Woodfin Grady, 1850-1889, a sometime lecturer as was Riley and writer for the Atlanta CONSTITUTION newspaper. Grady who was only a year younger than Riley wrote him in the very year of Grady's death requesting Riley to visit. "I see from the papers that you have been sick from overwork and prostration," he says in his invitation.

Many people encouraged Riley in his battle with Crestillomeem. Yet, there was always this feeling of ambiguity within Riley. He knew he was an

alcoholic but he also knew he was fighting it mightily and accomplishing much
good. Riley eared his alcoholism.

In one of his prose pieces, "Jamesy," Riley describes what an old drunk of the Nineteenth Century would have lived like. Keep in the back of your mind that Riley might have been thinking of himself if he didn't control his alcoholism. In "Jamesy," Riley confronts a bootblack, a boy who shines shoes, and asks him about his father.

"Won't work," said the boy, bitterly, "He won't work -he won't do nothin' - on'y `budge!' And I have to steer him in every night, cos the cops won't pull him any more - they won't let him in the station-house mor'n they'd let him in a parlor, cos he's a plum goner, and liable to `croak' any minute."

"Liable to what?" said I

"Liable to jist keel over - wink out, you know - cos he has fits, kindo jim jams, I guess. Had a fearful old matinee with him last night! You see he comes all sorts o' games on me, and I have to put up for him - cos he's got to have whisky, and if we can on'y keep him about so full he's a regular lamb, but he don't stand no monkeyin' when he wants whisky, now you bet! Sis can handle him better'n me, but she's been a losin' her grip on him lately - you see Sis ain't stout any moren, and been kindo sicklike so long she humors him, you know, mor'n she ort. And he couldn't git on his pins at all yesterday mornin', and Sis sent for me, and I took him a pint, and that set him a runnin' so that when I left he made Sis give up a quarter he saw me slip her, and it jist happened I run into him that evening and got him in, or he'd a froze to death. I guess he must a kindo had 'em last night, cos he was the wildest man you ever see - saw grasshoppers with paper collars on, an' old sows with feather-duster tails, the durndest programme you ever heard of! And he got so bad onct he was a goin' to belt Sis, and did try it, and - and I had to chug him one or he'd a done it. And then he cried, and Sis cried, and I cri..., I ... Dern him! You can bet your life I didn't cry."

You simply can't say that Riley was unaware of what alcoholism could lead to. He knew this and feared its great excesses.

The reason may well have been Riley's great desire to accomplish something with his life. He was very ambitious and desired fame. What is even more interesting is that he took a route to fame that derived from his alcoholism. Knowing his vulnerability, he wrote about a life in which sensitivities, feelings for others, friendships, homelife, and love derived from a living "God of the humble" who redeemed such a vulnerable person.

While Riley suffered from alcoholism, his poetry saved him from becoming the bum in "Jamesy."

The amazing thing is that Riley's breakup with Nye did not, apparently, affect Riley's great popularity among his fellow Hoosiers.

Later the same year of Riley's great "fall," when Georgia's Richard Malcolm Johnston appeared in Indianapolis on Nov. 6, 1890 to lecture on his "Tales of the South," Riley was asked to introduce him, after which the Georgian stated, "I really feel grateful at being introduced by Mr. Riley, said the author of the "Dukesborough Tales"... There has long been a common tie between us, each having the same affection for the people of his early childhood, and each having endeavored in his way to save from oblivion their peculiarities - one through prose and the other through

RYE AND RILEY.

The Poet Breaks With Bill Nye To Go In With John Barleycorn.

The Unique Combination of Humorist and Bard Severed For Good and All.

Mr. Nye Says It Had To Be Done and Gives James Whitcomb "a Roasting."

The Sharp Trick By Which the Latter Secured a Good Supply of Whisky.

A LAMENTABLE AFFAIR.

The fact that the Nye and Riley combination, an inimitable one of the kind, has been broken up has become generally known, and much sorrow is expressed that it should have been dissolved on account of an uncontrollable appetite for strong drink on the part of Mr. Riley. The circumstances leading up to the culmination which was reached in this city Thursday night cover a period of several years, during which the most vigorous and persistent efforts have been made both by Mr. Nye and Mr. Walker, the manager of the combination, to keep the unfortunate victim from ruining his prospects by indulgence. The party are at the Galt House, with the exception of Mr. Riley, who left yesterday afternoon for New York; thoroughly disgusted and in a very bad frame of mind. When they came to Louisville last Thursday to fill an engagement, an order was issued that no liquor was to be sold to Mr. Riley, who occupied Room 320, but Mr. Riley was apparently "on to" this game, for he went into 319 and sent his orders from there, succeeding in getting very drunk, before he was detected. Mr. Walker and Mr. Nye have both been doing all they could to prevent a catastrophe, but it was evidently fighting against fate, and was bound to come. In referring to the matter yesterday, Mr. Nye said to a Courier-Journal reporter:

"Yes, this business has been going on for a long time, but not so badly as lately, since we found we could not control him. Mr. Riley carefully considered this matter—loss of reputation, loss of money, and all that—and concluded that he must have his spree—and he's having it. Mrs. Walker, wife of our manager, in passing his room this morning, saw, through the half open door, Riley lying on the floor with his head on a 'lounge. He was fully dressed, and has not had his clothes off for two or three days.

"And you have quit for good?"

"Yes. It was bound to come. I have been half way prepared for it for some time. No; there is no chance of fixing it up; that could not be done. Riley has been my friend for years. His friends have kept his falling quiet for a long time, and the newspaper boys talked to him often myself, and would do it again if he were sober enough to comprehend anything. But it's no use to try now. We are good friends yet. No, he has not had much to say. He did get furious Thursday because Mr. Walker watched him. Walker lost his dinner by keeping no drinks had been given at the hotel, and Riley started out with Walker following. After going down the street a piece, Riley turned on him and they had some rough words, but Walker, knowing his condition paid no attention to him. Walker got him back to the hotel and he went into a closet. We stationed ourselves where we could watch both entrances, and thought we had him; but he got hold of a boy and bribed him to go and get a bottle of whisky. A man who is determined to get drunk will have liquor somehow. It rests with him whether he gets it, and he generally gets it.

"It is a terrible thing. Riley was warned that publicity must come, but he said he would submit no longer; he wanted to get drunk and was going to do it. I told him that he was simply sacrificing his reputation for a drink, but it had no effect on him. It was simply an impossibility to keep him from it. That bottle he got loaded him to the guards. He drinks like no other man I ever saw. He drinks until it is a physical impossibility for him to hold any more, and it takes weeks for him to get over it."

"The prohibition as to drinks has been removed, I suppose?"

"Oh, yes. He's his own master now. He takes his meals anywhere. He ate nothing at all Friday, and to-day had breakfast sent to the bar-room. He doesn't care. He's happy, and will probably stay here till he gets through with his spree. Well had about seventy nights more in our season—were about half through. We had to go through the South and to California, but all that's off now. One man's appetite for whisky ruined it all. Our last season was remarkably successful, and this one was far better. We turned people away in Chicago, Cincinnati and other places, and have had packed houses everywhere. It makes a man feel pretty badly to have to throw all the bright prospects we had away."

"What will be your course now?"

"I shall go back to New York, and may take a fresh start. I have been answering telegrams to-day from people who want me to go out with somebody else. I don't think I'll do it, however. I have been doing double work this season, and will really be glad of a chance to rest up a little. Besides, I have other work on hand, some of which should have been done a year ago. As for 'writing,' that has been difficult. I have had to revel Sundays, when I should have rested. The idea was that we should have a day off every week; but the booking was so close we couldn't do it."

"Yes, there is great deal of difference between Riley and his rest and Riley in some other degree of perfection, and there is not a man in this country who can so bring out his own work. He was the star of the concern, and I was quite content that it should be so. He is a remarkable man. I know how he will feel after this. He will sober up and feel repentant, but it will be too late. It is calculated to make a man feel badly—yes, it is sad to think that a man you have traveled with and roomed with for years, until he seemed like a brother, should be so far above his appetite for drink. He is certainly a brilliant man—one of the most brilliant I ever knew. Do I think he might go into the speciality business: No, I do not. Riley is too proud for that—and if he did, no one could manage him."

Mr. Nye appeared much cut up about the matter, and was very sorry it had occurred, but said it had to come to that end, despite his efforts and those of Mr. Walker. He thought he would turn his attention to other work and let the platform alone for a while.

Mr. Riley was not in a condition to say anything. As one of the chambermaids

Louisville, Kentucky Courier Journal Feb. 1890

the more exalted medium of poetry. There are three poets who have sung of those in humble life. Two of them we know though they have passed away and were of foreign lands. One of a foreign language. Beranger sung as sweetly as any linnet of the people of his native France, and the other is Robert Burns. The third is a neighbor to you, and you are familiar not only with his work but with his presence. I can say of him, as was said of the great Beranger, not a speck will ever be put upon the heart or honor or good sense or genius of James Whitcomb Riley." {applause.}

Who was this Riley as Crestillomeem struck again? What did he look like? What was his reputation? We have the record of Hamlin Garland, a writer and some say the literary arbiter of the 1890's who published an interview he had with Riley from a visit recorded in a McCLURE'S MAGAZINE article.

Riley is described at age 40 as "a short man, with square shoulders and a large head. He has a very dignified manner — at times. His face is smoothly shaven, and though he is not bald, the light color of his hair makes him seem so. His eyes are gray and round, and generally solemn, and sometimes stern. His face is the face of a great actor — in rest, grim and inscrutable; in action, full of the most elusive expressions, capable of humor and pathos. Like most humorists, he is sad in repose. His language, when he chooses to have it so, is wonderfully concise and penetrating and beautiful. He drops often into dialect, but always with a look on his face which shows he is aware of what he is doing. In other words, he is master of both forms of speech. His mouth is his wonderful feature: wide, flexible, clean-cut. His lips are capable of the grimmest and the merriest lines. When he reads they pout like a child's, or draw down into a straight, grim line like a New England deacon's, or close at one side, and uncover his white and even teeth at the other, in the sly smile of "Benjamin F. Johnson," the humble humorist and philosopher. In his own proper person he is full of quaint and beautiful philosophy. He is wise rather than learned — wise with the quality that is in proverbs, almost always touched with humor. His eyes are near-sighted and his nose prominent. His head is of the "tack hammer" variety, as he calls it. The public insists that there is an element of resemblance between Mr. Riley, Eugene Field and Bill Nye.

Strangely in the original 1878 version of Riley's great autobiographical poem, "The Flying Islands of the Night," one does not find his mother to be listed in the cast of characters. The original poem proposes that it is enough for Riley to have the spirit of Nellie in the beyond to sustain him.

However, as the breakup with Nye occurred and Riley found his capacity to endure long periods of platform engagements more difficult, Riley evoked his mother's memory more and more for strength.

Finally we find that Riley's mother, Elizabeth, is added to the 1891 book version of "The Flying Islands of the Night," as a source of sustaining resolve against alcoholism. Elizabeth becomes AEo of the revised and expanded poem which comes to reflect new cryptic information about Riley's life as his autobiography needs revision due to new developments in his life.

AEo, "an ideal mother," (as was Elizabeth, his own mother) provides an archetypical figure for Riley. We find the type in a short story by Riley, EZ, (standing for Ezra). Here the mother, a Methodist as Elizabeth was, looks after her child who has received a knot the size of an Easter egg administered by an alcoholic father in his intoxication and despite the mother's frailty by taking a ballbat to the bar in Greenfield where he has been imbibing the "budge," the common name for corn whiskey. Finding her son who has gone to the bar to try to bring his father home knocked out, she acts. The boy notes, "When I come to, things was lively, I tell you. My mother is a little woman - don't weigh over ninety pounds -but if you'd a seen her yesterday, you'd 'a' thought she weighed a ton. Ever been into Dutchy's? Know

what a nice spread of glassware he has behind his bar? Know that mirror that he smears with soap pictures, birds an' things? All gone. They tried to hold mother, half a dozen of 'em did, but they couldn't do it. The old man had sneaked off somewhere-first time she'd ever follered him - an' he felt ornery. She told Dutchy that she'd begged him time 'n again not to sell liquor to father, an' then she went for the glassware. .." AEo overcomes liquor all right. She takes on Crestillomeem for the life of her son.

This is the role Riley relied on his mother's memory to take in his own life after the Louisville incident. In the first book of "The Flying Islands of the Night" revised in 1891 for sale in 1892, Riley included this archetypical character, AEo, within his autobiographical piece.

Her role in the revised poem was as it was in Riley's life. Riley's mother was evoked along with Nellie's memory to help him avoid Crestillomeem. With Elizabeth as well as Nellie behind him, Riley had no fear of his enemies. He could withstand the press's attacks on him from his Louisville debacle and all its gossip.

AEO! AEO! AEO!

AEo! AEo! AEo![1]
Thou dost all things know -
  Waving all claims of mine to dare to pray
Save that I needs must: - Lo
  What may I pray for? Yea,
  I have not any way,
An Thou gainsayest me a toler-
ance so. -
  I dare not pray
    Forgiveness - too great
    My vast o'ertoppling weight
    Of sinning; nor can I
    Pray my
Poor soul unscouraged to go. -
Frame Thou my prayer, AEo!

Riley writing in his boyhood home (East Room, upstairs) in 1893. Moving back to his boyhood home may have helped him get back in touch with his mother AEo.

1. Riley had a strong belief that his mother, Elizabeth, was not dead but still with him. The death of Riley's mother brought on terrific loneliness and sorrow but also a new belief that the dead really do live close to one they loved in human life. Riley surrounds the initial of her name with the Greek letters alpha and omega to stand for her timeless presence with him. He once had a vision which he recounted to his secretary, Marcus Dickey, as found in Youth of James Whitcomb Riley, saying: "I was alone," said he, "till as in a vision I saw my mother smiling back upon me from he blue fields of love - when lo! she was young again." After the breakup with Nye and Riley's advancing age, he needs his mother as well as Nellie (Dwainie) for weapons against Crestillomeem.

What may I pray for? Dare
I shape a prayer,
  In sooth,
  For any canceled joy
  Of my mad youth,
  Or any bliss my sin's stress did destroy?
What may I pray for - What? -
That the wild clusters of forget-me-not
  And mignonette
  And violet

Be out of childhood brought,
  And in mine hard heart set
  A-blooming now as then? -
   With all their petals yet
Bediamonded with dews -
Their sweet, sweet scent let loose
  Full sumptuously again!

What may I pray AEo!
  For the poor hutched cot
  Where death sate squat
Midst my first memories? - Lo!
My mother's face - (they, whispering, told me so) -
  That face! so pinchedly
  It blanched up, as they lifted me -
   Its frozen eyelids would
   Not part, nor could
  Be ever wetted open with warm tears.
  ...Who hears
The prayers for all dead-mother-sakes, AEo!

Leastwise one mercy: - May
I not have leave to pray
All self to pass away -
  Forgetful of all needs mine own -
  Neglectful of all creeds; - alone,
  Stand fronting Thy high throne and say:
   To Thee
  O Infinite, I pray
   Shield Thou mine enemy!

One must say that being Riley's enemy was not a very dangerous status. If Riley blamed his former manager, Amos Walker with the bad publicity about his being an alcoholic from his Nye breakup, his revenge against Walker was taken in a remarkable way. Walker owned a sartorial wardrobe and prided himself on "outdressing" Riley. Waiting until Amos died, Riley dressed in his finest and hurried to the Walker home and rang the bell. When the widow opened the door, Riley made a courtly bow, plucked a gardenia from his lapel, handed it to her and left without saying a word.

Riley's enemy throughout his life was Crestillomeem.

Three anecdotes will close this section on Crestillomeem in the life of Riley. The first two were written in the memoirs of Walter Dennis Myers, James Whitcomb Riley's attorney in his later years.

RILEY AND HIS OLD SWEETHEART OF MINE, CRESTILLOMEEM AFTER HE MOVED TO LOCKERBIE STREET TO LIVE WITH THE HOLSTEINS

"The poet came to visit his friends, Major and Mrs. Holstein, for a week end on Lockerbie Street and stayed for the rest of his life. After Major Holstein died, his widow took care of Mr. Riley like a child. She understood him and knew how to manage him without irritation as no one else did.

Their house was "L"-shaped. "Uncle Jim's" room in the "L" had a porch overlooking an old-fashioned sloping cellar door which opened upward and, when not closed, was held open by a chain fitted into a hook in a rainspout extending from the roof and anchored by a tile connection into the sewer.

"Uncle Jim" loved an occasional nip of bourbon, which Maggie Holstein well knew. This, he obtained in a tavern a few blocks away, run by a good Irish friend. One day he came home on unsteady feet. Maggie deduced that he had had too many nips. She took him to his room and locked him in.

He craved just another nip or two. The only way to get out was by way of the porch above the cellar door and its sturdy rainspout. Down the rainspout he slid without trouble until the hook for the door chain entrapped him by piercing the seat of his trousers. This development had not entered his calcula- tions. He wriggled, scooted, twisted and squirmed until the seat was torn out of his pants. A freed man at last, he limped around to the front door and rang the

Riley boarded at the home of Maggie Holstein.

doorbell. When Maggie appeared, he bowed as low as his crippled chivalry would allow and breathed softly, "I thank you, Mrs. Holstein, for the use of your rear exit."

At the first glance, Maggie exploded, "Rear exit, indeed! Look at your rear...rags and tatters. You come in here and put on another pair of pants."

"That's kind and thoughtful of you, my dear Maggie, but I'm on my way to an old sweetheart of mine. You see..."

"I don't see," interrupted Maggie, "and you're on your way back to your room and a change of pants; and the room is going to be locked, good and tight, inside and porch side. As for that old sweetheart of yours, she's in her bottle down at Paddy O'Neil's and she's going to stay there. Why haven't you as much sense as Paddy? He dishes it out over the bar all day, yet never touches a drop."

"He's shy, Maggie. He's shy. That's why. And he's like you ... no romance in his soul. I caught him reading that Straus store ad: `Today is the day they give babies away with a half a pound of tea." He thinks that's poetry. It's enough to make Shakespeare break down and write another romantic tragedy and entitle it `The Wiles of Women." What's the world coming to?"

"Come on," commanded Maggie. "March! You're on the way back to your room."

"Uncle Jim" bowed low, nearly toppled over and mumbled, "As you wish. Thanks for the use of your front entrance. You are right, as always ... a torn seat in your pants is not the way to a woman's heart."

He tried what he thought was song, "Flow Gently, Sweet Afton."

"Oh, Jim, shut up! That's not romance. Too much like the baa of an old bachelor billie goat," said Maggie.

"Right you are again," agreed Uncle Jim. "Let's go and get a bachelor baby with a half pound of tea. Babies don't baa like billie goats. Only kids do that."

The poet staggered upstairs and into his room. Thereupon, Maggie locked the doors."

CRESTILLOMEEM LANDS RILEY IN COURT
AFTER HE SIGNED A PROMISSORY NOTE WHILE DRUNK

"How I hate the god-dam, red-eyed law!" snorted James Whitcomb Riley as he plopped down into a big chair in the Columbia Club upon his return from the courtroom. He had been joined as a co-defendant on a promissory note filed as a claim against the estate of an old-time friend by one who also pretended to be the friend of both the deceased and Mr. Riley. "And my father was a lawyer," he continued, "who called it the god-dam, red-eyed law, too, a good many times. Maybe that was why he took a nip or so of red-eye whenever he went to try a case."

Mr. Riley was addressing me. I was his lawyer.

"Do you think the Judge'll get mad and send me to jail for contempt for cussing on the witness stand? You see, he pulled his hand down over his walrus mustache and I couldn't make out whether he was laughing at me or taking a cud of tobacco out of his mouth. This much I'm sure of, that room-ful of ginks was laughing at me and the Judge never pounded his gavel.

"You see, I was mad. Sometimes I get mad pretty easy, and when I do, I fly off the handle and let loose and cuss. I always aim to be gentle and respectful of the dignity of the law. But when I fly off the handle and let loose and cuss. I always aim to be gentle and respectful of the dignity of the law. But when I fly off the handle, hell! I can't help but cuss, dignity or no dignity. Yet, I'd hate to be sent to jail and blowed up in the newspapers after I quit white-washing chicken coops and pale fences and kind...a...well, made a pretty good go of it. Not many people get their stuff put out in books that people seem to like to read.

But dammit to hell! Being sorry won't cure the chicken pox or the measles or a fellow with a stomach for Sunday School.

"The Judge never seemed like a Sunday School stomacher at the Club. I've heard him cuss, too."

He paused reflectively.

"The trouble is, I cussed in what Pappy used to call open court."

Mr. Riley's cussing in open court stemmed from a happening of many years before. It was then the next to the last day before hanging for murder was abolished and electrocution was substituted.

It had been the custom for Mr. Riley to meet with three friends at the Columbia Club weekly. One of the friends was a society doctor who turned into a promoter. After saving the lives of many socialites, he founded the Columbia Club and the city's two best hotels. He became a millionaire. Another was a ne'er-do-well whose sole claim to fame was that he married the only daughter of the richest man in town. Then, she died young. Her father went broke and he became a scheming hanger-on who lived by his wits. The last of the four was the Sheriff, a born politician, one of whose legal duties it was to execute criminals adjudged to be hanged.

The Sheriff pulled out his watch and jumped to his feet. "Sorry, boys. Gotta go. Must hand a murderer this afternoon after he's monkeyed around in the courts six years. This'll be the last hangin' in the state. Hereafter, it'll be electrocution in the Pen at Michigan City," he explained.

"You mean to say you're going to hang somebody and take his life," queried Mr. Riley, adding, "I thought you were a friend of mine."

"I'm the Sheriff. It's my job, ain't it?" replied the Sheriff.

"Joe, I don't want anybody as my friend who has the blood of another man on his hands," shouted Mr. Riley.

"Listen, Jim. You don't understand," replied the Sheriff. "I don't do the hanging, personally that is. There are three ropes on the gallows. Only one drops the trap. There are three deputy sheriffs. They draw lots for seats. Each picks up a sharp knife beside him. when I say, `Cut," they cut. Nobody ever knows which rope dropped the trap. See? I couldn't possibly do it."

Mr. Riley argued that giving the order was the same thing as cutting the rope. Verbal controversy was endangering the fate of an old friendship.

The Doctor broke in after gulping the last of several nips of what Mr. Riley called red-eye.

"Jim, you're drunk," he drawled.

"Shut up! You're the only one polluted here," snapped Mr. Riley.

"Nuts," negated the Doctor.

"Let's prove who's polluted," challenged Mr. Riley. "Next door is the Marion Trust Company. We'll get a blank promissory note with two straight lines. We'll sign. He who signs the straightest is the least drunk."

The doctor agreed. Notes were obtained and signed. Mr. Riley's inimitable signature was neat, clear and on the line. The Doctor's name was scrawled all over the bottom of the note. Beyond doubt, according to the terms of the test, Mr. Riley was the least intoxicated.

After one glance, the Doctor crumpled up the note, stuck it in his coat pocket and without another word left the room.

The Sheriff went to the hanging.

The years sped by. The Doctor died. Liquor had taken toll of his brilliant mind. In his will, the ne'er-do-well was named as executor of his estate.

But there was no estate. The Doctor died insolvent, leaving a widow and two little sons, penniless. I was attorney for the estate, partly because the old lawyer (Editor's note, John W. Kern, lawyer and one-time Mayor of

Indianapolis) with whom I started practice could not afford to waste time on matters bringing in no fees, partly because Mr. Riley's brother-in-law was a client of the office, and Mr. Riley's nephew was my college friend.

Diligent search disclosed no property until the executor reported that he had found a paid-up life insurance policy for twenty-five thousand dollars, payable to the estate, in the inside pocket of one of the Doctor's coats in an old suitcase. He reported nothing more and resigned as executor. At the same time, the executor must have found the note signed by Mr. Riley and the unfortunate Doctor. For, two months later this executor, who had resigned, filed the note with his name as payee and five thousand dollars payable, inserted by typewriter, as a claim. Mr. Riley was joined as a defendant.

The executor said that he had hesitated to file the claim against the estate of an old friend, but that the money was justly due and he was in dire need and the surviving family would have twenty thousand dollars less established claims anyhow.

At once, I interview Mr. Riley and his brother-in-law, Mr. Eitel, and was given the story of the execution of the note.

The claim was set down for trial. The attorney for the executor who had resigned, able but extremely gruff and unpleasant, put the note in evidence, attempted to prove the signatures by Mr. Riley and rested. On cross-examination, I used Mr. Riley to establish the circumstances surrounding execution. The former executor's attorney re-examined, and this is a part of the record:

Q. "Mr. Riley, I hand you claimant's Exhibit 1, the instrument in suit, and ask you ..."

A. "Wait a minute. You hand me what?"

Claimant's attorney: "The instrument in suit."

Witness Riley. "I always thought an instrument was a monkey wrench, a screw driver, a butcher knife, or something like that and not an old, crumpled-up piece of paper."

Q. "A fellow who makes his living out of writing ought to know what a paper instrument is. Now I hand you this instrument, claimant's Exhibit 1, ask you to examine it and state whether or not at the time you signed it you did not know that it had something to do with a business transaction."

A (In a gentle tone of voice) "Sure it's my signature, put there as I swore to just a little while ago. I signed no note to pay money."

Q. "When you signed, you knew it had something to do with a business transaction, didn't you? Now, don't fiddle-faddle about it."

A. "Mr. Lawyer, I don't know anything about business. My brother-in-law, Henry Eitel, sitting right there behind you, he's a banker and he tends to all my business. And I never would have signed this thing you call an instrument if we hadn't been hoisting a few." Mr. Riley's voice was low and gentle."

Q. "I move to strike out the answer as not responsive to the question. I asked the witness nothing about hoisting a few."

The Court: "Motion sustained. It may be stricken."

Q. "Very well. Reporter, read the question to the witness. Now, Mr. Witness, answer that properly. You should understand English. You make your living writing it."

(Mr. Riley's face flushed. He was getting angry. Imitating the lawyer, he answered:)

A. "Read the answer to the previous question, but add I never would have signed the thing you call an instrument if we hadn't been drinking red-eye."

Q. "Red eye? What do you mean, red-eye?"

A. "Whisky to you. Maybe bootleg."

The reporter read the previous question and Mr. Riley's answer.

The attorney: "I move to strike out the answer."

The Court: "Sustained."

The attorney: "You're just trying to be perverse."

The witness, interrupting: "Perverse! That's the kind of verse I never write."

Q. "Your Honor, direct the witness to answer my questions and quit elaborating. Now...now, reporter, read the question again, and you...you poet-taster, you, answer it properly."

A. "Reporter, read my answer again and add that I never would have signed this thing he handed me if Doc and I hadn't been drinking red-eye."

The answer was stricken out once more. The Judge explained that the law sometimes requires what seems trivial to the laity. Clearly, Mr. Riley was boiling with restrained rage.

Q. "Riley, for the last time, now I ask, when you signed Exhibit 1, the instrument in suit: you knew it had something to do with a business transaction, now didn't you? Answer that yes or no. Don't try to be a stubborn jackass."

A. "No. Now you listen to me: For the last time, I'm telling you I don't know a god-dam thing about business, and I'm god-dam proud of it. My brother-in-law, Henry Eitel, there behind you, he's a banker and a god-dam good one. He tends to all the god-dam business I have. Besides, I never would have signed this god-dam thing you keep on calling an instrument if Doc and I hadn't been drinking red-eye to beat hell."

The attorney spread his drooping hands side-wise and groaned in despair, "What's the use?"

The Judge said, "That means no more questions, I presume. I'll take the matter under advisement and ultimately decide against the claimant."

"Court's adjourned."

The Judge strode to his chambers, breathing a sigh of relief. Mr. Riley took me with him back to the Club, worrying lest the Judge send him to jail for "cussing in open court."

The Judge didn't send Mr. Riley to jail. Neither did he decide in favor of the claimant.

When advised about the decision, Mr. Riley soliloquized, "There's sense in the go-dam red-eyed law after all, like my Pappy so often used to say."

RILEY GETS DRUNK AT A HOTEL PARTY
IN FLORIDA IN THE LAST MONTHS OF HIS LIFE

Crestillomeem was with Riley from adolescence to his grave. The final anecdote I will close with is from Dr. Carleton B. McCulloch, who was Riley's physician for the last years of his life.

About a year before Riley died, Dr. McCulloch took Riley to Miami, Florida. Riley was partially paralyzed by this time, and was accompanied by a nurse, a housekeeper, a sister and two nieces, all women of prudish virtue. Carl G. Fisher, an Indianapolis promoter who built Miami Beach, and James Allison met Riley and asked him to come to their hotel for a party they were giving. The five women all were standing around saying "No." "You know Mr. Riley's failing," they suggested. But eventually, the men promised they would keep Riley absolutely abstemious.

Riley took permanent residence in Indianapolis with the Holsteins after the summer of 1893. This home was built in approximately 1860 by Mrs. Holsein's father John Nickum, a prosperous Hoosier Deutsch grocer. The home was built on what had been the farm of Geogre Lockerbie, a Scot, who had cleared the place of forest.

However, when they got Riley to their rooms, they handed him about six cocktails in quick succession, and by the time of the fish course, he was disgracefully stiff. He was in even worse condition by the time they got him back to his hotel room, dumped him in bed, and rapped on the nurse's door and fled.

The next afternoon they went over to see how Jim was doing. He was sitting at one end of the hotel's veranda staring out to sea. The five female companions, with about fifteen other women in a crowd, started buzzing at each other when the two approach. Allison and Fisher asked Riley how he was feeling but all Riley could do was grunt and look dead ahead. The conversation didn't go well. After fifteen minutes, Allison and Fisher ran out of small talk, and in a moment of silence, Riley said, "You see all those women over there?" he asked. Allison and Fisher allowed they did. "They think I'm sorry," the old man said.

RILEY'S DEPRESSION AND ALCOHOLISM
AS AFFECTING HIS CREATIVITY

There is a great body of psychiatric information which has begun to appear on subject of the creativity of writers. The general conclusion is that creative writers as well as visual artists have a much higher prevalence of pathological personality traits and alcoholism. In particular, depressive disorders, but no other psychiatric condition, affect writers almost twice as often as men with other high creative achievements. (The British psychiatric study upon which I base this considered only male writers.) 48% of such writers had passed through major depressive episodes.

That Riley was among those creative people suffering horrible depression and alcoholism is not novel. What is novel is that Riley's strategy for dealing with these behavioral influences, as revealed in his autobiographical poem "The Flying Islands of the Night", worked in such a salutary manner.

Dear Tom,

Riley was very fortunate to have as loyal and thoughtful a reader as you. You obviously persevered through one tough poem.

I gave up on it. It was way too tedious. This is why I have delayed writing you — it took me a long time to officially surrender.

Delerious? Yes. Intoxicated? I doubt it. His gamesmanship with the words, the old english style, and overuse of alter egos flittering about seem to call for too much patience. I would hope he'd be more blunt if he were stoned.

Mark Brunke

Mark Brunke author of "Alcohol and Creative Writing" Psychological Reports, Oct. 1992.

SPRAIVOLL

An Inspirer of Sweet poetry from the Message of the "Christ Hymn"

AN INSPIRER OF SWEET POETRY FROM
THE MESSAGE OF THE "CHRIST HYMN"

Who was Riley's great singer of poetry?

This is Spraivoll, "the tune fool." It is Riley's most enigmatic and engagingly distant self. She wears a Godly robe and her utterances sparkle and shine as rain and lightning. She is the Riley who sang God's praise as a kenotic choir member and drew energy from the silence of prayer. She is the Riley of "Jucklet's Prayer in Contemplation of AEo" (from "The Flying Islands of the Night"):

JUCKLET'S PRAYER TO AEO

"May

I not have leave to pray

All self to pass away -"

She was the kenotic Riley emptied of all his selves and any pretensions he might have or hope to have. She sang in despair of Riley's depression and alcoholism and out of the depths of Riley's anguish over the death of his mother, the hurt of the fate of living in an age he could not see reconciled with the truths of the American Civil War, and the death of Nellie Cooley.

Hope was a woman to Riley. Women gave Riley all the "hope" he knew about in the world. He turned himself into a woman to assume this special "inspired" role of Spraivoll in "The Flying Islands of the Night."

To live on, Riley needed hope for the future. This was a commodity that Incarnation Theology dealt in. In the year after Riley wrote "The Flying Islands of the Night," he expressed what sustained him.

HOPE (1879)

Hope, bending o'er me one time, snowed the flakes
Of her white touches on my folded sight,
And whispered, half rebukingly, "What makes
My little girl so sorrowful to-night?"

O scarce did I unclasp my lids, or lift
Their tear-glued fringes, as with blind embrace
I caught within my arms the mother-gift,
And with wild kisses dappled all her face.

That was a baby dream of long ago:
My fate is fanged with frost and tongued with flame:
My woman-soul, chased make through the snow,
Stumbles and staggers on without an aim,

And yet, here in my agony, sometimes
A faint voice reaches down from some far height,
And whispers through a glamouring of rhymes, -
"What makes my little girl so sad to-night?"

The poem "Hope" was originally enclosed in a letter of September 18, 1879, to Elizabeth Kahle. Upon sending her the poem, Riley added, "Here is a little poem that wrote itself. I hardly know if I fully comprehend it, but something tells me you will like it, for all its strangeness, and I trust you will." The poem was a favorite of Riley's great friend and spiritual advisor, Rev. Myron Reed, a kenotic minister of the First Presbyterian Church in Indianapolis, Indiana. Riley poured not only all of the masculinity but also all of the femininity he could imagine

Riley's friend, Lew Wallace.

into "logos" fantasizing about the American Nineteenth Century experience. There is nothing strange about this approach. The root of American thought derives from the Neo-Platonic concept whereby truth derives out of "feel" rather than the Platonic vanity that truth can be learned through objective rationality. Much of Christianity's power is in this understanding as is confirmed by Paul.[1]

From the martyrdom of Jesus on the cross, the true kenotics of the Nineteenth Century derived their key concept of Hope. As the Scottish kenotic apologist A.B. Bryce wrote in

His novel, BEN HUR: A TALE OF THE CHRIST (1880) was the age's great kenotic depiction of the humiliated Jesus of the "Christ Hymn" who cures Ben Hur's mother and sister of leprosy, and yet refuses Ben Hur's offer of an army to save Him from being crucified. Here our boy of the oppressed Jewry (Ramon Novarro of the 1925 movie version) battles a might Roman, Massala (Francis X. Bushman) in a widely publicized chariot race.

THE HUMILIATION OF CHRIST, "(Jesus) had announced Himself as the King, not only God's servant, but God's Son, the Hope of those who waited for the consolation of Israel." Hope was necessary for a people coming to understand their biological antecedents were in evolutionary forms - arboreal to slime- dwellers. Hope was in an act of degradation - the descent of Christ into an evolving world.

As Incarnation Theology struck into the American heartland from Germany no longer do we find American Protestants of the American heartland worshipping a regal God on a distant, glorious throne governing life through discoverable Newtonian laws of mechanics. Now we find Christian Protestants relying on the humble Christ of Philippians. For example, in Riley's hometown we have the Elder A.J. Branham recounting the start of a Greenfield (Indiana) Protestant church. "In April 1854, Brother James L. Thornberry of Kentucky held a two week meeting (in Greenfield), which resulted in quite a number of additions to the church. It was at this meeting that I was brought from darkness to light, and from the power of Satan to God; and from that day to this I have never regretted the casting of my lot with the poor, despised Nazarene and his humble followers." (As reported in the Hancock DEMOCRAT, July 25, 1889).

Prayer to a humiliated God became Riley's private habit as a foil to his alcoholism and delirious episodes. He prayed to a God who accepted crucifixion as glory. This was a God who healed the sick and loved the humble. This was a God of the vulnerable, tormented and tremens shaking alcoholic like Riley and so many of his circle of friends. This was a God who did not avoid taking the form of an evolving life form such as humanity.

In a Nineteenth Century world in which natural selection principles were deemed to order society by social Darwinists, where is there comfort? Why not merely succumb to existential terror? Does not fate govern all? Is not death the answer to every evolutionary life? Riley's time was faced with a revolutionized fundamental pattern of thought. The biblical God who created the world according to a Genesis account of a seven day creation was no longer for purchase. Intellectuals such as Robert Ingersoll were touring the country in Riley's time announcing the Bible was "hokey folklore." Was hope gone too?

Incarnation theology answered social Darwinism. A Mid-Western American Methodist kenotic theologian of Riley's day, R.J. Cooke, D.D, spoke thus.

CHRIST AS THE ANSWER TO THE LOWLY ORIGIN OF MAN

"Whatever physical science may have to say as to the lowly origin of man, here is what he is. God does not have to force himself into human nature, and when in it find himself unable to manifest himself in a throughly revealing capacity in the human, nor is the human unable to bear the weight, the presence of deity. But because man is spirit, because he has intelligence, and reason, and will, and affection, because he is a moral being, Infinite Spirit, Infinite Wisdom, and Infinite Love can adjust himself to the spirit of man -laying every power and quality of God alongside of every corresponding faculty in the human soul without violence to the soul - and thus manifest himself as God in the flesh. The astounding revelation dawns on us for the first time that the human may embody the eternal."

Cooke finds the principle of the Incarnation embedded in literature by which kenosis teaches the "infinite worth of man." Not just literature, and the laws, but also the society of the Christian nations are said to depend upon this truth, that it modified Roman law, that it motivated the struggles for freedom in Western civilization, that it abolished slavery and is behind reforms, underlies civilization, political and social institution. He finds the principle working in the struggles for wealth and power, in conflicts between labor and capital, alignments of class against class, within which the reaffirmation of the infinite worth of man is bound to prevail. Human progress will not bow to introduction of the machines of the Industrial Revolution because people are children of God and the human whose form in which God came kenotically is a form of life in redemption.

Kenotic literature is urged because the "ache of humanity is heart-ache. There is need then for the reaffirmation of the infinite worth of man; need for the incoming power of some transfiguring idea on the common life, some heaven-born vision of the innate glory of humanity, which will once more exalt man above the level of the brainless, soulless machine at his side - above the beast of burden, above the degrading passion for power and material grandeur as the highest ends - and dignify the man. "

Spraivoll began writing poetry to answer the call for a kenotic literature.

Spraivoll did not live so long as Riley's other selves. She abruptly departed after Riley achieved fame and wealth in the late 1880's. While she sang, the American people listened enraptured. No poet had embraced the idea of the Philippians "Christ Hymn" before so completely. Riley's poetry became more and more kenotic until one finds him subsuming all of the structures, meters and figures of poetry into characterizations of humility and service within his "Benjamin Johnson of Boone" poetry.

The great poetry of James Whitcomb Riley was thoroughly kenotic in the forefront of the great popularization of this theological movement of Riley's day. Riley empties himself to write poetry in the American experience of his day.

Spraivoll is the Riley who sings with the newfound understandings Riley gained from the Incarnationists. She is the Riley who engages his epoch and takes to song but often turns them into hymns.

The first clearly identifiably kenotic of Riley's poems is "Old Fashioned Roses."

OLD FASHIONED ROSES (1879)

They ain't no style about 'em,
And they're sort o' pale and faded
Yit the doorway here without 'em
Would be lonesomer, and shaded
With a good 'eal blacker shadder
Than the morning-glories makes
And the sunshine would look sadder
Fer their good old-fashion' sakes.

I like 'em 'cause they kind o'
Sort o' make a feller like 'em!
And I tell you, when I find a
Bunch out whur the sun kin strike 'em,
It allus sets me thinkin'
O' the ones 'at used to grow
And peek in through the chinkin'
O' the cabin, don't you know!

A Hoosier backyard of Riley's era. From the author's Ora Myers glass negative collection of Hancock County, Indiana subjects.

And then I think o' mother,
And how she ust to love 'em -
When they wuzn't any other,
'Less she found 'em up above 'em!
And her eyes, afore she shut 'em,
Whispered with a smile and said

We must pick a bunch and putt 'em
In her hand when she wuz dead.

But, as I wuz a-sayin',
They ain't no style about 'em
Very gaudy er displayin',
But I wouldn't be without 'em, -
'Cause I'm happier in these posies,
And hollyhawks and sich,
Than the hummin'-bird 'at noses
In the roses of the rich.

The proposal of this poem is that the humble has value. Thereafter to Riley there was no poetry by Spraivoll which did not evoke humiliation if not degradation.

The poem is far more radical that we could now hardly imagine. We recall that Riley's age was sometimes called the age of Hubert Spencer and those who treated the humble things with contempt and marked such with a destiny of extinction. The inferior species, the humble "old-fashioned roses," must be eradicated in favor of superior new varieties as a result of the "survival of the fittest." In the background of the age, we hear John D. Rockefeller, a contemporary American and one of its most prominent citizens, declaring his opinion in a Sunday School address

THE GROWTH OF AMERICAN BUSINESS LIKENED
TO AN AMERICAN BEAUTY ROSE

"The growth of a large business is merely a survival of
the fittest...The American Beauty rose can be produced
in the splendor and fragrance which bring cheer to its
beholder only by sacrificing the early buds which grow
up around it. This is not an evil tendency in business.
It is merely the working-out of a law of nature and a
aw of God."

God favors the rich and efforts of those trying to get rich. Riley is saying here that the less adaptive humble rose is preferable to Rockefeller's "American Beauty." A new voice was being raised in the American culture.

Riley derives such a conclusion through the medium of temperance Christianity empowered from the German theologians of the Mid-Nineteenth Century. Every experience Christ encountered, they taught, involved humility. Nothing else was real. Humiliation is predicable to the divinity of Christ. There is infinite moral value to every humiliation encountered in life because this reminds one of the contrast between the Godly and human states of the form of Christ.

Longfellow, near the end of his life, approved this poem when recited to him by Riley on Dec. 31, 1881 at Craigie House, Cambridge. Longfellow's ill heath stopped him from attending Riley's Tremont Temple reading of his poetry so Riley went to meet Longfellow. Although one cannot say that transcendentalism in its twilight years was thus passing the torch to Riley's kenoticism in the field of poetics, one can say that a poet cognizant of the sensibilities of his time acknowledged another. It was often said at the time that this meeting of Riley and Longfellow marked the passage of national poet from one man to the next, the popular transcendentalist of the early Nineteenth Century to the popular kenotic of the post Civil-War American Protestant nation.

From the date of publication of "Old Fashioned Roses" in the Indianapolis Morning HERALD, Riley was read on both sides of the Atlantic Ocean, and shortly thereafter began unceasing platform lecturing. In lecturing, Riley explained his use of dialect in this poem by saying it permitted him to convey "worth of character and truthfulness to life," stating the language of this poem was "the language of an old-timer, who once took the trouble to explain to me his love of the flowers about his doorway." About this old man, Riley added, "Colleges may disown him but God does not. Poetry is purity....Where purity abounds, poetry abounds." Holding a bible, Riley added, "This Book of Books says the pure in heart shall see God. Our old man in the doorway was poetic because his heart was pure. He had the poetry of character, and will, I believe, as certainly see God as the fishermen saw Him, who walked with Jesus by the Sea of Galilee."

SPRAIVOLL AS THE ANSWER TO A RIDDLE

Riley's autobiographical poem, "The Flying Islands of the Night" contains a riddle spoken by a voice later identified as Spraivoll, the poetical Riley.

When kings are kings, and kings are men -
And the lonesome rain is raining! -
O who shall rule from the red throne then,
And who shall cover the scepter when -
When the winds are all complaining?

When men are men, and men are kings -
And the lonesome rain is raining! -
O who shall list as the minstrel sings
Of the crown's fiat, or the signet-ring's,
When the winds are all complaining?

Rain, to the Riley contemporary to this poem meant "renewal" (SEE: Riley's poem, "The Rain") and wind meant despair of the night. (SEE: Riley's poem "Bells Jangled").

The answer to the riddle is Spraivoll.

The drift is this. When Riley is being revived from his alcoholism and he no longer drinks "red eye" so as make despair complain and flee, all of the play characters of Riley except Crestillomeem will utter poetry from the mouth of Riley's poetic self, Spraivoll. The minstrel Jucklet will utter entertaining narrative poetry. Amphine will utter romantic poetry. Krung will utter official poetry. And Spraivoll herself will utter the most special of all, Riley's kenotic poetry.

This poem was singled out for criticism by Riley's friend, Benjamin Parker. Shortly after the publication of "Flying Islands of the Night" the Indianapolis Saturday HERALD printed a criticism of it on September 14, 1878, by Benjamin Parker, the poet-editor of the New Castle MERCURY and a poet in his own right:

"Some of the friends of the MERCURY have said to us: "Let us have an end of this talk about Riley. We are tired of it, and the fellow's head will burst wide open if the editors are going to write about him so much." We are not unconscious of the danger, but Riley keeps intruding himself and the public seems to be pleased with his intrusions, and therefore he remains a growing quantity, a noticeable quantify if you please. The last of these intrusions, or if not the last the lengthiest, is a piece of nightmare or "thing-um-me-jig" rhyme called "The Flying Islands of the Night," which occupies a whole page of the Saturday Herald of August 24. What is it? Well we don't know. It is a waif of nothing on a warp of nought. It is a drama in which beings appear that never existed anywhere except in Riley's brain, and they inhabit the countries the very names of which are foreign to anything else on the earth except Riley's fancy. They are not fairies, nor elfish things, such as used to inhabit earth and hold high carnival in the corollas of wood flowers, but they are new creations. We can't describe the poem and we shan't try. It is full of pretty pictures, delicate creations of the most sensitive genius, but no practical soul can ever guess what they mean. Take this for example:

> When kings are kings, and kings are men -
> And the lonesome rain is raining -
> O who shall rule from the red throne then,
> And who shall wield the scepter when -
> When the winds are all complaining?

> When men are men, and men are kings -
> And the lonesome rain is raining -
> O who shall list as the minstrel sings
> Of the ermine robes and the signet rings
> When the winds are all complaining?"

Beautiful, isn't it? but what does it mean? Well, what does Poe's "Ulalume" mean? It means the same that this does, an expression of the beautiful in melody and rhythm, that is so exquisite that of itself it constitutes a living excellence. But Mr. Riley wants to call a halt in that direction now. One or two successes in nonsense rhyme is all that any man can achieve. The public is patient, but practical, and too much of that sort of things puts it out of humor, and once out of humor it is hard to woo back. We also wish softly but firmly to suggest to Mr. Riley that certain tricks, which the public is beginning to understand, by which he seeks to give himself notoriety must now be abandoned. He has the elements of the true poet in him. He has been very successful in illuminating them, and has made an excellent start. Now he must depend upon the merits of what he produces to sustain and increase the reputation already achieved. Tricks and subterfuges will serve him no longer, and he must turn his back upon them."

Riley's "The Flying Islands of the Night" was the most misunderstood poem in American literature. A poem about one's soul is necessarily ambiguous.

While other persona wrote poetry, Spraivoll's poetry was the most special. Spraivoll's poetry was written primarily out of Riley's vulnerability to life coming from his disabling alcoholism and the death of his soulmate Nellie. This poetry is the work of a hopeless man living in a lifeless world. In the strange transforming way that vulnerability permits, Riley wrote much of his kenotic poetry. Just as Jucklet wrote for the Indianapolis Saturday HERALD, and Amphine wrote for the Kokomo TRIBUNE, Spraivoll wrote for the Indianapolis JOURNAL which published over half of Riley's poetry and specifically the Benjamin Johnson of Boone series.

Kenotic poetry met the need Riley had sought since childhood to participate in the pure soul of art.

And yet it also gave him a new perspective that inspired special poetry.

Where was "home" in Riley's Nineteenth Century? Was "home" simply an adaptive shelter in a "tooth and claw" environment as the social Darwinists proposed? Riley evoked a more kenotic idea. He pictured a human situation though wrecked by vulnerability in which there was shelter with God, at a home not made by human hands, beyond time in God's reality. Here was no place where reality required struggle with reality. The kenotic idea of home was a place of rest from ambition and adaptive behavior. Riley wrote this poem:

WE MUST GET HOME (1881)

We must get home! How could we stray like this? -
So far from home, we know not where it is, -
Only in some fair, apple-blossomy place
Of children's faces - and the mother's face -
We dimly dream it, till the vision clears
Even in the eyes of fancy, glad with tears.

We must get home -for we have been away
So long, it seems forever and a day!
And O so very homesick we have grown,
The laughter of the world is like a moan
In our tired hearing, and its songs as vain, -
We must get home - we must get home again!

We must get home! With heart and soul we yearn

To find the long-lost pathway, and return!...
The child's shout lifted from the questioning band
Of old folks, faring weary, hand in hand,
But faces brightening, as if clouds at last
Were showering sunshine on us as they passed.

We must get home: It hurts so, staying here,
Where fond hearts must be wept out tear by tear,
And where to wear wet lashes means, at best,
When most our lack, the least our hope of rest -
When most our need of joy, the more our pain -
We must get home - we must get home again!

From the author's Ora Myers glass
negative collection of Hanock County,
Indiana subjects.

We must get home - home to the simple things -
The morning-glories twirling up the strings
And bugling color, as they blared in blue -
And-white o'er garden-gates we scampered through;
The long grape-arbor, with its undershade
Blue as the green and purple overlaid.

We must get home: All is so quiet there:
The touch of loving hands on brow and hair -
Dim rooms, wherein the sunshine is made mild -
The lost love of the mother and the child
Restored in restful lullabies of rain, -
We must get home - we must get home again!

The rows of sweetcorn and the China beans
Beyond the lettuce-beds where, towering, leans
The giant sunflower in barbaric pride
Guarding the barn-door and the land outside;
The honeysuckles, midst the hollyhocks,
That clamber almost to the martin-box.

We must get home, where, as we nod and drowse,
Time humors us and tiptoes through the house,
And loves us best when sleeping baby-wise,
With dreams - not tear-drops - brimming our clenched eyes, -

Pure dreams that know not taint nor earthly stain -
We must get home - we must get home again!

We must get home! There only may we find
The little playmates that we left behind, -
Some racing down the road; some by the brook;
Some droning at their desks, with wistful look
Across the fields and orchards - further still
Where laughs and weeps the old wheel at the mill.

We must get home! The willow-whistle's call
Trills crisp and liquid as the waterfall -
Mocking the trillers in the cherry-trees
And making discord of such rhymes as these,
That know not lilt nor cadence but the birds
First warbled - then all poets afterwards.

We must get home; and, unremembering there
All gain of all ambition otherwhere,
Rest - from the feverish victory, and the crown
Of conquest whose waste glory weighs us down. -
Fame's fairest gifts we toss back with disdain -
We must get home - we must get home again!

Mowing the grass in Riley's era. From the author's Ora Myers glass negative collection of Hanock County, Indiana subjects.

We must get home again - we must - we must! -
(Our rainy faces pelted in the dust)
Creep back from the vain quest through endless strife
To find not anywhere in all of life
A happier happiness than blest us then...
We must get home - we must get home again!

Riley's poetry began to attract more and more attention in America as his themes became more kenotic. His poems addressed what Cooke's Incarnation Methodism saw as "world chasm" in "modern life between the rich and the poor, the cultured and uncultured, the employer and the work- man. The gulf wider than the Atlantic that separates men in church, in busi- ness, in society, can never be bridged nor wide class antagonisms ever be reconciled till the higher descends to the lower in divine sympathy and

Christlike compassion for humanity. There is no salvation, social or moral, in any city or nation where the Church of the democratic Christ has become an exclusive aristocracy, where the scholar, the culture, the refined, avoid the dens of ignorance, the haunts of vice, the gloomy alleys where poverty hides its rags, or refuses to shake the grimy hand of honest toil. The higher must touch the lower.

This to us is the meaning of the kenosis in the Incarnation. This is the method of Christ. By this method may society be redeemed and by this method may men be led as Farrar says to the larger life, as Virgil led Dante from the lower hells, in whose sulfurous air no angel ever plumed his wing to the bright lift of the stars and the shimmer of the sea."

Riley's poetry sought a medium whereby the "higher" might engage the "lower."

We have an imaginary encounter of Riley with himself as Benjamin F. Johnson, the most kenotic personas of Riley's pseudonyms. Only subtly do we come to realize that this persona, under whose published name appears "The Old Swimmin'-Hole" and "When the Frost is on the Punkin," is among his other attributes nothing less than Darwin's "ape." Ben Johnson at least has hair all over him like this "ape" from whose descent all folk of Riley's time reacted with horror. Riley in his subtlety and wit causes the very most despicable bogey-man of his Nineteenth Century time to become the vehicle for his most kenotic poetry. Riley enjoyed this kind of wittiness.

The piece opens with Riley becoming introduced to Johnson's poetry through letters, the first of which revealingly said, "I make no doubt you will find some purty sad spots in my poetry, considerin'; but I hope you will bear in mind that I am a great sufferer with rheumatizum, and have been, off and on, since the cold New Years. In the main, however, I allus aim to write in a cheerful, comfortin' sperit, so's ef the stuff hangs fire, and don't do no good, it hain't a-going to do no harm, - and them's my honest views on poet-ry."

It is on a later day when Riley claims he was feeling too gloomy and depressed to write, (and getting ready to get "wild"), that he claims Benjamin Johnson came to knock on his door. Riley echoes the Matthew 7.7 text where Jesus reminds us "Ask and it will be give to you, search and you will find, knock and it will be opened to you. Everything anyone asks for gets received, or looks for gets found, or comes from knocking on a door for entry gets opened up."

"Come in!" (Riley) snarled, grabbing up my pencil and assuming a frightfully industrious air; "Come in!" ...

"Sir, howdy," said a low and pleasant voice. And at once, in spite of my perverse resolve, I looked up. I someway felt rebuked.

The speaker was very slowly, noiselessly closing the door. I could hardly face him when he turned around. An old man, of sixty-five, at least, but with a face and an eye of the most cheery and wholesome expression I had ever seen in either youth or age. Over his broad bronzed forehead and white hair he wore a low-crowned, wide-brimmed black felt hat, somewhat rusted now, and with the band grease-crusted, and the binding frayed at intervals and sagging from the threads that held it on. An old-styled frock coat of black, dull brown in streaks, and quite shiny about the collar and lapels. A waist-coat of no describable material or pattern, and a clean white shirt and collar of one piece, with a black string-tie and double bow, which would have been entirely concealed beneath the long white beard but for its having worked around to one side of the neck. The front outline of the face was cleanly shaven, and the beard, growing simply from the under chin and throat, lent the old pioneer the rather singular appearance of having hair all over him with the luxurious growth pulled out above his collar for mere sample.

I arose and asked the old man to sit down, handing him a chair decorously.

"No, no," he said - "I'm much obleeged. I hain't come in to bother you no more'n I can he'p. All I wanted was to know ef you got my poetry all right. You know I take yer paper," he went on, in an explanatory way, "and seein' you printed poetry in it once-in-a-while, I sent you some of mine - neighbors kindo' advised me to," he added apologetically, "and so I sent you some - two or three times I sent you some, but I hain't never seed hide-ner-hair of it in your paper, and as I wus I wus in town to-day, anyhow, I jest thought I'd kindo' drap in and git it back, ef you ain't goin' to print it - `cause I allus save up most the things I write, aimin' sometime to git 'em all struck off in pamphlet-form, to kindo distribit round 'mongst the neighbors, don't you know."

The three poems by which Benjamin Johnson of Boone chose to introduce himself to the world as related by Riley in his prose piece, "A Caller from Boone" were "The Old Swimmin'-Hole," "The Hoss," and "When the Frost is on the Punkin'."

THE OLD SWIMMIN'-HOLE (1882)

OH! the old swimmin'-hole! whare the crick so still and deep
Looked like a baby-river that was laying half asleep,
And the gurgle of the worter round the drift jest below
Sounded like the laugh of something we onc't ust to know
Before we could remember anything but the eyes
Of the angels lookin' out as we left Paradise;
But the merry days of youth is beyond our controle,
And it's hard to part ferever with the old swimmin'-hole.

Oh! the old swimmin'-hole! In the happy days of yore,
When I ust to lean above it on the old sickamore,
Oh! it showed me a face in its warm sunny tide
That gazed back at me so gay and glorified,
It made me love myself, as I leaped to caress
My shadder smilin' up at me with sich tenderness.
But them days is past and gone, and old Time's tuck his toll
From the old man come back to the old swimmin'-hole.

Oh! the old swimmin'-hole! In the long, lazy-days
When the humdrum of school made so many run-a-ways,
How plesant was the jurney down the old dusty lane,
Whare the tracks of our bare feet was all printed so plane
You could tell by the dent of the heel and the sole
They was lots o'fun on hands at the old swimmin'-hole.
But the lost joys is past! Let your tears in sorrow roll
Like the rain that ust to dapple up the old swimmin'-hole.

There the bullrushes growed, and the cattails so tall,
And the sunshine and shadder fell over it all;
And it mottled the worter with amber and gold
Tel the glad lilies rocked in the ripples that rolled;
And the snake-feeder's four gauzy wings fluttered by
Like the ghost of a daisy dropped out of the sky,
Or a wounded apple-blossom in the breeze's controle
As it cut acrost some orchurd to'rds the old swimmin'-hole.

Oh! the old swimmin'-hole! When I last saw the place,
The scene was all changed, like the change in my face;
The bridge of the railroad now crosses the spot
Whare the old divin'-log lays sunk and fergot.
And I stray down the banks whare the trees ust to be -
But never again will theyr shade shelter me!
And I wish in my sorrow I could strip to the soul,
And dive off in my grave like the old swimmin'-hole.

"The Old Swimmin'-Hole" is a poem which upholds the simple things as those things which make life really worth living: children, sunshine, a natural pool in a stream, the sight of wondrous and fantastic natural creatures freshly seen, a warm wind, friendship. The joy of life does not come from making others tremble. Nor is the great feeling of living coming from the proximity of assailing natural forces. The simple pleasure of companionship in natural bounty is enough to make life worth living.

Swimmin' holes were places of relaxation. In Indiana, there are few large bodies of water. The spot

The original "old Swimmin' Hole" on Greenfield, Indiana's Brandywine Creek. "The bridge of the railroad now covers the spot/Where the old divin' log lay sunk and forgot." Legend attributes the naming of this crick to three Revolutionary War veterans who stopped at its banks on their way to seek homes. They likened it to the Brandywine Creek in Pennsylvania where they had fought with General George Washington during the Revolutionary War. The settlers in the area decided to honor their recollection with the name.

Riley refers to was simply a deep and wide place in a small creek. Children were taught to swim by throwing them in the water over their heads. Girls were taught to be "afraid of the water" in those days. If they saw a minnow, tadpole, or -heaven forbid - a snake, they were expected to shriek and scream and head for the banks. Although the boys often wore no clothes at all, the men wore bathing suits resembling light-weight baseball outfits and women wore gathered tunics over bloomers.

Riley's poetry such as the humble "The Old Swimmin'- Hole" burst into an age of social Darwinism where persons were not to be seen as children at play. Nor were persons to be conceived as having any role outside each's function. The concept of "function" was key in social Darwinism which Riley's kenoticism opposed so vehemently. Persons were said to be functional aspects of society whose roles, natures and activities were a part of the mutual dependence of an "organism" (likened to a biological organism in evolution) of the society in which the person lived. This was the doctrine of "Society as an Organism," in Herbert Spencer's PRINCIPLES OF SOCIOLOGY. Riley suggested that a person was of the character of a child of God in a memory of innocence, a kenotic idea.

In another Riley poem, "Ike Walton's Prayer," a man prays not for gold and jewels, and lands and livestock, but for a humble home with a woman who would make the place a home in love. He prays not for riches, estates or castle halls, but for simple things: children, sunshine, gentle breeze, fragrance of blossoms and songs of birds. The vision is also in opposition to that of the social Darwinist who saw persons as biologically evolving forms seeking maintenance levels of existence.

There is a recollection of Tolbert F. Reavis, a visitor to Riley from Missouri, that sheds some light on the character of Benj. Johnson of Boone.

Reavis was traveling through Indianapolis on a warm September afternoon in 1911 and, though a stranger, decided to visit with Riley at his home on Lockerbie Street. Reavis was admitted and ushered in to a large old-fashioned drawing room where Riley sat on a comfortable arm-chair crossed in a grey suit and clean shaven. Riley greeted him cordially and asked him to be seated. After "small talk" about where the man lived (Missouri), Reavis told him he admired his work and asked him about several poems. Most of them turned out to be poems that Riley said were from "Old Ben Johnson of Boone." Riley explained the man's character as "opinionated, hard headed old farmer with a lot of good horse sense, and a man who admired natures and had great respect for the propriety of things."

The horse was a most admirable creature to Benjamin Johnson of Boone. I should add that the "hoss" was not an object of admiration to Riley. In reality he became deathly afraid of them.

THE HOSS (1882)

The hoss he is a splendud beast;
    He is man's friend, as heaven designed,
And, search the world from west to east,
    No honester you'll ever find.
Some calls the hoss `a pore dumb brute,' And yit,
    like Him who died fer you,
I say, as I theyr charge refute,
    `Fergive; they know not what they do!'

No wiser animal makes tracks
    Upon these earthly shores, and hence
Arose the axium, true as facts,
    Extoled by al, as `Good hoss-sense!'

The hoss is strong, and knows his stren'th, -
    You hitch him up a time er two
And last him, and he'll go his en'th
    And kick the dashboard out fer you!

But treat him allus good and kind,
    And never strike him with a stick,
Ner aggervate him, and you'll find
    He'll never do a hostile trick.

A hoss whose master tends him right
    And worters him with daily care,
Will do your biddin' with delight,
    And act as docile as you air.

From the author's Ora Myers glass negative collection of Hanock County, Indiana subjects.

He'll paw and prance to hear your praise,
    Because he's learnt to love you well;
And, though you can't tell what he says,
    He'll nicker all he wants to tell.

He knows you when you slam the gate
    At early dawn, upon your way

Unto the barn, and snorts elate,
　　To git his corn, er oats, er hay.

He knows you, as the orphant knows
　　The folks that loves her like theyr own
And raises her and "finds" her clothes,
　　And "schools" her tel a womern-grown!

I claim no hoss will harm a man,
　　Ner kick, ner run away, cavort,
Stump-suck, er balk, er `catamaran,'
　　Ef you'll jest treat him as you ort.

But when I see the beast abused,
　　And clubbed around as I've saw some,
I want to see his owner noosed,
　　And jest yanked up like Absolum!
Of course they's differunce in stock, -
　　A hoss that has a little yeer,
And slender build, and shaller hock,
　　Can beat his shadder, mighty near!

Whilse one that's thick in neck and chist
　　And big in leg and full in flank,
That tries to race, I still insist
　　He'll have to take the second rank.

And I have jest laid back and laughed,
　　And rolled and wallered in the grass
At fairs, to see some heavy-draft
　　Lead out at first, yit come in last!

Children at barn with dog litter and cats. From the author's Ora Myers glass negative collection of Hanock County, Indiana subjects.

Each hoss has his appinted place, -
　　The heavy hoss should plow the soil; -
The blooded racer, he must race
　　And win big wages fer his toil.

I never bet - ner never wrought

Upon my feller man to bet -
And yit, at times, I've often thought
    Of my convictions with regret.

I bless the hoss from hoof to head -
    From head to hoof, and tale to man! -
I bless the hoss, as I have said,
    From head to hoof, and back again!

I love my God the first of all,
    Then Him that perished on the cross,
And next, my wife, - and then I fall
    Down on my knees and love the hoss.

Riley posed that Benjamin Johnson had his own set of values and central interests and one of his main ones was his "hoss."

The third of the three poems is probably the one I have seen most anthologized into selected verses of the Nineteenth century of James Whitcomb Riley's poems.

It is the third of the Benjamin Johnson poems that Riley chooses to include in his introduction to the series in "A Caller from Boone." Ben Johnson's letter accompanying the poem states it was "wrote off on the finest Autumn day I ever

A "turn of the century" (Nineteenth) illustration of the setting of "When the Frost Is on the Punkin." Illustrator R.J. Campbell.

laid eyes on! I never felt better in my life. The morning air was as invigoratin' as bitters with tanzy in it, and the folks at breakfast said they never saw such a' appetite on mortal man before. Then I lit out for the barn, and after feedin', I come back and tuck my pen and ink out on the porch, and jest cut loose. I writ and writ till my fingers was that cramped I couldn't hardly let go of the penholder. And the poem I send you is the upshot of it all. Ef you don't find it cheerful enough fer your columns, I'll have to knock under, that's all!"

Angels cannot beat him into delirium to steal his mind. Instead he will invite them to a harvest setting on a rural farm in "When the Frost Is On the Punkin."

WHEN THE FROST IS ON THE PUNKIN (1882)

When the frost is on the punkin and the fodder's in the shock[1],
And you hear the kyouck and gobble of the struttin' turkey-cock
And the clackin' of the guineys[2], and the cluckin' of the hens,[2]
And the rooster's hallylooer as he tiptoes on the fence;
O, it's then's the times a feller is a-feelin' at his best,
With the risin' sun to greet him from a night of peaceful rest,
As he leaves the house, bareheaded, and goes out to feed the stock,
When the frost is on the punkin and the fodder's in the shock.

They's something kindo' harty-like about the atmusfere
When the heat of summer's over and the coolin' fall is here -
Of course we miss the flowers, and the blossums on the trees,
And the mumble of the hummin'-birds and buzzin' of the bees;
But the air's so appetizin'; and the landscape through the haze
Of a crisp and sunny morning of the airly autumn days
Is a pictur' that no painter has the colorin' to mock -
When the frost is on the punkin and the fodder's in the shock.

The husky, rusty russel of the tossels of the corn,
And the raspin' of the tangled leaves, as golden as the morn;
The stubble in the furries - kindo' lonesome-like, but still
A-preachin' sermons to us of the barns they growed to fill;
The strawstack in the medder, and the reaper in the shed;
The hosses in theyr stalls below - the clover overhead! -
O, it sets my hart a-clickin' like the tickin' of a clock,
When the frost is on the punkin and the fodder's in the shock!

Then your apples all is gethered, and the ones a feller keeps
Is poured around the celler-floor in red and yeller heaps;
And your cider-makin' 's over, and your wimmern-folks is through
With their mince and apple-butter, and theyr souse and saussage, too! ...
I don't know how to tell it - but ef sich a thing could be
As the Angels wantin' boardin', and they'd call around on me-
I'd want to 'commodate 'em - all the whole-indurin' flock -
When the frost is on the punkin and the fodder's in the shock!

1. In the fall, corn cut by hand was bundled with ears in the air to dry prior to husking and hauling to a corncrib for storage. The stalks, when dry, would be chopped and fed to livestock during the winter months.
2. Many farmers in frontier days considered guineas to be "watchdogs." When a stranger turned in the lane the guineas set up a tremendous howl in high pitched, loud babble.

The kenotic content of this poem is the proposal that the earthly state of Christ permits communication with the human properties of God. A person does not need to be divine to participate in the ultimate life of humanity. What the reality of the human condition encounters is also what God encounters and sanctifies. God like the persona of the poem will appreciate the experience and satisfaction that a harvest has proven successful to the mid-western American farmer. The Incarnation of Christ through kenosis has opened up the possibility of ultimate satisfactions in simple human achievements and work goals. Working through the summer and getting the crops in entitles one to have human satisfaction in all of nature because doing this is a sanctified human need that Christ would warrant participating in the human condition.

There is satisfaction in life expressed here. The farmer has not merely participated in a struggle for existence. He has happiness that he is a human being. He likens it to position where contact with God would be warranted. He is not in a phase of life. He lives in a state of ecstatic dialogue with a human God.

The writings of James Whitcomb Riley are very often Protestant Christian in spirit and subject matter. Sometimes the themes of this thrust are misunderstood as platitudes or sentimentalism. This is not the case and those who think so miss the point entirely about not only the writings of James Whitcomb Riley but also his age.

Riley's poetry became his century's "best sellers" starting with his first book, "The Old Swimmin'-Hole and 'Leven More Poems" first published in July, 1883.

A typical Riley poem from this little but "revolutionary" book of poetry consciously composed in defiance of social Darwinism and dedicated to its literary evolutionary "dead end" is "On the Death of Little Mahala Ashcraft." Here is a poem glorifying the life of a non-reproducing female of no significance whatsoever to any evolutionary scheme of the human race or life itself. And yet Riley finds her life to be worthy because she lived humbly.

ON THE DEATH OF LITTLE MAHALA ASHCRAFT (1882)

"Little Haly! Little Haly!" cheeps the robin in the tree;
"Little Haly!" sighs the clover, "Little Haly!" moans the bee;
"Little Haly! Little Haly!" calls the killdeer at twilight;
And the katydids and crickets hollers "Haly!" all the night.

The sunflowers and the hollyhawks droops over the garden fence;
The old path down the garden walks still holds her footprints' dents;
And the well-sweep's swingin' bucket seems to wait fer her to come
And start it on its wortery errant down the old beegum.

The beehives all is quiet; and the little Jersey steer,
When any one comes nigh it, acts so lonesome-like and queer;
And the little Banty chickens kindo' cutters faint and low,
Like the hand that now was feedin' 'em was one they didn't know.[1]

They's sorrow in the waivin' leaves of all the apple trees;
And sorrow in the harvest-sheaves, and sorrow in the breeze;
And sorrow in the twitter of the swallers 'round the shed;
And all the song her redbird sings is "Little Haly's dead!"

The medder 'pears to miss her, and the pathway through the grass,
Whare the dewdrops ust to kiss her little bare feet as she passed;
And the old pin in the gate-post seems to kindo'-sorto' doubt
That Haly's little sunburnt hands'll ever pull it out.

Did her father er her mother ever love her more'n me,
Er her sisters er her brother prize her love more tendurly?
I question - and what answer? - only tears, and tears alone,
And ev'ry neghbor's eyes is full o' tear-drops as my own.

"Little Haly! Little Haly!" cheeps the robin in the tree;
"Little Haly!" sighs the clover, "Little Haly!" moans the bee;
"Little Haly! Little Haly!" calls the killdeer at twilight,
And the katydids and crickets hollers "Haly!" all the night.

---

1. By Hoosier custom, farm wives' and daughters' chores included feeding the chickens, scattering chicken feed, ground grain, from a feed tin or vessel. Women and girls earned "pin

money" by selling eggs not consumed to a "huckster" who drove a merchandise wagon through the countryside or to a general or grocery store at a general store or in town.

Why is this poem kenotic? To a kenotic, there is magic in the death of a humble person, certainly this young child. She was a survivor of unfitness. "Haly" was not simply selected out by life for extinction, she is exalted into memory because of her degradation into death. A humble life is swallowed up in the victory of the life in the being of God's person, Christ. To a Nineteenth Century kenotic, the Christian knows no separation from God's earthly incarnate life which the survivor shares in earthly state. Flesh and blood, the evolutionary form, simply holds no heirship to God's servile life while on earth. Little Haly simply is too much a part of life to die.

1. Romans 9.16. In the coiny Greek: "ara oun ou tou thelontos oude tou trexontos alla tou eleontos Theou." ("So, it all depends not on what folks want or reach for, but on what is God's feel.")

Something like these thoughts must have been in the discussions of Myron Reed and Riley about the time he sat down to pen his Benjamin Johnson of Boone poems, wherein Riley emptied himself of himself, and lived the thought of the humble farmer whose spiritual capacity was that of priest and in his own deep yearnings, understandings and gropings for the infinite, the conclusion that in the lowly origin of man, here is what humanity is, spirit, intelligence, reason, good will, affection, morally in correspondence with the same faculties of his God without capacity to injure his soul, do violence to the souls of others, just as God was in the flesh.

While Darwinism became misconstrued as the seed of racism, industrialism's disregard for employees' welfare, laissez fairism, greed justification, bullyism and imperialism, the doctrine was, after all an intellectually complete theory. The actual working out of such Nineteenth Century ideas was the product of a faddish social philosopher and British founder of modern sociology, Herbert Spencer. His SYNTHETIC PHILOSOPHY, essays and his popular writings, such as THE STUDY OF SOCIOLOGY, published in 1872-73 in serial form in the POPULAR SCIENCE MONTHLY and distributed throughout the United States provided great support for social Darwinist ideas. Spencer's ideas were taught in the great universities such as at Yale by Spencer's greatest American protege, William Graham Sumner. His ideas were great points of reference regarding "the normal course of social evolution." Humanity was absolutely incapable of controlling its own destiny. Evolution was deemed universal and a process whereby homogeneity was reduced to heterogeneity just as the earth was formed in its diversity of material and energy from a nebular mass.

Spencer's ideas formed the basic matrix of ideas of the period in which Riley wrote. His ideas challenged and replaced the idea that the earth was only a few thousand years old created by a God during a single week in which the entire universe was formed and human beings were its culminating success. In Spencer's view, as society moved toward heterogeneity, progress was achieved by the method of survival of the fittest. Injustices were not avoidable whereby resources were gobbled up by the wealthy, profits of enterprises were amassed by the wealthy industrialists, and women and children were denied rights. Spencer opposed any social aid such as poor laws, state-supported education, regulation of housing or the professions, sanitary or health laws, or governmental involvement in the economic life of the nation. These were some of the Spencerian tenants popular in the nation as Riley began to contemplate the aims of his own writing career in the 1870's and, with the weapons of temperance Christianity, his alcoholism. In the interest of social survival, Spencer contended classes of superior citizens should be encouraged in favor of the inferior and no laws should intervene. Spencer's ideas gained great currency especially with the rich and powerful in the United States. Until Riley's popularization of kenoticism, there was no opposite force.

Spencer's ideas found God favoring the rich and the efforts of those trying to get rich. Western culture had never before found any basis for such ideas and the cultural life of the United States was shaken to its core. We read of the assertion of the railroad magnate Chauncey Depew commenting that the guests at the most exclusive social engagements in New York represent the survival of the fittest of the thousands who came to America in search of fame, fortune and power and that it was their "superior ability, foresight, and adaptability" that caused them to rise to the top in the competitive arena of New York business. American society was considered a stage of heterogeneity in which natural order principles had selected a wealthy class for survival. Absolute freedom for individual enterprise was the framework whereby society must progress. Economic and social brutality was acceptable because it was grounded in the self- adjusting doctrine of biological selection. Reform at a governmental level was wrong because nature selected the proper social environment for evolutionary progress. Herbert Spencer's ideas were the most prominent in sociological circles during the years of Riley's work and carried the weight of authority. Riley's poetry and lectures can be seen in fundamental opposition to the idea of America based on "tooth and claw" society. The Hoosier Deutsch child who never grew up spoke a poetic voice softly and innocently stating otherwise.

Here was all the answer to Darwinism that was necessary. The Pauline insistence that God became Incarnated in the man, Jesus of Nazareth, did not subject God to the forces of Darwinism, but rather were the product of a mind which valued humility and service to others. McLeod Campbell, a theologian who was deposed from a Presbyterian ministry in Scotland in the 1830's for a kenotic Christology, published a mature statement of his thought, THE NATURE OF THE ATONEMENT (1856) which became a standard text in American Protestant Seminaries. Beautifully written, it is still reckoned to be a kenotic theological classic and a harbinger of modern thinking on the subject. Although kenotic theology was generally condemned by the established church, which continued to hold out that Jesus of Nazareth was a figure in glory and Godlike stature, kenotic thought grew. Its advocates included many of the newly German trained theologians in the Union Theological Seminary in New York City where young ministry candidates learned from their German professors of kenotic theologies in the 1870's and 1880's.

There is a long list of ministering friends and counselors who constitute a very special group of people who seem to be Spraivoll's support group.

Perhaps they started out with Riley's own grandmother, Margaret Riley. During the adolescent years and later until his alcoholism became so rampant, they seem to be few in number. Possibly the most important step into Spraivoll's kenotic poetry came from fellow alcoholic, Luther Benson. Then they seem to descend upon Riley with great kenotic influence. Among the first was Reverend George C. Harding, owner and editor of the Indianapolis Saturday HERALD, one of Indiana's most distinguished editors. He published many of Riley's poems and "The Flying Islands of the Night" and took a great interest in Riley's literary bent. Myron Reed was perhaps the most important. Riley met him when delivering a Decoration Day poem at Crown Hill Cemetery in Indianapolis and Reed became an important friend to Spraivoll until his death.

It was men of God who took over Riley's life and cast it within the anchoring song of the Philippian's "Christ Hymn." Friends felt Myron Reed was one of the most unusual of Riley's friends. Although two very different types of men, they united into a friendship very close. They were often seen together. They went abroad together into the Burns county in Scotland. Riley wrote "Our Kind of a Man" upon Reed's departure from Indianapolis for a pulpit in Denver, Colorado as a tribute.

OUR KIND OF MAN (1884)
I

The kind of man for you and me!
He faces the world unflinchingly,
And smites, as long as the wrong resists,
With a knuckled faith and force like fists;
He lives the life he is preaching of,
And loves where most is the need of love;
His voice is clear to the deaf man's ears,
And his face sublime through the blind man's tears;
The light shines out where the clouds were dim,
And the widow's prayer goes up for him;
The latch is clicked at the hovel door
And the sick man sees the sun once more,
And out o'er the barren fields he sees
Springing blossoms and waving trees,
Feeling as only the dying may,
That God's own servant has come that way,
Smoothing the path as it still winds on
Through the golden gate where his love have gone.

Myron Reed from portrait by T.C. Steele.

II

The kind of a man for me and you!
However little of worth we do
He credits full, and abides in trust
That time will teach us how more is just.
He walks abroad, and he meets all kinds
Of querulous and uneasy minds,
And, sympathizing, he shares the pain
Of the doubts that rack us, heart and brain;
And, knowing this, as we grasp his hand,
We are surely coming to understand!
He looks on sin with pitying eyes -
E'en as the Lord, since Paradise, -

Else, should we read, Though our sins should glow
As scarlet, they shall be white as snow? -
And, feeling still, with a grief half glad,
That the bad are as good as the good are bad,
He strikes straight out for the Right - and he
Is the kind of a man for you and me!

Riley once said, "He was eternally seeing and reading the book of life as it was opened before him. He had a rare gift of discernment." Myron Reed was described by Meredith Nicholson in OLD FAMILIAR FACES as "a tall, dark Indian-like man quietly holding his horse in Circle Park." Reed had been a Captain in the Cavalry in the Civil War.

An acquaintance of both Riley and Reed recounts an evening of the two on January 25th in the early 1880's. Both were on a program of the Indianapolis Caledonian Society designed to commemorate the birthday of Robert Burns. An address by Myron Reed and a poem by Riley were the main entertainment while songs, instrumental music, recitations, dances in Scottish costume were additions. During one point in the program, young ladies came forward to sing "Bonny Doon."

After the program, Reed, Riley and the acquaintance (whose memoir is signed only as Senex Contrib.), left, with Riley steering the way. The talk was of Burns, his sympathy with all suffering, his hatred of oppression, the events of his life, etc. The account continues,: "At the corner of Washington and Pennsylvania streets there was in those days a popular cafe where, among other things, they served oysters in all styles. Riley proposed that we go down - it was in a basement - and continue the talk over

Robert Burns. 1759-1796. Riley was often considered the "Hoosier Poet" just as Burns was considered the "National Poet" of Scotland. Burns was the son of a poor nurseryman and was himself a small farmer and a revenue officer. He shared Riley's "weakness." Painting by Alexander Nasmyth from the Scottish Naitonal Portrait Gallery.

a hot oyster stew; the snow, the cold and the wind seconded the motion, so we went down. The writer had met Reed in company on several occasions; he now saw and heard him at close range in a time of relaxation and found the high opinion he had formed of his qualities of mind were quite equaled by those of his heart.

He says, "The oppressed and downtrodden could always find an advocate in him; distress and suffering challenged a sympathetic hearing and help from him, nor was he straitened in his exhibition of these, for, like Goldsmith's village preacher who -

Please with his guests the good man learned to glow

And quite forget their vices in their woe. his broad charity took in humanity in all its aspects and suffering and distress in all living things... when Riley told some droll stories, accentuated and set off by his impersonations and Reed had laughed heartily at them, one of them reminded him of a comrade in the civil war, whose freakish behavior was an unfailing source of amusement to him, although it did not affect all his comrades thus. Reed stated, "On the march, he pushed his cap up on the back of his head, stretched his long neck, lengthened his step, and did everything he could to evince an eagerness to get forward; at night when we went into camp, he would call out, `Captain, how many miles did we march today?' Then in a gruff tone he would answer himself, `Fifteen.' `Fifteen?' `Why that's no march: we must do better than that! The big show can't start til I get there, and we'll never get there at this rate!' He assumed the part of a veteran of all the wars his country had waged, and some foreign ones; and that his campaigns had converted his body into steel and leather, punctured by many scars received in battle. In that character, he would pull himself rigidly erect, his blouse tightly about him and cap down, till the bill touched his nose, nearly obscuring his rolling eyes, and speak gruff tones.

Once, overhearing a comrade complaining of the long toilsome march they had had that day and how his feet were almost blistered, he turned upon him, saying, `Son, did you think that this was a school picnic with fans? Why this is just the a.b.c. You would have had reason to cuss had you been with us on our march through the wilderness to Quebec, or when we marched with Doniphon from St. Jo across the Santa Fe after cleaning up the Mexicans and adding two more territories to the Union; cut loose and marched 600 miles into old Mexico joining old `Rough and Ready' at Buena Vista. Talk about the march of the Ten Thousand, it was just a walk before breakfast compared with ours.'...

Another time, when one found fault with the rations, `Vet,' as we called him, looked at the complainer in indignant astonishment. `Say, son, when you drew your rations? Sowbelly and hard-tack are the grub for soldiers.' After a year or two of this diet you can eat whetstones with relish. When your teeth wear out you can smash your hard-tack with a rock before eating it.' Here he gave a demonstration, smashing his hard-tack and devouring it with the meat, with assumed gusto..."

Eventually, Reed stopped and looking thoughtful for a moment, said, "God alone knows. `Vet' may have been a reincarnation of some old warrior who was wandering about seeking visibility and companionship."

"Riley and I saw Reed home at about 11."

As Reed was dying and just before his death on January 30, 1899, he repeated the word, "Riley," over and over.

A POETRY OF FRONTIER SONG AND DOGGEREL WOVEN AND WARPED IN CADENCED MYSTERY.

Let us now turn to the subject of where Spraivoll's poetry came from.

Riley's poetry was founded on frontier song and doggerel cadenced in the scoring and intervals of music. Like music, Riley's poetry carried affective energy. This was intentional. Music empowered Riley's poetry. Since this is so, we need to enquire - what is the root of music?

Since the teachings of Plato and Aristotle, music has been considered a primary actor of human behavior. A listener becomes involved with music involuntarily. Plato's theory of

Riley set to music by two of America's composers of his era, Hoagy Carmichael (who grew up near Riley's Lockerbie Street home) and John Philip Sousa. The "Messiah of Nations" was Riley's poem "America" which he wrote on the day after the assassination of President William McKinley of Indiana's neighbor state Ohio. It was also sung by great choruses of voices in Riley's era. One such use was when a chorus of hundreds sang it when the Indianapolis Soldiers and Sailors Monument was dedicated. The lyric was the only sheet music in history that could not be purchased. Riley's publisher, the Bowen-Merrill Co., gave it away to all who wished it.

"ethos" proposed that music was behavioral expression. It evoked response toward the good or the bad. Music and poetry of its genesis pass judgment. Frontiersmen may not have known of a theoretical basis for their "likes," but they did strongly seek after the thematics of musical expression. The affective agent of music has never been fully identified. Plotinus, a Neo-Platonist, argued that music influenced the soul. Music bears spirituality and touches such values, a concept which was adopted into church music theory. During one "dark" period in a time of ignorance, the church examined music to probe whether its enchant-

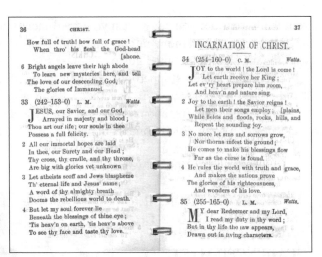

ment might be a matter of sorcery. Riley was dealing with a very powerful medium. He used it forcefully. Thousands of Americans in his time could recite his poetry. Front pages of every American newspaper carried it. The Nineteenth Century in America heard much singing and the songs taught much. Riley sang his share.

Pages from a "Hoosier" Baptist Hymnal of 1887. The music of the hymns is "understood" and referenced by number. Standard hymn tunes were numbered and the poems were sung to them. This hymnal was published in the poet's hometown of Greenfield, Indiana, by the D.H. Goble Printing Co. Riley's poetry similarly carried the music of frontier song and popularly known meter.

In the Hoosier lyric tradition, poems were similar to songs and not necessarily written with musical annotation. An example is a Baptist hymnal published in Riley's hometown of Greenfield, Indiana in 1887 by D.H. Goble. It is a hymnal without music. The little book contains 321 poems for use as hymns. Many Middle West Christians of the Nineteenth Century objected to musical scoring since the Bible contained none even in its Psalms. Other frontier Protestant church congregations banned choirs or refused to hire paid ministers or those with seminary training. Song on the frontiers of Nineteenth Century America might invoke strict biblical and religious discipline as a way of life and Godly emotion. Much poetry in Hoosier newspapers was basically "hymn without music." Protestant frontiersmen believed in carrying Godly music in their hearts, and poetic expression of it on their lips. Meter, as Riley used in his poetry, was learned in the churches by all congregants. Unscored hymns carried notations such as sm (short meter) etc. behind the name of the poem to be sung. Another example of meter is found in numerical metrical designation. For example, "Guide Me O Thou Great Jehovah" was listed in the Goble hymn book as being for "8's", "7's", and "4's." This meant that the poem could be sung to three different tunes depending upon the one begun by the initiator. Poetry, hymns and song were composed in a very strong oral tradition at the time of the writing of James Whitcomb Riley's poetry. The medium of song was poetry.

Music carried Riley's spirit. He once told fellow author Meredith Nicholson, "To throw your legs over the tail of a band wagon and thump away - there's nothing like it!" He played a bass drum in a band. Music carried him through the sadness of his adolescence. Riley was noted for playing the violin and guitar in particular. Music was the rhythm of Riley's expression just as surely as music was the well-spring he tapped to speak a common language in the same way the hymns of all peoples do.

At 18 James Whitcomb Riley started taking up fiddling and banjo. He sang tenor. One day

Instruments played by Riley included this banjo and guitar on display at the Riley birthplace, Greenfield, Indiana. The flute was the instrument played by John Riley, the poet's brother.

Riley bought an old violin, on the bottom saying Paolo Albani, Botzen, 1650. Working on farm in late teenage years. Riley loved to play it while his father demanded he help with hoeing instead of going with friends. When given the choice, Riley chopped a few weeds, then flung his hoe into the next lot, jumped over a fence and took off to town with curses. He came back an hour later to apologize. He simply was not going to give up music.

Music was how Riley expressed himself and told his love to his married friend, Nellie Cooley. Jim and Nellie were always together. They were a team. When a local merchant, John Ward Walker, bought a piano for his new imposing home built in 1871 near a huge wooded hill known as "Walker's Hill" on State Street in Greenfield, Jim and Nellie came to entertain with it according to a newspaper account of the event. Jim Riley played his violin and Nellie played the new piano at the first social event of many which were held at the Walker home. This residence became an entertainment location for many groups particularly for local Greenfield Methodist Episcopal Church functions. When Nellie came to play the piano, Jim Riley accompanied her with his violin with the secret of their attachment heavy in their hearts. Their love grew on the wings of music.

Riley turned the musical rhythms of his life with Nellie into his writings.

What is frontier song and doggerel? Examples may help. Doggerel is "occasional" poetry. It is poetry that makes no pretence of dignity and strikes for common emotion. Some call it "burlesque" or "bastard" verse. Its poetic feet are irregular and the unlearned often compose it. An example from an epitaph for a deceased horse follows:

JOHNNY KONGAPOD

Here lies Johnny Kongapod
Have mercy on him Gracious God
As he would on you if he were God
And you were Johnny Kongapod.

While there is much subtlety in the writing of James Whitcomb Riley, it should not be supposed that his verse derived from anything other than frontier American song and doggerel. In this, his poetry was not so different than other poetry of the time. Poetry was a much different medium in Riley's day on the American frontier than in modern times. A vestige of the type poetry Riley wrote survives as lyric of popular music. This is not to say that Riley did not study the poetry of others within English and American traditions and use his wits to craft poetry of great complexity of thought. Nevertheless, to the end of his life, Riley wrote as he had learned from frontier song and doggerel and simply could not imagine poetry outside the context of this framework.

His poetry was set to music with ease. Among Riley's poetry set to music or recorded are approximately one hundred fifty titles. Some of the poems have attracted multiple composers as did "A Life Lesson," "The Prayer Perfect" and "Little Orphant Annie" which appear to be the most often reduced to musical scores.

Riley's poems set to music include "America" (also known as "The Messiah of Nations" with music by John Phillip Sousa -other composers will not hereafter be listed), Baby Bye, Babyhood, The Bee-Bag, Billy and His Drum, Billy Goodin, The Boy Patriot, The Brook song, Childhood, A Christmas Glee, Christine's Song, Coffee Like His Mother Used to Make, Cradle Song, The Daring Prince, The Days Gone By, The Dead Lover, The Dead Wife, Dearth, the Diners in the Kitchen, Don't Cry, A Dream of Autumn, Dwainie- A Sprite Song, Ever a Song Somewhere, Extremes, The First Bluebird, Fool Younguns, The Funny Little Fellow, The Gobble-Uns'll Git You Ef You Don't Watch Out!, Good-By Er Howdy-Do, Granny's Come to Our House, Griggsby's Station, Heigh-Ho! Babyhood, Her Beautiful Eyes, Her Beautiful Hands, A Humble Singer, I Want to Be a Soldier, I Will Walk With You, My Lad, If I Knew What Poet's Know, An Impetuous Resolve, In the Orchard Where the Children Used to Play, It, The Jolly Miller, The Kingdom of a Child, Last Night and This, A Leave-Taking, Leonainie, A Life-Lesson, Light of Love, Little Girly-Girl, Little Orphant Annie, The Little Red Apple Tree, The Little Red Ribbon, The Little Tiny Kickshaw, Lockerbie Street, The Lost Lover, Lullaby, Make Me a Song, The Man in the Moon, Max and Jim, Maymie's Story of Red-Riding-Hood, Ms. Hammond's Parable, A Mother Song, My Fiddle, My Mary, O Heart of Mine, O, I Will Walk with You, My Lad, An Old Sweetheart of Mine, The Old Trundle Bed, Our Own - A Chant, Out to Old Aunt Mary's, Pansies, Parental Christmas Presents, A Pet of Uncle Sidney's. The Pixy People, The Prayer Perfect, A Primrose, The Raggedy Man, The Ribbon, The Ring and the Rose, A Riley-Album, Say Farewell and Let Me Go, A Scrawl, A Sea Song from the Shore, She "Displains" It, The Silver Lining, Some Scattering Remarks of Bub's, A Song, A Song and a Smile, A Song of the Road, There Is Ever A Song Somewhere, There, Little Girl, Don't Cry, The Tree Toad, Uncle Sidney, Uncle Sidney Says, Uncle Sidney's Logic, A Very Youthful Affair, The Weather, When Evening shadows Fall, When Our Baby Died, When She Comes How Again, when the Frost Is On the Punkin, Where Shall We Land, Wind of the Sea, and the Winky-Tooden Song. This listing of titles was made in the early 1940's. No listing of more current titles is available that I am aware of. The listings do not include Riley in collections of music. Nor does it include the Riley phonograph albums made toward the end of Riley's life when such items became technologically possible.

Since Riley believe poetry to be connected to music he hated the free verse of Walt Whitman, a contemporary poet for whom Riley had nothing but contempt. When asked, Riley condemned him saying he walked around with his shirt unbuttoned. Riley's frontier American mentality could not recognize Whitman's poetry as having musical genesis. Whitman's poetry simply could not be sung within the metered stanzas of pioneer Hoosier song and Riley did not conceive Whitman's work to be poetry.

The American poetry of Riley exists within a tradition that goes back to the time of Homer whose Iliad and Oddysey were sung by traveling folk artists. Song, in folk traditions, seems to often be the basis of poetic expression over the history of humanity.

It is not without meaning that Riley chose to call the poetic Riley in "The Flying Islands of the Night," the "tune- fool." Frontier songs were the basis of Riley's meter. Riley understood the thirst-quenching water of poetry to come from this well.

Riley recognized his musical and poetic nature to be combined as his self who wrote poetry in his autobiographical poem, "The Flying Islands of the Night." We find the following dialogue therein:

WHO IS SPRAIVOLL UNLESS CADENCED MYSTERY?

Jucklet

The voice of Spraivoll, an mine ears be whet
And honed o' late honeyed memories
Behaunting the deserted purlieus[1] of
The court.

1. A purlieu refers to land on the border of a forest where a serf in medieval times had the right to hunt without permission of a sovereign's forest laws or their punishment for unauthorized hunting. Figuratively, it is a place where one can range or a safe place to haunt or wander. Crestillomeem

And who is Spraivoll, and what song
Is that besung so blinding exquisite
Of cadenced mystery?

What did writing within such a definition of poetry mean'.
Riley's was a poetry he described as "cadenced mystery."
The form caused Riley's poems to immediately prove pleasurable to hear and familiar to grasp. They also thus had a form which could bear Godly encouragement in a desperate time-the kenotic themes which I feel gave Riley's works particular value. Frontier songs did this as one finds

in doggerels.

It should not be supposed there is no discipline in doggerel poetry. Doggerel can be honed as any other more formal form of poetry. Although Riley achieved great national fame as a poet and his poetry was known, in part, by thousands of people, his public poetry never strove to escape the doggerel metrical theories of frontier song. I have to qualify this by saying that the "personal Riley" was quite capable of using other verse as when Riley chose the Chatterton pentameter for his autobiographical poem, "Flying Islands of the Night." Riley not only composed his poetry from song rhythms but he also disciplined himself through doggerel poetry. One finds this particularly in his advertising poetry. Here are examples from his Anderson "Democrat" days:

ADVERTISING DOGGEREL

The farmer sat in his easy chair
Smoking his pipe of clay,
While his hale old wife with a sprightly air
Was clearing her throat to say,
"Read aloud," to the child that sat
On his grandfather's knee with the Democrat.
     Or:
     The Anderson Democrat
        is a
     Good Little Paper
      and you
   Ought To Be Kind To It
It Ain't the Best Paper In The "State."
      No, it
     Is Simply
     Good.

Frontier Hoosier songs of the first half of the Nineteenth Century were not so different from others sung on the American frontier north and south or anywhere West of the Appalachians. Among the favorites were "Skip to My Lou," "Old Sister Phoebe," and this one entitled "Thus the Farmer Sows His Seed:"

THUS THE FARMER SOWS HIS SEED

Come, my love, and go with me,
And I will take good care of thee.
I am too young, I am not fit,
I cannot leave my mamma yit.
You're old enough, you are just right
I asked your mamma last Saturday night.

Frontier songs often were accompanied by dances. This one could be sung while dancing a Virginia reel:

WEEVILY WHEAT

O Charley, he's a fine young man,
O Charley, he's a dandy,
He loves to hug and kiss the girls
And feed 'em on good candy.

The higher up the cherry tree,
The riper grow the cherries,
The more you hug and kiss the girls,
The sooner they will marry.

My pretty little pink, I suppose you think
I care but little about you.
But I'll let you know before you go,
I cannot do without you.

It's left hand round your weevily wheat.
It's both hands round your weevily wheat.
Come down this way with your weevily wheat
It's swing, oh, swing, your weevily wheat.

A patriotic song sung at nearly every Fourth of July celebration in the frontier places was as follows:

HAIL COLUMBIA

Hail! Columbia, happy land!
Hail! ye heroes, heav'n born band,
Who fought and bled in freedom's cause,
Who fought, and bled in freedom's cause.

And when the storm of war is gone,
Enjoy the peace your valor won;
Let independence be your boast,
Ever mindful what it cost,
Ever grateful for the prize,
May its altar reach the skies.

In the decade in which Riley was born, poetry provided a form of common expression and was certainly not solely the province of poets. As an example, there is the poetry of the martyred President, Abraham Lincoln, written on the American frontier prior to the American Civil War.

THE BEAR HUNT

Abraham Lincoln, "poet". Shown in Brady photograph of Feb. 9, 1864

A wild bear chase didst never see?
  Then hast thou lived in vain -
Thy richest bump of glorious glee
  Lies desert in thy brain.

When first my father settled here,
  'Twas then the frontier line;
The panther's scream filled night with fear
  And bears preyed on the swine.

But woe for bruin's short-lived fun
  When rose the squealing cry;
Now man and horse, with dog and gun
  For vengeance at him fly.

A sound of danger strikes his ear;
    He gives the breeze a snuff;
Away he bounds, with little fear,
    And seeks the tangled rough.

Or press his foes, and reach the ground
    Where's left his half-munched meal;
the dogs, in circles, scent around
    And find his fresh made trail

With instant cry, away they dash,
    And men as fast pursue;
O'er logs, they leap, through water splash
    And shout the brisk halloo.

Now to elude the eager pack
    Bear shuns the open ground,
Through matted vines he shapes his track,
    And runs it, round and round.

The tall, fleet cur, with deep-mouthed voice
    Now speeds him, as the wind;
While half-grown pup, and short-legged fice
    Are yelping far behind.

And fresh recruits are dropping in
    To join the merry corps;
With yelp and yell, a mingled din -
    The woods are in a roar -

And round, and round the chase now goes,
    The world's alive with fun;
Nick Carter's horse his rider throws,
    And Mose Hills drops his gun.

Now, sorely pressed, bear glances back,
    And lolls his tired tongue,
When as, to force him from his track

An ambush on him sprung.

Across the glade he sweeps for flight,
    And fully is in view -
The dogs, new fired by the sight
    Their cry and speed renew.

The foremost ones now reach his rear;
    He turns, they dash away,
And circling now the wrathful bear
    They have him full at bay.

At top of speed the horsemen come,
    All screaming in a row -
`Whoop!' `Take him, Tiger!' `Seize him, Drum!'
    Bang - bang! the rifles go!

And furious now, the dogs he tears
    And crushes in his ire -
Wheels right and left, and upward rears,
    With eyes of burning fire.

But laden death is at his heart -
    Vain all the strength he plies,
And, spouting blood from every part,
    He reels, and sinks, and dies!

And now a dinsome clamor rose, -
    `But who should have his skin?'
Who first draws blood, each hunter knows
    This prize must always win.

Bears were a constant threat to settlers
and were often subjects of their poetry.
From "The Crockett Almanac", 1841.

But, who did this, and how to trace
    What's true from what's a lie, -
Like lawyers in a murder case
    They stoutly argufy.

Aforesaid fire, of blustering mood,

> Behind, and quite forgot,
> Just now emerging from the wood
>   Arrives upon the spot,
>
> With grinning teeth, and up-turned hair
>   Brim full of spunk and wrath,
> He growls, and seized on dead bear
>   And shakes for life and death -
>
> And swells, as if his skin would tear,
>   And growls, and shakes again,
> And swears. as plain as dog can swear
>   That he has won the skin!
>
> Conceited whelp! we laugh at thee,
>   No mind that not a few
> Of pompous, two-legged dogs there be
>   Conceited quite as you.

The earliest poetry of Riley is close to being as doggerel as Abraham Lincoln's "The Bear Hunt" and has the same phrasings and metric cadences as frontier songs generally.

RILEY'S "THE SAME OLD STORY" (1870, age 20)

The same old story told again -
  The maiden droops her head,
The ripening glow of her crimson cheek
  Is answering in her stead.
The pleading tone of a trembling voice
  Is telling her the way
He loved her when his heart was young
  In Youth's sunshiny day;
The trembling tongue, the longing tone,
  Imploringly ask why
They cannot be as happy now
  As in the days gone by.

And two more hearts, tumultuous
  With overflowing joy,
Are dancing to the music
  Which the dear, provoking boy
Is twanging on his bowstring,
  As, fluttering his wings,
He send his love-charged arrows
  While merrily, he sings:
"Ho! ho!, you dainty maiden,
  It surely can not be
You are thinking you are master
  Of your heart, when it is me."
And another gleaming arrows
  Does the little god's behest,
And the dainty little maiden
  Falls upon her lover's breast.
"The same old story told again,"
  And listened o'er and o'er,
Will still be new, and pleasing, too
Till "Time shall be no more."

Riley with Henry Eitel interviewed at the Riley birthplace in Greenfield by Hamlin Garland, journalist and author.

Poetics had an important role to play in the Hoosier frontier with its rhymes and songs.

Song was a feature of every aspect of frontier life. Nothing was beyond its scope. The Hoosier regiments to the Mexican War in the mid-1840's sang as they went into battle. This was in the decade of the 1840's in which Riley was born. A refrain to one of the Hoosier regimental battle songs with many verses was:

A MEXICAN WAR "HOOSIER" REGIMENTAL BATTLE SONG

Fire! Fire! how they tumble-
Shout, shout for the State,
Whose young bosom sent thee
To war with the great!

To understand the subject matter of frontier poetry of song and dogger-el, it is necessary to look at the ground where such poetry grew.

Hamlin Garland, a fellow writer and admirer of Riley, came to Greenfield to visit him in 1892. Here is his account of the Hoosier Poet's birth town as he saw it then.

A VISIT TO RILEY IN HIS NATIVE TOWN

"In 1892 I visited Riley at his native town of Greenfield, Indiana, and the town and country gave moving evidence of the wonder-working power of the poet. To my eyes it was the most unpromising field for art, especially for the art of verse. The landscape had no hills, no lakes, no streams of any movement or beauty. Ragged fence-rows, flat and dusty roads, fields of wheat alternating with clumps of trees - these were the features of a country which to me was utterly commonplace..." (As found in a 1920 lecture read at the American Academy of Arts and Letters, entitled "Commemorative Tribute to James Whitcomb Riley.")

It seems curious that Hamlin Garland, whose formative years were spent on a family farm in Iowa, and whose best writings are about the economic troubles of Midwestern farmers, the drudgery of their existence, and the depredations practiced against them by moneylenders, would find Riley's Midwestern hometown of Greenfield such a drag.

Garland's point was that the genius of a person creates poetry and liter-ature from out of the stuff of life no matter how backwoods or ordinary it may seem to others. Again speaking of Riley, Garland continued, "...from this dusty, drab, unpromising environment Riley had been able to draw the honey of woodland poesy, a sweet in which a native fragrance as of bass-wood and buckwheat bloom mingled with hints of an English meadow and the tang of a Canada thistle."

What Hamlin Garland saw, echoed in the works of James Whitcomb Riley, was what Riley conveyed as one of the themes of what a home is. It is something plainly and unabashedly common. Since it is common, it bears with it characteristic proportionality and democratic distribution to all class-es, races and peoples. Every American is thought to deserve a home. It is something the most common of attributes to which each person has entitle-ment. In every ethical community, the most common family should be con-ceived as having a home according to James Whitcomb Riley. There is no social division which precludes this. Riley's poetry was of this teaching. It did not need to more specifically say so.

As Garland said, "He taught us once again the fundamental truth which we were long in learning here in America, that there is a poetry of common things, as well as of epic deeds. His immense success with the common, no-literary public is to be counted for him and not against him. either consciously or unconsciously his verses were wrought for the family. He never forced the erotic note. Surrounded by Americans, he wrote for Americans. To me his restraint is a fine and true distinction.

His verse sprang from a certain era of western development. It is a humble crop gathered from the corners of rail fences, from the vines which clamber upon the porches of small villages, and from the weedy side-walks of quiet towns far away from the great markets of the world..."

Riley's poetry is a poetry of home and the home of even the most common family.

On a more personal note, what impression did Riley give to Hamlin Garland in 1892? "In person Riley was as markedly individual as his verse. He was short, square-shouldered, and very blond, with a head which he was accustomed to speak of as "of the tack-hammer variety." His smoothly shaven face was large and extremely expressive, the face of a great actor. Though grim in repose it lighted up with the merriest smiles as he read or as he uttered some quaint jest. His diction when he wished it to be so was admirably clear and precise, but he loved to drop into the speech and drawl of his Hoosier characters, and to me this was a never-failing delight. I have never met a man save Mark Twain who had the same amazing flow of quaint conceits. He spoke "copy" all the time." Such was the way Riley struck a man who was not just a fellow writer but one of the foremost "realists" along with Stephen Crane in American fiction.

It would also be good to describe the Hoosier character out of which Riley's poetry flowered. The unfortunate side of Riley's poetry is brought out by this kind of analysis. Riley's characterizations are so good, his capacity to personify and breath life into an archetypical persona, that the characterizations really overshadow everything else. The benefit to Riley was that he could write over and over again and create a massive volume of poetry easily because he understood character types so very well. The problem is reaching the "meat" or substance. What is the theme of all this voluminous spewing out of character interaction?

The big picture reveals it as the individual poems do not. Riley is the poet who has given us to know about American life, what to expect of it, how to be fulfilled in it, and disappointed, but how to make it through life in it. This is particularly pronounced where Riley speaks with his kenotic poetic voice. Riley's prayer was to master a kenotic poetic style.

In my day in this, the late Twentieth Century, I recall Riley dismissed occasionally by literary friends and fellow authors as a "sentimentalist" because Riley wrote of humble characters, their lives and their settings in rural America where I live. Riley's poetry entered into the "heart" of such characters. He had them fighting for life and survival- feeling life's disappointments, having a pioneer wife die, being crippled or maimed or dead - in their humble non- notable non-adaptive existences but being transformed into heroic proportion by the fact of their very humility and vulnerability of their lives. This expresses the "splagxnon" of Riley, his inmost guts and feeling, a matter of hugely different aspect than sentimentalism.

The critics who see only "sentimentalism" in Riley's poetry miss the stem upholding the leaves. They simply do not take into account, nor understand, the late Nineteenth Century in America. Many of the very characters I have mentioned-before Riley wrote of them-were the type of American most would have dismissed as persons to be selected out or disregarded in their miserable lives because they were simply on the downside of evolutionary trends. Charles Darwin's speciation theory is the dominant scientific idea of Riley's era. Its proposals moulded thought after the American Civil War. Together with the impact of industrial development and laissez faire government, the framework of Post Civil War American culture lacked even the slightest aspect of humanism when James Whitcomb Riley's poetry began appearing on the front pages of American newspapers and his stories began to make their rounds in lyceum circuits. The poetry of James Whitcomb Riley and he, himself, became his epoch's great radical phenomena.

The poem, "To My Friend, William Leachman," and the other poems in Riley's first volume, THE OLD SWIMMIN' HOLE" AND `LEVEN MORE POEMS, hit America like a bombshell. All of America began to look at their neighbors differently. Maybe people shouldn't simply be seen as ape-descendants. The advent of Incarnation Theology, though not popularly named as such, was at hand. Folk drew the line at the Philippian's Christ Hymn against the Robert Ingersoll's who attacked the Bible.

If there is vulnerability in life, as Riley's own alcoholism rendered him vulnerable, nevertheless the situation was within the encounter of God with humanity. No special claim to wealth or wisdom or status gave access to this

God. Prayer was enough. God's standard of caring for humanity derived from an ethic confirmed on a cross of persecution where God too became weakened, fearful, filled with anxiety, and died.

RILEY'S PRIMARY AUDIENCE

Q: WHO ARE THE HOOSIER PEOPLE?
A: A FRONTIER HOME-SEEKING GOD-FEARING TRIBE OF HUMBLE WANDERERS.

Then we need to address the poetic audience of Riley. What is a Hoosier?

The term "Hoosier" descriptive of Riley's people of the frontier and his poetry came from a poem of great currency in the first half of the Nineteenth Century which described the people of Indiana. Poetry was very much a part of the daily lives on the American frontier. James Whitcomb Riley had his own theory where the word "Hoosier" came from. He stated, "The stories commonly told about the origin of the word Hoosier are all nonsense. The real origin is found in the pugnacious habits of the early settlers. They were very vicious fighters and not only gouged and scratched, but frequently bit off noses and ears. This was so ordinary an affair that a settler coming in to a bar on a morning after a fight, and seeing an ear on the floor, would merely push it aside with his foot and carelessly ask, "Who's ear?"

Hoosiers were the earliest frontiersmen who settled in the Ohio Valley north of the Ohio River in the early Nineteenth Century. They are the people of a poem by John Finley of Richmond, Indiana. In one of its first recorded usages in the 1833 Indianapolis JOURNAL, John Finley described folk living in backwoods Indiana cabins in a poem.

THE HOOSIER NEST

Blest Indiana! In whose soil
Men seek the sure rewards of toil,
And honest poverty and worth
Find here the best retreat on earth,
While hosts of Preachers, Doctors, Lawyers,
All independent as wood-sawyers,
With men of every hue and fashion,
Flock to the rising Hoosier nation.

Men who can legislate or plow,
Wage politics or milk a cow -
So plastic are their various parts,
Within the circle of their arts,
With equal tack the Hoosier loons,
Hunt offices or hunt raccoons.

...Suppose in riding somewhere West
A stranger found a Hoosier's nest
In other words, a buckeye cabin
Just big enough to hold Queen Mab in,
Its situation low but airy
Was on the borders of a prairie,
And fearing he might be benighted
He hailed the house and then alighted.
The Hoosier met him at the door
Their salutations soon were o'er;
He took the stranger's horse aside
And to a sturdy sapling tied.
Then, having stripped the saddle off,
He fed him in a sugar trough.
The stranger stooped to enter in,
The entrance closing with a pin,
And manifested strong desire
To seat him by the log heap fire,
Where half a dozen Hoosieroons

From the author's Ora Myers glass negative collection of Hancock County, Indiana subjects.

With mush and mil, tincups and spoons
White heads, bare feet and dirty faces
Seemed much inclined to keep their places,
But Madam, anxious to display
Her rough and undisputed sway,
Her offspring to the ladder led
And cuffed the youngsters up to bed
Invited shortly to partake
Of venison, milk and Johnny-cake
The stranger made a hearty meal
And glances round the room would steal
One side was lined with skins of varmints

> The other spread with divers garments,
>> Dried pumpkins overhead were strung
>> Where venison hams in plenty hung
>> Two rifles placed above the door,
> Three dogs lay stretched upon the floor,
>> In short the domicile was rife

Then we should examine an example of the poet considered the first great master of Hoosier poetry, Sarah Boulton. Riley himself acknowledged her reputation in a poem "Song of a Life-Time" and knew her well. In the poem he speaks of her quality of "melodiousness" and "mien" by which he meant Hoosier expression of character and manner. One of her well known poems follows:

PADDLE YOUR OWN CANOE

Voyager upon life's sea, to yourself be true,
  And where'er your lot may be, paddle your own canoe!
Never, though the winds may rave, falter, nor look back;
  But upon the darkest wave leave a shining track.

Nobly dare the wildest storm, stem the rudest gale,
  Brave of heart and strong of arm, you will never fail.
When the world is cold and dark, keep an aim in view;
  And toward the beacon mark paddle your own canoe.

Every wave that bears you on to the silent shore,
  From its sunny source has gone to return no more,
Then let not an hour's delay cheat you of your due;
  But, while it is called to-day, paddle your own canoe.

Would you wrest the wreath of fame from the hand of fate;
  Would you write a deathless name with the good and great;
Would you bless your fellow-men, heart and soul imbue
  With the holy task, and then paddle your own canoe.

Would you crush the tyrant wrong, in the world's fee fight,
  With spirit brave and strong, battle for the right;

And to break the chains that bind many to the few -
   To enfranchise mind enslaved - paddle your own canoe.

Nothing great is light won, nothing won is lost;
   Every good deed, nobly done, will repay the cost.
Leave to heaven, in humble trust, all you will to do;
   But, if you'd succeed, you must paddle your own canoe.

Riley's heritage was tied up part and parcel in frontier songs and poems. His later writing can be seen as deriving from this wellspring.

As did almost everyone else in Indiana, Riley's mother and father both wrote poetry of the frontier song variety. In a short article entitled a "Retrospective View of the Hancock County Bar," George Richman, a Hancock County historian writing in 1916, recalls Reuben A. Riley, as a "(legal) practitioner for almost a century...Mr. Riley was not only an able, conscientious lawyer, but he took a general interest in public affairs. Some of his poems and speeches that still remain in print show him to have been gifted along several lines." A poem of Reuben's survives:

THE CRUCIFICTION (Sic)

`Tis evening, at the supper now,*
   The Savior breaks the scared bread,
And pours the wine; with solemn vow
   Proclaims Himself the Church's Head.

`Tis night, on Olive's somber brow
   The stars are hid that twinkled there;
Alone the suffering Savior bows,
   With none His agony to share.

`Tis midnight, and the trial past,
   The Savior to the Jews betrayed,
A pris'ner in their hands at last
   To smite, imprison, and degrade.

`Tis morning, and among the great,
   Their spite, and jealous anger burns:

They mock Him with a robe of state,
　And crown Him with a crown of thorns.

`Tis noonday, and the Christ condemned
　To bleed and perish on the tree;
Yet angels do their Lord attend -
　Sinner, He died for you and me!

While on the cross the Savior hung,
　The pall of night at noonday spread,
The quaking earth with anguish wrung,
　The bursting tombs gave up their dead.

The veil was rent, the lightnings fell.
　From out the darkness hear the cry
Of Him who conquered Death and Hell.
　"Eloi Lama Sabachthani."

The tomb receives His mangled corpse -
　They set the seals, and Roman guard;
With taunting jeer, and muttered curse,
　The tomb is sealed, and watched, and barred.

Yet at the promised morning's dawn
　The seals were loosed, the guardsmen fell:
He `rose, triumphant marching on,
　In chains led captive Death and Hell.

The trembling earth, the bursting tomb,
　And songs of saints and seraphim
Proclaim the risen Lord has come;
　The world shall bow and worship Him.

As He ascends from earth above
　To Heaven, our promised home,
In trusting faith we live, and love,
　Our risen Lord again will come.

The poem is an artful account of the crucifixion united initially by anaphora, the droning and heavy repetition of the "'Tis" constructs. The poem bears a familiar meter to much of the son's poetry and is thematically consistent. It also sounds close to the hymn, "'Tis Midnight and On Olive's Brow." Frontier poetry never got far away from the

A newspaper press of Riley's era. The Hancock DEMOCRAT published in Greenfield, Indiana.

thoughts of hymns. Reuben's poetry was of the newspaper variety as was the early poetry of James Whitcomb Riley. We do not know much of it because the early newspapers the father wrote for were not so well preserved as those bearing the son's poetry.

We can trace the appearance of James Whitcomb Riley's writings back through time to the first newspaper pieces Riley published.

Riley was first a newspaper poet as was his father.

The custom of printing poetry on the front pages of newspapers ended probably in the 1880's in Indiana but not before Riley had mastered the form and found great success in it. The "Jay Whit" poetry - an early pseudonymn of Riley's- in the Indianapolis Saturday MIRROR is the first. There were four poems in this group. The first of them was mistakenly published as a poem of "Jay White" instead of "Jay Whit" as Riley intended. The others were correctly attributed to "Jay Whit." They included "Man's Devotion," March 30, 1872, "A Mockery," April 13, 1872; "Flames and Ashes," April 20th, 1872; and "Johnny" May 25th, 1872. Riley also sent the MIRROR "A Ballad/With a Serious Conclusion" which was published anonymously on May 11th, 1872.

His greatest pre-kenotic poetry and prose was published in the Indianapolis Saturday HERALD as early as June 1875. His first contribution was under the old pen name, "Jay Whit," and was entitled "Red Riding-Hood." Occasional poems were sent to the Saturday HERALD in late 1877 and then began Riley's major work, the Respectfully Declined Papers of the Buzz Club (Numbers 1 through 6). No. 1 was published, May 11, 1878; No. 2 was published June 15, 1878; No. 3 was published July 6, 1878; No. 4 was published August 24, 1878; No. 5 was published September 28, 1878; and the final installment, No. 6, was published November 16th, 1878. Riley wrote about the "Flying Islands," which was his long autobiographical and narrative "astronomical play/poem" in the September 14th Issue. Riley then contributed occasional poetry to the Herald during 1879 and one poem in 1880. A series of "Robert Burns" inspired poetry appeared in this paper from Riley in 1885.

The No. 4 of the Respectfully Declined Papers has proven to be the most important of Riley's submissions to the HERALD. In this issue was Riley's original composition of "Flying Islands of the Night."

The poetry submitted to the HERALD is Riley at his most rebelliousness. Where did this come from? In my epoch, psychologist's play with such questions as the relationship of age within a child's birth order to receptivity to original ideas. They conclude those born later than other siblings tend to be ideologically rebellious rather than accept dominant theoretical positions. Since I have often posed social Darwinism as Riley's foil, it is interesting to enquire where both Riley and Darwin were in birth order. Riley and Darwin were later-borns. Darwin's evolutionary theory required opposition to the strong and pervading nineteenth-century belief in the biblical story of creation. Riley's kenotic poetry required opposition to the scientific biological truth that evolutionary theory rendered impossible or unlikely a human God.

RILEY FAMILY POETRY

Long before Riley became famous, his family wrote poetry which confirms that poetry was a common form of expression within Riley's family.

Cornelia Loder who lived with the Riley's while teaching in the Greenfield schools in 1877 kept an autograph album. She sought entries from the Rileys and their guests. Here are little poems written by the Riley family from

The children of the Riley family. Left to right: John, Mary, Elva, Hum. Standing: the poet. (From Julia Wilson Riley photograph album. Courtesy of The Riley Old Home Society, Greenfield, Indiana.)

that album. Reuben Riley wrote,

If, through life's eventful race,
  Our duties be well done,
He'll still vouchsafe His grace,
  And Angels guard us home.
          June 11th, 1877

  Ms. Loder recalls "Cap" Riley, as he was sometimes called, was a lawyer with considerable oratorical skills from a platform but not much of a money-maker. Her opinion was that he was too upright a man to engage in more lucrative activities of legal practitioners. She says that the home was not at all poverty ridden. The Rileys had not only a respectable home but all of the common advantages available to a respectable small-town family. In appearance, Reuben Riley bore a remarkable likeness to John Wilkes Booth. He told Ms. Loder that after the assassination of President Lincoln he once had barely escaped arrest because of this resemblance. Ms. Loder also remembered the stepmother as being patient and kind. Her role of foster mother was difficult but she filled it "efficiently and the children usually were respectful of her." Her Quaker "thee" and "thou" and various other old fashioned ways of speech and manner contrasted strangely with the joyous humanity of the first Mrs. Riley. When she lived at the home, the children still grieved keenly for Elizabeth Riley. As her entry in the autograph album, the stepmother, Martha Lukens Riley wrote:

To Cornelia
This little emblem of respect
I gave my valued friend to thee
Treat not its motto with neglect
it is dear girl remember me.
But say if Heaven should early doom
For all is just by His decree,
My bosom to the silent tomb,
Wilt thou drop one tear for me
June 7th, 1877   Thy True friend, Mattie C. Riley.

Cornelia Loder depicts the Riley children in the household as an active, happy group, mingling freely in the normal social life of the town. The youngest Riley son, wrote his name "Hum Riley" in the album with many decorative elaborations. Riley had begun teaching his younger brother such flourishes as he was passing on his sign painting art to him.

  Elva's entry in the 1877 album read, In the dimly outlined vista of the future when alone In a mood of retrospection, you let your memory road, You must not forget Old Greenfield, and the Castle in the grove. You Will not forget the "romance," you must not forget the love (Editor's note, the reference here is to a boyfriend of Cornelia's) of the many friends you left there, but keep in memories store One bud of recollection if you can keep no more. The Will in the fourth line was a play on a young man's name. Elva signed herself as "La fille du chateau."

Mary, at twelve, wrote:
I'm small I know, but then I may
Make some noise in this world of ours.
My compliments to you I give
As plentifully as this day's showers
Come down from out the weeping skies.

Mary was the last survivor of the Riley family and lived until 1936.

From this album one definitely concludes the entire Riley family was used to rhyme and each could express himself or herself in it. Riley made no contribution in this album because it was circulated in the Spring of 1877 when Riley had gone to Anderson to work for the newspaper, the Anderson Democrat.

LONGFELLOW AND OTHER POETS WHO INFLUENCED RILEY

We have often commented on Riley's early love of Longfellow to whom Riley composed several poems. In one of his letters, Riley says of Longfellow, "The poetry of Longfellow is artless and subdued and very tender, yet deep as the love, the hope of any human heart, is deep." Only after his

Henry Wadsworth Longfellow, 1807-1882. Riley was much encouraged by Longfellow's early praise but modified the Longfellow style in the late 1870's to write uniquely American kenotic poetry. Nevertheless, Riley said of him, "Longfellow is my poetic Bible," and "His is the sweetest human mind that ever existed."

thirties, does Riley find his own confident vision of the spirit of his age. Longfellow then seems less relevant to American poetry to Riley.

Riley looked to Longfellow in his twenties for encouragement. The incident is one recorded in every biography of Riley and is substantially as follows:

In the fall of 1876, Riley sent a small sheaf of his poems to Longfellow asking for criticism and suggestions. The were "Destiny," "If I Knew What Poets Know" and "The Iron Horse." Longfellow's reply, dated at Cambridge on November 30, arrived in Greenfield on December 5. Riley was delighted, we know, from a firsthand report by the boarder Cornelia Loder: "He came into the hall waving a letter to Elva, his sister, and saying, `Some day you will be proud to be called the sister of the Hoosier Poet.'" Longfellow had taken the pains to criticize one of the poems, "Destiny", pointing out Riley's inexact use of the word, "prone." The word means "face downward", Longfellow explained, and Riley should have used "supine." But more important still, Longfellow had written that Riley's work showed "true poetic faculty and insight."

From this contact by letter in 1876, many have come to call Riley the student of Longfellow and his early years "Riley's Longfellow Period." This biographer believes Riley's poetry grows out of frontier song and doggerel and takes its schema and inspiration more directly from the influence of Dickens. Great study of many poets, Longfellow among them, no doubt influenced Riley.

Nevertheless we must examine Riley's relationship with Longfellow carefully because Riley's love of Longfellow was very intensive from Riley's earliest days. We have further information from Henry Wadsworth Longfellow Dana, the grandson who has written about his grandfather and Riley:

RILEY AND LONGFELLOW CONNECTIONS

"When Longfellow went abroad in 1868-1869, Riley, as a 19-year-old youth, followed the poet's travelings in the Greenfield COMMERCIAL. When the Norwegian violinist, Ole Bull, came to America, Longfellow described how "erect the rapt musician stood." And when Ole Bull played at the Academy of Music in Indianapolis on April 16, 1872, Riley in turn cried: "Why, it was music the way he stood!"

When an editor paid Longfellow $3,000 in 1874 for "The Hanging of the Crane," some jealous would-be writer said the poem was "flapdoodle." But Riley defended Longfellow, quoting the lines in which he had described the azure eyes of children:

"Limpid as planets that emerge
Above the ocean's rounded verge,

Soft shining through the summer night!"
From Longfellow's "Morituri Salutamus" of the next year, 1875, Riley
is said to have gleaned the key for his own life:
"Study yourself; and most of all note well
Wherein kind nature meant you to excel."
In his popular lectures, Riley gladly paid a fine tribute to Longfellow:
"The happiest forms of poetic expression are cast in simplest phraseolo-
gy and seeming artlessness...Longfellow has furnished many notable examples, first among which I would class the poem, "The Day is Done." It is like
resting to read it. It is like bending with uncovered head beneath the silent
benediction of the stars."

In much the mood of Longfellow's "The Day is Done," Riley wrote his
own poem, "In the Dark," especially when we include the three final stanzas of the original version.

It was this poem, the original manuscript version of "In the Dark," together with "A Destiny" (later called "The Dreamer") which he had published in
HEARTH AND HOME for April 10, 1875, and one or two other manuscript
and printed poems that Riley decided to send to Longfellow in order to get
his opinion of them. This was a crisis in his life and he turned to Longfellow
as the one person whose help he most needed. If only Longfellow would
give a word of approval he would have decided to devote the rest of his life
to literature.

Accordingly with some trepidation, on Nov. 27, 1876, James Whitcomb
Riley, then 27 years old, sent to Longfellow, then nearly 70, a letter in which
he said:

"I find the courage to address you as I would a friend since by your works
you have proven yourself a friend to the world: I would not, however,
intrude upon you now, did I not feel that you alone could assist me."

Almost immediately upon receiving the letter "there was really no (10
days suspense") Longfellow wrote to Riley on Nov. 30, 1876, saying of the
poems which he had sent him:

"I have read them with great pleasure, and think they show the true poetic faculty and insight."

As soon as this letter reached the post office at Greenfield and Riley
found it there and opened it, he was, as he said "in a perfect hurricane of
delight." He walked not through the streets of Greenfield but through some
enchanted city, where the pavements were of air; where all the rough sounds
of a stirring town were softened into gentle music; where everything was

happy; where there was no distance and no time."

Two years later, on Sept. 2, 1878, Riley wrote to Longfellow expressing to him "my warmest thanks" for the great good your influence and kindness have done me."

This time he enclosed a long poetical drama, "The Flying Islands of the Night," and a number of other poems.

Again, Longfellow replied promptly, on Sept. 5, 1878:

"I have received the poems you were kind enough to send me, and have read the lyric pieces with much pleasure...Among these poems the one that pleased me as much as any, if not more than any, was "The Iron Horse!"

It was interesting that the poem Longfellow selected for particular praise is one in which the poet of the Middle West exalted above any "Arab steed" the locomotives and their trains which were making Indianapolis one of the great railroad centers of the country.

Once more Longfellow's encouragement helped Riley, and who may deny that the faith the younger poet had in him, unlike the earlier harsh criticisms of Poe, gave Longfellow in turn a new lease on life so that much of his best and apparently effortless verse was written during the few remaining years.

A few years afterwards, on Dec. 31, 1881, less than three months before Longfellow's death, the Indiana poet came to make a personal visit on the New England poet at the Craigie House in Cambridge. That evening, New Year's Eve, Riley wrote:

"Just think o' me a-shakin' hands with Longfellow -which I did this very afternoon. I was advised not to go -that he was ill, and was not permitted by his physicians to see anyone, but I went, in the old spirit of desperation that is a good thing to have sometimes. I shan't try to tell you anything of his home - the house he lives in - but I knew it when in sight, and hurried on and up to it and rang the bell. (There's an old-fashioned brass knocker, highly polished, still set in the middle of the door.) The bell is at the side, and hard to find. The plain-looking woman that answered it said that Mr. Longfellow was not permitted to see anyone. And I asked her at least to present my card, on which I had written that Jas. W. Riley, of Indiana, wanted to offer his respects, if entirely agreeable, &c. There was some little delay- but, in the language of the tree toad, "I fetched him! O, I fetch him!" - And he seemed actually delighted, and pranced around and showed off his study and the famous Washington Room & all. Lord! What a lovable old man he is! He very highly commended some views I expressed regarding the higher worth of dialect, and clapped his hands over the "Old-fashioned Roses" which I repeated in illustration of the real purity and sweetness which might be found in the Hoosier idiom. I can't begin to tell you the great interest he expressed - and encouraging me again and again. I told him he was the first real poet who offered me encouragement of any kind - and in reply he said he was glad he did, and now could most heartily offer the same again, and more of it."

The Next Day, New Year's Day, 1882, in writing to his first publisher about his visit on the previous afternoon to Longfellow, he added:

"He was very, very gracious, and complimented me beyond all hope of expression. Can't tell you anything now, wait till I return, with the laurel on me brow."

Five days later he wrote to another friend:

"Have grappled hands with Longfellow, and he admitted me despite physician's orders, and likes me and says it."

Eleven weeks later came Longfellow's death. This was a great blow to Riley. The next month he wrote for the Indianapolis JOURNAL of April 29, 1882, an article called "An Hour With Longfellow," in which he gave a further account of his conversation with him:

"His talk, although varied, was mainly of our native poets and their work. He knew them all - even the humblest. And it was a surprise to us to find him well acquainted with even the local characteristics and dialects of the West. His theme gradually deepened into graver and more serious channels and he spoke of the higher mission of poetry - its kinship with all the purer emotions and aspirations of the human heart - and I remember as, with growing fervor, his fascinating topic swept him on he broke abruptly, saying: "But the idea grows too fragile for the touch of analysis - the thought loses all palpable embodiment and is veiled and almost lost in the midst of its own spiritual loveliness."

In January, 1883, some nine months after Longfellow's death, Riley was able to come again to Cambridge and visited the grave of Longfellow on top of Indian Ridge in Mount Auburn Cemetery. Like the author of "The Children's Hour," Riley himself was to enter into the "Child World" and it was appropriate that on this occasion he brought with him a group of children bearing roses to lay on Longfellow's tomb. Of this event he wrote a poem, which has heretofore only been published in part, but which is here printed apparently for the first time in its entirety:

THE POET AND THE CHILDREN
AT THE GRAVE OF LONGFELLOW

Because that he loved the children,
  If for nothing else, we would say
This is a grand old poet
  Who is sleeping here today.
Awake, he loved their voices,
  And wove them into his rhyme;
And the music of their laughter
  Was with him all the time.

Kindly, and warm and tender,
  He nestled each childish palm
So close in his own that his touch was a prayer,
  And his speech a blessed psalm.

Though he knew the tongues of nations
  And their meanings all were dear,
The prattle and lisp of a little child
  Was the sweetest for him to hear.

He has turned from the marvelous pages,
  Of many an alien tone -
Haply come down from Olivet,
  Or out through the gates of Rome, -

Set sail o'er the seas between him
  And each little beckoning hand
That fluttered about the meadows
  And groves of his native land -

Fluttered and flashed on his vision,
  As, in the glimmering light
Of the orchard lands of his childhood, The blossoms of
  pink and white

And there have been smiles of rapture
   Lighting his face as he came,
Hailing the children hailing him,
   And calling each by name.

And there have been sobs in his bosom,
   As out of the shores he stepped,
And many a little welcomer
   Has wondered why he wept.

Elizabeth Riley's sewing box carved by
Reuben Riley on display at the Riley birthplace, Greenfield, Indiana.

"That was because, O Children" -
   In fancy his voice comes slow
And solemn and sweet through the roses
   You have heaped o'er the below, -

"That was because, O Children,
   Ye might not always be
The same that the Saviour's arms were wound
   About in Galilee."

So because that he loved the children,
   If for nothing else, we would say
This is a grand old poet
   Who is sleeping here today. ...

At the time of Riley's visit, Longfellow had said to him, "We are all of one common family." Both poets were strong believers in democracy. For both there was no rich nor poor, nor high nor low, in poetry. In a sonnet called "Possibilities," Longfellow had raised the question: "Where are the poets?" and had said:

"Perhaps there lives some dreamy boy, untaught,
In schools, some graduate of the field or street,
Who shall become a master of the art."

Such lines appealed to the young poet, who had not had the advantage - or was it a disadvantage? - of university training, and to none more than

James Whitcomb Riley. He, in turn, loved to point to Longfellow as an example of "the art to conceal art." To a friend who was struggling to compose poetry, Riley wrote:

"One of the finest attributes of poetry-making is to conceal all effort. It can be done. Read any master to find that out. Longfellow above them all. He writes with the most painstaking care and slowness, and yet his verse all seems as though it made itself. There's the art of it."

Again he wrote:

"Study Longfellow, and be artless and subdued and very tender - yet deep as the love - the hope of any human heart is deep."

Ten years after Longfellow's death, Riley published in 1892 his sonnet called "Longfellow," beginning:

"The winds have talked with him confidingly;
The trees have whispered to him; and the night
Hath held him gently as a mother might,
And taught him all sad tones of melody."

In 1907, the centennial of Longfellow's birth was celebrated...At that time Riley wrote a sonnet called, "Longfellow; 1807 - February 27 - 1907."

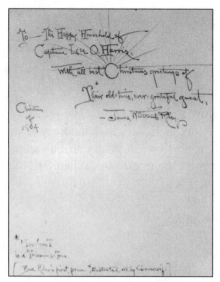

Two Riley hand-drawn Christmas cards sent to his teacher Lee O. Harris. (From the Barton Rees Pogue glass positive collection.)

This began:

> "O gentlest kinsman of humanity!
> Thy love hath touched all hearts, even as thy song
> Hath touched all chords of music that belong
> To the quavering heaven-strung harp of harmony."

From this time onward until his death in the house on Lockerbie Street in Indianapolis on July 22, 1916, James Whitcomb Riley himself had come to hold as a poet something of the position in the hearts of the common people of America that Longfellow held before him."

One of Riley's legacies from Longfellow is his range of stanza patterns including couplets, triplets, simple quatrains and ballad meters, the varied patterns of the ode and the elegy, sonnets, and blank verse. Longfellow was a marvellous poetic craftsman. However, Longfellow's poetry echoes artistic sensibility rather than Riley's musical ethos. We find this difference stated in Longfellow's own writings. In "The Singers," Longfellow gave poetry a threefold purpose: to charm, to strengthen and to teach. He wrote in "Michael Angelo: "Art is the gift of God, and must be used \Unto His glory. That in art is highest\ Which aims at this." Longfellow and Riley shared a fast brotherhood of moral concern. Like Longfellow, Riley was beholden to the past; but while the past inspired Longfellow to piety and a desire to preserve out of it what was lovely and good, Riley used the past as a field where innocence exists and hope in a redeeming God of humility survives. By way of national reputation, I would say that Riley and Longfellow each become identified with the Nineteenth Century as no other poets did, first Longfellow, then Riley.

Riley apprenticed to Lee O. Harris in poetics. One finds Harris as a primary influence. Riley wrote a poem to him entitled, "Master and First Song-Friend - Lee O. Harris."

Before we dismiss Lee O. Harris as merely Riley's teacher, we should be made aware that Harris made himself into a great disseminator of knowledge generally throughout the country. In the 1880's and until his death, he was the editor of "Home and School Visitor." Greenfield was its place of publication. The magazine was begun in Jan. 1881 and published for many years by D.H. Goble or by the later D.H. Goble Publishing Co. for distribution to township schools - mostly "one room" -dotting the countryside neighborhoods of Indiana and many other Western states. The growth of the

"Visitor" under Harris's editorial supervision was phenomenal. By May, 1886, its edition states, "We cannot give a better idea of (the "Visitor's") growth than by stating that for the three years past the number used in schools was 5,000, 10,500 and 18,000 respectively." Greenfield's little publication came to be used by schools all over the Midwestern United States. One of its editions claims its use "in every state and territory and in many foreign countries." That same edition claimed a publication of 22,000 per month so it must have become very widely dispersed. "Home and School Visitor" was originally published by a Hancock County School Superintendent whose name was Aaron Pope and Captain Lee O. Harris, Riley's teacher who was by now the Greenfield Principal of Schools. Aaron Pope was a tragic but brilliant man who died at the age of thirty-seven. Professor Pope (as he was called) had been a teacher in several township schools and also at the McCordsville graded school before becoming Hancock County School Superintendent. He died of a heart attack in June, 1882 shortly after the publication started and the enterprise was sold to D.H. Goble, then a Greenfield implement dealer who undertook its publication using the good offices of Lee O. Harris as Editor. The first format of "Home and School Visitor" was like a newspaper with advertising. It then took the form of a magazine. The first issue contains the news that electric lights had been introduced on Wall Street in New York. There are many poems, some for memorizing, many stories, with those for the lower one room school grades in larger print, "natural history" or what we would call science, stories about historic figures, "how to" articles explaining how common products were produced, current events, and other subject matter.

Will H. Glasscock, an early historian of Greenfield, wrote a book called YOUNG FOLK OF INDIANA in which he included Lee O. Harris under the caption "History, Story and Song." In describing Harris's youth, Glasscock wrote: "His ear was ever close to Nature's heart and he heard and felt its beatings in harmony with the promptings of his own life and soul." Among Harris's writings is a novel about a hobo called, THE MAN WHO TRAMPS, and a volume of poetry entitled INTERLUDES. Few remember that Riley himself did the artwork for Harris's novel. A letter from Riley to Harris at the James Whitcomb Riley Museum in Greenfield, Indiana confirms this revelation.

It might be well to examine one of Harris's own compositions to note Harris's poetic style. His poem, "Song of the Rain," was on the front page of the Indianapolis Saturday HERALD of January 26, 1878.

SONG OF THE RAIN

Where folded about by the shadows,
My spirit is nursing its pain,
I sit all alone in the darkness,
And list to the song of the rain.

And often I hear in its music
The patter of feet that are still;
And then I forget for a moment,
The mound on yon desolate hill.

And, thrilled with the bliss of her presence,
My heart leaps to welcome its guest;
I open my arms to receive her,
And clasp only grief to my breast.

I wrap myself up in the shadows
That woe o'er my spirit has spread,
And moan all alone in the darkness
And weep with the rain for my dead.

But now, as I hear at my window
The touch of those fingers so light,
That weave in the warp of the silence
The woof of their music to-night,

So sweet is the sound and so restful
The charm which its melody brings,
That sorrow has folded her pinions
To listen while memory sings.

And all that my heart has been dreaming
The rain in its music repeats,
While thoughts that like bees have been roaming
Come bearing their burden of sweets.

New hope, like a carrier pigeon,

Though weary and torn by the blast,
Escaping the snare of the fowler,
Flies home with her message at last.

Now faith paints the bow of her promise
On tear-drops that sorrow has shed,
And love is beguiled from her mourning,
And turns from the grave of her dead.

And thus, as I list to the fingers
That harp on my window to-night,
I look through the gloom and the darkness
With faith in the dawning of light.

In point of comparison of teacher (Harris) to student (Riley), I juxtapose Riley's "The Rain," published in the same newspaper, the Indianapolis Saturday HERALD in the next year on July 12, 1879:

THE RAIN

The rain sounds like a laugh to me -
  A low laugh poured out Rapidly.
My very soul smiles as I listen to
  The low, mysterious laughter of the rain,
Poured musically over heart and brain
  Till weary care, soaked with it through and through,
Sinks; and, with wings wet with it as with dew,
  My spirit flutters up, with every stain
Washed from its plumage, and as white again
  As when the old laugh of the rain was new.
Then laugh on, happy rain; laugh louder yet;
  Laugh out in torrent-bursts of watery mirth;
Unlock thy lips of purple cloud and let
  Thy liquid merriment baptize the earth,
And wash the sad face of the world, and set
  The universe to music dripping-wet.

Just as the Harris poem was really not about the rain, but about the death of a young woman, so is the Riley poem really not about rain either. Riley does not however take an unrelated tack about the fact of rain. He looks to its own essence. Rain falls to permit growth and creation to be sustained. This seems to Riley a thing like laughter: a spontaneous and life-affirming activity, favorable to life itself. The rain is, in this sense, "happy rain." Since rain has this role of revival, let it also be thought of as "baptizer," Riley suggests. The drift of Riley's mind is toward the essential and ultimate. A world of meaninglessness, anxiety, depression, fate, and death finds simple rain as challenger. The humble rain changes the drift of life to the direction of survival and comfort. While the thought is really rather humorous in any kind of overall scheme of things, nevertheless, how about a universe set to music "dripping wet?" Riley suggests. This catachresis takes the function of rain far beyond any simple possibility one might imagine and so serves to take the poem into the realm of its true subject: the rejuvenation of the world through simple acceptance of humble life situation, a kenotic idea. We have here not just an echo of literary figure of speech as in such usages as "to take arms against a sea of troubles." Instead we have a poem of a simple subject, rendered essential, thematic and finally, and this is most important, a point of salvation. The difference between the poetry of the teacher (Harris) and student (Riley) is dramatic.

Many other early poets influenced Riley. Riley wrote poems of acknowledgment to Robert Herrick, John Greenleaf Whittier and also Alfred Lord Tennyson. Riley's first poem, "A Backward Look," that we still have was published in 1870 under the nom de plume "Edyrn," the name of a very minor knight in "Geriant and Enid" in Tennyson's IDYLS OF THE KING. This first poem was published in the newspaper, the Greenfield COMMERCIAL, at an unknown date and one of its original stanzas read:

> They got me to climb for the bluebird's nest
>   By telling me they'd give me half the eggs,
> And I got to the limb by tuggin' my best
>   And fell to the ground and broke one of my legs.

As most of Riley's poems, great revisions occurred as the poems were printed, republished and reprinted.

Dickens is noticeable although not as a poet. In fact, Riley doesn't try to hide this influence at all. One of his great poems of the "Poetical Gymnastics" series is simply titled, "God Bless Us Every One" in the

Indianapolis Saturday HERALD published July 26, 1879. We know its origin as a saying of the crippled child, "Tiny Tim" in Charles Dickens' A CHRISTMAS CAROL,

GOD BLESS US EVERY ONE (1879)

God bless us every one!!! prayed Tiny Tim -
Crippled and dwarfed of body, yet so tall
Of soul we tiptoe earth to look on him
High towering over all.

He loved the loveless world, nor dreamed, indeed,
That it, at best, could give to him the while
But pitying glances, when his only need
Was but a cheery smile.

And thus he prayed, "God bless us every one," -
Condensing all the creeds within the span
Of his child-heart; and so, despising none,
Was nearer saint than man.

I like to fancy God in Paradise,
Lifting a finger o'er the rhythmic swing
Of chiming harp and song, with eager eyes
Turned earthward, listening. -

The anthem stilled -the angels leaning there
Above the golden walls - the morning sun
Gustave Dore' Engraving of
Of Christmas bursting flower-like with the prayer, - Dickens' "Christmas Carol" (1861).
"God bless us every one."

Riley chose to open his 1895 volume of SKETCHES IN PROSE AND OCCASIONAL VERSES with "God Bless Us Every One." He really saw himself in "Tiny Tim." His alcoholism was as disabling as Tiny Tim's. To Riley, God listens when one says in a seemingly loveless world, "God Bless us Every One!" I note that Riley often closed his dedicatory addresses and public functionary appearances with this benediction.

Riley acknowledged his appreciation of many poets by poetry. For John

Keats, Riley wrote "A Ditty of No Tone." calling Keats' poetry "sun-washed" (natural, evocative of nature) and "luxurious in rhyme." Something which captures fragrance of wild flowers, drone bee "flight", shower and sunshine. In one of his letters Riley states "Keats knew of the nectar of his language."

Riley's love of Robert Burns is referenced elsewhere. A poem to Burns is "As We Read." Riley says Burns was a poet who "outheld his hands lovingly to his people in dreams of sweet pathos and "sweet" themes."

Riley eulogized Ralph Waldo Emerson as one who "drew" to the principles he acclaimed and held a "simple faith" in the direction of the voyage of life.

Riley was born on Edgar Allan Poe's date of death and he always felt a special presence of Poe. In fact, Poe, indirectly brought him initial fame. William Lyon Phelps, Yale's English Professor who knew Riley intimately commented, "His immense admiration for Poe's genius was tempered by his regret over Poe's pessimism."

William Cullen Bryant inspired a Riley poem. Riley said his poetry was like music in "clearest utterings," a poetry of "pride, purity and strength."

Other poets who were Riley's friends and to whom he wrote poetry include Carmen: "To Bliss;" Madison Cawein: "A Southern Singer;" Rudyard Kipling; Joel Chandler Harris; Benjamin Parker; Robert Lewis Stevenson and Lew Wallace.

Clara Louise Bottsford, Riley's one-time fiance, wrote in the romantic mode. Her poem "Lancelot" for example appeared in the Indianapolis Saturday Herald of December 11, 1880 on the front page, as had Riley's "Poetical Gymnastics" column in the prior year. The lengthy poem describes Lancelot's feelings on his way into Guinevere's presence for a tryst. Lancelot feels "gloom" as he enters his "Queen of Passion's" room to do her bidding and "meet my doom!" He asks himself

Am I
The mighty Lancelot - to die
The meanest of the table round? -
I, Knight of Arthur's, fettered, bound,
The willing slave of even his queen -
Not his....nor any one's I ween,
But mine!...God's pity I am tired.

In August 1880 - to an aspiring writer - Riley explained how he wrote to market his writing. He urged writing for "today" and a general readership who are neither profound nor classical scholars. "...and not only avoid phrases, words or reference "of the old time order of literature," but "avoid, too, the very acquaintance of it - because we are apt to absorb more or less of the peculiar ideas, methods, etc. of those authors we read..." Then, also, "when I am forced to say a commonplace thing it is my effort, at least, to say it as it never has been said before - if such a thing can be done without an apparent strain." Writing it he tries to imagine himself competent to do so and then lays it aside for a day or so to resurrect it in

Book production at the Mitchell Printing Co. plant in Greenfield, Indiana.

another mood and to tear it shreds if needs be.

In reviewing another poet's work he could be devestatingly blunt. As to the following poetry stanza, he offered comment.

> "Fair home, where needs no solar ray
>   To smile away the night;
> Where shines an everlasting day, -
>   The risen Lamb the light."

"The first line with "solar ray" in it! My God! what has "solar ray" to do with poetry! The second line pure poetry in idea, phrasing, everything; and the next two commonplace -the last one absolutely awful! Kill Mr. Buck for me, please. Gather the revered gentleman to his fathers. - Crucify him! - for it's an absolute shame that a man who could write poetry, only carpenters at it, and builds a poem, as he would a pig- pen out of unwieldy planks and clap-boards. Kill the gentleman I tell you! tramp on him as you would a bald "woolly worm!""

Riley was a poet among many, many such artisans in Post Civil War Indiana. A very partial list of published Hoosier poets of the Nineteenth Century is compiled here to prove the point that many, many persons wrote poetry in Indiana during the Nineteenth Century: Albert Carlton Andrews, Marie L. Andrews, Albion Fellows Bacon, Mrs. Albion Fellows Bacon, R.G. Ball, Granville M. Ballard, M.E. Banta, Margaret Holmes Bates, Bessie Johnson Bellman, Horace P. Biddle, G. Henry Bogart, Sarah T. Bolton, Allan Simpson Bottsford, Ethel Bowman, Minnie T. Boyce, Louisa Vickroy Boyd, Robert H. Brewington, Albert Fletcher Bridges, Mattie Dyer Britts, M. Sears Brooks, Alice Williams Brotherton, Jerome C. Burnett, Clarence A. Buskirk, Kate M. Caplinger, Emma N. Carleton, Mary Howard Catherwood, Emily Thornton Cahrles, M. Louisa Chitwood, Noah J. Clodfelter, Jethro C. Culmer, Will Cumback, George W. Cutter, Hannah E. Davis, Ida May Davis, Richard Lew Dawson, Charles Dennis, William T. Dennis, John B. Dillin, May W. Donnan, Amanda L.R. Dufour, Julia L. Dumont, John Gibson Dunn, Sidney Dyer, Elijah Evan Edwards, Alfred Ellison, Henry W. Ellsworth, Orpheus Everts, John Finley, Mary Hockett Flanner, Elizabeth E. Foulke, William W. Foulke, Willis Wilfred Fowler, Strickland W. Gillilan, Jerome Bonaparte Girard, Samuel B. Gookins, Jonathan W. Gordon, Frank W. Harned, Lee O. Harris, William Wallace Harney, Irene Boynton Hawley, John Hay, Enos B. Heiney, Charles L.Holstein, Edwin S. Hopkins, Benjamin Davenport House, Horace F. Hubbard, Ben R. Hyman, Narcissa Lewis Jenkinson, Robert Underwood Johnson, Annie Fellows Johnston, Dulcina M. Jordan, David Starr Jordan, Isaac H. Julian, Esther Nelson Karn, Isaac Kinley, Jesse G. Kinley, Josie V.H. Koons, Mary-Hannah Krout, Harvey Porter Layton, Francis Locke, Richard K. Lyon, Zella McCoy, William W.H. McCurdy, Silas B. McManus, Arthur W. Macy, James B. Martindale, James Newton Matthews, Josephine W. Mellette, Freeman E. Miller, Joaquin Miller, Hattie Athon Morrison, Mary E. Nealy, William P. Needham, Rebecca S. Nichols, Meredith Nicholson, John C. Ochiltree, Richard Owen, Daniel L. Paine, Benjamin S. Parker, Edwin E. Parker, Oran K. Parker, Gavin Payne, William W. Pfrimmer, John James Piatt, Robert E. Pretlow, Herman Rave, Maude M. Redman, Joseph S. Reed, Peter Fishe Reed, Alonzo Rice, Renos H. Richards, John Clark Ridpath, Cornelia Laws St.John, Olive Sanxay, Henry J. Shellman, John W. Shockley, A.E. Sinks, Hubbard M. Smith, Evaleen Stein, Solomon P. Stoddard, George Stout, Juliet V. Strauss, Martina Swafford, Henry W. Taylor, Howard S. Taylor, John N. Taylor,

Minetta T. Taylor, Tucker Woodson Taylor, E.S.L. Thompson, Maurice Thompson, Laura M. Thurston, Oliah P. Toph, Newton A. Trueblood, William B. Vickers, Lew Wallace, Susan E. Wallace, W. DeWitt Wallace, Luther Dana Watterman, L. May Wheeler, Louisa Wickersham, Elizabeth Conwell Wilson, Forsythe Wilson, and Bruce H. Woolford.

Riley liked to call his poetry "poem-songs." Once Riley was asked for a contribution for a school newspaper in his hometown. Riley responded with a letter:

Miss Helen Downing:

Dear Friend and Fellow Citizen, - It is just impossible for me to write a suitable article for "The High School BUDGET," in the time you give me, being now a child no more.

... As to the old song-rhymes of mine you desire to print - Yes, put `em in "The BUDGET" if they're worthy...

That is how Riley described his poems...as song-rhymes.

By far, the great majority of Riley's works, even his poems, are not preserved. That so many are seems close to a miracle and is a mark of Riley's poetic draw as well as the closeness of poetry at that time to the life of the American people.

Almost from the first of his newspaper career, Riley wrote many newspaper articles and editorials which did not carry his name. One of the particular fields to which his writing was entrusted was editorials. A letter to Lee O. Harris of December 25, 1895 mentions that an editorial he wrote appeared in that day's Journal which made his soul "blush to the roots of its hair."

Here is a poem clearly written with music in mind. Minnie Belle Mitchell recalls that Riley's poem "The Old Times Were the Best," was actually written in his early youth when Riley was in the company of young people, include herself, practicing for one of the many entertainments Riley did. Angie Williams, later Angie Downing, was playing the piano when Riley left for a time and when he returned he had with him the poem "The Old Times Were the Best." Later he gave a copy to Angie to put to music.

A POETRY ECHOING NATURE WITH HER OWN VOICE

I close with a dissenting opinion from the poet Donald Culross Peattie who felt Riley's poetry was not so much musical and doggerel as "natural." He finds that Riley's better poetry "tries to echo Nature with her own voice." Riley is a poet who speaks for American Nature. "His fame as a versifier has helped to rob him of the title he ought to have, "the poet of wisest Nature."

"Poets themselves may resent the suggestion that Riley is more than a versifier. Yet what is poetry if it is not the essence of things, the thought-distilled, mood-condensed sweet sap of the tree of life? When a scientist has boiled down Nature to a quintessential, he hands you what he quite inaccurately calls a law. But when a poet does that, he stocks your memory with an unforgettable line that gets more about the subject into less space than prove can ever do. The man who said he was "knee-deep in June" is a Nature poet of the first rank."

Peattie continues, "Poems like "There little girl, don't cry", however sincere and popular, have done the reputation of Riley no lasting good. The truth is that like Burns he wrote in two different languages, and was two different men in them. The dialect poems are, on the whole, the good poems as Burns' were. Humor keep them off the rocks of sentimentality. And why should humor, which has long been accepted in the drama as a sparkling vessel for truth and art, reduce a poet to the rank of a minor? For no reason except that about poetry we are in a state of deadly earnestness, or in the doldrums of a decaying gentility...

In the matter of dialect, it is immaterial whether Riley employed the speech that all Hoosiers used, or the colloquial language of Indiana today. There are few Scotchmen who speak the idiom of Burns. It is only essential that the dialect should be the best medium for the subject that could have been chosen. And to my ear, at least, not only does Riley write the way the western child and farmer still often speak, but in setting style to subject his sense of pitch is nearly absolute. He vies with the grand masters of regional American literature, the Mark Twain of HUCKLEBERRY FINN, the Lowell of the BIGELOW PAPERS, and the Harris of UNCLE REMUS.

To one who was born in the Middle West, and has tried to write about its Nature, ...Riley's descriptions of birds on a hot summer day is still unsurpassed for that distillation of essence in the local speech which is poetry "come native with the warmth."

> "Pee-wees' singin', to express
> My opinion, 's second class,
> Yit you'll hear 'em, more or less;
> Sapsucks, gittin' down to biz,
> Weedin' out the lonesomeness;
> Mr. Bluejay, full o' sass,

In them baseball clothes o' his,
Sportin' round the orchard jes'
Like he owned the premises!"

That expresses my opinion of pee-wees, too. Sapsuck is precisely what my Illinois neighbors call the bird I have to set down in my naturalist's records as Sphyrapicus varius. And if any poet can do a better delineation of that cheap dandy of a bird, the bluejay, by all means let him seize his pen."

(Mr. Peattie's references are primarily to Riley's "Deer Creek" poetry. I must add that the place where such imagery arose, the Deer Creek of Indiana's White County lends itself to poetry as do few places of the country. To get the sense of it, your biographer walked this area in great satisfaction. Taking the "boardwalk" in Delphi's "Riley Park" along Deer Creek will raise the most depressed spirit into a sense of timeless peace.)

SPECIAL KENOTIC POEMS

James Whitcomb Riley's reputation as a poet rests most securely upon his early Benjamin Johnson of Boone poetry. They are his best and represent a high point of American poetry. They are written after his "Declaration of Independence" from his earlier mentor Henry Wadsworth Longfellow as contained in Riley's "USE AND ABUSE OF THE POETIC THEME" published in the Kokomo TRIBUNE of April 5, 1879. They are uniquely American in subject matter and heartland spirit and meter arising as they do from frontier song and doggerel. They are also deeply representative of the American experience of Civil War, Reconstruction and cultural dialogue between the Darwinism of Riley's age, to include its social Darwinism "offshoot," and the kenotic theological tide striking into America from Germany in the Nineteenth Century. We simply cannot fail to include in a biography of James Whitcomb Riley the poetry which contains his finest work and point out its kenotic content.

As an example, Riley, wrote of the farmer who had experienced so much rain he couldn't plant his corn in the year 1882. This was "Thoughts fer the Discuraged Farmer." It was Riley in his kenotic years. James Whitcomb Riley took upon himself such subjects literally close to home to the Hoosier people. Yes, the world does have a source of encouragement when a farmer couldn't get his corn in. Poems began appearing from the hand of a "Benj. F. Johnson of Boone" growing out of Riley's understanding of life following his worse bouts with Crestillomeem.

Who was the poet Benjamin F. Johnson of Boone?

It was James Whitcomb Riley, we remember, in his most thoughtful 30's and still at an early stage of his career. He used the name for a series of poems in 1882 which ran in the Indianapolis JOURNAL. Although the poems were written early in Riley's published career, they contain ones now famous. The first one of them was "The Old Swimmmin'-Hole." Another later one was "When the Frost Is on the Punkin." There were twelve in all.

The Benj. F. Johnson series of poems permitted Riley to portray the thoughts and philosophy of a plain old dust- bitten and clod-hopping

RES. OF GEORGE W. SMITH, BOONE TP. MADISON CO. IND.

Engravings of two Hoosier farms of Riley's epoch.

RES. OF H.T. BATES. FALL CREEK TP. MADISON. CO. INDANA.

Hoosier farmer who wrote with inspiration as flush as bitters with tanzy in it.[1]

1. Bitters gave Western heartland pioneers a "bite" to the taste of their food and tanzy was a plant with a very strong aroma used as a garnish like parsley.

THOUGHTS FER THE DISCURAGED FARMER (1882)

*The summer winds is sniffin' round the bloomin' locus' trees;
And the clover in the pastur is a big day fer the bees,
And they been a-swiggin' honey, above board and on the sly,
Tel they stutter in theyr buzzin' and stagger as the fly.*

*The flicker on the fence-rail 'pears to jest spit on his wings
And roll up his feathers, by the sassy way he sings;
And the hoss-fly is a-whettin-up his forelegs fer biz,
And the off-mare is a-switchin' all of her tale they is.*

A Hoosier cornfield of the late Nineteenth Century. John A. Howland photography collection.

*You can hear the blackbirds jawin' as they foller up the plow -
Oh, theyr bound to git theyr brekfast, and theyr not a-carin' how;
So they quarrel in the furries, and they quarrel on the wing -
But theyr peaceabler in pot-pies than any other thing:
And it's when I git my shotgun drawed up in stiddy rest,
She's as full of tribbelation as a yeller-jacket's nest;
And a few shots before dinner, when the sun's a-shinin' right,
Seems to kindo-sorto' sharpen up a feller's appetite!*

*They's been a heap o' rain, but the sun's out to-day,
And the clouds of the wet spell is all cleared away,
And the woods is all the greener, and the grass is greener still;*

It may rain again to-morry, but I don't think it will.
Some says the crops is ruined, and the corn's drownded out,
And propha-sy the wheat will be a failure, without doubt;
But the kind Providence that has never failed us yet,
Will be on hands onc't more at the 'leventh hour, I bet!
Does the medder-lark complane, as he swims high and dry
Through the waves of the wind and the blue of the sky?
Does the quail set up and whissel in a disappinted way,
Er hang his head in silunce, and sorrow all the day?
Is the chipmuck's health a-failin? - does he walk, er does he run?
Don't the buzzards ooze around up thare jest like they've allus done?
Is they anything the matter with the rooster's [1] *lungs er voice?*
Ort a mortul be complanin' when dumb animals rejoice?

Then let us, one and all, be contentud with our lot;
The June is here this morning, and the sun is shining hot.
Oh! let us fill our harts up with the glory of the day,
And banish ev'ry doubt and care and sorrow fur away!
Whatever be our station, with Providence fer guide,
Sich fine circumstances ort to make us satisfied;
Fer the world is full of roses, and the roses full of dew,
And the dew is full of heavenly love that drips fer me and you.

1. Nothing was so sure to a Hoosier, as the rooster's cry as the sun arose in the morning. Brahma chickens were the popular breed of the Nineteenth Century because they were meaty and survived long Hoosier winters with minimal attention.

This poem centers on a special mind which acknowledges God's descent from ultimate being into flesh. This mind bears the peace of God and withstands discouragement and depression. Riley cultivated this mind not only to overcome his own discouragement and depression but also to write a poetry of that "mind." It is a state of content at being in the form of humanity subject to degradation. Crestillomeem had drug him down into this degradation and the mind of Christ set him free. To the kenotic, Christ halted the influx of His own life with God, not to dissolve the mutual indwelling of God with God's child, but rather to participate in life as a human. The state of mind further acknowledges that Christ changed equality with God into a state of dependence and need. God would know that this farmer of Riley's poem needed his crops so everything would turn out just fine. "With

Providence fer guide, Sich fine circumstances ort to make us satisfied," the farmer thinks. The Incarnation was God becoming flesh to know what was necessary.

"Thoughts for a Discouraged Farmer," was a favorite poem of James Whitcomb Riley through the coming years. In 1909, the same year Riley suffered a stroke that left his right hand "cold," he was asked to be the guest of honor at a reunion group's meeting in Indianapolis. It was the first meeting of the "Hancock County Society" and Riley was asked to recite one of his poems. The one he chose to recite was "Thoughts for a Discouraged Farmer." Audiences had loved this poem for over a quarter of a century.

Considered one of Riley's best poetics was:

THE BROOK-SONG (1882)

Little Brook! Little brook!
You have such a happy look -
Such a very merry manner, as you
swerve and curve and crook-
And your ripples, one and one,
Reach each other's hands and run
Like laughing little children in the sun!

A Hoosier meadow. Oliver Wendell Holmes, the great jurist, and lover of Riley poetry once lauded Riley's great enthusiasm about "Indiana soil," and called him the "delineator of lowly humanity who sings with so much fervor, pathos, humor and grace."

Little brook, sing to me:
Sing about a bumblebee
That tumbled from a lily-bell and grumbled mumblingly,
Because he wet the film
Of his wings, and had to swim,
While the water-bugs raced round and laughed at him!

Little brook - sing a song
Of a leaf that sailed along
Down the golden-braided center of your current swift and
strong,
And a dragon-fly that lit
On the tilting rim of it,
And rode away and wasn't scared a bit.

And sing - how oft in glee
Came a truant boy like me,
Who loved to lean and listen to your lilting melody,
Till the gurgle and refrain
Of your music in his brain
Wrought a happiness as keen to him as pain.

Little brook -laugh and leap!
Do not let the dreamer weep;
Sing him all the songs of summer till
He sink in softest sleep;
And then sing soft and low
Through his dreams of long ago -
Sing back to him the rest he used to know!

The poet Riley proposed a kenotic view of nature which differed markedly from the "tooth and claw" picture of it posed by the social Darwinists of his time. Nature was not an environmental selector of those who might survive to reproduce and increase a species differentiating genetic pool. Nature was simply the situation as was humanity itself- situs of humanity's habitation. From the beginning of history, humanity has long to understand the dim cave in which the human shadow is cast and have searched for signs of it in nature. The kenotics proposed that nature was a place, however temporary, for rest rather than struggle for survival. Natural setting, the environment, was intended to nurture, feed and house a humanity in the quest of a life of service. It is intentional human nature, as happened with Christ, that one hunger, thirst, sleep, and feel weariness, and the function of nature out of the bounty of God's love to provide relief. Just as heaven is a place of rest, so is the earth. As the kenotic Lutheran theologian Chemnitz proposed, the natural situation of humanity in nature is merely a mix of "visibility, tangibility, and existence in loco" and in a natural setting with the same essential chemistry which through accidence became the body of Christ. The substance of nature was the same matter which became the natural humanity which Christ received from the Virgin Mary, having hands, feet, sides, flesh, bones in which body Christ chose to ascend into heaven and will return in jugment as he was seen to ascend in the kenotic view.

Another poem, almost as illustrative of Riley's kenoticism of this period, is Riley's "A Hymn of Faith."

A HYMB OF FAITH (1882)

O, THOU that doth all things devise
    And fashon fer the best,
He'p us who sees with mortul eyes
    To overlook the rest.

They's times, of course, we grope in doubt,
    And in afflictions sore;
So knock the louder, Lord, without,
    And we'll unlock the door.

Make us to feel, when times looks bad
    And tears in pitty melts,
Thou wast the only he'p we had
    When they was nothin' else.

Death comes alike to ev'ry man
    That ever was borned on earth;
Then let us do the best we can
    To live fer all life's wurth.

From the author's Ora Myers glass negative collection of Hancock County, Indiana subjects

Ef storms and tempusts dred to see
    Makes black the heavens ore,
They done the same in Galilee
    Two thousand years before.

But after all, the golden sun
    Poured out its floods on them
That watched and waited fer the One
    Then borned in Bethlyham.

Also, the star of holy writ
    Made noonday of the night,
Whilse other stars that looked at it
    Was envious with delight.

The sages then in wurship bowed,

From the author's Ora Myers glass negative collection of Hancock County, Indiana subjects

From ev'ry clime so fare;
O, sinner, think of that glad crowd
That congergated thare!

They was content to fall in ranks
With One that knowed the way
From good old Jurden's stormy banks
Clean up to Jedgmunt Day.

No matter, then, how all is mixed
In our near-sighted eyes,
All things is fer the best, and fixed
Out straight in Paradise.

From the author's Ora Myers glass negative collection of
Hancock County, Indiana subjects

Then take things as God sends 'em here,
And, ef we live er die,
Be more and more contenteder,
Without a'astin' why,

O, Thou that doth all things devise
And fashon fer the best,
He'p us who sees with mortul eyes
To overlook the rest.

Nineteenth Century kenotic ideas saw the possibility of personal participation in Godly life no matter what he or she faced. The example was the
life image of Christ, a genuinely human personality. This Christ was Jesus,
the man, born in "Bethlyham." Nevertheless though Jesus was a human
being, God was also in Him so there was relief for the kenotic "Ef storms
and tempusts dred to see\Makes black the heavens ore." Conditions faced by
humanity were within a scheme of salvation of a Christ in a peculiar loving
relation to God. There was no need to fear a life for love was the motive of
the Incarnation and love was the sole measure of its depth. Riley's point in
"A HYMB OF FAITH" is to adopt God's free relation to the world and
accept the world's situation because God did and yet see through the world
to adopt its essential attributes centering on a love perspective. The vulnerable human relates to the human incarnate God spiritually but confidently
through instinctive faith. Belief comes because it is impelled by the human

condition to seek clear fulfillment withheld from mortal life. We have no confident assurance through ourselves but we have it through the relationship of God when on earth to God. We have no authority by ourselves to evaluate as among ourselves, except as we have the capacity from God, who qualifies us in a new agreement, not written down, but instinctively. From Riley's "We Must Believe,"

"We must believe: For still all unappeased our hunger goes,
From life's first waking, to its last repose"

It was the "foolishness" done of God in becoming Incarnate that gives the ultimate knowing about God from a Nineteenth Century kenotic point of view. This "foolishness" avoided a robbery by Christ of God's love but made it available to a degraded humanity.

MY PHILOSOFY (1882)

I ain't, ner don't p'tend to be,
Much posted on philosofy;
But thare is times, when all alone,
I work out idees of my own.
And of these same there is a few
I'd like to jest refer to you -
Pervidin' that you don't object
To listen clos't and rickollect.

I allus argy that a man
Who does about the best he can
Is plenty good enugh to suit
This lower mundane institute -
No matter ef his daily walk
Is subject fer his neghbor's talk,
And critic-minds of ev'ry whim
Jest all git up and go fer him!

From the author's Ora Myers glass negative collection of Hancock County, Indiana subjects

I knowed a feller onc't that had
The yeller-janders mighty bad, -
And each and ev'ry friend he'd meet
Would stop and give him some receet
Fer cuorin' of 'em. But he'd say
He kindo' thought they'd go away

Without no medicin', and boast
That he'd git well without one doste.

He kep' a-yellerin' on - and they
Perdictin' that he'd die some day
Before he knowed it! Tuck his bed
The feller did, and lost his head,
and wundered in his mind a spell -
Then rallied, and, at last, got well,
But ev'ry friend that said he'd die
Went back on him eternally!

It's natchurl enugh, I guess,
When some gits more and some gits less,
Fer them-uns on the slimmest side
To claim it ain't fare divide;
And I've knowed some to lay and wait,
And git up soon, and set up late,
To ketch some feller they could hate
Fer goin' at a faster gait.

From the author's Ora Myers glass negative collection of Hancock County, Indiana subjects

The signs is bad when folks commence
A-findin' fault with Providence,
And balkin' 'cause the earth don't shake
At ev'ry prancin' step they take.
No man is grate tel he can see
How less than little he would be
Ef stripped to self, and stark and bare
He hung his sign out anywhare.

My doctern is to lay aside
Contensions, and be satisfied:
Jest do your best, and praise er blame
That follers that, counts jest the same.
I've allus noticed grate success
Is mixed with troubles, more er less,
And it's the man who does the best
That gits more kicks than all the rest.

Doing "one's best" as Riley terms is taking of the infinite into the finite realm as the Incarnate Christ did and a person can. A kenotic view upon how humanity can manifest as God in the flesh uttered from the mouth of a humble farmer. The kenotic assumed that human nature could spiritually correspond to the human nature of the Incarnate Son of God. As the kenotic late Nineteenth Century Methodist theologian R.J. Cooke stated, There could be "essential likeness and kinship between God and man. Whatever physical science may have to say as to the lowly origin of man, here is what he is. God does not have to force himself into human nature, and when in it find himself unable to manifest himself in it through lack of revealing capacity in the human, nor is the human unable to bear the weight, the presence, of deity. But because man is spirit, because he has intelligence, and reason, and will, and affection, because he is a moral being, Infinite spirit, Infinite Wisdom and Infinite Love can adjust himself to the spirit of man - laying every power and quality of God alongside of every corresponding faculty in the human soul without violence to the soul - and thus manifest himself as God in the flesh. The astounding revelation dawns on us for the first time that the human may embody the eternal." (From THE INCARNATION AND RECENT CRITICISM. Peripherally it should be noted how reactive to Darwinism kenotic thought and movement really was, that is the idea that even a lowly and humble person was exalted because God chose humble humanity form. Riley's poetry was, of course, its chief literary expression and his Benjamin Johnson poetry, the best of his kenotic poetry.)

As a further idea, kenotics hoped for Christian unity. The Nineteenth Century kenotic movement was intended as a union movement between Lutheran and Reformed elements in Germany. It eschewed contention. The idea swept into America and found fertile ground for Protestant churches of every denomination combating the pessimism, scepticism, and doubt about a united Christianity and its benefit as characterized by the immensely popular oratory of such as Robert Ingersoll, a popular orator.

MY FIDDLE (1882)

My fiddle? - Well, I kindo' keep her handy, don't you know!
Though I ain't so much inclined to tromp the strings and
switch the bow
As I was before the timber of my elbows got so dry,
And my fingers was more limber-like and caperish and spry;

Yit I can plonk and plunk and plink,
   And tune her up and play, And jest lean back and
laugh and wink At ev'ry rainy day!

My playin' 's only middlin' - tunes I picked up when a boy -
The kindo'-sorto fiddlin' that the folks call "cordaroy"[1];
"The Old Fat Gal," and "Rye-straw," and "My Sailyor's on the Sea,"
Is the old cowtillions I "saw" when the ch'ice is left to me;
   And so I plunk and plonk and plink,
      And rosum-up my bow And play the tunes that makes
   you think The devil's in your toe! I was allus a-
romancin', do-less boy, to tell the truth,
A-fiddlin' and a-dancin', and a-wastin' of my youth,
And a-actin' and a-cuttin'-up all sorts o' silly pranks
That wasn't worth a button of anybody's thanks!
   But they tell me, when I used to plink And plonk and
      plunk and play, My music seemed to have the kink O'
      drivin' cares away!

That's how this here old fiddle's won my hart's indurin' love!
From the strings acrost her middle, to the schreechin' keys above -
From her "apern," over "bridge," and to the ribbon round her throat,
She's a wooin', cooin' pigeon, singin' "Love me" ev'ry note!
   And so I pat her neck, and plink
      Her strings with lovin' hands, -
   And, lis'nin' clos't, I sometimes think
      She kindo' understands!

1. "Cordaroy" means "makeshift" or "stopgap" in Hoosier idiom. As best I can trace it, the term visualizes Hoosier country roads which in summer were covered with dust so thick that James Whitcomb Riley once described them "as thick as butter on country bread" and passable, but which in the Fall and Winter time might be half way up to the horse-drawn wagon axles in mud. A Hoosier pioneer-style improvement was to "firm up" these roads at their worst spots with "corduroy" logs.

A kenotic poem of satisfaction in dependence upon the assumption of the servile state of humanity. Hey, you can even enjoy fiddling because you can accept the human state because Christ did. Christ took on the form of a human and accepted its life in humiliation. His end in becoming a person was so that He might wear that form of existence which is at the greatest possible distance from and the greatest contrast to the life of God. There is the possibility of joy in this fact coming from its participation with the life of the earthly God. The theme is particularly and generally a Nineteenth century one as well. We note that James Russell Lowell asserts that reverence for life is the very primal essence and life of poetry. "From reverence the spirit climbs on to love, and thence beholds all things." Nevertheless the source of the satisfaction is that it is sanctified because it is human to enjoy pickin' and grinnin' which is otherwise an irrelevant activity than as a human being does it.

THE CLOVER (1882)

Some sings of the lilly, and daisy, and rose,
And the pansies and pinks that the Summer-time throws
In the green grassy lap of the medder that lays
Blinkin' up at the skyes through the sunshiny days;
But what is the lilly and all of the rest
Of the flowers, to a man with a hart in his brest
That was dipped brimmin' full of the honey and dew
Of the sweet clover-blossoms his babyhood knew?

I never set eyes on a clover-field now,
Er fool round a stable, er climb in the mow,
But my childhood comes back jest as clear and as plane
As the smell of the clover I'm sniffin' again;
And I wunder away in a barefooted dream,
Whare I tangle my toes in the blossoms that gleam
With the dew of the dawn of the morning of love
Ere it wept ore the graves that I'm weepin' above.

And so I love clover - it seems like a part
Of the sacerdest sorrows and joys of my hart;
And wherever it blossoms, oh, thare let me bow
And thank the good God as I'm thankin' Him now;
And I pray to Him still fer the stren'th when I die,
To go out in the clover and tell it good-by,
And lovin'ly nestle my face in its bloom

While my soul slips away on a breth of purfume.

Another poem extolling something common and humble. In a kenotic frame of reference, the clover symbolizes humble life such as Jesus gave up His nature as God to manifest. Freedom is a sub-theme of the poem. Being humble and thus acceptable to Godly reckoning brings freedom to enjoy life. Benjamin Johnson, an old Hoosier farmer, tends to deal with this world as a place of blessing. He is finding his life laden with the happiness from simple things. He can accept poverty because he can smell his clover. To a social Darwinist of Riley's epoch Benjamin Johnson is thus inexplicable. That he is in poverty is understandable because his values are not oriented within the struggle for existence. Poverty would cease if persons acted prudently, industriously and wisely and brought their children up to exercise those same virtues. Morals and social values are the result of historical and institutional foundations rather than either intuitive or Christian in character. Much of morality is simply restatement of property rights. The social Darwinist, Yale's William Graham Sumner in his FOLKWAYS espouses these views. Riley is not picturing a person who seems to be struggling with existence very much as long as he can smell the clover and he finds life virtuous and redeeming among the clover blossoms which are a gift from a God who sets the bounds of Benjamin Johnson's morality on the basis of service to others.

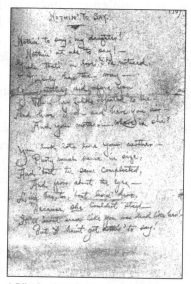

A Riley handwritten draft of "Nothin to Say."

NOTHIN' TO SAY (1883)

Nothin' to say, my daughter!
Nothin' at all to say!
Gyrls that's in love, I've noticed, giner'ly has their way!
Yer mother did, afore you, when her folks objected to me -
Yit here I am and here you air! and yer mother - where is she?

You look lots like yer mother: purty much same in size;
And about the same complected; and favor about the eyes:
Like her, too, about livin' here, because she couldn't stay;
It'll 'most seem like you was dead like her! - but I haint'
got nothin' to say!

She left you her little Bible - writ yer name acrost the page-
And left her ear-bobs fer you, ef ever you come of age;
I've alluz kep' 'em and gyuarded 'em, but ef yer goin' away -
Nothin' to say, my daughter! Nothin' at all to say!

You don't rickollect her, I reckon?
No: you wasn't a year old then!
And now yer - how old air you? W'y, child, not "twenty"!
When?
And yer nex' birthday's in Aprile? and you want to git
married that day?
I wisht yer mother was livin'! - but I haint't got nothin' to say!

Twenty year! and as good a gyrl as parent ever found!
There's a straw ketched on to yer dress
There - I'll bresh it off - turn around.
(Her mother was jes' twenty when us two run away.)
Nothin' to say, my daughter! Nothin' at all to say!

This is not a theological exposition of the Incarnation but rather a poem of affirmation of life itself. The ongoing evolutionary drift of the generations is not something to be regreted. It is acceptable without objection and there is "nothin'" more to say about it. The drama of life is lived within the context of the total world submissiveness to God in which God's own child is the absolute agent for total submission. God's life with people continues on through time.

This poem was the most prominent American poem of the year 1887. It was first published in the Indianapolis JOURNAL on July 31, 1887 and then printed to a more national audience in the CENTURY MAGAZINE issue of August, 1887. Riley recited it at a Chickering Hall poetry reading in New York City on November 29, 1887 before other poets and a great audience when his fellow poet James Russell Lowell called upon Riley to give further readings of his poetry. It introduced dialect as an appropriate speech to express the humble kenotic message. This poem and many others were published in Riley's book AFTERWHILES, one of his most enduring volumes of poetry with great holiday sales at Christmas time throughout the country.

THE BEAUTIFUL CITY (1883)

The Beautiful City! Forever
  Its rapturous praises resound;
We fain would behold it- but never
  A glimpse of its glory is found:
We slacken our lips at the tender
  White breasts of our mothers to hear
Of its marvelous beauty and splendor; -
  We see - but the gleam of a tear!

Yet never the story may tire us -
  First graven in symbols of stone -
Rewritten on scrolls of papyrus
  And parchment, and scattered and blown
By the winds of the tongues of all nations,
  Like a litter of leaves wildly whirled
Down the rack of a hundred translations,
  From the earliest lisp of the world.

We compass the earth and the ocean,
  From the Orient's uttermost light,
To where the last ripple in motion
  Lips hem of the skirt of the night, -
But the Beautiful City evades us -
  No spire of it glints in the sun -
No glad-bannered battlement shades us
  When all our long journey is done.

Where lies it? We question and listen;
  We lean from the mountain, or mast,
And see but dull earth, or the glisten
  Of seas inconceivably vast:

From the author's Ora Myers glass negative collection of Hancock County, Indiana subjects

The dust of the one blurs our vision,
  The glare of the other our brain,
Nor city nor island Elysian
  In all of the land or the main!

We kneel in dim fanes where the thunders
  Of organs tumultuous roll,
And the longing heart listens and wonders,
  And the eyes look aloft from the soul:
But the chanson grows fainter and fainter,
  Swoons wholly away and is dead;
And our eyes only reach where the painter
  Has dabbled a saint overhead.

The Beautiful City! O mortal,
  Fare hopefully on in thy quest,
Pass down through the green grassy portal
  That leads to the Valley of Rest;
There first passed the One who, in pity
  Of all the great yearning, awaits
To point out the Beautiful City,
  And loosen the trump at the gates.

A poem of Nineteenth Century kenotic hope. The Beautiful City is the dialoguing Neo-Platonic Jerusalem to "come down" referenced in the book of Revelation. Regarding this along with other poems, Riley once told a reporter that he "did not make them. God made them," adding, "all that I do is to fit the words to them. I am a sort of a mental camera, that catches the stories. I develop the plate - and there you are. And just here I must protest against the opinion of our dear Longfellow who claims that it is sheer laziness in a poet to refrain from writing because he is not in the mood. As I see it, he who attempts to write when not in the mood prostitutes his powers."

The kenotic content of the poem is its reminder of the promise of a second coming in a world ruling time by the incarnate Christ. The event will render all the world's ruling principles and authority and power null and void. The poem prescribes a regimen of hope, never to give up that the world will continue until contrariness to God is eventually and inevitably stepped underfoot by the appearance of the incarnate Christ who will "loosen the trump (proclaim entry with trumpets) at the gates."

The poem became one of the most popular of Riley's epoch. I think it must be seen in relationship to the dominant vision of the age.

AWAY (1884)

I can not say, and I will not say
That he is dead. - He is just away!

With a cheery smile, and a wave of the hand,
He has wandered into an unknown land,

And left us dreaming how very fair
It needs must be, since he lingers there.

And you - O you, who the wildest yearn
For the old-time step and the glad return, -

Think of him faring on, as dear
In the love of There as the love of Here;

And loyal still, as he gave the blows
Of his warrior-strength to his country's foes. -

Mild and gentle, as he was brave, -
When the sweetest love of his life he gave

To simple things: - Where the violets grew
Blue as the eyes they were likened to,

The touches of his hands have strayed
As reverently as his lips have prayed:

When the little brown thrush that harshly chirred
Was dear to him as the mocking-bird;

And he pitied as much as a man in pain
A writhing honey-bee wet with rain. -

Think of him still as the same, I say:
He is not dead - he is just away!

The kenotic content of this poem is very similar to the thought of "On the Death of Little Mahala Ashcraft." I cannot help but include it in this series however since it was so important from a popular standpoint in the Nineteenth Century. Probably every Protestant minister in America used it at one point or another in counseling, sermon or burial service. About the writing of this poem, Riley said, "I was confined to my bed. I was ill and weak and all alone. My eyes were inflamed, and so I just rolled over and wept with the weather." The occasion of the poem was the death of General Wm. H. H. Terrell, who was an aide to Indiana's embattled Civil War Governor Oliver Morton. Riley remembered the General gave "the sweetest love of his life to simple things." While walking in a garden after a shower, Riley once saw the General stoop to pity "a honey-bee wet with rain." The kenotic content of the poem is its center in the promise of life after death from the incarnate Christ. The poem recalls the teaching of Paul who argued, "If God when on earth preached that there was a rebirth after death, how can any among you be saying that the dead aren't reborn into new life after death? If there's no life after death, then God when on earth could not now exist as he once did as an earth dweller, arose and arisen."

BEREAVED (1890)

Let me come in where you sit weeping, - ay,
Let me, who have not any child to die,
Weep with you for the little one whose love
    I have known nothing of.

The little arms that slowly, slowly loosed
Their pressure round your neck. the hands you used
To kiss, - Such arms - such hands I never knew.
    May I not weep with you?

Fain would I be of service - say some thing,
Between the tears, that would be comforting, -
But ah! so sadder than yourselves am I,

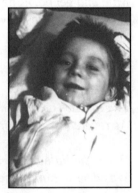

From the author's Ora Myers glass negative collection of Hancock County, Indiana subjects

Who have no child to die.

The writing of "Bereaved" began with a strange premonition which so vividly impressed Riley one night that he was unable to sleep. He arose and wrote the poem rapidly in about twenty minutes. Usually, Riley's compositions were labored, taking days or even months to rewrite and polish. On this occasion, he stated his heart was heavy with a sadness he could not relate to any known cause as he addressed his lines to the unknown parents in the poem. Later he received word of the death of the child of his lecturing partner, Bill Nye and Riley at once dedicated this poem to Mr. and Mrs. Nye. Had they been the subject of his strange foreboding?

The poem is kenotic in its presentation of the mind of the Incarnate Christ in grief over the human condition. This poem is demonstrative of such grief as is found in childlessness. The poet had no children. About the genesis of this poem, Riley wrote, "I was awakened far in the night as by a summons, and in seeming answer I arose and the poem came trickling through my tears. What was it that woke me I can not tell. Was it the pitying gaze of fathers and mothers keeping their lonely vigil through the night? Was it the cry of empty arms for the touch of vanished fingers? Was it an angel ray of light, a celestial petition from the land of dreams and sleep? I do not know."

SPECIAL POEMS OF NATURE
THE "DEER CRICK" OR "DELPHI" EPOCH

A famous body of Riley poetry was written in an epoch in which Riley escaped from not just the lyceum circuit, but also Indianapolis and Greenfield by frequent visits to Delphi, Indiana, where his friend, Dr. Wycliffe Smith lived. This was in the mid-1880's. The "Deer Creek" poems reflect Riley's opportunity to wander "Deer Crick" country of Carroll County which bordered orchards, clover fields and forested areas.

The poem "On the Banks of Deer Crick" was written for the Delphi TIMES at a time when Riley was not feeling well. Riley went to the banks of Deer Crick (Creek in Hoosier dialect) across from Jackson's hole or Wilson's cave where he could rest before reading poems at the old Delphi Opera House that evening. While taking in the scenic wonder of the place, he scribbled the poem "On the banks o' Deer Crick..."

ON THE BANKS O' DEER CRICK (1885)

On the banks o' Deer Crick! There's the place fer me! -
Worter slidin' past ye jes' as clair as it kin be: -
See yer shadder in it, and the shadder o' the sky,
And the shadder o' the buzzard as he goes a-lazin' by;
Shadder o' the pizen-vines, and shadder o' the trees -
And I purt' nigh said the shadder o' the sunshine and the breeze!
Well! - I never seen the ocean ner I never seen the sea. -
On the banks o' Deer Crick's grand enough fer me!

On the banks o' Deer Crick - mil' er two from town -
'Long up where the mill-race comes a-loafin down, -
Like to git up in there - 'mongst the sycamores -
And watch the worter at the dam, a-frothin' as she pours:
Crawl out on some old log, with my hook and line,
Where the fish is jes' so thick you kin see 'em shine
As they flicker round her bait, coaxin' you to jerk,
Tel yer tired ketchin' of 'em, might nigh, as work!

On the banks o' Deer Crick! - Allus my delight
Jes' to be around there - take it day er night! -
Watch the snipes and killdees foolin' half the day -
Er these-'ere little worter-bugs shootin' ever' way! -
Snake-feeders glancin' round, er dartin' out o' sight;
And dewfall, bullfrogs, and lightnin-bugs at night -
Stars up through the tree-tops - er in the crick below, -
And smell o' mussrat through the dark clean from the old by- o!

Er take a tromp, some Sund'y, say, 'way up to "Johnson's Hole,"
And find where he's had a fire, and hide his fishin'-pole:
Have yer "dog-leg" with ye, and yer pipe and "cut-and-dry" -
Pocketful' o' corn-bread, and slug er two o' rye...
Soak yer hide in sunshine and waller in the shade -
Like the Good Book tells us - "where there're none to make afraid!"
Well! - I never seen the ocean ner I never seen the sea. -
On the banks o' Deer Crick's grand enough fer me!

The "Deer Creek" poetry was the hallmark of one of Riley's favorite platform lectures entitled, "Characteristics of the Hoosier Dialect," and it was fantastically popular all around the country beginning in 1884.

One of the poems he wrote for this "lecture" as it was billed was "Knee Deep in June." Although the poem was tailored for his platform entertainment, he later had it first published in the Indianapolis JOURNAL of June 14, 1885 under the title "Long About Knee Deep in June." Then, it was included in the immensely popular book AFTERWHILES in 1887. It was made available for sale at the Indianapolis NEWS office in Indianapolis in that year and the first edition of 1,000 did not last a month. It sold for $1.25. "Knee Deep in June" probably received more critical acclaim than most of Riley's poems. Among those who have commented on "Knee Deep in June" was James Russell Lowell, one of the Cambridge group of poets, who remarked that, "Nothing that the poets have written in this country for years has touched me so deeply as 'Knee Deep in June.'"

KNEE-DEEP IN JUNE (1885)

I

Tell you what I like the best -
'Long about knee-deep in June,
'Bout the time strawberries melts
On the vine, - some afternoon
Like to jes' git out and rest,
And not work at nothin' else!

II

Orchard's where I'd ruther be -
Needn't fence it in fer me! -
Jes' the whole sky overhead,
And the whole airth underneath -
Sort o' so's a man kin breathe
Like he ort, and kind o' has
Elbow-room to keerlessly
Sprawl out len'thways on the grass
Where the shadders thick and soft
As the kivvers on the bed
Mother fixes in the loft

Deer Creek looking toward the slate bluffs east of Delphi. Courtesy of Carrol County Museum.

Allus, when they's company!

III

Jes' a-sort of lazin' there -
  S'lazy, 'at you peek and peer
    Through the wavin' leaves above,
    Like a feller 'ats in love
And don't know it, ner don't keer!
Ever'thing you hear and see
  Got some sort o' interest -
  Maybe find a bluebird's nest
Tucked up there conveenently
Fer the boy 'at's ap' to be
Up some other apple tree!
Watch the swallers skootin' past
Bout as peert as you could ast;
  Er the Bob-white raise and whiz
Where some other's whistle is.

"Boardwalk" along the Riley Park, Delphi, Indiana.
Courtesy of Carrol County Museum.

IV

Ketch a shadder down below,
And look up to find the crow -
Er a hawk, - away up there,
'Pearantly froze in the air! -
  Hear the old hen squawk, and squat
  Over ever' chick she's got,
Sudden-like! - and she knows where
  That-air hawk is, well as you! -
  You jes' bet yer life she do! -
    Eyes a-glitterin' like glass,
    Waitin' till he makes a pass!

V

Pee-wees' singin', to express
  My opinion, 's second-class,
Yit you'll hear 'em more er less;

Sapsucks gittin' down to biz,
Weedin' out the lonesomeness;
Mr. Bluejay, full o' sass,
 In them baseball clothes o' his,
Sportin' round the orchard jes'
Like he owned the premises!
 Sun out in the fields kin sizz,
But flat on yer back, I guess,
 In the shade's where glory is!
That's jes' what I'd like to do
Stiddy fer a year er two!

VI

Plague! ef they ain't somepin' in
Work 'at kind o' goes ag'in'
 My convictions! - 'long about
 Here in June especially! -
 Under some old apple tree,
 Jes' a-restin' through and through,
I could git along without
 Nothin' else at all to do
 Only jes' a-wishin' you
Wuz a-gittin' there like me,
And June wuz eternity!

Road out of town, Delphi, Indiana courtesy of Carroll
County Historical Society.

VII

Lay out there and try to see
Jes' how lazy you kin be! -
 Tumble round and souse yer head
In the clover-bloom, er pull
 Yer straw hat acrost yer eyes
 And peek through it at the skies,
 Thinkin' of old chums 'at's dead,
 Maybe, smilin' back at you
In betwixt the beautiful
 Clouds o' gold and white and blue! -

Month a man kin railly love -
June, you know, I'm talkin' of!

VIII

March ain't never nothin' new! -
Aprile's altogether too
  Brash fer me! and May - I jes'
  'Bominate its promises, -
Little hints o' sunshine and
Green around the timber-land -
  A few blossoms, and a few
  Chip-birds, and a sprout er two, -
Drap asleep, and it turns in
  'Fore daylight and snows ag'in! -
But when June comes - Clear my th'oat
  With wild honey! - Reach my hair
In the dew! and hold my coat!
    Whoop out loud! and th'ow my hat! -
  June wants me, and I'm to spare!
  Spread them shadders anywhere,
  I'll get down and waller there,
    And obleeged to you at that!

After accompanying Dr. Wycliffe Smith on a horseback ride, Riley penned:

FROM DELPHI TO CAMDEN (1884)

I

From Delphi to Camden - little Hoosier towns, -
But here were classic meadows, blooming dales and downs;
And here were grassy pastures, dewy as the leas
Trampled over by the trains of royal pageantries!

And here the winding highway loitered through the shade
Of the hazel covert, where, in ambuscade,
Loomed the larch and linden, and the greenwood-tree
Under which bold Robin Hood loud hallooed to me!

Riley's first poem published in an Indianapolis newspaper was on its front page. "Man's Devotion" by "Jay Whit," a Riley pseudonym.

Here the stir and riot of the busy day
Dwindled to the quiet of the breath of May;
Gurgling brooks, and ridges lily-marged and spanned
By the rustic bridges found in Wonderland!

II

From Delphi to Camden, - from Camden back again! -
And now the night was on us, and the lightning and the rain;
And still the way was wondrous with the flash of hill and
plain, -
The stars like printed asterisks - the moon a murky strain!

And I thought of tragic idyll, and of flight and hot pursuit,
And the jingle of the bridle and the cuirass and spur on
boot,
As our horses' hooves struck showers from the flinty boulders set

In freshet-ways of writing reed and drowning violet.

And we passed beleaguered castles, with their battlements a-frown;
Where a tree fell in the forest was a turret toppled down;
While my master and commander - the brave knight I galloped with
On this reckless road to ruin or to fame was - Dr. Smith!

POETRY FOR NEWSPAPER PUBLICATION

Any artist lies imprisoned within his media of expression. These bounds are as iron bars to genius. The best an artist accomplishes is to ecstatically raise the language of his or her media to its highest pitch and intensity.

James Whitcomb Riley's media was the Nineteenth Century "local sheet" the predecessor to today's newspaper. We have seen the mundane operation of these organs as we traced how the hoax poem "Leonainie" came to be published. Through most of his life, Riley was a "newspaper poet." The one newspaper he came to be most associated with was the Indianapolis JOURNAL, now the Indianapolis STAR. Riley wrote, however, for many newspapers in many capacities. He wrote advertising and editorial copy as well as his more famous poetry. He also covered news events and was assigned to special projects such as his five-part serial on "What Our Bright College Boys Are Doing" published during the last 1891 to January 1892. There is not a major Riley poem which was not first published in a newspaper before printing in a book.

There simply is no current reference to the poetry published in the newspapers of the American Nineteenth Century. The practice of placing poetry on the newspaper front pages - of anywhere - in newspapers has long ago vanished. Riley's media has, in short, passed into history. Without experience with the media, it is hard to understand its message. Nevertheless we must try if we are to have any chance at all of understanding the Post Civil War American scene and particularly its mood and dynamic.

Riley was apprenticed into newspaper journalism at a time when country journalism was intensely personal in cast and flavor. Editors of local newspapers were vehement in their beliefs, many of them of a political nature. Politics caused great candid and savage debate - a product of the great divisions in the country caused by the American Civil War just a decade earlier in history. Elections were especially bitter in the Hayes-Tilden election of 1876. Many Hoosiers refused to accept that Hayes won and called him a "de jure" President. No doubt some of Riley's journalistic work was of a political nature. The newspapers of his day were highly partisan and Riley wrote for many of them to include their editorials.

Riley had trouble with this. Throughout his life, Riley had great suspicion about the political process. Remembering the lynching incident from his young manhood, Riley was suspicious of aroused people. Politics was also tied to racism in Indiana in Riley's memory especially during election times. Greenfield's black community were Republican and at the time the county voted basically Democrat. It was a rare election in which Greenfield's blacks were not harassed in some way. In the 1872 campaign, a political speaker of the Democrat parties, Thomas A. Hendricks, came to Greenfield to speak for Greeley and evoked racism according to George Knox, Greenfield's black barber as stated in his memoirs, saying "he could stand everything but one thing and that was the "nigger." Shortly after the black lynching in Greenfield in 1875, in the 1876 presidential campaign, clubs were organized, Grant and Lincoln clubs by the Republicans and Tilden and Hendricks clubs by the Democrats. On the Monday before the election in November, the Democrat Club held a county rally numbering by George Knox's estimate about 25,000 and the club members gathered in Greenfield shouting things like "Hurrah for Tilden and Hendricks!" and occasionally "God damn the Republicans and nigger lovers." Wagons were decorated with slogans like, "Clean the Radicals out," "Clean the black Republicans out," "White husbands or none." George Knox remembered a group coming into his barbershop and one jumping up on his stove and Knox asked him to get off and was told, "Don't give me any of your black sass." Some took razors and cut Knox's leather straps and another kicked his dye stand over. Knox stated, "I had gone through the army, passed through exciting times, had experienced the quick terror of the midnight whisper, "the enemy is upon us" (during the Civil War in Northern service), but even on the battle field of Mission Ridge, that bloody spot, where men were being killed in platoons all around me, heads and legs torn off, cannon and minie balls flying as thick as hail, at no time did I suffer in feelings, as on that awful day." George Knox was James Whitcomb Riley's great friend and first employer. Riley was on his side politically.

Riley was able to avoid the most heated of these political conflicts by seeking to live at the soul level where his play characters could breathe. Not until the Benjamin Harrison campaign for the Presidency do we find Riley personally speaking out for a candidate. Benjamin Harrison was his man in that election largely because he was a good personal friend.

If pressed, Riley would not say he was either a Democrat or Republican. To probe more deeply, Riley was asked about his father's politics since political affiliation was often a family matter. Reuben Riley of course had been both a Democrat and Republican and other "splinter" parties. Once when asked whether his father was a Democrat or Republican, Riley replied: "I don't know, I haven't seen him since breakfast."

Riley hated such politicizing. Riley mentioned that he was forced to do editorial work of this nature in a letter to Elizabeth Kahle of August 9, 1881.

Riley actually felt politicians were a rather comical lot.

A LOCAL POLITICIAN FROM AWAY BACK (1887)

Jedge is good at argyin' -
No mistake in that!
Most folks 'at takles him
He'll skin 'em like a cat!
You see, the Jedge is read up,
And b'en in politics,
Hand-in-glove, you might say,
Sence back in '56.

Elected to the Shurrif, first,
Then elected Clerk;
And buckled down to work;
Practised three or four terms,
Then he run for jedge -
Speechified a little 'round
And went in like a wedge!

From the author's Ora Myers glass negative collection of Hancock County, Indiana subjects

The first newspaper Riley contributed to was The REPUBLICAN. This was a newspaper begun by T. B. Deems about 1870 in Greenfield, Indiana, and survived for approximately three months. No copy of this newspaper survives.

For a far longer period Riley wrote for The Greenfield COMMERCIAL. The COMMERCIAL was begun by Amos C. Beeson in 1867. In 1870, Beeson sold this Pro-Republican newspaper to Lionel E. Rumrill who terminated it in December, 1872. Riley published most poetry in the Greenfield

COMMERCIAL anonymously. One poem was a spoof of a Bret Harte style and revolved around a girlfriend of Riley's, Lucy Atkinson. Riley called on her as did a young jewelry salesman of Greenfield. Riley and the jewelry salesman did not consider themselves rivals for the attention of Lucy because neither saw each other at Lucy's home. One day, Lucy sent Riley a note to come to her home at six o'clock p.m. that evening. Riley did so but somewhat later than six. When Riley arrived, he saw Lucy in a bridal dress with happy friends around in an obvious marriage party. A two-horse carriage was tied at the gate ready to take the married couple off. The woman was Lucy. Riley had been invited to a surprise wedding of his girlfriend to another man.

To commemorate this occasion, Riley wrote a poem in the style of Bret Harte's "Truthful James." It was published in The Greenfield COMMER-CIAL on January 14, 1871 in "The Poet's Corner" section of that newspaper. The name of the poet was listed as Brat Heart.

AN UNEXPECTED RESULT

Of late I'm becoming persuaded to smile
At some things turning out, once-in-awhile;
In the way that they do! I'll aim to explain,
In order to make my meaning more plain,
In the following crude vernacular strain:

"Never go back on a woman, John!
Unless you think she's a drawin' you on."

"Drawing me on! Now look here, Dick
Show me the girl that can do that trick
Before you venture on calling me `sick."!
It's all set up - she wants to tell
Me "something" to-night - now look here - well -
I'm going to cut her - I want you to see
How much more she thinks of me
Than of that damned jeweler - how'll that be?"
"Be? - mighty bad, for a woman to fix
And dress and get ready by half-past six,
Don't play off on her, John! If you can,

Get ready and go! act like a man -
Some other time you can work this plan!
And besides that you want to know
What she wants by begging you so
To come there early. If I were you
I'd marry that woman, that's what I'd do,
As certain as one and one make two!
Or ain't you much on the marry now?
Well, she's a mighty fat take anyhow!"

"Well now, you can bet she ain't so slow,
Hang it! I won't play off on her so!
Where's my overcoat? I'm going to go!
And you needn't sit up till I come in,
For I am right on the `woo' and the `win!'"

"All right, John, my bully old brick!
Play it right fine, and talk mighty slick,
Good night, success to you!"

"Good night, Dick!"

"Not back a'ready! Why, what's up now?
Going to go back on it? What's the row?
Are you going crazy - Ouch! look here, say,
Don't step on my corns in that lubberly way!
You're the cussedest fool 'at I've seen today!"

"Well, I reckon I am! Say, Dick, look here -
Come here to the window and it will appear
To you in a stronger light - I'm a fool,
And a damned one too! Oh, I'm perfectly cool!
I mostly resemble what's most like a mule.
Don' you see 'em turning the corner there?
See those carriages? That with the pair
Of grays hitched to it? The happy twain
Who sit inside, it is very plain,
Are married and going off on the next train!"

"Well, what of that?"

               "Why, that's the girl I
kindly consented not `whirl
For your sweet sake - and I'll defer
Stating particulars - but for her,
She may go to hell with her jew - el - er!"

Of late I'm growing persuaded to smile
At some things turning out once-in-awhile,
In the way that they do. I've tried to explain,
In order to make my meaning more plain,
In what some may term a "sarcastic vein."

Toward its last days Riley was the COMMERCIAL's local editor, solicitor and writer of advertisements. He filled the literary department with poetry and astonished the editor and public as well with advertisements like the following:

Write me a rhyme of the present time;
And the poet thus begun:
A cheap bazaar for a good cigar
Is the store of Carr and Son."

The wares of the Mr. George Dove's shoe shop were presented this way:

"It's my opinion," said Farmer Gray,
As he drove in town one Christmas day,
`Of all the gifts there's none that suits
A boy as well as a pair of boots.'
So he drove to Dove's and made the purchase."

"O where - tell me where
Shall I buy my winter ware?
And a voice answered, There!
At the store of Hart and Thayer,
Where

> *They deal so fair*
> *And square*
> *You'll be tickled, I'll declare."*

A year and half after his mother's death, Riley sent a poem to his brother John, then living in Indianapolis, to see if his brother could get it published. John was able to do so at the Indianapolis Saturday MIRROR but only after recopying because Riley's penmanship was very bad. Riley sent this poem to his brother on February 9th and awaited expectantly until the first, "Man's Devotion," was published on March 30th. Riley used the pen name Jay Whit but the newspaper mistakenly printed it as "Jay White."

Again Riley sent poetry in. Riley drove himself crazy after sending "A Ballad" to the Mirror. He wrote his brother "This suspense is terrible! - daily I may be seen with solemn expression following the mail-bag from the depot, as though' it were some dear-little-fat-corps of a relative who had perhaps remember me in his will- but alas!... "

When the poem "A Ballad" was finally published, it was edited and Riley was heartsick. Prepositions and articles were changed. Riley saw these as insults to the "ballad style." "It hurts me more that the poem was my favorite, and I had built an airy castle for it!" he said.

Riley's early contributions to this newspaper were thus: 1872: March 30, "Man's Devotion" by Jay White (sic); April 13, "A Mockery" by Jay Whit; "Flames and Ashes" by Jay Whit; May 11, "A Ballad" anonymous; May 25, "Johnny" by Jay Whit.

After the Greenfield COMMERCIAL ceased operation, many of Riley's writings then appeared in the older Greenfield newspaper, The Hancock DEMOCRAT. The reason was one of his best loafing buddies was Almon Keefer, several years his elder, but a compositor at that newspaper. Keefer had been in Riley's father's Civil War unit and was a bachelor himself. The Hancock DEMOCRAT is a great source of information about the writings and career of James Whitcomb Riley. This is the newspaper, for example, which published Riley's obituary of Nellie Millikan Cooley and his poetry to her. An Editor of the DEMOCRAT, John Mitchell, was also a close Riley friend and companionable social alcoholic with an arrest for public intoxication in Greenfield close to the time of Riley's own in his younger years.

Another of the first newspapers publishing Riley poetry was the Greenfield NEWS. Riley once said when he covered an event for the NEWS, it became a "Hartpence local." This referred to William Hartpence, a Civil War veteran who returned to Greenfield in December, 1874, purchased the plant of the Greenfield NEWS, and published it as a Republican weekly newspaper to which Riley contributed. The Greenfield NEWS began in 1874 under the ownership of Will T. Walker and Lionel E. Rumrill. A year later Walter Hartpence purchased the newspaper and continued it until the NEWS ceased publication in the Spring, 1875. Riley felt responsible since he was one of the few who contributed to the doomed newspaper.

Riley's efforts at the Greenfield NEWS were recounted by William Hartpence as follows: "When I took possession of the NEWS, Riley was contributing a serial bit of fiction, entitled "Babie McDowell." This I continued for some weeks, when needing space for increased advertising, by my direction, Riley dexterously "killed" his principal characters and ended the story. I preserved the file of the NEWS very carefully and they are neatly bound in first-calls style in marbled board full size of page. They show Riley's name at the head of the local department of the paper. This volume is now more carefully than ever preserved by my son. Bert E. Hartpence, Harrison, Ohio.

My knowledge of James Whitcomb Riley began in 1861 when I was a printer in the Hancock DEMOCRAT office, that was at that time housed in a little brick annex on the west side of the old courthouse in Greenfield. "Jim" as everybody called him until he came into fame, was then a yellow-haired, freckled faced boy of the normal type, with a predilection for chewing tobacco, which, I think, he inherited from his father, Reuben A. Riley."

The NEWS he was writing for part time and without pay folded in the Spring 1875. Riley celebrated the event by joining company with a friend, Oliver Moore, to make a circuit as "Delineator and Caricaturist" shortly afterward. This attempt to start an entertainment career, bombed as otherwise related.

As an older man, Riley recalled his first serious journalistic writing as occurring after his return from the "medicine show" escape from his hometown. The account appears in the Biographical Edition of his poetry and was ostensibly edited by his nephew, Edmund Eitel:

"...he became the local editor of his home paper (The Greenfield NEWS) and in a few months "strangled the little thing into a change of ownership." The new proprietor transferred him to the literary department and the latter, not knowing what else to put in the space allotted him, filled it with verse. But there was not room in his department for all he produced, so he began, timidly, to offer his poetic wares in foreign markets. The editor of The Indianapolis MIRROR accepted two or three shorter verses but in doing so suggested that in the future he try prose. Being but a humble beginner, Riley harkened to the advice, whereupon the editor made a further suggestion; this time that he try poetry again. The "Danbury (Connecticut) NEWS," then at the height of its humorous reputation, accepted a contribution shortly after "The MIRROR" episode and Mr. McGeechy, its managing editor, wrote the young poet a graceful note of congratulation. Commenting on these perilous times, Mr. Riley once wrote, "It is strange how little a thing sometimes makes or unmakes a fellow. In these dark days I should have been content with the twinkle of the tiniest star, but even this light was withheld from me. Just then came the letter from McGeechy; and about the same time, arrived my first check, a payment from "Hearth and Home" for a contribution called "A Destiny" (now "A Dreamer in A Child World"). The letter was signed, `Editor' and unless sent by an assistant it must have come from Ik Marvel himself, God bless him! I thought my fortune made. Almost immediately I sent off another contribution, whereupon to my dismay came this reply: `The management has decided to discontinue the publication and hopes that you will find a market for your worthy work elsewhere.' Then followed dark days indeed, until finally, inspired by my old teacher and comrade, Captain Lee O. Harris, I sent some of my poems to Longfellow, who replied in his kind and gentle manner with the substantial encouragement for which I had long thirsted."

Riley's first full-time employment came at Anderson, Indiana when Riley was hired by the Anderson DEMOCRAT. This tour ended Riley's wandering days about Indiana as a painter and member of the Graphics or with its members. In the Anderson DEMOCRAT of April, 1877, a box in the newspaper stated the following:

WORD

"It is our endeavor to serve the best interest of our patrons, and with this in view, we have secured the services of Mr. J. W. Riley, who has attained quite a reputation as a poet and writer. His productions have already attracted the attention of such men as Longfellow, Whittier, Trowbridge and many other notables; and being convinced of the high order of his talent in that direction, we believe we not only benefit ourselves and patrons by the acquisition of his services, but that he is also supplied with a congenial position, and one in which he will develop the highest attributes of his nature. Feeling that we have already the hearty endorsement of a kindly public, we leave

Mr. Riley to close the homily.

Todisman and Groan (Proprietors)

In making my salam to the Anderson public, I desire first to extend my warmest thanks to those who have interested themselves in my behalf, and whose kindly influence has assisted me to an office I will ever feel pleasure in occupying. And in the fulfillment of the duties that devolve upon me, it shall be my warmest endeavor to merit the trust and confidence that has been so generously relegated. That the position is one that is fraught with a thousand trials and vexations, shall not deter me from the steadfast purpose of right and justice; and while I shall at all times exercise the lighter attributes which go to make up the interest of a weekly, it shall be my care, as well, to wend away all petty slurs that shake the growth of dignity, and in fact, to nurture jealously the character of the paper, and assist in my humble way in giving to its individuality the stamp which "bears without abuse the grand old name of gentleman." Treating the kindly indulgence of the public for any discrepancy of inexperience, I am, Very truly,

J.W. Riley."

Elijah B. Martindale. Proprietor of the Indianapolis JOURNAL who offered Riley employment even after his "Leonainie" disgrace and public intoxication arrest record, thus saving him from poverty and despair.

At the Anderson DEMOCRAT, Riley took charge of the advertising end of the paper: soliciting, make-up, proofreading, reporting of locals, starting at eight dollars a week. Soon he began inserting his own poetry such as his parody of the Whittier poem that Riley called "The Other Maud Muller," "A Man of Many Parts," "The Frog" and a parody of the Coleridge poem, "The Ancient Mariner" that Riley called "The Ancient Printerman," "Craqueodoom" in the style of Joseph Drake's "The Culprit Fay," and a parody of Lewis Carroll's "Alice in Wonderland" poem of the same name called "Father William." I suppose "Leonainie" is in this same line of imitation pieces for apprenticeship into a greater poetry.

Newspapers did not pay for poetry when Riley first began to hope for monetary rewards from his writing. The newspapers did pay for prose pieces. To accommodate both his need for money and his interest in poetry,

Riley wrote prose pieces but included poetry within them so that he did in fact get paid.

From the start through advertising rhymes, doggerels and occasional more serious poetry, James Whitcomb Riley came to sharpen his poetic skills as a newspaper contributor and poet. Although there are original poems published in many, many newspapers throughout the country, three are newspapers of particular significance. Each was a major publisher of original Riley poetry. Riley's longstanding career was however with only one of these newspapers, the Indianapolis JOURNAL.

How did Riley become a newspaper poet and not simply a journalist? From the start he was hired on because of his poetic bent.

Of all the people who gave James Whitcomb Riley a start in his writing career none was more helpful than Judge Elijah B. Martindale. He should be credited with initially giving Riley the chance to write poetry regularly for newspapers. The Judge gave Riley employment at The Indianapolis JOURNAL, which would be about the only truly steady job Riley ever had. The offer of this job literally snatched Riley out of a period of great despair and drunkenness. Riley actually started at the JOURNAL in November, 1879 after returning from a stint accompanying the temperance lecturer, Luther Benson, through a circuit in Northern Indiana. Riley started out at the JOURNAL at a regular weekly salary of twenty-five dollars. Riley contributed to the JOURNAL earlier but only sporadically. The editor said Riley "would stamp up and down our reportorial rooms moaning for the sight of sunflowers." Riley would get homesick and leave a note on the editor's desk, "Going down home for a day or two to smoke my segyar." Then he was simply gone.

The only picture I have seen of Judge Martindale has him posed as Napoleon with his right hand thrust inside his coat. He was a heavy man with receding hairline and a huge brushlike mustache with its ends curled as if by wax below the line of his mouth. His appearance is very self-assured and his eyes look like those of a man who can see through steel. I have not seen a picture of him after he filed personal bankruptcy in the later 1870's, having previously transferred the JOURNAL and other major assets to this children. Here was a man who almost literally took Indianapolis as a pup and tamed it during the post-Civil War period, giving it the habits that continue now in its maturity.

Judge Martindale grew up near Shirley, Indiana, although he was born in the country in Wayne County August 22, 1828. His father was a pioneer preacher of the Christian Church and moved to a country farm near Shirley when the Judge was four. Like so many persons who amounted to something that I have found in Hoosier history, he learned industry by living and working on a family farm. He was the tenth of fifteen children. His education was the scanty one of the period with only brief seminary attendances in the dead of winter. At sixteen, in 1844, he decided to become a saddler and was apprenticed to learn to make horse saddles which took him to age twenty or so.

While he had been a saddler apprentice, he had also become a great reader and particularly found himself most interested in the law. In his early twenties he decided to become a lawyer, moved to New Castle, and hung out a shingle. He also married there and would eventually be the father of ten children. For twelve years he practiced law in our neighbor county seat. For one term he was a Prosecuting Attorney but he became of interest to us, as a James Whitcomb Riley influence, in 1861 when he was appointed the Judge for Hancock County. Here he came to know of the Riley family of Greenfield. Reuben Riley, the poet's father, had been a very active member of the Greenfield bar. The Judge's position was more technically Judge of the Court of Common Pleas for Hancock, Henry, Randolph, Delaware, and Wayne Counties which was all one big venue in those days. This brief stint - he was judge only a year - earned him the title Judge ever after. He moved to Indianapolis in 1862 and began a legal practice there.

From the start, the Judge took Indianapolis on as a development project. Cattycornered from the City-County Bldg is the Martindale "Block" or building, the northeast corner of Market and Pennsylvania Streets, which he had built and he also was a prime mover of the platting of most of Indianapolis of that period so that lots could be sold on easy terms for new settlers to move there. He represented many commercial and manufacturing interests and always encouraged them to expand and grow to build up our Hoosier capital. He was a visionary who saw the prime city of Indiana as needing not just employment opportunities and homes of brick and wood but also a poet of the love of the home. This seems why he brought James Whitcomb Riley to Indianapolis -to nourish the heart and soul of his adopted city.

In 1876, the Judge bought the Indianapolis JOURNAL, then the leading Republican newspaper in the state. He managed this newspaper for only a four year period and sold it on the eve of the political campaign of 1880 after a personal bankruptcy had caused him great distress. His period of ownership and that of his children into whose name the JOURNAL was placed for "safekeeping," was, however, critical in the life of James Whitcomb Riley.

During the Judge's first year as owner of the JOURNAL he happened to come to Greenfield, a town he knew well, for the funeral of a young lawyer, Hamilton Dunbar, who had been a "star comer" of his court when he had been judge. It was September, and the meeting would prove to be one of the most important dates in Riley history.

The tragically dead young lawyer, Hamilton Dunbar, had been a school-mate and good friend to James Whitcomb Riley and Riley had written a poem, "Dead in the Sight of Fame" which Riley read at a meeting of the Greenfield bar honoring the memory of Hamilton Dunbar. Judge Martindale was very impressed by Riley's poem. A week later, the Judge wrote to ask Riley to come to Indianapolis to talk to him. Riley did not do so, but he did send the Judge some poems that Riley offered the Judge's newspaper to publish.

The next February, the Judge sent Riley $10 for the poems and repeated his invitation for Riley to come see him, writing a letter as follows:

The JOURNAL
Indianapolis, Feb. 27, 1877.

Jas. W. Riley
Greenfield, Ind.
My dear Sir:

I want to thank you for the article and poem sent The JOURNAL. I am sure you have a future and will help with The JOURNAL to make it what-ever your application and industry deserves. I hope you will call on me when you are in the city. I may be able to make some suggestions and afford you encouragement. I like to help young men who help themselves.

Truly yours.
E.B. Martindale

The Judge and his newspaper, the JOURNAL, were to remove Riley from his home in Greenfield to Indianapolis at the most bitter time in Riley's life when the only other course which was probably open to Riley was that of becoming an unemployed Greenfield town drunk.

Of the Judge's later life, little is important to us in following the life of James Whitcomb Riley. The Judge went on to establish and become the owner of a major Indianapolis industry, the Atlas Works, a foundry and machine factory, and was active in many social and public causes until his death.

The first time Riley used his full name for a poem was for a poem published in the Indianapolis JOURNAL of April 17, 1881 entitled "The Ripest Peach." When asked why he had used his full name then, he said there were many James Rileys in Indianapolis and he was tired of getting letters from their girls.

Although Riley was employed by the JOURNAL until 1888, he contributed poems long after that. The JOURNAL used Riley for humorous items and poems. Riley told how he produced them. "I had a peculiar position...My editor-in-chief was one of the most indulgent men in the world and let me do pretty much as I pleased. I wrote when I felt like it, and when I

An illustration of a person I imagine as looking like "John Walker". Drawing by Frank Beard. The "John Walker" series of poems from this era of Riley's poetic career seems to have been "Crestillomeemy."

did not, nothing was said. At first when called on for a certain thing by a certain time I grew apprehensive and nervous, but I soon solved the problem. I learned to keep a stack of poems and prose on hand, and when there was a big hold in the paper and the called for `copy' I gave them all they wanted.

Riley was closely connected to the Indianapolis JOURNAL. The newspaper employed Riley and regularly published Riley poetry for many years from January 10, 1877 with "Song of the New Year," to December 29, 1901 with "To the Mother."

There is an example of the enthusiasm with which The JOURNAL published Riley poetry after he reached fame. The newspaper was literally willing to stop its presses to put in a Riley poem toward the end of his long period of contribution to that newspaper. James Whitcomb Riley had very deep feelings that caused him to write poetry under great inspiration and excitement.

One night during 1890, Riley wrote a poem to describe his feelings about war.

Riley wrote the poem "Song of the Bullet" from his Lockerbie Street home when most Hoosiers, not so poetic or maybe inspired, were in bed. He liked to write in the middle of the night.

The managing editor of The Indianapolis JOURNAL, then Indiana's most prominent newspaper, Harry New, related that Riley brought the poem in at 10'o clock in the morning in great disarray and very excited. Riley said he had just written it and if The JOURNAL wanted to run it they could. The managing editor told the famous Hoosier Poet that the next day's newspaper had already been made up and he would give the poem very prominent treatment in the next issue. Riley replied that he would let The JOURNAL have the poem if they would publish it the next morning or not at all.

So great was the occasion of publishing anything from "The Hoosier Poet" that you can imagine what Indiana's most important newspaper did. It stopped the presses to print the poem as James Whitcomb Riley had asked. Since Riley has been dead for so many years it might be well to give his words as remembered by that editor as best he could recall, when Riley had brought in that poem. "I have done something good," he said. "I had gone to bed and to sleep. It came to me and woke me up. I got up and put it down. It is good. There it is. You may have it." When the Editor had said he couldn't possibly publish it in the next morning's newspaper since Riley had brought the poem in to him at 1 am, that's when Riley said publish it for the morning paper or not at all.

Thinking about it, the poem gives a view of war that the struggling country was trying to deal with.

The imagery and message of the poem combine to produce its powerful impact on the reader. The poem became very well known and was printed in many newspapers around the country.

It is simply not possible to say that Riley wrote for only the The Indianapolis JOURNAL. Riley was a journalistic "gadfly." He apparently was willing to write news, edit such material, garner advertising, and/or do any and everything else for a newspaper which published his poetry.

One finds him editing the Kokomo TRIBUNE "Home Department" in 1879 in order to secure for himself an organ to originally publish his seventeen "John C. Walker" poems of this era and other poetry. Following the "fame" from Leonainie, the John C. Walker poems were the next stepping stone to Riley's rise in prominence as a poet. These poems, all of which were first published in the Kokomo TRIBUNE, were copied far and wide in the United States.

Great speculation arose. Who was this John C. Walker? In July, 1879, the Mishawaka ENTERPRISE published the following article directed to the

Kokomo TRIBUNE: "Will wage a year's subscription to the ENTERPRISE that your "John C. Walker" whose charming little poems have been such a brilliant feature of your paper, is none other than J.W. Riley, Indiana's rising young poet, in disguise."

For the most part they were as entertaining as any poetry ever written. John C. Walker wrote verse that was "The Ginoine Ar-Tickle" which was the title of his poem in the "Home Department" of the Kokomo Saturday TRIBUNE of November 8, 1879.

THE GINOINE AR-TICKLE (1979)

Talkin' o' poetry, - there're few men yit
`Ats got the stuff biled down so's it'll pour
Out sorgum-like, and keep a year and more
-Jes' sweeter ever' time you tackle it!
W'y all the jinglin' truck `at has ben writ
For twenty year and better is so pore
You caint find no sap in it any more
`N you'd find juice in puff-balls! - AND I'D QUIT!
What people wants is facts, I apperhend;
And naked Natur is the thing to give
Your writin' bottom, eh? And I contend
`At honest work is allus bound to live.
Now thems my views; cause you kind reecommend
Sich poetry as that from end to end.

Charles H. Philips, placed him in charge of his Kokomo TRIBUNE column, "Home Department."

James Whitcomb Riley knew Charles Philips, the eldest son of Theophilus C. Philips, owner and publisher of the Kokomo TRIBUNE from Riley's Graphics days of wandering about Indiana. Philips's father had been appointed postmaster of Kokomo by President Lincoln and was a staunch Republican as well as Editor and Owner of the Kokomo TRIBUNE. The famous John Walker Poems eventually were all published first in The Kokomo TRIBUNE. After the Leonainie incident, the next step in general public awareness of Riley came through the publication of his poetry and prose in the Kokomo TRIBUNE where Riley took employment as Editor of the TRIBUNE's Home Department in March 1879.

The Kokomo TRIBUNE, at this point in its history, was among the finest publications in the west and strived to duplicate the quality of "magazine" journalism. Many of the finest Hoosier writers contributed to it and it prided itself on having "sixty" literary contributors who were the finest writers in Indiana. "John C. Walker" soon took top honors as the finest of them all.

The first of Riley's poetry to the Kokomo TRIBUNE was after Riley's contribution of the "Edgar Allan Poe" hoax poem, "Leonainie," to the rival Kokomo DISPATCH. About a month after this publication, Riley sent to the Kokomo TRIBUNE his hoax of the hoax, called "Leoloony" contributed anonymously but published by the Kokomo TRIBUNE September 1, 1877. He also wrote an anonymous parody of "Leonainie" for the Indianapolis Saturday HERALD which was published September 1, 1877.

Not until January, did Riley begin his vast output of significant poetry sent to the Kokomo TRIBUNE. It began with Riley's tribute to Luther Benson, the temperance lecturer who had "pulled him out of his alcoholic bout" after the condemnation of Riley for pulling the Edgar Allan Poe hoax. Benson had literally rescued Riley from oblivion and the obscurity of being a public drunk. Within this time period had come Riley's firing from his job at the Anderson DEMOCRAT and his arrest for public intoxication in his hometown of Greenfield.

The beautiful kenotic poem "T.C. Philips" followed in July, and a tribute to a child of Kokomo named after the ill- fated poem, Leonainie, before the John C. Walker series of poems began. Occasional anonymous poems from the pen of James Whitcomb Riley were also published within the period 1879 and March 19th, 1881 when the last was printed. The most significant was a poem, "The Beetle," which was as widely reprinted in the national press as the John C. Walker poems.

The poem suffered a title change as it began a long career of re-publication and re-issuance and became known as the "Dusk Song." Its refrain is:

"O'er garden blooms
  On tides of musk,
The beetle booms adown the glooms
  And bumps along the dusk."

James Whitcomb Riley's friend, Dan Paine, a critic for the Indianapolis News in August, 1879, wrote Riley, "That infernal Beetle has been booming and bumping about my ears all day. The poem is just crammed with subtle beauties. Do you know there is as much imagery and poetry in the work you have turned out this week as would suffice many a man, who breaks into the magazines at a round price, for half a year. And you are doing it for nothing." From 1877: September 1, "Leoloony." to March 19, 1880, "Kate Kennedy Philips."

Some were telling Riley his poetry was too good to contribute to weekly papers, but the counsel of Myron Reed, Riley's spiritual mentor in matters of his alcoholism and life in general, was different. Reed encouraged Riley to "keep" as close as possible to the people of his age and time. They were to be the "balance" of his poetry. Reed insisted Riley stay attuned to the country people of the Hoosier state. Only by knowing his own people could Riley become acquainted with himself and the well-springs of his own poetics. Reed insisted Riley weigh his own life first and inform it with the life of those with whom he lived. Avoid at all costs gratifying your desire to live in the vanity of city literary life, Reed warned. In the meantime, the poems contributed to the Kokomo TRIBUNE were picked up on the newspaper exchanges and widely reprinted.

Riley occasionally used his own name in the "Home Department" columns as with his poem "Tired.

TIRED (1879)

"Oh I am tired!" she sighed as her billowy
 Hair she unloosed in a torrent of gold
That rippled and fell o'er a figure as willowy,
 Graceful and fair as a goddess of old:
Over her jewels she flung herself drearily,
 Crumpled the laces that snowed on her breast,
Crushed with her fingers the lily that wearily
 Clung in her hair like a dove in its nest.
  -And naught but a shadowy form in the mirror
  To kneel in dumb agony down and weep near her!
"Tired?" - of what? Could we fathom the mystery? -
Lift up the lashes weighed down by her tears,
And wash, with their dews one white face from her
  history,
 Set like a gem in the red rust of years?
Nothing will rest her - unless he who died of her
 Strayed from his grave, and in place of the
  groom,

From the author's Ora Myers glass negative collection of Hancock County, Indiana subjects

Tipping her face, kneeling there by the side of
her,
Drained the old kiss to the dregs of his doom.
-And naught but that shadowy form in the
mirror
To kneel in dumb agony down and weep near
her!

Another newspaper publishing Riley poetry was The Indianapolis Saturday HERALD. This was the weekly newspaper which published "The Flying Islands of the Night" in the "Buzz Club" series, and Riley's "Poetic Gymnastics" series. The newspaper accepted Riley poetry from an earlier period of time than The Indianapolis JOURNAL. Poetry in the HERALD began with a Jay Whit poem on June 26, 1875, "Red Riding-Hood" and ended on December 19, 1885 with "At Last Meeting."

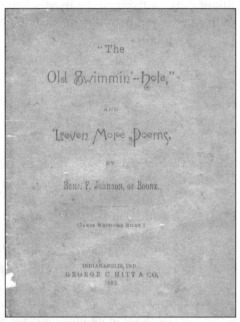

James Whitcomb Riley was a writer in prose as well as a poet. Riley wrote news articles and editorials by the hundreds. Riley took newspaper assignments to report events like other staffers. There is a record of Riley's assignment to report on what he called a "wind fight" one time. This was an oratorical contest. Routine assignments continued during the days he was at the JOURNAL. Few of them are identified as Riley's work. Many

Cover of Riley's first book, 'THE OLD SWIMMIN'–HOLE," AND 'LEVEN MORE POEMS By Benj. F. Johnson of Boone, (James Whitcomb Riley). The Indianapolis JOURNAL's George Hitt is listed as the Publisher since he took the book down to Cincinnati, Ohio to be printed. Riley is the "& Co." (Courtesy of the Riley Old Home Society, Greenfield, Indiana.)

of his editorials were written for the Indianapolis JOURNAL, which we remember was the chief newspaper in Indiana. If such things mould public opinion or

express it tangentially if in no other way, Riley's writing had to be influential. Although we cannot identify this sort of work, we can pose that it was of the same gentle, humanitarian and generous point of view as his other writing.

Some mention should also be made about Riley's interest in another media. Sound recordings were just being invented and becoming popular in Riley's era. Riley had planned on releasing nine records in his own voice to the public, but only four were issued: 1) "Out to Old Aunt Mary's," 2) "Little Orphant Annie," 3) "The Happy Little Cripple" and 4) "The Raggedy Man." Five other recordings were made but not marketed: 1) "Goodbye, Jim," 2) "When the Frost is on the Punkin," 3) "An Old Sweetheart of Mine," 4) "On the Banks of Deer Crick" and 5) "The Rain" (it is not known which rain poem this was to be, perhaps "Wet Weather Talk" or "A Sudden Show." These unreleased recordings have been lost to the history of literature. The records appeared in 1914 and 1915 on rolls in the thick Edison style but also on the regular Victrola variety.

BOOKS OF POETRY

When Riley began his literary career, Indiana was within a generation of being the American frontier. Literature in Indiana was a growing interest but no poets wrote poetry in book form. Riley was the first great published poet in book form. It made him a very wealthy man. That any book of his ever got published is almost miraculous. The business planning for it was simply beyond his capacity. In 1879 and 1880 Riley and one of his many female poet-correspondents, Mary Hartwell Catherwood, planned a book to be entitled THE WHITTLEFORD LETTERS. This never happened.

The very first book Riley published was a great success. Its title was THE OLD SWIMMIN' HOLE" AND `LEVEN MORE POEMS. George Hitt, Riley's friend and general manager of the Indianapolis JOURNAL, assumed responsibility for its publication. Hitt took Riley's early Benjamin Johnson of Boone poems to Cincinnati in the hopes of finding a publisher who would print them. The publisher Hitt found said he would print the book if somebody would pay for it. The publisher would not publish it at his own expense. Hitt said he would pay for it. The initial publisher is listed on the volume as Hitt and Co. The "and Co." was Riley who also partially contributed to the book's cost of publication.

Hitt's response to the Indianapolis Public Library about how the book was handled reads:

"My dear Mr. Dickerson:

Replying to your inquiry of the 9th instant, concerning the number and disposition of the first edition, published in July, 1893, of Riley's THE OLD SWIMMIN' HOLE" AND `LEVEN MORE POEMS, it affords me pleasure to say that (1) the number printed was 1,000 copies; and (2) that they were disposed of, promptly, as my record shows, as follows:

Gifts to the State press and elsewhere for advertising and publicity purposes,	103 copies
Riley took for his close friends, presumably to be autographed,	25 copies
Sold at the Journal counting room @ $.50 each	130 copies
Sold to the local bookstores and elsewhere, at the dealers' price of $.33 and a third	739 copies
	1,000 copies

Within three months the edition was exhausted and Merrill, Meigs and Co., immediately reset the matter, with a red line around each page, for a second edition that also appeared in 1883. With this publication, however, I had nothing to do.

/SS/ George C. Hitt

As indicated, later Riley was published by Merrill Meigs and Co. which became the Bowen-Merrill Company. In November, 1883, the Merrill, Meigs firm, basically lawbook publishers, reprinted THE OLD SWIMMIN' HOLE" AND `LEVEN MORE POEMS. Eventually over 500,000 were printed.

Hamlin Garland gave a wonderful account of the impact of the book. He says, "One day in 1885, while calling upon my friend Charles E. Hurd, the Literary Editor of the Boston TRANSCRIPT, I noticed upon his desk a curious little volume bound in parchment entitled THE OLD SWIMMIN' HOLE" AND `LEVEN MORE POEMS by Benjamin F. Johnson of Boone. Hurd, observing my interest, handed the book to me, saying, "Here is a man you should be interested in. He comes from out your way." (Hamlin Garland, this writer who resided in Boston, had grown up in Iowa.) "This was my introduction to "The Hoosier Poet." I read in this booklet `When the Frost in on the Punkin,'` My Fiddle,' and other of the pieces which later became familiar through Riley's readings on the platform and I tasted in them a homely flavor which no other American poet had given me. I became almost at once an advocate of the man and the book. I wrote to the author and thereafter read every line of his writings so far as I could obtain them. I felt that in James Whitcmob Riley America had a writer who voiced as no one else had voice the outlook of the MIddle Western farmer."

The Riley first Edition books published during his lifetime were:

1. THE OLD SWIMMIN' HOLE" AND `LEVEN MORE POEMS by Benj. F. Johnson, of Boone. (James Whitcomb Riley), 1883.

2. THE BOSS GIRL, James Whitcomb Riley, 1886 (Published 1885)

3. AFTERWHILES, James Whitcomb Riley, 1888 (published 1887).

4. OLD-FASHIONED ROSES, James Whitcomb Riley, 1888.

5. NYE AND RILEY'S RAILWAY GUIDE, 1888. (This book was given many alternate titles.)

6. PIPES O'PAN AT ZEKESBURY, 1889 (Published 1888).

7. RHYMES OF CHILDHOOD, 1891 (Published 1890).

8. NEIGHBORLY POEMS, 1891.

9. THE FLYING ISLANDS OF THE NIGHT, 1892 (Published 1891).

10. GREEN FIELDS AND RUNNING BROOKS, 1893 (Published 1892)

11. POEMS HERE AT HOME, 1893.

12. ARMAZINDY, 1894.

13. THE DAYS GONE BY, 1895.

14. A TINKLE OF BELLS, 1895.

15. A CHILD-WORLD, 1897 (Published 1896).

16. RUBAIYAT OF DOC SIFERS, 1897.

17. THE HOMESTEAD EDITION, (which included first edition materials in several of its volumes), 1898, (later volumes in 1902 and 1908.)

18. THE GOLDEN YEAR, 1898.

19. RILEY LOVE-LYRICS, 1899.

20. HOME-FOLKS, 1900.

21. THE BOOK OF JOYOUS CHILDREN, 1902.

22. AN OLD SWEETHEART OF MINE, 1902.

23. HIS PA'S ROMANCE, 1903.

24. OUT TO OLD AUNT MARY'S, 1904.

25. A DEFECTIVE SANTA CLAUS, 1904.

26. RILEY SONG'S O'CHEER, 1905.

27. WHILE THE HEART BEATS YOUNG, 1906.

28. MORNING, 1907.

29. THE RAGGEDY MAN, 1907.

30. THE BOYS OF THE OLD GLEE CLUB, 1907.

31. THE ORPHANT ANNIE BOOK, 1908.

32. RILEY SONGS OF SUMMER, 1908.

33. THE LOCKERBIE BOOK, 1911.

34. THE RILEY BABY BOOK, 1913.

35. BIOGRAPHICAL EDITION (The Complete Works of James Whitcomb Riley), 1913.

36. RILEY SONGS OF FRIENDSHIP, 1915.

37. THE OLD SOLDIER'S STORY, 1915.

38. THE HOOSIER BOOK, 1916.

39. MEMORIAL EDITION, 1916. (slightly edited version of Biographical Edition with seven poems not published previously).

Of all the books published, THE FLYING ISLANDS OF THE NIGHT was revised the most. Illustrators varied. Publishers groped to try to make something of it and Riley loved to review its mystery. He added this and that as the different editions were published.

When "The Flying Islands of the Night" was reduced to book form for the first time, Riley added the following stanza regarding his book. He did not call the book a "soul journey" or an "accomodation" or a recollection of his life with Nellie Cooley. Instead he merely said the book contained his "heart."

`TIS MY HEART

It was an age ago - an age
Turned down in life like a folded page. -
See, where the volume falls apart,
And the faded book-mark - `tis my heart, -
Nor mine alone, but another knit
So cunningly in the love of it
That you must look, with a shaking head,
Nor know the quick one[1] from the dead.

1. "the quick one" was "the living" in the original poem, "Glimpse."

Why was "The Flying Islands of the Night" ever re-published after its initial appearance?

My suspicion is that "The Flying Islands of the Night" was such a compelling poetic output that it would not die. The Editor of the Indianapolis HERALD wrote Riley that he was going to publish "Flying Islands" again by a letter of June 8, 1885. He says he is writing to do the decent thing to let him know although he doesn't have to.

Riley held off this re-publication of "The Flying Islands" by its originating newspaper, apparently, by contributing other poetry in its place. Riley seems not to have wanted the old poem of his "tremens" dredged up.

A drawing to illustrate "An Old Sweetheart of Mine" by Howard Chandler Christy for a 1902 Book Edition of that poem.

What may have caused his change of attitude may have been the great outbreak of publicity anyway about his alcoholism that erupted as a result of the break-up of the Riley-Nye comedy team. Crestillomeem was not just on the public's mind about Riley, she was also on Riley's mind. Riley chose to deal with her again.

On the other hand, the new editions - the Homestead Edition later in the '90's also revised "The Flying Islands" - increasingly obfuscating the point of the poem although some of the additions do seem recoverable. As an example, what is the meaning of the change to the poem of the following: A stanza of "Chorus of Floating Heads:" "Plumed as the spherey things, we are the host that swings\ And swarms, with a war of wings and a wonder of songs\ Blest with the tumult of glad, gold-throated trumpetings\ That trill to the heavenmost starry heights where the laugh of the storm belongs." (Among the changes to reach this point: Cross out "With a wonder of night" and replace with "Plumed as the spherey things," replace "thoughts" with "songs," remove the plural of "trills" to "trill," and change "peeks" to "heights.") It should be noted that what is happening is Riley is moving the poem into "safer" abstraction.

The poem was generally criticized. One critic of the Pittsburgh

Commercial GAZETTE wrote, "You can hardly realize that it emanated from the same brain that gave birth to "The Raggedy Man,' `When the Frost Is on the Punkin,' and `Good- by, Jim.' This work will not be as satisfactory to the general readers as his others, although some admire it most of all."

A later volume of contained the most beautifully illustrated edition called the "Franklin Booth Edition," after its illustrator.

While the first Riley books were not noted for illustration, the ones published after the 1890's were. As Riley's earlier biographer, Marcus Dickey, has said: "The end of the`nineties marked the beginning of a series of illustrated books, which were received enthusiastically by the book trade and the Riley public...The milestones in his popularity were marked by the appearance of the illustrated books -Child Rhymes and Farm Rhymes and others in the Deer Creek volumes illustrated by Vawter, the crowning success being An Old Sweetheart of Mine in 1902, illustrated by Howard Chandler Christy. This had a tremendous vogue and was followed with equal success by Out to Old Aunt Mary's, Home Again with Me, The Girl I Loved, and other titles in the Christy-Riley series.

Edward Eggleston, "Father of Hoosier Dialect Leterature."

Of the many illustrators, we remember Will Vawter as being the one most closely associated with Riley. As a young man growing up in Greenfield and suffering from the same alcoholism that plagued Riley, Vawter and Riley shared great empathy.

THE GOLDEN AGE OF HOOSIER LITERATURE

As can be seen, in the 1890's Riley began to publish his great output of books annually. The time marked the commencement of what is sometimes called the "Golden Age of Hoosier Literature." The state had only a brief literary tradition which actually began only shortly before the American Civil War prior to this. The first Hoosier writer of note was Julia Dumont, a school teacher, who published LIFE SKETCHES FROM COMMON PATHS in New York in 1856. She is considered the first Indiana author with a national reputation. Most find her characterizations wooden and scenes of Hoosier life artificial. Nevertheless her pupil, Edward Eggleston, was influenced to take Hoosier experiences as the stuff of his narratives. Eggleston's THE HOOSIER SCHOOLMASTER first published in 1871 has become a classic of frontier life in community. It remains the most vivid picture of Indiana in its unsophisticated adolescence. In the next decade, the Indiana writers James Whitcomb Riley, in poetry, and Lew Wallace, in prose, were two figures very prominent in American literature. Riley's poetry of Hoosier domesticity was particularly popular with the realists.

By the 1890's Hoosier writers included George Barr McCutcheon, author of GRAUSTARK; William Vaughn Moody, employed at the University of Chicago as a Professor of Literature; Gene Stratton-Porter, a housewife near a farm in Fort Wayne; Theodore Dreiser, born near Terre Haute in 1871; Newton Booth Tarkington, soon to be the author of the acclaimed PENROD and other novels; and Charles Major, a Shelbyville writer of romance such as WHEN KNIGHTHOOD WAS IN FLOWER and THE BEARS OF BLUE RIVER.

There were many writers who could be flushed up in every county of the state. George Ade, an Indiana author, once told a story of a traveling lyceum lecturer who had heard the writing was very popular in Indiana at this time. The lecturer, hoping to ingratiate himself with his audience, invited all the authors in his audience to come on stage and sit with him. The entire audience stood up and started forward as Ade told it.

Riley's great wealth derived from sales of books after the great platform successes of the 1880's had caused him to become famous.

He had considered this source of income however from an early age. The fall of 1876, Riley was planning with Benjamin S. Parker of New Castle and Captain Lee O. Harris, at Parker's suggestion, a collection of verse to be published for the holidays. The project did not materialize but the three corresponded about it extensively. Eventually, Riley's conception of writing books of poetry paid very handsomely. In the warmly humanistic way that was Riley's, much of Riley's wealth has been used to help establish a hospital for children in Indianapolis among other eleemosynary undertakings.

All of his writing to the very end was Nellie Cooley's as well as his own. His heart had gone with Nellie into her grave. From "The Flying Islands of the Night." The night of death will permit him to live again with Nellie.

SONG[1]

Fold me away in your arm[2], O Night -
  Night, my Night, with your rich black hair! -
Tumble it down till my yearning sight
And my unkissed lips are hidden quite
  And my heart[3] is havened there, -
    Under that mystical dark despair -
    Under your rich black hair.

Oft have I looked in your eyes, O Night -
  Night, my Night, with your rich black hair! -
Looked in your eyes till my face waned white
And my heart laid hold of a mad delight
  That moaned[4] as I held it there
    Under the deeps[5] of the dark despair -
    Under your rich black hair.

Just for a kiss of your mouth, O Night -
  Night, my Night, with your rich black hair! -
Lo! will I[6] wait as a dead man might
Wait for the judgment's dawning light
  With my lips in a frozen prayer -
    Under this loveable dark despair -
    Under your rich black hair.

1. This poem was originally published as "Night" in the Indianapolis Saturday HERALD of June 28, 1879 in Riley's front page column of weekly verse called "Poetic Gymnastics." "Night" did not find itself included within "Flying Islands" until the HOMESTEAD EDITION of the poem of 1898.
2. Originally in the plural. The image of Riley embracing and embraced in the arms of his dead inspiring Nellie in death is lost by this reduction from the plural to the singular. On the other hand, the "Night" is perhaps more clearly associated with the death of Nellie in its singularity of "arm."
3. As originally published in 1879, this word was "soul."
4. The word "moaned" was originally "shrieked" as published in 1879.
5. The word "deeps" was originally "waves."
6. As originally published in 1879, the words were reversed, with the rhetorical "will I" becoming the fatalistic "I will."

By its inclusion in "The Flying Islands of the Night," Riley assimilates the experience of his despair over the death of his "Nellie" into his anticipation of a reunion in the afterlife. One can easily imagine Riley right now having gone right on living after his death playing duets with Nellie at the piano as these lines are read.

MR. BRYCE

A HUMOROUS MAN LECTURING ACROSS THE COUNTRY WITH A "SAD FACE" NOBODY SEES

MR. BRYCE

A HUMOROUS MAN LECTURING ACROSS THE COUNTRY WITH A "SAD FACE" NOBODY SEES

There is a "special" Riley role that was perhaps his most professional "self." This was Riley the "Platform Lecturer," Mr. Bryce. Riley describes himself this way in the Buzz Club series published in the Indianapolis Saturday HERALD IN 1878 as his platform career was unfolding. The Buzz Club series, of course, included the first appearance of Riley's "The Flying Islands of the Night." At the second meeting of this "fictional" Buzz Club, a new character is introduced as Mr. Bryce.

Mr. Bryce sounds an awful lot like James Whitcomb Riley. He also sounds like a "Jucklet" clone or maybe a "histrionic Jucklet." What is Riley up to this time?

Mr. Bryce is described as "a sad faced, seedy gentleman of slender architecture, and a restless air indicative or a highly sensitive temperament. He wore no badge of age, save that his beardless face was freaked about the corners of the eyes, nose and mouth with wrinkles not quite thick enough for mature years and yet too deeply etched to indicate either a brief or gentle contact with the acrid cares of life. His dress, although much worn, and sadly lacking in length of leg and sleeve still held a certain elegance that retained respect. But without dilating further as to details of description, or retrograding to rehearse the incident through which the genial Mr. Hunchley formed the queer young man's acquaintance in a concert hall a night or two preceding... Mr. Hunchley's introduction, "Gentlemen, I

Riley as "Mr. Bryce." A photograph of Riley popularly know as "The Debonair Lecturer." (Neg. C7171, IMCPL-Riley Collection, Indiana Historical Society.)

have the very great honor of introducing to your notice a gentleman of whose intrinsic talents the world is yet to hear when the plaudits of a nation shall infest the atmosphere. A gentleman, a genius and an artist all combined in a music-box of nature and a masterwork of mind. A drawing star whose brilliance shall permeate the gloom of - of histrionic history, and - and - but why continue in a vein of prophetic possibilities whose length is simply boundless."

Mr. Bryce was Riley's new "self" as a "Platform Lecturer."

With hindsight, let us examine how Mr. Bryce did for himself. Mr. Bryce had four most special platform occasions which we will mention briefly before tracing this life of Riley. The first was Riley's great success on the platform at Kokomo, Indiana in the year of the writing of "The Flying Islands of the Night." He had floundered around before this and failed time after time as a platform entertainer. The Boston engagement in 1882 at the Tremont Temple was the second great platform event. Riley was a success in this first major booking by the famous Boston James Redpath Agency and this brought him instant national attention. The third major platform appearance was one for a Copyright League engagement at New York's Chickering Hall in 1886. The greatest poets of America read to this audience and James Whitcomb Riley was the most enthusiastically received. His reading on the first day was so successful that James Russell Lowell, the organizer of the event, asked Riley to re-take the stage the second day which Riley did with equal success. The final significant reading was in 1890 when Riley returned to Indianapolis and was given a reception by the Indianapolis Literary Club after his breakup with Nye in Louisville, Kentucky. The breakup was due to Riley's public alcoholism and this event triggered the feeling in Riley that he was still valued as Mr. Bryce despite his shame. He never did lecture much after that and Mr. Bryce slowly "fades away." However, Mr. Bryce did not retire in shame and degradation but was saved from this by Hoosier friends who forgave him his alcoholism because of his literary and public platform achievements.

A NEWCOMER AFTER FLYING ISLANDS SOUL-SELVES

If we assume that Riley wrote "The Flying Islands of the Night" to give his soul-selves an opportunity for inner dialogue, poor Mr. Bryce was left out. Bryce was not dead. He was a future Riley when Riley might be able to perform on the lyceum circuit or lecture on platforms successfully.

Riley, as Mr. Bryce, was not out of Riley's mind. Later, in the sixth meeting of the Buzz Club, "Mr Bryce arose, bowed, fluttered his hands, and said: "As I believe I expressed myself on a former occasion, I lay no claims to that immortal gift of song, yet I trust that what I shall offer you to-night may serve at least the purpose for which it is designed, namely, that of pleasing rather as a sketch of character than as a work of art. And although I feel that it must, too, fall short of the requirements of strict imitation, it was projected in that spirit, and weak as it is, and all unworthy to be classed as even that, as such I must present it, reserving, however, the right to claim it as my own in case the model remains undiscovered. And with this little whiff of pleasantry, Mr. Bryce bowed his smiling face an instant from sight, and lifting it again, grown old and wrinkled as by enchantment, and then in a voice grown husky as with age and little use, he read, or rather recited, with moat life-like simplicity, the homely romance of "Farmer Whipple -Bachelor."

Riley is planning a "lecture" that will be successful after all of his prior ones which were dismal failures. He wants Mr. Bryce to be born out of his experiences. It happened.

Later, after Mr. Plempton delivers his Indian piece "Unawangawawa; Or the Eyelash of Lightning," Mr. Bryce says, "I would like to examine your sketch...the fact is, that, as a character reading, you understand, this contains the elements of a public hit, and if you'll allow me to take it I'll engage to bring down the applause of thousands! Ah!it's a - it's a - simply a literary bonanza, and I'd give my best "makeup" to be its author!"

Mr. Bryce, the Riley who is a platform lecturer is born.

A "FRESH START" YEAR ON THE PUBLIC PLATFORM

Let us recall Riley's year of the writing of "The Flying Islands of the Night."

In 1878, following his writing of "Das Krist Kindel," his public condemnation for writing the Edgar Allan Poe forgery "Leonainie," arrest for public intoxication and loss of his job as a journalist on the Anderson DEMOCRAT, Riley began a counterattack on his life which depended upon success as a platform lecturer. On January 24, 1878, he wrote the Editor of the Kokomo DISPATCH, Oscar Henderson, the publisher of "Leonainie" to propose a lecture there. It was arranged for Valentine's Day and was a rousing success. The people of Kokomo wanted to see the person who had caused their town's name to be broadcast nationally as the site of the newspaper perpetrating the "Leonainie" hoax. The Editor of the rival newspaper, The Kokomo TRIBUNE, also assisted with publicity.

The Kokomo TRIBUNE reported this first great success of Riley on the lecture stage as follows:

J.W. RILEY, THE POET

SPLENDID SUCCESS!

LARGEST AUDIENCE OF THE SEASON AND EVERYBODY DELIGHTED.

One of the largest audiences that has assembled in the Opera House for a year past, was that which greeted Mr. J.W,. Riley, on last Thursday evening... The auditors are unanimous in their opinion that Mr. Riley's reading afforded the best entertainment we have had for months.

We are pleased to commend Mr. Riley to our brethren of the press, and can assure them that they cannot be too loud in their praise of him. It is his intention, we believe, to visit most of the leading cities of the State during the next few months, and if we are not very much mistaken, it will not be long until Mr. Riley will rank high up among the best readers of the day, with Miss Helen Potter, them so successful person in that line of entertainment who is now before the people."

Riley totted up receipts of about seventy dollars which meant that approximately three hundred people were in the audience.

The people of Kokomo were so delighted with Riley that they took up a petition to have him repeat his lecture on the following night. The petition was published in the Kokomo Tribune together with Riley's reply:

Gentlemen: I have no engagement for this evening and could remain but fearing that a church organization kindly postponed a social in consideration of my appearance last evening my remaining to-night - the occasion of that meeting - would not reflect a proper courtesy. But heartily appreciating the honor you do me, and willing and eager to respond, I will select the first favorable date, and designate the same as soon as chose.

Very Gratefully Yours,   J.W. Riley

Kokomo JOURNAL, Feb. 16, 1878.

J. W. RILEY, THE POET

Splendid Success !

Largest Audience of the Season, and Everybody Delighted.

One of the largest audiences that has assembled in the Opera House for a year past, was that which greeted Mr. J. W. Riley, on last Thursday evening. And for intelligence, and culture, the audience has never before been equaled in this city—our best people were out and close attention to each word spoken was given to the speaker.

Mr. Riley gave a select reading of an hour and a half, which delighted those present more than any other entertainment we have had for many a day. It would be our pleasure to review the entertainment fully, giving expression to the perfect naturalness of each rendition, but we have no space left to do so. We shall do this at another time.

Mr. Riley has reason to be proud of his greeting in this city. Coming among us a comparative stranger, after our people have been dissatisfied with several entertainments of the winter, he has reason to be gratified greatly by the large audience which complimented him. A few of his friends who knew him well ...

Another testimonial was printed in the same newspaper, "We, the teachers of the Kokomo city schools, who attended the entertainment given by Mr. Riley last evening, take this method of thanking him for the many laughs which we are sure erased some wrinkles, though our eyes filled with tears during the rendition of "Dot Leedle Boy of Mine." Surely "Benson was out-Bensoned." Come again at any early day.

S/ named teachers.

Riley, Henry W. Longfellow, John G. Whittier, James R. Lowell, and Walt Whitman, were the five poets honored with stamps in the 1940 "American Poets Issue" by the United States Post Office. Riley was the "ten center." The poets' hometowns were given great publicity. The "one cent" Longfellow stamp was issued in Portland, Main Feb. 16; the "two cent" John Greenleaf Whittier in Haverhill, Mass. Feb. 16; the "three cent" James Russell Lowell stamp was issued in Cambridge, Mass. Feb. 20; and the "five cent" Walt Whitman in Camden N.J. Feb. 20th; – before Greenfield, Indiana got its turn with a "First Day of Issue" of the Riley stamp on Feb. 24th. Shown are Arthur Downing on the left, President of the Riley Old Home Society and Greenfield Postmaster Marshall Winslow on the right. The stamps went on sale nationally two days later. At the time, stamp collecting was a very popular hobby and there were said to be 10 million stamp collectors in the United States alone waiting for such philately. A special machine was installed in the Greenfield Post Office which could cancel 900 letters a minute and the post office did not close until after midnight.

The Tribune proclaimed that "J.W. Riley is to-day the most popular person who has appeared before a Kokomo audience for a year."

This entertainment was a real turning point in Riley's career. Much of the success came about through the ghost of the "Leonainie" hoax. Other readings followed in places like Tipton and Noblesville.

Riley scheduled other appearances. He joined the Greenfield Literary Club in March of 1878 and read his poetry many times before this group. One of the recorded times was this same month when he read his poem "Fame" at Presbyterian Church meeting of the Greenfield Literary Club. He also lectured in Tipton and Noblesville this same month. Then he gave "Recitations" to the Indianapolis Literary Club on April 5th of the next month before Indianapolis civic and state leaders. In May, he performed at a "Complimentary Benefit by The Greenfield Literary Club at the Masonic

Hall. The next month, May, he recited poetry in New Castle. One of his bigger "breaks" came on Memorial Day when Riley was asked to read one of his poems at Decoration Day at Indianapolis. On this date, May 30th, 1878, Riley met Myron Reed, Pastor of the Indianapolis First Presbyterian Church who became Riley's closest friend in his life. Myron Reed is listed for the first time in the Minutes of the General Assembly of the Presbyterian Church USA in 1878. The last time he was listed was 1883. These dates bracket Rev. Reed's ministry in Indianapolis as Pastor of the 1st Presbyterian Church. The appearance of Myron Winslow Reed into the life of James Whitcomb Riley was nothing short of being providential.

In August, Riley was picked up by the Western Lecture Bureau for sponsorship for lyceum touring for the next year.

In this same August, Riley sent to and had published in the August 24th Saturday HERALD his "The Flying Islands of the Night in his Buzz Club series.

The year continued to be busy. In October, Riley appeared with Sarah Bolton, "the grand lady of Hoosier poetry," at a meeting of the Pioneer Association of Indiana at the State Fair. The poem he delivered, "Old Cabin," was published in the Annual Report of the Indiana State Board of Agriculture and became his first poem published in a book. He then read at the Indianapolis "Old Settlers Meeting" also held during State Fair time on Oct. 3, 1878. We know of Riley reciting at an Old Settler's Reunion at Oaklandon in November and many other programs around the state. Then in December, Riley read at Tipton, Noblesville, and gave a reading at the Greenfield Masonic Hall for the benefit of a Miss Sproule. At some point along in here, Greenfield started becoming known around the state as the birthplace of James Whitcomb Riley, the lecturer.

Riley's need for money to support himself and his alcoholism drove him into great despondency. He was writing but was earning very little. His platform career found him getting invitations but the rewards were little enough. Sign painting was being avoided because it simply took up too much time. The straits of Riley's finances are revealed in the following letter sent to collect a debt:

To Samuel Richards of the Anderson Presbyterian Church, Riley wrote on Feb. 16, 1879 a "confidential letter" asking help in getting the church to reimburse him for the $5 expenses he had been promised for giving a lecture there. Riley detailed he had borrowed the money to go up to Anderson to give the program but never got reimbursed by the church. He said "I can't complain, either, because it don't (sic) amount to much- it's little - very little - but when a fellow hasn't anything, it's a big thing for him to lose."

James Whitcomb Riley's platform appearances were just as much in the tradition of the early Hoosier Circuit riding preachers as in other traditions. Yes, his lectures were noted for their humor and entertainment but they also spread the humanistic message of Riley's poetry concerning humility, neighborliness, faith and accommodation to the needs of others. Just prior to his years on the platform, Riley apprenticed in the platform by accompanying the temperance Christian circuit riding speaker Luther Benson. The Hoosier tradition of traveling with a message for folk goes back to the days of frontier circuit riding preachers. A circuit rider was the only preacher that the early settlers had contact with. He would travel from one settlement to another on horseback.

An example of such a traveling public performer was the Elder of the Methodist Church, Reuben D. Robinson, who was a circuit rider interviewed in a Fort Wayne newspaper, the SENTINEL, of Dec. 28, 1880 when he was head of the Kokomo Conference. He related his career of travel. After Elder Robinson graduated from the university at Greencastle, (now Depauw University), he was going to be a medical doctor but he changed his mind and decided to concern himself with spiritual rather than physical ills of people. In 1845, he was given a license to become a Methodist minister. The first circuit he had included Tipton County and parts of Howard, Carroll, Clinton, and Boone counties. The settlements were only connected by blazed trails. He kept a journal of those experiences.

The salary of a Methodist minister was one hundred dollars a year. That was what it was supposed to be but he was lucky to collect most of it. The salary did not so much matter because he had no expenses and was given a home wherever he went. In fact, the people he served had everything except money. Money was something they didn't have much use for. The streams had fish, the forest had game, wild fruit was for the picking and bees gave an abundance of honey. He remembers Hoosier life as being very primitive until the railroads came. Every woman knew how to use a spinning wheel and hand looms for making cloth were in every thrifty household.

There were no church buildings in his circuit. He held services in the various houses of the people of a settlement neighborhood. He remembered preaching in houses standing in a chimney corner with the only light coming from the roof. Many houses had no windows or doors. When he had a service, the congregation was always very large. He says people came from ten miles every direction in those days. It was not uncommon for a Hoosier to walk up to four miles for even common needs.

Indoor services were only held in the winters. In the summers the woods were better places. He said that "Groves have been the scenes of the strongest religious meetings ever conducted. Much of Wesley's and Whitefield's success may properly be attributed to the fact that they spoke in the open air."

People expected the minister of that era to carry news. There were no newspapers in the areas of circuit riders. The only source of information to the early settlers was the preacher and the school teacher.

Kokomo, which was in his circuit, had a remnant of an Indian village nearby. The Elder visited this village by a blazed trail. As soon as the chief was persuaded he wasn't there to buy or sell, the circuit rider was treated with great hospitality. The chief's name was Sharpandorsh. They had just returned from a visit to the far west, but the chief did not like that country. He had visited an Osage tribe. When the circuit rider asked him what he though of the Osage, he answered, "Him heap ugly."

There is much more, but generally I was interested in the testimony of this man of God about the tradition of public lecturing in Indiana because Mr. Bryce chose to join it. Mr. Bryce became a circuit rider too. He just did it a little more on the sly as a "Jucklet clone" would be likely to do such a thing.

At about the time of the writing of "The Flying Islands of the Night," Riley most seriously considered the life of a platform lecturer. While entertaining during medicine show performances and other acts of minstrelcy, Riley played around with entertaining people with stories and verses from others. And so he sang and played music on his guitar and banjo and told stories through Indiana and Ohio. Riley's early efforts were not headline events. Becoming Mr. Bryce was a major effort since no one had ever taken the frontier Hoosier dialect on a lyceum circuit stage before.

We remember that Dickens was Riley's most influential source of inspiration and Riley wished to do what his idol Dickens had done by way of public platform lecturing. He saw many others do the same. It is the humanist impulse such as possessed by both Dickens and Riley to want to embrace humanity in person.

As an older man, Riley gave the following information to his nephew Edmund Eitel for inclusion in his Biographical Edition about his public platform career.

"In boyhood I had been vividly impressed with Dickens' success in reading from his own works and dreamed that some day I might follow his example. At first I read at Sunday- school entertainments and later, on special occasions such as Memorial Days and Fourth of July's. At last I mustered up sufficient courage to read in a city theater, where, despite the conspiracy of a rainy night and a circus, I got encouragement enough to lead me to extend my efforts. And so, my native state and then the country at large were called upon to bear with me and I think I visited every sequestered spot north or south particularly distinguished for poor railroad connections. At different times, I shared the program with Mark Twain, Robert J. Burdette and George Cable, and for a while my gentlest and cheeriest of friends, Bill Nye, joined with me and made the dusty detested travel almost a delight. We were constantly playing practical jokes on

The "Tower of Flowers" erected at Greenfield, Indiana's courthouse for the October 1949 James Whitcomb Riley Birthday Centennial. The undergirding was of steel. School children contributed a majority of the flowers many of which were mailed to Greenfield from around the country. To the right was a huge portrait of Riley and spectators can be seen in the front of a stage where hourly performances were scheduled.

each other or indulging in some mischievous banter before the audience. On one occasion, Mr Nye, coming before the footlights for a word of general introduction, said, `Ladies and gentlemen, the entertainment to-night is of a dual nature. Mr. Riley and I will speak alternately. First I come out and talk until I get tired, then Mr. Riley comes out and talks until you get tired!' And thus the trips went merrily enough at times and besides I learned to know in Bill Nye a man blessed with as noble and heroic a heart as ever beat. But the making of trains, which were all in conspiracy to outwit me, schedule or no schedule, and the rush and tyrannical pressure of inviolable engagements, some hundred to a season and from Boston to San Francisco, were a distress to my soul. I am glad that's over with."

We return to Riley's early twenties. Hearing both Bret Harte-who used dialectical materials- and Robert Ingersoll perform on lecture platforms in 1883 were key events in Riley's life. Here were two prime "stars" of the stage. Riley wanted the fame of similar conquest.

Riley worked at recital numbers while with traveling medicine shows. Riley did not come to be a humorist easily. He practiced every day. As an example, "The Bear Story," a Riley favorite was the product of recitations for many years from almost the first of his "medicine show" career. Although this was a year after Riley had left Doc. Townsend, Mack wrote Riley in Dec. 1876, that Doc was still trying to say Riley's "Bear Story," but always got it mixed up.

Lyceum poets and lecturers were professional stage people among their other talents. Those that were poets often talked of the need to read formal verse with a "good ear" which is to say a poem is open to many readings and often depends upon the skill of the reader. For Riley to succeed as a platform lecturer, he needed a good "ear" but also "readable" material. As a frontiersman born in a log cabin, he was most comfortable with the Hoosier dialect. Reading in dialect requires a particular "good ear." Each dialect, of course, imposes on verse a regular recurrence of durations, stresses, and voweled syllables intended to parcel a line into equal divisions of time. There was, however, little literature within this body of dialect. The Hoosier dialect's foot bears a different temporal period than any other dialect. Its "fit" into meter required a special metrical scheme of regularity. For Riley, this was no problem, because his poetry was based upon frontier song and doggerel anyway. The combination into oral performance was something which was however unique when heard outside of his own native region. The effort on Riley's part, however, was very draining since it became necessary for Riley to produce his own material if he wished to succeed as a dialectical reader. Much depends upon dialectical meter which is nothing but regional rhythms of speech learned from birth and formally organized. Because of Riley's poetic approach this product had also a musical quality as well as formal dialectical versification.

Riley learned to assume roles in his life as on stage. Not every play character Riley dreamed up worked. Riley assumed only a few roles and played them well. One play character he needed to survive was Mr. Bryce, the platform lecturer. Whatever else he did, he gave time to perfecting this role.

Let us try to figure a birthdate of Mr. Bryce.

Perhaps Mr. Bryce was born in Spring 1874 when Riley went to visit in Mooresville to paint signs and live with Aunt Ann and Uncle Jim Marine. Riley decided, while there, to go to Monrovia for a first stage performance. He was twenty- five but willing to try his hand on the platform. Arriving at Monrovia on a Tuesday, he engaged a church for his performance and prepared and hung posters around the town indicating he was a "Comedian." Shortly before the performance the trustees of the church cancelled him saying they didn't know he was a comedian when they agreed to let him use their premises for a show. Then he engaged the local school house for Thursday night and had to wait. In the meantime, a town official came to him and said he had to buy a license if he intended to sell tickets. Having no money, Riley was forced to explain he was having a "free show" to get around this obstacle. The night of the show, Riley rendered "Tradin' Joe" and "Farmer Whipple" and sang such songs as "Silver Thistle" and "Kathleen Mavourneen." He got cat calls when he tried to sing "The Mocking Bird" in his own variation. At the end of the show, the village blacksmith got up and said, "You fellows have had your fun with this young man and I think you've hurt his feelings. He has done his best to please you, and he has given us a pretty good show. I move we pass the hat." After doing so, the hat contained beans and pebbles, nails and screws, tobacco quids, buttons, pieces of a door-knob and a wish-bone and forty-eight cents. Then he tried a program at Charlottesville, Indiana after returning back home. Both flopped.

Late September in 1874, Riley was asked to go to Roberts Park Methodist Church in Indianapolis to entertain children at a "sociable." He told "The Bear Story." We find Riley, late in 1874 contributing poems and stories and news items without pay to the Greenfield NEWS, but at the same time traveling with his friend, Will Othell, for other little entertainments. On Christmas Eve he appeared at a social entertainment at the Indianapolis Third Presbyterian Church and read "Dot Leedle Boy."

DOT LEEDLE BOY (1874)

Ot's a leedle Gristmas story
  Dot I told der leedle folks
Und I vant you stop dot laughin'
  Und grackin' funny jokes! -
So help me Peter-Moses!
  Ot's no time for monkey-shine,
Ober I vast told you somedings
  Of dot leddle boy of mine!

Ot vas von cold Vinter vedder,

Ven der snow vas all about -
Dit you have to chop der hatchet
    Eef you got der sauerkraut!
Und der cheekens on der hind leg
    Vas standin' in der shine
Der sun shmile out dot morning
    On dot leedle boy of mine,

He vas yoost a leedle baby
    Not bigger as a doll
Dot time I got acquaintet -
    Ach! you ought to heard 'im squall! -
I grackys! dot's der moosic
    Ot make me feel so fine
Ven first I vas been marriet -
    Oh, dot leedle boy of mine!

He look yoost like his fader! -
    So, ven der vimmen said,
"Vot a purty leedle baby!"
    Katrina shake der head...
I dink she must 'a' notice
    Dot der baby vas a-gryin',
Und she cover up der blankets
    Of dot leedle boy of mine.

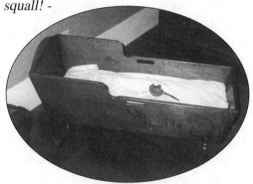

The cradle of James Whitcomb Riley with home-made rattle at the Riley birthplace, Greenfield, Indiana.

Vel, ven he vas got bigger,
    Dot he grawl und bump his nose,
Und make der table over,
    Und molasses on his glothes -
Dot make 'im all der sveeter, -
    So I say to my Katrine,
"Better you vas quit a-shpankin'
    Dot leedle boy of mine!"

No more he vas older
    As about a dozen months
He speak der English language

Und der German - bote at vonce!
Und he dringk his glass of lager
    Like a Londsman fon der Rhine -
Und I klingk my glass togeder
    Mit dot leedle boy of mine!

I vish you could 'a' seen id -
    Ven he glimb up on der chair
Und shmash der lookin'-glasses
    Ven he try to comb is hair
Mit a hammer! - Und Katrina
    Say, "Dot's an ugly sign!"
But I laugh und vink my fingers
    At dot leedle boy of mine.

But vonce, dot Vinter morning,
    He shlip out in der snow
Mitout no stockin's on 'im. -
    He say he "vant to go
Und fly some mit der birdies!"
    Und ve give 'im medi-cine,
Ven he catch der "parrygoric" -
    Dot leedleboy of mine!

From the author's Ora Myers glass negative collection of Hancock County, Indiana subjects

Und so I set und nurse 'im,
    Vile der Gristmas vas come roun',
Und I told 'im 'bout "Kriss Kringle,"
    How he come der chimbly down:
Und I ask 'im eef he love 'im
    Eef he bring 'im someding fine?
"Nicht besser as mein fader,"
    Say dot leedle boy of mine. -

Und he put his arms aroun' me
    Und hug so close und tight,
I hear der gclock a-tickin'
    All der balance of der night!...
Someding make me feel so funny

Ven I say to my Katrine,
"Let us go und fill der stockin's
Of dot leedle boy of mine."

Vell - Ve buyed a leedle horses
Dot you pull 'im mit a shtring,
Und a leedle fancy jay-bird -
Eef you vant to hear 'im sing
You took 'im by der topknot
Und yoost blow in behine -
Und dot make much spectakel
For dot leedle boy of mine!

Und gandies, nuts und raizens -
Und I buy a leedle drum
Dot I vant to hear 'im rattle
Ven der Gristmas morning come!
Und a leedle shmall tin rooster
Dot vould crow so loud und fine
Ven he sqveeze 'im in der morning,
Dot leedle boy of mine!

From the author's Ora Myers glass negative collection of Hancock County, Indiana subjects

Und - vile ve vas a-fixin' -
Dot leedle boy vake out!
I t'ought he been a-dreamin'
"Kriss Krinle" vas about, -
For he say - "Dot's him! - I see 'im
Mit der shtars dot make der shine!"
Und he yoost keep on a-grying' -
Dot leedle boy of mine, -

Und gottin' vorse und vorser -
Und tumble on der bed!
So- ven der doctor seen id,
He kindo' shake his head,
Und feel his pulse - und visper,
"Der boy is a-dyin."
You dink I could believe id? -

Dot leedle boy of mine?

I told you, friends - dot's someding,
  Der last time dot he speak
Und say, "Goot-by, Kriss Kringle!"
  - dot make me feel so veak
O yoost kneel down und drimble,
  Und bur-sed out a-gryin',
"Mein Gott, mein Gott in Himmel! -
  Dot leedle boy of mine!"

Der sun don't shine dot Gristmas!
  ...Eef dot leedle boy vould liff'd -
No deefer-in! for Heaven vas
  His leedle Gristmas gift!
Und der rooster, und der gandy,
  Und me - und my Katrine -
Und der jay-bird - is a-vaiting
  For dot leedle boy of mine.

From the author's Ora Myers glass negative collection of Hancock County, Indiana subjects

This was an early Riley poem. The poem was nevertheless one written to perform not to be written out. Riley needed dialectical poetry because he felt audiences wanted it. He used it often on stage.

Many of these early entertainments were church related. In some respects, Riley was trained as an entertainer for Godly work by his Methodist Church. From his earliest manhood, he went to Sunday School at the Methodist Church in his hometown and illustrated lessons for the children in bright-colored chalk. In Spring 1875, Riley served as temporary secretary of the Sunday School of Greenfield's Bradley Methodist Church of which he became a probationary member one Sunday morning at regular church service. On May 8 he was still on the rolls but later came the marginal note. "Dropped. Never received into full connection." Nevertheless Riley's first entertainments were almost entirely church related.

The Greenfield schoolteacher, Cornelia Loder, notes Riley was already recognized as a platform entertainer when in 1877 she made "her home with (the Rileys) one week before school." She lodged at the home of the Rileys when she was hired to teach in the Greenfield grade schools under Superintendent John Binford in the summer of 1876. She recalled the

Greenfield Academy building which Reuben turned into a residence as a tall, old, dignified, block-shaped, frame structure with a flat roof and a cupola belfry. The home stood in a grove of trees. It was very imposing with pillar ornaments on the front giving it the impression of height and great dignity. The family called it the "Old Castle," or the "Castle in the Grove." James Whitcomb Riley went to school there to Lee O. Harris in earlier years.

Loder recalls Riley entertained at the county's teacher's institute for free. She remembers that the teachers had requested James Whitcomb to give his "Bear Story" at the institute. This "more serious" stage in which he planned a platform career required much time. Riley wrote that even a boy he was always "ready to declaim, and took natively to anything dramatic or theatrical." But now, at this period of his life in his mid-twenties he was in demand at local entertainments. He frequently went to school "last days" to entertain. These were the Friday afternoons at the end of the school week when parents were invited to come in and see what their children had accomplished during the week. Riley was asked to come in as a guest for these events and read his own poems.

Riley was already recognized as a literary entertainer. Miss Loder recalled "making my home with them one week before school began in order to attend the teacher's institute. The teachers had requested James Whitcomb to give his Bear story at the institute, and Elva (the sister) said to me `I wish Jim wouldn't do that. It sounds so silly." I had never heard it before and could see why everybody wanted to hear him tell it." She also commented hearing that Riley never told the story twice the same way.

Riley recited some other poems which were not original during this period in his platform career. One was "The Lily Bud" by Anna Poe. Riley touched simple Christian emotions in his platform work from the earliest stage of his career and concentrated all of his creative effort on such evocations. The story line of "The Lily Bud" has two brothers who live on adjoining farms not speaking to each other for a long time. A little baby came into one of the homes. The other brother happens to be working near that home one day and cannot resist the desire to see the baby and steps through the back door up to the cradle. The brother/father sees him and steps to his side and peace is made between them. The story is a simple referent to the Matthean recollection whereby Jesus teaches it is not just murder but also anger toward a brother that must be resolved if one is to fulfill a life consonant with the law of Christian love. Mary Riley, the poet's sister, once recollected the hours of labor that Riley devoted to getting his performance of poetry right while residing with the family at the Greenfield Academy residence.

Riley on a 1904 "reading" tour at Portland, Indiana. His secretary, Marcus Dickey is in the back seat with Elwood haynes, inventor. This was the first "Haynes" automobile. Photo courtesy, Riley Museum, Greenfield, Indiana.

She recalled, "It was his custom to shut himself up in his room at night, and work till 3 or 4 o'clock in the morning, reading aloud to himself, over and over, the recalcitrant lines of whatever poem he was at the time engaged in writing.

Even then, his voice had that strange arresting quality that so greatly moved audiences in his later years, when he read his poems from the lecture platform. However, if his voice occasionally woke me from sleep, it was to me merely the comforting tones of the voice I loved - the voice of a brother whose tender care of me had replaced the loss of our sweet mother. I immediately went back to sleep undisturbed by its sound.

The rest of the family was less enraptured, though, and I can remember my other brothers rising in righteous wrath, and tiptoeing to his door to protest in angry whispers. Jim would apologize, and, for awhile his voice would remain as low and droning as a bumble bee. But he'd forget again shortly and resume his absorbed and dramatic intonations in a normal voice, and then I'd hear our father (Reuben Riley) go to his door and remonstrate. The strongest expletive father ever used was `By George," but the mildness of the expression was contradicted by the stern tone, and I quaked for Jim as I heard father say: `By George, I want an end to this!'"

As a consequence of his "night activities," Riley often slept over at other places or at his paint shop, when he had that facility which he called `The Morgue.'"

Out of what inspiration does one create a program of public readings? To what emotions of an audience does one seek to strike a sympathetic chord? My gut feeling is that the audience of every age bears its own agenda. A speaker during Civil War times must have questioned what was the Civil War all about? Likewise, after that event, - when Riley took the stage at great public "lectures" - an audience must have questioned how the life of the United States should be re-ordered after the Civil War. Such questions are rarely put in direct terms. Signals about such things come from themes and hints of how people are posed as behaving. When Homer sang of the Trojan War to Helennistic audiences, he was subtly moulding the thoughts and highlighting appropriate behavior for the proud people that the Greeks became.

This is what happened when James Whitcomb Riley took the stage and began giving the American people kenotic poetry and heroic yet domestic character types to consider such as the vulnerable and humble Mahala Ashcrafts, William Leachmans, Herr Weisers, the Little Orphan Annies, Raggedy Men and the boy of Riley's famous "Bear Story." They were not however roles of fate such as the Helennists were given by Homer, but rather roles of dependence.

Many of Riley's early years on the stage were given over to accommodating what the platform stage and the needs of the audience permitted. Riley tried mimicry and it usually failed. His "Benson Out-Bensoned" - a caricature study on Riley's own great temperance counselor - was dropped. As to Riley's great capacity to imitate the style and oratorical manner of Robert Ingersoll on the stage, very little came of it. In fact, this imitation was a failure. Although Riley's imitation was amusing and true to its subject, audiences did not like it. Riley abandoned it and the subject matter that went along with it but was keenly disappointed because he thought he did a rather good imitation of the man.

The needs of making a living influenced his programs greatly. I don't mean he lectured to preach kenotic themes. They were simply his to say....and yet "I am simply compelled to ask a fair price," Riley wrote to a committee in 1879, "since it is through this means that I hope to gain a revenue sufficient to forward my literary studies." Committees were the agents who sponsored lectures in the entertainments halls of the nation.

In fact, Riley's platform material did not need to include such things as his Benson caricature or Ingersoll imitation. His popular lecture series beginning in 1879 left out all such things, and centered more on his own poetic expressions. Two of his more popular compositions on the "lecture circuit" for that year were "Farmer Whipple, Bachelor," and "An Old Sweetheart of Mine." These poems were magical as he performed them. It was said that Riley made his audiences see, feel, touch and taste poetry. Riley himself was a magnet who radiated affection for his hearers. Many persons attending Riley lectures reacted with great emotion. Not uncommonly were actual tears shed.

In this year of 1879, when Riley was thirty, he raised his entertainment contract from fifteen dollars to twenty five dollars for each performance around Indiana. Handbills were passed out before these performances calling Riley "the Poet Laureate of Indiana, - a feast of reason and a flow of soul," things like that. It was all for fun and entertainment but when one sums up what happened out of it one must reckon that Riley was praising sensitivity about life and values centered around strengthening the American home.

Many of Riley's first appearances were at church groups during his first years of platform lecturing. He called himself "a poet and delineator." In a handbill kept by a storekeep in Shirley, Indiana, in the possession of the Riley Old Home Society Museum in Greenfield, Indiana, there is the announcement of a two-night benefit supper and program sponsored by the Presbyterian Church in old "Bell's Hall" in Knightstown. James Whitcomb Riley was engaged into the program on the second night as a substitute for "Mrs. Jarley's Wax Works," a drama performed by Knightstown, Indiana, ladies assuming various roles. The advertisement does not indicate what share of the second night's income Riley got. The admission to the church supper on the second night- including the cost of the Riley recitation- was 15 cents on Feb. 12, 1880. The admission the first night with the "Mrs. Jarley's Wax Works" program was 35 cents. One suspects Riley came very cheap in those days. The recollection of Dr. Omar H. Barrett, then 80, of Knightstown in the Indianapolis STAR of September 3, 1939, was that the poet again appeared in Knightstown some time later with the audience paying $1.50 each to hear him and the hall was sold out in advance.

Dec. 1880 ended another bad year financially for the elderly Captain Reuben Riley. In 1873 he was forced into court on a promissory note he had given earlier to tide the family through. The creditor, William C. Burdett, refused to wait any longer for the elderly Riley to pay him back. Unable to pay, a judgment for $605 was entered against Reuben Riley in the summer term of the Hancock Circuit Court with another $630 tacked on due on Christmas day of that year. The Captain did not pay on the judgment and the Riley family home, the Seminary, had to be sold at the courthouse door October 18, 1879 with John W. Campbell purchasing it by a judgment sale subject to the right of the elderly Riley to pay it off and regain title and live in it in the meantime. Campbell paid the Sheriff $892 for this right and later the Sheriff conveyed his deed to Campbell on Dec. 28th, 1880. This year Reuben applied for a Civil War Veteran disability pension. The Riley family stayed in the home without title.

The family fortunes continued to ebb downward. The pressures on the alcoholically impaired James Whitcomb Riley must have seemed insurmountable. The poet's elderly brother, John, was chronically and sometimes critically ill, unable to work much, and returned to Greenfield. Riley's equally alcoholically impaired brother, Hum, and sister, Mary, suffering from spinal meningitis and barely walking dragging her foot, were still needing food and shelter from the parent, Captain Riley, whose mental health was broken by the Civil War and whose law practice had fled. The ruinous and hopeless political campaign Reuben Riley had waged on behalf of the liberal National Greenback Party seeking election to Congress set the family back even further financially. There seemed no answer. Riley's regular employment on the Indianapolis JOURNAL made him the only functional member of his family.

Program of a memorable event at Dickson's Grand Opera House

The answer to the problems of the poet was - at least in part - more income. Riley looked to going on the platform stage in the lyceum circuit as a means of earning enough money to live on for him and his beleaguered family. Riley did, eventually, become very wealthy, but the going was slow and the large incomes of the poet did not arrive until his book publishing days in the 1890's and thereafter. Eventually audiences would pay $1,000 a performance to hear Riley, but these days were far in the future as Riley began his act of Mr. Bryce.

Describing the Riley of the 1880's and 1890's Riley's friend, Booth Tarkington in a Saturday Evening Post article of August 2, 1941, spoke of "the eloquence of his large nose and comedian's long upper lip...That was when we saw him on the stage of a theater and he gave `readings' from his poems. Then he turned himself into other people — a middle-aged Indiana farmer, an old Civil War veteran, half a dozen different types of children — and cast a spell of such moving reality upon the transformations that the artist himself was utterly forgotten, though we, his audience, sat roaring with laughter, or weeping, at his will. Never in a life somewhat experienced in such spectacles have I seen any other comedian or tragedian so accurately lead an audience where he would."

A RILEY ENTERTAINMENT OF 1880

Now let us enquire about this lyceum business that brought Riley such great fame.

The greatest promoter of Riley was Major James B. Pond who - with George Hathaway - bought out the Redpath Bureau in Boston owned by James Redpath. The two ran the Redpath Lyceum Bureau for four years and then Major Pond moved on to New York. The bureau sponsored lectures. Repertoires of the speakers was very diverse: travel, science, current politics, reform, labor, anti-slavery, education, legal topics, foreign matters, biography religion. The engagements bore titles such as those of the lecturer, Wendell Phillips, "Street Life in Europe," "The Lost Arts," "The Times, or a Lesson of the Hours," "Temperance," "Woman," "The Indian" or "In Early Days," etc. etc. Promoting such lectures was a substantial business in this pre-radio and pre-television era. The traveling entertainers of the platform provided the great entertainments for the country in the 1880's when Riley took the stage.

What was Riley's entry card into this business?

The answer is found in Riley's friendship with an entertainer already on the Redpath Agency list. This was Robert Burdette who was billed as "The Hawkeye Man" because he was the Editor of the Burlington (Iowa) HAWK-EYE newspaper.

Riley met Burdette in Spencer, Indiana when the two were between platform appearances in December, 1879. Riley had just appeared at Bloomington, Indiana and Burdette, the more established platform speaker, had just completed an engagement with a lecture on "The Rise and Fall of the Mustache" at Spencer. They struck up an instant friendship. Both began comforting each other over their meager audiences of the night. Riley's at Bloomington, he said, was no more than the janitor. Burdette said there was not a lady in the house when he performed. Soon the two decided to take the same train to Indianapolis the next day. At Indianapolis, Burdette made the first of annual visits to Riley.

The common gossip was that Burdette and Riley encouraged each other into great bouts of intoxication. Lotta Cooper recalled in her book CLARA LOUISE that "Robert J. Burdette was equally brilliant and equally submersible, so that either of them, when it came time to "take the platform," were likely to be found incapacitated for public appearance and their managers were in despair."

There are "wild" accounts of the two together.

The two grown men played like children when they got together. A record of one of these visits survives. Riley recorded in a letter that Burdette came to visit him in April, 1881 and seemed to go stark raving mad. Riley took the bait and went mad too. Soon they started playing circus. Burdette became the master of the arena and rode chairs around the room and did contortion acts and feats of strength. Soon Burdette became an elephant and Riley was urged to be his animal trainer and exhibitor, steering Burdette (the elephant) around the room as in a ring, planting him on his hind legs and spinning him around and around, and finally allowing his "master" to put his leg almost on him as Riley lay on the floor confidently he was not trampled.

The two also romped around Indianapolis together on Burdette visits. They claimed they were "hunting material" or were making "character studies." Really they were just having fun loitering together, drinking together and enjoying each other's company. On one occasion, Burdette heard Riley give "The Object Lesson" to friends at the JOURNAL office, became convinced Riley could succeed with his own lyceum bureau, the famous James Redpath agency of Boston, and with this conviction wrote them a letter from June 7th, 1881 with an accompanying letter to Riley as follows:

"My dear Riley, I have closed a letter to the "Redpath Lyceum Bureau" No. 36 Bromfield street, Boston, and you are the subject of the letter. I told them I would write you and have you send on your press notices. Now, my dear frater, sit down and write them a nice little letter, and send them every good thing that has been printed about you, and see if we can't work into the "Redpath" lists. I told them I would only lecture 3 months next winter, and recommended you as the rising star on the humorous platform. Good bye, my dear boy, and God bless you. I'm awfully busy or I'd write a longer letter. Ever yours."

Riley became a Redpath lecturer through this recommendation by Robert Burdette.

Mr. Bryce needed nurturing and the play character's maturity came slowly. There is a joyous letter sent to Elizabeth Kahle from Riley on August 9, 1881 in which he says, "I have just received word from the Redpath Lyceum Bureau that my name will be on their lists, and for me to at once prepare my circular, and send a circular containing my programme, press-anities and personal letters of favor and compliment from such celebrities as Governors, Senators, Authros, etc.. as I may be able to interest in my behalf. These will be headed by one from Mr. Burdette, of the Hawkeye, who has already been of vast service to me, and of whose friendship I am assured for many reasons."

In 1881, Riley became a regular lecturer for the Redpath Bureau of Boston. He developed into a veteran. Riley's friend Henry S. Miller said Riley told him he always felt stage fright when he first arose to give readings but if he lay both his hands down on a table he got assurance. He needed to do that for sure on his first big trip to the East Coast from frontier Indiana. A famous Riley trip to see his youthful mentor, Henry Wadsworth Longfellow, was planned. On his first lecture in Boston, Riley was bashful and probably would not have visited Longfellow except that General "Dan" Macaulay, one-time Mayor of Indianapolis and believer in Riley took him in hand and literally took charge of him. He drove him out to see Longfellow. The visit was short due to Longfellow's health but warm. Longfellow remembered Riley and the two talked of poetry.

The Boston engagement is fully described in Riley's hometown newspaper, the Hancock DEMOCRAT of February 9, 1882.

"J.W. Riley, the young Hoosier poet, has returned to Indianapolis crowned with laurels."

The article recounts that at one of his Boston stage presentations, the audience was 2,500, an astonishing number of people to gather for a literary performance in those days. James Whitcomb Riley was 32 at the time and was active on the entertainment circuits of first Indiana and then the rest of the country. When he tackled Boston, James Whitcomb Riley was welcomed there by Henry Wadsworth Longfellow and was given a reception at the Papyrus Club of that city which had the reputation of being a very ritzy place where snobby writers and intellectuals went.

A current publication, THE WESTERN WORLD, contained a biography of the young Greenfieldian which was quoted in this front page article as follows:

"When contemporaneous writers speak well of a brother, the world may pretty safely conclude that he has merit. Maurice Thompson says of the subject of this sketch: "Riley is a rare bird. He has genius and among the young writers is far the ablest. If the fruit holds the flower and beauty of the blossom, Riley will not be unnumbered among the national celebrities." Speaking of one of the poems, another brother poet, B.S. Parker, says, "It is full of delicate creations of the most sensitive genius. Longfellow, Trowbridge, and Marvel, and other stars in American iterature, wrote complimentary things of him and sent him encouraging letters. Hence it is fair to infer that his position in the future will be one of eminence.

James Whitcomb Riley, poet, humorist, and dialect reader, is purely a Hoosier production, born in the interior of Indiana, in the town of Greenfield, which until with the last three years, has been his home. His father is still a resident lawyer of that place. Riley tells the story of his early schooling in the following quaint style. "My first teacher was a fat old lady with kind spectacles, who taught twenty scholars in one room of her little dwelling and kept house and her blind husband in the other. And just back of the cool dim room was a little Dame-Trot-kitchen where she invariably took me after a whipping and gave me two great white slabs of bread, cemented together with layers of butter and jam and as she always whipped me with the same slender switch as she used for a "pointer," and cried every lick herself, you've no idea how much punishment I could stand. When old enough to be lifted by the ears, that office was performed by a pedagogue whom I promised to whip, sure, if he'd just wait till I got big enough and he is still waiting. There was but one book at the school in which I found a single interest - McGuffey's old leather bound fourth reader. It was the tallest book known and to boys of my size, it was a matter of eternal wonder how I could belong to the big class in the fourth reader. At sixteen I couldn't repeat the simplest school-boy 'speech' without breaking down, and rather than undertake it deliberately chose to take a whipping"

This was how Riley described what his Greenfield education was.

The Boston trip was one arranged for by Riley's new agent for booking platform entertainments, the Redpath Bureau of Boston. Riley signed with them the prior year, in August, 1881. Then his brother, Hum, died in Greenfield. Riley was despondent and thinking constantly of death. No one in his family had decent health. His mother was dead and his father was not the same since his Civil War service. James Whitcomb Riley kept up his employment at the Indianapolis JOURNAL newspaper and took the Redpath booking for a reading at Boston as a means of climbing out of the doldrums of his lonely life. The prospect of speaking at the Tremont Temple in Boston, where Dickens had recently read, gave him something to look forward to and he poured his energy into preparing for this performance. He needed this success and got it.

Years of travel and lecturing followed with national fame growing. Riley came to rely more and more upon alcohol to relieve his loneliness and depression. Riley performed on the stage beautifully but between performances he found the travel to be draining and depressing.

Here was Riley's formula for success:

"In my readings I had an opportunity to study and find out for myself what the public wants, and afterward I would

Riley at age 35.

endeavor to use the knowledge gained in my writing. The public desires nothing but what is absolutely natural, and so perfectly natural as to be fairly artless. It can not tolerate affectation, and it takes little interest in the classical production. It demands simple sentiments that come direct from the heart. While on the lecture platform I watched the effect that my readings had on the audience very closely and whenever anybody left the hall I knew that my recitation was at fault and tried to find out why. Once a man and his wife made an exit while I was giving "The Happy Little Cripple" - a recitation I had prepared with particular enthusiasm and satisfaction. It fulfilled, as few poems do, all the requirements of length, climax and those many necessary features for a recitation. The subject was a theme of real pathos, beautified by the cheer and optimism of the little sufferer. Consequently when this couple left the hall I was very anxious to know the reason and asked a friend to find out. He learned that they had a little hunchback child of their own. After this experience I never used that recitation again. On the other hand, it often required a long time for me to realize that the public would enjoy a poem which, because of some blind impulse, I thought unsuitable. Once a man said to me, "Why don't you recite "When the Frost Is on the Punkin?" The use of it had never occurred to me for I thought it `wouldn't go.' He persuaded me to try it and it became one of my most favored recitations. Thus, I learned to judge and value my verses by their effect upon the public. Occasionally, at first, I had presumed to write `over the heads' of the audience, consoling myself for the cool reception by thinking my auditors were not of sufficient intellectual height to appreciate my efforts. But after a time it came home to me that I myself was at fault in these failures, and then I disliked anything that did not appeal to the public and learned to discriminate between that which did not ring true to the hearts of my hearers and that which won them by virtue of its simple truthfulness."

I think it clear to assume that Riley had mastered his lecture craft by the time of this Redpath Agency booking in Boston.

It was in 1883 that THE OLD SWIMMIN' HOLE AND 'LEVEN MORE POEMS first appeared in book form. Riley was hesitant at first to use them in his lectures because they were "special" but eventually did so.

Some of his more famous Hoosier dialect poems were simply written to illustrate one of his most successful platform programs entitled, "Characteristics of the Hoosier Dialect." This poetry is now thought of as the "Deer Crick" poetry by many. It was fantastically popular all around the country starting around 1884. One of the poems he wrote for this "lecture" was "Knee Deep in June."

We have some idea of the image Riley projected of himself as a platform lecturer from his letters. For one thing, he misrepresented his age claiming to be five years younger than he really was. His cavalier attitude and wit are truly Mr. Bryce.

In a letter to Alonzo Hilton Davis of Apr. 16, 1885, Riley described himself saying,

I WAS THIRTY-ONE YEARS OLD LAST SPRING... "I was thirty-one years old last spring, - I am a blonde of fair complexion, with an almost ungovernable trend for brunettes. Five feet six in height -though last state fair I was considerably higher than that -in fact I was many times taken for old High Lonesome, as I went about my daily walk. Used to make lots of money but never had any on hand. It all evaporated in some mysterious way. My standard weight is a hundred and thirty-five, and when I am placed in solitary confinement for life, I will eat onions passionately, birdseed I never touch. I whet my twitterer exclusively on fishbone. My father is a lawyer, and lured me into his office once for a three-months sentence. But I made good my escape, and under cover of the kindly night, I fled up the Pike with a patent medicine concert-wagon, and had a good time for two or three of the happiest years of my life. Next, I struck a country paper and tried to edit, but the proprietor he wanted to do that, and wouldn't let me, and in about a year I quit tryin' and let him have his own way, and now it's the hardest thing in the world for me to acknowledge that he is still editor and a most successful one. Later I went back home to Greenfield, Ind., near Indianapolis, - east, and engaged in almost everything but work and so became quite prominent. Noted factions and public bodies began to regard me attentively, and no grand jury was complete without my presence! I wasn't, however, considered wholly lost til I began to publish, poetry brazenly affixing my own name to it...."

Riley entered into a "bad contract" in 1885 that was supposed to last for five years. In April 1885, Riley signed a five year contract with the Western Lyceum Agency. Riley's take was one-half the receipts. Soon the contract became a bonanza to the manager. Riley said of himself regarding this business deal, "I signed the papers. In those days I believed implicitly in men. My faith and ignorance were such that had a man brought me my death warrant I would have signed it without reading.

The contract proved very profitable for the managers and very draining for Riley. Eventually it was transferred to Major James Pond. The terms were modified after Riley started receiving four hundred dollars a week. Under the new contract his manager became Major Pond. Riley was to receive sixty dollars a night, one third of which went to the Western Agency although it did nothing. Despite the great sums as one for sixteen hundred dollars in Chicago with 500 people turned away at the door, Riley continued to be paid forty dollars. One thousand six hundred dollars was the take for one of the nights. Riley remarked: "An oyster would know that was not a square division of the profits." Riley's drinking got heavier and heavier. He was constantly traveling and becoming more disillusioned about his contract and life in general by the show. Being famous wasn't so attractive any more. He wrote:

"Fame, says I, go `way from me -
Please go `way and lem me be,
I'm so tired out, and so
Dam' infernal sick of "show"
That the very name of you
Palls, and turns my stomach, too"

Riley travelled extensively for over two decades and yet he was forever confused by train schedules. Nor did Riley ever learn how to get around in the cities where he lectured. Riley had to be taken by hand from the station to his hotel and then to the lecture hall. He was led around as one does a blind man. Repeat this by the nearly one hundred places a year where he lectured for the many years and the drain of the travel alone becomes very daunting. He lost track of his clothes. "Nine times out of ten, when I travel with a trunk, the thing is lost...I go about the country with a grip, and I keep a tenacious hold on it all day, but I never feel quite safe about it at night. If there is ever a horrible railway accident and among the debris is discovered a valise with an arm attached to it, they may bury it without further identification as the fragments of the Hoosier Poet.

A recollection by Kate Milner Babb, described Riley in the 1880's on two occasions when he was giving entertainments in town halls throughout the state. He was in the Bloomington town hall for one entertainment when she was in college. She remembered his changes of expression, how the "slender young man" changed his mien to a wrinkled old farmer with his voice until, if one's eyes were shut, he would be sure that several persons were on the stage. She called the period the end of the "elocutionist era" when traveling stage shows ventured from town to town but said "no elocutionist I had ever heard could compare with him." She remembered the next time he came to Bloomington, he was with Bill Nye who introduced their organization as the "poet and his liar." He spoke at the Indiana University chapel and had a large audience unlike the small one at the town hall.

One must always make distinctions in Riley's poetry. A major distinction is in his dialect poetry in which he is writing the way he would say a piece if he were on the platform. The dialect thus is more inflectional and explanatory of the regional distinction than a recast of language. An example is the "Doc Sifers,:" dialectical poem of 1887. A stanza is written, "Of all the doctors I could cite you to in this-'ere town Doc Sifers is my favorite - jes' take him up and down! Count in the Bethel Neighberhood, and Rollins, and Big Bear, And Sifers' standin's jes' as good as ary doctor's there! .."

Four years after Riley's Boston platform appearance, he made his initial appearance before a New York City audience. The entertainment was given in aid of an international copyright law, and the country's most distinguished men of letters took part in the program. It is probably true that no one appearing at that time less known to the vast audience in Chickering Hall than James Whitcomb Riley, but so great and so spontaneous was the enthusiasm when he left the stage after his contribution to the first day's program, that the management immediately announced a place would be made for Mr. Riley on the second and last day's program. It was then that James Russell Lowell introduced him.

ASSESSMENT OF RILEY

"Ladies and gentlemen: I have very great pleasure in presenting to you the next reader of this afternoon, Mr. James Whitcomb Riley, of Indiana. I confess, with no little chagrin and sense of my own loss, that when yesterday afternoon, from this platform, I presented him to a similar assemblage, I was almost completely a stranger to his poems. But since that time I have been looking into the volumes that have come from his pen, and in them I have discovered so much of high worth and tender quality that I deeply regret I had not long before made acquaintance with his work. To-day, in presenting Mr. Riley to you, I can say to you of my own knowledge, that you are to have the pleasure of listening to the voice of a true poet."

Before this performance, Lowell was quoted as remarking to a friend, "Why have I not heard of Riley? Tell me all you know about him. I sat up last night till two o'clock reading his verse. Nothing that the poets have written in this country for years has touched me so deeply as "Knee-Deep in June."

Riley's platform appearances continued to increase in frequency. Before joining with Bill Nye we have a record of Riley's itinerary for one Hoosier tour from May 30th into July, 1887. The trip started at Lebanon, and then went to Crawfordsville, Attica, Covington, Terre Haute, Rockville, Vincennes, Evansville, Washington, Columbus, Sullivan, Mitchell, Anderson, Fairmont, Bluffton, Hartford City, Goshen, Huntington, Rochester, North Manchester, Goshen, South Bend, Shelbyville, New Castle, and Cambridge City by July 1st.

Such trips were under the contract with the Western Lyceum Agency, with A.J. Walker his personal manager and traveling companion. This person noted the poet's every move. His arrival times and departure times to the minute, every stay, who he stayed with, what exact amount of money was received, and the name of the train and its line they traveled to the next town.

Riley needed new material since he was returning to the same cities. He believed in dialect and wrote much. We find in the August, 1887 Century Magazine the statement that of all dialectical poetry being written, Riley's use of it in "Nothin' to Say," is an illustration of the only possible excuse for this sort of work," in that "the tender and touching little poem does not depend on the dialect" -but that - "The feeling, the homely pathos of the verse makes it of value, and the dialect is simply its strongest and most fitting expression."

Riley did not realize how lonely his life would be. Riley as Mr. Bryce teamed up with Crestillomeem mightily. He recalled "a dreary midnight at a little station down on the Old Jeff. Road. It was a raw cheerless night. The utter darkness of everything on the outside gave to the stranger a sense of blank desolation...The lonely ticking of the instrument in the office was unbearable...No agent to tell you the train was four hours late. Wait there in those grim, hysterical conditions till three o'clock in the morning as I did and perhaps it will not seem so unclassical in a poet to uncork a calabash,

take a few potations and climb on the train three sheets in the wind." This was an occasion when his managerial agent had not watched him closely.

For 1888, Riley went to New York to make arrangements to team with Bill Nye on the platform stage. Nye and Major Pond were to be the owners of the combination and Riley who always said, "I'm no business man," was to receive $500 a week and his hotel and travelling expenses."

The Nye-Riley combination started in Newark, N.J., November 13, 1888. It was really a trial balloon. The receipts for the engagement were not

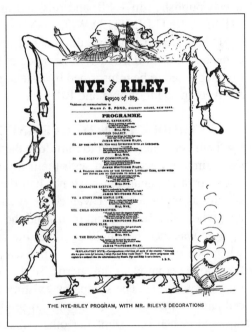

A Nye-Riley program with illustration by James Whitcomb Riley.

much. Both Riley and Nye were from the West. Riley was from Indiana and Nye from Wyoming. Neither had a great reputation in the East. The two blamed Major Pond, their agent, for this initial bust. The next evening the two opened at Orange New Jersey. Major Pond came despite being ill but again there was a very small turnout. At first Nye said he would not go on. Finally after "persuasion" from Major Pond, Nye went on stage. The show was a great success but not much money, only $54 came in.

The third entertainment called for them to appear at an Actor's Fund entertainment along with others. Riley and Nye were the hit of the show over all the other entertainers and from that point, Major Pond stated, "applications began to come in from all over the country, East, West, North and South." The first week's business was in the red but this did not bother Riley at all. Pond stated, "Nye's humorous weekly syndicate newspaper articles made him a drawing attraction, and Riley's delightful readings of his dialect poems made the entertainment all that the public desired."

Riley and Nye developed a friendly working relationship. The two even conspired to produce a humorous book. NYE AND RILEY'S RAILWAY GUIDE contained almost everything except time tables or train routes when it was published in 1888, and reissued under various names, as ON THE SHOESTRING LIMITED WITH NYE AND RILEY.

Others shared in their enjoyment of each other. Mark Twain saw it and explained it in an introduction he made of the two in Boston. This introduction happened to be transcribed by a stenographer employed by Major Pond, the lyceum agent of Nye and Riley.

INTRODUCTION TO NYE AND RILEY PERFORMANCE

"I am very glad indeed to introduce these young people to you, and at the same time get acquainted with them myself. I have seen them more than once, for a moment, but have not had the privilege of knowing them personally as intimately as I wanted to. I saw them first, a great many years ago, when Mr. Barnum had them, and they were just fresh from Siam. The ligature was their best hold then, but literature became their best hold later, when one of them committed an indiscretion, and they had to cut the old bond to accommodate the sheriff. In that old former time this was Chang, that one was Eng. The sympathy existing between the two was most extraordinary; it was so fine, so strong, so subtle, that what the one ate the other digested, when one slept the other snored, if one sold a thing the other scooped the usufruct. This independent and yet dependent action was observable in all the details of their daily life - I mean this quaint and arbitrary distribution of originating cause and resulting effect between the two: between, I may say, this dynamo and this motor. Not that I mean that the one was always dynamo and the other always motor - or, in other words, that the one was always the creating force, the other always the utilizing force; no, no, for while it is true that within certain well-defined zones of activity the one was always dynamo and the other always motor, within certain other well- defined zones these position became exactly reversed. For instance, in moral matters Mr. Chang Riley was always dynamo, Mr. Eng Nye was always motor; for awhile Mr. Chang Riley had a high, in fact an abnormally high and fine, moral sense, he had no machinery to work it within; whereas Mr. Eng Nye, who hadn't any moral sense at all, and hasn't yet, was equipped with all the necessary plant for putting a noble deed through, if he could only get the inspiration on reasonable terms outside. In intellectual matters, on the other hand, Mr. Eng Nye was always dynamo, Mr. Chang Riley was always motor: Mr. Eng Nye had a stately intellect, but couldn't make it go; Mr. Chang Riley hadn't, but could. That is to say, that while Mr. Chang Riley couldn't think things himself, he had a marvellous natural grace in setting them down and weaving them together when his pal furnished the raw material. Thus working together, they made a strong team; laboring together, they could do miracles; but break the circuit, and both were impotent. It has remained so to this day; they must travel together, conspire together, beguile together, hoe, and plant, and plough, and reap, and sell their public together, or there's no result. I have made this explanation, this analysis, this vivisection, so to speak, in order that you may enjoy these delightful adventurers understandingly..."

Nye and Riley teamed up in ways other than alternately performing on stage. Here is an original poem Riley wrote for Nye to include in his comedic act called "The Autumn Leaves Is Falling":

Lo! the autumn leaves is falling,
Falling here and there -
Falling in the atmosphere
And likewise in the air....

In Nye's performance of the poem he would read the poem from a scroll which he unrolled as one does a manuscript. The scroll was ornate with a blue ribbon around it and Nye used his trembling hands to sustain his hold on the scroll and even wore a pair of white cotton gloves on this skit to protect this precious scroll. Nye claimed his reading of "Autumn Leaves" would cause the audience to not only toss pansies, violets and flowers on the stage in gratitude but also potatoes and turnips and tropical shrubs. Nye would read one stanza and retire behind the curtain. After an uproar of laughter he would come back with another stanza, etc.

The two appeared in all of the major cities of the country until April,

1889. At that time, Riley was so ill he did not continue the tour. A long list of bookings had to be cancelled. The stars returned to their homes, and settlements with disappointed committees and local managers absorbed all the profits.

In the next year, Major Pond reported trying it again "and in the season 1889-90 did a tremendous business in Washington and in the South. The combination was a more profitable attraction than any opera or theatrical company."

Riley and Nye were each other's coaches about their performances. They talked at length about improvements to be made. How the voice, gesture, and posture of each might be improved. They learned from each other as friends and never considered the other critical.

TALENT AS A READER

Meredith Nicholson assessed Riley's talent as a reader as hardly second to his creative genius. He attributed them to "the most careful study and experiments; facial play, gesture, shadings of the voice...So vivid were his impersonations and so readily did he communicate the sense of atmosphere, that one seemed to be witnessing a series of dramas with a well-set stage and a diversity of players. He possessed in a large degree the magnetism that is the birthright of great actors; there was something very appealing and winning in his slight figure as he came upon the platform. His diffidence (partly assumed and partly sincere) at the welcoming applause, the first sound of

(The Columbus Press, January 16, 1889.)

NYE AND RILEY—THEIR SPLENDID ENTERTAINMENT LAST EVENING.

"Tell of the things jes' like they wuz—
They don't need no excuse."

The vast concourse of cultured people who assembled last evening at the First Congregational Church—filled every seat, packed the aisles, and stood in every vacant place—was an appropriate tribute of appreciation of two men who have done much to make this world happier.

Nye and Riley! What an inimitable couple they are! The drollery of Nye is delightful and the versatility of Riley captures everybody. One could not write of their entertainment with justice unless he could find words which in cold type would mean as much to the risibilities of readers and the hearts of men as did the words of Nye and Riley as they were spoken in tones of voice which type can never imitate.

(The Pittsburg, Pa., Post, December 18, 1888.)

AN EVENING WITH THE WITS.

Lafayette Hall was packed like a box of dried herring, and everybody who had room enough to laugh did so to the limit. Even Bill smiled in a surprised way, evidently startled at the result of his spontaneous wit. It had escaped him unawares. The bubble was blown unbidden.

Somebody has said that Bill Nye cannot lecture. Somebody don't know. His lank form, and polished dome of thought, as he fondly terms his joke box, combine upon the stage the sort of success that succeeds in making sides sore. But if Nye's dry wit and nasal drawl are funny, James Whitcomb Riley's Hoosier sonnets are that, and more. If the sonnets lack anything, his superb mimicry supplies it. Between these two funny men a couple of thousand people were all torn up by mirth last night.

(The New York Herald, February 22, 1889.)

HUMORISTS AT STEINWAY HALL.

Every seat was filled and every inch of standing room occupied in Steinway Hall last night by spectators who laughed until they were threatened with pleurisy and lockjaw at the eccentric yarns of Bill Nye and the dialect recitations in verse of James Whitcomb Riley, the "Hoosier poet." If their reception last night could be taken as a measure of continued metropolitan success they certainly have "struck it rich."

(The Boston Herald, March 1, 1889.)

TICKLED BOSTON'S FUNNY BONE.

The entertainment given by Messrs. Bill Nye and James Whitcomb Riley at Tremont Temple last evening attracted an immense house, and proved to be highly enjoyable. The programme was a splendid one, and a more mirth provoking one has rarely, if ever, been presented in this city. "Mark Twain" came up especially from Hartford to introduce the two readers, and his illusions to them as Chang and Eng of Barnum fame was capitally worked up and carried out.

Press summaries of the Riley-Nye team in Columbus, Ohio; Pittsburg, Pennsylvania; New York City, New York; and Boston, Massachusetts. (From a lyceum circuit program – Courtesy, Spcial Collections Dept., Rare Books, Alderman Library, Univ. of Virginia.)

his voice as he tested it with the few introductory sentences he never omitted - these spoken haltingly as he removed and disposed of his glasses - all tended to pique curiosity and win the house to the tranquillity his delicate art demanded. ...Riley's programs consisted of poems of sentiment and pathos, such as "Good-bye Jim" and "Out to Old Aunt Mary's," varied with humorous stories in prose or verse which he told him inimitable skill and without a trace of buffoonery. Riley usually appeared with other platform artists. Richard Malcolm Johnston, Eugene Field and Robert J. Burdette were sometimes paired with Riley, but he was most known for joint appearances with Edgar W. ("Bill") Nye."

The poem referred to as "Good-Bye Jim" became more formally known as "The Old Man and Jim." It became one of the most popular poems ever written with a Civil War subject.

THE OLD MAN AND JIM (1888)

Old man never had much to say -
  'Ceptin to Jim, -
And Jim was the wildest boy he had -
  And the old man jes' wrapped up in him!
Never heerd him speak but once
Er twice in my life, - and first time was
When the army broke out, and Jim he went,
The old man backin' him, fer three months[1];
And all 'at I heerd the old man say
Was, jus' as we turned to start away, -
  "Well, good-by, Jim:
    Take keer[2] of yourse'f!"

'Peared-like, he was more satisfied
  Jes' lookin' at Jim
And likin' him all to hisse'f-like, see? -
  'Cause he was jes' wrapped up in him!
And over and over I mind the day
The old man come and stood round in the way
While we was drillin'[3], a-watchin' Jim -
And down at the deepot[4] a-heerin' him say'
  "Well, good-by Jim:

Take keer of yourse'f!"

Never was nothin' about the farm
  Disting'ished Jim; Neighbors all ust to wonder why
  The old man 'peared wrapped up in him:
But when Cap. Biggler he writ back
'At Jim was the bravest boy we had
In the whole dern rigiment, white er black, [5]
And his fightin' good as his farmin' bad -
'At he had led, with a bullet clean
Bored through his thigh, and carried the flag [6]
Through the bloodiest battle you ever seen. -
The old man wound up a letter to him
'At Cap. read to us, 'at said:
  "Tell Jim Good-by,
    And take keer of hisse'f!"

Jim come home jes' long enough
  To take the whim
'At he'd like to go back in the calvery [7] -
  And the old man jes' wrapped up in him!
Jim' lowed 'at he'd had sich luck afore,
Guessed he'd tackle her three years more.
And the old man give him a colt he'd raised,
And follered him over to Camp Ben Wade, [8]
And laid around fer a week er so,
Watchin' Jim on dress-parade -
Tel finally he rid away,
And last he heerd was the old man say, -
  "Well, good-by, Jim:
    Take keer of yourse'f!"

Tuk the papers, the old man did
  A-watchin' fer Jim -
Fully believin' he'd make his mark
  Some way - 'jes wrapped up in him! -
And many a time the word 'u'd come
'At stirred him up like the tap of a drum -

At Petersburg,[9] fer instance, where
Jim rid right into their cannons there,
And tuk 'em, and p'inted 'em t'other way,
And socked it home to the boys in gray,
As they scooted fer timber, and on and on -
Jim a lieutenant and one arm gone,[10]
And the old man's words in his mind all day, -
  "Well, good-by Jim:
    Take keer of yourse'f!"

Think of a private, now, perhaps,
  We'll say like Jim,
'At's clumb clean up to the shoulder-straps[11] -
  And the old man jes' wrapped up in him!
Think of him - with the war plum' through,
And the glorious old Red-White-and-Blue
A-laughin' the news down over Jim,
And the old man, bendin' over him -
The surgeon turnin' away with tears
'At hadn't leaked fer years and years,
As the hand of the dyin' boy clung to
His father's, the old voice in his ears, -
  "Well, good-by, Jim:
    Take keer of yourse'f!"

1. When the Civil War broke out, few expected the South to last long. Volunteers were called initially for three months. The main result of the service of the "three months" soldiers was the work of the Ohio and Hoosier regiments sent into the western counties of Confederate Virginia which resulted in the breaking off of the area into a new political unit, then State, now called West Virginia. The deployment saved the vital Ohio River for the North.

2. "care" in Hoosier vernacular.

3. Learning to march and respond to commands about

The Petersburg trenches where "Jim" lost an arm during a rebel assault and died after surger. Petersburg was one of the last battles of the Civil War as Riley's readers were aware. (From HARPER'S WEEKLY)

weapons.

4. Civil War era soldiers moved by train whose stations were called depots.

5. "black" referred to African-Americans who served in Northern ranks along with Caucasian-Americans (whites) unlike the Southern Army which allowed African-Americans to serve on the battlefields only as servants to officers.

6. Carrying a unit flag was dangerous because it make the bearer a choice target. To carry the flag meant the bearer was deemed very brave. The bearer led the charging troops who followed wherever the flag was carried.

7. Calvary troops rode horses often initially supplied by the cavalryman's family.

8. Camp Ben Wade

9. Petersburg was about the last battle of the Civil War. The listeners or readers of this poem would realize that Jim had just about made it to the end of the war. The Southern capital of Richmond was close to Petersburg so if Petersburg fell as it did on Richmond and the Southern government fell too.

10. Without antibiotics to fight infection, many soldiers who required surgery died during the American Civil War. The prognosis was never optimistic, if one suffered a wound and an arm or leg had to be amputated.

11, A shoulder strap was the epaulet which an officer wore. This marked Jim as such a notable soldier that he was given a battlefield commission.

Rank and file Union soldiers.

Any anthology of poetry that does not include this poem as one of the key ones concerning the Civil War period is simply a failure. The poem was first published in Riley's famous volume, "Poems Here at Home," of 1893. The alternate title, "Good Bye Jim," was used when the poem was issued in its own book with illustrations by Howard Chandler Christy in 1913.

Another special piece of Mr. Bryce was "The Old Soldier's Story" composed and rehearsed in Macon, Georgia, at the Lanier House there in 1888. It has become especially associated with Riley. Its composition occurred after Riley refused to go with Nye on an informal outing with a local committee sponsoring the two at a reading. Riley said he was too tired. As his secretary describes Riley's own explanation, "When we (Riley and Nye) went down to dinner, I made up my mind I would tell Nye another stale story, such a story as I knew he had been feeding on that afternoon. I had, unbeknownst to him, been rehearsing the story for several days. I began to tell him as earnestly as though it was newer than the hour, the oldest story I ever heard. I heard a clown tell it in the Robinson and Lake Circus when I was a boy, and the first eternity only knows how old it had to be before a clown would be allowed to use it. Nye heard it long before he ever heard me tell it - the old man's story of the soldier carrying his wounded comrade off the battlefield. Well, I dragged the story out as long as I could, just to weary Nye; told it in the forgetful fashion of an old man with confused memory; told the point two or three times before I came to it; went back again to pick up dropped stitches in the web; wandered and maundered, made it as long and dreary as I knew how. Nye received the narrative with convulsions of merriment. He choked over his meat and drink until he quit trying to eat and just listened, giggled, chuckled and roared. He declared it was the best thing he had ever heard me do and insisted that I put it in our program....A week later, at Louisville, Kentucky, I think it was, I told the story to a thousand people. In theatrical parlance, the galleries fell, the house went wild and I had to tell it again."

I include here "The Old Soldier's Story" from a version recorded in Riley's rendition before the New England Society in New York City.

THE OLD SOLDIER'S STORY

"Since we have had no stories to-night I will venture, Mr. President, to tell a story that I have heretofore heard at nearly all the banquets I have ever attended. It is a story simply, and you must bear with it kindly. It is a story as told by a friend of us all, who is found in all parts of all countries, who is immoderately fond of a funny story, and who, unfortunately, attempts to tell a funny story himself - one that he had been particularly delighted with. Well, he is not a story-teller, and especially he is not a funny story-teller. His funny stories, indeed, are oftentimes touchingly pathetic.

"The Coffee Call," by Winslow Homer (1864) from his American Civil War "Campaign Sketches."

But to such a story as he tells, being a good-natured man and kindly disposed, we have to listen, because we do not want to wound his feelings by telling him that we have heard that story a great number of times, and that we have heard it ably told by a great number of people from the time we were children. But, as I say, we can not hurt his feelings. We can not stop him. We can not kill him; and so the story generally proceeds. He selects a very old story always, and generally tells it in about this fashion: -

I heerd an awful funny thing the other day - ha! ha! I don't know whether I kin git it off er not, but, anyhow, I'll tell it to you. Well! le's see now how the fool-thing goes. Oh, yes! - W'y, there was a feller one time - it was during the army and this feller that I started in to tell you about was in the war and - ha! ha! there was a big fight a-goin' on, and this feller was in the fight, and it was a big battle and bullets a-flyin' ever' which way, and bombshells a- bustin', and cannon-balls a-flyin' 'round promiskus; and this feller right in the midst of it, you know, and all excited and het up, and chargin' away; and the fust thing you know along come a cannon-ball and shot his head off - ha! ha! ha! Hold on here a minute! no, sir; I'm a gittin' ahead of my story; no; no; it didn't shoot his head off - I'm gittin' the cart before the horse there - shot his leg off; that was the way; shot his leg off; and down the poor feller drapped, and of course, in that condition was perfectly he'pless, you know, but yit with presence o' mind enough to know that he was in a dangerous condition ef somepin' wasn't done fer him right away. So he seen a comrade a-chargin' by that he knowed, and he hollers to him and called him by name - I disremember now what the feller's name was...

Well, that's got nothin' to do with the story, anyway; he hollers to him, he did, and says "Hello, there," he says to him; "here, I want you to come here and give me a lift; I got my leg shot off, and I want you to pack me back to the rear of the battle" - where the doctors always is, you know, during a fight - and he says, "I want you to pack me back there where I can get meddy-cinal attention er I'm a dead man, fer I got my leg shot off," he says, "and I want you to pack me back there so's the surgeons kin take keer of me." Well - the feller, as luck would have it, ricko'nized him and run to him, and throwed down his own musket, so's he could pick him up; and he stooped down and picked him up and kindo' half-way helt him betwixt his arms like, and then he turned and started back with him - ha! ha! ha! Now, mind, the fight was still a-goin' on - and right at the hot of the fight, and the feller, all excited, you know, like he was, and the soldier that had his leg short off gittin' kindo' fainty like, and his head kindo' stuck back over the feller's shoulder that was carryin' him. And he hadn't got more'n a couple o' rods with him when another cannon-ball come along and tuk his head off, shore enough! - and the curioust thing about it was - ha! ha!- that the feller was a-packin' him didn't know that he had been hit ag'in at all, and back he went - still carryin' the deceased back - ha! ha! ha! - to where the doctors could take keer of him - as he thought. Well, his cap'n happened to see him, and he thought it was ruther cur'ous p'ceeding's-a soldier carryin' a dead body out o' the fight -don't you see? And so he hollers at him, and he says to the soldier, the cap'n did, he says, "Hullo, there; where you goin' with that thing?" the cap'n said to the soldier who was a-carryin' away the feller that had his leg shot off. Well, his head, too, by that time. So he says, "Where you goin' with that thing?" the cap'n said to the soldier who was a-carryin' away the feller that had his leg shot off. Well, the soldier he stopped -kinder halted, you know, like a private soldier will when his presidin' officer speaks to him - and he says to him, "W'y," he says, "Cap, its a comrade o' mine and the pore feller has got his leg shot off, and I'm a-packin' him back to where the doctors is; and there was nobody to he'p him, and the feller would 'a'died in his tracks - er track ruther - if it hadn't a-been fer me, and I'm a packin' him back where the surgeons can take keer of him; where he can get medical attendance - er his wife's a widder!" he says, "'cause he's got his leg shot off!" Then Cap'n says, "You blame fool you, he's got his head shot off." So then the feller slacked his grip on the body and let it slide down to the ground, and looked at it a minute, all puzzled, you know, and says, "W'y, he told me it was his leg!" Ha! ha! ha!"

Comedians who tried to repeat Riley's success were unsuccessful. His hesitations, chuckles and bewitching laughter as he proceeded, his "ha-haing" as the narrator etc. were part of its telling lost to history.

Mark Twain, a fellow humorist of the epoch, who heard Riley tell it before three thousand people in the Tremont Temple, Boston, wrote of Riley's "Old Soldier's Story," in his chapter "How To Tell a Story:" "In comic-story form the story is not worth the telling. Put into the humorous-story form it takes ten minutes, and is about the funniest thing I ever listened to - as James Whitcomb Riley tells it. He tells it in the character of a dull-witted old farmer who has just heard it for the first time, who is innocent and happy and pleased with himself, and as to stop every little while to hold himself in and keep from laughing outright; and does hold in, but his body quakes in a jelly-like way with interior chuckles and at the end of the ten minutes the audience laughed until they are exhausted, and the tears ran down their faces. The simplicity and innocence and sincerity and unconsciousness of the old farmer are perfectly simulated, and the result is a performance which is thoroughly charming and delicious. This is art - and fine and beautiful, and only a master can compass it; but a machine could tell the other story."

I detail an example of the performances of Riley and Nye. This one was from Gilmore's Opera House, in Springfield, Massachusetts, of February 26, 1889:

PROGRAMME

I. Simply a Personal Experience - Bill Nye
II. Studies in Hoosier Dialect - James Whitcomb Riley
III. At this Point Mr. Nye Will Interfere With an Anecdote -
  Bill Nye
IV. The Poetry of Commonplace - James Whitcomb Riley
V. One of the Author's Literary Gems, Given Without Notes
  and No Gestures to Speak of - Bill Nye
VI. Character Sketch - James Whitcomb Riley
VII. A Story from Simple Life - Bill Nye
VIII. Child Eccentricities - James Whitcomb Riley
IX. Something Else - Bill Nye
X. The Educator - James Whitcomb Riley

Major Pond has recorded one of the entertaining times that Riley and Nye had with each other.

RILEY PLAYING DEAF

"I remember when we (Pond, Nye, Riley) were riding together, in the smoking compartment, between Columbus and Cincinnati. Mr. Nye was a great smoker and Mr. Riley did not dislike tobacco. An old farmer came over to Mr. Nye and said:

"Are you Mr. Riley?" I heard you was on the train."

"No, I am not Mr. Riley. He is over there."

"I knew his father, and I would like to speak with him."

"Oh, speak with him, yes. But he is deaf, and you want to speak loud."

So the farmer went over to him and said in a loud voice:

"Is this Mr. Riley?"

"Er, what?"

"Is this Mr. Riley?"

"What did you say?"
"Is this Mr. Riley?"
"Riley, oh! yes." "I knew your father."
"No bother."
"I knew your father."
"What?"
"I knew your father!"
"Oh, so did I."

Riley's platform partnership breakup with Bill Nye in Louisville, Kentucky in January 1890 was mentioned earlier as one of Crestillomeem's tricks and we refer to it here only because it was so damaging to the psyche of Mr. Bryce. Riley had been found publicly intoxicated in public and the press filled the newspapers with it.

Would Riley ever dare to show his face again? He referred to himself as a "fallen skyrocket." In the flurry of the publicity, Riley decided to make a statement. He said, "I desire to stand before the public only as I am. My weaknesses are known, and I am willing for the world to judge whether in my life or writings there has been anything dishonorable. I do not say that in this blight which has fallen on me, I am innocent of blame. I have been to some degree derelict and culpable. The whole affair is to be regretted and for the present I have to accept the responsibility. I have always been a firm believer in the doctrine that ruin, where undeserved, can be but temporary, and now I have an opportunity to see my belief tested. I do not desire to say anything harsh of anybody, and for the present, at least, am content to wait for better things. I am sustained by the renewed expressions of affection from my friends."

Would Mr. Bryce's mistake be forgiven?

The question was answered when the Indianapolis Literary Club decided to hold a reception for Riley "in the face" of all the bad press. At this reception the most noted persons of Indianapolis expressed great affection and forbearance for what had happened. Riley's great lawyer friend William Fishback was one of those speakers and he publicly assured Riley of the Club's great regard. Judge Livingstone Howland also spoke and commented that if Fishback was touched by Riley's poetic powers, then Riley had to be a poetic genius. By the close of the reception Riley had regained his peace of mind that he could appear in public again. In fact he recited two pieces, "Tradin' Joe" and "The Little Man in the Tin Shop." The word went out in the press that Riley was not down for the count. The Chicago MAIL reported that Riley was still the "king on his native heath, despite derogatory reports." Other press around the country echoed like sentiments.

The American public continued to talk about the Riley- Nye breakup for many months. In the meantime, Nye had picked a new partner who did not suffer from Riley's alcoholism. The man's name was Burbank and when the Nye-Burbank team arrived in Indianapolis on April 8, 1891, Riley introduced them to their Indianapolis audience and also got on stage and entertained right along with them. A reporter quoted Nye more than a year after their breakup, "He hoped that now the press of the country would attack some other great national issue - the silver issue, for instance - to the exclusion of the Nye-Riley question." (As quoted in the Indianapolis JOURNAL of April 8, 1891.)

The same article continues:

"The Indianapolis public never has anything but the warmest of welcomes for James Whitcomb Riley and his portion of the entertainment was insufficient for the demands of last night's audience which would gladly have listened to much more than he could have offered. The inimitable prose description of the "general store" in a country town and his amiable discussion in rhyme of the tastes of a number of characters easily recognized as having their counterpart in every village, furnished much amusement and were rapturously applauded. His sketch of the story-telling bore was equally as well received, their being an accompaniment of laughter to almost every sentence of the story. Mr. Riley also recited something he has never before given to the public - a poem entitled "Decoration Day on the Place" and which is a fitting companion piece to "Good-bye Jim." At the conclusion of his closing number the applause was so loud and long continued that Mr. Riley was compelled, after returning his thanks for the demonstrations of favor, to inform the audience that he had nothing further of a suitable nature to offer and to suggest that the programme was quite long enough."

DECORATION DAY ON THE PLACE (1891)

It's lonesome - sorto' lonesome, - it's a Sund'y-day, to me,
It 'pears-like-more'n any day I nearly ever see! -
Yit, with the Stars and Stripes above, a flutterin' in the air,
On ev'ry Soldier's grave I'd love to lay a lily thare.

They say, though, Decoration Days is giner'ly observed
'Most ev'rywheres - espeshally by soldier-boys that's served. -
But me and Mother's never went - we seldom git away, -
In p'int o' fact, we're allus home on Decoration Day.

They say the old boys marches through the streeets in colum's grand,
A'follerin' the old war-tunes they're playin' on the band -
And citizuns all jinin' in - and little childern, too -
All marchin', under shelter of the old Red White and Blue. -
With roses! roses! roses! - ev'rybody in the town! -
And crowds o' little girls in white, jest fairly loaded down! -
Oh! don't The Boys know it, from theyr camp acrost the hill? -
Don't they see theyr com'ards comin' and the old flag wavin' still? -
Oh! can't they hear the bugul and the rattle of the drum? -
Ain't they no way under heavens they can rickollect us some?
Ain't they no way we can coax 'em through the roses, jest to say
They know that ev'ry day on earth's theyr Decoration Day?

We've tried that - me and Mother, - whare Elias takes his rest,
In the orchurd - in his uniform, and hands acrost his brest,
And the flag he died fer, smilin' and a-ripplin' in the breeze
Above his grave - and over that, - the robin in the trees!

And yit it's lonesome - lonesome! It's a Sund'y-day, to me,
It 'pears-like- more'n any day I nearly ever see! -
Still, with the Stars and Stripes above, a-flutterin' in the air,
On ev'ry soldier's grave I'd love to lay a lily thare.

Later that year, on October 8, 1891, Riley gave this same poem in Chicago at a banquet of the society of the Army of the Tennessee. After Riley's delivery, it was said the audience arose as one man and waved their napkins until the assembly hall appeared to be a sea of waving linen. A Chicago INTER OCEAN editorial says of the event, "The really great hit of the evening was James Whitcomb Riley's tribute to the men who did the actual fighting. There was not a commonplace sentence spoken by him and the poem with which he closed deserves a place in the little classics of American literature."

Riley was not always acclaimed by the literary reviewers of his time.

Perhaps his greatest detractor was Ambrose Bierce, the critic of the San Francisco EXAMINER at the time Riley made his first lecture tour to the Pacific coast late in 1892. James Whitcomb Riley was from nowhere to Bierce. Reviewing Riley's readings at San Francisco, Bierce laid into Riley bad. Ambrose was said to do this every now and then on his "bad hair days." Bierce admitted he hated dialect poetry with a passion. He called Riley the leader of "the pignoramous crew of malinguists and cacophonologoists who think they get close to nature by depicting the sterile lines and limited motions of the gowks and sod hoppers that speak only to tangle their tongues, and move only to fall over their own feet." Riley was "The Bard of Hoop-Pole County, Indiana."

Bierce wrote of Riley:

"Riley has not written a line of poetry. His pathos is bathos, his sentiment is sediment, his diction is without felicity, his vocabulary not English - in short, Mr. Riley writes through his nose....I already know that Mr. Riley was precious to the gowlage of Indiana-by-the sea...First stanza of a poem o' his'n entitltyed `Up and Down Old Brandywine,' which appears, plague-spotted with `half tones' in the way of COSMOPOLITAN.

Of Riley's `rot,' `O, critic mine, I ne'er did scrawl or
        preach;
He speaks it, doubtless - write it he does not;
For tongue and pen have different proprieties of speech,
And the stuff that Riley wrongly writes is WROT."

Of course, Ambrose Bierce didn't like anybody and nobody much liked him either. Bierce built his curiously powerful reputation on being an obnoxious semi-dilettante whose criticism of others was cleverly fun to read.

Intermittent short tours continued until 1903. In the fall of that year Mr. Bryce made his last "reading" tour which started and ended in Indiana. Frankfort, Indiana was the first stop. The tour then continued through several cities in Indiana and Michigan to Detroit. Then the tour struck into Ohio to Toledo and Dayton and Cincinnati and on to Pittsburg, Pennsylvania. The final stops were in the west in Illinois, Iowa and into Kansas where Riley's largest audience ever was at Topeka at that city's Toler Auditorium. On the way back to Indiana, Riley gave a reading at Kansas City, Missouri before terminating the tour at Logansport in Indiana on December 14, 1903. Then Mr. Bryce died of fatigue and Riley could simply not resurrect him again.

Riley had conceived of the character Mr. Bryce in his Buzz Club series of 1878 in the same series in which "The Flying Islands of the Night" appeared. Riley described this role to be "a gentleman, a genius and an artist all combined in a music-box of nature and a masterwork of mind. A drawing star whose brilliance shall permeate the gloom of - of histrionic history, and - and- but why continue in a vein of prophetic possibilities whose length is simply boundless."

The year 1903 saw the "simply boundless" career of Mr. Bryce come to its bound. The "run" had been long and successful even if it was "fatiguing" and shared with Crestillomeem as well as Spraivoll, Dwainie and AEo.

Riley's body being prepared for transport to the Indiana statehouse under the watchful eye of Greenfield undertaker, Chancy F. Pasco (center).

KRUNG

THE PROBLEM OF FAME; A KING OF POETRY WHO IS ALSO DEPRESSED, ALCOHOLIC AND LIVING AS DEAD SELVES

BECOMING A COMFORTING "PEOPLE'S POET" OF AN ESTRANGED PEOPLE AS AN ACT OF A SOUL-SELF

Riley wanted to be Krung the most of any soul-self he play-acted in his life. Riley had so needed comfort himself that he wished to trade in this commodity with his own estranged American people. Krung is the Riley "reputable man" worthy of public fame and honor. He was a man entrusted with singing music to the souls of others. With the help of his "soul partners" encouraging him in the sight of God - Nellie and his mother, Elizabeth - Riley wished upon himself the soul-self role of becoming the American "People's Poet." My gut feeling is that Riley wished this because he saw the American people as so adrift after the American Civil War. His work was "humanizing."

This goal was reached in his own lifetime. It was necessary for him to be a poet to carry this role off. In his epoch, unlike ours, poets were given roles in the common lives of the bourgeois. A poet was allowed to comfort others just as priests had once done in society or ministering angels had been thought to do for the wayward human spirit. In Riley's day, for example, it was customary for a poet to eulogize the dead with a poem. A great bulk of Riley's poetry is funerary. Krung filled his poetry of this genre with comforting messages of comfort and kenotic hope.

He felt himself a "vessel" in these writings. He wrote in the world of the reality of the Incarnation which broke through into his expression. Once his friend Lee O. Harris's daughter Anna Randall died and Riley was up all night composing a poem for her services. There was one word he was not satisfied with but he finally had to turn the poem in to the minister. A little later he thought of the word he wanted but the funeral had begun. Riley concentrated on the desired word and had it in mind when the Presbyterian minister read his poem. Low and behold the minister did not read the written word but the one supplied in its place by the poet's mind. Riley was convinced that the spirit world helped him in his mission to comfort the needful.

Riley became Krung because his kenotic folk-songs struck the souls of so many others. Riley's poetry was literally on the lips of the nation. His poetry carried the message of Incarnation Theology "Hope," a commodity vitally needed in an America assuming more and more responsibility for world order as well as struggling with the need for a ground of peace within its borders. In the year before Riley's death, the President of the United

States, Woodrow Wilson, took time out from worries over World War I threatening to draw America in and the German submarine fleet in the Atlantic which had sunk the American ship LUSITANIA in the May before to send a birthday greeting for a dinner for Riley. "I wish that I might be present to render my tribute of affectionate appreciation to him for the many pleasures he has given me, along with the rest of the great body of readers of English. I think he has every reason to feel on his birthday that he has won the hearts of his countrymen. Woodrow Wilson." The nation's Vice President, Charles Fairbanks, had organized this particular birthday dinner in Indianapolis for Riley October 7, 1915 and was its toastmaster. In his last years, Riley was treated with greater honor than any poet in history.

James Whitcomb Riley as "Krung". Taken at Washington D.C., Jan. 11, 1910, when Riley read the poem, "General Lew Wallace," at the unveiling of Wallace's statue in Statuaary Hall, the capital. The speakers were Indiana's Governor Marshall, Senator Albert J. Beveridge, Riley, and Rev. Lloyd C. Douglas, author of *The Magnificent Obsession.* Later that year, on July 10th Riley suffered a stroke which rendered his left side paralyzed for the rest of his life. Riley with his poetry and Wallace with his portrayal of the "humble Christ" of his novel *Ben Hur* were the two primary kenotic authors of the Nineteenth Century.

Where did Riley's strange yearning to become Krung and comfort a people reeling from a civil war come from?

I think it was an odd legacy from his father. His father was such a glorious "wounded" figure. Reuben Riley was a true Civil War hero. He had an unstained reputation for high moral standing. At every choice of paths, Reuben took the turn on the "high road."

...and yet, Reuben Riley was a complicated man too. To the son, Reuben might be a shining knight, but he was a penniless one who simply was too weak to re-enter the lists after the American Civil War. Reuben could not support his family.

It seems impossible to understand James Whitcomb Riley without trying to understand that he was a child of the American Civil War and more specifically of his father, Reuben Riley, who participated and was "broken" in it as were so many other Americans. The whole fabric of the American nation was rent by that event. Someone needed to start doing some "stitching."

James Whitcomb Riley, as Krung, was born in West Virginia at the minor Civil War Battle of Rich Mountain, Virginia. It was at this minor battle that Reuben Riley, the poet's father, saw combat so shocking to his sensibilities that he suffered post-traumatic stress syndrome the rest of his life. This impoverished his family. A loving father, Reuben was not a breadwinner thereafter. The Riley family lost its comfortable middle-class home that Reuben had built before the war. The family

LATE CAPTAIN R. A. RILEY. OF GREENFIELD.

Drawing by Will Vawter, Greenfield-born artist, of the Poet's father. Reuben Riley, near the time of his death in December, 1893.

moved from place to place - wherever shelter could be found.

And yet this sad invalid combat veteran of a father of Riley's was nevertheless a great warrior, national savior and symbol of his country to James Whitcomb Riley's eyes. Reuben Riley in fact had a public presence that in many ways overcame his personal disabilities. He was strangely and enigmatically both a much admired and woefully pitied person after the American Civil War. How could Riley measure up to such an enigmatic father figure? If one once participates in battle to serve not just his nation but also a perceived will of God that slavery be ended by war since it could not be ended by peace, how can he be approached to be a father?

And yet the son wanted to achieve or surpass the small glory that Reuben Riley achieved in his life. The boy wanted to whip his father. Perhaps all male children do.

We cannot judge Krung on the same ruler with the other Riley acted soulselves because Krung is so very unique.

Krung would become the "wealthy" Riley and his father's child. None of the other members of Riley's "self" cast dreamed of having a cent. Spraivoll preferred to live in a humble estate. Krung would be the fastidious dresser where the other selves in Riley's cast of characters had to wear what could be borrowed. Jucklet's wardrobe was sometimes depleted when his overcoat was required as security for payment of food or lodging when Riley's pockets were empty in his wandering days. Crestillomeem was oblivious to it all.

The genius who can write to become famous and not be subject to alcoholism of Riley was in "Krung." Krung organized the realm of Riley for the public. Krung represents the Riley of "Fame." He is not a figure of power but rather of notice by the public. He is an "officially reputable person." Someone not only his father, but someone who Riley's admired Abraham Lincoln, as well as the American people, would be proud of. Krung always held to the right above the wrong as in "John Walsh." Krung knew that there is a recoil from the dregs of alcoholism as in "Dead Selves." Krung had a sense about fame and its possibility which had to do with redemption.

Riley wrote the following poem to explore the subject:

FAME (1877)

I

Once, in a dream, I saw a man
  With haggard face and tangled hair,
And eyes that nursed as wild a care
  As gaunt Starvation ever can;
And in his hand he held a wand[1]
  Whose magic touch gave life and thought
  Unto a form his fancy wrought
And robed with coloring so grand
  It seemed the reflex of some child
Of Heaven, fair and undefiled -
A face of purity and love -
To woo him into worlds above:
And as I gazed with dazzled eyes,
  A gleaming smile lit up his lips
  As his bright soul from its eclipse
Went flashing into Paradise.
Then tardy Fame came through the door
And found a picture - nothing more.[2]

Riley would eventually join other Hoosier writers of Indiana's "Golden Age of Literature". Left to right, James Whitcomb Riley, George Ade, Meredith Nicholson, and Booth Tarkington.

... And this is Fame! A thing, indeed,
That only comes when least the need:
The wisest minds of every age
The book of life from page to page

Have searched in vain; each lesson conned
Will promise it the page beyond -
Until the last, when dusk of night
Falls over it, and reason's light
Is smothered by that unknown friend
Who signs his nom de plume, The End.

1. The magic wand to the painter is his brush.
2. Fame came to the painter after his death. Riley's first biographer, Marcus Dickey, said of this poem: "the poetic deity comes tardily through the door to crown a homeless, lifeless artist and sculptor."

What glory was it that fame might bring?

Let us look at the father's accomplishments to gauge the son's.

Reuben Riley brought together the first military company to be recruited in Indiana after the fall of Fort Sumter.

Reuben Riley was a "mover" and "chomped at the bit" to enter the Civil War on the side of the Union.

At the very outbreak of violence at Fort Sumter, the newspaper in Riley's hometown of Greenfield, The Hancock DEMOCRAT, roared with this announcement:

"Attention Fellow Citizens! Reuben A. Riley, Esq., is making an effort, with the assurance of success, to recruit a company to represent old Hancock in the struggle for the maintenance of law. We hope that he will be as successful in the field as in the forum." Thereafter, Riley went around the county with a fife-and-drum

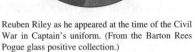

Reuben Riley as he appeared at the time of the Civil War in Captain's uniform. (From the Barton Rees Pogue glass positive collection.)

corps to recruit and got a Captain's Commission from his friend Governor Oliver P. Morton.

Military records show Reuben Riley mustered in at age 42 as Captain, Co. I, 8th Regiment, Indiana Infantry (3 months service in 1861). Riley was enrolled in Greenfield, Indiana on April 18, 1861 and mustered onto the company roll on April 22, 1861. Upon leaving Greenfield, the women of the town presented Reuben Riley with a battle flag they sewed for his company to carry to remember the home folks.

From the Official Records of the War of the Rebellion we find that Reuben Riley's Eighth Indiana Volunteer Regiment joined an Ohio regiment and two other Hoosier Regiments on a frontal attack of Rich Mountain under the command of the Union General Rosecrans. The Report of George B. McClellan, the overall commander of the "Army of Occupation of Western Virginia" of July 14th to his Headquarters details a 4 o'clock in the morning movement by Reuben's attacking force. "The men were ordered to break through the heavy brush and thickets at the foot of the lofty summit to reach Hart's farm at the top about five miles away and once there to sweep down the other side to attack rebel entrenchments from the rear."

The report states, "(Rosecrans) had taken the enemy's position at Hart's farm, from which it appeared that he, with great difficulty and almost superhuman efforts on the part of his men, had forced his way up the precipitous side of the mountain, and at about 1 p.m. reached the summit, where he encountered a portion of the enemy's force, with two guns in position behind earth and log works - affording protection to their men. The attack was commenced by the enemy with heroic spirit and determination. They opened fire upon the advance of our column with volleys of musketry and rapid discharges of canister, killing several of our men, and at first throwing them into some confusion. They, however, soon rallied, and returned a brisk and accurate fire, which told with terrible effect in the enemy's ranks - killing and wounding nearly every man at their guns. The troops then advanced, continuing their well-directed fire, until they drove the enemy from their position, and caused them to take flight down the turnpike towards their entrenchments at the base of the mountain. The troops then encamped on the battle-field at about 2 o'clock p.m. and remained there until the following morning..."

If there was a Civil War battle which the North vitally needed to win it was the battle of Rich Mountain in the mountainous western portion of Virginia. Western Virginia, as the Virginia region west of the Alleghenies was called, was a region in foment. Historically a part of the Confederate State of Virginia, it wanted out. Twenty-five of its county governments wished to secede from Confederate Virginia. Nevertheless, it was occupied by troops loyal to the Confederate state government at Richmond. These troops had to be booted from the region if the local people could choose up sides for the North. The reason the early battles in West Virginia were important was strategic and geographic. If the North was to maintain commerce between East and West, the Baltimore and Ohio Railroad must be protected. This goal required driving the Confederates as far south of its route as possible. If Western Virginia remained Confederate, the Baltimore and Ohio Railroad would not be secure. To win West Virginia, Rich Mountain must be taken. It was the Southernmost strongpoint of the Confederates in western Virginia. The troops of the Confederate General Robert Garnett occupied this mountain as a camp and another twelve miles to the north at Laurel Mountain. From these two sites, the Southern General Garnett commanded all the major east- west, north-south roads in western Virginia.

General George McClellan took personal command of the "three months" federal troops, mainly Ohio and Indiana militia, on June 22d. Dividing them, McClellan orchestrated a feint at Laurel Hill and with his main body attacked Rich Mountain on the night of July 11th. After a brief engagement, the Confederates retreated down the mountain. A Dispatch from Beverly, Virginia of July 13th reports the rebels moving rapidly to Cheat Mountain Pass after burning the bridges at Huntsville and the Cheat Mountain Bridge. At Rich Mountain, one hundred and thirty-one dead were found, some from Georgia and South Carolinians but chiefly Eastern Virginians. On the morning of July 13th, the Southern Commander, Col. Pegram, sent a letter to Gen. McClellan offering to surrender himself and command of six hundred men still left on the site. Most of them were captured as they tried to join their comrades at the other Confederate camp at Laurel Mountain. The Laurel Mountain camp of the Confederates was soon abandoned and the Southern troops groped out of Virginia-leaderless since their general died from a mortal wound in his back - with the three month's federal troops at their heels for the short time left in their enlistments.

Years later, on June 23rd, 1880, in a disability pension application, Reuben Riley described what happened to him at the battle of Rich Mountain of July 11, 1861. "During the progress of the battle, this deponent (Reuben describes himself) received a severe concussion from an exploding shell which was fired by the enemy and exploded very near and to a little above and to the left of his head, staggering and nearly knocking him down. That Lieut. Col Bryant of the 10th Indiana Vol. Fifty was directly under the explosion, fell, was carried off the field insensible and now entirely recovered. That the immediate effect of said concussion was a feeling of numbness followed by coldings and after reaction a roaring as the right ear and severe pain in the right side of the head. That the roaring in the right ear has continued ever since and the pain in the right side of the head and the coldings and numbings of the right side of the body at intervals ever since, that his hearing in the right ear is almost entirely destroyed and the sight of his right eye was clouded and greatly impaired thereby and his nervous system so impaired as to render him unable to perform severe physical or mental labor."

One of the soldiers under Reuben Riley's command has left an account of Reuben's activities at Rich Mountain stating he was with Reuben Riley's company, but on picket duty, all the night before the battle, "in the march in the rear of Camp Garnett of Rich Mountain and in the battle and lay on the battlefield the night after the battle. During the night after the battle Capt. Riley was very ill, weak, cold and scarcely able to walk, that at about midnight this deponent and a cousin (Aaron Hutton, who was afterward killed in battle) placed Capt. Riley on a guttapindia (?) blanket, using another as a covering and lying down one of us on either side of him, on our arms at the head of his Company, And by the natural warmth of our bodies, restoring warmth to him and aiding to that extent in restoring warmth to him and bringing up reaction to and in him. And that he was for a long time after in bad health, just able to walk about....and ever since his last discharge has been in comparative poor health and most of the time an invalid."

/s/Lafayette Slifer

Reuben Riley was mustered out at Indianapolis, Indiana on August 6, 1861 and paid forty two cents to get home.

On August 5, 1861, Hancock County, Indiana, gave a glorious reception to Cpt. Riley's three month men who had just returned from saving West Virginia for the Union. Cpt. Riley responded to the welcome

Reuben Riley's Civil War sword. Courtesy, Riley Museum, Greenfield, Indiana.

address made by Judge Gooding. Riley gave accounts of how his men had passed the time after leaving Camp McClellan. He also described the battle of Rich Mountain. The reception was given in Pierson's Grove on the outskirts of the little village of Greenfield. One can imagine how proud James Whitcomb Riley must have been of his father and how closely he listened when his heroic and wounded father spoke about saving the Union and standing up for Abraham Lincoln.

Over a year later, about August 16, 1862, we find Reuben Riley raising another company from Hancock County young men and entering the regular army again. This time, 80 Hancock Co. men enlisted with Reuben as Captain for three years. Riley was off to war despite his disability from three months duty the year before. One of 2nd Lieutenants was Lee O Harris. Also the Greenfield Saxhorn Band which included William Hart enlisted as a body and the night before they left for Civil War they serenaded the town with a concert playing "Sweet Alice" and "Hazel Dell."

This time Reuben Riley had enlisted for three years. Events would intervene. Army records show Reuben Riley mustering in to the roll of Co. G., 5th Ind. Cav. October 30, 1962. Initially he was appointed as a 2 Lieutenant but was soon promoted because he had been a Captain in three months service. His service with his Cavalry unit operating in Kentucky was however only short days. The month later, November, he was assigned to be a member of court martials in Indianapolis, Indiana and served on these boards until June 16, 1863, the next year.1

Now, in the next summer, that of 1863, Reuben Riley was finally with the troops. His Fifth Indiana Cavalry, with its thousand horsemen, was centered around Glasgow, Kentucky screening the movements of Confederate forces which might wish to thrust North when Reuben arrived. Reuben joined it about the time it was given the mission to interdict the cavalry of General John Hunt Morgan. A great chase was begun when Morgan slipped through Kentucky and crossed the Ohio into Indiana. Reuben Riley was simply not able to function as a cavalryman in this chase. Living in the saddle was not like riding his horse to the courthouse.

A legend in the Riley family had

General John Hunt Morgan, a Tennessean who led Confederate cavalry on a raid across the Ohio River and into Indiana at the time of the battles of Gettysburg and Vicksburg, probably in the vain hope of diverting federal forces into defensive positions in the north. Reuben Riley was among the federal cavalry following Morgan on his mad dash north. The strain of this chase ended Reuben Riley's army career and put him into an officer's hospital in Louisville before his eventual disability discharge. Three young townsmen of close to Riley's age, called up in the emergency from Greenfield, were also killed from this "northern invasion."

Reuben Riley at the Battle of Vicksburg where he captured his own brother, a Confederate surgeon named Dr. John Riley, serving with the Texas forces and arranged to have his brother sent to Alton, Illinois to help care for the wounded soldier's there. This apocryphal story was often told by Dr. John Riley's son, Dr. Joseph Shelby Riley. Vicksburg fell on July 4, 1863. While it was possible therefore that Reuben participated in the Vicksburg campaign, his own war record and particularly his recount of his activities in applying for "leave" militate otherwise. It was not the battle of Vicksburg that did Reuben in but rather the chase of Morgan by the 5th Indiana Cavalry through Kentucky, over the Ohio River into Indiana and then on into Ohio.

It must have been about this time as well that James Whitcomb Riley discovered an "enemy" Confederate being harbored by his beloved grandmother, Margaret Riley, in Greenfield. Riley describes his horror at finding his own uncle in a letter to a cousin, Joe S. Riley, of December 30, 1895 preserved by the Randolph County Historical Society Museum:

AN ENEMY WITH GRANDMOTHER

"(I) visited...Grandmother living alone in her own little - Dame Crump - cottage across the town from my father - then away from home, a Captain, in his country's service - Judge, I ask, of this boy's state of mind, when he discovered this Southern brother of his own father, smoking a very sequestrated but peaceful pipe with the good old mother who adamantly answered my juvenile curiosity regarding her peculiar guest, that it was "John Slick" - an old relative of their Pennsylvania people. - Though, at once, I guessed it was my own father's brother - an escaped prisoner here in the heart of the North - in fair safety, again meeting his old mother from whom he had been separated for years and years. Tacitly therefore I bore about a brave secret for one of my tender years and patriotic training vividly twas I recall his constrained interest in this "son James of Reuben's" - as the very dear, gentle, and utterly lovable old mother and grandmother put it." The man's name was really Dr. John Schleek Riley, the poet's uncle. (Slick, Schleek, etc. Like all Hoosier Deutsch names there simply is no consistent English form.)

The chase of Morgan must have also made a deep impression upon Riley because several of his friends were called up instantly to provide defense for the hometown and three were killed.

One thinks of Greenfield as being so peaceful and lazy in June. The rigors of trying to make it through the winter are over. In Civil War times, the crops were mostly planted. Maybe there was a little cultivating to do. The Agricultural Fair was the big event in the county. It was held in June during that era. Probably three young men by the names of William Hart, Ferdinand Hafner and John Porter were going about their own business. Certainly, they were not imagining the terror that would soon strike town. These three men were not in the Union Army most of which was massed around Gettysburg or in Tennessee. They had absolutely nothing to do with the Civil War. Yet, the next month would find all three dead during service against a Confederate Army which invaded Indiana and was rumored to be on its way up to nearby Indianapolis to arrest the governor and free the Confederate soldiers in prison at Camp Morton there. One of those who witnessed this historic time in Hancock County was James Whitcomb Riley. Riley was 13 when Greenfield received the news that Indiana was invaded by a Confederate army believed heading his way.

What did Riley experience? How did the three civilian young men just slightly older than he was die in service against Morgan's raiders? How did others become wounded and suffer as well? Another unlikely victim of Morgan's Raid was also a man who would become Circuit Court Judge in afteryears, a man whose name was David Gooding. He was wounded in action against the Southern terrorist guerilla army even though he held no military office. Gooding, who became an "emergency" Private (in Army rank terms) in the Hancock County Home Guard had recently been a former State Senator from the county before getting thrown into the mix of trying to defend our state and county.

Morgan's Raid struck into Indiana in the summertime of the year 1863 with two brigades of cavalry, variously estimated at between 3000 and 11,000 troops, and a battery of cannon. No one knows exactly why. Some say Morgan was trying to create a diversion. Some say he was trying to get away from Union cavalry troops of which Reuben Riley was one who followed him north through Kentucky. One of these troops was Reuben Riley, the father of the poet. The reason no one knows why is that General John Hunt Morgan never filed an official report of his invasion of Indiana with the Confederate War Department. Probably that was because he was captured and thrown in prison for awhile in Ohio before escaping and returning to Confederate lines to fight again.

I suppose one of the factors that was in Morgan's mind was the fact that the Civil War wasn't particularly popular right about then in Indiana. I have heard it said that Morgan hoped to "stir up the copperheads," and maybe even hoped to enlist some new recruits. Support of the war was at a very lob ebb in Indiana when Morgan's Raid hit in the summer of 1863. Abe Lincoln had been forced to institute a draft to keep the Union Army up. The draft enrollers were not popular. One of them got himself killed going to a farmer's house across the Rush County line from Hancock County to talk about signing up a farmer's sons there.

What was Greenfield like? Greenfield only had about 700 people in it and Indianapolis, the state capital, was not much larger and had only one telegraph office. Most of Indiana citizens were rural dwellers and small farmers.

If General Morgan thought he might be received sympathetically in Indiana, however, he was very mistaken.

The Home Guard of the Hoosier county where he landed, that is Harrison County, put up a little fight quickly and suffered four dead.

When General Morgan took his troops across the Ohio River on July 9th, 1863, it is an understatement to say that all hell broke loose in Riley's Hancock County. One company of militia was raised in Greenfield on the single day of July 10th and another on the next. These two units are about the strangest bunch of people one would ever expect might have been. Our newspaper editor, William Mitchell, became a sergeant in one. Henry Gates, whose name lives on above a current downtown Greenfield building, was a corporal in another. The three young men who would lose their lives to the futile quest for glory by the daredevil Confederate General Morgan were also in this mix.

Morgan's Raid

The response to the news of the Confederate invasion of Indiana was explosive. The Governor didn't hear about it until about 3 on that Thursday afternoon after Corydon was captured. Then he issued urgent orders for all businesses to close and for the white male citizens to take up arms.

Hancock County had several informal companies of Home Guards during Civil War times. The Greenfield unit, called the Hancock Guards, drilled where Greenfield's Central Park is now located behind the Post Office which was then kind of a blue grass meadow.

But it was the New Palestine Home Guards, called the Anderson Guards, who were the first to be called to emergency duty. They got the call on the next day that they were henceforth to be Company D of the 106th Indiana Regiment, mustered into federal service on July 10th, the day after Corydon fell to the rebels. The unit was commanded by Captain Thomas Tuttle and was eventually sent to Cincinnati.

At first General Morgan headed due north in a straight line toward Indianapolis burning bridges as he went. After capturing Corydon, the Confederates struck next at Salem on July 10th, the same day the New Palestine guard was federalized, but the line of attack was not in simple columns. They stole horses systematically. The rebels would dispatch the men from the head of each regiment on each side of the road to five miles into the country seizing every fresh horse they could find and then fall in the rear of the column with fresh horses, In that way they would sweep Indiana of its horses for ten milers at a time and could literally ride an average of 21 hours a day as they raced through Indiana.

On Friday, at Salem, the Confederates destroyed the railroad depot and robbed the stores but then turned and drove toward Madison instead of Indianapolis. But before reaching Madison, the Confederate army turned north again toward Vernon.

This was on the 11th, the day that Riley's older friends in the Greenfield Home Guards were federalized to become Company E of the 105th Indiana Regiment. The Greenfield unit was moved to Indianapolis by rail and then ordered to the southern part of the state to shore up the defenses at Vernon.

General Morgan approached Vernon but fiddled around there awhile before considering whether to attack that town. Eventually he decided not to and took off for Cincinnati, crossing the Indiana and Ohio state line at Harrison.

So how did the three Hancock County boys die during Morgan's Raid? After Morgan was in Ohio, a report was received that he had turned south and was going to strike back into Indiana to capture Lawrenceburg and from there cross into Kentucky. Two regiments of the new militia, including the Hancock Guard, were ordered to positions two or three miles northeast of Lawrenceburg at a place where there is a little town now called Lawrenceburg Junction. It was a narrow place in the valley west of the Miami River with a steep hill along one side of the highway. In marching out there, our boy's regiment came to where the road doubled sharply on

itself and climbed up the hillside. Some of the men in the rear not knowing
of this turn in the road, and nervous in the darkness and fearing attack, saw
the men at the head of the regiment outlined against the sky on the hill above
them apparently marching toward them and mistook them for Morgan's
men. A gun accidently went off and fire was returned.

Dead were the three Greenfield boys that Riley had known. Two of them
died in this crazy firefight. These were farmboys, John Porter and Ferdinand
Hafner. The third died later from lingering injury. This was William Hart.
He had been made lieutenant of the Hancock Guards after just getting off
active duty but his duty was not with an infantry unit but rather a band. At
the start of the Civil War, the Greenfield Band had been inducted wholesale
and had been made the regimental band of the Indiana 18th Regiment.
William Hart had been in this band before being discharged and he had been
working in his father's grocery store in Greenfield only a couple of days
before his death as a result of Morgan's Raid.

Soon Riley's own father would return home from the chase of Morgan.
Riley's father was a
casualty too of this
great daredevil fool
who so foolishly
invaded the north. If
there was any chance
of recovery of heath
for Reuben after his
initial three month's
duty, this second
"short" stint of less
than a year ended it.
Henceforth, Reuben

A magazine sketch of Morgan's Raiders in Salem, Indiana, July 10, 1963. The
poet's father, Reuben Riley, was part of the federal cavalry trying to catch up to
the raiders and lost what was left of his health as a result.

Riley was unable to practice law or do any other gainful work due to post-
traumatic stress syndrome.

One of the most puzzling aspects of the boyhood of James Whitcomb
Riley was the poverty of his adolescent home. Wasn't the poet's father a
wealthy Greenfield lawyer? Maybe he abandoned his law practice to enter
the federal army during the Civil War but when he was in the Army. Didn't
he achieve the rank of Captain and at least draw officer's pay? How could
Riley's family be so impoverished as the accounts reveal?

The National Archives contains a Board Proceeding which helps to understand this phenomenon.

Reuben Riley's was the 180th action that was considered by a Board of Officers convened under Special Order No. 285 of the War Department. Their meeting in the session which considered Reuben Riley's case was held in Cincinnati, Ohio on December 28th, 1863 to decide if Reuben Riley should be excused from further service in the Civil War. The board was under orders from the War Department to take up cases of "convalescents" who were absent from their units. Their job was to retire them, send them back to the ranks, or order them to "light duty" assignments.

The record states, "The Board then examined" which means they asked Reuben Riley why he had not been with his unit very much. (His military record shows many absences - some noted as being "without leave" after Reuben joined his cavalry unit in June, 1863,)

Their findings show:

"Captain R.A. Riley, 5th Indiana Cavalry, Company "G." Entered three month's service April 18th, 1861. Re-entered service October 30th, 1862. Age 44 years. Served while in three month's service in Western Virginia. Since reappointment, in Dept. of the Ohio. Was at battle of Rich Mountain. After being mustered in August, 1861, was ill for about a year with excessive discharge of urine, pain in loins, and numbness of lower extremities. About July 25th, 1863, having been previously well, had hemorrhage from stomach and bowels followed by jaundice and suppuration of axillary glands. Entered officer's hospital at Louisville, July 30th, 1863.

Has twenty days leave of absence from August 12th, 1863. States that he has forwarded surgeon's certificates at intervals of about twenty days as required.

Now, has inordinate diuresis, frequent nausea and vomiting and fixed pain in loins of right hip.

Appetite variable. Bowels regular. Is feeble. Can walk a mile at a moderate gait. Average weight in health, 155 lbs. Now weighs 125 lbs. Tendered his resignation September 25th, 1863.

The Board respectfully recommends that this officer be honorably discharged. /s/ J.F. Head, Secy. U.S.A. (and other board members.)

The surgeon's certificate of disability for this board indicated Riley suffered from "scrufulous diathesis producing superation of the axillary glands hence general disability and nervous prostration and that he is not able to endure the hardships of a military campaign. His last payment was in October 31, 1863.

Greenfield Ind Sept. 21st 1863 —

Adjutant General United States Army
Washington D. C.

Sir: For the following reasons
I tender my unconditional resignation
to take effect immediately.

1st. I am confident I have not
left me the physical health to render
the necessary exposure and fatigue
of Camp and field. I commanded
a Co. in the three months service, — was
at the Battle of Rich Mountain, and
from sickness, exposure, and fatigue
developing a scrofulous tendency, I remained an invalid for about one
year there after. The exposure and
fatigue of the long and unintermitting
march after Gen. John Morgan
in his late Raid, through Ky. Ind. & Ohio
brought on severe sickness, followed
by the same scrofulous diathesis, and
I have now been for fifty one days
unfit for service, or Camp life, and
without the hope of soon, if ever, becoming so. (See Surgeons Certificates marked
A. & B. ~~herin attached~~)

2nd. I have no desire to tax an already

Reuben Riley's resignation letter.

To recapitulate the record, Reuben Riley was apparently with his Civil War unit he enlisted with initially only about a month. He served the rest of his time on Court Martial duties from roughly Nov. 12 through May in Indianapolis and probably lived at his home in Greenfield. Eventually, he returned to his unit for at most three or four weeks. Sick, he entered a hospital in Louisville and obtain a Surgeon's Certificate that he was not constitutionally able to serve in the field and got leave to return to Greenfield. He resigned his commission in Sept., 1863 and he was given an honorable discharge in Dec. 1863.

I think this record helps us to understand the phenomenon of the poverty in which James Whitcomb Riley lived during his teenaged years. His father was simply a very sick man who had been rendered so by entering military service at a far greater age than most of the other officers. During the Civil War most of the major officers were in their thirties with obvious notable exceptions. The men of the lesser ranks were usually even younger. Apparently, Reuben Riley was taken away into a great wave of desire to serve the "North" and entered into regular Army service which his age and constitution simply did not permit.

Reuben Riley's career as an Army Officer after his initial three month service is certainly not notable. He served viably only a fraction of the three years he was committed to serve. Even that short initial time of service resulted in illness and hospitalization. He was back home in Greenfield after about ten months of being a soldier.

Once discharged, why didn't he just pick up where he left off?

We do know that he had been a wealthy lawyer before the Civil War. Records at the Recorder's Office of Hancock County, Indiana show extensive land holdings, etc.

Now however came a period when Reuben Riley even lost his family home. The boyhood home of James Whitcomb Riley was foreclosed on during this period. The Rileys had to live wherever they could. Not until the 1890's did the poet himself recover his boyhood home by re-purchase.

I think there is enough evidence from this Board record to conclude that the reason for the family impoverishment was that Reuben Riley simply returned from the Civil War with shattered health and was not able to resume the life in legal practice and in court as before. The "why" he would do such a thing is more revealing. Reuben Riley, even beyond the age he should have, volunteered to serve his President, Abraham Lincoln. The great sacrifice of a comfortable life with his family and for his family followed.

After Reuben's return to Greenfield this time, the young James Whitcomb Riley might not have seen war as so glorious an adventure. Seeing his father rendered an invalid did not spell glory. In the meantime, the adolescent Riley ran errands for Soldier's Aid Society. When troops went through town on the railroad, Riley's boys group posted letters and filled canteens with milk. The boys prepared themselves with marching and drilling. Riley was still too young to serve in the army by the time the war ended.

After the Civil War, Riley's father could do little except hope that his son, James Whitcomb Riley, would receive an education to make something of himself. Instead, Riley quit school. Riley's father beat him when he quit, further alienating the father and son.

Why was Reuben this way? He explains how he felt after the Civil War in a speech of September 14, 1878 delivered in Franklin, Indiana, as reported in the Hancock DEMOCRAT. The speech was for campaign purposes when Reuben Riley undertook an abortive campaign for Congress from Indiana's then 6th District on the National Greenback Party ticket.

SPEECH FOR THE NATIONAL GREENBACK PARTY

"Fellow citizens - Having no National Greenback paper in this Congressional District through which to reach you and having politely challenged each of my competitors, Capt. William R. Myers, the Democratic nominee and Gen. Wm. Grose, the Republican nominee, to meet me in joint discussion through the district, which they both, for reasons best known to themselves, declined. I am therefore, compelled to come before you alone and to write and publish my speech, circulate and ask you to read, reflect and conscientiously vote as you believe to be right.

My friends and fellow citizens, previous to the last war I had been very active in my profession; and immediately before and during the dissensions that led to the war, I was also active as a politician. In 1854, rather than sanction what I regarded as a conspiracy to make human slavery universal and freedom sectional, embodied in the Kansas-Nebraska bill, I voluntarily sundered my position and life long connection with the Democratic party, and went out into political chaos to organize the defeat of that conspiracy. Not because I believed a true Democratic party could do such iniquity, but because the conspirators had obtained possession of the organization and machinery of the party. They had surprised and captured the garrison and controlled the citadel. It was necessary to dislodge them in order to preserve the life of the nation. The Whig party had antagonized the Democratic on everything but slavery, and that was now the only issue and its leaders had gone over to the conspirators and the party to its grave. The tremendous exigencies of the hour caused fearless, patriotic and determined men to unite for the preservation of the nation's life, and of that union the Republican party sprang into life like Minerva from the brain of Jupiter, fully matured and armed to contest successfully the bloody field with Mars. Of their number I was one. I helped to organize the Republican party. That conspiracy after four years of war, agony and blood was defeated and the life of the nation saved and for this salvation the nation is indebted, not to the professional politicians, but to the intelligent, patriotic soldier boys from all parties, who enlisted and fought freedom's battles to their crowning victories, not as politicians, but as patriots and in the sinews of war furnished not as loans or bonds but by the direct exercise of its sovereign that power of the government in the shape of the greenbacks. May heaven's choicest blessings descend upon those patriots and statesmen.

I returned home near the close of the war worn out, broken down in health, an invalid, without reasonable hope of long surviving, expecting to retire from active life and to spend the remnant of my days in retirement, seeking amusement and entertainment by indulging my taste for mechanism, history and Belle-letters; but the mal-administration of the government, the consequent bankruptcy and suffering all around, my sympathy with the sufferings and distress, my detestation of fraud and injustice, the threatening perversion of the government, and the unanimous call of national friends to lead in this Congressional District, what many regard as a forlorn hope, against official conspiracy, betrayal and political heresy, has called me forth again to battle for purity, justice and the right..."

Strangely, James Whitcomb Riley succeeded at the pursuit of Belle-letters that his father said he wanted to master after the Civil War but apparently couldn't. The young Riley really carried to fruition his father's intentions for his own life. Krung achieved goals of Reuben Riley.

Edmund Eitel stated his grandfather, Reuben Riley, suffered "shell shock" and was partially deafened and paralyzed in the Civil War in an article for Harper's Magazine, Feb. 1918 number. He suffered "serious injury."

"He returned home with the best of his vitality spent as a sacrifice to his country. He lost his farm and the comfortable old Greenfield homestead and moved his family from one rented house to another. At this time his wife died.

What really happened to the Riley birthplace and home?

James Whitcomb Riley's birth home is traced from deed records in the Hancock County Courthouse with the earliest ones for the year 1851.

Riley's boyhood home in Greenfield as re-purchased by the poet in deed dated Feb. 23, 1893. Note the natural gas streetlight in front of the home. (Courtesy of The Riley Old Home Society, Greenfield, Indiana.)

An Indenture of 1870 gives more authoritative history of the Riley Home loss than any other record. The document details how Reuben Riley purchased the Riley boyhood home at public auction at the Court House door in Indianapolis December 12, 1846. Reuben Riley's marriage to Elizabeth Marine had occurred the preceding year at the home of her parents in Randolph County, and he and his bride had come to Greenfield to settle. He paid $274.75 for his property, the remainder to be paid on a five year credit with seven per cent annual interest.

Reuben owned the property which he had himself so vastly improved until March 25, 1864 when he sold his interest to Jeremiah S. Boyer who in turn sold the property July 11, 1865 to Gabriella A. Hart. It seems that Reuben Riley also owned a farm at this time, a place of 198 acres west of Greenfield.

The farm netted him $5,955. It was possibly this money that Reuben lost in speculation on Western lands. His poor health might have been the reason that he could not oversee any such transactions, and thus invested unwisely. At any rate we know that there was a period in the life of the Riley family when they were, in the later words of the poet, "very poor." It will be noted that James Whitcomb Riley was fifteen years old at the time the "old homestead" was sold, a very sensitive age. Gone was Riley's home with its yard where apple trees ripened, quince and locusts had furnished shade, where the garden had yielded food for the family table and where his mother had grown flowers especially the red roses Riley always loved.

At first the family lived with Reuben's mother Margaret on Greenfield's South Street.

Now Riley spent most of his time at Nellie Millikan's and drew and painted with her mother. He tried portraiture. We know of one of these as being of John Davis, Riley's friend from youth and a member of the Greenfield Cornet Band with Riley. Riley called him "Durbin," and the name stuck. Riley made a pencil sketch "once when he was playing a horn in the band, and afterwards painted his portrait. The portrait remained in the home of John Davis on the south wall of his home throughout "Durbin's" life according to a recollection of his brother William B. Davis.

Perhaps the most shocking incident to Riley's hopes to be the reputable and famous man his father wanted was the marriage of Nellie Millikan to another man. Nellie Millikan and George Cooley were married on February 22, 1865. George Cooley was a wounded Civil War veteran as was Reuben. Soon two children were born to the couple. The only problem was that Riley loved Nellie very much. Without her, Riley had no choice for a marriage partner with whom he wished to have a family.

The family were living with Margaret Riley when Greenfield learned that Richmond was taken by General Grant's victorious Army of the Potomac. The war seemed close to ending. Riley remembered this event as one marked by bonfires in the streets and a "monster confligration" on the Courthouse commons. The ladies organized a Grand Hop for the whole town. Then General Robert E. Lee surrendered his Army of Northern Virginia on Palm Sunday, April 9, 1865 at Appomattox Court House, Virginia.

Greenfield did not find out the war had ended until the next morning, April 10th. Greenfield went wild again with celebration. Bells rang from all the churches. Bonfires were re-lit. Gunpowder was freely used. Businesses closed down for the day. The citizens thronged the streets greeting each other with the great joy that the Civil War was over. People felt safe at last. The Hancock DEMOCRAT expressed the general sentiment that "The country, in spite of rebel sympathizers at home and abroad, and difficulties that can not be told, was redeemed, regenerated and disenthralled, and stood up among the nations of the earth, more powerful than when the great struggle began." That evening, homes in Greenfield were beautifully illuminated all along the National Road. A band was constituted to play martial music. A stand was erected at Walker's Corner near the Hancock County courthouse where speakers, including Reuben Riley, marked the occasion. Riley listened to his father speak on the plat- form. Krung watched for clues as to how Riley should one day become Mr. Bryce and speak from a plat- form.

Then, on Sunday, April 30, 1865, the body of the assassi- nated President Abraham Lincoln passed through Riley's hometown

The assassination of Abraham Lincoln as depicted in the April 29, 1865 Edition of Harper's Weekly.

of Greenfield by train on the way to burial in Illinois. The funeral train chug chugged along the Indiana Central Railway line through town preceded by another locomotive running security in case the tracks were booby trapped. Many Greenfield folk gathered at the Greenfield depot hoping to see the grand coffin of the slain President but the train did not stop. One can imagine the young poet-to-be at age 15 standing with his friends as the martyred President's body was transported through town on the black-draped train.

Reuben Riley gave a eulogy to the crowd which had gathered at the Greenfield train station. Not all of Riley's Greenfield eulogy of Lincoln, following his assassination, survives, but this does: "Never in the history of recorded time has the transition from free exultant forgiving universal joy been so quick, so sudden, the universal gloom, sorrow. We rejoice with joy unspeakable at the realized salvation of our government. We are stricken with horror dumb with dark forebodings, almost despair, at this blackest crime against the nation - against humanity - the assassination of Abraham Lincoln." With this Reuben sat down and openly wept.

James Whitcomb Riley's response was much different. Krung had listened to his father once again triumph in a platform oration. But also Jucklet was listening and wondering what it meant to be Reuben Riley's child. How could James Whitcomb Riley survive? This was always Jucklet's question. There were mountains of questions in the boys mind.

What happened to his father's life?

Was his father's sacrifice of his health and prosperity done for any purpose?

How could Riley cope with his life?

Should he himself take up his father's idealism?

What do you do when you go from living in a happy home to an unhappy one?

What do you do when your father is functional and goes off to war and returns home an invalid?

The pent up emotions of the war needed resolution. Krung could not be born for many years in Riley's life.

When Riley imagined how his father sacrificed so much to restore the Union, the fact was that Indiana did not seem so different after the war than before. Where Riley lived, Lincoln had lost his 1860 election. A Lincoln advocate was politically a "loser" in Hancock County. Riley's recollections of violent politicking were vivid and always negative. When a friend insisted to Riley he was going to run for an office in Riley's later years, Riley commented, "They'll burn your barn," and "They'll kidnap your children." He truly meant these comments as a warning and painful reminder of the political struggles in his hometown where his own father had suffered loss of legal courtroom battles because of Hoosier politics. It is reported that on one occasion Reuben Riley was fined the amount of his attorney fee for representing a client for alleged "courtroom comments" by a judge of the opposition party. The story goes that the Riley family had no food on the table from that experience. Standing up loyally for Lincoln, as he felt he must, was a trial to the soul for Reuben Riley.

After the war Reuben Riley was different. His black hair was gray, His arm paralyzed. His hearing was hard. His law practice never recovered. In 1865 Reuben wanted to go to Kansas where he invested in land but Elizabeth wouldn't. He lost his home to meet debts. Elizabeth was forced to move her family here and there in abject poverty.

Riley changed from portrait artist to house painter under the financial pressure. On the Census taken June 27th, 1870 Riley was listed as a "painter." He did occasional painting of fence, barn, house. He claims to have found himself "with a five-ought paintbrush in his hand one day under the eaves of an old frame house that drank paint by the bucketful, learning to be a painter." In apprenticeship to a house painter, he acquired the art of "marbling" and "graining" - long abandoned embellishments of domestic architecture.

In a letter of January 29, 1879, Riley told his correspondent Elizabeth Kahle, "I was once stark, staring mad to be an artist, but unlike yourself, I never realized the sweet fruition of my dreams.

"My crayon cupids, reddening into shape,

Betrayed my talents to design and - scrape" nothing more. So I leant my easel in the corner like a pair of tongues and gave my pictures to the poor - determined that henceforward, like little Tom Tucker, I would sing for my "supper" - though at times I sadly fear that in running away from the thunder, I have run into the lighting, for with good Chispa, I am left to exclaim, - "Alas and alack-a-day! Poor was I born, and poor do I remain. I neither win nor lose. Thus I wag through the world, half the time on foot, and the other half walking!"

---

1. I had always heard that Reuben Riley's court martial duties were against civilian "Copperheads" (also called "Sons of Liberty") prosecuted because they were trying to undermine the Northern cause in Indiana through sabotage and sedition. The National Archives was contacted but could not confirm on what court martials Riley served. Such cases are kept

on a name index of defendants into an alpha-numeric filing system.

As long as Riley was subjugated by his alcoholism, he had no chance of reaching fame. Krung was the "famous Riley," but alas! only a potential when Riley originally wrote "The Flying Islands of the Night" in 1878. Having an alcohol problem stood in Riley's way to fame.

In Act I of his autobiographical poem, Riley has Jucklet finding Krung drunk and totally dominated by Crestillomeem, Riley's alcoholism. This was Riley still subjugated by Crestillomeem and stymied in his quest for fame.

KRUNG SAFE COUCHED

Safe couched midmost his lordly hoard of books1
I left him sleeping like a quisied babe
Next the guest-chamber of a poor man's house;
But ere I came away, to rest mine ears,
I salved his welded lids, uncorked his nose
And o'er the odorous blossom of his lips
Re-squeezed the tinctured sponge, and felt his pulse
Come staggering back to regularity.
And four hours hence his Highness will awake
And Peace will take a nap.

Riley is trying to sleep off a drunk here. But the moment is not merely incidental. Riley was far too often intoxicated in his wanderings during his years following the death of his mother, the years of painting signs and assisting at traveling medicine shows after the escape from the Greenfield where Kemmer was lynched, and following the death of Nellie Cooley, the only woman Riley ever fully loved.

How highly did Riley regard himself in these years? Perhaps not very highly. This impression derives from "A Ballad," also published in the The Saturday MIRROR just prior to Riley's departure from his home in Greenfield with Doc McCrillus's patent medicine show. The father in this poem is absent in war service as was Riley's father absent in the Civil War although Reuben Riley military career was brief and his record lackluster at best and the mother of the narrator, a boy, hears the mother say,

    "Thus I went playing thoughtfully-

For what my mother said -
'You look so like your father!'
Kept ringing in my head..."

One might wonder if Riley's mother compared Riley to his father in such a way. Likely, Elizabeth Marine Riley doted on her children with all of the passion she would have otherwise devoted to a relationship with the children's father while Reuben Riley was away in the Civil War. The thematic conclusion to "The Ballad" comes when the father does eventually gruffly return unrecognized to the boy who says:

"I don't look like my father,
  As you told me yesterday -
I know I don't - or father
  Would have run the other way."

Here is the sound of a young man who does not feel he can measure up to his father and who does not even deserve to look like him. Such a boy will never become a Krung. One would risk calling this a feeling of very substantial comparative inferiority but not necessarily an immoderate view of his own capabilities.

Although Riley feigned no interest in politics as Krung, he was often not only aware but also involved in politics as a young man. The band he played in serenaded political meetings and many other connections existed not the least of which was his father's ongoing political ambitions and interests.

Living in a Democrat county as Hancock County was in the 1870's, Riley knew the problems of being a Republican as his family was.

In the 1870's few Republicans were elected to office in Hancock County but one time a man named Columbus Jackson, a Greenfield retailer, was elected as township trustee as a Republican and by a definite margin. To celebrate the victory, Riley wrote a song and rounded up members of his band, the Davis Brothers Band, and marched to Mr. Jackson's store on West Main Street. The song is sung to the tune, "Columbia, the Gem of the Ocean." Mr. Jackson came out of his store to timidly acknowledge the singing and, when convinced he was not being "pranked" by Riley as many feared in Greenfield, he passed out a box of cigars to the band.

The song went:

Columbus, the gem of the Jacksons! The pride of
  the rich and the poor;
The popular choice of all factions,
  By twenty five ballots or more.

Riley grew up a "Child of Co. G." Pictured are Civil War veterans and members of the Grand Army of the Republic some of whose members were in Riley's father's Civil War company.

> Behold the reward of your labors,
>> Where order and law stand in view,
> And harken to your jubilant neighbors,
>> Who sing you the red, white and blue!

CHORUS
> Who sing you the red, white and blue,
>> Who sing you the red, white and blue -
> Then harken to your jubilant neighbors,
>> Who sing the red, white and blue!

Riley tried to learn the law with his father. Riley commented to his nephew Edmund Eitel about this period "At this time it is easy to picture my father, a lawyer of ability, regarding me, nonplussed, as the worst case he had ever had. He wanted me to do something practical, besides being ambitious for me to follow in his footsteps and at last persuaded me to settle down and read law in his office. This I really tried to do conscientiously, but finding that study of law was unbearable, I slipped out of the office one summer afternoon, when all out-doors called imperiously, shook the last dusty premise from my head and was away.

Riley's first hint of the possibility of fame arose from recitals at Dedication Day Ceremonies. On these occasions Riley recited original poetry which he had composed out of memory of the experiences he had witnessed or heard about in Civil War times. My strong suspicion is that the Civil War greatly influenced Riley as a boy. The following is a poem written by Riley which he read at Decoration Days beginning with one at New Castle, Indiana.

THE SILENT VICTORS (1876)

I

Deep, tender, firm and true, the Nation's heart
* Throbs for her gallant heroes passed away,*
Who in grim Battle's drama played their part,
* And slumber here to-day -*

Warm hearts that beat their lives out at the shrine
* Of Freedom, while our country held its breath*
As brave battalions wheeled themselves in line
* And marched upon their death:*

When Freedom's Flag, its natal wounds Scarce healed,
* Was torn from peaceful winds and flung again*
To shudder in the storm of battlefield -
* The elements of men, -*

When every star that glittered was a mark
* For Treason's ball, and every rippling bar*
Of red and white was sullied with the dark
* And purple stain of war;*

When angry guns, like famished beasts of prey,
* Were bowling o'er their gory feast of lives,*
And sending dismal echoes far away
* To mothers, maids and wives: -*

I.N. Fred, Hoosier soldier in his Civil War uniform. Fron tintype.

The mother, kneeling in the empty night,
* With pleading hands uplifted for the son*
Who, even as she prayed, had fought the fight -
* The victory had won:*

The wife, with trembling hand that wrote to say
  The babe was waiting for the sire's caress -
The letter meeting that upon the way, -
  The babe was fatherless:

The maiden, with her lips, in fancy, pressed
  Against the brow once dewy with her breath,
Now lying numb, unknown, and uncaressed
  Save by the dews of death.

II

What meed of tribute can the poet pay
  The Soldier, but to trail the ivy-vine
Of idle rhyme above his grave to-day
  In epitaph design? -

Civil War dead on Maryland battlefield. Alexander
Gardner photograph.

Or wreathe with laurel-words the icy brows
  That ache no longer with a dream of fame,
But, pillowed lowly in the narrow house,
  Renowned beyond the name.

The dewy tear-drops of the night may fall,
  And tender morning with her shining hand
May brush them from the grasses green and tall
  That undulate the land. -

Yet song of Peace nor din of toil and thirst,
  Nor chanted honors, with the flowers we heap,
Can yield us hope the Hero's head to lift
  Out of its dreamless sleep:

The dear old Flag, whose faintest flutter flies
  A stirring echo through each patriot breast,
Can never coax to life the folded eyes
  That saw its wrongs redressed -

That watched it waver when the fight was hot,
  And blazed with newer courage to its aid,

Regardless of the shower of shell and shot
  Through which the charge was made; -

And when, at last, they saw it plume its wings,
  Like some proud bird in stormy element,
And soar untrammeled on its wanderings,
  They closed in death, content.

III

O Mother, you who miss the smiling face
  Of that dear boy who vanished from your sight,
And left you weeping o'er the vacant place
  He used to fill at night, -

Who left you dazed, bewildered, on a day
  That echoed wild huzzas, and roar of guns
That drowned the farewell words you tried to say
  To incoherent ones; -

Be glad and proud you had the life to give -
  Be comforted through all the years to come, -
Your country has a longer life to live,
  Your son a better home.

O Widow, weeping o'er the orphaned child,
  Who only lifts his questioning eyes to send
A keener pang to grief unreconciled, -
  Teach him to comprehend

From the author's Ora Myers glass
negative collection of Hancock
County, Indiana subjects

He had a father brave enough to stand
  Before the fire of Treason's blazing gun,
That, dying, he might will the rich old land
  Of Freedom to his son.

And, Maiden, living on through lonely years
  In fealty to love's enduring ties, -
With strong faith gleaming through the tender tears
  That gather in your eyes,

Look up! and own, in gratefulness of prayer,
  Submission to the will of Heaven's High Host: -
I see your Angel-soldier pacing there,
  Expectant at his post. -

I see the rank and file of armies vast,
  That muster under one supreme control;
I hear the trumpet sound the signal-blast -
  The calling of the roll -

The grand divisions falling into line
  And forming, under voice of One alone
Who gives command, and joins with tongue divine
  The hymn that shades the Throne.

IV

And thus, in tribute to the forms that rest
  In their last camping-ground, we strew the bloom
And fragrance of the flowers they loved the best,
  In silence o'er the tomb.

Union Civl War soldier.

With reverent hands we twine the Hero's wreath
  And clasp it tenderly on stake or stone
That stands the sentinel for each beneath
  Whose glory is our own.

While in the violet that greets the sun,
  We see the azure eye of some lost boy;
And in the rose the ruddy cheek of one
  We kissed in childish joy, -

Recalling, haply, when he marched away,
  He laughed his loudest though his eyes were wet, -
The kiss he gave his mother's brow that day
  Is there and burning yet:

And through the storm of grief around her tossed,

One ray of saddest comfort she may see, -
Four hundred thousand dons like hers were lost
  To weeping Liberty.

But draw aside the drapery of gloom,
  And let the sunshine chase the clouds away
And gild with brighter glory every tomb
  We decorate to-day;

And in the holy silence reigning round,
  While prayers of perfume bless the atmosphere,
Where loyal souls of love and faith are found,
  Thank God that Peace is here!

And let each angry impulse that may start,
  Be smothered out of every loyal breast;
And, rocked within the cradle of the heart,
  Let every sorrow rest.

Riley was sufficiently known as a public reciter to be asked by the Hancock County Bar Association to compose and read a piece at a lawyer's funeral. This event was a critical moment in Riley's life since one of those present at the reading was Judge Elijah Martindale who was the owner of The Indianapolis JOURNAL. The poem evokes the tragedy of a rising young lawyer who is young and dead leaving behind a family:

DEAD IN SIGHT OF FAME (1876)

DIED - Early morning of September 5, 1876, and in the
gleaming dawn of "name and fame," Hamilton J. Dunbar.

Dead! Dead ! Dead!
  We thought him ours alone;
And were so proud to see him tread
The rounds of fame, and lift his head
  Where sunlight ever shone;
But now our aching eyes are dim,
And look through tears in vain for him.

Name! Name! Name!
  It was his diadem;
Nor ever tarnish-taint of shame
Could dim its luster - like a flame
  Reflected in a gem,
He wears it blazing on his brow
Within the courts of Heaven now.

Tears! Tears! Tears!
  Like dews upon the leaf
That bursts at last - from out the years
The blossom of a trust appears
  That blooms above the grief;
And mother, brother, wife and child
Will see it and be reconciled.

After hearing Riley, Judge Martindale believed Riley had prospects as a poet. This memorial poem and reading resulted in the letter which the Judge wrote Riley to come to Indianapolis to talk with him at the Indianapolis JOURNAL office. This eventually became Riley's newspaper and Riley was often known as "The JOURNAL's Poet."

To many, the Riley of this period of his life was a "no-good." He couldn't hold a job. In 1876, at age 26, James Whitcomb Riley was totally unlucky in love and had never settled down. He was an alcoholic without means to support himself except through occasional painting jobs. All of his attempts to court a woman were unsuccessful. Most of the women he dated took one look at Riley's prospects and his track record and quickly married someone else. Nellie was married to another man. Life was really very hard on Riley.

And yet when Judge Martindale heard Riley recite a memorial poem at the funeral of Hamilton Dunbar, in Greenfield and pondered its words, something "clicked" in the judge's mind.

Indiana needed a culture as well as material growth and progress. Here was a true poet with obvious literary genius. The Judge would make it his "project" to bring Riley to Indianapolis to write for the JOURNAL, Indiana's leading newspaper. Perhaps no person in his right mind would have done so, but the Judge was no ordinary person. The frontier needed culture. Here was a frontier boy who wrote poetry.

As James Whitcomb Riley's star rose, his father's set ever more quickly. Reuben Riley attempted to run a Congressional District race as a candidate of the Greenback Party in 1878. The results were disastrous. The results show William Myers, the Democrat, winning with 16,167 votes, William Grose, the Republican, losing with 15,548, and the poet's father, Reuben Riley, coming in a distant third but with 2,043 votes, enough votes to have made the difference in the election. The Greenback Party was historically speaking a splinter party formed from Republican Party. Reuben Riley's candidacy seems to have swung the 6th District to the Democrats. But how well did Reuben Riley run in Hancock County? That is not quite so clear a victory for Reuben Riley. In his home county, Reuben Riley garnered only 225 votes, compared to 2,125 for his Democrat opposition and 1,370 for the Republican. The home folks did not back their local candidate.

As with the other "selves" of Riley's life as depicted in "The Flying Islands of the Night," Riley as Krung was a major beneficiary of Riley's accommodation and resolve to live in dialogue to those who loved him who were now dead - Nellie Cooley in particular.

Riley describes his life preceding the writing of his autobiographical poem as one of separation from his mother and his married lover in "The Flying Islands of the Night." These facts-together with life in a small town which lynches black folk-produce his alcoholism and period of delirious poetical writings. The period preceding "Flying Islands" is one of despair and alcoholism, after which he repented of his life, referring to this period to Marcus Dickey, his secretary, "My steps are turning gladly toward the light, and it seems to me sometimes I almost see God's face. I have been sick - sick of the soul, for had so fierce a malady (alcoholism) attacked the body, I would have died with all hell hugged in my arms. I can speak of this now because I can tell you I am saved."

The reappearance as Krung in Riley's Autobiographical poem, "The Flying Islands of the Night," in Act III, the final stanzas. describes Riley's salvation from alcohol.

THE RESTORATION OF KRUNG

Through AEo's[1] own great providence, and through
The intervention of an angel whom
I long had deemed forever lost to me,[2]
Once more your favored Sovereign, do I greet

And tender you my blessing, O most good
And faith-abiding subjects of my realm!
In common, too, with your long-suffering King,
Have ye long suffered, blameless as he:
Now, therefore, know ye all what, until late,
He knew not of himself, and with him share
The rapturous assurance that is his, -
That, for all time to come, are we restored
To the old glory and most regal pride
And opulence and splendor of our realm.

1. As originally published in the "Buzz Club" series of 1878, the word "AEo's" was "God's." Riley changes the later attribution for his providential change in luck first to his mother, AEo, Elizabeth, the poet's mother.

2. The "angel," the dead Nellie Cooley, Riley's inspirational married friend.

(Turning with pained features to the strangely stricken Queen)
There have been, as ye needs must know, strange spells
And wicked sorceries at work within
The very dais boundaries of the Throne.
Lo! then, behold your harrier and mine,
And with me grieve for the self-ruined Queen
Who grovels at my feet, blind, speechless and
So stricken with a curse herself designed
Should light upon Hope's fairest minister.[1]

1. Differing from the originally published "Buzz Club" papers in 1878, there is inserted in a bold hand here the line of Krung's "Remove her from my sight" on the manuscript at the Lilly Library at Indiana University, Bloomington, Indiana.

(Motions attendants, who lead away Crestillomeem - the King gazing after her, overmastered with stress of his emotions.

James Whitcomb Riley's salvation in kenotic ideas produced great success.

Krung was primarily the Riley of Indianapolis rather than his hometown of Greenfield, Indiana. Riley had far too bad a reputation in Greenfield for him to be much of a Krung there. As close to "fame" as Riley could get in this period of "The Flying Islands of the Night" was to have a poem of his read at the Decoration Day at the New (now Park) Cemetery in 1879. For Riley to really be Krung he had to make a more permanent arrangement in a fresh field, not simply transient escapes, from Greenfield, the hometown of his boyhood.

Living in Greenfield, it was simply not possible for Riley to become Krung, the official poet, the poet laureate of the Hoosier people. His exploits, alcoholism, occasional arrests, playful or serious, were so well known that they could not be overcome. The days when Riley's friend, Benjamin Harrison as President, was seriously considering naming him the country's official Poet Laureate were far in the future.

We can date the serious emergence of Krung to the year 1879, late in that year, when Riley moved to Indianapolis.

In November, 1879 he wrote one of his friends from Indianapolis where he had gone to live while working for the JOURNAL, "I have been coming to anchor here...I am bothered about getting settled in this infernal city. I am not used to it, and I don't believe I ever will be.. Lots of features about it that are lovely, but the racket and rattle of it all is positively awful - no monotony on God's earth like it."

Almost immediately, Riley assumed the play character of Krung once he was in Indianapolis. His poetry could take on an official aspect when Riley was Krung. A Riley poem, "Grant," published on the front page of the Indianapolis JOURNAL, welcomed U. S. Grant to Indianapolis on Dec. 9, 1879. ("What words of greeting will be best\To frame a welcome for the guest\Whose hero heart and friendly hand\Have found a home in every land!...)

Not until the close of 1879, long after the early narratives such as "An Old Sweetheart of Mine" (written while Nellie was still alive), the autobio- graphical "The Flying Islands of the Night," and the columns of John C. Walker and "Poetical Gymnastics" had Riley moved to Indianapolis.

To a Greenfield resident of Riley's day, Indianapolis was a "big neigh- bor city" but nothing like a megalopolis.

When the Civil War began, Indiana's chief city was not Indianapolis, but Madison, far to the South and on the Ohio River. Yes, Indianapolis was made the state capital in 1823, but that did not turn the wilderness where the capital was designated into a city. Indianapolis was simply another stop on the same stagecoach line that went through Greenfield on the National Road. Nor did the waves of settlers traveling on the dusty wagon trains pause at Indianapolis more than any other place on the National Road. In fact the lure of gold kept many of them heading on West to California.

It was the railroad which caused Indianapolis to grow in population. The first train pulled into Indianapolis in 1847. The first Union Depot was built on South Illinois Street in 1853. The Hoosier capital was the first city in the country to plan for a railroad station where all railroads converged. Madison, nestled along the curvy Ohio River at the base of 400 foot steep cliffs, could not compete with Indianapolis as a railroad center. Indianapolis was on a level plain making railroad traffic easy.

It was the Civil War that caused Indianapolis to become Indiana's first city in fact. Indianapolis became the main recruiting station for the mobilization of thousands of Hoosier troops to enter that conflict. It was in Indianapolis that the Hoosier governor, Oliver Morton, set up an Arsenal that was the start of Hoosier industrialization, producing huge supplies of ammunition for the north. Industries and factories sprang up everywhere around the railroad hub of Indianapolis. Businessmen, tradesmen and large groups of immigrants turned Indianapolis into a whirlpool of activity.

It was about this time that Judge Martindale left his bench in the judicial district including Greenfield to go to Indianapolis. His training as a lawyer and judge enabled him to participate in Indianapolis's huge growth spurt around the time the Civil War ended when Indianapolis began its bloom with industries such as meat packing plants such as the huge Kingan Packing House, mills, buggy and wagon shops and saw works, and a huge building spree. The Martindale Block in Indianapolis was built by him. This was only one of the two and three story business "blocks" that went up in Indianapolis around this time. It is said 1,600 homes were constructed in the Spring of 1865 in Indianapolis, 9 miles of streets and 18 miles of sidewalks for the old lamplighters to traverse lighting up their gas street lights. The German language was spoken almost as the English in the Indianapolis of those days with newspapers flourishing in each.

An "escritoire" or partable writing desk circa 1870-80. The writing surface folds into a box. Riley wrote on such an instrument even while traveling. Courtesy, Riley Museum, Greenfield, Indiana.

In the years following the Civil War, Judge Martindale, born on a farm from around Shirley, grew in prominence in the tumultuous Hoosier capital city and eventually bought the chief newspaper in Indiana, the Indianapolis

JOURNAL.

Riley attributed his move to Indianapolis to Myron Reed in a conversation with his secretary, Marcus Dickey. He changed his residence, he claimed, after reading a letter from Reed saying, "There is a certain disadvantage in living in the town where you were born and raised - they will call you by your given name. Whatever you may become, people will grade you down to where you were; they will remember you as a boy. Their applause will not be generous or unanimous. If you have every done anything ridiculous - and you have -it is remembered. Come West, young man, come to Indianapolis. Leave your mistakes behind."

James Whitcomb Riley began using his middle name, Whitcomb, in the 1880's. This not only lent his name dignity but signals that Riley envisioned Krung and fame was someone and something within reach. The Whitcomb had always been a part of his name but it was not a name that "fit" the itinerant alcoholic sign-painter, Riley. Riley moved into his "name" after figuring out his life while writing "The Flying Islands of the Night."

Who was Riley named for? James Whitcomb had been Hancock County's first prosecutor in 1828. He was also governor when Reuben was in the state legislature in 1844 and 1846. By 1849. Reuben's friend, James Whitcomb, had been elected a Senator by the legislature and Reuben named his son after him, James Whitcomb Riley.

Especially after Riley's move to Indianapolis and employment with the JOURNAL, Riley's poetry took on an official aspect. The poet came to represent the national recovery mood of America following the American Civil War and become associated with its memorable occasions. The presence of James Whitcomb Riley invoked his kenotic poetry. I believe this was the reason for his being the choice to recite poetry at every important public occasion within the State of Indiana and at the important ones, those particularly in which a President was involved, during his last years. One finds poetry dedicated to Lincoln, Grant, Harrison, McKinley and Roosevelt in his works and particularly at the times of their deaths when national eulogistic poetry was required. Riley assumed the task of Poet Laureate of the American people during these last years and did it as inspired to do so by his prayer to AEo.

As the 1880's progressed, great honor began to be paid to Riley following his successful national platform touring.

Krung began a modest rise to success after Riley's official move to Indianapolis. He did not leave Greenfield entirely behind but returned as frequently as his constantly embarrassed financial situation allowed. Krung's first great date of triumph occurred after his successful lecturing engagement in Boston. His hometown newspaper, the Hancock Democrat stated, "He has made a special study of the Hoosier dialect for years, and as a result, produced in it some very fine effects. His "Tom Johnson's Quit," which appeared in June, 1878, has been copied from ocean to ocean. He is a master of pathos, the equal of Carlton and Hay, and equally happy in his choice of subject. As a sketch writer some of his character studies, notably "The Boss Girl," "The Tale of a Spider," and "An Adjustable Lunatic," are worthy of a Dickens, a Hawthorne or a Poe..."

Krung is the Riley of the extremely precise and scripted handwriting. Only when Riley was at the point of "fame," the goal of Krung, did Riley's handwriting assume the extremely precise and engraving-like script so recognizable in the handwriting of the 1880's on. The earlier handwriting, mostly in letters to friends in the years of larking, is barely readable. One commentator ascribes the extremely crafted handwriting of Riley's later years to Riley's desire to be clear. He hated typographical errors made in printing of his work. Thus, he evolved a handwriting that was meticulous and cognizable in every detail. Nevertheless, Riley's writing is painstaking and artistic only in his year's of fame.

One of Riley's goals clearly had public action in mind. Riley was a source of inspiration for the building of a monument to Civil War veterans. His poem, "A Monument for Soldiers" was written to help create public interest in the project and was published in the Indianapolis JOURNAL.

A MONUMENT FOR THE SOLDIERS (1884)

A MONUMENT for the Soldiers!
 And what will ye build it of?
Can ye build it of marble, or brass, or bronze,
 Outlasting the Soldiers' love?
Can ye glorify it with legends
 As grand as their blood hath writ
From the inmost shrine of this land of thine
 To the outermost verge of it?

And the answer came: We would build it
 Out of our hopes made sure,

And out of our purest prayers and tears,
  And out of our faith secure:
We would build it out of the great white truths
  Their death hath sanctified,
And the sculptured forms of the men in arms,
  And their faces ere they died.
And what heroic figures
  And the sculptor carve in stone?
Can the marble breast be made to bleed,
  And the marble lips to moan?
Can the marble brow be fevered?
  And the marble eyes be graved
To look their last, as the flag floats past,
  On the country they have saved?

And the answer came: The figures
  Shall all be fair and brave,
And, as befitting, as pure and white
  As the stars above their grave!
The marble lips, and breast and brow
  Whereon the laurel lies,
Bequeath us right to guard the flight
  Of the old flag in the skies!

A monument for the Soldiers!
  Built of a people's love,
And blazoned and decked and panoplied
  With the hearts ye build it of!
And see that ye build it stately,
  In pillar and niche and gate,
And high in pose as the souls of those
  It would commemorate!

The American Civil War and the experience of its aftermath in the lives of humble Americans was a major theme of Riley's poetry. Illustration of Howard Chandler Christy of a Riley Civil War poem.

Eventually, on Dec. 31, 1900, Riley read this poem when the new Indianapolis Columbia Club was dedicated on the Indianapolis Circle at a New Year's Day Eve banquet. The poem had done well for the fund raisers for the Civil War monument which was built and dedicated on the Indianapolis Circle two years later.

Krung achieved the second of his most notable successes on a second particular occasion after his Boston triumph in 1882 at New York in 1887.

In 1887, Riley gained greatly in reputation by appearing with James Russell Lowell, Mark Twain, Edward Eggleston, Richard Henry Stoddard, Henry Cuyler Bunner, and George W. Cable at benefit readings in New York City. Lowell was the presiding author and one of the most distinguished American men of letters as well as diplomat. The occasion was intended to arouse support for the passage of international copyright laws and the event was sponsored by the American Authors' Copyright League.

The Soldiers and Sailors Monument, Indianapolis-the result of Riley's call for "A Monument to the Soldiers."

Although there were "readings" elsewhere the most important were scheduled for New York at Chickering Hall on November 28 and 29, 1887.

The event organizer, Robert Underwood Johnson, detailed his participation in a book, REMEMBERED YESTERDAYS, published in Boston in 1923. Riley was added to the program during the workup on the suggestion of one of the "readers," Bunner, who said "Don't fail to get Riley." When the program was arranged, Riley was placed last on the list for November 28th. This was considered a less than desirable spot. People might be expected to want to leave early to catch the commuter trains.

As the program worked out, Riley's readings of "When the Frost Is on the Punkin'" and "The Educator," turned out to raise the greatest appreciation of all the readings. In fact, after Riley closed he was given a standing ovation and asked to do an encore. His encore was "Goodbye, Jim." Not only the audience but the rest of the authors joined in the applause. Riley was deluged with established figures such as Lowell, Parke Godwin, George William Curtis and others waiting to shake his hand. As a final gesture, Lowell announced to the audience that Riley had agreed to speak at the next evening's readings to further great applause.

On the second evening, Lowell again presided and read his own poetry. Then Richard Malcolm Johnson, Charles Dudley Warner, Thomas Nelson

Page, William Dean Howells, Frank R. Stockton, and George William Curtis read from their work before Riley was introduced to close the program. Once again, after Riley read, the audience was aroused to repeated applause. More than $4,000 was raised for the American Authors' Copyright League which subsidized lobbying in Washington.

One of the authors at the readings, Thomas Nelson Page, summed up his impression of the occasion in a letter. Page was a well established writer of short stories and essays and, a Virginian, the author of an important children's book of the South, TWO LITTLE CONFEDERATES. The letter was written to event organizers of a reception for Riley including Elijah Walker Halford that Page missed since he got the invitation after the reception had been held, and reads:

"Riley is one of the few geniuses it has ever been my fortune to know. On the two occasions when I have met him in public, he has easily won the palm against such men as Lowell, Clemens, Eggelston, and many others, who were the picked champions in the Literary field. But far better than this, I rank the qualities which through his native modesty have kept him sweet and unaffected while they dazzled and entranced all others. He has the very soul of a poet, and we are all proud of him. His books lie before me now, and are my constant friends, as in them I find the very flavor of the apple-blossoms, and find my youth embalmed.

I beg to testify that we love him down in this old State (referring to Virginia) and I bespeak for him a glorious future."

In 1888, Riley delved into one of his few public political efforts for his friend Benjamin Harrison who was then running for President. At the time of the Harrison campaign of 1888, Riley recited his "The Frost is on the Punkin'" which was loudly applauded and on the spur of the moment he recited as an encore the following lines, composed while sitting to wait for the applause to subside. He arose to his feet, adjusted his black-bowed "nippers" (glasses) to his nose, rubbed the palms of his hands together till the cheering had subsided and then recited the following:

"And there's still another idy I orto here append
  In a sort o' Nota Bena for to taper off the end
  In a manner more befittin' to a subjec' jes in view,
  Regardin' things in politics an' what we're goin' to do
  Along a little later when affairs at Washington,
  `At's been harassin' us so long, has to Harrison:

We're goin' to give the man a seat and set him there
kisock
When the frost is on the punkin and th' fodder's in the
shock.

His home state began to recognize in Riley a notable son of national fame. A dinner was given to his honor at Indianapolis's Denison Hotel sponsored by the Western Association of Writers on October 19, 1888. The toastmaster of the occasion, W. Dudley Foulke, reviewed not just Riley's success in the decade just prior but also the literary advances in the West, stating " No man had done more to promote this progress than the gentleman in whose honor the entertainment was given..." and proposed a toast to James Whitcomb Riley.

Riley closed brief remarks with his Dickensonian, "God bless us every one."

KRUNG CONTEMPLATES HIS ALCOHOLIC SELF AS CRESTILLOMEEM

It was Krung who most benefited from Riley's accommodation to life on the basis of his "spiritual" married life with Nellie Cooley. In the "Flying Islands of the Night," Krung overcomes his alcoholism. He leans heavily on the throne, as though oblivious to all surroundings, and, shaping into speech his varying thought, as in a trance, speaks as though witless of both utterance and auditor.

ON THE LOVE OF AN INTOXICATING QUEEN

(Speaking of his alcoholism as Crestillomeem,)

I loved her[1], - Why? I never knew. - Perhaps
Because her face was fair; perhaps because
Her eyes were blue and wore a weary air; -
Perhaps... perhaps because her limpid face
Was eddied with a restless tide, wherein
The dimples found no place to anchor and
Abide: perhaps because her tresses beat
A froth of gold about her throat, and poured
In splendor to the feet that ever seemed

Afloat. Perhaps because of that wild way
Her sudden laughter overleapt propriety;
Or - who will say? - perhaps the way she wept.
Ho! [2] *have ye seen the swollen heart of summer*
Tempest, o'er the plain, with throbs of thunder
Burst apart and drench the earth with rain? She
Wept life that. - And to recall, with one wild [3] *glance*
Of memory, our last love-parting [4] *- tears*
And all...It thrills and maddens me! And yet
My dreams will hold her [5]*, flushed from lifted brow*
To finger-tips, with passion's ripest kisses
Crushed and mangled on her lips...O woman! while
Your face was fair, and heart was pure, and lips
Were true, and hope as golden as your hair,
I should have strangled you!

1. The "her" is Crestillomeem as his alcoholic possessor. This is a poem of the hold of alcoholism. This poem was not in the original Buzz Club papers series of 1878. As this poem, called "Delilah," originally was published in the Indianapolis Saturday HERALD of September 6, 1979 in Riley's front page column entitled "Poetical Gymnastics," the treacherous deceiver was referential to the Delilah who trimmed Samson's head of hair and thus deprived him of his strength to perform acts of righteousness.

This work was originally in quatrain form with alternate rhyme and line indentation. The poem was included in the first edition of the published whole of "The Flying Islands of the Night" in its inexplicable "blank verse" in stylistic conformity with the inexplicable subject, alcohol addiction.

2. The "Ho," Riley's catchword for intoxication, is substituted here for "O" in the original poem "Delilah."
3. The poem "Delilah" uses the word "swift" instead of "wild."
4. "our last love-parting" was "Our time of parting," in the original poem, "Delilah."
5. "And yet my dreams will hold her," was "For yet in dreams I hold her," in the original poem, "Delilah."

(As Krung, ceasing to speak, piteously lifts his face,   Spraivoll[1] all suddenly appears, in space left vacant by the Queen, and kneeling, kisses the King's hand. - He bends   in tenderness, kissing her brow -then lifts and seats her at his side. Speaks then to throng.)

1. Having conquered alcohol, Riley can now assume the role of poet.

Riley did go on to win his fame. In 1889, selections of the Riley's poetry were published in England under the title "Old Fashioned Roses." Riley's international reputation is dated from this event. Academic recognition of Riley came as early as 1891 when Henry Augustin Beers wrote in his INITIAL STUDIES IN AMERICAN LETTERS that Riley was a national poet.

The Riley who was Krung was a great letter writer. He sat down at his little desk in Lockerbie Street and wrote letter after letter in his older years. Most of these letters were I suppose written out of loneliness and harken toward impossible friendships with other notable people of his time.

A KRUNG POEM OF THE CIVIL WAR

In Riley's time one of his poems, "Armazindy," became known as a Civil War Epic.

There is a ford across Sugar Creek in Riley's home county of Hancock County, Indiana - I have seen photographs of it- which was said by Riley to be a place near where a real "Armazindy Ballenger" lived. I cannot locate the spot. I suspect it is on one of the county roads which cross Sugar Creek.

"Armazindy" was, of course, a genuine heroine to most Americans of the 1890's. The Riley poem "Armazindy" was originally composed for a Grand Army of Republic (Civil War veteran's group) meeting or "encampment" in 1893, but became the title poem of a book of poetry Riley published in 1894.

It is a story of a small Indiana girl, 14, who struggles to fill the place of her soldier father killed by an accident in coming home from the Civil War. The poem is in Hoosier dialect.

The story line is simple. Armazindy takes over the operation of the Ballenger family farm after her father dies and her mother, a consumptive, dies soon after. She is left with the care of twins and a palsied aunt who cannot feed herself.

> *Jes' a child, I tell ye! Yit*
> *She made things git up and git*
> *Round that little farm o' hern! -*
> *Shouldered all the whole concern; -*
> *Feed the stock, and milk the cows -*
> *Run the farm and run house! -*

This little girl grows up fast. She learns to cope. She deals with "hands." She takes no charity. She becomes a respected neighbor while raising her siblings, running the farm, and generally dealing with life.

When in a few years she meets a thrasher, Sol Stephens, she falls in love except that another girl of a more conventional family, Jule Reddinhouse, takes him away from her by writing Sol's family that Armazindy was merely getting Sol to marry her so Sol would take care of Armazindy's obligatory family, the

An 1890's thrashing scene used to illustrate the poem "Armazindy." (From the Barton Rees Pogue glass positive collection.)

twins and aunt. Jule ends up eloping with Sol and she and Sol leave Armazindy behind.

Armazindy merely resumes her life and "shet her jaws square" to resume her laborious duties as before the tragic hope of life with Sol began.

As the story continues, Jule and Sol have two children but being the wife of a thrasher is not really what Jule was very thrilled about so Jule ran off leaving Sol with the children. Then Sol takes to alcohol and soon dies in an accident, falling into a belt on his thresher.

Before Sol dies, he asks that Armazindy be fetched. She comes. The next thing you know, guess who is left to take care of and rear Sol's children with Jule? If you guessed Armazindy, you would be right on.

Riley describes her:

"Clear and stiddy, 'peared to me
as her old Pap's ust to be."

So what are we to make of this poem?

First of all it was a popular success but subject to criticism. I suspect the poem suffers from problems of reference to us. Today, many people would dismiss "Armazindy" and such poems as overly sentimental, possibly because the subject matter seems irrelevant. In our current American scene there could literally never be an Armazindy Ballenger. Social legislation does much more to provide for desperate situations. We should remember though that Riley's fight was with the social Darwinists of Riley's day who controlled the country's political agenda with their demand that government not interfere with the natural evolutionary order on behalf of the poor and homeless. This poem was on Riley's kenotic agenda. We can hardly imagine today a girl such as Armazindy.

Armazindy was a call for government action. In many respects Riley hated the status quo as when it neglected the needs of the Civil War veterans and their families. It was part of Riley's natural reaction against a legal system which so often failed to carry out Lincolnesque justice. Both Lincoln and Riley read the law although Lincoln was much the more committed learner. The law had no "hold" on a Riley who saw his county jail broken into and a black man removed for lynching just at the time he was making a final choice of profession.

THE DEATH OF KRUNG'S MENTOR, REUBEN RILEY PERMITTED RILEY TO BECOME A BELOVED FAMOUS PERSON

A critical event in the life of James Whitcomb Riley was December 6, 1893 when Reuben Riley died, age 74. The cause of death according to his death certificate on file in the Hancock County, Indiana, Health Department is listed as "La Grippe" ill for 10 days complicated by typhoid pneumonia for 5 days. Riley's great example as Krung had always been his father. Riley had reacted to his father's life at almost every point sometimes positively and sometimes negatively. Now Riley was on his own to visualize how to live as Krung.

What mark should he make as the famous Krung?

The choice was his.

Krung became the King-Poet described by Meredith Nicholson as "The Poet Who All the People Loved." Riley could not have followed his father's style of fame and done such a thing. Reuben was a Riley. The poet once said of his family that the Rileys had composite characteristics. Physically they were unusually zestful. When afflicted they were strengthened. Despite their natively tender and compassionate natures, they were grim and piteous. But most of all: "God is not as intolerant nor as impetuous as some of us Rileys" as Riley said of the family in a letter to a cousin.

That was not to be Riley as Krung would have it.

Riley was to act toward his state and nation in such a way as to promote the kenotic points which had saved him from his "weakness" so that all people he came across could share in that salvation.

A quote from a nationally distributed novel about Riley, The Poet, by Meredith Nicholson, will indicate how well he succeeded:

"Down the long aisle of trees the tall shaft of the soldier's monument rose before (Riley). He had watched its building, and the memories that had gone to its making had spoken to his imagination with singular poignancy. It expressed the high altitudes of aspiration and endeavor of his own people; for the gray shaft was not merely the center of his city, the teeming earnest capital of his State, but his name and fame were inseparably linked to it. He had found within an hour's journey of the monument the material for a thousand poems. As a boy he had ranged the nearby fields and followed, like a young Columbus, innumerable creeks and rivers; he had learned and stored away the country lore and the country faith, and fixed in his mind unconsciously the homely speech in which he was to express these things later as one having authority. So profitably had he occupied his childhood and youth that years spent on "pave ground" had not dimmed the freshness of those memories. It seemed that by some magic he was able to cause the springs he had known in youth (and springs are dear to youth!)- to bubble anew in the crowded haunts of men; and urban scenes never obscured for him the labors and incidents of the farm. He had played upon the theme of home with endless variations, and never were songs honester than these. The home round which he had flung his defenses of song domiciled folk of sim-

Riley relaxing at the site of the "Old Swimmin' Hole" with Tom Randall and Hamlin Garland visiting Riley as a reporter for Harper's magazine. This scene became the subject of a mammoth art copying project by William . Bixler of Anderson, IN. Bixler painted the scene shortly after taking art classes then reproduced it a reputed 5,000 times between 1912 a1918. Most of the paintings were gifts to American schoolrooms which contributed pennies to pay for the statue of James Whitcomb Riley his hometown. In this way, an original oil painting illustrating a Riley poem "The Old Swimmin' Hole" found its way into rally thousands of American classrooms in the Twentieth Century. (From the Barton Rees Pogue glass positive collection.)

ple aims and kindly mirth; he had established them as a type, written them down in their simple dialect that has the tang of wild persimmons, the mellow flavor of the pawpaw."

Riley sang his kenotic hymns and became much beloved.

It should not be assumed that Riley was a stuffy perfectionist as Krung. He had the benefit of family to provide him comfort and joy. Harriet Eitel Wells recalls "In the bicycle days of the 90's when mama (Elva May, Riley's sister) and Uncle Jim were learning to ride, they decided to go together for their first spin. They left our house, then at Meridian and Ninth Street, to go north. A few minutes later we looked up the street to see how they were progressing. There they sat! - mama on the grass plot on one side of the street; uncle on the grass plot on the opposite side of the street. It seems that one had said something to the other and they turned their heads. Presto! The accident followed.

Riley kept a "tea hour" when he lived in the Eitel home. Harriet Eitel recalls "The tea hour in our home always meant the assembling of a group of congenial friends and writers, with Uncle Jim, seated in his big leather chair, the dominant spirit and holding everybody spellbound as he related some story or recited some lovely poem. In that day there seemed to be leisure for a group of friends with talent of varying kinds to meet frequently. One book would remind Uncle of another, and that of still another, and he would go on talking, reading, or reciting with every one fascinated, and afraid to move for fear he would stop. Many a time when such a group was in the room I thought that I should withdraw so as to write down their wonderful conversation. But it was all so interesting I could not tear myself away. We delighted in naming the chairs (of the Eitel home) after the writers who sat in them. For instance, one we called John Fox Jr., one Madison Cawein, another Thomas Nelson Page, and so on."

In 1898, Riley was introduced to an audience in Boston by Julia Ward Howe, the author of "The Battle Hymn of the Republic." She commented about the Civil War, "'We felt our Pilot's presence with his hand upon the storm as we went sailing on.' With that Pilot we walked the troubled waters. Our Ship of State groped through the smoke of war to the day of your hymn - the day of peace."

The public figure of Riley as Krung did not disappear after the death of Riley's father. We still find Riley speaking frequently to favorite audiences of veterans, pioneer groups, dinners and some entertainments.

We also find Riley writing Krung poetry. Krung wrote "A Peace-Hymn of the Republic" first given in Louisville, Kentucky, September 12, 1895 for the Twenty-Ninth Encampment of the Grand Army of the Republic. The piece bore obvious reference to the "Battle Hymn of the Republic," a poem by Julia Ward Howe.

A PEACE-HYMN OF THE REPUBLIC (1895)

There's a Voice across the Nation like a might ocean-hail,
Borne up from out the Southward as the seas before the gale;
Its breath is in the streaming Flag and in the flying sail -
    As we go sailing on.

'Tis a Voice that we remember - ere its summons soothed as now -
When it rang in battle-challenge, and we answered vow with vow, -
With roar of gun and hiss of sword and crash of prow and prow,
    As we went sailing on.

Our hope sank, even as we saw the sun sink faint and far, -
The Ship of State went groping through the blinding smoke of War -
Through blackest midnight lurching, all uncheered of moon or star,
    Yet sailing - sailing on.

As One who spake the dead awake, with life-blood leaping warm -
Who walked the troubled waters, all unscathed, in mortal form, -
We felt our Pilot's presence with His hand upon the storm,
    As we went sailing on.

O Voice of passion lulled to peace, this dawning of To-day -
O Voices twain now blent as one, ye sing all fears away,
Since foe and foe are friends, and lo! the Lord, as glad as they. -
    He sends us sailing on.

Not until April, 1898 - when Riley again gave a reading at the Tremont Temple in Boston, did Riley have a chance to share a podium with Ms. Howe. On an evening's performance for the Woman's Club House

Corporation bene-
fit at Boston, Riley
came to the stage
with Julia Ward
Howe leaning on
his arm. At this
sight, the audience
broke out into an
applause of very
long duration.
Riley was intro-
duced by her and
Riley replied of his
pleasure to be
introduced by the
writer of "The
Battle Hymn of the
Republic," to
which Ms. Howe
replied, "We felt
our Pilot's presence

Riley took permanent residence in Indianapolis with the Holsteins after the summer of 1893. This home was built in approximately 1860 by Mrs. Holstein's father John Nickum, a prosperous Hoosier Deutsch grocer. The home was built on what had been the farm of George Lockerbie, a Scot, who had cleared the place of forest.

with His hand upon the storm as we went sailing on. With that Pilot, we walked the troubled waters. Our Ship of State groped through the smoke of war to the day of your hymn - the day of peace."

The poet's hometown was the scene of a great event in the year 1896 when Riley was welcomed back to Greenfield rather as a conquering hero would have been. Riley stipulated that he wanted Captain Lee O. Harris to share the podium with him and he did so. Riley was welcomed to Greenfield at the train station by the remaining members of the Davis Brothers Old Band. Then the group headed to the Old Masonic Hall for a program. Every available space was filled with extra chairs filling the orchestra. The walls were also lined with onlookers. Riley recited his own verse and it was said "never was there an audience that gladdened his heart like this one." Riley said,

"After a long absence and most devious wandering, I am fervently rejoiced and touched by this welcome to my old home 'the dearest spot on earth to me' and made so not only by sacred reason of its being the place of my nativity, but especially because it has ever held the first, the best and the most forbearing friends I ever knew or ever needed. I feel grateful, too, with tenderest emotion of heart and mind, to be associated on the program with my old friend and master, Captain Harris, the inspiration of my earliest literary dreams and the steadfast help and influence of my life effort. But how to justly thank you and thank him- as I thank my lucky stars, is a staggering proposition..."

Riley then attended a dinner at the home of Dr. and Mrs. C.K. Bruner greeting old friends and spent the night at his cousin's home, the Hough's.

Greenfield had shown its pride in its native son.

The Riley of the later years had his own way of regarding the realities of his past life. He stated these principles in a speech he gave welcoming his friend and former President of the United States, Benjamin Harrison, back to Indiana after Harrison's presidential years in a speech to Indianapolis's elite Commercial Club of which both were members on April 22, 1897. Speaking of Harrison, he stated:

"The details of the trials of that earlier time and scene the young aspirant of today of course knows little of nor does that history as fitfully chronicled by reminiscent contributors to the home papers evoke its just measure of serious consideration. Only the sturdy and heroic participants themselves can realize the import of that earlier history - only the comrades of that epoch and environment - the old friends - the old neighbors. To them the simple glories of that primitive past yet exceed all its trials and ordeals, and draw them into closer comradeship to- day. To them that past is sacred, and as they meet strike hands and fall into hearty discussion of the bygone years, it is always with a warmth of interest that in the cheeriest mirthful greeting sounds yet a minor note along the current of the laugh and in the merriest twinkle of the eye shows a certain shadowy, tender, yet insistent threat of rain. It is the fitting reverence remembrance pays to the youth-time of that friendship now grown to such ripe and sound maturity. So steadfastly on until this hour has it fared with our old friend and neighbor..."

Riley did not dwell on the past. It was something to be shared with sympathetic friends who understood why the things of the past had happened. That was all. Maturity erased its stings.

A warm picture of Riley as an older man comes to us from the recollection of his niece, Mrs. Harry Miese. She remembered him as a perfectionist. "I remember his careful lesson to us on exactly how to close and fold an umbrella. When he found he could write despite his lack of formal education he bought grammars and worked until he was perfect. Uncle Jim said to me once: `I enjoy anything that's perfectly done.'" She also recalled he loved red neckties and red socks but he never wore them because they were too loud. He kept them in a drawer in his room and took them out to look at occasionally. "My uncle often said, and he believed it too, that anyone could do anything they had faith to do. He liked food and always said he hoped there would be `too much butter' on his sandwiches."

Riley hated to be late for an event. His niece, Hariett Eitel Wells, recalls he sometimes came down at 4 P.M. dressed in formal attire for an evening out so he would not be late. He pinned his shirt collar with long straight pins so it would not slip up.

In the spring and summer of 1898, Riley's country was at war with Spain. The Spanish-American conflict was brief and telling. Spain lost the last vestiges of its 400 year old empire. More importantly the United States drew together in a union that had been shattered for a generation by the American Civil War. Riley celebrated this victory with a poem published in the December ATLANTIC MAGAZINE. It was another famous Krung poem.

THE NAME OF OLD GLORY (1898)

I

Old Glory! say, who,
By the ships and the crew
And the long, blended ranks of the gray and the blue, -
Who gave you, Old Glory, the name that you bear
With such pride everywhere
As you cast yourself free to the rapturous air
And leap out full-length, as we're wanting you to? -
Who gave you that name, with the ring of the same,
And the honor and fame so becoming to you? -
Your stripes stroked in ripples of white and of red,
With your stars at their glittering best overhead -
By day or by night
Their delighfulest light
Laughing down from their little square heaven of blue! -
Who gave you the name of Old Glory? - say, who -
*   Who gave you the name of Old Glory?*

The old banner lifted, and faltering then

In vague lisps and whispers fell silent again.

II

Old Glory, - speak out! - we are asking about
How you happened to "favor" a name, so to say,
That sounds so familiar and careless and gay
As we cheer it and shout in our wild breezy way -
We - the crowd, every man of us, calling you that -
We - Tom, Dick and Harry - each swinging his hat
And hurrahing "Old Glory!" like you were our kin,
When - Lord! - we all know we're as common as sin!
And yet it just seems like you humor us all
And waft us your thanks, as we hail you and fall
Into line, with you over us, waving us on
Where our glorified, sanctified betters have gone. -
And this is the reason we're wanting to know -
(And we're wanting it so! -
Where our own fathers went we are willing to go.) -
Who gave you the name of Old Glory - Oho!-
      Who gave you the name of Old Glory?

The old flag unfurled with a billowy thrill
For an instant, then wistfully sighed and was still.

III

Old Glory: the story we're wanting to hear
Is what the plain facts of your christening were, -
For your name - just to hear it,
Repeat it, and cheer it, 's a tang to the spirit
As salt as a tear; -
And seeing you fly, and the boys marching by,
There's a shout in the throat and blur in the eye
And an aching to live for you always - or die,
If, dying, we still keep you waving on high.
And so, by our love

Riley accepted membership in the American Academy of Arts and Letters by letter dated February 2, 1911 joining his literary friends William Dean Howells, Samuel Clemens, Henry James, Joel Chandler Harris, Julia Ward Howe, and Charles Adams, and others such as Carl Schurz, Theodore Roosevelt, Woodrow Willson, Augustus Saint-Gaudens, Winslow Homer and John Singer Sargent.

For you, floating above,
And the scars of all wars and sorrows thereof,
Who gave you the name of Old Glory, and why
    Are we thrilled at the name of Old Glory?

Then the old banner leaped, like a sail in the blast,
And fluttered an audible answer at last. -

IV

And it spake, with a shake of the voice, and it said: -
By the driven snow-white and the living blood-red
Of my bars, and their heaven of stars overhead -
By the symbol conjoined of them all, skyward cast,
As I float from the steeple, or flap at the mast,
Or droop o'er the sod where the long grasses nod, -
My name is as old as the glory of God.
    ...So I came by the name of Old Glory.

On the following January, Riley was asked to recite the poem at the Indiana statehouse where the State accepted a gun captured from the Spanish fleet by Admiral Dewey and also to receive the battle flag of the naval vessel, the Indiana. The scene was mayhem as the state legislators of Indiana and a huge crowd milled around in the statehouse. Then Riley was introduced to give his poem by Admiral George Brown. Riley offered it as a "homely poem to the dear flag, a homely tribute by a voice from the crowd." Most of the people present were familiar with "The Name of Old Glory" which had quickly achieved national prominence as the patriotic poem of the Spanish American War. Then Riley gave it. The crowd filled with patriotic emotion. When Riley finished the crowd rose with applause. It was one of the great moments in the history of the Hoosier state.

William Dean Howells was the literary arbiter of the 1890's. Of the critics contemporary with James Whitcomb Riley his voice was most listened to. Howells was the champion of literary realism. He hated romance. He tested every writer by whether he treated life as it really was. "The truth should always be told. It may be indecent, but it cannot be vicious. The imagination can only work with the stub of experience, for experience is life. The difference between realism and romanticism is that the realist takes nature as he finds her; the romanticist colors nature for his own use."

In 1899, Howells visited Indianapolis and was particularly anxious to see James Whitcomb Riley during his visit. He not only lectured in Indianapolis, but was escorted through a tour of the city by Booth Tarkington later a two time Pulitzer Prize win-

An Empire style sofa with "Crazy Quilt" purchased by Riley circa 1890 to furnish his Greenfield home. Riley was known to "nap" on this couch in the afternoons. Courtesy, Riley Museum, Greenfield, Indiana.

ning author of the city. Tarkington was then thirty and already the author of the novel, The Gentleman from Indiana. Riley was a close friend of the Tarkington family and was invited to a dinner at the home of Mary Booth (Tarkington) Jameson, nicknamed Haute, during the Howells visit. Riley was the star of the brightest magnitude in the Hoosier literary constellation at the time. He was much sought after as a public reader and when he recited "The Old Man and Jim" or "Out to Old Aunt Mary's" audiences simply responded with unabashed tears. By this time Riley's kenotic poetry such as The Old Swimmin'-Hole and 'Leven More Poems, had long reached "best seller" class and this and other published works provided much income for Riley. Unfortunately, illness kept Riley from this dinner and so the next day, Howells made a call on Riley at his Lockerbie Street home. They conversed privately for about an hour.

Only seven months before this visit, Howells had written "I think Mr. Riley a very great artist, with insight as subtle as the best of the new English poets, and sympathy as generous." The critic of realism greatly admired Riley who he called "the poet of our common life." He had concluded that Riley's poetry was of such sweetness, sincerity, and purity that "some may not yet prize it aright."

We know of Howells' impression of Indianapolis. As he crossed the northern places of Indiana en route to Detroit and wrote of his visit. He was pleased with his reception in Indianapolis and his lecture. People had stuffed him with praise, he wrote his wife from the train. He also thought the physical appearance of Indianapolis was notable. He called it "a stately and beautifully livable city. He was particularly impressed with the new, "distinctly noble" Civil War monument in the heart of the capital which gave the city "a very European effect." Of the people he had met, Riley and former President, Benjamin Harrison, were the two he stated stood out most vividly.

Among the many honors Krung received were the following. In 1902, Yale College, New Haven, Connecticut conferred upon Riley at age 52 the honorary degree of Master of Arts. On taking his degree at Yale in 1902, William Lyon Phelps, a friend and English Professor at the university, commented that Riley received more applause than all the other candidates put together.

As the noted journalist, Lester Negley, Sr., put it, Riley was a poet of "stated occasions." One of Riley's great moments as Krung was when, on May 15, 1902, he participated in the dedication of the central shrine of Indianapolis, the Indiana Soldiers and Sailor's monument. This obelisk arising from a base of sculpted heroically configured statuary was located in the epicenter of the Hoosier city as set aside by the original city plan of Indianapolis as the capitol of the Hoosier people. It was on a circle. The circle had originally been envisioned as the place where the Indiana governor's official residence would be located but Indiana governors would not live under such conditions of scrutiny. The occasional nickname of Indianapolis as the "Circle City" derives from the important place which this monument's location on the Indianapolis circle occupies.

Riley wrote a special poem, "The Soldier," for the occasion. The morning of the dedication began at 8 a.m. when a "parade of flags" was staged and survivors of Indiana regiments of the Mexican, Civil and Spanish-American wars marched around the circle carrying their flags. At 10 a.m. General Lew Wallace, Civil War general and kenotic author of BEN HUR, presided at the dedication service where Riley read his poem after a men's chorus of 200 voices had sung.

Krung had been active in the effort to raise money to build the monument. He had written a very popular poem called "A Monument for Soldiers" which was used to build popular support for the project.

In 1903 Wabash College at Crawfordsville, Indiana presented Riley at age 53 with an Honorary Master of Arts. The next year, in 1904, the University of Pennsylvania, Philadelphia, Pennsylvania honored Riley at age 54 with a degree of Doctor of Letters. Riley's final degree -Honorary Doctor of Laws - was granted in 1907 by Indiana University, Bloomington, Indiana at

Riley's age 57.

Krung received many honors. He was truly the famous person who Riley had only hoped to be when he wrote "The Flying Islands of the Night." Riley was elected a member of the American Academy of Arts and Letters, New York City, New York in 1911. This was a prestigious position for the poet born in a log cabin in Greenfield, Indiana. This same year, Riley was awarded a gold medal for poetry by the National Institute of Arts and Letters for his contribution to American poetry. Riley was the third person to receive the award and the first poet so honored. The medal bears the likeness of Apollo, the sun god, symbolizing creative force and on the reverse a Grecian lamp representing the light shed on civilization by the fine arts. In

Riley is welcomed by his townsfolk. Riley Day in downtown Greenfield, Indiana on October 9, 1912

acknowledging the honor, Riley stated, "Nothing has ever filled my cup so brimming as your generosity in conferring upon me the medal of the institute in the department of poetry. I have been a humbler and, I hope, a better man since that bestowal. You not only honored me beyond any imaginable deserving, but my state and mine own people as well. The institute medal was given annually to the United State citizen for distinguished original creative work in the field of sculpture, history, poetry, architecture, drama, painting, fiction, essays, biography, or music.

And now came the great days when Krung was honored with birthday celebrations. On October 7, 1911, Riley Day was observed in schools of Indiana and New York City. On this same day, October 7, 1911, the anniversary of his birthday he came to Greenfield on an invitation of the teachers and pupils of the Greenfield schools. After that visit, on Oct. 9, 1911, Riley, partially paralyzed, sent the following letter to the pupils of Greenfield, Ind.

Indianapolis, Indiana, Oct. 9, 1911

To the Pupils of the Greenfield Schools, Greenfield, Ind.

Dear Friends of Mr. Riley:

Being unable to write to you himself, my uncle has asked me to express his gratitude for the appreciative birthday greetings you sent to him on behalf of the teachers and pupils of the Greenfield schools. Your greetings were especially welcome, more dear than any of the many others, because they recall the happy days of his youth in Greenfield, many memories of the old home, and the loyalty of the people of Greenfield.

He asks me to return to his friends, one and all, his gratitude, appreciation and love. Very truly yours,

/s/Edmund Eitel

This same month of October, 1911, on the motion of Riley's Greenfield friend, Minnie Belle Mitchell, the Indiana State Federation of Women's Clubs proposed a statewide Indiana celebration of Riley Days in honor of Riley for the next year.

The tribute of school children across the country came. The school children of practically every section of the country had programs in his honor.

Minnie Belle Mitchell has described the very first Riley Day which was held October 7th, 1912:

"The first birthday celebration was held in Indianapolis, the home of the poet. Two thousand school children formed a great procession and passed his home in Lockerbie Street. Mr. Riley, seated on the lawn with a group of friends, greeted the children. Mrs. A.L.New, of this city and myself were among the invited guests. Moving pictures were made of the poet greeting the long line of children. A reproduction of his favorite poem "Out to Old Aunt Mary's" from the original manuscript was given to each child.

Then Mr. Riley came to Greenfield - back to the friends of whom he said - Oh, Home-Folks! you're the best of all 'At ranges this tereschul ball- Greenfield, too, was celebrating the Hoosier's poet birthday with the poet in its midst. It was a wholesome, homey reception that greeted Mr. Riley. The town was decorated from end to end, the stores closed their doors and school children from over the county paraded the streets. People from all over the state came -old boyhood friends and those who knew him only through his books.

Riley Day during "Made in Anderson Week", June 3rd, 1913. Anderson honors Riley.

From early morning the crowd restlessly awaited the coming of the royal guest and finally when it heard the old band begin to play in the far distance, "Hail to the Chief: - or was it playing "Lilly Dale" like a voice from the poet's far distant youth? Then the poet's car came in sight passing slowly and cautiously through throngs of people - thousandsof them, cheering and calling his name. the car soon reached a double line of children and each child was armed with flowers of every hue. As Mr. Riley passed, the flowers were tossed into his car literally covering him with blossoms.

Mr. Riley's car was parked at the Court house curb where a group of his oldest and closest friends awaited him. Mayor Ora Myers introduced the honored guests: Hon. William R. Hough, a cousin, delivered the address of welcome; Captain Henry Snow talked on "Old Times in Greenfield"; John F. Mitchell told of boyhood days and William A. Hough used the poet himself as the subject of his remarks.

A happy feature of the occasion was the presentation of a silver loving cup, purchased by the school children of Prof. Frank Larrabee. Mr. Riley, deeply touched, responded as follows: "I thank you. Sometimes I think I ought to apologize to the people of Greenfield in that I may not seem to appreciate all they do for me. Not being able to arise I shall only say that I cannot tell you how my heart is touched. It is a great thing, and if later we claim the reward we all hope for, heaven will indeed have to surpass itself to find more than I have here. I thank you."

Riley's mail was enormous and he received mail at three places, his house, the publisher's, and the office of a trust company where a desk was reserved for him. He enjoyed receiving mail and made sure not a single letter escaped his notice. He duly inscribed books sent him in the mail for autograph from all over the country.

1913 was the famous "Made In Anderson Day," where Riley was invited to the city that had harbored him most in his 20's and where "Leonainie" was written among many other poems. Riley's automobile was met at Pendleton by the city notables and a great cavalcade proceeded on climaxing in a grand parade and readings at Anderson's Grand Opera House. Children brought flowers to the footlights. Riley responded, "Citizens of Anderson, and you, little children who have so wonderfully greeted me, I have no words to express to you what is in my heart at this moment. This is the happiest day of my life. I thank you for your generous welcome, I thank you for your beautiful flowers. With all my heart, I thank you - I thank you."

Krung continued to write public poetry for many persons as the years progressed.

A friend of Daniel L. Marsh, Reverend Doctor W.W, Hall, held evangelistic meetings in Riley's boyhood home, Greenfield, Indiana, in the fall of 1914, less than two years before Riley died. Riley wrote him a poem which he entitled "The Evangelist," with this greeting:

"These lines are a greeting to you and an epitome of your first sermon in Greenfield. You are at liberty with them." The lines are found in Marsh's,

THE FAITH OF THE PEOPLE'S POET:

Hail, Harbinger of God's Good News!
Good News' to pulpits and to pews: -
Oh, hear His voice in - `Peace Be Still,'
And dwell entwined in His sweet will.
`The Purpose?' Ah, with glad accord,
Put on the armor of the Lord,
And forth to battle! - all as one, -
The fight! The fight! Is now begun!

`The Plan?' - `Tis writ with pencil pure, -
Line and dimension straight and sure: -
Inquire of Him - `Lord, what to do?'

Then let Him have His way - in you.

`The Motive?' that all tongues confess
To Him - our Hope and Righteousness!
Tho' now the view be darkly dim, -
Through faith we'll win the world to Him!

`And Victory?' It will be won!
God's Promise - through His Promised Son!
We'll sing it in the realms above -
Enraptured by Enraptured Love!

Riley's generosity continued when he contributed real estate valued at approximately $100,000 north of St. Clair square to form part of the site of the new Central Indianapolis library building. Riley's private gifts to the needy and charitable causes were substantial but never disclosed.

On September 8, 1915, the Governor of Indiana, Samuel M. Ralston, issued a proclamation designating October 7, 1915, the 66th anniversary of the birth of Riley, as "Riley Day" in Indiana and urged all people of the state "to arrange in their respective communities, appropriate exercises in their schools and at other public meeting places; that they display the American flag at their homes and places of business on that day in honor of James Whitcomb Riley, Indiana's most beloved citizen."

Riley's huge popularity during his lifetime caused his name to have great commerical value. Some of the products sold across America bearing indicia of him are shown.

This proclamation simply must be more fully quoted since it contains rhetoric among the finest prose in public literature:

PROCLAMATION OF RILEY DAY OF SEPT. 8, 1915

"Whether the arch above his head was at times one of sunshine or one of cloud, all recognized that in the depths of his soul there was love for his fellowman and adoration for his God. Whether he was painting signs or writing verses, the people were his study. He familiarized himself with their manners and customs and characteristics, and with melody and sweetness and a singular fit of invention, he told them things about themselves they did not know. This is why they have always loved him.

Riley in September, 1913.

More than any other citizen of Indiana, James Whitcomb Riley has carried the fame of his native state into the schools and homes of the world. It is not strange therefore that there should be a widespread feeling among our people that the anniversary of his birth should be celebrated in honor of his poetic genius and his literary achievements, and in recognition of his contributions to society.

He is the children's poet, and he has become such because he has so much of the spirit of the One who said, Suffer little children to come unto me. All Indiana will rejoice therefore to see her children afforded an opportunity to place their heart wreaths upon his brow and strew their flowers about his feet.

Now, therefore, I, Samuel M. Ralston, as Governor of the State of Indiana, hereby designate and proclaim the seventh day of October, A.D., 1915, the anniversary of the birth of James Whitcomb Riley, as Riley Day; and I urge all the people of the state to arrange in their respective communities, in their own way, appropriate public exercises in their schools and at their other public meeting places; and that they display the American flag at their homes and places of business on this day, in honor of Indiana's most beloved citizen."

What Indiana did for Riley was not done before. No poet in history had been accorded such honor. Krung was truly arrived in this last year of Riley's life. A Boston newspaper, The Christian Science MONITOR, took note of this action and said, "You have to think of Riley in his right setting,

doing much the same humanizing work as a poet that Lincoln did as a statesman, and with the same instruments - pathos, humor, and sincere love of
men as men."

This last birthday of Riley was not just celebrated in Indiana. Informal
celebrations were held in Chicago, St. Paul and at the Panama Exposition,
San Francisco while formal
celebrations were held in
West Virginia, Jacksonville,
Florida, Washing D.C., and
Pittsburgh were three thousand teachers joined in the
exercises while eighty thousand children were enter-
tained with "The Old
Swimmin'-Hole" and "The
Raggedy Man."

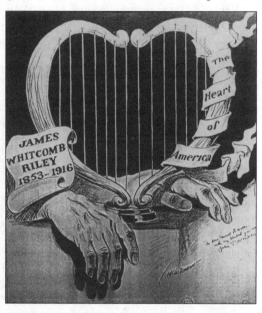

A last dinner was held for
Riley in Indianapolis at the
Claypool Hotel. The arrangements for this gala dinner
were extensive and its chair-
man was the Vice President of
the United States, Charles
Fairbanks. He was also the
toastmaster for the evenings

A final newspaper tribute published upon his dath, titled "The Master
Musician Is Dead."

entertainment. The speakers included Governor Samuel Ralston, Colonel
George Harvey, John Finley, Young Allison, Albert Beveridge, William
Allen White, George Ade, and Senator John Kern. The Union soldiers of
Indiana presented Riley with a silk flag. Many other acts of friendship were
given. Letters were read from many. Among them was one from William
Dean Howells, "Give him my dearest love and all such honor as one of the
least may offer one of the greatest of our poets.") Another from President
Woodrow Wilson ("I wish that I might be present to render my tribute of
affectionate appreciation to him for the many pleasures he has given me,
along with the rest of the great body of readers of English. I think he has
every reason to feel on his birthday that he has won the hearts of his countrymen.")

Riley Day has remained celebrated in Riley's hometown of Greenfield,

Indiana, to the time of this writing as the Twentieth Century closes. More about this event is chronicled in your author's HISTORY OF HANCOCK COUNTY, INDIANA, IN THE TWENTIETH CENTURY.

Riley went to Florida that winter as he had the previous ones in his last years and returned to Indiana in the Spring.

Krung's last appearance came June, 1916. This was just one month before he died. Riley agreed to pose on the lawn of his Lockerbie Street brick home for the shooting a film that was to be used in promotion of Indiana's Centennial Celebration of 100 years of statehood in 1916. Riley did this at the special request of the Governor despite his paralysis and bad health. It was filmed by Harry Cobur and at this appearance, Lester C. Nagley, Sr., took his own photos, one of which was the shot of Riley and the children which was used as the basis for the mural of Riley in the Hancock County Courthouse.

Riley's bronze coffin weight twelve hundred pounds being carried from the Lockerbie Street home. (From the Barton Rees Pogue glass positive collection.) At the time of his death, Riley was contemplating a move to a mansion he was building for himself. The unfinished structure located at the northeast edge of Indianapolis was subsequently disposed of for use as a tuberculosis sanitarium and call "Sunnyside."

Krung's death followed. On Saturday night, at ten minutes to eleven, July 22d, 1916, before Riley retired for the night, he asked a nurse staying with him for a glass of water. While waiting, Riley attempted to turn on his side and gently died.

Krung's death was greatly mourned. Flags over Indiana drooped to half-staff. In Washington, the Speaker of the House, Champ Clark, commented to the press and President Wilson telegraphed his sorrow to Edmund Eitel. Krung's body lay in state under the Indiana statehouse dome prior to the funeral. Riley's body was eventually laid to rest on the high knoll of Crown Hill Cemetery in Indianapolis.

Riley died one of the wealthiest poet in literary history. His estate was valued at $283,182.70 exclusive of book rights which were subject to secret agreements never disclosed. Riley's legacies provided income sufficient to support his heirs, his one surviving sister, Mary Elizabeth Payne, then living in New York, and his nephew and niece, Edmund H. Eitel and Elizabeth Whitcomb Eitel, of Indianapolis, the children of Riley's sister Elva, for the rest of their lives. In fact, Riley had provided very substantial income to all of these during his lifetime. No last will and testament was ever found.

In the Riley notice of death in the New York SUN, a critic commented: "He took by divine right the place of an American poet which has not been occupied since Longfellow's tenancy ended." The Greenfield contingent to the Riley viewing at the Statehouse had worn ribbons, "Greenfield and Hancock County. The Home of Riley - He Still Lives."

How the world felt about the death of Riley may have been best expressed by one of Riley's successors in the use of dialect poetry, Michigan's Edgar Allen Guest.[1]

JAMES WHITCOMB RILEY

There must be great rejoicin' on the Golden Shore today,
An' the big and little angels must be feelin' mighty gay;
Could we look beyond the curtain now I fancy we should see
Old Aunt Mary waitin' smilin' for the coming that's to be.
An' Little Orphant Annie an' the whole excited pack
Dancin' up and down and shoutin': "Mr. Riley's comin' back!"

There's a heap of sadness in the good old world today;
There are lumpy throats this morning now that Riley's gone away.
There's a voice now stilled forever that in sweetness only spoke
An' whispered words of courage with a faith that never broke.
There is much joy and laughter that we mortals here will lack,
But the angels must be happy now that Riley's comin' back.

The world was gettin' dreary, there was too much sigh and frown;
In the vale o' mortal strivin', so God sent Jim Riley down,
An' He said, "Go there an' cheer `em, but don't make your plans to stay
Coz you're needed up in heaven. I am lendin' you to man
Just to help `em with your music, but I'll want you back again.

An' Riley came an' mortals heard the music of his voice
An' the caught his songs o' beauty an' they started to rejoice;
An' they leaned on him in sorrow an' they shared with him their joys
An' they walked with him the pathways that they knew when they were
boys;
But the heavenly angels missed him, missed his tender gentle knack,
Of makin' people happy, an' they wanted Riley back.

There must be great rejoicin' on the street of Heaven today;
An' all the angel children must be troopin' down the way;
Singin' heavenly songs of welcome an' preparin' now to greet
The soul that god had tinctured with an everlastin' sweet;
The world is robed in sadness an' is draped in somber black,
But joy must reign in Heaven, now that Riley's comin' back!

1. From a booklet issued by Horace Ellis, then State Superintendent of Public Instruction of the State of Indiana issued in 1917 in the Riley Museum, Greenfield, Indiana. Guest was an Englishman born in Birmingham of that country on August 20, 1881 who was brought to the United States at the age of ten. He was educated in Detroit, Michigan and wrote greatly admired books of verse. He also was on the editorial staff of the Detroit FREE PRESS and wrote a syndicated column carried in major American newspapers. One of his famous poems begins: "It take a heap o'livin' in a house to make it home."

A "victrola" or "record player" with "record" or "phono-graphic recording" of Riley reciting "The Raggedy man." Courtesy, Riley Museum, Greenfield, Indiana.

BUD

RILEY AS A CHILD TUCKED ALL INSIDE - "THE CHILDREN'S POET"

RILEY AS A CHILD TUCKED ALL INSIDE
THE "CHILDREN'S POET"

Perhaps the one "fragmented" Riley self not mentioned in "The Flying Islands of the Night" or in the Buzz Club series was the part of himself as "Bud." That is because Bud was Riley as a "tucked-away-inside" elfin child: innocent, hopeful and unwearied. He was a child who never surrendered to life but stayed strong and knew the truth of dreams.

Two great circumstances seem to have permitted Riley to become the child he wished to be more overtly in his older age. The first was fame. Fame permits a person to be who he wants to. The second was the death of the father, Reuben Riley in 1893, the strong disciplinarian who would never have approved such odd behavior as a man acting the child.

Bud Riley going on six. (Neg.C7169, IMCPL-Riley Collection, Indiana Historical Society.)

When it came time that Riley's child-self could spring forth, Bud was waiting to appear. Bud was Riley who could not grow up. Why? Perhaps it because the world of Riley's childhood was so fascinating and charming that

Will Vawter's illustration of the poem, "Little Orphant Annie" for the book, RILEY CHILD-RHYMES WITH HOOSIER PICTURES, published in 1905. Vawter illustrated more than a dozen Riley books including five collections issed by Bobbs-Merrill after Riley's death.

he simply did not want to escape it. From his childhood memory comes "Little Orphant Annie."

LITTLE ORPHANT ANNIE [1] (1885)

INSCRIBED
WITH ALL FAITH AND AFFECTION

To all the little children: - The happy ones;
and sad ones;
The sober and the silent ones; the boister-
ous and glad ones;
The good ones - Yes, the good ones, too;
and all the lovely
bad ones.

Little Orphant Annie's [2] *come to our house to stay,*
An' wash the cups an' saucers up, an' brush the crumbs away,
An' shoo the chickens off the porch, an' dust the hearth, an'
sweep,
An' make the fire [3], *an' bake the bread, an' earn her board-*
an-keep;
An' all us other childern, when the supper-things is done,
We set around the kitchen fire an' has the mostest fun,
A-listenin' to the witch-tales 'at Annie tells about,
An' the Gobble-uns 'at gits you
>   *Ef you*
>>   *Don't*
>>>   *Watch*
>>>   *Out!*

Wunst they wuz a little boy wouldn't say his prayers [4], -
An' when he went to bed at night, away up-stairs,
His Mammy heerd him holler, an' his Daddy heerd him bawl,
An' when they turn't the kivvers down, he wuzn't there at all!
An' they seeked him in the rafter-room, an' cubby-hole, an' press,
An seeked him up the chimbly-flue, an' ever'-wheres, I guess;
But all they ever found wuz thist his pants an' roundabout: -
An' the Gobble-uns 'll git you
>   *Ef you*
>>   *Don't*
>>>   *Watch*
>>>   *Out!*

An' one time a little girl 'ud allus laugh an' grin,
An' make fun of ever' one, an' all her blood-an'-kin;
An' wunst, when they was "company," an' ole folks wuz there,
She mocked 'em an' shocked 'em, an' said she didn't care!
An' thist as she kicked her heels, an' turn't to run an' hide,
They wuz two great big Black Things a-standin' by her side,
An' they snatched her through the ceilin' 'for she knowed
what she's about!
An' the Gobble-uns 'll git you

Ef you
   Don't
      Watch
         Out!
An' little Orphant Annie says, when the blaze is blue,
An' the lamp-wick sputters, an' the wind goes woo-oo!
An' you hear the crickets quit, an' the moon is gray,
An' the lightnin'bugs in dew is all squenched away, -
You better mind yer parunts, an' yer teachurs fond an' dear,
An' cherish them 'at loves you, an' dry the orphant's tear,
An' he'p the pore an' needy ones 'at clusters all about,
Er the Gobble-uns 'll git you
   Ef you
      Don't
         Watch
            Out!

1. The poem was first published under the name "The Elf Child" in the Indianapolis JOURNAL of November 15, 1885. It was composed in "The Crow's Nest" of the Reuben Riley home known as "The Seminary" in Greenfield, Indiana.

2. As originally published the waif's name was Little Orphant "Allie." "Allie" was the nickname of Mary Alice Smith the given name of the child described. She was an orphan taken into the Riley home during Riley's childhood before the Civil War. She delighted the Riley children with her imaginative stories and odd ways. When she fed the chickens, she was a queen, she said, throwing gold to the peasants. She pressed her cheek lovingly on the steps of the curving stairway and reported that she could hear fairies and elves whispering underneath. This was Little Orphant Annie. Her mother was dead and she wanted to go to "the Good world where my mother is." The real Mary Alice Smith married the farmer Wesley Gray and settled down south of Philadelphia, Indiana. In her later years, "Little Orphant Annie" was in great demand for visiting

Mary Alice Smith, "Little Orphant Annie," in her older age. She came from Liberty, Indiana where she had lived in the hills. Her mother died, her father left her, and an uncle, John Rittenhouse, from Greenfield came down in a wagon to fetch her to his hometown. She got work at the Riley's. For many years after she left the Riley's, her whereabouts were unknown. Then on September 30, 1882, Riley published a prose piece in the Indianapolis JOURNAL: "Where is Mary Alice Smith?" She was soon found after a search by Riley's nephew Edmund Eitel. In January, 1888, Riley brought her to the stage of the Grand Opera House in Indianapolis to great applause at the conclusion of his readings and repeated the whole story of the little slender orphan dressed in black who was dropped off at the Riley Home and told the Riley children about elves and goblins.

Hoosier schools to talk to the enthralled children about her years at the Riley home. She called Riley a "tease" and said he drew ugly pictures of his playmates to annoy them and many other remembered tales.

3. Up to the mid-Nineteenth Century, cooking was done in a large open fireplace on the Hoosier frontier. Big coal-burning cast-iron stoves replaced fireplace cooking around the time of the American Civil War in the early 1860's. 4. Riley's childhood in the 1850's was a time of great religious enthusiasms on the American frontier.

A pallet of straw located in the alcove where Little Orphant Annie slept at the Riley Home, Greenfield, Indiana.

There might have been more serious reasons why Riley enjoyed contemplating his life in youth so much. Was it because he was a Hoosier Deutsch child in a transitional "mixing pot" culture? Or was it because depression had deprived Riley of any chance to mature as would another adult? Or had he felt the death of loved ones too deeply to recover? Or was it because his humanitarian and kenotic ideas had given him the peace to become the child again?

I think Riley recalled his childhood so fondly because he had been through so much loneliness and heartache. Rudyard Kipling, the author of the British CHILD'S GARDEN OF VERSES, may have thought this too when he wrote Riley a poem:

TO J.W.R.

"Your trail runs to the westward,
And mine to my own place;
There is water between our lodges,
And you cannot see my face.
And it is well - for crying
Should neither be written nor seen,
But if I call you Smoke-in-the-Eyes,
I know you will know what I mean."

Both ached for the lost child in themselves.

Riley replied to Kipling's poem with his own entitled:

TO RUDYARD KIPLING
"If there be sweet in any song I've sung,
  'Twas savored for thy palate, O my child!
For thee the lisping of the children all -
  For thee the youthful voices of old years -
For thee all chords untamed or musical -
  For thee the laughter, and for thee the tears."

Riley acknowledged tears went into his children's poetry as well as laughter.

In his last years Riley could become a child and "The Children's Poet" perhaps the most joyous appellation he would have. Bud lived in a friendly "Child-World." Riley became Bud and went to live with him there in his dreams.

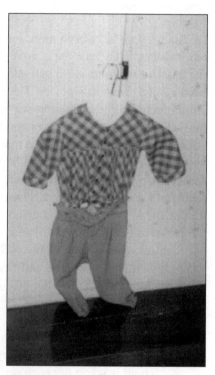

Riley chose to become Bud when even fame was already available. Riley ultimately was not satisfied with being Krung. The possibility of finding peace as an innocent child can have was too great a draw. Riley had always wished to be Bud.

Although Riley wrote children's poems most of his literary life, he only drew on the "Bud" inside him. Not until 1893 when Riley's father died could Bud be brought out in the open as Riley's companion in real life. This event liberated Riley to become the child of innocence Riley really was but

A "roundabout" or boy's everyday clothes at the time of Riley's boyhood.

could never be in reality. Soon came the book A CHILD-WORLD published in 1896 which brought back memories of Riley's life in Greenfield, Indiana when it was a village of three hundred souls where life was fun and meanness was not contemplated.

The father's expectation of the son was always that he would take to his own legal profession, marry and raise a family. Riley never did any of these things. By the time the father died, Riley was a child who had outlived most of the life strategy of "The Flying Islands of the Night." Riley had always wanted to live in a world of dreams. Riley once said, "My father did not have a large library, but a choice one, and among those books there were some he forbade me to read. There were books of fairy tales and mythology. Soon as he was out of the room, however, I was again sporting with the elves and fairies. It was a wonderful world, because I thought it was real." This world did become totally real after the father died. His was the only hand to shushhhhhh the dreaming.

The rebirth of Bud released a great force of creative energy. Riley's identity as the child permitted him to "make believe" about everything.

Bud was innocent and good. When the child was absent from him, he was not whole. He was as the child in this poem published in the Indianapolis JOURNAL on September 26, 1880:

A PHANTOM

Little baby, you have wandered far away,
And your fairy face comes back to me to-day,
But I can not feel the strands
Of your tresses, nor the play
Of the dainty velvet-touches of your hands.

Little baby, you were mine to hug and hold;
Now your arms cling not about me as of old -
O my dream of rest come true,
And my richer wealth than gold,
And the surest hope of Heaven that I know!
O for the lisp long silent, and the tone
Of merriment once mingled with my own -
For the laughter of your lips,
And the kisses plucked and thrown
In the lavish wastings of your finger-tips!

Little baby, O as then, come back to me,
And be again just as you used to be,

For this phantom of you stands
  All to cold and silently,
And will not kiss nor touch me with its hands.

Bud came back.

Riley regained the spirit of himself as a child. He felt himself in the past in the presence of the living. He once stated to his secretary late in life, "You don't believe in ghosts? Well, I do. The lad I was when I stood in the solitude of the woods, by Tharpe's Pond, comes to associate with me at night. He is not a tangible being, not a body you can touch with a finger, but a vivid presence here in my room nevertheless. He is the ghost of my boyhood self, and when he lingers round, my heart is warm, and I revel in past emotions and bygone times." About this child he had no insecurities. He could play with all other identities. Riley's use of pseudonyms is legion. His letters end with signatures outlandishly fake. Sometimes he signs himself as Jamesy O'Reilly or Uncle Sydney. Names meant very little to Riley and he really didn't think them very important. When he submitted the poem "Lord Bacon" to a newspaper he ascribed it to his business manager, Amos J. Walker. In October, 1905, late in his life, he submitted poems entitled, "Three Southern Singers" as being from John Challing. More readily known pseudonyms are "Edyrn," "Jay Whit," "John C. Walker," "Doc Marigold," and "Harrison Driley." He thought nothing of turning his identity into the Irish as "Jamesy O'Riley" or "Jamesy O'Reilly."

This was not a man in identity crisis. James Whitcomb Riley simply never settled on who he wanted to be until he made up his mind that he really wanted to be the child, "Bud" most of all.

Once when Riley was praised for being the poet who put the real child into American literature, he replied "I have only been trying to do the little fellow simplest, purest justice." He said, "There is always beside me the little boy I used to be, and I can think his thoughts, and live his hopes and his tragedies now, just as much as I could when I looked like him."

There is a story about this Bud. He not only lived in Riley's imagination, he lived in Riley's reality as well. Riley took walks with him.

In his later years those who knew him, remarked how he delighted to go for imaginary walks with "Bud." "Bud" was of course Riley's own nickname as a child in Greenfield. Cane in hand he would venture off onto Lockerbie Street and head toward downtown Indianapolis in the company of the make-believe boy, "Bud." "But" skipped ahead of him usually as he walked usually about two or three feet. They stopped at a store and Riley bought tobacco and red cinnamon drops for Bud. Riley ate them both. When he ate the cinnamon drops his lips got boyishly and glorious crimson.

As he walked, he conversed with Bud. "There's a beautiful horse, Bud," Riley would say to his youthful companion "Bud." The talk would be of things both understood. "Wonderful morning, Bud," Riley would say.

One day Riley and "Bud" turned from East Street into Market Street just as an automobile was coming around the corner just ahead of Riley. The man was scared to death. When he told a friend about this, Riley said, "I got back to the curb all right but he almost got `Bud.'"

The world that Bud lived in was a past world of his own youth in Hancock County. What would those days have been like? What was Greenfield like before the Civil War?

We have the benefit of the witness of Lee O. Harris as to this world. Riley's instructor, Lee O. Harris, described the scene when James Whitcomb Riley was born and grew up in the 1850's in Hancock County, Indiana. I quote the first stanza of Harris's "The Harvest Days of the Olden Times," first published in the Indianapolis SENTINEL.

THE HARVEST DAYS
OF THE OLDEN TIMES

"Oh! the harvest days of the olden time!
The ring of the sickles to merry rhyme!
The wealth that fell at the reapers feet,
With the tinkling sound of a music sweet!
My soul is wrapt in a dream today
And over my senses, from far away,
There comes a rustle of grain, combined
With the drowsy voice of the summer wind,
And my heart o'erflows with a song of praise
     For the days - the days
The harvest time of my boyhood days..."

Harris was writing about recollections of the everyday experience of the folk at harvest time in Hancock County before the Civil War.

What would harvest time have been like in Hancock County in the 1850's to write about? Can we picture this land which Bud described in A Child-World?

Most of Hancock County was still being cleared. Few farms were over 50 acres. The land was plowed with wooden mold-board plows to put in crops between stumps. The stumps didn't bother the farmers though because the crop work was mostly done by hand except for help from oxen pulling a few implements. Rail fences separated fields and the timber was used for fuel in the home fireplaces. The ashes from this made lye for soap. Crops at harvest time were mostly for home consumption. Neighbors didn't see each other very much. For mail, you went into Greenfield to the Post Office for pick up. Then, as today, corn was the principal crop. An average farmer would have had two oxen, a saddle horse, a couple of family cows, possibly a razor back pig or two, and a few chickens. The livestock ran in the woods and corn, oats and wheat was planted by hand. We remember that Greenfield was not a town when Riley was born. It was unincorporated forest with inhabitants on a National Road huddling together in log cabins. An early memory of Riley was his father returning home with a deer he had hunted slung over his saddle for venison.

The harvest time that Lee O. Harris was describing was all done by hand. The family cut their corn with corn knives. I should say the stalks were cut in the fields and hauled near the house for hand husking during the winter. Sometimes neighbors would gather in the Hancock County farm neighborhoods for a "husking bee." In those days, corn harvesting was often "two step." The first step was when the corn was "topped" with cutting the stalks just above the ears to get the most palatable part of the stalks for livestock feed.

While the settlers of this virgin land of frontier Indiana were busy subsisting, the children were given free rein to go to Kingry's Mill, a grist mill, about a mile downstream on Brandywine Crick. The favorite "Swimmin' Hole" was on the way. The boys and girls were said to play Robin Hood up and down the crick. Riley was said to be a small child, not so strong as the others, but clever with ideas for games. He was fascinated with a pirate named Captain Kidd and many fairy tales and mythological figures. His imagination fed many of the children's activities and he was popular as a playmate because he could bring others into his imaginative scenarios.

We might think of this pioneer life as difficult. No, that is not the way our Hoosier pioneer ancestors considered their lives. Providence gave these people their fifty acres and strong hands to cut those stalks and husk the ears of corn. Were they happy? Were they as happy as we, their descendants?

The second stanza of Harris's poem:

"I stand again where the breezes toy
With the tangled locks of the farmer boy:
I hear the chorus of tuneful birds,
The twinkling bells of the grazing herds,
The happy shout and the joyous song,
And the gladsome laugh of the reaping throng:
The shout, the song, and the merry peal -
Attuned to the ring of the flashing steel -
They come me now through the dream maze
                    From the days - the days
The harvest time of my boyhood days..."

Is Harris glossing over the times he recalls? Is this romanticism? Is this some sort of gross resort to emotion? Where are the disappointments when the ax handle broke, the army worms ate the crops, men could expect to marry early and often because their wives died in childbirthing, or when childhood diseases cut life expectancy to a few years? To some extent, I suppose, "selective memory" of the good times permitted folk to strive and want to go on despite it all. On the other hand, hey! there were and are today joyous touches of life by a providential hand. Harris chose those moments to recall in his poetry.

What about the children? The families took the child care and education of their family youth to themselves. Riley's "Uncle Mart" Riley lived with Reuben and Elizabeth and built a treehouse for Riley and his brother. A swing was dangled from a tree for him to do "skyscrapers." Uncle Mart read to Riley from Nathaniel Hawthorne's TANGLEWOOD TALES when that book came out in 1853. He was also read to by Almon Keefer from a book of sea adventure called, TALES OF THE OCEAN.

Bud has his juvenile idiosyncracies that caused folk to love the old man Riley all the more.

In describing his fictional "Poet" in his novel about Riley of the same name, Meredith Nicholson said, "A certain inadvertence marked the Poet's ways. His deficiencies in orientation, even in the city he knew best of all, were a joke among his friends. He apparently gained his destinations by good luck rather than by intention.

Incurable modesty made him shy of early or precipitate arrivals at any threshold. Even in taking up a new book he dallied, scanned the covers, pondered the title-page, to delay his approach, as though not quite sure of the author's welcome and anxious to avoid rebuff. The most winning and charming, the most loveable of men - and entitled to humor himself in such harmless particulars!

The affairs that men busied themselves with were incomprehensible to him.

According to Meredith Nicholson, with his intimate Riley "had a fashion of taking up without prelude subjects that had been dropped weeks before." A child doesn't care much about time sequences.

Riley's nephew Edmund H. Eitel once stated, "The vivid presence of the poet's youth must have always been with him for he once referred to the part these memories played in the writing of many of his poems. He called these memories his "Dream Youth." Perhaps the psychologist might explain that this `Dream Youth' was a world in itself, created out of his recollections and developed in his

One of Bud's play areas. The dining room at the Riley boyhood home, Greenfield, Indiana with the "cubby hole" (a small enclosed space) at the right rear next to the cabinet. "Wunst they wuz a little boy wouldn't say his prayers, –/An' when he went to bed at night, away up-stairs, /His Mammy heerd him holler, and' his Daddy heerd him bawl, 'An' When they turn't the kivvers down, he wuzn't there at all! /An they seeked him in the rafter-room, an' cubby-hole..." (from the poem, "Little Orphant Annie") This is the cubby-hole of the poem.

poetic imagination. There was a very definite door to this world. That door was the memory of a deeply felt spiritual experience of childhood."

If we are correct in our assumption that Riley did not seek nor achieve maturation as an adult, but essentially stayed the Hoosier Deutsch child, then "Bud" would provide the most realistic of the heterogeneity of Riley's personality mix. Bud is the child who actually became alive and was the reality of James Whitcomb Riley toward the end of Riley's life. He was a real person if only to James Whitcomb Riley. He was the person who authored the children's poetry which gave Riley great fame. The real Riley was this Hoosier Deutsch child never grown up.

Bud's life was an imaginary sphere where Riley could avoid the realities of a world of Social Darwinist thought, depression and alcoholism.

William Lyon Phelps says of him:

"HE CARED ONLY FOR POETRY"

"He cared only for poetry, never talked about anything else. He took no interest in politics, and he never voted but once. When he later discovered that by reason of his unfamiliarity in making out the ballot, he had voted for the opponent of the friend who had induced him to go to the polls, he vowed never to vote again. He was extraordinarily neat and precise; his clothes were immaculate, his handwriting was a work of art....He always took infinite pains with his verse, considered carefully its technique and the weight of every word. He hated free verse with such uncompromising ardor that he was unable to see anything in Walt Whitman...There was absolutely no taint of vulgarity in the man; his profanity was lyrical. He had a heart of gold, and a genius for friendship. Having missed me one day at the train, he wrote, "I could have wept, had not the Almighty given me the blessed fit of cussin'...(Of Bill Nye, the humorist): The two humorists traveled together - Riley could never travel alone, as he could never find the right train or get off at the right place, having no notion of locating....(His letters) reflect his chronic modesty; he often felt that publishers and lecture bureaus paid him more than he earned. ..His affection for children and his understanding of them, shown not only in his verse but in the natural "equal" way he treated them, were beautifully expressed immediately after his death in a cartoon by Westerman, which appeared in the OHIO STATE JOURNAL, at Columbus. At the foot of a staircase there is crowded group of children looking up, and calling "Good night, Mr. Riley, good night, good night" One of the smallest children, overwhelmed by tears, is being led away. (Verse) was his natural medium of expression...He never got over the torture that afflicted him for hours preceding his appearance (at public lectures). He would eat nothing all day, would groan and wail and lament, could not bear to be left alone; and yet the instant he stepped out on the stage, there was no sign of the nervousness or of the agony that had tormented him. I remember once, a few hours before he was due to appear, trying to reason with him. "Why, Jim, there's nothing to be afraid of. You have done this hundreds of times, always done it well. Nobody is going to hurt you. You haven't even got to think up anything to say. All you are going to do is to repeat your own poems. Come on, let's have something to eat, and you'll feel better." He looked at me in amazement. "Eat? My God, hear him talk. Hear him say eat. I haven't eaten a mouthful all day." The professor comments, "I am certain that if he had known he was to be hanged, he would not have suffered so acutely."

William Lyon Phelps is talking here of a child, not an adult.

Riley himself recognized that the boy lived in him and that he was really this child, Bud, wrote a poet on that exact subject entitled, "The Old Man," sometimes called, "Salutation - To Benj. F. Johnson" (Riley's early pseudonym) which closes,

"So to-day, as lives the bloom,
And the sweetness, and perfume
Of the blossoms, I assume,
    On the same mysterious plan
The Master's love assures,
That the selfsame boy endures
In that hale old heart of yours,
    Old Man."

The real Riley, the only "ginoine ar-tickle," is the Hoosier Deutsch child filled with kenotic peace who needn't become an adult. We find this Riley in letters which Riley wrote to a child Dory Ann (Edith Thomas Medairy) covering a period of many years. In those letters Riley typically signed his name "Bud."

In older age, Riley acquired a player piano and when visited by a friend he inserted a favorite "roll" and danced around the room snapping his fingers in time to the music. The boy in him was always very near the surface of his character.

In his older age, "Bud" kept Riley going. One sees this in two letters written the same day to an Aunt and a separate letter to her niece both living in New York. In the letter to the Aunt, a poet friend Miss Edith M. Thomas, Riley relates the death of friend, "Youth - Youth - Youth! come down this way again! Then the Dread Shadow even could not blur the glory of the summer as it does. The fourth member of our household had gone on - the fourth in three years and this last a dear old and already sainted Mother! So

I could not write - nor can I yet, - only in this allusion to reaffirm yet newer, firmer belief in a wholly compensating hereafter. -Simply for all mother's sakes it must be so..."

Then to the little girl, "You needn't think you're so big if have been to Bennington! Maybe this afternoon I'm going to get to go 'way out to Millersville, and eat supper there, `fore we drive back, and have chicken and white gravy which Uncle Sidney laughs and calls it "kitepaste", an' hot biskits or salt risin' bread, and "milk that's purt-nigh puore cream for the child," as Mrs. Tilley she allus says."... This Bud had quite forgotten the fact that fate sometimes cuts into the innocent pleasures of childhood.

The Riley who wrote from the standpoint of Bud had characteristic themes as identified by the English poet Rudyard Kipling in a letter he wrote to Mrs. Charles Holstein in 1893 - "children and loafing and home life. They are all three of `em pretty new to a Gipsy (sic) like myself, and I love to hear them sung as they should be."

The idea of these themes derive from the dreams of Riley's own inner essential immature persona. The process is probably similar to his picture of himself in composition in "Tale of a Spider:" "Although by no means of a morbid or misanthropic disposition, the greater portion of my time I occupy, in strict seclusion, here at my desk - for only when alone can I conscientiously indulge certain propensities of thinking aloud, talking to myself, leaping from my chair occasionally to dance a new thought round the room, or take it in my arms, and hug, and hold, and love it as I would a great, fat, laughing baby with a bunch of jingling keys." Riley is that Hoosier Deutsch baby, a child who still can converse with the angels.

RILEY AND PALMISTRY

Bud allowed Riley to do childish and fun things. Riley came to love to have his palm read. A set of Riley's handprints has been preserved in the book LION'S PAWS by the palmistry reader Nellie Simmons Meier. Ms. Meier claims that her readings were the only ones that James Whitcomb Riley ("our close friend") really "listened to." She describes his hands as "always immaculate." "Mr. Riley was ultra fastidious with regard to his hands and the texture of the skin was remarkably fine." She notes his two hands were very different. The left one, which a palmist calls a "natural" hand (to a right-handed person), reveals a diffident, shrinking, secretive, timid nature, while the "right hand" is the hand of a self-reliant person with great initiative - the hand of a self-made man. The left hand shows a "long droop" at the "head line" indicating to her great imagination which Riley manifested in great "gloomy forebodings" as well as in his humor, while the "head line" in the right hand is modified to reveal Riley had much less difficulty with depression as the years passed.

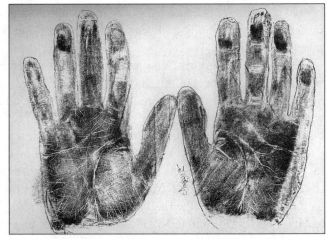

The inked handprints of James Whitcomb Riley preserved by the palmist Nellie Simmon Meier. She noted most his whimsy evident from the development of the "mount of Mercury" and the "sign of Mercury" faintly visible under the fourth finger in the left hand and also his touch for fantasy established by the "mount of the Moon" with a large whorl "whose sword is sharp enough to cut the line twixt fact and fancy."

She notes: "The qualities that made him a poet were easily found. His smooth fingers showed inspirational qualities, and the pads or cushions on the inside of the nail phalanges reveal him to be supersensitive to everything that went on around him. The mount of Venus was well developed and smooth, indicating a deeply emotion nature responsive to mental contacts and material conditions...The length of the first phalange of the finger of Mercury with the pointed tip showed his gift of expression in speaking or writing...His heart line was the saddest kind of a heart line, for when he lost faith and belief, which he gave in extremes, the awakening disappointment brought a poignant suffering, which found its outlet in his work and enriched his poems...On the mount of the Moon was a whorl, a mark that looked like a thumb print which, with a similar print under and connecting the fingers of Saturn and Apollo, told of extraordinary intuitive powers. On his left hand under the fourth finger there was the unusual "mark of mercury" showing whimsy to the highest possible degree. She adds that Riley commented about the spiritual world during a "reading," saying:

"I always think it wonder when I go to the circus, to see a man riding around the ring on a bare-backed horse, keeping a number of colored balls passing from his hands into the air and back again and again, without dropping one. But the Great Power has been keeping the rainbow balls of many universes moving through space as He rides in a circuit."

So ends our recollection of Riley's connection with the strange science, if one may call it that, of palmistry.

Riley's attitude toward children has become a great controversy. Some believed he sincerely did not love children at all. Often he seemed undemonstratively dignified in the presence of children. This was not coldness. The role of "Children's Poet" caused some people to believe he should act clownish or silly to gain the attention of children. Riley did not do that. He had to make friends with a child in his own way and that way was not an artificial

American heartland children of Riley's epoch. He thought of America as "room for the children to play and to grow." John A. Howland photography collection.

or gurglingly effusive way. Children never misjudged him.

Not all childlike behavior was acceptable to Riley. Bill Nye stated that Riley simply could be cool sometimes to a human pest who determined to abuse a casual acquaintanceship from selfish motives of exploitation. Nye is quoted as saying, "a 2-year old child, with its natural sincerity, would be knowing him (Jim) at his best inside ten minutes. Like most men who have learned to despise what is fraudulent and false, he flies to the unbought love of children."

Riley's genius for making adult friends was no less active in making friends with children. It merely expressed itself in an unorthodox and unconventional manner. His genuine love was for the love of childhood.

Meredith Nicholson's assessment of the children's poetry is that "Much of his verse for children is autobiographical, representing his own attitude of mind as an imaginative, capricious child" and he gives the best example as lines from "That-Air Young-Un:"

THAT-AIR YOUNG-UN (1888)

"Come home onc't and said at he
Knowed what the snake-feeders thought
when they grit their wings; and knowed
Turkle-talk, when bubbles riz
Over where the old roots growed
where he th'owed them pets o' his -
Little turripuns he caught
In the County Ditch and packed
In his pockets days and days!"

Riley's poetry celebrates the freedom and selfhood of children. Loyalty and obligation to parents are not its keymarks but rather the license to be young and grow up with the privilege of being a child developmentally in its sphere. The child is deemed entitled to be loved as an intimate spiritual experience in a world which may be perceived as immoral or impersonal. Riley's poetry poses that each child is entitled to be loved regardless of the family's status, wealth, resources, and practices.

This perception of children is certainly not akin to the current American model of childhood. If one accepts the characterization of my century's child psychologist, Jerome Kagan, a child is urged through childhood toward becoming "psychologically mature." As stated in his THE NATURE OF THE CHILD, "In American families, the primary loyalty is to self-its values, autonomy, pleasure, virtue, and actualization. Most parents accept this criterion for maturity and try to arrange experiences that will make it easier for their children to attain the ideal." A child raised in the current American family is simply not permitted to go "truanting" as the Riley child was. The current ideal of self-grasping and personal gain also seems difficult to conform to the Riley social model of an order based on justice, mercy and compassion.

Riley's child would remain an innocent rather than grow to maturity hardened into ways a child would consider unjust.

Perhaps Riley's most lasting sobriquet is as the "Children's Poet." For "Riley Day," on the centennial of his birth in October 7, 1949, the Governor of Indiana officially christened him so.

RILEY DAY PROCLAMATION OF OCT. 7, 1949
TO ALL TO WHOM THESE PRESENTS
MAY COME, GREETING:

WHEREAS, all who live in Indiana or who have their ancestral roots in Hoosier soil have a special appreciation of the poetry of James Whitcomb Riley because it is the poetry of home, of fields and woodlands, and of the people who made our great state; and

WHEREAS, in the minds and hearts of Hoosiers there has been no other like Mr. Riley who has known so well their native land, their philosophy of life, and their common sense and heritage, or who has possessed the down-to-earth wisdom of the country store, the warmth and humanity of good talk among friends, and the gift of humor and storytelling, or who so greatly found in the daily things of life the elements of goodness and beauty; and

WHEREAS, to all within the state and to millions beyond its borders, James Whitcomb Riley is known as "The Children's Poet" because he was one who could look on life with the freshness that makes the world to a child a place of wonder and delight, and because he lives forever in his poetry and in a great memorial hospital that has saved or bettered the lives

Children honor Riley on Riley Day 1913. (Lester C. Nagley photo. Courtesy of The Riley Old Home Society, Greenfield, Indiana.)

of many of the countless little ones for whom he wrote; and

WHEREAS, in the eventful year, the centennial of his birth, when the children of our state have walked in the ominous shadow of a dread disease, Indiana knows how much it owes to him whose warm heart inspired others to make living brighter for childhood; now

THEREFORE, as Governor of the State of Indiana and in accordance with a resolution of the General Assembly of Indiana, I proclaim October 7, 1949, the 100th anniversary of the birth of the poet, as

RILEY DAY
throughout the length and breadth of the state...
Henry Schrieker, Governor

The children's poetry is almost all a matter of recollection from the poet's childhood. It is written however, or sometimes revised in Riley's latter years. The poet acknowledges this time disparity in many ways none of which seem to matter to children. For example, he dates his "The Diners in the Kitchen" as being from a "session" with his Uncle Sydney in 1869.

Many of Bud's poems were first collected in book form in A CHILD-WORLD. That does not mean that the poems were all written then. "The Bear Story," for example, was first published very late in the poet's career. The story had been polished from tellings as early as Riley's rambling journeys with Doc McCrillus. The poem was first told at Cadiz, Indiana when Riley was with the Doc's medicine show, Riley was entertaining and ran out of songs to sing. The children loved it. Riley then retained it and gave it at the Roberts Park M.E, Church in Indianapolis at a social for children in 1874. Before writing the story down, Riley had told the story for twenty years during his "lectures" around the country and as part of his platform entertainments. First published for the Christmas season of December, 1896, the book A CHILD-WORLD had sold 30,000 copies according to the publisher's journal BOOKMAN by June 1897 and subsequently went into further printings.

All of America of that era came to know "The Bear Story." No story in American literature is more captivating...or rambling. The Alex referred to was Riley's brother Hum (Humboldt Alexander Riley) tragically alcoholic and dead at 25. Riley attributed its idea to an evening gathering in the Riley family when everyone was required to tell a story. This was in the era before there were electronic entertainments and families invented such entertainments at home for diversions. Riley's brother, Hum, was five years old at the time and the little guy invented the rambling adventure.

THE BEAR STORY

That Alex "ist maked up his-own-se'f"

W'y, wunst they wuz a Little Boy went out
In the woods to shoot a Bear.[1] So, he went out
'Way in the grea'-big woods - he did, - An' he
Wuz goin' along -an' goin' along, you know,
An' purty soon he heerd somepin' go "Wooh!"
Ist thataway - "Woo-ooh!" An' he wuz skeered,
He wuz. An' so he runned an' clumbed a tree -
A grea'-big tree, he did, - a sicka-more[2] tree.
An' nen he heerd it ag'in: an' he looked round,
An' 't'uz a Bear - a grea'big shore-'nuff Bear!-
No: 't'uz two Bears, it wuz -two grea'big Bears-
One of 'em wuz -lst one's a grea'-big Bear. -
But they ist boff went "Wooh!" -An' here they come
To climb the tree an' git the Little Boy
An' eat him up!
*   An' nen the Little Boy*
He 'uz skeered worse'n ever! An' here come
The grea'big Bear a-climin' th' tree to git
The Little Boy an' eat him up- Oh, no! -
It 'uzn't the Big Bear 'at clumb the tree-
It 'uz the Little Bear. So here he come
Climbin' the tree - an' climbin' the tree! Nen when
He git wite clos't to the Little Boy, w'y, nen
The Little Boy he ist pulled up his gun
An' shot the Bear, he did, an' killed him dead!
An' nen the Bear he falled clean on down out
The tree - away clean to the ground, he did -
Spling-splung! he falled plum down, an' killed him, too!
An' lit wite side o' where the Big Bear's at.

An' nen the Big Bear's awful mad, you bet! -
'Cause - 'cause the Little Boy he shot his gun
An' killed the Little Bear. - 'Cause the Big Bear
He - he 'uz the Little Bear's Papa. - An' so here
He come to climb the big old tree an' git

The Little Boy an' eat him up! An' when
The Little Boy he saw the grea'-big Bear
A-comin', he 'uz badder skeered, he wuz,
Than any time! An' so he think he'll climb
Up higher - 'way up higher in the tree
Than the old Bear kin climb, you know. - But he -
He can't climb higher 'an old Bears kin climb, -
'Cause Bears kin climb up higher in the trees
Than any little Boys in all the Wo-r-r-ld!

An' so here come the grea'-big Bear, he did, -
A'climbin' up - an' up the tree, to git
The Little Boy an' eat him up! An' so
The Little Boy he clumbed on higher, an' higher,
An' higher up the tree - an' higher - an' higher -
An' higher'n iss-here house is! - An' here come
The old Bear -clos'ter to him all the time! -
An' nen - first thing you know, - when th' old Big Bear
Wuz wite clos't to him - nen the Little Boy
Ist jabbed his gun wite in the old Bear's mouf
An' shot an' killed him dead! - No; I fergot, -
He didn't shoot the grea'-big Bear at all -
'Cause when he shot the Little Bear, w'y, nen
No load 'uz any more nen in the gun!

But th' Little Boy clumbed higher up, he did -
He clumbed lots higher - an' on up higher - an' higher
An' higher - tel he ist can't climb no higher,
'Cause nen the limbs 'uz all so little, 'way
Up in the teeny-weeny tip-top of
The tree, they'd break down wiv him ef he don't
Be keerful! So he stop an' think: An' nen
He look around -An' here come the old Bear!
An' so the Little Boy make up his mind
He's got to ist git out o' there someway! -
'Cause here come the old Bear! - so clos't, his bref's
Purt' nigh so's he kin feel how hot it is
Ag'inst his bare feet - ist like old "Ring's" bref

When he's be'n out a-huntin' an' 's all tired.
So when th' old Bear's so clos't - the Little Boy
Ist gives a grea'-big jump fer 'nother tree -
No! - no, he don't do that! - I tell you what
The Little Boy does: - W'y, nen - w'y, he- Oh, yes! -
The Little Boy he finds a hole up there
'At's in the tree - an' climbs in there an' hides -
An' nen th' old Bear can't find the Little Boy
At all! - but purty soon the old Bear finds
The Little Boy's gun 'at's up there - 'cause the gun
It's too tall to tooked wiv him in the hole.
So, when the old Bear find' the gun, he knows
The Little Boy's ist hid round somers there, -
An' th' old Bear 'gins to snuff and sniff around,
An' sniff an' snuff around - so's he kin find
Out where the Little Boy's hid at. - An' nen - nen -
Oh, yes! - W'y, purty soon the old Bear climbs
'Way out on a big limb - a grea'-long limb, -
An' nen the Little Boy climbs out the hole
An' takes his ax an' chops the limb off!...Nen
The old Bear falls k-splunge! clean to the ground,
An' bu'st an' kill hisse'f plum dead, he did!

An' nen the Little Boy he git his gun
An' 'menced a-climbin' down the tree ag'in
No! no, he didn't git his gun - 'cause when
The Bear falled, nen the gun falled, too -
An' broked It all to pieces, too! - An' nicest gun! -
His Pa ist buyed it!- An' the Little Boy
Ist cried, he did; an' went on climbin' down
The tree - an' climbin' down - an' climbin' down! -
An' sir! when he 'uz purt' nigh down, - w'y, nen
The old Bear he jumped up ag'in - an' he
Ain't dead at all -ist 'tendin' thataway,
So he kin git the Little Boy an' eat
Him up! But the Little Boy he 'uz too smart
To climb clean down the tree. - An' the old Bear
He can't climb up the tree no more - 'cause when

He fell, he broke one of his - He broke all
His legs! - an' nen he couldn't climb! But he
Ist won't go 'way an' let the Little Boy
Come down out of the tree. An' the old Bear
Ist growls round there, he does - ist growls an' goes
"Wooh! -woo-ooh!" all the time! An' Little Boy
He haf to stay up in the tree - all night -
An' 'thout no supper neever!- Only they
Wuz apples on the tree! - An' Little Boy
Et apples - ist all night - an' cried - an' cried!
Nen when 't'uz morning the old Bear went "Wooh!"
Ag'in, an' try to climb up in the tree
An' git the Little Boy - But he can't
Climb t' save his soul, he can't! - An' oh! he's mad! -
He ist tear up the ground! an' go "Woo-ooh!"
An'- Oh, yes! - purty soon, when morning's come
All light - so's you kin see, you know, w'y, nen
The old Bear finds the Little Boy's gun, you know,
'At's on the ground. - (An' it ain't broke at all -
I ist said that!) An' so the old Bear think
He'll take the gun an' shoot the Little Boy: -
But Bears they don't know much 'bout shootin' guns:
So when he go to shoot the Little Boy,
The old Bear got the other end the gun
Ag'in' his shoulder, 'stid o' th' other end -
So when he try to shoot the Little Boy,
It shot the Bear, it did - an' killed him dead!
An' nen the Little Boy clumb down the tree
An' chopped his old woolly head off. - Yes, an' killed
The other Bear ag'in, he did - an' killed
All boff the bears, he did - an' tuk 'em home
An' cooked 'em, too, an' et 'em!
                —- An' that's all.

1. The bear.
2. Sycamore tree. This was a humorous note since the audience knew the sycamore tree was very slippery and almost impossible to climb.

It was said Riley came across a little girl with a broken doll on a step in

Anderson, Indiana in 1880 and after returning to his boarding house room, he wrote this poem:

A LIFE-LESSON (1880)

There! little girl; don't cry!
They have broken your doll, I know;
And your tea-set blue,
And your play-house too;
And things of the long ago;
But childish troubles will soon pass by. -
There! little girl; don't cry!

There! little girl; don't cry!
They have broken your slate, I know;
And the glad, wild ways
Of your schoolgirl days
Are things of the long ago;
But life and love will soon come by, -
There! little girl; don't cry!

From the author's Ora Myers glass negative collection of Hancock County, Indiana subjects

There! little girl; don't cry!
They have broken your heart, I know;
And the rainbow gleams
Of your youthful dreams
Are things of the long ago;
But Heaven holds all for which you sigh. -
There! little girl; don't cry!

Riley wrote the following poem for The Indianapolis JOURNAL for its October 31, 1880 issue and it was subsequently published in the national children's magazine, ST. NICHOLAS in its November, 1880 issue. Eventully it found its way into Riley's book, RHYMES OF CHILDHOOD published in 1891 to much national acclaim.

A NONSENSE RHYME (1880)

Ringlety-jing!
  And what will we sing?
Some little crinkety-crankety thing
  That rhymes and chimes,
  And skips, sometimes,
As though wound up with a kink in
    the spring.

  Grunkety-krung!
  And chunkety-plung!
Sing the song that the bullfrog sung, -
    A song of the soul
    Of a mad tadpole
  That met his fate in a leaky bowl;
And it's O for the first false wiggle he
    made
In a sea of pale pink lemonade!
    And its O for the thirst
      Within him pent,
      And the hopes that burst
      As his reason went -
When his strong arm failed and his
    strength was spent!

  Sing, O sing
  Of the things that cling,
And the claws that clutch and the
    fangs that sting -
    Till the tadpole's tongue
    And his tail upflung
Quavered and failed with a song
    unsung!
    O the dank despair in the
      rank morass,
      Where the crawfish crouch in
      the cringing grass,

And the long limp rune of the loon wails on
    For the mad, sad soul
    Of a bad tadpole
        Forever lost and gone!

    Jinglety-jee!
    And now we'll see
What the last of the lay shall be,
    As the dismal tip of the tune, O
        friends,
    Swoons away and the long tail
        ends.
        And it's O and alack!
            For the tangled legs
            And the spangled back
                Of the green grig's eggs,
                And the unstrung strain
                Of the strange refrain
That the winds wind up like a strand
of rain!

Hoosier children on a yard swing and bike of Riley's era. From the author's Ora Myers glass negative collection of Hancock County, Indiana subjects.

        And its O,
        Also,
    For the ears wreathed low,
Like a laurel-wreath on the lifted brow
Of the frog that chants of the why and
    how,
    And the wherefore too, and the
        thus and so
    Of the wail he weaves in a woof
    of woe!
Twangle, then, with your wrangling
    strings,
The tinkling links of a thousand
    things!
And clang the pang of a maddening
    moan
Till the Echo, hid in a land unknown,

Shall leap as he hears, and hoot
  and hoo
Like the wretched wraith of a
  Whoopty-Doo!

Children soon came to love the imaginative picture of this poem:

The NINE LITTLE GOBLINS[1] (1880)

They all climbed up on a high board-fence -
Nine little goblins, with green-glass eyes -
Nine little goblins that had no sense,
And couldn't tell coppers[2] from cold mince pies[3];
And they all climbed up on a fence, and sat -
And I asked them what they were staring at.

And the first one said, as he scratched his head
With a queer little arm that reached out of his ear
And rasped its claws in his hair so red -
"This is what this little arm is fer!"
And he scratched and stared, and the next one said,
"How on earth do you scratch your head?" And he laughed like
the screech of a rusty hinge -
Laughed and laughed till his face grew black;
And when he choked, with a final twinge
Of his stifling laughter, he thumped his back
With a fist that grew on the end of his tail
Till the breath came back to his lips so pale.

And the third little goblin leered round at me -
And there were no lids on his eyes at all, -
And he clucked one eye, and he says, says he,
"What is the style of your socks this fall?"
And he clapped his heels - and I sighed to see
That he had hands where his feet should be.

Then a bald-faced goblin, gray and grim,
Bowed his head, and I saw him slip

His eyebrows off, as I looked at him,
And paste them over his upper lip;
And then he moaned in remorseful pain -
"Would - Ah, would I'd me brows again!"

And then the whole of the goblin band
Rocked on the fence-top to and fro,
And clung, in a long row, hand in hand,
Singing the songs that they used to know -
Singing the songs that their grandsires sung
In the goo-goo days of the goblin-tongue.

And ever they kept their green-glass eyes
Fixed on me with a stony stare -
Till my own grew glazed with a dread surmise,
And my hat whooped up on my lifted hair,
And I felt the heart in my breast snap to,
As you've heard the lid of a snuff-box[4] do.

And they sang: "You're asleep! There is no board-fence
And never a goblin with green-glass eyes! -
'Tis only a vision the mind invents
After a supper of cold mince pies. -
And you're doomed to dream this way," they said, -
"And you shan't wake up till you're clean plum[5] dead!"

1. The Hoosier folklore of goblins may have been inspired by the many misshapen or hump-backed people or even dwarfs of Riley's time. In those days, tragic accidents, rough circumstances, malnutrition and lack of medical care caused more disfigurements among people.
2. Coppers are pennies, small monetary coins, which were made from copper in Riley's day.
3. Mince meat was standard fare in pies in frontier Hoosier times. When hogs were butchered, the meat of the head and neck (nothing was wasted) was called "mince meat." To the shredded meat was added applesauce or canned cherries, or raisons and suet or beef fat and often corn whiskey.
4. A snuff-box was a small box containing a tobacco product inhaled through the nose carried by fashionable gentlemen.
5. "Clean plum" is Hoosier vernacular meaning totally.

The following poem encounters the fright and shock a child feels at an erratic act of nature. The poem was written following an earthquake in

Indianapolis on August 13, 1886 measuring 3.4 on the Richter scale. Indiana "rides" on a forty mile long high angle fault known as the "Fortville Fault" which is one of only three known faults which rend the North American plate. The displacement is approximately sixty feet on the surface but it marks a clear path and cuts deep.

WHEN THE WORLD BU'STS THROUGH (1886)

(Casually Suggested by an Earthquake)

Where's a boy a'goin',
An' what's he goin' to do,
An' how's he goin' to do it,
When the world bu'sts through?
Ma she says, "she can't tell
What we're comin' to!"
An' Pop says "he's ist skeered[1]
Clean - plum - through!"

S'pose we'd be a-playin'
Out in the street,
An' the ground 'ud split up
'Bout forty feet! -
Ma says "she ist knows
We 'ud tumble in";
An' Pop says "he bets you
Nen[2] we wouldn't grin!"

S'pose we'd ist be 'tendin'
Like we had a show,
Down in the stable
Where we mustn't go, -
Ma says, "The earthquake
Might make it fall";
An' Pop says, "More'n like
Swaller barn an' all!"

Landy! ef we both wuz

Runnin' way from school,
Out in the shady woods
Where it's all so cool! -
Ma says "a big tree
Might sqush our head";
An' Pop says, "Chop 'em out
Both - killed -dead!"

But where's a boy goin',
An' what's he goin' to do,
An' how's he goin' to do it,
Ef the world bu'sts through?
Ma she says "she can't tell
What we're comin' to!"
An' Pop says "he's ist skeered
Clean - plum -through!"

Hoosier dining room scene in Riley's era. From the author's Ora Myers glass negative collection of Hancock County, Indiana subjects.

1. just scared
2. then

Another Riley children's favorite is this poem of a helpful and caring "handyman." A poem common in children's programs of Riley poetry:

THE DINERS IN THE KITCHEN (1902)

Our dog[1] Fred
Et[2] the bread.

Our dog Dash
Et the hash[3].

Our dog Pete
Et the meat.

Our dog Davy
Et the gravy.

Our dog Tuffy

Et the coffee.

Our dog Jake
et the cake.

Our dog Trip
Et the dip.

And - the worst,
From the first, -

Our dog Fido
Et the pie-dough.

1. A Hoosier dog was not only a pet, but often a hard working-farm animal who located domesticated animals in woodlots and herded them. One of the most common Nineteenth century breeds was a collie, originally bred in the Scottish Lowlands and Northern England.
2. A Hoosier variant for "ate," or "consumed."
3. Hash is a dish, mainly meat cut up into small pieces, previously cooked, served in gravy.

This poem represents how a child felt at the breakout of a house fire:

FIRE AT NIGHT[1] (1902)

Fire! Fire! Ring! and Ring!
Hear the old bell bang and ding!
Fire! Fire! 'way at night, -
Can't you hear? - I thin you might! -
Can't hear them-air clangin' bells? -
W'y, I can't hear nothin' else!
Fire! Ain't you 'wake at last! -
Hear them horses poundin' past -
Hear that ladder-wagon grind
Round the corner! - and behind,
Hear the horse-cart, turnin' short
And the horses slip and snort
As the engines clank-and-jar
Jolts the whole street, near and far,
Fire! Fire! Fire! Fire!

Can't you h'ist[2] that winder higher?
La! they've all got past like "scat!"...
Night's as black as my old hat -
And it's rainin', too, at that!...
Wonder where their old fire's at!

1. The poem of a child's excitement as a horse-drawn fire truck goes by.
2. "hoist" or "lift"

A poem of children's disappointments:

ALMOST BEYOND ENDURANCE (1903)

I ain't a-goin' to cry no more, no more!
  I'm got ear-ache, an' Ma can't make
    It quit a-tall[1];
      An' Carlo bite my rubber-ball
  An' puncture it; an' Sis she take
An' poke' my knife down through the stable-floor[2]
An' loozed it - blame it all!
But I ain't goin' to cry no more, no more!

An' Aunt Mame wrote she's comin',
    an she can't -
  Folks is come there! - An I don't care
    She is my Aunt!
    An' my eyes stings; an' I'm
    Ist coughin' all the time,
An' hurts me so; an' where my side's so sore
  Grampa felt where, an' he
  Says `Maybe it's pleurasy![3]"
But I ain't goin' to cry no more, no more!

An' I clumbed up an' nen failed off the fence[4],
  An' Herbert he ist laugh at me!
An my fi'-cents
It sticked in my tin bank, an' I ist store
  Purt' nigh my thumbnail off,

a-tryin to get
It out - nen smash it! - An' it's in there yit!
But I ain't goin' to cry no more, no more!

Oo! I'm so wickud! - An' my breath's so hot -
Ist like I run an' don't res' none
But ist run on when I ought to not;
Yes, an' my chin
An' lip's all warpy, an' teeth's so fast,
An' 's a place in my throat I can't swaller past -
An' they all hurt so!
An' oh, my-oh!
I'm a-startin' ag'in -
I'm a-startin ag'in, but I won't, fer shore! -
I ist ain't goin' to cry no more, no more!

1. In an epoch before pain-killing medicines, children suffered afflicting childhood conditions and often fatal childhood diseases.
2. Hoosier Deutsch barns were often three floors.
3. pleuresy is a disease causing pain in the chest or side thought to be the result of taking a chill in Riley's day, an inflammation of the pleura into the pleural cavity.
4. Wire mesh fence was introduced in Indiana in the 1890's which invited children to climb the fences as never before.

RILEY AND "RAGGEDY ANN" - AMERICA'S MOST ENDURING CHILD'S DOLL

Johnny Gruelle, whose artist father was a friend of James Whitcomb Riley, created a doll eighty years ago whose name came from two of Riley's most famous poems: "The Raggedy" from "The Raggedy Man" and the "Ann" from "Little Orphant Annie." Struggling to support several members of his family, Gruelle was a cartoonist for the Indianapolis STAR who took refuge in flights of fancy. When his work did not take up his full time, he enjoyed making drawings and inventing adventures for his little girl's rag doll, "Raggedy Ann."

He was hired to do a full page cartoon called "Mr. Twee Deedle" in which the first drawing of Raggedy Ann appeared, just as a background figure.

His hobby grew into sixteen books, and there were thirty more in the "Raggedy Ann" series by his son, Worth and brother, Justin after Johnny's death in 1938. In the preface of his book, "Raggedy Ann Stories" Gruelle

tells the story which
has become legend.
His little daughter,
Marcelle, liked to
play in her
Grandma's attic,
`way out in the coun-
try, and had grown
tired of whirring the
old spinning wheel
there and flopped
down to rest on an
old horsehair sofa.

The FAMOUS STORY BOOK DOLLS

The Raggedy Se-
ries Story Books
are ● shown on
page 765.

Beloved
playmates,
the very
dolls
the chil-
dren have
read about.
Ann has yarn
hair, apron, cot-
ton dress and
bloomers. Andy has yarn hair, cap, tie, plaid
shirt and overalls. Belindy has bandana cap,
two-piece dress and bloomers. Very soft and
light. Splendidly made of fine materials. Nothing to break. Our price very special. Usually
sells elsewhere for $2.50.

Our Price
$1.95 EACH

18N3056—Raggedy Ann.
Ht., 16½ in. Shpg. wt., 1¾ lbs.
18N3058—Raggedy Andy.
Ht., 16 in. Shpg. wt., 1½ lbs.
18N3061—Beloved Belindy.
Ht., 14 inches. Shpg. wt., 1½ lbs.

For Parcel Post, Express and Freight Rates, See Index for Pages

In 1928, a Beloved Belindy, Raggedy Ann, or Raggedy Andy doll could be had for $1.95 from the Sears Roebuck catalogue.

During the Twentieth Century when mail order purchases were frequent, Raggedy Ann dolls were available from the catalogue of retail giant, Sears Roebuck and Co., of Chicago.

"I wonder what is
in that barrel, `way
back in the corner," she thought to herself.

Standing on a couple of trunks, she yanked out of the barrel some interesting relics: old tintypes, old pictures, a little white bonnet. Then she came
upon an old rag doll, with only one shoe button eye, a painted nose, and a
smiling mouth. Grandma rejoiced with Marcella at the find of her old rag
doll; and quickly went to her sewing machine for another black, shiny shoe
button which she sewed on to match the other. The doll joined Marcella's
doll family and became her very favorite. Of course she was somewhat different from the doll that emerged later on commercially.

It seems that a New York bookstore undertook to sell Johnny's book,
"Raggedy Ann Stories," and had a stack of them in a show window which
were not selling. Someone had the idea that a rag doll to accompany the display might help to sell the books. Thus, it was that probably Johnny's sister, Prudence produced a doll for the purpose.

The result was electrifying. There were more demands for the doll than
for the books. It was priced at $2.50. A business woman, Molly Goldman,
saw an opportunity to profit from the popularity of the dolls and began to
manufacture them in 1934. Gruelle sued Mrs. Goldman, but the lawsuit
broke his health. However, others had started to make the dolls, some in
Norwalk, Connecticut under the direction of Gruelle himself. These early
dolls, some with brown, some with orange, some with red hair dressed in
blue flowered material like the original doll, or green, are not worth hundreds of dollars. Gruelle had moved to Connecticut sometime after 1910.

Johnny Gruelle, born in Arcola, Illinois in 1880, typified the American Dream, for he was rewarded for his hard work, perseverance, and creativity. The pathos in his life came from the death of his daughter, Marcella, when she was sixteen.

RILEY IN THE NATION'S HEART

Riley's children's poetry caused Riley to be given a special place in the nation's heart. The people of America recognized Riley for his concerns about them which were their own as well. This regard caused an appreciation of Riley which was something very new in literary history. Never before was a poet lauded by his country and state as

The James Whitcomb Riley Hospital for Children was originally conceived as a small hospital to correct child deformities and treat diseases of children. It was erected by popular subscription at a cost approaching $3,000,000 and received the first patient in 1924. Since then it has grown into a national medical center with expertise in the relief of suffering and needy children.

was Riley. This was the thrust of an editorial in the Christian Science MONITOR of October 7, 1915 which stated that Indiana honored Riley as Massachusetts had never honored Ralph Waldo Emerson or Henry Wadsworth Longfellow, or New York for William Cullen Bryant. The MONITOR then went on to draw a comparison between Riley and Lincoln. "You have to think of Riley in his right setting doing the same humanizing work as a poet that Lincoln did as a statesman, and with the same instruments - pathos, humor, and sincere lover of men as men."

The humble message of the Philippian's Christ Hymn had reverberated through Riley's chords of rhyme through the curtain of time. Time appreciated the favor.

CONCLUSION

I take this opportunity to assess what I consider to be Riley's place in the greater world of literature.

I find his kenotic poetry of humilty to be his greatest contribution. I do not state this because his "Old Swimmin Hole and `Leven Other Poems" sold thousands of copies in his epoch or represented America's vision of itself in humility before God or "hope" for itself. I like his kenotic poems because they are a poetry for the "unfit to survive," written "in the face" of the social Darwinists of his Nineteenth Century who saw the poor and humble as merely those being selected out by evolutionary forces. Riley participated in an American recovery from its experiences with the American Civil War as well. I think he deserves credit for giving

Reputedly, James Whitcomb Riley "front and back." Trick photo taken at Knightstown, Indiana. (From the Julia Wilson Riley Photograph album. Courtesy of The Riley Old Home Society, Greenfield, Indiana.)

America an innocent dream. Riley's poetry gave America hope t o cheer its participation in life. No age in history was faced with questions about humanity and life more bluntly than the Nineteenth Century. Evolutionary theory permitted a definition of humanity undreamed of before. Industrialism brought concern about the role of workers in society. Civil War amendments to the United States Constitution demanded equality of all people and an end to racism and sexism. The menu of all of this was terribly hard to stomach and digest. And yet the poetry of Riley entered into the dynamics of the age too. Humanism and the value of even the humblest life was at stake. Riley carried its banner.

I ask myself how in the world could Riley have sat down in the midst of all his problems in the same year of his castigation for forging an Edgar Allan Poe poem, shortly after an arrest in his hometown for intoxication, and firing from his job on the Anderson DEMOCRAT, and separated from his Nellie by her husband spiriting her away to write as the Hoosier Deutschman he was, "Das Krist Kindel?"

DAS KRIST KINDEL (1877)

I had fed the fire and stirred it, till the sparkles in delight
Snapped their saucy little fingers at the chill December night;
And in dressing-gown and slippers, I had tilted back "my throne" -
The old split-bottomed rocker - and was musing all alone.

I could hear the hungry Winter prowling round the outer door,
And the tread of muffled footsteps on the white piazza floor;
But the sounds came to me only as the murmur of a stream
That mingled with the current of a lazy-flowing dream.

Like a fragrant incense rising, curled the smoke of my cigar,
With the lamplight gleaming through it like a mist-enfolded star; -
And as I gazed, the vapor like a curtain rolled away,
With a sound of bells that tinkled, and the clatter of a sleigh.

And in vision, painted like a picture in the air,
I saw the elfish figure of a man with frosty hair-
A quaint old man that chuckled with a laugh as he appeared,
And with ruddy cheeks like embers in the ashes of his beard.

He poised himself grotesquely, in an attitude of mirth,
On a damask-covered hassock that was sitting on the hearth;
And at a magic signal of his stubby little thumb,
I saw the fireplace changing to a bright proscenium.

And looking there, I marveled as I saw a mimic stage
Alive with little actors of a very tender age;
And some so very tiny that they tottered as they walked,
And lisped and purled and curled like the brooklets, when
they talked.

And their faces were like lilies, and their eyes like purest dew,
And their tresses like the shadows that the shine is woven through;
And they each had little burdens, and a little tale to tell
Of fairy lore, and giants, and delights delectable.

And they mixed and intermingled, weaving melody with joy,
Till the magic circle clustered round a blooming baby-boy;
And they threw aside their treasures in an ecstasy of glee,
And bent, with dazzled faces and with parted lips, to see.

`Twas a wondrous little fellow, with a dainty double-chin,
And chubby cheeks, and dimples for the smiles to blossom in;
And he looked as ripe and rosy, on his bed of straw and reeds,
As a mellow little pippin that had tumbled in the weeds.

And I saw the happy mother, and a group surrounding her
That knelt with costly presents of frankincense and myrrh;
And I thrilled with awe and wonder, as a murmur on the air
Came drifting o'er the hearing in a melody of prayer: -

By the splendor in the heavens, and the hush upon the sea,
And the majesty of silence reigning over Galilee, -
We feel Thy kingly presence, and we humbly bow the knee
And lift our hearts and voices in gratefulness to Thee.

Thy messenger has spoken, and our doubts have fled and gone
As the dark and spectral shadows of the night before the dawn;
And, in the kindly shelter of the light around us draw,
We would nestle down forever in the breast we lean upon.

You have give us a shepherd - You have given us a guide,
And the light of Heaven grew dimmer when You sent him from Your side -
But he comes to lead Thy children where the gates will open wide
To welcome his returning when his works are glorified.

By the splendor in the heavens, and the hush upon the sea,
And the majesty of silence reigning over Galilee, -
We feel Thy kingly presence, and we humbly bow the knee
And lift our hearts and voices in gratefulness to Thee.

Then the vision, slowly failing, with the words of the refrain,
Fell swooning in the moonlight through the frosty window-pane;
And I heard the clock proclaiming, like an eager sentinel

Who brings the world good tidings, - "It is Christmas - all is well!"

This poem not only marks Riley's genial Hoosier Deutsch heritage within the transitional frontier culture of America but also some "touch" of destiny. There is some inspiration in Riley that I leave to others to place in words. I simply cannot further explain what I mean.

Wellwishers outside the Indiana Statehouse waiting to see Riley's body lying in state inside. (From the Barton Rees Pogue glass positive collection.)

I do think however that Riley's poetry was a poetry of humility, mystery and love and a proper reflection of its appropriation of the "Christ Hymn" with which it dialogued.

Just as the Philippian's "Christ Hymn" - a basic reference to the kenotics of Riley's age - is essentially poetry as well as song, so does its message, to be grasped, require poetic expression even more than metaphysical theological argument. The theologians discoursed and argued about its themes within the framework of the theological controversies of the Nineteenth Century, but it was in the poetry of James Whitcomb Riley that the point of Incarnation was made and triumphed in the United States in the Nineteenth Century. It was the poetry of James Whitcomb Riley that echoed the message calling for harmonious neighborliness, accommodation, racial toleration and the reconciliation possible because a "humiliated" Christ lived and thought enough of humanity to choose to live as one. Riley's poetry stands for the proposition that the unfortunate, the erring, the broken are subjects not just of kindness but also mercy. I like that thought. Maybe, I think we all kind of depend on it.

I also like the thought that Riley's poetry challenged the vision of Americans. Instead of the John D. Rockefellers and the railroad magnates or their ilk being the "great ones" of the Nineteenth Century, Riley's vulnerable and humble characters, the honest and tranquil Herr Weisers, the friendly and loyal William Leachmans, and the tragic but redeemed Mahala Ashcrafts for the adults -the Little Orphant Annies, Raggedy Men and the imaginative boy of Riley's famous "Bear Story" for the children-stormed into the American consciousness.

And so Riley's poetry remains in the American dream for us his children of the future - to sing to our souls of the old things, the wholesome things, the good things.

Staff of the Riley Museum Larry Fox, & Camilla Miller, Docent.

Carrying on the Riley Tradition: Standing, Mayor Pat Elmore, Top L to R: Ann Osborne, Curator; Terese Fargo, hostess, Lee Ann Petropoulos, Riley Old Home Society Pres.; Ellen Clift, Hostess. Bottom row L to R: Clark Ketchum, Parks Superintendent, Joan Ream, Hostess

We close with Riley's thought for us all.

The Prayer Perfect

Dear Lord! kind Lord!
 Gracious Lord! I pray
Thou will look on all I love
 Tenderly today!
Weed their hearts of weariness
 Scatter every care
Down a wake of angel-wings
 Winnowing the air.

Bring unto the sorrowing
 All release from pain!
Let the lips of laughter
 Overflow again;
And with all the needy
 O, divide, I pray
This vast treasury of content
 That is mine today

  — James Whitcomb Riley

Reproduced by
The Riley Old Home Society of Greenfield

ACKNOWLEDGEMENTS

In the news account of Riley's death, the absence of any real Riley biography was noted on its page one by the New York TIMES, which commented under the headline, "Early Life a Mystery," "James Whitcomb Riley was born at Greenfield, Indiana, probably in 1853. The poet made a secret of his age. A good deal of his early life is legendary for the reason that Riley refused to consent to have a biography published. A few years ago some of his admirers in Chicago, after consulting most of his early friends who were still living, wrote an account of his life and submitted the proofs to him.

The poet was greatly disturbed and protested, asking his friends to let him alone. He said his life was too commonplace to interest any one. He revised the proofs, however, but doctored the biography so that no specific or direct statement and no dates were left standing. He decided to allow it to be published that way, but later changed his mind, bought up the rights to the book, and had it destroyed. When friends in his later days pressed him to write a biography, he said: "No, no; it seems too conceited."

Did Riley leave no biography? My own conclusion is somewhat different from the conclusion of the New York TIMES. I think Riley wrote his own life into his cryptic poem "The Flying Islands of the Night" and wished to leave it at that. I have tried to follow the play/poem's themes in this extension of his life as much as I could. Riley revised the poem several times to include later experiences which permit us to go beyond Riley's depressed and alcoholic "Crestillomeem" dominant period of his late 20's. Thank the God who looks out for America for this.

I often thought of this book as a "payback" to a dead man who has always been the source of much inspiration to me as his writings have been to many Americans. Particularly when writing my CHILDREN OF A NEW ABRAHAM, (my "logos" of America), I often found myself encouraged by Riley's writing to "reach" into the vulnerability of human life to extract its existential as well as ordinary value. I thank you James Whitcomb Riley-the thanks of a grateful student to an old, beloved friend.

Now I shall make other acknowledgments.

The University Press of Kentucky gave me specific permission to quote from SLAVE AND FREEMAN, the writings of George Knox. Mrs. Richard H. Dickson, a member of one of Indiana's "first families," gave me permission to use a memorandum written by her father, Walter Dennis Myers, an attorney of James Whitcomb Riley. The Indiana State library, its newspaper division,"Indiana Room" and reference section were often very helpful as were their contemporaries at the Indianapolis Public Library. The Indiana Historical Society is due much credit, particularly for their permission to use Millikan family photographs and other materials and visuals. Susan Sutton of that society was a great resource. Paul Henderson provided basic research for the "Leonainie" poem/hoax. A great section in "Jucklet" came from an unpublished manuscript of his. Acknowledgment is made to Felix Post, author, and the Royal College of Psychiatrists, Belgrave Square, London for specific permission to quote material from their 1996 Article in the BRITISH JOURNAL OF PSYCHIATRY entitled "Verbal Creativity, Depression and Alcoholism." Likewise, Mark Brunke, chatted with me while giving his permission to quote from his article "Alcohol and Creative Writing," in Psychological Reports 71(2):651-8, 1992 Oct. As always I owe much to the insights of my friends, Calvin Porter, New Testament Professor at Christian Theological Seminary, Indianapolis, and the same institution's theologian Edward Towne, as well as my Greek Orthodox brother, the "missionary to the Hoosiers," Charles Ashanin who first acquainted me with the literature of the Protestant Incarnation movement of the Nineteenth Century some years ago. Many libraries and librarians - Carol Graf comes to mind of the Kokomo-Howard County Public Library, county historians-especially Joe Skvarenina (of Hancock) and Monisa Wisener (of Randolph)-and journalists have been my friends in this undertaking. The Anderson Public Library's "Indiana Room" is a "ginoine ar-tickle" for Riley materials and I spent many happy days there. I have sought permission to use more recent materials under copyright and specifically thank the Lafayette JOURNAL AND COURIER for Delphi background material. I deeply appreciate the experience of walking in Delphi's Riley Park and driving the area to Camden as Riley and Dr. Wycliffe Smith did. Also I acknowledge

The National Archives and many college libraries, particularly those of Indiana University, both at Indianapolis and Bloomington, the Universities of Harvard, Virginia and Wyoming (which has the great Bill Nye collection), and particularly the Lilly Library at Indiana University, Bloomington, Indiana which lovingly preserves much Rileyana. Letters are sometimes quoted from the Lilly Library's Riley Letters Collection. Others are from copies of almost all of Riley's correspondence purchased from the Leslie Payne estate by my friend, Robert Tinsley, or from publications of various sorts. All of the staff and its great director, Susan Wagonner, of the Greenfield (Indiana) Public Library have been very helpful. Marcia Hunt of that library found John T. Hatfield's book THIRTY THREE YEARS, A LIVE WIRE. Larry Fox, Archivist of the James Whitcomb Riley Museum in Greenfield, Indiana, read the manuscript and offered valuable suggestions. He also helped me with illustrations from the life of Riley in the Riley Museum as did the great docent of that museum, Camilla Miller. Many photos derive from the Barton Rees Pogue glass positive collection which I wished to help preserve. In publishing these glass impressions, I wish to remember another Greenfield native son, the poet, Barton Rees Pogue. Pogue was born in 1883 on North Spring Street, Greenfield. He first was on the faculty at Taylor University in Upland, Indiana before going into public entertainment in the new media of radio at that time. He wrote numerous poems for broadcast on Cincinnati's famous channel, WLW. Pogue was very proud of his "hometown" connection with Riley and composed a visual program about Riley for schools from which these glass negatives derive. Camilla Miller provided me with illustrations from the Howland photography collection. I also thank the Riley Old Home Society for the photographs from the Julia Wilson Riley family album and other illustrations. Kenneth Ross of The Department of History, Presbyterian Church (U.S.A.) in Philadelphia assisted greatly in helping me determine the course and extent of Incarnation Theology into the American heartland and background information on Riley's friend, Myron Reed. I have tried to use materials from those who knew Riley as much as possible. Such people included Booth Tarkington, Minnie Belle Mitchell, George Ade, Meredith Nicholson, Hamlin Garland, William Neff, George Richman, Marcus Dickey,

William Lyon Phelps, Edmund Eitel, Riley relatives, and many others. I include material from a genealogy of James Whitcomb Riley by Patricia Jean Zumwalt, Livingston, TX, based in part on the pedigree work of Hannah Foster Dowling. Ms. Dowling born 1907 of Dayton, Ohio, used as sources material "from my grandfather" Jesse A. Foster of Preble Co., Ohio - a Riley relative, cemetery stones, and correspondence with Sam Riley of Texas and Jim Smith Berry of Cincinnati, Ohio. Philip Kabel's writings provided much information on the Riley family history from Randolph County. I am indebted to Arville L. Funk, Corydon, Indiana for background on Morgan's Raid. Death records relating to James McClanahan were obtained from Saint John's Health System Medical Records Department, Anderson, Indiana, the Madison County Board of Health and other sources. Anna Chittenden information was primarily provided by the Indiana Archives Section of the Indiana State Library which maintains records of the former Central State Hospital where Ms. Chittenden was committed by Court order. Much more information on William Bixler is contained in a wonderful article in the Milwaukee, WI JOURNAL of May 15, 1941. Phyllis Arthur and Tina Nehrling of the Riley Children's Theatre unwittingly helped me select the poetry for children included in the "Bud" Section. The quotes from the press on Luther Benson are from the book, Banta, INDIANA AUTHORS AND THEIR BOOKS. The literature on German Settlers in Indiana is surprisingly scarce considering the huge number of the Hoosier Deutsch. GERMAN SETTLERS AND GERMAN SETTLEMENTS by Dr. William A. Fritsch of Evansville, Indiana is among the best sources. Riley is proudly mentioned in this publication. The list of contemporary Hoosier poets with Riley was compiled from Benjamin Parker and Enos Heiney's POETS AND POETRY OF INDIANA, 1900. The Russo BIBLIOGRAPHY OF JAMES WHITCOMB RILEY was extremely helpful in locating background materials but I have also concentrated on "local sources" most heavily. The greatest of these was my mother, Dorothy June Williams. She wrote extensively on James Whitcomb Riley. Before her death, she and I wrote A HISTORY OF HANCOCK COUNTY, INDIANA IN THE TWENTIETH CENTURY which contains much Riley material. She is also the author of the "Riley Home History" and many other writings. Her weekly newspaper columns in the Greenfield Daily REPORTER, the Hancock JOURNAL and the Hancock County AD-NEWS as well as my own (covering a total period of close to half a century) have gone into this book. Other references are found in the text. I do not name all those I should acknowledge. As always whenever military actions during the American Civil War come up, I leaf through the mountainous OFFICIAL RECORDS OF THE WAR OF REBELLION at the Indiana State Library Reference Room. The material on the little known Civil War Battle of Rich Mountain comes mainly from those records. Many anonymous newspeople who interviewed Hartpence, McCrillus, Haute Jameson, the Davis boys, and many, many other people in Riley's life are not named here but should have been. Their published newspaper articles in numerous newspapers and journals have constituted the main body of this book. There are simply too many. THE LOVE LETTERS OF THE BACHELOR POET JAMES WHITCOMB RILEY TO MISS ELIZABETH KAHLE of the Boston Bibliophile Society, 1922, was interesting although I still wonder why Riley wrote Miss Kahle the letters. I have quoted from some of these. I have perused earlier biographies of Riley with great admiration. In fact, however, I started this project by taking a COMPLETE WORKS of Riley's poetry with me for a stay on the island of Rhodos, my favorite place, with Venice, in all the world. Riley and I had a marvelous time in the Mediterranean as we became more acquainted than ever before. Perhaps this biography will offer somewhat different conclusions about Riley's life based upon local history and folklore sources primarily. Riley was so famous that even to this day "local" stories about him survive. I have files full of reference materials should anyone wish to contact me about some specific fact. Biographies are not of course footnoted but I have "cheated" where necessary.

Angela McMahan at the typesetters, the Greenfield (IN) DAILY REPORTER, and Gary George, are the wonderful layout specialists. Angela you are so very appreciated by all of the "Riley" family for your help with this work of preservation. My fine assistant Bill Allford was always interested. In the middle of this project, Becky Mayhugh joined my office and has helped immeasurably.

Now I am tired and shall rest a minute.

INDEX

Cornelia, 427; Logansport, IN, 548; Longfellow, Henry Wadsworth, 187, 382, 429-31; Lowell, James Russell, 462, 532; lung tester, 158; Lyceum, 524; Lyceum circuit, 523; lynching incident, 306-15; "Made in Anderson" event, 227, 612; Major, Charles, 499; Marcel, Adrian, 196; Marine, Elizabeth, 83, 198-203; Marion, IN, 211; Marine, John, 84; Marvel, Ik, 304, 482; Martindale, Elijah B., 483-487, 583; Masonic Hall, Greenfield, IN, 59, 210; McClanahan, Jim, 109, 110, 207, 219, 224-31, 287, 290; McClellan, George, 558; McCrillus, Dr. Samuel, 266, 274-82, 291-93, 576; McCulloch, Dr. Carleton B., 371; McCutcheon, George Bar, 499; McKinley, President William, 405; Merrill, Meigs and Company, 494; Methodist Church, 305; Miller, Henry, 109,206; Millikan, Jesse, 178; Millikan, Rhoda Houghton, 98, 178, 184; Mitchell, Minnie Belle, 58, 446, 610; Monrovia, IN, 513; Moody, William Vaughn, 499; Moore, John, 306; Moore, Oliver, 481; Morgan, John Hunt, 560-5; Morgue, The, 322, 520; Morton, Oliver P., 88, 466, 556; Murphy, Elizabeth Fisher, 242; Murphy, Frank, 287; Murphy, pledge, 16; Musselman, Catherine, 205; Myers, Kate, 219; Myers, Ora, 611; National Greenback Party and Reuben Riley, 585; National Institute of Arts and Letters, 609; Nature poetry, 446-8; Neill's school, 89; Negley, Lester Sr., 608; New Castle, IN, 509; New England Society, 541; New Palestine (IN) Home Guards, 564; Newspaper poetry, 474-93; Nicholson, Meredith, 7, 221, 244, 403, 629, 630; Nickum, John, 372, 602; Nye, Bill, 533; Nye, Edgar Wilson, 8; Ohio, Lima, 317; O'Neil, Paddy, 366; O'Reilly, Jamesy, 626; Othell, Will, 514; Page, Thomas Nelson, 593; Palmistry, 633; Paine, Dan, 490; Parker, Benjamin, 383; Pedigree, 78-84; Peattie, Donald Culross, 446; Peru, IN, 68,205; Phelps,William Lyon, 608, 631; Philadelphia, IN, 622; Phillips, Charles, 235- 37, 489; Philips, Theophilus C., 489; physical description, 361, 529; Pioneer Association, 509; Platform Lecturer, 504; Poe, Edgar Allan, 105, 115, 297-300, 443; Poems set to music, 408-9; Poet, Children's, 2; Pond, James B., 8, 524; Porter, Gene Stratton, 499; poverty of family, 272, 565-9; Press summaries, 536; Proclamation of Riley Day, 613-614; prose, 492; Racism, 306; Rafter room, 88; Raggedy Ann, 652; Ralston, Samuel M., 614; Randall, Anna, 552; Redpath Bureau, 524, 526; Redpath, James, 8; Reed, Rev. Myron, 219, 377, 401-5, 491, 509, 589; Richards, Myra, 6; Richman, George, 24; Riley Day, 610;

Riley, Elizabeth, 269-70, 362, 577; Riley, Elva May, 273; Riley Hospital, 654; Riley, Hum ,428; Riley, John A., 16; Riley, Martha Lukens, 428: Riley, Mary, 223, 274, 523; Riley, Margaret, 82, 401, 561; Riley, Reuben, 79, 89, 114, 424, 476, 522, 554, 560-85, 569-71, 574, 598; Riley's Declaration of Independence from prior American poetry, 334-5; Roberts Park Methodist Church, 514; Robinson, Reuben D., 510; Rockefeller, John D., 381; Rowell, Adda, 203; Rumrill, Lionel E., 481; Sargent, John Singer, 13; Schrieker, Henry, 638; "Seminary," The, 106, 273; Shelbyville, IN, 499; Shirley, 522, 588; Sisters and brothers, 84; Skinner, John, 222, 317, 318; Smith, Mary Alice, 622; Smith, Wycliffe, 240; Smoot, Walter, 231; Sneathen, "Smallpox", 240; Snow, Tom, 115; spirit writing, 220; Social Darwinism, Riley and, 399-401; Society of the Army of the Tennessee, 547; Soldiers and Sailors Monument, Indianapolis, IN, 405, 590-2, 608; song as basis of Riley poetry, 405; sound recordings, 493; Sousa, John Philip, 405; South Bend, IN, 206, 287; Spanish American War, 604; Spencer, Herbert, 399; Stafford, William, 224, 339, 344; Stamp Issue, American Poets Postage, 508; Stein, Evaleen, 243; Stein, Orth, 243; Stevenson, Robert Lewis, 247; stroke, 452; suicide, 331; Sumner, William Graham, 399,461; Swope, Elmer, 87; Take Radway's Ready Relief Prank, 69; Tarkington, Booth, 212, 499; Tarkington, Hautie, 221; Taylor, H.S., 238; Tea hour, 600; temperance, 282-6, 300-3; Temple, Tremont, Boston, MA, 505; Tennyson, Alfred Lord, 441; Terrell, William H.H., 466; The Old Swimmin' Hole and 'Leven More Poems, 529; Townsend, Doc, 266, 315-9; tremens, 350; Twain, Mark, 534, 543; Uncle Sydney, 626; Vawter, Will, 4, 498; Walker, A.J., 364, 532; Walker Block Building,194; Walker, Horace, 357; Walker, John, 224, 253, 339, 487, 488, 490; Walker, Will T., 481; Wallace, Lew, 377, 499; Wallace, Zerelda, 282; Warsaw, IN, 204; Weiser, Herr, 241; Wells, Harriet Eitel, 97, 600; Western Association of Writers, 594; Western Lecture Bureau, 509; Western Lyceum Agency, 530; Wheeler,Ella, 219; Whit, Jay, 426, 473; Whitcomb, James,589; Whitman,Walt, 409; Whittier,John Greenleaf, 441; Wick, William, 87; Wills, Elizabeth T., 283; Wilson, President Woodrow, 10, 553; Windsor, IN, 78; Winslow, Marshall, 508; Wizard Oil Company, 316; Wordsworth, William, 157; wunk, 21.